Zen Pathways

Zen Pathways

*An Introduction to the Philosophy
and Practice of Zen Buddhism*

禅道の千路

BRET W. DAVIS

閑風

OXFORD

UNIVERSITY PRESS

OXFORD
UNIVERSITY PRESS

Oxford University Press is a department of the University of Oxford. It furthers
the University's objective of excellence in research, scholarship, and education
by publishing worldwide. Oxford is a registered trade mark of Oxford University
Press in the UK and certain other countries.

Published in the United States of America by Oxford University Press
198 Madison Avenue, New York, NY 10016, United States of America.

Library of Congress Cataloging-in-Publication Data
Names: Davis, Bret W., author.
Title: Zen pathways : an introduction to the philosophy and
practice of Zen Buddhism / Bret W. Davis.
Description: New York : Oxford University Press, 2022. |
Includes bibliographical references and index.
Identifiers: LCCN 2021035257 (print) | LCCN 2021035258 (ebook) |
ISBN 9780197573686 (hardback) | ISBN 9780197573693 (paperback) |
ISBN 9780197573716 (epub)
Subjects: LCSH: Zen Buddhism—Philosophy. | Zen Buddhism—Doctrines.
Classification: LCC BQ9268.6 .D386 2021 (print) |
LCC BQ9268.6 (ebook) | DDC 294.3/420427—dc23
LC record available at https://lccn.loc.gov/2021035257
LC ebook record available at https://lccn.loc.gov/2021035258

DOI: 10.1093/oso/9780197573686.001.0001

With nine deep bows of gratitude, I dedicate this book to the memory of

Tanaka Hōjū Rōshi (1950–2008)
and
Ueda Shizuteru Sensei (1926–2019)

Tanaka Rōshi fulfilled his vow to become an "educator of educators." For a decade he guided me in my practice. Time and again I entered the electrifying atmosphere of his interview room to be tested on kōans. Often swiftly dismissing me and my muddles with the ring of a bell, his compassionate severity allowed me to undertake an "investigation into the self" more rigorous and more revealing than I could have imagined. That decade of doing sanzen with him changed my life. Tanaka Rōshi wrote very little. He taught with the living words of his speech, with his piercing gaze, and with his ear-to-ear smile. He exemplified Zen for us with the crispness of his movements and with the purity of his motives. May some of the spirit of his holistic pedagogy flow through these pages to benefit its readers and all who are, in turn, touched by their lives.

For nearly a quarter of a century I had the great privilege of learning directly from Ueda Sensei in both scholarly and Zen contexts. He modeled for me what it means to walk the parallel paths of Zen and philosophy, allowing them to illuminate and enrich each other without compromising the distinct nature and rigor of either one. Ueda Sensei's profoundly insightful philosophical interpretations of Zen inform many pages of this book. Tanaka Rōshi's successor and my current teacher, Kobayashi Gentoku Rōshi, asked Ueda Sensei to formulate the Zen layperson's name (kojigō) that I was given: Kanpū 閑風 (literally "peaceful wind"). Ueda Sensei used one of the characters from his own given name: the kan in Kanpū is another reading of the character for shizu in Shizuteru 閑照 (literally "peaceful illumination"). I am deeply honored to carry forth part of his name along with his mission of relating, without conflating, the Eastern and Western paths of Zen and philosophy.

Figure 0.1 Author with Tanaka Hōjū Rōshi in Shōkokuji monastery, Kyoto, November 2004

Figure 0.2 Author with Ueda Shizuteru Sensei at his home in Hieidaira, August 2012

Gateless is the Great Way.
It has thousands of different pathways.
                            —Wumen, *The Gateless Barrier*

Your journey begins here.
                    —Printed on a piece of trash sojourning on a sidewalk
                                                    in Baltimore

Contents

Preface

Why Write or Read This Book?

Why write or read a book on Zen when it is claimed that Zen is "not based on words and letters"? Well, since there is no first word in Zen, there can be no last word. Precisely because, for Zen, it is not the case that in the beginning was the Word, there can be no book or collection of sayings that says it all. That is why every new Zen teacher leaves a record of his or her teachings. That is why every new encounter can become a new kōan. Every new context calls for a new text, a text that tries to leave some life in the printed words, to leave at least a vivid trace of the living words that are—as Zen master Dōgen puts it—"expressive attainments of the Way" (*dōtoku*). The reader is invited to revive the verbiage.

For more than a century now, Zen Buddhism has been in the process of transmission from Japan and other parts of East Asia to the United States and other Western countries. The modern Western recontextualization of this age-old tradition has, appropriately, called forth many new texts—as did the eastward transmission of Buddhism from India to China in ancient times.

But do we really need yet another introduction to Zen? After all, there already exist many shelves of books on Zen, more than a few of which are written by authors who are—either as scholars or as teachers—more qualified than I am to write about Zen. Nevertheless, as a philosophy professor who studied with the contemporary representatives of the Kyoto School in Japan for many years, as a scholar who is fluent in Japanese and proficient in reading Classical Chinese, and most importantly as a longtime lay practitioner who has been authorized to teach Rinzai Zen, I hope that this book makes a unique contribution, one that will be welcomed especially by readers who are interested in both the philosophy and practice of Zen.

Toni Morrison famously said, "If there's a book you really want to read but it hasn't been written yet, then you must write it." I hope that there are some students, scholars, lifelong learners, and philosophically minded Zen practitioners who will appreciate my attempt to write the book that I wish had been there for me to read more than thirty years ago, when I started down the parallel pathways of Zen and philosophy. Now, I wish someone else had written this book so that I could use it in my college courses on Asian and comparative philosophy and religion.

I should mention that my Zen training has for the most part been undertaken in Japan, where I resided for thirteen years, and where I continue to spend much time during sabbaticals as well as summer and winter breaks. Since I have not been affiliated with any of the Zen establishments in North America or Europe, I feel somewhat "outside the loop" when I read accounts—such as Rick Fields's *How the Swans Came to the Lake: A Narrative History of Buddhism in America*, Helen Tworkov's *Zen in America: Five Teachers and the Search for an American Buddhism*, and James Ishmael Ford's *Zen Master Who? A Guide to the People and Stories of Zen*—of the incredible efforts that have been made over the last half century to transmit Zen to North America. When I read such books, or articles in such magazines as *Tricycle: The Buddhist Review*, and when I visit the established Zen centers in the United States, I feel like I've arrived unfashionably late to a party that is already in full swing; perhaps a bit like a Japanese monk who returned to Japan after spending years in China learning Zen in the fourteenth century, only to find that a couple of earlier generations of Chinese and Japanese monks had already done the heavy lifting of transmitting Zen from China to Japan. In any case, I hope that my unusual mixture of academic and Zen training has enabled me to belatedly add a minor new voice to the booming cross-cultural chorus involved in the ongoing movement of Zen Buddhism around the world: in the past from India to China to Japan, and onward in the present to the United States, Europe, and elsewhere.

Allow me to introduce myself in just a little more detail, so that readers have a better sense of whose voice is speaking through the printed words of this book. While living in Japan for much of my twenties and thirties, and during numerous stays since returning to the United States in 2005 to begin my career as a philosophy professor, I have endeavored to follow in the giant footsteps of Kyoto School philosophers and lay Zen masters Nishitani Keiji and Ueda Shizuteru, who spent their lives commuting between the academic study of philosophy and religion at Kyoto University and the holistic practice of Zen at the nearby Rinzai Zen monastery of Shōkokuji. After graduating from college in 1989, I spent half of the next seven years studying philosophy in a PhD program at Vanderbilt University in Nashville, Tennessee, and half studying Japanese, practicing Zen and karate, and teaching English mainly at a Buddhist university in the vicinity of Osaka, Japan. After going back to the States for a couple of years to finish my coursework at Vanderbilt, in 1996 I returned to Japan to live for eight and a half more years, this time in Kyoto. There, I studied Buddhism at Otani University for a couple of years, and then undertook doctoral studies and postdoctoral research in Japanese philosophy at Kyoto University. I also taught philosophy, religion, and ethics courses at universities in the area. All of this study and teaching was done entirely in Japanese, which is also the language I have spoken at home for the past three decades. Alongside my academic activities in Kyoto, I commuted regularly to, and sometimes lived in, the monastery at Shōkokuji in order to prac-tice Zen. For a decade I worked on kōans under the direction of Tanaka Hōjū Rōshi, and after he passed away in 2008, I have continued this practice under the direction of Kobayashi Gentoku Rōshi. In 2010, I was officially authorized by Kobayashi Rōshi as a teacher (*sensei*) and director of a Zen center (*dōjōchō*).[1] In fact, with Tanaka Rōshi's permission and encouragement, in 2005 I founded, and since then have directed, The Heart of Zen Meditation Group, which meets in a remodeled "meditation chapel" at my home institution in Baltimore, Loyola University Maryland.

This book is the hybrid fruit of, on the one hand, more than three decades of practicing and more than a decade of teaching Zen, and, on the other hand, more than three decades of studying and two decades of teaching Western, Asian, and cross-cultural philosophy. The bridge builders between these two disci-plines, in whose footsteps I have tried to follow—albeit starting from the Far West rather than from the Far East—are those Kyoto School philosophers who have both practiced and reflected on Zen. Especially important for me have been the central figures of the first three generations of the Kyoto School: Nishida Kitarō (1870–1945), Nishitani Keiji (1900–1990), and Ueda Shizuteru (1926–2019).

Nishida understood the essence of religion to be the direct self-awareness obtained through delving deeply into the basic fact of existence. And he un-derstood the essence of philosophy to be an intellectual reflection on that self-awareness.[2] Human beings, Nishida thought, need both.

Another prominent Kyoto School philosopher and influential lay Zen teacher, Hisamatsu Shin'ichi (1889–1980), expressed the relation between philosophy and religion as follows:

> Philosophy seeks to know the ultimate; religion seeks to live it. Yet for the whole human being, the two must be nondualistically of one body, and cannot be di-vided. If religion is isolated from philosophy, it falls into ignorance, supersti-tion, fanaticism, or dogmatics. If philosophy is alienated from religion, it loses nothing less than its life. . . . Religion without philosophy is blind; philosophy without religion is vacuous.[3]

When Hisamatsu says "religion," he mainly means Zen practice and the expe-rience of awakening to the "formless self." In fact, he was quite scathing in his critiques of Christianity, Pure Land Buddhism, and other religions that preach salvation based on faith in a higher power outside the self. By contrast, D. T. Suzuki (1870–1976), along with many Kyoto School philosophers—including Suzuki's lifelong friend Nishida, and also Nishitani, Ueda, and Hisamatsu's stu-dent Abe Masao (1915–2006)—were interested not only in pointing out var-ious differences but also in pursuing parallels between Zen and the profoundest theological, buddhological, and mystical teachings of Christianity and Pure Land Buddhism.

Some readers may wish to think of Zen teachings and practices in terms of "spirituality" rather than "religion," insofar as "religion" connotes for them institutional establishments and dogmatic creeds more than liberating and enlightening personal experience. Yet if we think of "religion" etymologically as re-ligio, and if we understand this to imply a way of reuniting with the ground and source—or source-field—of our being, then perhaps they might feel more comfortable with the term. In any case, the present book is less concerned with the history and sociology of Zen as an institutional religion and more concerned with elucidating and philosophically interpreting its most enlightening and liberating teachings and practices.

To be sure, a lot of mischief, hypocrisy, and abuse has also gone on in Zen institutions, as is sadly the case with other religious traditions. One can and should read books that investigate such matters. Although this book is written more for philosophically minded spiritual seekers than for critically minded sociologists and historians, I do make an effort to take the latter kind of research into consideration, and also to point out what I see as certain potential shortcomings and pitfalls of Zen practice and philosophy (such as those involving erroneous anti-intellectualism or harmful antinomianism) that must be heeded and avoided.

The word "spirituality," it should be remarked, has its own problems. It cannot be applied to Zen if it indicates a concern with the spirit as opposed to, or as separable from, the body and the material world. Yet if "spirit" is used—as it sometimes is—as a holistic word for what encompasses and pervades our whole body, heart, and mind, then Zen can indeed be understood in terms of spirituality. Zen practice is holistic. It engages the whole psychosomatic person, which, moreover, it does not dualistically separate from the whole universe.

Buddhism has always been an exceptionally philosophical religion. Indeed, it is for this reason that Zen masters have often felt the need to push back against what they saw as an overemphasis on intellectual reasoning and textual study in the Buddhist tradition. Their counterbalancing stress on embodied-spiritual practice over merely cerebral intellection remains an important lesson for many of us today. However, the counterbalancing pendulum has sometimes swung too far in the opposite direction, with some teachers and especially their epigones suggesting that philosophical thinking and scholarly studies are not only unnecessary but even antithetical to Zen. Especially in some of his early writings, the pioneer Zen spokesperson in the West, D. T. Suzuki—himself, ironically, an avid and prolific scholar—at times left readers with that impression. However, as will be discussed in Chapter 21, in his later work Suzuki increasingly stressed the need to articulate a "Zen thought" and even a "Zen logic" rather than resting content with only "Zen experience." It is important to bear in mind that those past Zen masters who tried to wean their students from an overreliance on the intellect were often themselves learned and sharp thinkers. The thirteenth-century Japanese Zen master Dōgen, for example, was an ingenious philosopher and erudite scholar. At the same time, as will be discussed in Chapters 20 and 22, Dōgen too stressed the importance of regularly putting aside texts, putting on hold intellectual reasoning, and wholeheartedly engaging in embodied-spiritual practices, especially the silent practice of seated meditation.

Those Kyoto School philosophers who were also dedicated Zen practitioners—Nishida, Hisamatsu, Nishitani, Abe, Ueda, and so on—have done the Zen tradition, and the world at large, an indelible service in reconnecting the embodied-spiritual practice of Zen with rigorous philosophical thinking, and also with pioneering a dialogue between Buddhist and Western philosophy and religion. That is why, as a student who was committed to philosophy yet not wholly satisfied with its exclusively intellectual approach, and who thus took up a parallel practice of Zen, I was drawn to follow in their footsteps and to commute between the university and the monastery. What I offer in this book is the fruit of that commute: an introduction to Zen that pays due attention to both its practical roots and its philosophical leaves.

Tips for Using This Book, and Conventions Used in It

Although it is based on decades of academic research along with practice and teaching, I have endeavored to write this book in an accessible and engaging manner. It is primarily addressed to college students and other newcomers with a philosophical as well as practical interest in Zen (even though I certainly also hope that seasoned scholars and practitioners will find in its pages fresh takes on familiar teachings). For this reason, I have tried to keep the main text uncluttered with scholarly references to terms and texts. For those who are interested in delving deeper into an issue addressed in the main text, the notes provide references and suggestions for further thinking and reading. Although I encourage students to study—and appreciate scholars who work in—multiple languages, and although my own study and practice of Zen have been undertaken largely in Japanese, given the introductory nature of this book I have limited my references mainly to sources in English, except in cases where I am quoting from or drawing directly on a non-English source that has not been translated. I have noted cases where I have modified or redone existing translations, either to make them more faithful to the original or to make them fit with the conventions and style of this book. In cases where only a non-English source is cited for a quotation, translations are my own.

In the main text, Chinese, Japanese, Sanskrit, and other non-English terms are used sparingly. I have transliterated terms using the English alphabet and, except for macrons over certain Japanese vowels, I have not used diacritical marks. When original-language equivalents are provided for some key terms, and when it may not be clear from the context which language the terms are from, I use the following abbreviations: P. = Pali, Sk. = Sanskrit, Ch. = Chinese, Jp. = Japanese, Gk. = Greek, Ln. = Latin, and Gm. = German. To keep things simple, I use Sanskrit (e.g., Nirvana, *anatman*) rather than Pali (e.g., Nibbana, *anatta*) versions of equivalent terms, even when referring to teachings and texts from the Pali canon. For Chinese terms and names, the now standard Pinyin (instead of the older Wade-Giles) method of transliteration has been used. East Asian names are written in the order of family name first, except in cases where authors have used the Western order. In such cases, the original language order will be given in parenthesis after the first appearance of the name—for example, Shunryu Suzuki (Jp. Suzuki Shunryū) and D. T. Suzuki (Jp. Suzuki Daisetsu).

I use the familiar Anglicized Japanese term "Zen" throughout rather than "Chan," "Seon," or "Thien" when referring to the Chinese, Korean, and Vietnamese pronunciations of the same sinograph: 禪, simplified in modern Japanese as 禅. East Asian countries all adopted the sinographs, or Chinese characters, from China in ancient times. The Japanese language still uses them today. Sinographs for many key terms in Chinese and Japanese are provided in the index, as are diacritics for some key Pali and Sanskrit terms. Although there is no distinction between lowercase and uppercase letters in these languages, I frequently capitalize key terms in order to emphasize their importance and indicate respect—*not* in order to reify or deify their referents.

The chapters in this book are like summary snapshots of my current understanding of what I consider to be the most important and interesting topics in Zen practice and philosophy. I hope that readers will approach each chapter as an initiation and as an invitation to further study and practice, a portal through which they can access a field of inquiry and discussion. Scholars, practitioners, and other readers who want to broaden and deepen their study of Zen, or students who want to dig further into a specific topic for a research paper, can mine the notes of the chapters that address the topics in which they are most interested for sources and suggestions for further reading.

In the back of the book can be found discussion questions for each chapter. Professors may want to use these for assignments; general readers may want to peruse them in order to pique their interests and prep their minds before reading each chapter; study groups may want to use them to stimulate discussion of the main ideas in each chapter.

The chapters have been organized such that the book unfolds as a comprehensive introduction to the practice and philosophy of Zen. At the same time, each of the relatively brief chapters has been written such that it can be read on its own. Each chapter focuses on a single issue or cluster of ideas, which its title is meant to display. This means that readers don't necessarily need to read the whole book; they can easily zero in on the topics that most interest them by browsing the table of contents in the front of the book or the discussion questions in the back—or they can use the index to research specific terms and explore the ways in which they are discussed in various contexts across the book. Professors should be able to easily select a set of chapters to fit with the content of their courses and within the space available on their syllabi.

For example, readers interested mainly in practical instructions for meditation can focus on Chapters 3, 4, and 22. For readers interested in attaining a more accurate and in-depth understanding of topics that are popularly associated with Zen in the West (including meditation, oneness, karma, being in the zone, art, and kōans), I recommend Chapters 1, 3, 8, 15, 17, 19, and 22. Readers interested in a Zen interpretation of basic Buddhist teachings and in Zen's relation to other schools of Buddhism can focus on some or all of Chapters 5–7, 10–12, 15, and 23. Readers interested in interreligious dialogue between Zen and Christianity can focus on some or all of Chapters 1, 7–15, 21, and 23. Readers interested in specific areas of philosophical inquiry such as metaphysics, epistemology, ethics and society, or nature, art, and language can focus on a relevant selection from Chapters 2, 3, 8, 9, 11, 14–16, and 18–21.[4] Readers interested in the nature of the self (i.e., philosophical anthropology) can focus on Chapters 2, 7, 8, 9, 11, and 24. Those who want to cut to the chase and get a quick preview of the path of Zen as an "investigation into the self" can start with Chapter 2; then, if they want to get a fuller overview of the entire path of Zen, they could jump from there straight to Chapter 24.

Acknowledgments

Most of the first draft of this book was written during a sabbatical leave granted to me by Loyola University Maryland for the academic year 2018–19. That earlier and briefer version became the basis for a series of lectures recorded and released in video and audio formats under the title *Real Zen for Real Life* by The Teaching Company as part of their Great Courses series. I thank The Teaching Company for permission to publish a substantially reworked and expanded version of this material in the form of a book. I also thank The Teaching Company for, in the first place, convincing me to attempt to address a wider audience in a more direct and personal manner than I am used to doing in my more exclusively academic writing. I sincerely thank Peter Ohlin at Oxford University Press for taking an interest in and supporting the project, and Madeleine Freeman, Leslie Johnson, Koperundevi Pugazhenthi and others involved at OUP and Newgen for their congenial and careful work on its production.

Readers of this book may be surprised to learn that my personality inclines me to keep my most intimate thoughts and experiences to myself. Because of that inclination, combined with my enculturation in the self-effacing and reticent ethos of Japan, I have, up until this point, been hesitant to write directly about my practical experience of Zen. Yet, after my much more extroverted mother passed away in 2009, and then after I turned fifty a few years ago, I decided it was time to stick my neck out of my introverted shell and—as my brother Peter likes to say—to put myself out there, for better or for worse. I don't know if I have managed to find the appropriate middle way between the unwholesome and un-helpful extremes of being "stingy with the Buddha Dharma," on the one hand, and spreading "the stench of Zen" by flaunting my personal experience, on the other, but I have tried, with the hope that including some personal anecdotes and other autobiographical references along the way will make the book more engaging and thus more impactful.

I am accustomed to composing scholarly articles, and writing this book for a wider readership of students and lifelong learners has enabled me to find a more candid and straightforward voice, one that is somewhere in the triangulated middle of the academic voice I use when addressing other scholars, the peda-gogical voice I use in the classroom with college students, and the more inti-mate teaching and testimonial voice I use in meditation meetings with fellow practitioners. I thank my academic colleagues around the world, the many students I have been privileged to teach at Loyola University Maryland and in

Japan, and the members of The Heart of Zen Meditation Group for allowing me to cultivate these three voices. I now hope that the synthesis of these voices forged in the writing of this book manages to speak to the integrated body-heart-mind-spirit of its readers.

It is not possible to adequately acknowledge all the people who have aided me as I've walked and crisscrossed the paths of Zen and philosophy. I can only single out a few people and a few of the ways in which they have influenced and enabled me on this journey. I have dedicated this book to Tanaka Hōjū Rōshi and Ueda Shizuteru Sensei, who, as I stated on the dedication page, were pivotal to my practice and study of Zen, and thus to my life. The other Zen teacher to whom I am profoundly indebted is Kobayashi Gentoku Rōshi. After Tanaka Rōshi passed away in 2008, Kobayashi Rōshi became the abbot of the monastery at Shōkokuji in Kyoto. Having long known him as a monk, and for many years as the head monk at Shōkokuji, since 2008 I have continued my practice under his guidance during my periodic sojourns in Kyoto and during his mostly annual visits to Baltimore. Given that I am an academic philosopher by profession, Kobayashi Rōshi has made sure that my practice does not get overly mired down in "bookish Zen" (*moji Zen*).

The monks at Shōkokuji alongside whom I have had the privilege to practice over the last quarter of a century are too many to mention by name—most of whom, in any case, I only know by their monastery nicknames. The fellow lay practitioners and scholars of Zen with whom I have practiced and studied in Japan are also too many to list, though I would like to single out a few. Horio Tsutomu, one of Nishitani Keiji's last students, tutored me regularly on Nishitani's texts at Ōtani University while I was taking classes in Buddhist studies there from 1996 to 1998, before he graciously encouraged me to transfer to Kyoto University. A very accomplished lay practitioner, Professor Horio made the introductions necessary for me to begin my practice at Shōkokuji in 1996 as a member of the lay practitioner group, Chishōkai, whose past members have included eminent Kyoto School philosophers such as Nishitani Keiji, Tsujimura Kōichi, Ueda Shizuteru, Hanaoka Eiko, and Ōhashi Ryōsuke. It was inspiring to sit for many years in the same *zendō* (meditation hall) and even on the same well-worn cushions as these path-making predecessors, and an honor to sit alongside fellow inheritors of this lineage such as Akitomi Katsuya, Minobe Hitoshi, and Mizuno Tomoharu, as well as other "Way-friends" (Jp. *dōyū*) such as Steffen Döll, Yoshie Takami, and many others. I'd also like to mention in this context Professor Kataoka Shinji, a Chishōkai *daisenpai* (great predecessor) whom I never met, though I lived for a time in the same room of the head monk's quarters at Shōkokuji that he once occupied. A renowned lay Zen master and a professor of education at Kyoto University, it was Professor Kataoka who inspired Tanaka Rōshi to set out to become an "educator of educators." For most of the years I lived in Kyoto, Matsumoto Naoki served as the leader of Chishōkai. He and I spent many moons practicing together, including many long nights sitting side by side under the moon doing *yaza* (night sitting) during intensive meditation retreats (*sesshin*).

Again thanks to Professor Horio's mediation, I was able to participate in the last two annual meetings of the landmark Kyoto Zen Symposia in 1997 and 1998. It was there that I first met a number of leading scholars who would, over the years, become my good friends as well as mentors; these include John Maraldo, Mori Tetsurō, Thomas Kasulis, James Heisig, Rolf Elberfeld, Graham Parkes, Thomas Yūhō Kirchner, Matsumaru Hideo, Michiko Yusa (Jp. Yusa Michiko), and Fujita Masakatsu. Professor Mori does his Zen practice elsewhere, but I was able to study many Kyoto School and Zen texts with him and other members of the Kufūkai research group he leads. Although Professor Fujita is not a Zen practitioner, I learned a great deal from him about Nishida and other Kyoto School philosophers while I was a PhD student and later a postdoctoral research fellow in the Department of Japanese Philosophy at Kyoto University between 1998 and 2004.

Before moving to Kyoto in 1996, I lived in Osaka from 1990 to 1994. During those years I spent many evenings, weekends, and vacations "temple hopping." Among the places where I got my Zen practice under way was Shinshōji International Zen Training Monastery in Fukuyama, where I often spent several days, and sometimes several weeks, learning the basics of monastic life. One of the places I regularly attended meditation meetings near my home in Osaka was Shitennōji, an ancient temple complex founded by the legendary Prince Shōtoku in the sixth century. At the time, I was teaching at Shitennōji Buddhist University, where all classes begin with a brief meditation.

Nowadays, I must admit, I don't begin all my classes at Loyola University Maryland that way. However, I do offer students in my courses on Asian philosophies the option of doing a "meditation path," which requires them to regularly meditate on their own and with The Heart of Zen Meditation Group, and to reflect on their experience in relation to assigned readings. I am very grateful to Loyola for supporting my use of this experiential pedagogy, and, moreover, for providing me with the use of a chapel that has been beautifully renovated in a Japanese style with tatami mats and meditation cushions. My senior colleague Drew Leder has been a constant source of encouragement and support, as well as a co-conspirator in engaging our students in this holistic pedagogy, as has more recently my junior colleague Jessica Locke. Drew has also inspired and assisted me in incorporating an alternative "service-learning path" in some of my classes. To be able to discuss Buddhist texts and teachings together with some students who are meditating and others who are doing community service—is this not how it should be? It is certainly teaching me a lot.[5]

Let me thank by name some of the current regular participants in The Heart of Zen Meditation Group: Ethan Duckworth, Ed Stokes, Janet Preis, Mickey Fenzel, Janet Maher, Steve DeCaroli, Jeffrey McGrath, John Pie, Rhonda Grady, Bess Garrett, Susan Gresens, Phil Pecoraro, Carl Ehrhardt, Cheryl McDuffie, David Gordon, Bu Hyoung Lee, Ilona McGuiness, Drew Leder, and Rick Boothby. Former students who have continued or come back to sit with us include, among numerous others, Coleman Anderson, Patrick McCabe, Alex Kasinskas, Samantha Kehoe, Daniel Napack, and Will Stann. Among the many hundreds of other students who have participated in The Heart of Zen Meditation Group over the years, let me single out one of the very first: Luke Dorsey. Luke was one of my first students at Loyola and, to this day, maybe the most enthusiastic one. He even visited me in Kyoto one summer when I was staying in the monastery of Shōkokuji. I remember him patiently kneeling for nearly two hours listening to a talk by Ueda Sensei, of which he could understand not a word. I also remember taking a walk with him on the Kamo River and getting attacked from behind by a hawk trying to steal our ice cream sandwiches. After he graduated, Luke continued to attend our weekly meditation meetings in Baltimore—until he went to bed one New Year's Eve and never woke up. His picture adorns our group's altar, along with a picture of Michael Prenger, a buoyant and sturdy ship captain and a contagiously committed meditator who sat with us for several years prior to his passing, and a picture of Father Greg Hartley, a joyful Jesuit priest who ran a Zen meditation group at Loyola before I started teaching there in January 2005, and who suddenly died from a heart attack a month after I arrived. The "Heart" in the name of our group is, in part, a tribute to the legacy of Fr. Hartley.

Beyond Loyola, let me thank Kōshō Itagaki, Tetsuzen Jason Wirth, Shūdō Brian Schroeder, and Jien Erin McCarthy, together with whom I founded CoZen, a loosely organized group dedicated to bringing Zen practice and academic philosophy into a fruitful partnership. Participants in the CoZen Symposia I have led at Istmo—an idyllic retreat center in Panama run by my brother Sean and his wife, Ayesha—have included fellow philosopher-practitioners Carolyn Culbertson, Brad Park, Gereon Kuperus, and Matt Swanson, in addition to many of the CoZen and Heart of Zen Group friends already mentioned.

Among family members, as always, I'd like to thank my children, Toshi and Koto, as well as my brothers, Peter, Chris, and Sean. For this book, I'd like to single out the two most important women in my life: my mother, Barbara Stephen Davis (1938–2009), and my wife, Naomi Tōbō Davis. My mother was an open-minded spiritual seeker as well as a devout Christian. She always and unreservedly supported my philosophical pursuits and wandering ways, even when my spiritual quest led me to fly far away from the nest in which I was raised. Whatever regrets she had about our Episcopal church's failing to fully satisfy my search seemed to be redeemed by the vicarious joy with which she shared my journey into Zen practice. The connections I have more recently been able to make between some of the profoundest teachings of Zen and Christianity are inspired by her trust that, in due time, the bird will return to replenish the nest with foreign yet strangely familiar fruits.

I met my wife, Naomi, a few months after first moving to Japan in 1990, and she has been my daily source of sustenance—emotional as well as culinary—ever since. Naomi has not only passively endured but indeed actively enabled my long absences for monastic as well as academic reasons. Two episodes tell the story. About six months after we starting dating, I suddenly showed up at the office building where she worked, basically to beg her for money. Granted, I needed the dough for a noble purpose: to buy a train ticket to get to a Zen monastery and to make a donation to cover a month of training there. Nevertheless, I don't think this beggar boy managed to impress her upwardly mobile co-workers as a real catch of a boyfriend. And yet she stuck with me. Many years later, in 2006, with our two-and-a-half-year-old son Toshi in tow and our baby daughter Koto still in her belly, Naomi got left with her parents in Osaka while I spent the summer training at the monastery of Shōkokuji. And still she stuck with me. Before and after that, she has held down the fort on innumerable such occasions. When I was considering whether to take on the project that led to this book, it was Naomi who reminded me not only of Kobayashi Rōshi's support but also of Tanaka Rōshi's wish that I would help convey the spirit as well as teachings of Rinzai Zen to the wider world. While I am far from fulfilling his wish, I promise to continue along this path, and I hope that this book will serve others as a set of trail markers.

1

What Really Is Zen?

Recovering the Beginner's Open Mind

A Zen Master Gets Kicked Out of a "Zen" Restaurant

What we have made of "Zen" in the popular culture of the United States and other Western countries has often strayed quite far from its Asian roots. For example, a restaurant can spend tens of thousands of dollars on crafting a "Zen" atmosphere for its Western clientele, but if an actual Zen master from Japan were to dine there, would they even recognize him for what he is?

A few years ago, I took a visiting Japanese Zen master to an Asian-style restaurant in Las Vegas that claims to provide "spiritual dining" and even "vibe dining." Although I was skeptical about the spiritual vibe of the place, it turned out that they did serve delicious traditional Asian cuisine as well as innovative fusion dishes. The beautiful interior design was centered on an impressive twenty-foot-high statue of the Buddha, with other exquisite Buddhist images adorning the surrounding walls. Everything was rather amusing and enjoyable until . . . we got kicked out. I mean we got literally, physically, thrown out of the place.

The problem started when, after paying our bill, I left the Zen master alone in the dining hall while I went to use the restroom. Not surprisingly, he took the opportunity to take some pictures of the giant Buddha statue and the other Buddhist images. His fellow monks and temple parishioners back in Japan would surely be interested in seeing how figures from their tradition had been transplanted to this iconic American city. Yet by taking photographic mementos he was evidently violating the sacrosanct rule that "what happens in Vegas stays in Vegas."

I emerged from the restroom to find the Zen master being verbally accosted by a bouncer. I tried to intervene, telling the bouncer that my companion understood little English. The bouncer snapped back at me that he seemed to understand well enough when he was told the first time to stop taking pictures, and yet he continued to do it anyway. The irate man was in no mood to listen to my explanation that a smile and nod do not necessarily indicate understanding. I felt both alarm and disbelief when, together with the Zen master, I was forcibly

Zen Pathways. Bret W. Davis, Oxford University Press. © Oxford University Press 2022.
DOI: 10.1093/oso/9780197573686.003.0001

taken by the arm and pushed out the front door. The Zen master himself, unsurprisingly, remained calm throughout the ordeal and was both apologetic and amused after I explained to him what had just transpired.

What really is Zen? Does it have anything to do with the "journey into sensual bliss" advertised by this restaurant? Or does Zen have more to do with the sublime quietude and rustic naturalness of the Grand Canyon and Monument Valley that we experienced in the following days? Is it also found in the beauty of the sleek and simple design of an iPhone or the chic interior design of a loft apartment? Certainly, it has something to do with the alert yet unanxious state of mind demonstrated by the Zen master as he was being incomprehensively kicked out of a purportedly "Zen" restaurant.

The word "Zen" has been adopted into our everyday English vocabulary, yet part of its appeal is its residual unfamiliarity—its exotic and mystical ring. Around the world, in fact, foreign words often carry a peculiar rhetorical power, giving listeners the sense that the speaker knows more than they do about something important and profound. In Japan, advertisers and specialists in this or that field often pepper their speech with words borrowed from English. Such loan words seem especially meaningful precisely on account of the fact that people don't know exactly what they mean.

My favorite example—or, I should say, my least favorite example—of this rhetorical ploy is the use of the English expression "informed consent" by medical professionals in Japan. By not translating this technical term into Japanese when they are addressing, for example, an elderly man with little knowledge of English, they are, ironically, betraying precisely the principle the term is meant to convey, insofar as they are getting him to nod in acquiescence to something he doesn't really understand. Analogously, the use of the word "Zen" in the West is misleading, and even ironically contradictory, when it is intended to connote something foreign, exotic, mystical, or otherworldly, for in fact, Zen practice aims to bring us down to earth, to the here and now of our real lives, rather than to feed our fantasies of distant lands populated with sages dwelling in mysterious mists on magical mountaintops—and speaking like Yoda in *Star Wars*.

The allure of such Orientalist escapism is both exemplified and called into question by some of the books that initially sparked my own interest in Zen and other Asian religious traditions.[1] Somerset Maugham's *The Razor's Edge* and Hermann Hesse's *Siddhartha* are some of the books that inspired me as a restless twenty-year-old ready to head out in search of . . . I knew not yet what. Reading engaging novels like these, or maybe just seeing the movie versions, can, of course, be the occasion for embarking on a more serious "journey to the East." They may inspire one to read more scholarly books, to take up the practice of meditation, and perhaps even to live in an Asian country like Japan where one can study and practice Zen Buddhism in its traditional temples and monasteries, as I did for much of my twenties and thirties.

Another great novel I read between classes in college was Robert Pirsig's *Zen and the Art of Motorcycle Maintenance*. This book helps bring Zen down to earth, inspiring us to think outside the box—or between the lines of a motorcycle repair manual—in dealing with the nitty-gritty tasks and curveball situations of life. For all its merits, however, Pirsig's book only scratches the surface of the actual practice and thought of Zen. This has not prevented it from spawning a prolific and still proliferating cottage industry of books by authors with even less familiarity with actual Zen practice and thought.

A quick search on Amazon.com today will turn up books with titles such as *Zen Golf, Zen and the Art of Poker, Zen and the Art of Fundraising, Zen and the Art of Faking It*, my favorite, *Zen Puppies*, and my least favorite, *Zen as F*ck: A Journal for Practicing the Mindful Art of Not Giving a Sh*t*. As interesting, helpful, cute, or provocative as these books may be, for the most part they are only tangentially related to the actual practice and thought of Zen Buddhism; in some cases, they are even antithetical to it.

Zen as a Practice of Emptying One's Cup

We may need to clear our shopping carts, and we will certainly need to clear our minds, if we are going to learn about real Zen. In fact, the real practice of Zen is largely about clearing our hearts and minds. Actually engaging in this practice is vital to understanding what it is all about. As we will see, Zen meditation is a profoundly spiritual practice of "clearing the heart-mind." Metaphorically, this can be understood as a practice of "emptying one's cup."

101 Zen Stories, a small book published in 1919 as one of the first introductions of Zen to a Western audience, begins, very appropriately, with the following story about the need to "empty one's cup."

> Nan-in, a Japanese [Zen] master during the Meiji era (1868–1912), received a university professor who came to inquire about Zen.
>
> Nan-in served tea. He poured his visitor's cup full, and then kept pouring.
>
> The professor watched the overflow until he no longer could restrain himself. "It is overfull. No more will go in!"
>
> "Like this cup," Nan-in said, "you are full of your own opinions and speculations. How can I show you Zen unless you first empty your cup?"[2]

To properly set out on the path to Zen, we must empty our cups—in other words, we need to open our minds.

In fact, the idea of emptying one's cup goes deeper than even this story might suggest, since Zen meditation itself can be understood as a practice of "emptying one's cup." In other words, not just the way *to* Zen but the Way *of* Zen itself is a matter of continually emptying one's cup, clearing one's mind, and returning to what in Zen is called the "beginner's mind." The eighteenth-century Japanese Rinzai Zen master Tōrei echoes the twelfth-century Chinese Zen master Dahui's exhortation: "Do not lose the heart and mind of a beginner for an instant!"[3]

The modern Sōtō Zen master Shunryu Suzuki (Jp. Suzuki Shunryū) tells us, "If your mind is empty, it is always ready for anything; it is open to everything. In the beginner's mind there are many possibilities; but in the expert's mind there are few."[4] So if you feel like a total beginner at all this Zen stuff, that's great! Don't lose that feeling! The beginner's mind is an open mind. A know-it-all is incapable of learning anything.

To be sure, as the German philosopher Hans-Georg Gadamer points out, some of our preconceptions may be useful, as long as we are ready to revise them in the process of learning. The problem is not that we have prejudices (in the literal sense of pre-judgments) per se; the problem is what Gadamer calls "the tyranny of hidden prejudices"—in other words, the implicit biases that aren't brought out into the light so that they can be called into question and revised if necessary.[5]

The Greek philosopher Plato points out the paradox that, in trying to learn about something new, we need to already have some knowledge of what we are looking for. Otherwise, how would we even know what to look for, and how would we know when we've found it?[6] But the problem Zen calls our attention to is that we tend to think we know all too much about what we are looking for. The problem is that have lost the beginner's mind: our original and innocent openness to the world; our ability to see things afresh.

Debunking Medieval and Modern Reconstructions

When we open a book on Zen, we need to ask ourselves: What is already in our cup? What preconceptions about Zen fill our minds and will perhaps get in the way of, or distort, our learning about it? For example, some Westerners may still associate Zen with the counterculture movement of the 1960s and 1970s. Nowadays, Zen may be associated more often with hipster culture, or more broadly with metropolitan, upper- or upper-middle-class, highly educated, and mostly white people who regularly practice yoga, drink a lot of smoothies and kombucha, and identify as SBNR: "spiritual but not religious." In Western pop culture the word "Zen" often gets tossed into a conversation as a cool way of saying "cool" in the sense of laid-back and peaceful. Our often superficial and trivializing cultural appropriations of the term have also resulted in odd expressions, such as taking a break in a "Zen Den" (i.e., relaxation lounge) in order to "find my Zen" (i.e., destress and collect myself). In the Western imagination, "Zen" has connotations of hip and cool, liberal and progressive; it is thought to be a fashionable and easygoing spirituality with just the right touch of esoteric exoticism and none of the stuffy and constrictive baggage of dogmatic institutional religions.

In Japan, by contrast, Zen is generally associated with the strict discipline of a rigorous spiritual practice and also with a traditional, ritualistic, and culturally conservative religious establishment. You may be surprised to learn that, in Japan, "Christianity" has connotations of being modern and even fashionable. That is why, even though only around 1 percent of the Japanese population identifies as Christian, roughly half of Japanese couples today choose to have a Christian wedding ceremony. While, to the chagrin of generations of missionaries, 99 percent of Japanese have no interest in being baptized, most love the imagery and pageantry of a Christian wedding ceremony. Christianity is more likely to be associated with a white wedding dress and a white priest-for-hire than with the religious beliefs symbolized by the cross that adorns the charming wedding chapel.

Analogously, the cultural appropriation of "Zen" in the popular culture of the West has often been as superficial as it has been enthusiastic. However, in Western universities these days the pendulum has swung in the other direction; the current academic trend is to use historical and philological scholarship to criticize the idealized spiritual and romantic image of Zen fashioned by earlier generations of writers. In erudite books with clever titles like *Chan Insights and Oversights*[7] and *Seeing Through Zen*,[8] this critical—and sometimes polemical—debunking is aimed not only at the ways in which authors like D. T. Suzuki and Alan Watts have presented Zen to Westerners; it is also aimed at the traditional self-conceptions and self-presentations of the Zen tradition throughout its fifteen-hundred-year history in Asia.[9]

Applying the historical-critical methods of modern biblical studies, scholars of Buddhism—buddhologists—have shown that canonical Zen texts were in fact written down and revised by later generations of monks and literati rather than being literal transcripts of the words of the masters. To begin with, the story of Bodhidharma, who is said to have brought Zen from India to China sometime around 500 CE, has been revealed to be largely a symbolic fabrication by later generations, even if in part based on an actual historical person.[10] Moreover, much of the foundational Zen lore regarding the words and acts of the golden age of Zen masters in the Tang Dynasty (618–906 CE), it turns out, was edited and embellished by masters and other monks and literati in the Song Dynasty (960–1279). The narratives and teachings recorded in the *Transmission of the Lamp [of*

Enlightenment] literature[11]—from which the episodes and encounter dialogues that appear in the kōan collections were drawn—were subjected to revision not only for pedagogical purposes but also for the sake of pious hagiography and sectarian polemics.

Another classic case in point is the reconstructive origins of the canonical *Platform Sutra of the Sixth Patriarch*, which is attributed to the seventh-century Chinese Zen master Huineng but in fact seems to have first appeared around 780 CE, "over a century after the events it describes were supposed to have taken place."[12] The earliest versions of the autobiography and teachings of Huineng included in this text were in fact composed by Shenhui and other purported successors in the Southern School in order to differentiate their teachings from, and elevate them over, those of Shenxiu and other teachers of the rival Northern School. While the teachings presented in the *Platform Sutra*—the only Zen text to be audaciously designated a "sutra"—are indeed a "brilliant consummation" and "wonderful mélange of early Chan [i.e., Chinese Zen] teachings," they can hardly be attributed verbatim to the historical person Huineng.[13] However spiritually inspiring and philosophically rich such classical texts of the Zen tradition may be, we cannot read them as unbiased and unembellished historical records or as innocent of sectarian politics and other mundane motives.

What Is "Real Zen"? Engaging in a Hermeneutics of Both Faith and Suspicion

Well, then, what *does* it mean for us to talk about "real Zen"? As the subtitle of one of the best and most balanced books on this topic puts it: *Will the Real Zen Buddhism Please Stand Up?*[14] The author of that book, Steven Heine, does an admirable job of taking seriously both what he calls the "traditional Zen narrative" and modern "historical and cultural criticism" of Zen. I fully agree with Heine that we should take both of these approaches to Zen seriously. My intent in this book, however, is not just to take a balanced approach between repeating the traditional narratives from the inside and criticizing them from the outside. Rather, my emphasis will be on gleaning what remains viable and valuable in the traditional teachings of Zen after they have been put through the crucible of modern criticism and, moreover, as they are in the process of being transplanted into a modern Western cultural context. I am not just interested in academically learning *about* Zen; I am also—and, indeed, most of all—interested in personally learning *from* Zen. To borrow an expression from Gadamer, I want to take the "claim to truth" made by Zen teachings seriously, rather than assume that those teachings can be reduced to products of their historical and cultural contexts, or even to propaganda and rhetorical plays for attaining and maintaining power and prestige.[15]

Obviously, the Zen masters who appear in the lore of the tradition, and the monks and scholars who compiled, edited, and in some cases even pseudony-mously composed their words, were living in the real world of institutional and societal politics; mundane motives no doubt often clouded and sometimes corrupted their compassion-driven skillful means. Yet, to say that a sincere prac-tice of Zen requires "the passive submission to a hegemony, the unwitting con-traction of an intellectual pathology," is no more true than it would be to say that a sincere engagement in critical scholarship requires the passive submission to a cynical attitude, the unwitting contraction of a spiritual pathology.[16] Difficult as it may be, I think it is not impossible for the same person to be a scrupulous scholar and dedicated practitioner of Zen, and to let these two disciplines fruit-fully supplement and constructively critique each other.

The French philosopher Paul Ricoeur contrasts an affirmative "hermeneutics of faith," in which a reader attempts to retrieve and amplify the meaning implicit in a text, with a critical "hermeneutics of suspicion," in which a reader attempts to expose the clandestine motives and disguised meanings at work underneath the surface of a text.[17] Ricoeur argues that both interpretive approaches are nec-essary; his strategy is to take a "long detour" through the hermeneutics of sus-picion (especially that of Nietzsche and Freud) as a crucible through which the recovery of a purified hermeneutics of faith—a "post-critical, second naivety"—becomes possible. As a philosopher who is also a Christian, his overall project is to enable a "post-religious faith" by way of passing through an atheistic destruc-tion of idolatrous religion. For Ricoeur, this entails the renunciation of a religion centered on the image of an omnipotent Father who we are afraid will punish us and whom we petition to protect us. That false god of "accusation and consola-tion," Ricoeur contends, is dead or at least should be dying. But in the wake of the death of that god, he suggests, a revival of faith in a truly divine God of love and poietic creation becomes possible.[18]

Despite all the challenges and opportunities Zen Buddhism has faced in the modern era—including the rise of a more socially conscious and committed Engaged Buddhism, the breakdown of a clear distinction between monastics and lay practitioners, and the dissolution of gender discrimination in Western adaptations of Zen institutions (see Chapters 14, 16, and 18)—arguably there have not been any fundamental doctrinal challenges on a level comparable to the contemporary questioning of the very meaning of "God" by many progres-sive Christian theologians and philosophers.[19] A possible exception is a prefer-ence for metaphorical-psychological over literal-cosmological interpretations of Buddhist doctrines such as the Six Realms of Rebirth and the Pure Land by many modern Zen teachers, but even this is hardly without traditional precedent (see Chapters 12 and 23).

To find periods of radical doctrinal debate in the Buddhist tradition that are comparable in degree, if not content, to some of the debates occurring today among Christian theologians and philosophers, one may have to go all the way back to the split between the progressive Mahayana movement and the conservative schools that came to be called (critically and from a Mahayana perspective) "Hinayana" starting in the second and first centuries BCE (see Chapter 10), and to the debates given rise to by the "Third Turning of the Wheel of the Dharma" starting in the 3rd century CE (see Chapter 8).[20] Of course, there have been other major developments and debates in the history of the various traditions of Buddhism—for example, the incorporation of manual labor as a spiritual practice and the appreciation of the soteriological efficacy of nature in the Chinese formation of Zen (see Chapter 18), and the long-standing divergences (as well as convergences) between Zen and Pure Land Buddhism (see Chapters 10 and 12). As for the Buddha, although he was promoted to the status of a transcendent savior in some Mahayana Buddhist sutras and traditions, the ninth-century Chinese Zen master Huangbo taught that "the One Mind alone is Buddha"; his successor, Linji, went so far as to instruct us to "kill the Buddha" that we would encounter outside our own mind (see Chapter 11). Not surprisingly, the modern Japanese philosophers of the Kyoto School, steeped in Zen as well as in the most radical developments of Pure Land Buddhism, have been important dialogue partners for post-critical Christians in search of deeper understandings of the divine (see Chapter 21).

Even if Zen is not currently undergoing the same kind of core doctrinal crisis as Christianity is for some, we should pay attention to suspicious critiques as well as to sympathetic interpretations of the Zen tradition. Like Ricoeur, I think such critiques can help to purify the Zen tradition of problematic aspects and accretions, and thus allow for a more compelling contemporary understanding and appropriation of it. It is this kind of post-critical affirmative understanding and appropriation that is foregrounded in the present book, although sometimes critical concerns will also be raised—for example, in Chapter 15 when discussing the problem of "blaming the victim" that has sometimes tainted the teaching of karma; in Chapter 16 when discussing the inherent dangers in the teaching that enlightened persons may transgress the letter of the moral law in order to better express its spirit; and in Chapters 4 and 17 when warning of how Zen meditation and teachings of being in the zone of "no-mind" can be and have been misappropriated by corporate managers and military commanders.

As will be on display throughout this book, Zen has all along been an ironically "iconoclastic tradition." Some of its canonical stories include Bodhidharma (fifth–sixth centuries) telling Emperor Wu that he has gained no karmic merit from all of his meritorious activities, and that the most sacred truth is that that there is nothing sacred;[21] depictions of Huineng (seventh century) tearing up the sutras;[22] Linji (ninth century) encouraging his students to "kill the Buddha";[23] Ikkyū (fifteenth century) writing erotic poetry about his steamy love affair during the last decade of his life with a blind musician;[24] and "an older woman of Hara" (seventeenth century) boldly retorting "Hey, you aren't enlightened yet!" after she told the eminent master Hakuin of her luminously enlightening experience and he tested her by saying that "Nothing can shine in your asshole."[25] Contemporary Zen Buddhists should feel free to carry on this irreverent and iconoclastic tradition of destroying false idols of Zen—but only insofar as they have sufficiently imbibed its true spirit and are doing so in a genuine effort to keep it alive and let it thrive.

Of course, there will always be some sardonic scholars who are more interested in dismissively denouncing rather than critically reinvigorating the Zen tradition, and they will concentrate solely on suspiciously subjecting it to ideology critiques in Marxist, Freudian, Foucauldian, and other terms that are imposed upon it from the outside. Zen's appeals to direct experience and even its legendary iconoclasm, they will say, are disingenuous strategies for gaining and maintaining personal and institutional power and prestige.[26] Such polemicists hunker down in a hermeneutics of suspicion vis-à-vis Zen, although presumably—unless they are committed and consistent cynics—they too use a hermeneutics of faith when looking elsewhere for truths that they can live by.

By contrast, the main interpretive stance of the present book is that of trust—and growing confidence—that the teachings of the Zen tradition do in fact have something to teach us and that its practices are in fact worthy of being practiced. Although I do endeavor to heed what philologists, historians, and cultural critics have revealed by way of maintaining a critical distance and looking at Zen through the lenses of a hermeneutics of suspicion, my own approach to Zen—both in my life and in this book—is more that of a philosopher and practitioner who engages with Zen in search of truths that I can live by. I am, as it were, more interested in standing on—and leaping off from—the shoulders of spiritual giants than I am in chipping away at their feet in search of their Achilles heels in order to score scholarly points.

Nevertheless, taking Zen's lessons seriously need not entail taking Zen's lore literally. After all, the texts of the Zen tradition were not written as academic history books. John Maraldo's judicious and insightful *The Saga of Zen History and the Power of Legend* makes a compelling case for treating the traditional chronicles and lore of Zen as I do in this book—namely, as soteriological or liberating "legends" rather than as literal accounts of "history" in the modern academic sense uncritically assumed by many modern scholars "who seek only the facts behind the texts and devious motives behind the facts." Maraldo shows how such critics tacitly meld a deconstruction of the historical factuality of Zen stories with a presumption to be able to see into the storytellers' minds and unveil their "true intentions" and "clandestine agendas," which are generally claimed to be such mundane motives as securing prestige, power, profit, or patronage. Maraldo argues that when they pretend to be able to know the implicit intentions behind the printed words of Zen texts, these critics ironically presume to possess epistemic powers on par with the Zen masters they seek to deflate and dethrone: "When these sleuths suggest that certain traditional Chan writers were out to dupe their audience, or when they read authors as acting in bad faith, they verge on a mind-reading that surpasses any mere 'pointing to the human mind.'"[27]

Thankfully, not all historians of Zen presuppose a simplistic "fact versus fiction" dichotomy and proceed to reveal the facts and debunk the fictions. Indeed, Maraldo quotes the "patriarch of Chan studies, Yanagida Seizan," as writing:

> One who knows only how to repudiate and dismiss the stories as factually unhistorical is not qualified to read the lamp histories [of the Chan/Zen tradition]. . . . [The historian] can clarify the historically and socially religious nature of the people who fabricated them and can lay bare a historicity [*shijitsu*] of a different dimension than so-called historical fact.[28]

Maraldo also quotes a comparable passage from John McRae, a prominent historian of Zen who studied under Yanagida, and who called his teacher "the greatest scholar of Chinese Chan of the twentieth century." Despite the fact that, as Maraldo points out, McRae himself often seems to equivocate over whether to dismissively debunk or positively reappraise Zen narratives as fabricated histories, he forcefully endorses Yanagida's sensibly sympathetic stance when he writes of the *Platform Sutra*:

> A journalist would say that the entire work is a web of lies. It would be unfair to discount the *Platform Sutra* in this fashion; rather, it is the fictional quality of the text that renders it important, that makes it true. To be sure, almost all the details of the text's charming story are untrue, but the fact that it was the product of a fertile literary imagination—and that it was enthusiastically adopted by centuries of Chinese Buddhists—implies that it was more representative of the deepest religious sensibilities of the Chinese people than a journalistically accurate account could ever have been.[29]

I ask the reader to bear in mind that, throughout the present book, the stories of Zen are treated as *liberating legends* rather than as literal records of historical facts. Regardless of whether past practitioners made or maintained precisely such a distinction, we should read them more as praxis-parables than as historical chronicles. When reading a parable, it does not matter so much whether the events actually happened exactly as they are being told, or even if they happened at all.

It is true that the idea of a lineage of "mind-to-mind transmission" from Shakyamuni down to present-day Zen masters plays a central doctrinal and institutional role in the tradition, yet this idea need not be taken too literally. I concur with Maraldo when he writes that

> the ritual chanting of a Chan [and Zen] lineage may be understood to open an experience of continuity with "the buddhas and patriarchs of old," rather than as representing an acceptance of (mistaken) historical genealogy. What lineage chanting brings about is not naïve belief in a line of ancestor Chan [and Zen] masters, but a sense of the continuity and communality of practice.[30]

To be sure, many in the past and some still in the present do take the lineage legends literally, and contemporary practitioners should heed the lessons of recent historical scholarship on such matters. Still, it is important to bear in mind that the context and aims of the ancient chroniclers were never the same as those of contemporary academic historians, and the baby of spiritual practice should not be thrown out with the bathwater of discovered historical inaccuracies and disclosed political machinations.

However important a role lineage has played in the Zen tradition, it has never been a historically based religion in the same sense as are the Abrahamic faiths. To begin with, it should be pointed out that "Dharma transmission" in Zen is really a matter of "recognition" of spiritual awakening, not the literal transference of anything, such as a robe and bowl, an esoteric teaching or ritual, or even a secret handshake or bowing technique. What is most important to practitioners is awakening itself, not the recognition they receive, however important the latter may be for the purposes of establishing teaching credentials and preserving institutional continuity. After all, one of the greatest Japanese Zen masters and the revitalizer of the Rinzai Zen institution, Hakuin, apparently never officially received a "seal of certification" (*inka shōmei*) from any of the teachers he studied under, even though all Rinzai Zen masters today trace their transmission lineage back to and through him. (Note that "Dharma transmission" [*shihō*] in the Sōtō school occurs at a much earlier stage in training and thus implies a lower level of recognition and authorization. The various Zen schools employ different systems of ceremonial ranks and qualifications for teaching, and today these are undergoing further modifications, especially in the West.)

Moreover, although transmission lineages in Zen begin with the Seven Buddhas of Antiquity, the seventh of which is Shakyamuni Buddha, many Zen practitioners do not understand the core of their practice to depend on the historical existence of even Shakyamuni Buddha, much less the six mythical Buddhas that are said to have preceded him. If historical scholarship were to one day prove that Jesus was a fictional character made up by the authors of the New Testament, that would be doctrinally devastating to Christianity. Christians would have to fundamentally rethink their understanding of the Incarnation as a unique historical event. By contrast, many Zen Buddhists have said that even were it to be revealed someday that Shakyamuni Buddha did not exist as a historical person, the core teachings and practices of Zen Buddhism would remain unaffected.[31] Shakyamuni, after all, was one of countless Buddhas, and we are all endowed with the potential to become Buddhas ourselves. For Zen Buddhism, historical narratives do matter; stories of the "transmission of the lamp" of the awakened mind down through the ages constitute the narrative thread that holds the history of Zen together, supporting the continuity and authority of its institutional tradition. But what matters *most* to many sincere Zen practitioners, especially today, is how the teachings and practices embedded in those stories can illuminate and change our lives—not when, where, and by whom they were first taught and written down.

Real Zen, for Contemporary Westerners, Must Be Contemporary Western Zen

The "real Zen for real life" that I attempt to articulate in this book might be understood by some scholars to be more of an interpretive product of "Zen Buddhist modernism" than an exact replica of "traditional Zen Buddhism."[32] In some respects—such as in an emphasis on teachings and practices over lineages and institutions—I affirm that this is indeed the case. In other respects, however, it is not. Often I chart a course between the proponents and critics of Buddhist modernism. For example, I do not claim that Zen Buddhism is entirely compatible with, much less proven by, the latest developments in modern Western physical and cognitive sciences—even while I acknowledge that there are intriguing parallels and connections deserving of cooperative and critical dialogue.[33] Also, while I am myself a participant in the modern movement of Zen beyond the walls of the monastery and into lay life, in Chapter 3 I'll express some serious reservations about the secularization and instrumental uses being made of Zen and other forms of Buddhist mediation in the current mindfulness movement.

While I share some concerns with the critics of Buddhist modernism, and while I am certainly interested in correctly understanding what Zen Buddhism has meant for others in the past, I am most interested in what it can mean for us today. The living tradition of Buddhism has always been concerned with applying traditional teachings to the here and now of people's real lives, rather than with preserving those teachings as relics in a museum or transcribing them as chronicles in a history book. In modern times, can real Zen be anything but modern Zen? If real Zen is living Zen, then it must always be contemporary Zen. We do not live in ninth-century China or in thirteenth-century Japan. We have a lot to learn from Zen masters who did live then and there, but in the end we must apply their lessons to our lives here and now.

Moreover, just as Buddhism was Sinicized in China and Japanized in Japan, over time it should be, and is already being, Americanized in America. The pre-eminent scholar of Buddhist modernism, David McMahan, writes:

> We can surely dispense with the myth of the pure original to which every adaptation must conform. . . . Every extant form of Buddhism has been shaped and reconfigured by the great diversity of cultural and historical circumstances it has inhabited in its long and varied existence.[34]

The question is not *whether* but *how* Buddhism will change as it enters further into Western societies. Will it "bring novel conceptual resources to the West and the modern world that might indeed offer new perspectives on some of modernity's personal, social, political, and environmental ills," or will it "accommodate itself so completely to mainstream western values and assumptions that it no longer is an alternative to them and thus accedes the resources it has for critiquing them"?[35]

The celebrated modern Vietnamese Zen master Thich Nhat Hanh has contributed as much as anyone to the modernization and Westernization of Zen Buddhism, letting it flourish in a new time and place without compromising its core teachings. He wrote the following words of admonition and encouragement:

> Buddhism is not one. The teaching of Buddhism is many. When Buddhism enters one country, that country always acquires a new form of Buddhism. . . . Buddhism, in order to be Buddhism, must be suitable, appropriate to the psychology and the culture of the society that it serves. . . . I think we can learn from other Buddhist traditions, but you have to create your own Buddhism.[36]
>
> One cannot become a practitioner of Zen just by imitating the way of eating, sitting, or dressing of Chinese or Japanese practitioners. Zen is life, Zen does not imitate. If Zen is to fully take root in the West, it must acquire a Western form, different from Oriental Zen.[37]

That said, the difficulty is to carry out this Western appropriation and recreation in ways that are fruitful and, insofar as we are going to continue to call it Zen Buddhism, in ways that remain true to the core teachings and practices of that tradition as it originated and developed in Asian countries. Buddhism was first introduced to China around the first century CE, yet it took many centuries before it was not only properly understood but also creatively appropriated. Even if the speed and ease of transferring information and engaging in intercultural exchange have been greatly enhanced by modern technology, an "appropriate appropriation" of a deep and vast tradition like Zen Buddhism takes at least several generations. This is the ongoing project to which I am attempting to make a small contribution by writing this book.

Starting in the sixth century in China, Zen was formed by way of a creative synthesis of Buddhist teachings and practices imported from India with the Chinese traditions of Confucianism and especially Daoism. Centuries later, starting in the twelfth century, Zen was brought to Japan, where for eight centuries it has developed in conjunction with Japanese culture and Shintō sensibilities. Over the course of the last century, Zen has been imported to the United States and other Western countries, initially from Japan and later also from Korea, China, and Vietnam.

In the West, and in Asian countries such as Japan that have internalized a dialogue with Western culture and thought, Zen has continued its development, now in conversation with German Idealism, English Romanticism, American Transcendentalism, medieval Christian mysticism, modern psychology, and other such philosophical, religious, and scientific schools. The teachings of Zen have been deployed in opposition to both religious fundamentalism and anti-religious secularism. They have also been used to critique consumerism, technological destruction of and alienation from nature, and other perceived ills of the dominant and domineering worldviews and lifestyles of the modern West. All of this is now part of the ongoing development of Zen as a living and increasingly cross-cultural tradition.

Realizing Zen: Understanding and Actualizing It Here and Now

The modernization and even Westernization of Zen is thus not necessarily a bad thing. Indeed, Zen can only become real for many of us today insofar as we allow this Asian tradition to take root in our real lives in the modern Western and Westernizing world. The twentieth-century Japanese Zen philosopher Nishitani Keiji liked to use the English verb "to realize," since this word can mean both "to attain an understanding" and also "to make real" or "to actualize."[38] In this double sense, our task is to *realize* what Zen is. On the one hand, this means understanding what it has been, which requires opening our minds and trying our best to understand the teachings and practices passed down by Chinese,

Japanese, Korean, and Vietnamese masters. On the other hand, in order to fully realize what those teachings and practices can mean for us, we have to relate them to, and enact them in, our real lives.

It is true that, as contemporary critics are fond of pointing out, there is much magic and mischief to be found in the history and lore of the Zen tradition, just as there is in all religious traditions. As we attempt to figure out what Zen has meant for others and what it can mean for us, we have to constantly ask ourselves: What is the vital core, the beating heart of the teachings and practices of Zen? What are the teachings and practices that may well challenge and change the way we think and live? And what are the extrinsic limbs that happen to have grown out of, or been attached to, Zen in particular times and places? What aspects of the tradition may need to be altered, or even amputated, in order to fruitfully realize Zen here and now?

Stuff changes. That is certainly a core Zen Buddhist teaching. One of the unchanging laws of the universe is that everything changes—at least the law of impermanence is permanent! But change can be for the better or for the worse. Usually it is a mixed bag of both. In the case of the Asian-style restaurant in Vegas, the sushi innovations were great, but the attitude of the bouncer was, it is fair to say, not very Zen—or even very "Zen."

In this book, I invite the reader to dig beneath the chatter about "Zen" in our popular media and get at the "real Zen." But, again, what does it mean to speak of the real Zen? Is there some essential core of Zen that is true for all times and places? In a sense, the Zen tradition suggests that there is indeed: it is the same insight into the nature of the self and world that the Buddha experienced, that each subsequent Ancestor in the "mind-to-mind transmission" or "transmission of the lamp [of the awakened mind]" experienced, and that we, too, can experience. Zen kōans are the often enigmatic and paradoxical stories, dialogues, sayings, or questions assigned as topics of meditation and used to trigger and test a student's awakening. To attain such an awakening, we are told that we must "interlock our eyebrows" with past Zen masters and learn to see with their eyes.

And yet the Zen tradition also recognizes that its universal and timeless truths must manifest themselves differently by different people in different times and places. Zen is neither a matter of subjective opinion nor a matter of objective doctrine; it is a matter of universal truths manifesting in ways and words appropriate to particular times and places. What we are called on to do is to understand the real teachings and practices of Zen in a manner that is appropriate for us here and now.

The term "real" in our quest for "real Zen" thus cuts both ways. On the one hand, we are not trying to flee our present circumstances and transport ourselves back in time to another age or across the ocean to another land. Nor are we just interested in a detached study of the history of other people's beliefs and practices. We want to know what Zen can mean for our own lives. On the other hand, however, we want to set aside our prejudices and preconceptions in order to open ourselves to what Zen masters who lived in the past and in distant lands have to teach us. We will inevitably need to meet them in the middle, so to speak, but getting there requires that we question our presuppositions, not just about Zen but also about ourselves. We especially need to be open to the possibility that Zen may be able to teach us about ourselves.

In this book, I hope to inspire you to realize not only what Zen *has been* for others but also what it *can be* for you. Real Zen is about *your* real life, not just about the lives of people living far away or long ago. Nevertheless, we have much to learn from the teachings of legendary Zen masters, and also from the generations of often anonymous monastics and lay practitioners who refined and reformulated their teachings. The chapters in this book will not only explain the philosophical teachings of Zen but also offer instructions on how to put those teachings into practice, starting with the practice of meditation.

Practicing Zen While Engaging in Interreligious Dialogue

The practice of Zen can be, and has been, undertaken by persons of various religious and secular worldviews. Zen meditation, or *zazen*, is practiced today by many Jews, Christians, and people of other faiths, by people who do not consider themselves "religious" at all, and by many people who consider themselves "spiritual but not religious."

In *Buddhism Without Beliefs* and *Secular Buddhism*, the contemporary author and former Korean Zen monk Stephen Batchelor argues that the core teachings and practices of Buddhism do not depend on any religious beliefs or traditional rituals.[39] Accordingly, he thinks they are well suited to people who are looking for a spiritual path without all the religious traps and trappings. On the other hand, a modern Japanese Zen master, Yamada Kōun, used to tell his Christian students in effect: I don't want you to practice Zen to become a Buddhist; I want you to practice Zen to become a better Christian. Some of his Christian students are Catholic priests and nuns who became Zen teachers without ceasing to be Christians.[40] We'll reflect on Zen's relation to Christianity in a number of chapters of this book (especially Chapter 12 but also Chapters 7–11, 13–14, 21, and 23). We'll see how—as D. T. Suzuki and the philosophers of the Kyoto School have long pointed out—some of the most radical teachings of Christian mystics like Meister Eckhart resonate deeply with Zen.[41] And we'll see how some of the core teachings of the Bible itself, such as "Love your neighbor as yourself," do as well.

However, when D. T. Suzuki writes that "Zen is the ultimate fact of all philosophy and religion," his affirmation of these interreligious resonances raises eyebrows together with questions.[42] The claim he is making is that while other philosophies and religions reflect only a partial grasp of the truth, Zen presents us with the naked truth itself. This inclusive yet marginalizing form of religio-centrism is not unlike the theological reforms made in Vatican II, when the Catholic Church moved away from its exclusionary traditional doctrine of *extra ecclesiam nulla salus* (outside the church, there is no salvation) and acknowledged that other religious traditions do "reflect a ray of that Truth which enlightens all men." Nevertheless, the Church still maintains that the full light of that Truth and "the fullness of religious life" is found only in Christ.[43] According to the doctrine of *preparatio evangelica*, the true elements of non-Christian religions are affirmed as merely provisional preparations for receiving the full truth of the Christian gospel.[44]

Such *marginalizing inclusiveness* is certainly better than *damning exclusiveness*, yet it still privileges one religious tradition and sidelines others. Moreover, it tends to cover over the real, and perhaps even core, differences between traditions. It is for this reason that I cannot agree with the approach D. T. Suzuki takes when he writes:

> Zen is not necessarily the fountain of Buddhist thought and life alone; it is very much alive also in Christianity, Mahommedanism, in Taoism, and even in positivistic Confucianism. What makes all these religions and philosophies vital and inspiring, keeping up their usefulness and efficiency, is due to the presence in them of what I may designate as the Zen element.[45]

This view of other religions as less pure expressions of Zen is the mirror image of the theologian Karl Rahner's view of adherents of other religions as "anonymous Christians." Rahner means by this locution that while the virtues and truths that these people of other faiths manifest attest to the fact that they have received the grace of Christ outside the church, they have not yet recognized Christ as the source of that grace. Fellow theologian Hans Küng rejects the arrogance of identifying people as Christians who do not identify themselves as such, and yet he agrees that all good people of other faiths are destined to become Christians. More liberal theologians, such as Paul Knitter, go beyond acknowledging that other religions possess "elements of goodness and truth" and claim that they are legitimate ways to salvation (or liberation) in their own right. Critically discussing these official and unofficial Christian views, theologian John Cobb argues that the main aim of interaction among religions should no longer be conversion, or even just mutual understanding, but rather "mutual transformation." Christians can become better Christians, and Buddhists can become better Buddhists, if they listen to and learn from one another.[46]

As someone who is politically committed to liberal democracy, I think that, as a society, we should *legally* treat all religious beliefs and practices equally, so long as they are not encouraging or enabling people to harm others. Moreover, I think that care should be taken to place religions on an equal footing in academic contexts as well as in interreligious dialogue. I also think that believers and practitioners should engage in interreligious dialogue with an attitude of openness to the possibility of not only supplementing their own beliefs and practices but also changing them.[47]

Nevertheless, this does not mean that on a personal-existential level, as a philosopher and truth-seeker, I assume or maintain that all religions are equally valid or valuable. Nor do I assume that they are all, at bottom, saying the same thing—much less that any one of them has a monopoly on purely expressing that one thing. I study and practice Zen Buddhism because I experience it as illuminating and liberating. I remain personally engaged with this tradition because I continue to experience it as capable of leading me to truth and liberation, rather than, for example, because it is the tradition that I happen to have been raised in or the one that is most socially convenient for me to adhere to. At the same time, I continue to engage in dialogue with other religious and philosophical traditions in order to deepen and enrich my understanding of both Zen and those other traditions. I continue to engage in interreligious critical thinking and dialogue not only in order to understand others and their other traditions; I do so also, and even first of all, in order to deepen and enrich my understanding of the truth about myself and the world.

The Nature of This Book

The chapters of this book reflect my own back-and-forth movement between Eastern and Western traditions and cultures, which I hope will make the study and practice of Zen more accessible and engaging to you. In the end, it is up to you to appropriate the teachings and practices of Zen in terms and ways that make the most sense to you given your context and conditioning.

For some of you, this might entail considering how to relate Zen to a committed or complicated relationship you have with the religious tradition (or nonreligious or anti-religious climate) in which you were raised. Personally, in my early twenties I found myself drawn to Zen at the same time as I found myself unsatisfied with Christianity as I knew it. However, through the practice and study of Zen I found new eyes for the depth of some core Christian teachings that I had previously understood only in superficial or literalistic terms. In this book I will frequently reflect on the relation between Zen and Christian teachings, and will also often make reference to other religious, secular, and philosophical ideas.

Some of these ideas may be new to you, and I hope that the ones that are already familiar to you will appear in a fresh light when seen from the perspective of Zen Buddhist teachings and practices. (I once translated for a Japanese Zen master in Germany who picked out passages from the Bible and explained how he understands them as Zen kōans!)

I have written this book as a philosophy professor, as an academic scholar, and as a practitioner and teacher of Zen. You can read the book to learn about the teachings and practices of Zen, and you can also—to whatever extent you feel appropriate—use it to experiment with its practices, especially the practice of meditation. This book is an invitation to engage in the practice of Zen as well as to learn about its philosophical articulations and implications.

In the middle of Chapter 2, I'll ask you to pause to undertake a brief meditation. Chapter 3 will discuss the nature of Zen meditation, and Chapter 4 will provide practical instructions for beginning a routine practice of it. The different methods of meditation practiced in the Sōtō and Rinzai schools of Japanese Zen will be discussed in Chapter 22.

Although I have written the book as an organically integrated introduction to the whole of Zen practice and philosophy, I have also tried to make each chapter intelligible on its own. So if you don't have time to read the whole book, feel free to pick out those chapters that most appeal to you—in the Preface I gave some indications of how you might do this.

This first chapter has been largely preparatory. We have reflected on what some of our presuppositions about Zen may be so that we can "empty our cups"—that is, so that we can clear our minds and recover a beginner's mind. Most importantly, you have learned that emptying your cup, regaining and realizing the beginner's mind, is a crucial component of practicing any of the "thousand paths" of the Zen Way.

2

Previewing the Path of Zen

Know Thyself, Forget Thyself, Open Thyself

We talk about ourselves all the time: "I am this, I am that." We check our appearance in the mirror and we pose for selfies. Social media encourages us to
become almost obsessed with portrayals of our self-identities. And yet, for all
that, we rarely step back and deeply reflect on the question "Who really am I?"
For that matter: "What really am I?" In my concern with my appearances, and
with presenting my identity to others, have I perhaps been covering over, perhaps even suppressing, these more profound existential questions?

Who am I? What am I? These simple and direct yet somehow unnerving
questions are found in the titles of two books published by a celebrated modern
Zen philosopher, Ueda Shizuteru.[1] I was fortunate enough to study with
Professor Ueda in Japan, both in academic contexts and at Shōkokuji Monastery
in Kyoto, where, after meditation sessions, he gave monthly talks on Zen classics.

During the many years I lived in Japan, I of course learned a lot about Japanese
culture and customs. But studying and practicing Zen taught me first and foremost the importance of learning about myself. To begin with, I became more
aware of the various ways in which I present myself in different circumstances.
For example, I introduce myself in some contexts as a philosophy professor, in
other contexts as a practitioner and teacher of Zen, and in still other contexts
as a husband, a father, a brother, a US citizen, and so on. We all carry around a
number of identity boxes, and we habitually define ourselves and others with the
labels on these boxes. In fact, life in society requires that we do so.

Yet do any of these boxes, or even all of them added up together, exhaustively
define who we are? Are we just the sum total of all the labels we put on ourselves?
In this chapter, I'd like us to dig deeper than the kind of self-introductions you'd
find on a business card, webpage, or resume, deeper than how you might present
yourself to a new neighbor at a barbeque or to a stranger on an airplane. Even
deeper than you would to a psychologist. Toward that end, I will introduce you to
the path of Zen as a path that begins with the injunction to know oneself.

The fourteenth-century Japanese Zen master Daitō Kokushi called the practice of Zen an "investigation and clarification of the matter of the self."[2] Such an
investigation may at first seem unnecessary, because we all tend to assume that
we already know ourselves, and so we generally neglect to even ask the question,

Zen Pathways. Bret W. Davis, Oxford University Press. © Oxford University Press 2022.
DOI: 10.1093/oso/9780197573686.003.0002

much less succeed in finding the answer. Indeed, you might be thinking right now: "Of course there are a lot of things that I don't know much about, but I do at least know myself." Nevertheless, in this chapter I will invite you to reflect more deeply on the question of how well you really do know who or even what you are.

The injunction to know oneself can be found in many traditions, including the Western philosophical tradition that goes back to Socrates. According to Zen, however, to truly discover what the self is, we need a more direct path than mere intellectual reasoning. The best path to attain an intuitive knowledge of ourselves is a holistic practice of meditation. Later on in this chapter I will invite you to pause, put down this book, and undertake a brief and simple meditation. (In subsequent chapters you will learn in detail about how and why to practice Zen meditation.)

In this chapter, drawing on an ancient Daoist text that influenced the development of Zen Buddhism in China, I will introduce Zen meditation as a kind of "emptying" or "fasting" of the mind that cleanses our consciousness, freeing us from the "boxes" of hardened prejudices and preconceptions that normally constrict and contort our perceptions and thoughts. Reflecting on the experience of meditating in this manner, I'll talk about the problem of what I call "karmic editing." What I mean by "karmic editing" is the way our habits of mind restrict and even distort our perception of the world. I'll explain how this problem is addressed by Zen meditation as a clearing and cleansing of the heart and mind.

All of this will prepare us to reflect, at the end of this chapter, on a famous passage written by the thirteenth-century Zen master Dōgen. Dōgen says that the path of Zen begins as a practice of meditation that "turns the light of the mind around on itself." This leads—paradoxically yet demonstrably—to a profound "forgetting of the self" that opens us up to everything else that's going on in the world around us.

Know Thyself: A Teaching from Many Traditions

Some version of the spiritual quest as an "investigation into the self" can, in fact, be found in all the great philosophical and religious traditions of the world. In the *Daodejing*, the foundational text of Daoism—a tradition that greatly influenced the development of Zen in China—we read: "Those who know others are knowledgeable; [yet] those who know themselves are enlightened."[3] In India, the eighth-century Hindu sage Shankara instructed earnest students to meditate on the question "Who am I?"[4] Although he speaks of "God" rather than "Buddha," Gandhi—whom Martin Luther King Jr. called "the greatest Christian of the twentieth century" even though he was a Hindu[5]—speaks of the great spiritual search for the true self in words that could be easily mistaken for those of a Zen master:

> The purpose of life is undoubtedly to know oneself. We cannot do it unless we learn to identify ourselves with all that lives. The sum total of life is God.... The instrument of this knowledge is boundless, selfless service.[6]

In the Western tradition as well, both the importance and the difficulty of attaining self-knowledge have often been recognized. Benjamin Franklin wrote: "There are three Things extremely hard, Steel, a Diamond, and to know one's self."[7] In his poem "Gnothi Seauton," Ralph Waldo Emerson tells us to look for God not up in the heavens but deep within our own hearts—for in truth, he says, "God dwells in thee."[8] Emerson is practically quoting from the New Testament here: St. Paul says that "God's Spirit dwells in you."[9] In his *Confessions*, St. Augustine laments that he had been "searching for you outside myself and failing to find the God of my own heart."[10] The prophet Muhammad is reported to have said: "He who knows himself knows his Lord."[11]

In addition to Christianity, Emerson's Transcendentalism was influenced by Hindu philosophies that directly link the true self, the *Atman*, with the divine source of the universe, *Brahman*. But the title of Emerson's poem, "Gnothi Seauton," is neither Christian nor Hindu; it is an ancient Greek proverb that means "Know thyself." This proverb was inscribed in the forecourt of the Temple of Apollo at Delphi. Ever since Socrates made frequent references to it, "know thyself" has been used as a motto for philosophical inquiry in the Western tradition.

In Plato's dialogue *Phaedrus*, Socrates says that one should not waste one's time on investigating mythological stories of gods and other unusual creatures:

> I have no leisure for them at all, and the reason, my friend, is this: I am not yet able, as the Delphic inscription has it, to know myself; so it seems to me ridiculous, when I do not yet know that, to investigate [such] irrelevant things.[12]

This would be a good point at which to acknowledge that many Westerners are interested in Zen more out of a kind of curiosity about something that seems exotically foreign and mystical than out of a genuinely philosophical and spiritual quest for self-understanding. If such cultural curiosity—or what might even be dubbed "spiritual tourism"—were our sole motivation for learning about Zen, Socrates would rightly scold us and tell us that we should first and foremost strive to know ourselves.

Another lesson from Socrates also resonates deeply with Zen. Socrates reminds us that a genuine quest for self-knowledge begins with the realization that we don't already know who or even what we are. The journey to wisdom begins with an acute awareness of one's ignorance. This is the first lesson Socrates teaches in Plato's *Apology*. The oracle at Delphi had proclaimed Socrates to be the wisest man in Athens. He was puzzled by this and set out to prove the oracle wrong by finding someone wiser. Yet he came to realize that he was in fact wiser than others, because while they were ignorant but thought they were wise, he at least knew that he was ignorant.[13]

Socrates's teaching once again resonates around the globe with a line from the *Daodejing*: "To know that one does not know is best; not to know but to believe that one does is a disease."[14]

A Zen Master Quotes Socrates to a Western Philosopher

Another chapter of the *Daodejing* tells us, "Those who study [doctrines and rituals] increase day by day, while those who practice the Way, the *Dao*, decrease day by day."[15] Instead of accumulating more and more information, Daoist sages practice letting go of unnecessary mental and emotional baggage, clearing their minds and hearts of all excess clutter, until they are able to wander freely in attunement with the natural Way or *dao* of the world. Among the many teachings that Zen inherits from the Daoist tradition is this emphasis on a return to simplicity and naturalness.

I tell meditators that I hope they leave the meditation room each day with less, not more, than they came in with: less stress, less mental clutter and emotional agitation, fewer attachments and prejudices—in short, fewer of the things that close, rather than open, our hearts and minds.

In Chapter 1, I told the story of a university professor who visited a Zen master and was taught that he must first "empty his cup," that is to say, empty his mind of all his preconceptions about Zen if he wishes to truly learn about it. Moreover, we learned that this emptying of the mind, as a returning to the beginner's mind, is itself a principal teaching and practice of Zen.

There is another story that deserves retelling here. This one is found at the beginning of one of the first and still best philosophical introductions to Zen in the West, a book written by an elder friend of mine, Thomas Kasulis. The story is about a philosophy professor who goes to a temple in Japan to study Zen—and, yes, Tom has confirmed my suspicion that the story is in fact autobiographical.[16] The Zen master first asks the philosophy professor what it is that he thinks he has come to study; what is Zen? After the professor mumbles "something about Zen's being a way of life rather than a set of dogmas," the Zen master lets out a good-natured laugh and says:

> Everyone comes here to study Zen, but none of them knows what Zen is. Zen is . . . knowing thyself. You are a Western philosopher and you know of Socrates' quest. Did you assume that Zen would be something different?[17]

My own experience confirms the point. Soon after my twenty-third birthday, I sold my two most-prized possessions—my motorcycle and, believe it or not, my long hair—in order to scrape together enough money to buy a one-way ticket to Japan.[18] I went there to learn the language, culture, and philosophy, and, especially, to practice Zen in a traditional Japanese setting. Looking back, I had many preconceptions and even misconceptions about Zen—dreams of mystical experiences on mountaintops and such. At least in part, I was motivated by a youthful desire to escape the seemingly boring familiarity of my native culture and to seek adventure in an exotic land. In effect, I was *fleeing* rather than *finding* myself, insofar as I was yearning for the exciting and extraordinary rather than awakening to the here and now of what in Zen is called "the ordinary mind" or "the everyday even mind" (see Chapter 13).

Fortunately, the motivational fuel that drives such escapism and exoticism burns up fairly quickly during the long hours of meditation undertaken at Zen temples and monasteries, not to mention the very down-to-earth practices of weeding gardens and, yes, cleaning toilets. If any ulterior motives remain, they are briskly wiped away during the penetrating and uncompromising one-on-one interviews with a Zen master. Unsurprisingly, Westerners who are motivated by mere Orientalist curiosity, rather than a genuinely existential quest, do not last very long in such an environment. As the months and years of commuting regularly to temples and monasteries went by, I was gradually able to begin emptying my cup and getting down to the serious business of the practice of Zen as an "investigation into the self."

Zen as a Path of Meditation

Zen is not, in the end, a Japanese, Chinese, Korean, Vietnamese, or Indian path. It is a path for all human beings who are sincerely interested in coming to know themselves. This was the Japanese Zen master's point when he rhetorically asked whether the American philosophy professor thought that it would be any different from Socrates's quest.

Nevertheless, despite significant similarities, there are also some important differences between the path of Zen and that of other religions and philosophies: differences in method and so also in results. Zen does not ask one to pray to, or to believe in, an external God or Buddha. Like Socrates, it stresses the importance of seeking knowledge, rather than relying merely on faith, and first of all seeking knowledge of oneself.[19] Yet while there are intriguing accounts of Socrates standing motionless for hours, apparently absorbed in a meditative state,[20] for the most part Socrates's method was that of discursive, rational, dialectical inquiry, and he thought this is best done by disengaging the mind from the body.[21] The Zen path is a more holistic one whose embodied-spiritual or "psychosomatic" practice does not disengage the psychic from the physical dimensions of our being.[22]

Contrary to some popular opinions and partial teachings, Zen is not, in the end, opposed to rational thought.[23] But it does teach that we need to dig down beneath discursive reasoning by means of meditation, reconnecting intellectual knowledge to a deeper, more holistic wisdom. Arguments must be based on insights, otherwise they easily degenerate into self-serving sophistries or, at best, abstract theories having little impact on our lives. For the most enlightening, most life-changing insights, we need a method that engages the body, heart, and spirit as well as the mind. We need to root the intellect in an embodied-spiritual practice of meditation.

Ever since Shakyamuni Buddha attained enlightenment while meditating under the Bodhi Tree, meditation has played a vital role in all schools of Buddhism. It is especially central in Zen Buddhism. As a school of Buddhism, the Zen tradition traces itself back to Shakyamuni Buddha, who lived in India around 500 BCE. Legend has it that about a thousand years later, Zen was brought to China by a monk named Bodhidharma. Seven centuries after that, around 1200 CE, it was transmitted to Japan by Zen masters such as Eisai and Dōgen.

Buddhism has many traditions and schools (see Chapter 10), each of which is based on a particular "sutra" or set of sutras. All sutras claim to be the teachings of the Buddha, yet they were all were written down much later. Even the earliest sutras, the ones that make up the Pali Canon of the Theravada Buddhist tradition, which has thrived in Sri Lanka and Southeast Asia, were first written down four centuries after the Buddha died. The sutras that form the scriptural basis of the Mahayana Buddhist tradition, which has thrived in Central and East Asia, were composed starting in the first century BCE, many being translated from Sanskrit into Chinese by end of the second century of the Common Era. When these scriptures were brought from India to China, the different schools of Chinese Buddhism distinguished themselves from one another by claiming that one sutra or another is the pinnacle of the Buddha's teaching.

The Zen school, however, is different. While Zen Buddhists do study and chant many sutras and other texts, the Zen school is unique in that it does not claim to be based on any written teachings at all; rather, it is based on the Buddha's actual experience of enlightenment. This experience of enlightenment is said to be attainable by all human beings, insofar as the Buddha-nature or Buddha-mind is universal. In other words, all human beings have the same underlying nature and mind as the Buddha. Yet this Buddha-nature or Buddha-mind must be realized, awakened to, and actualized, and the best method for doing so is the one that the Buddha himself used: meditation. The Japanese word *zen* in fact means "meditation" or "state of meditative concentration." In Chinese, *zen* is pronounced *chan*. *Chan* is short for *channa*, which is how the Chinese pronounced *dhyana*, the Sanskrit word used in India for practices or rarified states of meditative concentration.

Thus, Zen is the school of Buddhism in which the practice of direct realization through meditation is central, rather than a particular doctrine or scripture. All the teachings of all the various schools of Buddhism, including the teachings employed by the Zen school itself, are thought to be nothing more and nothing less than "expedient means" or "skillful means" to help bring people to their own direct experience of awakening to the truth about themselves and the world. The most direct path to this experience is the practice of "seated meditation," or *zazen*.

A Taste of Meditation

Let me invite you at this point to jump in and actually get a taste of the experience of meditation.

Simply sit still, with a straight back, eyes partially but not completely closed. . . . Relax all your muscles. . . . Relax your mind. . . . Let the center of your awareness drop down into your lower abdomen. . . . Now breathe—deeply yet naturally. Thoughts will come and go. Just let them be. Don't pay them any attention. Don't feed them any energy, either by grasping on to them or by trying to force them to go away. Just breathe, just be.

Please put down this book and sit for as long as you feel comfortable, preferably for at least five minutes.

* * *

Let's now reflect on your experience. Most first-time meditators are initially taken aback by the uncontrollable swirling of their emotionally charged thoughts. This is your encounter with the first lesson of meditation—the realization of how much you in fact need to meditate!

Yet even in this very brief and simple meditation, perhaps you also began to sense that there is a calm and open awareness underlying those swirling thoughts. Little by little, as you settled into that calm openness of mind, perhaps you also began to hear the ensemble of subtle sounds that surround you: the hum of the air conditioner or the rustling of tree leaves; the ticking of the clock or the murmur of traffic noises; the birds chirping in the backyard or maybe even the rhythm of your own heartbeat.

Inspired by Zen, the avant-garde composer John Cage shocked the music world in 1952 when he composed a piece that entailed just sitting in silence at a piano or other instrument(s) without playing a single note for 4 minutes and 33 seconds. He wanted the audience to hear the music that is going on around us all the time.[24]

In your brief experiment with meditation, perhaps you started becoming attuned to what had been going on around you all the time and yet had not previously been allowed into your conscious mind, since you had been focused on particular sensations or feelings, or lost in thoughts about other times and places. The cup of our mind is usually filled to the brim with swirling memories, plans, imaginings, and worries. Even without going so far as to empty the cup, a few minutes of physical stillness and calm attentiveness can allow the muddy water of the mind to stop swirling, such that the water begins to clear and the murky thoughts and emotions begin to settle.

Becoming Aware of, and Thus Alleviating, the Problem of Karmic Editing

Cognitive scientists tell us that at any given moment we are consciously aware of only a tiny fraction of the enormous amount of data that is streaming in through our sense organs. At this moment, for example, you are probably not aware of the sensation of your shirt touching your back. Now that you have read this, you may have shifted the focus of your attention so that you have become aware of this subtle sensation. The point is that this sensation was already there; it's just that you were not consciously aware of it until you turned your attention to it.

Most of the time, our minds have tunnel vision. Our monkey-minds jump from one thing to the next, but cognitive scientists tell us that even the most jittery of multitaskers are paying attention to only one thing at a time. Of course, we cannot and would not want to be aware of everything all the time. That would be multitasking madness. The crucial question is: In what manner are we narrowing the field of our awareness? How is our focus getting determined? In effect, our habits of mind, our projects and prejudices, are always more or less unconsciously "framing" and "editing" the world of our experience.

This constant construction of the filter or grid—this shaping and tinting of the lenses—through which we experience the world is one of the basic meanings of what in Buddhism is called karma. We'll discuss karma in more detail in

Chapter 15. For now, let's just say that karma means that how we act in response to the present situation shapes how we are going to perceive—and so likely again respond to—similar situations in the future.

If I have the habit of waking up and groping my way to the coffeemaker every morning, tomorrow morning when I wake up I am going to perceive the hallway and stairway as an obstacle course to the kitchen. The toy at the bottom of the stairs and the broom leaning against the wall are going to be perceived at that moment as obstructions, rather than as things to play or clean with. As this example shows, not only do the habitually crafted lenses of my mindset drastically restrict what is allowed to enter my field of awareness, they are also constantly putting a "spin" on everything that is allowed to enter. The primary problem is that we usually remain unaware of this ongoing process of what I am calling *karmic editing*. We constantly assume that the restricted and reformed version of reality we experience simply is reality.

Even now, if you are like me, you may be thinking: "Yes, I get that other people—and those other news networks—are constantly putting a spin on things. They are telling themselves and others a distorted version of only one side of the story. They are both perpetrators and victims of karmic editing. I, on the other hand, am just seeing things as they are. My unbiased story is the whole truth and nothing but the truth!"

Meditation is, to begin with, a practice of emptying the mind of this conceit that our own edited version of reality is the only unbiased and therefore valid one. It is a matter of recognizing that we are always, more or less, caught up in the reels of karmic editing. The contemporary Sōtō Zen master Shohaku Okumura (Jp. Okumura Shōhaku) writes: "The world we live in is the world we create based on how our mind encounters the myriad dharmas [i.e., all the things we experience]." We cannot prevent our mind from creating our world, but we can wake up to the fact that this is what is happening, and by "letting go of rigid belief in the narratives and preferences of our minds" we can participate more freely and responsibly in this interpretive filtering process.[25] Although "in order to live we must make choices using our incomplete conceptual maps of the world . . . the practice of zazen can help us understand that our pictures of the world and our values are biased and incomplete, and this understanding allows us to be flexible."[26] Our experience of the world is always limited and perspectival, but it can be more or less egoistic or empathetic, more or less closed- or open-minded, more or less rigidly assertive or flexibly responsive.[27]

In taking up the practice of meditation, we are setting out on a path that, step by step, breath by breath, enables us to become aware of this entanglement and to participate more freely and responsibly in shaping the ways in which we experience the world.

Fasting the Mind and Forgetting the Self

The legendary Daoist sage Zhuangzi, whose writings were particularly influential on Zen, spoke of a meditative practice of "sitting and forgetting." He also referred to this as a practice of "fasting the mind."[28]

We need to unlearn our prejudices, our prejudgments about ourselves and others, so that we can open our minds to what is really there, so that we can become at least a little more aware of the "spin" imposed upon our experience of reality by our swirling thoughts and feelings and desires.

The problem is not that we don't have a grip on reality. The real problem is that we generally have too much of a grip on reality, in the sense that we are willfully grasping the world and forcefully trying to reshape it to fit into the boxes we have fashioned with our projects and prejudices. Meditation is a temporary relaxing of this grip—this hold on, this attachment to, our own edited version of reality. Meditation is a matter of "opening the hand of thought" or "releasing one's grip on thoughts," as the modern Sōtō Zen master Uchiyama Kōshō beautifully puts it.[29]

By sitting and forgetting, by emptying our cup, by fasting the mind, we learn to stop seeing things only from our own narrow, rigid, and, let's admit it, usually quite egocentric point of view.

Having gotten a taste of meditation in this chapter, in Chapters 3 and 4 you will be provided with detailed information and instructions regarding the nature of Zen meditation and how to practice it.

Turning the Self Inside Out

Let me conclude this chapter by quoting and commenting on a crystallized account of the path of Zen by the thirteenth-century Zen master Dōgen. He writes:

> To study the Buddha Way is to study the self.
> To study the self is to forget the self.
> To forget the self is to be enlightened by the myriad things of the world.
> To be enlightened by the myriad things of the world is to let drop off the body-mind of the self and the body-mind of others.[30]

Without any explanation, this passage, famous as it is, may strike one as enigmatic if not simply incomprehensible. However, I hope that this chapter has better prepared you to ponder it.

Here is what I think Dōgen is saying. The path of Zen begins as a quest to know oneself. Yet this investigation into the self leads, paradoxically enough, to a forgetting of oneself: to study oneself is to empty oneself of all the false ideas one has of oneself, to let go of all the attachments and labels and status symbols we habitually cling to and identify ourselves with.

Positively put, this *emptying* is an *opening*, an opening of oneself to others. In studying the self, we discover that *deep inside us lies an openness to the outside*. Discovering this openness dissolves the dualistic barriers of separation we have constructed between inside and outside, subject and object, self and other. This is what Dōgen means by the peculiar language of "dropping off the body-mind of the self and the body-mind of others."[31] We no longer feel the need to remain fixated on the rigid identifications of "self" and "other" that isolate us as separate minds and bodies and restrict our creative cooperation and compassionate interaction.

Dōgen writes: "Foolish people think that if they help others first, their own benefit will be lost, but this is not so. Beneficial action is an act of oneness, benefitting self and others together."[32] He also says that "when we reflect on the past and future of our body-and-mind, we cannot find the boundary of self or others."[33] We realize that our lives are intertwined, and that our default mode of thinking and feeling ourselves to be dualistically separated from others is, in fact, an egoistic delusion. And so we realize that the ceremonies of our lives should be experienced as cooperative endeavors to actualize our community.

We must be careful not to misunderstand Zen's conception of nondual community in terms of a homogeneous unity—a topic that will be addressed in Chapters 8 and 9. Dōgen recognizes that "the relationship of self and others varies limitlessly according to circumstances."[34] Yet it is never the case that "I" am a physical or mental *thing* that I should be obsessed about distinguishing from and opposing to other things. I am rather, at each moment, a unique opening to a world of interconnectivity.

The self, Zen tells us, is empty. This means that the self is empty of separateness and thus full of interconnectedness, empty of independent substantiality and thus full of interrelated activity (see Chapter 7). Emptiness here also means openness. To be open is to be responsive, and to be responsive is to be creative as well as compassionate. Creativity is not a forceful act of imposing one's project on the world; it is, rather, a responsive participation in events of interactivity. Great artists rarely claim sole authorship of their works; they speak of influence and inspiration, of losing themselves in the creative flow, of being spoken to by their materials and guided by their tools, and of gratitude to their supporters and their audience. Only in the midst of all these interconnections can an artist do his or her part in producing good art. This is true of all of us in all that we do. In the end we discover ourselves not by retreating from the interconnections that make up the world we live in but rather by fully engaging in them.

To be sure, meditation *retreats* play an important role in the practice of Zen. During such retreats, one steps back from the activities of one's life onto a meditation cushion for a few minutes a day, a few hours a week, or even a few weeks a year, and one practices "emptying one's cup" by "fasting one's mind" and "forgetting oneself." Yet, in the end, such retreats are not an escape from life (see Chapter 14). Rather, they are meant to allow one to get back in touch with the open source of creativity and compassion that is who one really is.

We have reached the conclusion of this chapter, and hopefully have managed to take a few steps backward toward retrieving the openness of the beginner's mind. Let me summarize what we have learned: The path of Zen is a way of taking up the ancient philosophical and religious quest to know oneself. It suggests, however, that the more we really come to know ourselves, the more we learn to forget ourselves. We learn to forget ourselves not in the sense of the superficial self-oblivion that preceded the quest but rather in the profound sense of the discovery, deep within, of an opening to the outside, an opening that in fact frees us from the rigid and absolute distinctions we are accustomed to making between inside and outside, self and other, and even egoism and altruism.

Going all the way inside, we are turned inside out.

The true self, it turns out, is an open mind and an open heart.

3

Zen Meditation as a Practice of Clearing the Heart-Mind

Figure 3.1 Zazen in meditation hall of Shōkokuji monastery, Kyoto, July 2018

This chapter and the following one will introduce you to the practice of Zen meditation. In this chapter, I'll talk about the importance and the meaning of meditation for Zen. In Chapter 4, I'll explain how to go about actually doing it.

Zen Pathways. Bret W. Davis, Oxford University Press. © Oxford University Press 2022.
DOI: 10.1093/oso/9780197573686.003.0003

The Significance of Meditation in Zen

As mentioned in Chapter 2, the importance of meditation for Zen is readily apparent in the fact that the word *zen* itself means "meditation." Zen (Chan in Chinese) is the school of Buddhism that more than any other prioritizes the practice of "seated meditation," called *zazen* in Japanese. The seminal thirteenth-century Japanese Zen master Dōgen at times went so far as to claim that "you no longer have need for incense-offerings, doing prostrations, calling on the name of Amida Buddha, penance disciplines, or reading sutras. Just sit in zazen and cast off your body and mind."[1] Dōgen tells us that he learned this exclusive emphasis on *zazen* in China from his teacher, Rujing.[2]

Now, this doesn't mean that Dōgen and other Zen masters don't encourage people to also engage in such secondary practices.[3] If you were to visit a Zen temple or monastery today, you'd witness a lot of activities other than silent meditation going on: walking meditation (*kinhin*), chanting, prostrations, one-on-one kōan interviews, working in the kitchen and vegetable garden, and so on. In later chapters, we will talk about some of these other important forms of Zen practice. Here, let us focus on the pivotal practice of seated meditation or *zazen*.

What is the point of doing *zazen*? In a word, it is to awaken to one's original heart-mind. The reason I use the hyphenated expression "heart-mind" is that in Chinese and Japanese the word for "heart" and "mind" is written with the same sinograph (Chinese character): 心, pronounced *xin* in Chinese and either *shin* or *kokoro* in Japanese. In effect, these languages and cultures do not tend to separate the locus of thinking and the locus of feeling. And so when I refer to "mind" in this book, please remember that this includes the "heart." For Zen, an open mind entails an open heart, and vice versa. A wise mind and a compassionate heart are, so to speak, two sides of the same *kokoro*.

The point of *zazen*, seated meditation, is to clear or purify the heart-mind. Or rather, the point is to realize—to discover and allow to freely function—the clarity and purity of the original heart-mind that is already there, buried beneath our karmic baggage of egoistic delusions and desires. This karmic baggage manifests as the distracting thoughts, emotions, and desires that will probably assail you as soon as you try to settle into a practice of meditation. The Sanskrit word for these unsettling mental and emotional "afflictions" is *klesha*, meaning the "impurities" or literally "coverings" that conceal the purity of our true nature. These "defilements" cloud over the original luminosity of our enlightening minds, smothering the warm glow of our originally compassionate hearts, and as a result we suffer from, and cause others to suffer from, "agonizing worries" (*bonnō*, the Japanese word for *klesha*). In liberating us from these unwholesome mental and emotional afflictions, *zazen* does not make us into anything we are not already. Rather, it lets us return to our originally clear and open heart-mind.

In the beginning, you will likely experience meditation as a struggle. It is a very odd struggle, since it is a struggle with yourself, a struggle between different parts of yourself, between the part of you that wants to meditate and the part of you that does not. When you introspect, you find that there are at least two of you in there! That is the first moment of self-discovery: the realization that the self is complicated and often at odds with itself. Zen meditation entails first of all facing up to this complicated and self-contradictory nature of the self. Ultimately it is about digging down to the deepest and truest part of ourselves, our "original mind," and clearing the way for it to function freely.

In ancient times the Zen school was known not only as the "meditation school" but also as the "Buddha-mind school." The word "Buddha" means "awakened one." It is not really a proper name but rather a description of anyone in any place and time who is fully awakened. In this book I'll often follow the custom of using the term "the Buddha" to refer specifically to Shakyamuni Buddha, the man named Siddhartha Gautama who attained enlightenment while meditating under the Bodhi Tree in northern India and founded the historical tradition of Buddhism some 2,500 years ago. We'll discuss various other meanings of the word "Buddha" in Chapters 10 and 11. Here the point is that "Buddha-mind" means a truly awakened mind or the original mind that we are trying to wake up to. Meditation is the most direct means of uncovering and enabling the free and fluid functioning of this Buddha-mind or Buddha-nature.

Bodhidharma's Definition of Zen

We are now ready to look at the classic answer to the question "What is Zen?" attributed to Bodhidharma, the semi-legendary figure who reportedly brought Zen from India to China in the late fifth or early sixth century CE. He is said to have characterized Zen with the following four phrases:

> Not relying on words and letters,
> A special transmission outside all doctrines;
> Pointing directly to the human heart-mind,
> Seeing into one's true nature and becoming a Buddha.[4]

What does this saying mean? Let's start with the fourth phrase and work backward. The word "Buddha," as we now know, means an "awakened one," someone who has woken up—in this case not from sleep but from a state of ignorance or delusion. Awakened to what? We're told that this awakening is a matter of seeing into the true nature of the self or the human heart-mind. Okay, but just what is the true nature of the human heart-mind? This is where the verbal explanation comes to an end. In the third phrase we are told that it must be "directly pointed to," and in the first and second phrases we are told that it cannot be grasped by relying on texts or doctrines. Another possible translation of the first line is "not establishing words and letters." In other words, while Zen masters have left us with many sayings and stories, none of them are written in stone. All their verbal or written teachings are but indirect pointers to the true nature of the self and the universe, the "one great matter" that really matters.

The real point of Zen cannot ultimately be either expressed or grasped in the form of scriptures or in formulaic doctrines. Ultimately, the point of Zen can only be "directly pointed to." It cannot be grasped through the mediation of words and concepts, which are, at best, secondhand traces of someone else's direct experience. It must be immediately experienced firsthand, and this is best done through the practice of meditation. Real Zen must be realized through *zazen*.

Of course, Zen practitioners do study Buddhist texts and chant Buddhist sutras. And Zen masters have left behind volumes of recorded sayings, poetry, and dialogues, as well as more theoretical and instructional texts. In Chapter 20 we will examine the understanding and role of language in Zen, and in Chapter 21 we'll discuss the relation between Zen and philosophy. Here let me just say that the Zen tradition has always affirmed that there is a vital—albeit provisional—role to be played by oral and written instruction. The point is not that texts and teachings are untrue, but rather that on their own they cannot fully capture or embody the truth. The point is not that intellectual understanding is unimportant, but rather that it is always partial and insufficient for attaining a truly liberating insight.

Three Levels of Wisdom: Received, Intellectual, and Experiential

One problem with relying on texts and teachings is that we mistake second- or thirdhand information for firsthand experience and understanding. The Buddhist tradition has long recognized there to be three levels of wisdom: that which arises from listening and reading, from rational reflection, and from holistic meditative practice.[5] We can paraphrase these as *received wisdom, intellectual wisdom,* and *experiential wisdom.*

Received wisdom is acquired through reading traditional texts or listening to a trustworthy teacher and committing those doctrines to memory. Attaining intellectual wisdom requires a more active and critical use of one's rational faculties, such that one comes to a clear understanding of why a teaching makes sense (or does not). As a professor, I want my students to start by carefully reading the assigned texts and attentively listening to my lectures. But then I also want them to move from received to intellectual wisdom. That is to say, I don't just want them to memorize the views of the philosophers we are studying; also, and even more importantly, I want them to intellectually grasp and critically evaluate their arguments.

Even in the best-case scenario, however, most of the learning that happens in our schools and universities stops at the level of intellectual wisdom. At best we prepare students to go out into the "real world" and, through real-life experiences, to take the intellectual knowledge they attained in the classroom and turn it into the kind of experiential wisdom that changes their lives and allows them to more positively affect the lives of those around them.

The Buddhist tradition, at its best, promotes a holistic practice that includes but is not limited to intellectual thinking. It encourages practitioners to engage in embodied-spiritual meditative practices and to let the teachings imbue their daily lives so that they sink in to the level of experiential wisdom. For it is only experiential wisdom that is truly liberating and life-changing.

What level of wisdom should you aspire to gain from this book? That of course depends on your level of interest and motivation. I hope that you will at least find its pages interesting enough that you retain some juicy bits of received wisdom to pass along during dinner-party conversations. Moreover, I hope that you find at least some of the teachings of Zen conceptually compelling enough that they end up contributing to your storehouse of intellectual wisdom. Beyond even that, I invite you to consider putting the teachings of Zen into practice in your daily life, and to do so via engaging in the practice of meditation. By putting the teachings into practice, they will, over time, become a matter of your own experiential wisdom. Keep in mind that real Zen can manifest itself only in your real life.

The present chapter is devoted to giving you a better intellectual understanding of Zen meditation. Chapter 4 will provide you with concrete instructions so that you can begin to develop a firsthand experiential understanding of the practice.

Zen Among Other Forms of Meditation

The practice of mediation in India goes back more than three thousand years, predating even the earliest scriptures of Hinduism. Chapter 6 of the most famous Hindu scripture, the *Bhagavad Gita*, gives explicit instructions for practicing *dhyana yoga*, the spiritual discipline of meditation. Inspired by Zen and other Asian traditions, some Christians have gone back to the Desert Fathers to recover meditative practices of prayer involving repeating a biblical phrase like a mantra. Trappist monks have developed a silent practice of centering prayer. Jewish Kabbalists and Muslim Sufis have their own practices of meditation. In

China, Daoists were practicing meditation long before Buddhism was introduced in the first century of the Common Era. The "mindfulness" boom today stems in part from Zen but mainly from a secularized version of a Theravada Buddhist method of meditation. "Mindfulness" is a translation of *sati*, which is in Theravada Buddhism is cultivated both in practices of "calming meditation" called Samatha and in practices of "insight meditation" called Vipassana. The latter is the primary source of modern secularized practices of mindfulness. (Theravada is the Buddhist tradition that has thrived in Sri Lanka and Southeast Asia, as distinct from Zen and other schools of Mahayana Buddhism that have thrived in Central and East Asia. For a sketch of these different traditions of Buddhism, see Chapter 10.)

There are many different methods of meditation, and different methods naturally produce different experiences. There are also different motivations to meditate. One can meditate just to relax and de-stress. Or one can meditate to improve one's concentration and focus. One might meditate to concentrate better on a secular activity, or to focus one's prayerful relation with God. Some mystics meditate in order to experience a *unio mystica* or mystical union with God.

One can meditate to escape from the travails of life, imaginatively transporting oneself to another time and place, or perhaps to a realm outside of time and space. Or, as in Zen, one can meditate to live life more fully, with fewer attachments, and with more freedom, flexibility, and concern for the well-being of all beings.

The Buddha taught two kinds of meditation: concentration and insight. On his path to enlightenment, he learned methods for attaining deep levels of meditative concentration from two teachers, but he was not satisfied with the temporary respite from suffering that these states of absorption provided. He continued to employ these methods of concentration, but used them in order to calm, stabilize, and focus the mind so that it could attain liberating insight into the true nature of the self and the world.

Whereas some schools of Buddhism distinguish more sharply between the preparatory practice of concentration and the liberating practice of insight,[6] Zen views concentration and insight as two sides of the same coin: when the mind is cleared, settled, and focused, it naturally attains insight and manifests its innate wisdom. The Sixth Chinese Ancestor in the Zen tradition, the seminal seventh-century Zen master Huineng, purportedly used the Chinese philosophical concepts of "body" or "substance" (*ti*) and "function" (*yong*) to explain the intimate relation between meditation and wisdom. He says:

Good friends, this Dharma teaching of mine is based on meditation and wisdom. But don't make the mistake of thinking that meditation and wisdom are separate. Meditation and wisdom are of one essence and not two. Meditation is the body of wisdom, and wisdom is the function of meditation.[7]

The Buddha taught the Eightfold Path as the way to enlightenment. Its eight limbs are grouped into three categories. The first category is wisdom, and it consists of (1) right view and (2) right intention. The second category is morality, consisting of (3) right speech, (4) right action, and (5) right livelihood. We will discuss Zen and morality in Chapter 16. Here, our interest is in the third category, which is meditation. It consists of (6) right effort, (7) right mindfulness, and (8) right concentration.

"Right effort" does not mean simply trying hard; it specifically indicates the meditative process of training the mind to let go of negative states of mind and cultivate positive ones.[8] Some Buddhist methods of meditation, such as Theravada Vipassana and Tibetan Lojong, involve detailed instructions for *gradually* removing negative states of mind, such as anger and jealousy, and producing positive ones, such as patience and compassion. Zen meditation, like the Mahamudra and Dzogchen meditation methods of the Tibetan schools, is meant to *suddenly* awaken us to our innate virtues of wisdom and compassion, from which we have become alienated through the Three Poisons of ignorance, avarice, and aversion—or, in stronger language, delusion, greed, and hatred.

The various schools of Buddhism employ a range of meditation methods. Some involve simple or elaborate words or images. Zen meditation, being a "sudden" rather than "gradual" form of meditation, is a stringently "cold turkey" approach. Rather than giving you different thoughts to hold on to, it asks you to "let go of thoughts" by "opening the hand of thought," as the modern Sōtō Zen master Uchiyama Kōshō wonderfully teaches.[9] Uchiyama Rōshi's Japanese phrase is *omoi no te-banashi*, which more literally means "releasing one's grip on thoughts." Thoughts may still arise, but we no longer grab and hold on to them. Nor do we push them away. We no longer either chase after them or try to chase them off. To open the hand of thought is to "wake up to the reality of life" by awakening to the big open mind beneath our egocentrically constricted judgments and feelings, wishes and worries. Such thoughts don't disappear forever, but now we see them for what they are. As Uchiyama Rōshi puts it, we see them as coloring the "the scenery of life," and a regular practice of *zazen* enables us to wake up to the reality of life "without being carried away by the scenery."[10]

There is nothing wrong with mental activity per se. The brain secretes thoughts like a sweat gland secretes sweat. To tell the untrained brain to just be quiet is like telling a nervous person's armpits to stop sweating. The inner voice yelling at the other voices to shut up just adds to the cacophony. Don't blame the hyperactive brain for excessively secreting thoughts, since that's just what it does as long as you keep feeding it mind candy. You have to teach it to calm down and invite it to rest in silence for a time. The problem is not really thinking as such; the problem is that we have gotten hooked on chasing after chains of thoughts, filling our minds with feelings about them. Our minds have become restless time-traveling machines driven back and forth by our regrets about the past and our anxieties about the future.

We'd like to kick the habit of this excessive and obsessive talking to ourselves, and so we are drawn to the meditation cushion. Once there, however, we find that we are scared silly of settling into the present moment and sitting in silence. Nevertheless, what brings us to the meditation cushion may be that we already sense that the peace of mind we seek is to be found in the depths of that silence. And what motivates us to keep meditating may be that we sense how, once we become at home in that silence, the thoughts and feelings and desires that originate from there will be all the more sincerely honest and deeply meaningful.

Even Dōgen, who is probably the most well-read, prolific, and linguistically adept of all Zen masters, instructs us to "put aside the intellectual practice of investigating words and chasing phrases" while we meditate. Rather than looking for answers in texts and from teachers, he says that the practice of meditation is a matter of learning "to take the backward step that turns the light [of the mind around] and shines it inward."[11]

In Chapter 22, we'll examine Dōgen's method of "just sitting," after which we'll also look at how kōans are used in meditation in the Rinzai tradition. Yet in the Rinzai tradition, in which I was trained, for a year or more before practitioners are assigned a kōan they are generally required to intensely practice the "counting the breaths" method of meditation that I'll introduce in Chapter 4. If you are interested in taking up a practice of meditation along with reading this book, I suggest that you start with that method.

The Subtraction Method of Zen Meditation

Zen meditation is a matter of "emptying" or clearing the heart-mind. It is a matter of "subtraction" rather than "addition." Although there is a lot of what I call Addition Zen being peddled and paraded around out there, serious practitioners are engaged in what I call Subtraction Zen. Real Zen, Subtraction Zen, is not about accumulating new tricks and trinkets, nor is it about putting on the robes and airs of a new persona; it is about shedding such acquisitive and self-aggrandizing desires and attachments.

Zen meditation is a matter of clearing out the clutter of our minds rather than acquiring more stuff to fill them with. It is for this reason that I tell newcomers at the end of their first session that I hope they got *nothing* out of the experience! In fact, I hope they get less than nothing. I hope they walk away with *less* rather than *more* than they came in with: less mental clutter, less emotional baggage, less stress and anxiety. I hope they walk away lighter and freer, more open-minded and open-hearted. These are not things: freedom and openness are the "no-things" that make a creative and compassionate life possible.[12]

At first, Zen meditation can seem downright boring and unproductive. After all, when one does *zazen*, one is not really doing much of anything at all. Indeed, the less the better! For it is our constant striving for immediately attainable results that is the problem. That is the lesson you should learn from any initial feelings of boredom and unproductivity during meditation. *Don't flee from boredom. Go all the way into it; go all the way through the bottom of boredom! The place of rest you seek lies beneath, not beyond, your restless mind.*

The Sanskrit word for enlightenment (*bodhi*) and one of its East Asian equivalents (Ch. *jue*, Jp. *kaku*) literally mean "awakening." To become enlightened means to wake up, to no longer be sleepwalking through life, to be awake and aware of what's going on, to no longer live in one's egocentric bubble or—to paraphrase the Presocratic Greek philosopher Heraclitus—in one's private dream world.

However, to properly wake up, first of all we need to have a good night's sleep. Did you sleep well last night? How many hours? Seven or eight? Did you get a lot done during those seven or eight hours? Perhaps you did actually work through some psychological issues while you were dreaming. But what about during the hours of deep sleep? How much did you get done during those hours? What? You got *nothing* done during your deep sleep? What a waste of time! I hope you don't do that often. What? You waste a few hours doing nothing in deep sleep every night? What a lazy bum!

I am joking, of course, but the joke has a point. I am trying to remind you of what Daoists call the "use of the useless."[13] We are so busy all the time, trying to get so much done, achieve so much. The Chinese character for "busy," 忙, literally means "the mind perishes." In other words, when one is too busy one loses one's mind.[14] Anyone who has ever been too busy—and who hasn't these days!—knows the feeling. And yet we keep doing it, unsure of how to get off the gerbil wheel.

When we get really busy, we might think that we surely don't have seven or eight hours a day to waste by doing nothing but lying down with our eyes closed. But how much could we get done if we didn't sleep? If we want to get things done, especially thoughtful and creative things, and do them well, often the best thing to do is to take some time off and get a good night's sleep. Or exercise. Or just take a walk and "clear one's mind." Indeed, isn't it after a good night's sleep, or after a workout or a walk, that we get our best ideas? Isn't that when the lightbulbs light up? Isn't that when we realize that our problems aren't so unmanageably huge and complicated after all? Isn't that when it dawns on us that the people around us also have problems, concerns, dreams, and ideas?

Zen meditation is a practice of pausing our busy lives so that we can clear out the busy mess of our minds. It is a practice of clearing, emptying, opening, cleaning, and purifying the heart-mind—or rather, it is a matter of waking up to its original openness and purity. Potentially more intense even than deep sleep and aerobic exercise combined, it is the ultimate way to clear the mind. It is the touchstone, the home base of dropping everything and doing absolutely nothing that allows us to run around the bases and do everything else in our lives with clarity, composure, compassion, contagious peace, and creative energy.

Subtraction and Vow: Two Sides of the Same Meditation Medallion

Since people typically begin a meditation practice with lots of ideas in their heads about what they are going to gain from it, I like to stress at the outset that Zen meditation is a matter of subtraction rather than addition. In order to get people to "empty their cups" and let go of egoistic expectations and inclinations to instrumentalize Zen, I may even tell them that Zen meditation is a matter of doing nothing and getting nothing out of it!

Before I lose any readers, let me stop stressing how useless and unproductive Zen meditation is. I'll assume that you've gotten the point of my saying that, at its core, Zen meditation is a method of subtraction, and so I can now divulge that there is also a whole lot to be gained from the periphery of the practice. Indeed, the medicine of Zen meditation has many wonderful "side effects."

Before I "warn" you about the wonderful "side effects," however, I need to tell you about the main aim of the medicine. The other side of the same coin of Subtraction Zen is what I call Vow-Vehicle Zen. By way of clearing our heart-minds, we free ourselves up for becoming pure vehicles of the great compassionate vow to enlighten and liberate all sentient beings from suffering. Through the study and practice of Zen, the motivation to commit oneself to this vow eventually emerges naturally, welling up, as it were, from the depths of the empty self and extending outward to the endlessly interconnected universe.

If you already think of yourself as a Mahayana Buddhist, then you will understand your meditation practice to be motivated by this Bodhisattva vow. Traditionally, Zen meditation is undertaken in the spirit of this vow, which both motivates and is deepened by the practice. *The Principles of Zen Meditation*, a classic eleventh-century Chinese text still used in Rinzai Zen monasteries today, begins with these words:

> Bodhisattvas who are learning wisdom should first of all arouse the great heart
> of compassion, initiate the immense vow, and diligently practice meditative

concentration. They should vow to liberate all sentient beings from suffering rather than seeking just their own personal salvation.[15]

Bodhisattvas are those who aspire to become Buddhas, not for their own sake but for the sake of liberating all sentient beings from suffering. Arousing the *bodhicitta*, the compassionate and enlightening mindset of a Bodhisattva, is the first step on the Buddha Way. As a Mahayana Buddhist, one should arouse this ultimate intention, this great Bodhisattva vow, each time one sits down to meditate.

Of course, such a vow should not, and indeed cannot, be forced on anyone. With a range of participants in mind—most of whom do not identify as Buddhists—I usually begin my instructions in The Heart of Zen Meditation Group with a stress on the subtraction side rather than the vow side of the Zen meditation medallion. By practicing the subtraction method of Zen meditation, by emptying one's mind of its clutter and confusion, eventually an insight into the openness of the original heart-mind, into the interconnectedness of all beings, and into the nonduality of the mind of wisdom and the heart of compassion will begin to dawn on one (and, even then, participants are welcome to conceptualize such insights in Christian or other non-Buddhist terms if they wish). Until that time, one can approach Zen meditation simply as a method of clearing the heart-mind, a method of ceaseless subtraction that paradoxically releases plenty of positive byproducts along the way.

A Zen Buddhist Critique of the McMindfulness Boom

I promise I'll introduce those positive "byproducts" or "side effects" of the practice of Zen meditation in a moment. Before I do, there is one more matter that needs to be addressed. Given the popularity of contemporary "mindfulness" practices, it needs to be emphasized that taking up a serious spiritual practice of Zen meditation should not be conflated with merely dabbling in techniques of mindfulness for the sake of acquiring psychological benefits, such as stress reduction—as legitimate and as valuable as those benefits may be. There are, of course, many dedicated and sincere teachers and practitioners of secularized and simplified (or complicated) methods of mindfulness meditation. Chief among them is Jon Kabat-Zinn, whose popular Mindfulness Based Stress Reduction (MBSR) is widely used today in hospitals, businesses, schools, and homes as a method of achieving and maintaining mental health and fostering psychological well-being.[16] It is important to recognize the good intentions of those who teach and practice these methods and the real psychological relief and spiritual realizations they bring.

However, the contemporary mindfulness boom—or, as one skeptical scholar ironically dubs it, "mindfulness mania"[17]—also has its astute critics, including many Zen teachers who warn not only of the shortcomings but also of the misuses of what has been dubbed "McMindfulness."[18] These Zen teachers denounce the commodification of truncated mindfulness techniques and their instrumental uses as "organizational WD-40" for the sake of increasing corporate profits or as psychological training tools for achieving military objectives. In general, the problem with secularized mindfulness techniques is that when they find it convenient, they abandon—or at least put out of sight on the sidelines—the crucial ethical and religious contexts in which these Buddhist meditative practices have traditionally been embedded. To be sure, foregrounding the proximate benefits of meditation and other practices has always been a "skillful means" employed in the Buddhist traditions.[19] Yet once these practices are uprooted from their original ethical and religious moorings, such mundane motivations for practice are no longer able to serve as gateways into deeper levels of motivation and understanding.

The modernization of Zen obviously should not entail the complete instrumentalization of its core practice of meditation. Indeed, instrumentalized Zen meditation is no longer really Zen meditation. Zen meditation is meant to bring an end to the delusory and destructive ego, not to serve it as a means for achieving its ends. Obviously, using truncated techniques of calming and focusing the mind merely for the sake of increasing the efficiency of "worker bees" in corporate cubicles is a questionable appropriation of traditional Buddhist meditative practices. Yet it is also the case that adapting these practices for unquestionably commendable therapeutic purposes should not be equated with engaging in Zen as a rigorous spiritual discipline. After all, if what one is looking for is a way to relax and destress, or to deal with more serious issues of anxiety or depression, surely it would be unwise to attend a very physically demanding and psychologically challenging Zen retreat (*sesshin*)! And it would be downright irresponsible and dangerous to recommend such a retreat to a psychologically unstable person—for example, someone suffering from PTSD or prone to psychosis—in need of psychotherapy or psychiatric treatment.[20] *Zazen* is by no means a "quick fix" panacea for all psychological ailments. While it does aim to uproot the core causes of our "normal" human spiritual dis-ease, any "abnormal" mental health issues should be addressed before one is ready to engage in the austere rigors of this spiritual discipline.

In short, just as one should not demand *too much* from *zazen* and expect it to serve as a short-cut cure for any and all psychological ailments, one should also not demand *too little* from *zazen* and turn this deeply spiritual discipline into a tool serving more shallow aims.

That being said, promoting an appreciation for the positive "byproducts" of *zazen* can be understood as an appropriate "skillful means," as long as this approach is not assumed to be a substitute for therapy and medicine, and as long as it is enabled to serve as a gateway into the deeper dimensions of the practice. Moreover, critiques of either the therapeutic limitations and potential dangers or the instrumentalization and commercialization of modern methods of mindfulness meditation should not completely detract from the potentially powerful and empowering effects experienced by most meditators.

The core of modern mindfulness methods is *non-judgmental awareness of what's happening in the present moment*. The various traditional Buddhist methods of meditation differ with regard to whether judgments—such as determining whether a thought or feeling is wholesome or unwholesome, conducive to alleviating or compounding suffering—are *intentionally* included in the practice of meditation, or whether the capacity for *naturally* making such judgments in everyday life is thought to be recovered by letting go of all judgments during the practice of mediation itself.[21] Regardless, something vital is lost when practices of mindfulness are transplanted from their original ethical and religious contexts into the contemporary context of neoliberal capitalism with its primary aim of profit based on maximizing productivity and consumption. Greed may be good for the mentality of unfettered capitalism, but greed is one of the Three Poisons of the mind in Buddhism, along with hatred and delusion. Such corporate exploitations easily lose the heart and soul of Buddhist mindfulness, which is meant to convert greed, hatred, and delusion into generosity, lovingkindness, and wisdom.

Watered-down and secularized methods of mindfulness can easily be co-opted so as to portray stress and mental distress as a private problem rather than a collective one, shifting the blame and responsibility from society and corporations to the individual. These secularized mindfulness methods are often sold to CEOs as a shrewd investment that will pay off in terms of worker productivity and thus corporate profits. As critics like Ronald Purser point out, a genuine "mindfulness revolution" would call into question the neoliberal culture based on corporate greed and selfish individualism, rather than serve as a stress-reducing pacifier and thus, in effect, as an enabler for perpetuating the status quo of the stress-producing system.[22] Mindfulness methods are also being sold to the military in order to increase not only psychological resilience and capacity for coping with PTSD but also accuracy and efficiency in killing enemies on the battlefield. By contrast, mindfulness practices in Buddhism take place in the context of moral precepts, beginning with the commitment not to kill.

In Chapter 16 and elsewhere I discuss the important role that morality plays in traditional Zen Buddhism, and throughout this book I discuss meditation in the holistic and deeply religious context of Zen Buddhist practice. I also argue that meditation and other forms of Zen practice can and should be used to enhance critical thinking and ethical action, but that they should never be thought of as a substitute for them. Although neither a critique of neoliberal capitalism and its appropriations of truncated and distorted forms of Buddhist meditation nor a critique of the ethical and political shortcomings of Zen teachers and institutions (especially their complicity with Japanese militarism in the first half of the twentieth century) is a focal topic of the present book, I do hope to dispel what I deem to be unnecessary traditional and modern anti-intellectual and politically disengaged distortions of Zen, and to demonstrate the complementarity of Zen practice with philosophical thinking and ethical action (see especially Chapters 14, 16, 17, and 21).

The current mindfulness movement in North America stems mainly from the Vipassana meditation techniques practiced in the Theravada Buddhist tradition of South and Southeast Asia,[23] especially as those techniques were abbreviated and streamlined by modern Burmese teachers and their students.[24] Yet modern Western methods of mindfulness also include elements of Tibetan Mahamudra and East Asian Zen forms of "nondual" meditation, especially the injunction to suspend judgmental thinking during the practice.[25] Some Zen texts and teachings in fact prefer to speak of a practice of "mindlessness" or of awakening a state of "no-mind," stressing the need to let go of the dualistic mind that purports to separate itself from physical or mental objects and pass judgments on them from the outside.[26]

In Zen, the judgmental mind is indeed suspended during meditation. One neither pursues thoughts nor labels them as good or bad. And yet this non-judgmental practice is done in the context of vowing to eliminate unwholesome states of mind for the sake of dedicating one's life to the liberation of all sentient beings from suffering. The practice of *zazen* is understood to enable an awakening and cultivation of the Four Divine Abodes or Immeasurable Mindsets of lovingkindness, compassion, empathetic joy, and equanimity. Nevertheless, while chanting such vows and learning about such virtues are significant parts of the entire practice of Zen Buddhism, the great gift of *zazen*—the core practice of Zen—is that the sprouts of these vows and virtues, and the capacity to think and act in accord with them, spring forth naturally from the soil of the heart-mind when it is allowed to awaken to its true nature through sitting in silence and stillness.

The Beneficial Byproducts of Zen Meditation

With that vision of the ultimate ethical and spiritual impetus and aim of Zen meditation in mind, let me now make good on my promise to provide some more mundane motives by introducing some of the beneficial byproducts of engaging in a regular practice of Zen meditation. These significant byproducts include the following benefits to physical, mental, and emotional well-being.

Improvement in posture and physical well-being. Our society has largely forgotten the importance of bodily posture for alertness, for digestion, and most importantly for one's psychophysical disposition. *Zazen* reminds the body, as well as the mind, of the beneficial effects of good posture. Moreover, *zazen* increases physical as well as mental flexibility, and in general it attunes our minds to the needs of the body, allowing the body to mindfully retune itself.

Increase in ability to concentrate. The power of "one-pointedness of mind" that is cultivated in a simple meditation practice, such as counting the breaths, can be applied to *any* activity. This ability to concentrate means that one is able to work or study or play more intently and more effectively in less time and with less wasted energy. For example, twenty minutes of meditation plus ninety minutes of relaxed yet focused preparation for a test or an interview is much more productive than two stressed-out and unfocused hours of preparation. Moreover, you'll be much less anxious and in a much clearer state of mind during the test or interview.

Decrease in stress level and increase in effectiveness. A regular practice of meditation definitely reduces the overall amount of stress in one's life. Although meditation is not a quick fix, it is a sanctuary for deep relaxation and revitalization that is ever available to those who have cultivated a regular practice. Much of our stress is self-created, or at least self-enhanced; we are often our own worst enemies when it comes to stress. Meditation allows us to distinguish between artificial anxieties and real problems, and to let go of the former while effectively addressing the latter, without evasion or procrastination. It allows one to become the peaceful eye in the midst of an orchestrated whirlwind of effective activity.

Increase in natural creativity and problem-solving ability. Although we humans are naturally creative beings, our artificial products of mind and matter tend to clog up the veins through which our creative energy flows. In meditation one wipes the slate clean, enabling one to come at things afresh, to bring novel ideas to projects and solutions to problems. Although it takes less time (and a smaller cushion), meditation is not unlike a good night's sleep in this regard. It is also not unlike physical exercise in the way it refreshes one, giving back more time and energy than it takes away. In fact, meditation is not unrelated to many of the regenerative activities we already engage in. In this respect, it is more like a concentrated and potentially much deeper and more liberating form of these regenerative activities.

Recovery of sincerity and improvement in interpersonal relations. Deep down, we know how to behave toward family, friends, colleagues, and strangers. We know that the best way to be loved is to love; the best way to have good friends is to be a good friend; and so on. Yet we have built up so many psychological barriers that prevent us from behaving how we should and how we really, deep down, want to act. And so we live with many internal conflicts and regrets and, if we let these accumulate, maybe even with secret feelings of self-loathing. In taking time for meditation, one first of all learns to be kind to oneself. One calmly notices all the negative thoughts and feelings that have been tying one up in knots. No longer feeding them any more mental and emotional energy, one lets these negative thoughts and feelings drift off like storm clouds in the open expanse of a blue sky. Little by little, one learns to identify with the unbounded openness of the blue sky rather than with the bounded negativity of the storm clouds. These clouds will eventually drift along or dissipate, so that one can return to being the sincere and kind person that one has, deep down, always been.

Letting the Heart-Mind Be Seated

Finally, a core benefit of the practice of Zen mediation is that it *awakens an inner confidence that is both firm and flexible.* This confidence entails the kind of firmness that does not inhibit flexibility but rather it makes possible—like the fulcrum supporting a seesaw or the tip on which a spinning top balances. The Daoist sage Zhuangzi says that, having long engaged in the meditative practice of "sitting and forgetting," of "fasting the mind," the sage dwells at the empty "hinge of the Dao" or "axis of the Way." "When this axis finds its place in the center," he writes, "it responds to all the endless things it confronts, thwarted by none."[27]

The genuine self-confidence that emerges from this forgetting of the self, from this emptying of the ego, does not lead to arrogance but rather enables one to freely confess one's ignorance and to feel entirely comfortable letting others be the center of attention when and where that is the appropriate thing to do.

The ninth-century Chinese Zen master Linji taught that the real problem with our lives is that we "lack self-confidence"; that is to say, we "lack faith in ourselves."[28] He tells his followers to not be just followers, and to stop looking for something or someone outside themselves that will enlighten and liberate them. He wants self-confident companions, not subservient sycophants. Linji says that anyone who has awakened a genuine self-confidence is able to become "master of every situation."[29] He does not that mean such persons would always need to be in the driver's seat or the center of attention, but rather that they would be able to *freely* follow as well as lead, to freely listen as well as speak, because they would no longer be slaves to their own deluded desires any more than they are to anyone else's.[30]

Tanaka Hōjū Rōshi, my teacher for many years in Kyoto, used to say that *zazen*, seated meditation, is really about letting the heart-mind be seated. He also used to say that the practice of Zen is about discovering the "unshakable central axis" of our inner being. People who have discovered this firm axis of flexibility at the core of their being are truly free rather than fixated; they are *free and responsible* in the literal sense of being *able to freely respond* to the situation at hand, rather than passively swung around this way and that by external conditions and the winds of fortune.

My children are now teenagers. As any parent of teenagers knows, peer pressure is a very real and difficult problem that kids deal with on a daily basis. But let's be honest: we adults are still dealing with, and often succumb to, peer pressure. We can call it "colleague coercion" if that makes it sound more sophisticated, but it is basically the same thing that our kids are dealing with. Nevertheless, it is true that teenagers are especially susceptible to peer pressure, because they are still in the midst of developing their adult identities. Like other parents, I want to help my kids any way that I can. Yet by trying to step in and help too much, we can end up stepping on their feet and not letting them learn to walk on their own. For example, it would not do any good if I followed my teenagers around everywhere and didn't let anyone pressure them into smoking or taking drugs. They need to learn to deal with such temptations on their own. For that, they need self-confidence more than anything.

How can we give our kids self-confidence? We cannot. We can only provide them with the tools needed to build self-confidence. There are many things that we parents do in this regard. At our house, one of the things we do is ask our kids to meditate for ten minutes in the morning before going to school. Of course, you can make a person sit on a meditation cushion, but you can't make them meditate. I've taught my kids the basics of the practice, but I can meditate for them no more than I can directly give them the inner confidence they really need.

Ultimately, self-confidence must be found within oneself. Not somewhere in one's swirling thoughts, since those are often just internalized forms of peer pressure. Thoughtfully replacing negative thoughts with positive ones may help, but the "non-thinking" of Zen meditation opens the door to a much deeper dimension of ourselves. It turns the light of the mind around and illuminates the depths of the self, and these depths include both the innermost openness to the outside that we discussed in Chapter 2 and the firm axis of flexibility at the core of the mind that we are discussing now. From out of these depths arises a true self-confidence, one that remains unshaken in the midst of inner as well as outer storms.

One of the greatest benefits of a regular practice of Zen meditation is the discovery and cultivation of the kind of firm axis of flexibility and core of self-confidence that allows one to sail with the winds of circumstance, rather than being blown over by them.

Hopefully, this chapter has managed to motivate you to practice Zen meditation. Chapter 4 will provide concrete instructions for actually engaging in the practice.

4

How to Practice Zen Meditation

Attending to Place, Body, Breath, and Mind

Figure 4.1 Zazen in tea room of Shōkokuji monastery, Kyoto, December 2019

Zen Pathways. Bret W. Davis, Oxford University Press. © Oxford University Press 2022.
DOI: 10.1093/oso/9780197573686.003.0004

In Chapter 3 we talked *about* Zen meditation, *zazen*. In this one, let's get down to business and learn how to actually *do* it. Traditional instructions generally include four steps in which one carefully attends to the place or environment, to bodily posture, to the breath, and to the mind.

Attending to the Environment

Let's start with attending to the place or environment. This includes not only where but also when and for how long to sit. I recommend that you begin with short ten-minute meditation periods, once or twice a day, and over several weeks gradually lengthen your meditation periods to twenty-five minutes, even if you can only find time to do this once a day. Even for an experienced meditator, it often takes ten or fifteen minutes to really settle into a meditative state, and so it is not surprising that the minimum length of time for a meditation period in temples and monasteries is usually twenty-five minutes.

Meditation periods in monasteries can be as long as fifty minutes or more, but this is appropriate only if it does not cause too much discomfort and if one is able to maintain concentration for that long. During intensive Zen retreats, called *sesshin*, practitioners sit for twelve hours or more per day. But don't let this scare you off, just as it should not scare off beginning joggers to know that some super-athletes run double marathons. Always start where you are. After all, where else *could* you start?

As for when to meditate, traditionally favored times are dawn and dusk. There is indeed something special about these twilight hours, these between-times that belong neither to the hectic daytime nor to the slumbering nighttime. Meditation is, after all, a practice of the Middle Way between stress and sloth; it cultivates a calm alertness between and beyond restless thinking and sleepy dullness. The earth and sky seem to emit their most meditative atmosphere at dawn and at dusk.

That being said, it is of course possible to meditate at any time of the day or night. So just find a time that works best for you. For me, it is first thing in the morning and at the end of the workday before dinner. Transition times in your daily routine are often good places to wedge in a meditation period. This also allows you to begin your next activity with a refreshed mind and disposition.

Finding and cultivating the right space for meditation is very important. Although it should not be too cold or too hot, it is best to have exposure to fresh air. Even in the winter I usually crack a window. Natural sounds or even the white noise of city streets will likely not disturb you, but loud sounds and especially voices will, so it is best to find as quiet a place as possible.

Good-quality incense that does not produce too much smoke can be very conducive. I recall riding my bicycle through the narrow streets of Kyoto and often getting a whiff of incense coming from someone's house. My back would immediately straighten and I'd be instantly brought into a meditative state of mind. Years of sitting in monastic settings with incense burning had apparently created a kind of muscle memory response. If you light a stick of incense each time you meditate, or if you sit in a certain spot in a certain room at a certain time of the day, you may find that these environmental factors help put you in the right frame of mind.

It is important that your meditative space be clean and uncluttered. The mind tends to reflect its environment, which is why you probably find that cleaning your room feels like you are also cleaning your mind. It is not surprising that Zen monks spend almost as much time cleaning as they do sitting in meditation.

You may wish to have an image in your meditation space, such as a figure of the Buddha or a Bodhisattva. Traditionally, a Zen meditation hall, called a *zendō*, is adorned with an image of Manjusri, the Bodhisattva who symbolizes wisdom, while the main hall of a Zen temple or monastery usually has an image of Shakyamuni Buddha. Avalokiteshvara, or Kannon in Japanese, the Bodhisattva who symbolizes compassion, is also frequently found in Zen temples. Of course, you could also have a figure from a tradition you identify with, such as a crucifix or cross for Christians or a Shiva figure for Shaivite Hindus. It may be helpful for you to bow to this figure before and after meditation. For Zen Buddhists, such images represent the wisdom and compassion that is to be discovered in their own hearts and minds. Bowing to these symbols reminds them that this self-discovery is what the practice of meditation is about (see Chapters 11 and 13).

Last but certainly not least, preparing the environment entails getting your cushions, bench, or chair ready. Various sitting positions are possible. The most important part of the posture is from the waist up, which will be the same whether you are sitting in a cross-legged or kneeling position, on the floor or on a chair.

If you are going to sit on a chair, it is best to have one that is not too high or too low and that has a flat seat with firm padding. If you are going to sit on the floor, it is best if you have a large flat square cushion, called a *zabuton*, as well as a smaller round or rectangular cushion, called a *zafu*. These can be easily ordered from online stores. It is also possible to fold a blanket or two into the shape of a *zabuton*, and to fold a beach towel or two into a *zafu*. Sofa cushions and pillows are not very appropriate because they are generally too soft and so don't provide enough firm support.

Attending to the Body

Now that you've attended to your environment, it's time to turn your attention to your bodily position. Be sure to wear loose and comfortable clothing that does not restrict your abdomen when you breathe in deeply or cut off the circulation in your legs if you are going to sit cross-legged on the floor. If you are going to sit on a chair, I recommend that you perch yourself on the front of the chair without leaning against the back, with your knees at a ninety-degree angle and with your lower legs perpendicular to the ground. If this is difficult for you, then you can sit all the way toward the rear of the chair so that your back is supported in an upright posture.

Let me now explain several cross-legged and kneeling positions. After that, I'll tell you what to do from the waist up, which will be the same for all sitting positions. A normal cross-legged—or, as my daughter calls it, "crisscross apple-sauce"—position is *not* good for meditation. This is for two reasons. One is that it doesn't provide a stable base. The other is that it does not support a naturally straight back, and so it cramps the deep-breathing space of your lower abdomen.

All the recommended cross-legged positions require some flexibility—and they also have the side benefit of increasing your flexibility the more you sit in them. You can think of your meditation practice as, in part, a practice of physical rehabilitation from all the stiffness and poor posture caused by years of what I call "couch-and-slouch karma." However, bear in mind that while minor discomfort can be considered part of the discipline of meditation, and can even help keep you focused, you should be careful to avoid any intense joint pain or excessive discomfort. Your body position should not distract you more than it helps you to get into a state of ultimately peaceful concentration.

For all the cross-legged positions, you should begin by placing just your buttocks on the small cushion, the *zafu*, which should be positioned toward the back of the flat cushion, the *zabuton*. You'll find that this allows the back to be naturally straight. It is important to use a *zafu* that is the right height. You can increase the height with a folded towel if need be.

The easiest of the cross-legged positions is the Burmese position. Take one leg and bend it all the way so that your heel is directly in front of or even slightly tucked under your crotch. Then bend the other leg and lay it flat on the floor directly in front of the inner leg, as close in as possible. Ideally, both knees should be touching the floor. Some meditators place small cushions under knees that don't want to go all the way down. Notice how much more stable you are now. That is because your two knees and your buttocks are forming a tripod, like the base of a pyramid, supporting your naturally straight back.

The stability of this tripod base becomes even more apparent if you move from the Burmese position into a half-lotus position. To do that, take your outer leg and lift your foot all the way up onto the opposite thigh and pull it in as snugly as you can. The closer in toward your body it is, the less torque there will be on your knee. If your flexibility is not quite there yet, you can lift your foot just up onto your calf, a position that is sometimes called a quarter-lotus.

Now, for the very flexible and ambitious, in order to go from a half-lotus to a full-lotus position, hold your top foot in place with your elbow, then slide out your other foot and lift it up onto your other thigh. Again, be sure to pull it snugly in toward your abdomen. You'll find that the half-lotus and lotus positions, while obviously demanding more flexibility, are very supportive of a good back position. With limbs all tucked together and the body upright and settled, the mind is invited to join this physical state of stability and concentration.

For many people, however, cross-legged postures are not viable options. You may want to try a kneeling position. In Japan, sitting on your heels with your legs folded under you is called *seiza*, literally "correct sitting." This is how one sits on formal occasions. I sometimes meditate in the morning in this position, and I usually eat dinner and even teach my seminar classes in this position. It is very conducive to clear thinking and healthy eating habits.

The drawback to *seiza* is that your legs will probably quickly fall asleep. In that case, there are two ways you can take the pressure off your legs in a kneeling position. You can take the *zafu*, turn it vertically, and slide it between your legs. Or you can acquire a wooden kneeling bench, which is placed over your calves. Many meditators find these supports to work very well.

Incidentally, legs falling asleep is just part of life in Japan. I've witnessed many Japanese people stumble in their kimonos as they try to stand up after sitting in *seiza*. I have personally stumbled my way around many meditation halls, including hopping on one leg to kōan interviews after long periods of sitting in lotus or half-lotus. Don't worry, I've tested the limits, and my legs have always eventually woken back up! But, again, there's no need to go to any ascetic extremes. Indeed, I do not allow hopping in my *zendō*. If someone's legs have fallen asleep, the rest of us patiently practice standing meditation until that person's legs are revived and ready to begin a period of walking meditation.

We have talked about what to do with your legs in all the recommended chair, cross-legged, and kneeling positions. Now let's talk about what to do from the waist up in all of these positions. The first thing you should do is establish a naturally straight back. To begin with, use your back muscles and straighten your back. I am sure that you could hold this artificially straight position for a few minutes, but eventually your back muscles would start aching. So we need to find a way to let your spine, not your muscles, do the work. Here's the technique I recommend. Leaving the back straight, bend forward from the hips until your buttocks starts to lift off the *zafu*, bench, or chair. Then rock back slowly onto the *zafu*, bench, or chair, releasing all of the tension in your back as you return to an upright position. Try this technique a few times, and you should find that it allows your back to remain straight, with a slight arch in your lower back, while also allowing you to relax your back muscles. Like a canvas supported by a tent pole, relax all the muscles in your shoulders and back and let your spine do the work of holding you upright.

Here's what to do with your hands. With your palms facing downward, hold your left thumb with your right hand. Then wrap your left hand around your gently clenched right hand. Now rest your clasped hands in your lap, snugly tucked up against your lower belly. Be sure to relax any tension in your hands and arms once they are in place. I suggest that you begin with this simple manner of placing your gently clasped hands in your lap. Later on, you may want to try a more advanced hand position that is commonly used by Zen practitioners: the Cosmic Mudra. To do that, place your right hand on your lap, palm facing upward. Then, place your left hand on your right hand, also palm facing upward. Finally, touch your two thumbs together so that your hands form a circle. While you meditate with your hands in this position, you'll find that when you are tense, your thumbs press together and point upward. When you are distracted, your thumbs drift apart. And when you are drowsy, your thumbs droop downward. However, when you manage to maintain a relaxed alertness, a concentrated mindfulness, your thumbs remain gently touching, effortlessly keeping the form of the Cosmic Mudra.

Once the hands are in place, the next thing to attend to is the head. Most of us sit with our chin slightly protruding outward. If you slide it back and forth, you'll see how sticking your chin out warps your entire posture. So it is best to slightly tuck your chin in when you meditate. Or, what amounts to the same thing, literally or imaginatively pull a tuft of hair on the crown of your head upward toward the ceiling. This sets the head in proper alignment with the spine.

Make sure the head is not tilted either to the left or to the right, and that it's not bending forward or back. Those of us who read a lot or work hunched over a computer will need to take special care not to allow the head to droop forward. Your ears should be over your shoulders, and the tip of your nose over your belly button. This may take some reconditioning, since we've built up a lot of bad body karma. Keep in mind that meditation is a holistic discipline, and you are rehabilitating your posture and flexibility at the same time as you are training your mind—and, moreover, you are realizing how interconnected body and mind actually are.

Next, let's talk about what to do with the eyes. In Zen meditation, one leaves the eyes open, though you can lower the eyelids halfway. Let your vision naturally settle on a spot on the floor about four or five feet in front of you if you are sitting on the floor, probably about six or maybe seven feet in front of you if you are sitting on a chair. Be sure that the spot is right in the middle, otherwise over time it will cause your body to lean left or right. And make sure that the spot is not too close or too far away, since over time that will cause your head to dip forward or lean back. You'll find that when the eyes wander, so does the mind. Bringing the eyes back to their "parking place" will help bring your mind back to the practice.

Closing the eyes completely would, to be sure, eliminate external distractions, and some meditators find it helpful to do so. However, there are several potential problems with closing the eyes. For one, it invites sleepiness, and anyone who has meditated for some time knows how powerful the "sleep demon" can be! The second problem is that closing the eyes activates the imagination, a boost for daydreamers but a distraction for meditators. The potentially most serious problem with closing the eyes is that it can foster a sense of retreating inside and cutting oneself off from the outer world. In Zen meditation, we are trying to re-connect with, not escape from, the rest of the world.

Attending to the Breath

The breath is the focus of many meditative techniques and spiritual traditions, and for good reason. Whether it is the Hebrew *ruach*, the Greek *pneuma*, the Latin *spiritus*, the Sanskrit *prana*, or the Chinese *qi*, the breath has often been associated with the psychophysical energy that enlivens all existence.[1] It is note-worthy that the breath-spirit is associated not just with the psychic as opposed to the physical, not just with the mental as opposed to the material. Rather, the breath-spirit is the unifier of these supposedly opposed dimensions of reality. The breath is the great mediator of the mental and material aspects of the psy-chosomatic self, and of the inner and outer dimensions of self and world. If we understand *spiritus* in this holistic sense, then Zen can indeed be understood as a kind of spirituality.

By meditating on the breath, you will discover that it conjoins and pervades the physical, emotional, and cognitive aspects of yourself. Deep breathing with the lower abdomen calms the emotions and clarifies the mind. Short breathing with the chest is an emergency mechanism for stressful situations—and it produces stress if done unnecessarily.

By meditating on the breath, you discover that it is a respirational exchange of inside and outside. If we attend to the breath, it is a constant reminder that we are not isolated individuals but are intimately connected with the world around us. Breathing in, we inhale the world; breathing out, we exhale the self. Or rather, the self just is this back-and-forth movement between inside and outside.

The first kōan I was given—a kōan that I am certain will keep on giving until I take my last breath—was "Where does the breath come from?" I cannot give you the answer. I would if I could, but it is impossible to give someone the answer to a kōan. The best one could do is to give someone the hollow husk of one's own answer. But that would in fact be the worst thing one could do—like breaking a tool before you hand it to someone, when that tool could have saved their life. Giving someone the hollow husk of an answer to a kōan would be like breaking the valve on an oxygen tank before handing it to someone who is suffocating. But I can tell you where to go to find the answer to the kōan "Where does the breath come from?" The best place to discover the source of the breath is on the meditation cushion.

Attending to the Mind

We'll talk about how kōans are used in conjunction with meditation in Chapter 22. To begin with, in meditation you should focus your mind on the breath. Before I was ever assigned a kōan, for years I practiced "counting the breaths" (Jp. *susokukan*) and then wordlessly "following the breaths" (*zuisokukan*).

The method of counting the breaths has for centuries been a basic practice of Zen meditation, and it is the practice I recommend you start with. It is also a practice you can always return to. I remember a Zen master telling me a long time ago that when he sits down to meditate, he often begins by stabilizing the mind using this method. If this practice is good enough for a Zen master, I recall thinking, then it's good enough for me! I still practice it regularly.

Here is how you do it. After you have gotten yourself physically situated, take a deep breath and then forcefully exhale all the stale air out of every crevice inside you. You can repeat this preparatory step two or three times if you wish. Then, with your mouth closed and your tongue pressed gently against the back of your upper front teeth, relax all the muscles of your lower abdomen and let yourself naturally breathe in deeply. Now breathe out more slowly through the nostrils until you have exhausted all the air. Then let your body naturally turn from exhalation back to inhalation. It is important to breathe naturally. As you relax your lower abdomen and mindfully attend to the breath, it will naturally deepen of its own accord. There is no need to force it. Eventually the breath may become at times very subtle and even shallow. At that point too, let it do what feels natural.

When you are ready, begin counting one number per breath, of course silently and to yourself. Exhaling, count one number for the duration of the outbreath. Like this: Exhaling, *one* . . . Relax and inhale. Exhaling, *two* . . . Relax and inhale. Exhaling, *three* . . . Keep this up until you have counted to ten with ten breaths. Then simply begin again with *one* . . .

If your mind wanders and you lose track of which number you are on, just gently yet firmly bring yourself back to the practice and begin again at one.

I should say not *if* but rather *when* your mind wanders. It will wander. Repeatedly. Don't get frustrated; it is all part of the practice. Don't think, "If I could just stay focused, then I could begin to meditate." Rather, as long as you are making an effort to stay focused, to bring the mind back again and again when it wanders, you are doing it. You are meditating. Always meditate with the understanding that there is no such thing as a bad meditation. Often, the harder a meditation period is, the more you get out of it. But the easy ones are good too. They are all good.

You might be thinking now, "Counting the breaths, and only up to ten—that sounds easy!" Once you try it, though, you'll realize how difficult it is *because* of its simplicity. And you'll realize how unnecessarily complicated the mind usually is. Remember, this is the first lesson of the experience of meditation. To begin with, it teaches you how much you need to meditate, because your mind is more out of control than a four-year-old juiced up on Halloween candy!

Meditators often speak about experiencing the "monkey-mind," since the hyperactive mind is like a monkey swinging from one branch to another, from one distracting thought or train of thoughts to another: "This reminds me of that, oh, and that brings to mind that other thing," and so on. Our minds fly off to other places and times, back into the past and out into the future, remembering, planning, obsessing, worrying, fantasizing, and so on. Counting the breaths is an excellent way to bring them back, again and again, purely and simply to the here and now.

"Okay," you might be thinking, "but isn't it boring, just counting from one to ten, and starting over again?" That thought is coming from the sloth-mind teaming up with the monkey-mind. While the monkey-mind makes us feel restless, jittery, and fidgety, his partner the sloth-mind makes us feel lazy, foggy, and drowsy. They work together like a wrestling tag team to distract us from meditating and to keep us on the pendulum swing between the extremes of being stressed out and zoned out. Many of us today spend most of our lives on this pendulum between stressing out and zoning out, with rare moments of meditative zoning in that are all too few and far between. To deal with stress we zone out with distractions, rather than zone in with meditation.

Meditation is neither exciting nor boring, but we are unfamiliar with this Middle Way, and so if it is not exciting, we think, it must be boring. So be it. Let's say to the monkey-mind: "Yes, meditation is boring. It is meant to be boring. As boring as possible. It is not meant to give you another juicy set of thoughts. It is meant to wean you from your habit of always chasing after juicy thoughts." To repeat what was said in Chapter 3: Don't flee from boredom. Go all the way into it; go all the way through the bottom of boredom! The place of rest you seek lies beneath, not beyond, your restless mind.

Zen meditation is, admittedly, a rather "cold turkey" approach. We humans are addicted to distracting thoughts. And that was true even before we had electronic enhancers for our multitasking monkey-minds. No matter how smart our phones get, they are not going to enlighten us. However, there is one wise way in which you can use your smartphone during meditation, and that is to set a timer, preferably one that ends with a nice bell sound—and yes, of course, there's an app for that! Traditionally, in a monastery the monitor keeps time with an incense stick, and you can of course still do that. In any case, it is best not to have a watch or clock in view, so that you can give yourself completely over to the timeless practice of being and breathing, here and now.

When the numbers are no longer needed to cultivate concentration, you can drop the counting and just follow the breaths. Eventually you can even drop the focus on the breath and "just sit" (Jp. *shikantaza*), abiding in wide-open awareness of all that is happening, neither grasping on to nor ignoring anything. At some point you may decide to seek the guidance of a qualified teacher and take up kōan practice. I'll introduce *shikantaza* and kōan practice in Chapter 22. At this point, let me provide a few more instructions on stilling the body and clearing the mind so that you can get started establishing a routine practice of Zen meditation.

Lead with the Body, with Physical Stillness

They say that when the going gets tough, the tough get going. But no matter how tough you are, you cannot muscle your way to peace. No matter how much willpower you have, you cannot force yourself into a deep state of stillness. You have to let this distilling process happen. You cannot control the process of spiritual fermentation; you can only supply the ingredients, cultivate the conditions, and let it naturally happen.

Trusting the process of meditation and having patience with this process are two of the most important requirements. I always tell myself and others, *lead with the body*. You cannot completely control the body, but you at least have more control over the body than you do over the mind. You can command the body to be still and have some success, but if you try to command the mind to be still, that usually just riles it up all the more. As with a small child throwing a tantrum, just give it space, a large and quiet space filled with attentive patience.

Even if we can sometimes get our minds to be relatively still for a few minutes, this does not straightaway pacify our turbulent emotions. When the mind stops racing for a minute or two, we might realize that, underneath the thinking mind, the emotional heart is anxious and unsettled. Through a prolonged practice of meditation, our emotions become calmer and brighter. Even then, however, the deepest dimension of ourselves—let's call it our spirit—is not yet fully at peace.

In a practice of meditation, we can best attain stillness and peace in this order: first the body, then the mind, then the heart, and finally the spirit. Lead with the body, with physical stillness. That may take a considerable amount of effort and commitment, but you can do it. Then, attending to the breath, trust in the process. Let the breath be the bridge that it is; let it circulate like a fluid connecting tissue between the different physical, psychological, and spiritual dimensions of your being.

As you attend to the breath, your physical stillness will create the condition for your mind to eventually calm down. Mental stillness, in turn, will allow the emotions to slowly settle and relax. Then, gradually—or perhaps even suddenly—you will one day attain the spiritual peace you deeply desire. This will happen at least periodically, and maybe someday more or less continually.

To a significant degree, physical stillness can be willed; we can control it. Mental stillness . . . not so much. We can at best hold the mind still for a few seconds, or perhaps for a minute or two. More effectively, we can use techniques like counting the breaths to cultivate a concentrated state of "one-pointedness of mind." It would be nice if we had even this much control over our emotions, but we don't. Emotional peace has to be cultivated still more indirectly, through physical and mental stillness.

What we most deeply desire, spiritual peace, is really impossible to attain by willpower. Indeed, the more we crave it and grasp for it, the further it seems to recede from us. The best we can do is create the conditions for it to happen. Lead with the body, with physical stillness, attend to the breath, and trust in the process of meditation.

Leading with the body includes committing to physical stillness for the duration of each sitting. Of course, if you have a severe leg cramp or a bumblebee lands on your nose, by all means move! But otherwise, it is important to commit to refraining from all *voluntary* movements during a sitting. *Involuntary* movements, like sneezing, are fine. Let them come and let them go, like anything else beyond your control. You'll find that they don't really disturb you or other meditators around you. Believe me, I've heard my share of involuntary bodily sounds being emitted from meditating monks. No one pays them any attention.

In a Zen monastery, *voluntary* movements, however, are strictly forbidden. Farting is fine, but sniffling will summon the "encouragement stick" from the monitor monk. So if you have a runny nose, be sure to blow it before the sitting begins. After that, during the meditation, try "calling its bluff"—I've found that it almost never actually drips down past my upper lip.

Of course, you don't have to meditate in a strict environment like a Zen monastery. But it is important to know that voluntary movements are distracting and that they can easily become addictive. Once you start to adjust your posture or scratch an itch, it easily becomes a habitual fidgeting. Like opening a big bag of potato chips, it's hard to know when to stop, or how many seconds to wait before going for another.

I discovered early on that there is a "master breaker switch" inside us that turns off all voluntary movements. Rather than turning off each of the switches in the house one by one as the need arises, just find the master breaker switch and turn it off as soon as a meditation period begins. Once I discovered this master switch, I found it to be incredibly and powerfully liberating. I had never realized how much I had been at the beck and call of my bodily whims. If you are allowed to move whenever you want, you may be free externally, but not internally. You are a slave to whatever urge your body throws at you to fidget, scratch, adjust, or otherwise move about and remain unsettled. Discovering this master switch frees you from your body's restlessness and, eventually, from your mind's distractedness.

Once you become capable of physical stillness, this sets in motion the process of attaining mental, then emotional, and finally spiritual peace.

Dealing with Distractions: Discovering the Mirror-Mind

Beginning meditators are likely to think, "If only I could get used to sitting still without so much physical discomfort, then I could really start meditating." However, once the leg and back pain subsides, the monkey-mind starts swinging from branch to branch, juicy thought to juicy thought, with even more impunity. You realize that the bodily aches had at least helped to keep you mentally focused!

Disciplining the mind proves to be more difficult than disciplining the body. This is especially the case because our efforts to control the mind generally end up adding fuel to the mental fire. Sending in the disciplinarian storm troopers just makes the stormy winds of the mind blow all the more turbulently. Now there are two of you in there causing trouble. To begin with, there is the busy mind that is doing everything it can to not settle down into meditative concentration; this is the unruly you that feeds off noise and distraction and is afraid of the depths of silence and stillness. And now, adding fuel to the fire, there is the disciplinarian you who wants to meditate and so goes chasing after the unruly you in order to pin this rascal down and force him to be calm and quiet. Anyone who has been around little kids knows that trying to force them to stop throwing a temper tantrum by shouting at them, or trying to catch them when they are running amok long after bedtime, can just make the situation worse. Like an out-of-control child, the mischievous monkey-mind feeds off such negative energy. Chasing a monkey will not make it stop swinging from branch to branch.

The seventeenth-century Japanese Zen master Bankei tells us, "Clearing away thoughts from the mind as they arise is like washing away blood in blood."[2] Trying to clear your mind is counterproductive, since the "trying" just adds another thought and more energy to the mental mayhem.

So, what can you do? First of all, relax and realize that dealing with distracting thoughts, like dealing with physical discomforts, is an important part of the practice of meditation. These are not prerequisites; they are part and parcel of the practice itself. So don't worry—when you are dealing with these issues, you are already meditating!

The modern Sōtō Zen master Shunryu Suzuki (Jp. Suzuki Shunryū) gives some very helpful advice. First of all, he tells us, every time you catch your mind wandering and bring it back to the practice, this is nourishing your practice, just like picking weeds and returning them to the soil nourishes the plant that they were previously taking nourishment from.[3] Returning again and again from mental tangents is what keeps the wheel of meditation in motion.

Another teaching Suzuki Rōshi gives in this regard goes even deeper and wider. He says: If you want to control your mischievous mind, don't try to control it. Don't try to pin it down or confine it to a mental jail cell. Do the opposite and give it a wide-open space in which to roam. Using another vivid metaphor, he says: "To give your sheep or cow a large, spacious meadow is the way to control him."[4] That wide-open pasture is an image for what he and other Zen masters call "Big Mind." All the thoughts and distractions of our small minds take place within a wide-open and non-judgmental field of awareness.

Meditation allows us to shift our self-identification from small mind to Big Mind. Small mind might still be up to its old tricks, but those tricks cease to disturb us the more we identify with the great expanse of Big Mind. In Big Mind, there is ultimately no difference between external and internal distractions. "Big mind," says Suzuki, "experiences everything within itself."[5] A dog barks, your neighbor meditator coughs, an uninvited memory or a delicious fantasy pops up—they are all just clouds passing through the wide-open blue sky of Big Mind.

If we chase after these distractions or try to chase them off, either way we end up just feeding them more energy and making the sky of the mind all the more cloudy. Just remind yourself that you are the wide-open sky, and let the clouds float in and out as they will. "When you are practicing zazen," Suzuki says, "do not try to stop your thinking. Let it stop by itself. . . . Things will come as they come and go as they go. Then eventually your clear, empty mind will last fairly long."[6]

Zen masters often speak of the "mirror-mind." They compare the clear mind to a mirror that just lets things show up as they are, and lets them go without leaving a trace when they pass. Eventually, the luminous blue sky of the mirror-mind will shine so brightly that cloudy thoughts will dissipate on their own. Bankei says:

You have to realize that your thoughts are ephemeral and unreal and, without either clutching at them or rejecting them, just let them come and go of themselves. They are like images reflected in a mirror. A mirror is clear and bright and reflects whatever is placed before it. But the image doesn't remain in the mirror. The Buddha-mind is ten thousand times brighter than any mirror and is marvelously illuminative besides. All thoughts vanish tracelessly into its light.[7]

In one of the most famous episodes in Zen lore, the lowly layman Huineng responds to an instructive yet still limited verse by the senior monk, Shenxiu, a response that proved him worthy of becoming the seminal Sixth Chinese Ancestor in the lineage of Zen.

Shenxiu's verse reads: "The body is a bodhi tree. / The mind is like a bright mirror on a stand. / At all times keep it polished. / Don't let it be covered by dust."[8] Shenxiu understands the purity of the mirror-mind to be tarnished by deluding thoughts, and so he thinks of meditation as a practice of repeatedly wiping away this defiling dust. The Fifth Ancestor, Hongren, praised this verse in public, telling his disciples to rely on it in their practice. However, in private, he told Shenxiu that it "shows your understanding has only reached the threshold and has not yet entered inside. . . . If you want to enter the door, you have to see your nature."[9] Soon thereafter Hongren found a worthy successor upon reading the verse composed in response by Huineng, at the time an illiterate layman working in the rice mill of the monastery.

According to one of the earliest versions of the *Platform Sutra*, Huineng's responding verse reads: "Bodhi originally has no tree. / The mirror also has no stand. / Our Buddha-nature is forever clean and pure. / Where is there any dust?"[10] Huineng does not question the aptness of thinking of the Buddha-nature or Buddha-mind as a mirror. Rather, he claims that the essential purity of the mirror-mind could never be defiled. He also suggests that the mirror-mind is non-judgmentally aware of thoughts and things as they present themselves, rather than preemptively judging them to be essentially either pure or impure.[11]

The purpose of meditation is not to polish the mirror-mind so as to keep it from being stained by impure thoughts. The point is to discover that the unstainable mirror-mind has been there all along, a discovery that allows it to function more freely. By awakening to the wide-open space of non-judgmental awareness, we activate our innate capacity to make unbiased and appropriate judgments in specific times and places.

The point of Zen is to let the mind respond freely to those thoughts and things without getting stuck, without getting attached to craving or loathing any particular thought or thing. As the *Diamond Sutra* tells us in the line that fully awakened Huineng: "Arouse the mind that does not linger anywhere."[12] In other words: Awaken the mind that does not get stuck on anything and so can freely circulate to wherever presently needs attention. The point is to be free and able to respond in the midst of dealing with thoughts and things.

Although Huineng warns us not to get fixated on any particular bodily posture, telling us that "the single practice of meditation means at all times, whether walking, standing, sitting, or lying down, always practicing with a straightforward mind,"[13] it nevertheless remains the case that the best posture in which to awaken to this straightforward mind is the one that we carefully cultivate and maintain in *zazen*, seated meditation.[14]

Kinhin: Walking Meditation

In between periods of sitting, walking meditation, called *kinhin*, is often practiced. In Rinzai and Sōtō Zen centers these practices differ in some respects. In Rinzai, one sits facing out into the room, whereas in Sōtō one sits facing the wall. And the walking meditation is done much slower in Sōtō than it is in Rinzai.

New participants in The Heart of Zen Meditation Group often say that they find the walking meditation to be both a surprisingly difficult and a surprisingly fruitful practice. Expecting it to be an easy break from struggling with their fidgety bodies and monkey-minds while trying to sit still, they sometimes find it even more difficult to simply walk slowly and attentively in circles around the room. There are several reasons for this. To begin with, we move quite a bit slower than they are used to walking to get from point A to point B. In the Sōtō school one walks *much* slower during *kinhin*, in "half steps," one breath per step. In the Rinzai school we typically walk at a fairly brisk pace. In the winter, between periods of sitting still in freezing temperatures in the monastery, we literally *run* in circles around the meditation hall in order to warm up.

Incidentally, this is one of many things that are done rather briskly in Rinzai Zen monasteries, which are known for the dynamic quality of their training. I sometimes have to remind people that doing something *mindfully* does not necessarily mean doing it *slowly*. In fact, the opposite is often the case: If a car swerves into your lane, you'd better quickly and attentively get out of the way! And a baseball player's Zone of Zen would not be worth much if he could only hit very slow pitches.

In The Heart of Zen Meditation Group, we take a middle-of-the-road approach to the speed of our walking meditation. We move at about half the speed one would normally walk. I encourage folks to walk *naturally yet mindfully*. That is what makes it both difficult and fruitful. Since we are used to walking inattentively, once we start to pay attention to our movements, our awareness easily turns into awkward self-consciousness. Walking meditation allows us develop an *unselfconscious mindfulness*, which opens the door to the fluidly nondualistic quality of heightened awareness experienced when one is in the Zone of Zen (see Chapter 17).

Here is how we shift from a sitting period into a walking period. A bell is rung, signaling the start of the transition. At that point, just move your eyeballs around a bit to bring your mind back into a more active state. Then the clappers are struck twice, once together and once on the floor. That signals that a walking meditation is about to begin. Now begin to move your body. Try to attend fully to each physical movement just as, while sitting, you had been attending fully to your breath. First bring your palms together in front of your upper chest, a gesture called *gasshō*, and bow while still seated. Then unfold your legs—take your time and massage them if they have fallen asleep.

Once everyone is standing and waiting with palms together in *gasshō*, the clappers are struck, signaling the beginning of the walking. After bowing, place your hands in the *shashu* position: left hand over right, clasped gently together and held before your chest so that your forearms are parallel to the ground.

Turn to the left, and proceed to walk clockwise around the room. Be sure to leave as much space as possible between you and the person in front of you. As a group, try to remain evenly spaced throughout the room. Set your pace by the leader of the meditation. If he or she speeds up or slows down, adjust your speed accordingly and stay evenly spaced. This attentiveness will keep your field of awareness wide and help you cultivate a mindful awareness of your interconnected rather than isolated self. Walking silently together is a wonderfully communal experience.

As you walk, put your mind in your feet. While you were sitting, your mind was placed in your lower belly, in an area called the *tanden*, just under your navel. We tend to place our minds in our heads, chasing around after thoughts, or in our chests, swirling around with our emotions. Once you get used to placing your mind in the *tanden*—the locus of deep breathing and nondual awareness—you will increasingly become capable of freely placing it anywhere. Zen meditation is a method of awakening the mind that does not get stuck anywhere, the mind that freely attends to the present activity in its shifting circumstances.

With your mind placed in your feet and freely flowing with each step, attend to the subtle sensations on the soles of your feet as they gently press down on, and then lift up off, the ground. Attend to all the subtle adjustments you effortlessly make in your ankles and elsewhere throughout your body to maintain your balance. Awaken to the wonder of walking—one of the myriad miracles of our mundane lives that we have become desensitized to and thus fail to appreciate.

Walking is one of the most common and supposedly simple movements we do. And yet when you do it mindfully, you discover its almost infinite complexity. At first, that discovery can also make it strangely difficult. Suddenly you may feel clumsy; it may feel surprisingly unnatural. It will take some practice to be able to walk *fully attentively yet utterly naturally*.

The other problem you may face during walking meditation is that the monkey-mind easily gets bored and tries to stir up trouble. Walking slowly around a room is not enough stimulation for it, especially if it has gotten used to a diet of binge-watching TV and obsessively scrolling through social media. It will demand some juicier mind candy than just walking slowly around a room. "At least give me a guided meditation!" the monkey-mind might demand. But, even if not quite as minimalistically "boring" as *zazen*, *kinhin* is still a "cold turkey" approach to weaning ourselves off our addiction to mind candy. The point is to return to the present, to the extraordinariness of the ordinary, not to exchange a worldly distraction for a spiritual one.

To be sure, this "cold turkey" approach can be tough. It is hard not to start daydreaming about dinner or start glancing at something or someone across the room. And so, to help keep the mind mindful of the here and now of each step, I have developed the following three-stage method, which I occasionally employ. Normally, after introducing each stage of the method, I let meditators walk for at least five minutes or so in silence.

Stage 1: As you walk, take each step as if it were the very first step you have ever taken in your life. Imagine you had never—until right now—been able to walk. With each brand-new step, completely forget about the previous step and take this one as if it were your very first. Be full of joyful awareness of just how wonderful it feels to actually walk. Practice this for five minutes or more.

Stage 2: As you walk, take each step as if it were the very last step you'll ever take. Reversing the last story, imagine that you are about to lose your ability to walk. You are perfectly able to walk now, but you have just been notified that for some reason you will soon lose this ability. Now, this step, this one you are about to take, is the last one you will ever take. Fully take it in, fully appreciate the experience. With gratitude to your legs for every step they have taken for you in the past, and with apologies for having always taken them for granted, take each step as if saying farewell forever to a loved one. Let your feet and the ground kiss each other goodbye. Practice this for five minutes or more.

Stage 3: As you walk, take each step as if it were both the first step you've ever taken and the last step you'll ever take. Drop all the narrative. It was, after all, just a fictional device used to cultivate a sense of what it means to take each step for the first and last time. In truth, each step *is* the first and last of its exact kind. Every step is unique—it is just that we fail to appreciate its uniqueness. We flatten everything out into generalities. It is just another step, we think, and we get bored. Walking is not boring. It is we who are boring. Wake up to the wonder of walking. Taking each step as if it were your first and last, waking up to the fact that, each time, it is in truth the first and last time that you will take *this* step—now, for once, here and now, you are just walking. That's walking meditation. Practice this for at least five minutes, or for however long you can attentively sustain it.

Kinhin is a nice, and even necessary, break from sitting still for long periods of time in *zazen*. That is indeed part of what *kinhin* is for. But it is hardly just a break. In fact, walking meditation should be understood as a gateway into the most difficult and important practice of all—the practice of daily life. Zen practice is divided into *practice-in-stillness* and *practice-in-motion*. Practice-in-stillness has one main form: *zazen*, seated meditation. Practice-in-motion, on the other hand, has innumerable forms. Every activity is an opportunity to engage in practice-in-motion. *Kinhin*, walking meditation, is, as it were, a matter of taking baby steps toward bringing the energized stillness and peaceful clarity awakened and cultivated in *zazen* into all the activities of our lives.

5

The Buddha's First and Last Lesson

The Middle Way of Knowing What Suffices

It is impossible to understand Zen Buddhism, of course, without learning about the main teachings of the Buddha, and starting with this chapter you'll be doing just that. The Buddha always geared his teachings to whomever he was addressing at the time. Following his example, I will be gearing my explanations of basic Buddhist teachings mainly to an audience of twenty-first-century Westerners interested in learning about Zen Buddhism and possibly in applying its teachings and practices to their lives.

The Buddha gave his first sermon to a group of wandering ascetics. Some weeks prior, they had abandoned him as their leader when they heard that he had given up the path of extreme asceticism. So, it is not surprising that the very first lesson he taught was the Middle Way between indulging and repressing sense desires.[1]

Given that this was the Buddha's very first teaching, it is surprising that there persists a popular Western misconception of Buddhism as demanding a complete denial of all desires. Yet, given that most of us live more or less on the hedonism side of the spectrum, it is perhaps no wonder that we misperceive the Middle Way as being closer to the extreme of asceticism than it really is.[2]

In order to understand the Middle Way, we need to start by understanding how the Buddha arrived at this insight through many years of his own experiences of, and experiments with, both extremes of hedonism and asceticism.

The Four Sights: Witnessing Suffering and Searching for a Way Beyond It

The person who became the historical Buddha, the awakened one, was Siddhartha Gautama, who was born in the sixth century around today's border between India and Nepal.[3] Commonly accepted dates for his life are 563–483 BCE, though some scholars now date his life about eighty years later than this. When Siddhartha was born, a Hindu priest prophesied that he would grow up to become either a universal monarch or a great spiritual liberator. His father was the ruler of a small kingdom, and, unsurprisingly, he wanted to make sure

Zen Pathways. Bret W. Davis, Oxford University Press. © Oxford University Press 2022.
DOI: 10.1093/oso/9780197573686.003.0005

that his son took the political path rather than the spiritual one. For that reason, he kept Siddhartha sheltered and shielded from all the miseries of life. And so, up until the age of twenty-nine, Siddhartha lived a life of extreme privilege and luxury. He was given all the delicious food and beautiful women he desired, and he was not exposed to any of the suffering caused by even such unavoidable matters as old age, sickness, and death.

However, on three unannounced excursions, Siddhartha witnessed three sights. On the first excursion, he saw a very old man, hunched over and barely able to walk. On the second excursion, he saw a very sick person whose flesh was covered with open sores. And on the third excursion, he saw a corpse being carried on a bier in a funeral procession.

Whenever I think about these sights, I recall my own experience of walking the streets in the sprawling cities and slums of India, where the suffering of humanity is so very painfully in plain view. I also recall walking by funeral pyres on the bank of the Ganges River. Yesterday, a living, breathing body; today, a burning corpse. I had often heard the phrase "Dust to dust, ashes to ashes," but there and then I was witnessing the fact. And it was much rawer and more real than the mummified and makeup-covered corpses I had seen at Western funerals—or even the ones I had seen in the back room of a funeral parlor on a field trip I took for a college course on death and dying.

The whole world is on fire, the Buddha tells us in "The Fire Sermon," a sermon that, according to T. S. Eliot, "corresponds in importance to the Sermon on the Mount."[4] The world of our experience is burning with the flames of craving, hatred, attachment, and the sufferings these deluding afflictions cause. "All is burning," the Buddha says, "burning with the fire of lust, with the fire of hatred, with the fire of delusion; burning with birth, aging, and death; with sorrow, lamentation, pain, grief, dejection and despair."[5] How can we figure out how to put out the fire if we don't even acknowledge that it is raging both in and all around us? Yet our society systematically keeps suffering out of sight, behind closed doors in hospitals, hospices, and funeral homes, tucked away in ghettos, locked up in prisons.

Siddhartha was profoundly disturbed by the sights of old age, illness, and death that he witnessed on his excursions outside his pleasure palace. In each case, he asked his attendant, "Could these things happen to me?" In each case the answer was, "Yes. Not only *can* they happen to you, they *will* eventually happen to you." The best that we humans can hope for is that we get the chance to grow old enough to lose our faculties before we get sick and die. The only certainty in life is that it will end. We can hope to witness and accomplish many things in life: to finish a project, to fulfill a dream, or to see our grandchildren graduate from college. However, the only thing we know for sure is that today we are one step closer to death than we were yesterday.

The young Siddhartha returned to his palace, but he could no longer enjoy its pleasures, knowing what he now did about life's inevitable sufferings. Nevertheless, Siddhartha was not destined to become a pessimist. This was fore-told by a fourth sight he had on yet another excursion he took outside the palace walls. He saw a "renouncer," a wandering mendicant, a spiritual seeker who, from the peaceful smile on his face, seemed to have already found something. This fourth sight inspired Siddhartha to leave home in search of a way beyond suf-fering—not just for himself but for everyone.

Leaving home required some great sacrifices. Prince Siddhartha gave up his social standing and all his possessions; he left behind all the pleasures and protections he enjoyed within the palace walls. He also left behind his family, including his wife, his son, and the aunt who had raised him—an act that was even more demanding, both for himself as well as for them. Eventually he did come back for them, and they joined his Sangha, his com-munity of practitioners. But in the meantime, it must have been very hard on all of them. As all traditions recognize, the spiritual search requires sacri-fice. Ultimately, one must give up everything; one must die to the old Adam to gain true life; one must abandon the ego to awaken to the true self (see Chapter 12).

Motivated to Liberate All Sentient Beings from Suffering

It is important to bear in mind that Siddhartha's search was not for himself alone. He wanted to find a path beyond suffering so that he could show it to others. He wanted to wake up, to become a Buddha, so that he could wake others up. The close connection between wisdom and compassion, between enlightenment and concern for others, is present from the beginning of the Buddha's path.

In facing up to our own sufferings, we become attuned to the sufferings of others. In learning to see the fire within us, we also learn to see the fire all around us. And by becoming more empathetic, we also become more compassionate. This is a recurrent theme in Buddhism. Even before leaving home in search of a path of spiritual liberation, after being awakened from his hedonistic slumbers by his encounters outside the palace walls, Siddhartha became keenly aware of the suffering of his father's slaves, who toiled under harsh conditions in the fields. He at once freed them, telling them: "You are free to go wherever you like and live in happiness." He also released the oxen from their harnesses, not being able to bear the sight of their suffering either.[6]

Buddhists are concerned with liberating from suffering all "sentient beings"—all beings who can feel, not just humans. Although the Buddha did not teach absolute vegetarianism, he did prohibit his followers from killing animals either directly or indirectly (by eating the meat of animals that had been killed especially for them).

In any case, if the Buddha had thought that *psychological* suffering could be relieved by just eliminating the causes of *physical* suffering, then it would have probably made more sense for him to have taken the path that would have led to becoming a universal monarch. That way he could have freed many more slaves and farm animals. But the fact is, even after he liberated his father's slaves and told them, "You are free to go wherever you like and live in happiness," they were not totally free and completely capable of living in happiness. Indeed, even we who live in "the land of the free" and are legally guaranteed the right to *pursue* happiness are by no means guaranteed to *catch* it.[7]

Physical freedom from external constraints is by no means a guarantee of spiritual freedom from internal bondage. In fact, people who are free to do whatever they want can end up just becoming a slave to their wants. We must attain internal as well as external freedom, and that requires spiritual discipline.

Studies show that, on average, rich people are no happier than middle-class folk. To be precise, a 2010 study carried out by researchers at Princeton University showed that an increase in wealth is likely to make people significantly happier on a day-to-day basis only up to an annual household income of around $75,000. Beyond that, there is no clear correlation between making more money and being a happier person each day, even if making more money does lead people to think that their life is going better.[8] It is of course important to think that one's life is going well along with actually feeling happy each day. But the bottom line is that wealth is not all there is to well-being. That should give us capitalist competitors and materialistic consumers cause to pause and reflect: do we want more money or more happiness? Because they are not the same thing.

Different Desires: Some Wholesome, Some Unwholesome, and Some Needing Moderation

Most of our activities are motivated by the pursuit of one or the other of what I call the Four P's: pleasure, profit, power, and prestige. We all want these; in fact, to be happy we all need at least a certain amount of all four. But are they all we need? Do they deserve all of our attention and energies?

In Hinduism, four legitimate aims of life are recognized. The first two are pleasure and wealth. The third is moral duty—in other words, doing our part to uphold the order of our household, our community, and the cosmos as a whole. Yet pleasure, wealth, and duty are not enough. Especially in our evening years, says the Hindu tradition, we should increasingly turn our attention to the ultimate aim of life: spiritual liberation. This is called Moksha in Hinduism.

Buddhism sometimes uses this term, but in general calls it Nirvana. The Hindu doctrine of the Four Life Aims is helpful insofar as it recognizes that we have different kinds of desires and that they are all natural and legitimate—as long as they are kept within their proper bounds and measure. There is nothing wrong with a moderate pursuit of pleasure and wealth, as long as this pursuit does not overshadow and override the higher aims of morality and spirituality.

This is a good point at which to clear up a common confusion about Buddhism. *The Buddha did not teach that all desire is bad.* Not at all. First of all, there are many positive desires that the Buddha thought we should cultivate, starting with the desire to liberate oneself and others from suffering. In Mahayana traditions such as Zen, the primary motivation to practice, the first great vow one lives by, is to liberate all sentient beings from suffering. The point of practice is not to eliminate all desire but rather to replace deluded cravings with the motivational power of this liberating vow.

The Buddha spoke of the Four Immeasurables or Immeasurable Mindsets: lovingkindness, compassion, empathetic joy, and equanimity.[9] These are called immeasurable because we can never have an excess of them; they are to be endlessly cultivated and equally directed to the innumerable sentient beings in the universe.[10] We are called upon to endlessly strive, without attachment or aversion, to bring happiness, relief from suffering, and shared joyfulness to all sentient beings everywhere. Such wholesome desires are to be engendered and multiplied rather than curbed and moderated. In Zen and other East Asian Buddhist traditions, lovingkindness (Jp. *ji*, the desire to make people truly happy) and compassion (Jp. *hi*, the desire to relieve people of suffering) are generally combined into one commonly used expression: *jihi*. Of course, there are some unwholesome desires that should be utterly abandoned. The desire to hurt others, hatred, jealousy, and so forth fall into this category. The Buddhist path can indeed be summarized as a way of transforming the Three Poisons of avarice, aversion, and ignorance, or greed, hatred, and delusion (in Sanskrit: *raga*, *dvesha*, and *moha*) into generosity, lovingkindness and compassion, and wisdom (*dana*, *maitri* and *karuna*, and *prajna*). Enlightenment converts the unwholesome desires of greed and hatred into the wholesome desires of generosity and love.[11]

Many desires, however, belong to a third category of those that we should learn to have the right amount of. These include, for example, desires for food, sleep, and sex. There is nothing wrong with the desire for food when, and to the extent that, the body needs nutrients. But an excessive desire for food is unhealthy. An excessive, inordinate desire is called a "craving." And it is craving, not desire as such, that the Buddha's Second Noble Truth says is the cause of suffering. (The Four Noble Truths will be discussed in Chapter 6.) Altruistic desires are to be engendered and cultivated, and egoistic cravings are to be prevented and eliminated. But the third category of desires, desires that are proper in the right amount, is the trickiest. This is where the Buddha's first teaching of the Middle Way comes into play.

Experimenting with Extremes Before Finding the Middle Way

On his way to becoming the Buddha, Siddhartha personally experimented with both extremes of indulging and quashing desires. Growing up in an overprotective pleasure palace, Siddhartha lived the life of hedonism, giving free rein to his sense desires. Turning decisively away from this life, for six years Siddhartha tested the limits of the path of extreme asceticism. If desires are the source of internal bondage, he thought, if they are the cause of my suffering, then I'll show them who's boss!

During this pre-enlightenment period of extreme asceticism, Siddhartha nearly starved himself to death. It is said that he could touch his spine through his stomach. Although I recently saw an image of this displayed at a Zen Buddhist temple in Kamakura, Japan, it is crucial to bear in mind that this is *not* an image of the Buddha. It is a depiction of Siddhartha before he became the Buddha, during the time when he wandered as far as one can go down the erroneous path of extreme asceticism. Images of Siddhartha after he became the Buddha generally depict him with a healthy body mass index. Admittedly, images of the Chinese Zen figure Budai, the so-called Happy Buddha or Laughing Buddha, seem to go too far in the opposite direction. The symbolic point of this plump figure is to counteract perceptions of Buddhism as world-negating and aloof from society. Budai's large belly symbolizes his abundance, while the sack he carries symbolizes, in part, his contentment with few possessions. His smiling face conveys the infectious joy he brings to others, including the village children he entertains as he wanders freely through the world. We'll meet Budai again at the end of this book (Chapter 24), where we'll see how the sack he carries also symbolizes his Santa Claus–like generosity.

Of course, images frequently get co-opted for other purposes. The first Buddhist image I encountered as a child was a statue of Budai at an all-you-can-eat Chinese restaurant in Texas. Needless to say, this all too Americanized version of a Chinese restaurant, where you are encouraged to eat all you can possibly fit into your expandable stomach, is not the best place to learn about the Middle Way.

In Japan, I learned the common saying *hara hachi bun me*, which means that you should eat until you feel 80 percent full. Although I've repeated this saying for three decades now, it is still easier said than done. We tend to eat with our mouths, so to speak, rather than with our stomachs—in other words, we often keep eating because something tastes good or because indulging in an extra helping of "comfort food" temporarily relieves stress, not because our stomach is still grumbling for more nutrition. Compounding the problem, in an all-you-can-eat restaurant we feel like we are being challenged to eat with our wallets as well as with our mouths. If we don't walk out feeling like our stomachs are about to burst, we feel like we got ripped off!

It is difficult to know when to stop, to know when one has had enough, just the right amount. Extremes are easier to pursue: either more is better, or less is more; either it's all-you-can-eat, or it's a celery-stick-a-day diet; either it's strict abstinence, or it's sex addiction; either be a workaholic, or live a life of leisure—the world seems to be constantly offering us such binary choices between extremes. The Buddha teaches us to say no to both extremes and to find the right balance between them.

The Middle Way Beyond the Pendulum Swing Between Extremes

The Buddha is not alone in advocating a Middle Way. In ancient Greece and medieval Christendom, one of the cardinal virtues was "temperance" or "moderation," *sophrosyne* in Greek and *continentia* in Latin: note the etymological connection with being "content," happily satisfied. In Chapter 2 we discussed the importance of the dictum "Know thyself," inscribed in the forecourt of the Temple of Apollo at Delphi. In fact, there is another dictum inscribed there: "Nothing in excess" (Gk. *mēden agan*). We seem to have lost a sense of this virtue of moderation. The tendency to excess, including to the spiritual arrogance the Greeks called *hubris*, is related to a lack of self-knowledge. Only if one knows one's limits can one know how much is enough and how much is excessive.[12]

We seem to have lost an understanding of this virtue of moderation. It is telling that many of my college students, even those with a devout Catholic upbringing, don't even know the meaning of the word "temperance." We live in a society that promotes excess. Admittedly, teaching temperance won't be the best stimulus for a capitalist economy—an economy that, after all, thrives not just on satisfying desires but on creating cravings. But reviving this teaching of temperance is nevertheless necessary in order for us to cultivate a more balanced lifestyle.

It is not by deleting all desires, any more than it is by multiplying them, that we can find balance in our lives. In a lecture to my students, Kobayashi Gentoku Rōshi, the current abbot of Shōkokuji monastery in Kyoto, compared the Middle Way to riding a bicycle. It is only by pushing down just the right amount and with just the right rhythmic timing on the left and right pedals that we can maintain our balance and move forward on down the road.

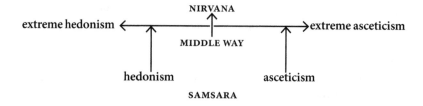

When I teach students about the Middle Way, I often draw a line on the chalk-board with arrows on each end pointing to the extremes of hedonism and ascet-icism. The Middle Way is found in the middle. Yet it is not just a middle point on a spectrum of inflating and curbing desire. Rather, it is a middle passageway; there is an opening in the middle that leads beyond our life of swinging between extremes on the hedonism-asceticism pendulum. We overwork, and then we crash on the couch. We stress out during the week, and then we zone out on the weekends. In this pendulum swing from one extreme to the other, we continually bypass this opening in the middle. Only if we find this passageway, the Buddha taught, can we pass from Samsara, a life of self-inflicted suffering, to Nirvana, a life of true peace and joy. If we try to get there by steering too far in the direc-tion of either hedonism or asceticism, we will hit a wall and won't be able to pass through this opening in the middle.

And so the Middle Way is not just about finding the right balance. It is about what you can do when you are balanced. It is not just about not falling over; it is about where you can go on that bicycle. It is about moving from a life of swinging between extremes to a balanced life filled with energy, joyful peace, creativity and compassion.

"I Only Know How to Be Content with What Suffices"

Let me conclude this chapter by commenting on a saying that concisely expresses the teaching of the Middle Way. One can find the saying carved into water basins in Buddhist temples around Japan. There is one in Kyoto at Ryōanji, the Zen temple with the most famous rock garden (see photograph at the end of Chapter 19). The striking beauty and spiritual depth of that garden are surely re-lated to knowing not only just the right placement but also just the right number of rocks to use. Not too many, just enough: fifteen, to be exact. A vast world of interconnected waters and mountains opens up in that rectangle of merely 248 square meters. The spirit can breathe in the quietude of that small, unclut-tered space better than it can in the middle of the hustle and bustle of a major metropolis.

Tucked away in an even smaller garden space on the other side of the temple is a water basin ingeniously crafted such that the center square that holds the water forms part of each of the four sinographs or Chinese characters that surround it: 吾唯足知. There is also a water basin with the same saying in Hasedera, a temple in Kamakura. In Chinese, the saying reads *wu wei zu zhi*. In Japanese, it reads *ware tada taru wo shiru*. The meaning is "I only know how much is enough" or "I only know what suffices."

Figure 5.1 Water basin at Hasedera, Kamakura

In fact, the character for "enough" or "sufficiency" also means "satisfaction" or "contentment." And so the saying could be more fully translated as "I only know how to be content with what suffices." It teaches us that true satisfaction does not come from pursuing excess any more than it comes from suffering insufficiency. Rather, true contentment comes from knowing just the right amount, from knowing what suffices. True happiness is not found by satisfying as many desires as possible, any more than it is found by suppressing all our desires. Rather, it is based on knowing how to limit our desires to just the right amount.

The saying carved on these water basins has ancient roots in Daoism as well as Buddhism. In the *Daodejing* we read: "One who knows what is enough, is rich."[13] And in one of the earliest collections of the Buddha's teachings, the *Dhammapada*, we read: "Contentment is the greatest wealth."[14] In *The Sutra of the Buddha's Final Instruction*—a text recognized in the Zen tradition as one of the Three Sutras of the Founder—on his deathbed the Buddha teaches his disciples:

> When people offer you food and drink or clothing or bedding or medicine, look at the amount and consider how much is enough. Take just what you need and do not pile up a surplus. . . . The person of few desires seeks nothing, wants nothing, and thus is free of affliction. . . . The practice of limiting one's desires brings the mind a sense of composure free of all anxiety. . . . To have but few desires is to have nirvana.[15]

Note that the Buddha is counseling us to *limit* our desires, not to *eliminate* them. Like the audience of the Buddha's final sermon, and unlike the ascetics who were the audience of his first sermon, most of us probably need to practice limiting our desires more than we need to learn to affirm their naturalness in the right amount. In any case, if we find the right balance, if we find the Middle Way of moderation, the result is not a mere state of psychological stability. The result, the Buddha promises, is nothing less than the passageway to Nirvana.

In an illuminating essay on this topic, Catholic priest and scholar of Buddhist and comparative philosophy James Heisig writes that what the Buddha is teaching us is that

> the mind converted to sufficiency is clear, transparent—and enjoyable. Learning to limit desire is not a lackluster, lowland path between the extremes of worldly gluttony and ascetic self-torture, but a high point from which both of these extremes look mediocre.[16]

The Buddha once explained practicing the Middle Way with the metaphor of tuning a *vina*, a string instrument like a sitar or a guitar. If the strings are too loose, they will make only a dull sound, if any at all. On the other hand, if the strings are wound too tightly, they will break. Only if they are tightened just the right amount will they be able to play beautiful music. Analogously, the Buddha said, "over-aroused persistence leads to restlessness, [and] overly slack persistence leads to laziness. . . . Thus you should determine the right pitch for your persistence." Only by tuning the pitch of our persistence, he teaches, can we free ourselves from the Three Poisons of ignorance, avarice, and aversion and thereby attain Nirvana.[17] In other words, we could say that by limiting but not eliminating our desires, by finding the right balance between overly severe discipline and merely lazy lenience, our lives can manifest a beautifully natural harmony.

6

The Buddha's Strong Medicine
Embracing Impermanence

The Four Noble Truths

In his first sermon, after he taught the Middle Way, the Buddha explained for the first time the doctrine that became the framework for his other teachings: the Four Noble Truths. These four truths are the fact of suffering, the causes of suffering, the possibility of ending suffering, and the way to achieve the end of suffering.[1] Their meaning can be spelled out as follows:

1. Human beings suffer, especially from a deep-rooted spiritual or existential unease.
2. This suffering is primarily caused by a feedback loop between craving and ignorance.
3. It is possible to put an end to these causes of suffering, and thus to attain the ultimate peace of Nirvana.
4. The way to do this is to follow the Eightfold Path, which consists of right view, intention, speech, action, livelihood, effort, mindfulness, and concentration.

Before we begin to further unpack the meaning of these Noble Truths, let me remind you that the Buddha always geared his teachings to whoever happened to be his audience at any given time. There is a saying in Zen that during his forty-five (or forty-nine) years of teaching, in truth the Buddha taught not a single word. The paradoxical quality of sayings such as this one is meant to provoke us into thinking more deeply. Only by way of patiently pondering the puzzle can we really get its point. In this case, the point is that the Buddha did not dictate a doctrine that would fully capture the truth for everyone everywhere at every time.

Buddhism is an inherently non-dogmatic religion. Its teachings are meant to liberate us from suffering, not to reveal absolute truths that are to be carved in stone and carried around like big heavy chips on our shoulders. All Buddhist teachings are heuristic "skillful means" for ending suffering.

Zen Pathways. Bret W. Davis, Oxford University Press. © Oxford University Press 2022.
DOI: 10.1093/oso/9780197573686.003.0006

The Parable of the Raft: Buddhism Itself Is a Means, Not the End

The Buddha made this point most clearly in the Parable of the Raft.[2] Here's the gist of the story: Imagine that you are on a camping trip, and you find yourself on the very dangerous side of a river, surrounded by vicious animals and poisonous plants. On the other side of the river is a safe and peaceful haven. Using your resourcefulness, you manage to fashion a raft from tree branches and reeds, and although it is difficult to paddle across, you eventually make it safely to the other shore.

Then you do something stupid. Overjoyed at the usefulness of your invention, you think: "This raft saved my life! This is the most wonderful possession in all the world!" And so you resolve to carry around this heavy, soggy contraption on your shoulders, not just for the rest of your camping trip but indeed for the rest of your life. "Wouldn't that be dumb," says the Buddha in effect. What then should you do? Well, the raft served its purpose, so now it is time to leave it behind—or, even better, see if you can figure out a way to send it back to the other shore so that another camper can use it to cross over.

In Buddhism, the expressions "this shore" and "the other shore" are often used to refer to Samsara and Nirvana. This shore is the realm of suffering, and the other shore is the realm of peace. What, then, is the "raft" that is used for crossing over from Samsara to Nirvana? This is the main point of the parable. The raft is the Buddha's teaching, the Buddha Dharma. In other words, the raft is Buddhism.

This means that, in this parable, the Buddha is in effect telling us not to attach ourselves to Buddhism! "The raft is for crossing over, not for clinging," he says. Buddhism is a means, not the end. If we attach ourselves to Buddhism, or to any religion, then we turn the medicine into poison. And the next thing you know we are beating others over the head with our soggy raft, forcing them to get on board, or telling them they need to bow down before it.

You may want to keep this Parable of the Raft in mind as you read this book. Are the teachings of Zen Buddhism useful to you? Do they help to ease your mind and enliven your spirit? If so, make the most of them! If some teachings don't, then you may have to leave them behind—or maybe just off to the side for now. Maybe they will make more sense to you later on. Keep in mind, however, that many of the teachings will be challenging, and they are meant to be challenging. So you may often find yourself thinking, "I don't want to believe that!" Ask yourself, "Why not?" It may turn out to be your knee-jerk reaction that is the problem. It may be the "not wanting to believe" rather than the teaching that is the real problem. It may be a deep-rooted desire that is preventing you from accepting the "strong medicine" or "tough love" of a teaching.

The Buddha's Tough Love: Pulling Out the Poison Arrow

In fact, upon his enlightenment, the Buddha at first thought that there was no point in trying to teach others what he had realized, since they would not have the ears or the desire to hear it. Like small children who need to be told that if they want their tummies to stop aching they should cut down on the candy, we adults are addicted to beliefs and habits that are actually the root of our own suffering. So, sometimes we should question our own resistances rather than the teaching that is triggering them. If a teaching doesn't challenge you, it probably also won't be able to transform or awaken you.

It may be that a certain teaching is not right for you, at least not at this time. Keep in mind that the Buddha, or any genuine Buddhist teacher, is interested in relieving suffering and helping you live better, not in convincing you to swear by a creed or heed a commandment out of sheer obedience or blind faith. Buddhism is a religion of awakening, of enlightenment, rather than of faithful obedience. The Buddha encouraged his followers to test whatever he taught them, to find out for themselves if it is true or not. To be sure, he also taught that obstinate doubt can become a hindrance, and faith—or, better, trust—does play an important role in Buddhism, as it does in any learning process. But, in the end, it is *understanding* the truth that will set you free, not just blindly believing in it.[3]

It should also be noted that the Buddha did not promote knowledge about anything and everything just for the sake of satisfying our intellectual curiosity. There is no time for that. First and foremost, we need to focus on the knowledge necessary to liberate us from suffering. In this regard, the Buddha taught the Parable of the Poison Arrow.[4] This is a story about a man who has been shot with a poison arrow. Wouldn't it be foolish, the Buddha says, if the man were to refuse to let the surgeon take the arrow out until he learned who shot the arrow, what the arrow is made of, and other superfluous information? Obviously, the only knowledge that is really important in that situation is the knowledge of how to get the poison arrow out as quickly and as safely as possible.

Analogous to a surgeon who knows how to remove a poison arrow, the Buddha presented himself as a kind of spiritual doctor who can teach us how to remove the Three Poisons of greed, hatred, and delusion that are causing us and those around us to suffer.

The Buddha as a Spiritual Doctor

The Four Noble Truths can be compared to what happens when you are ill and you go to the doctor. First, the doctor will ask you questions that will help you precisely present the symptoms that are plaguing you. Second, the doctor will diagnose the underlying cause or causes of those symptoms. Third, the doctor will give you a prognosis. (Note that in this case, the prognosis is good: the Third Noble Truth promises that we can be cured!) Finally, the doctor will give you a prescription, a path to recovery.

1. Presentation of symptom: *existential dis-ease*
2. Diagnosis of cause of dis-ease: *craving and ignorance*
3. Prognosis: *good; there is a cure*
4. Prescription: *follow the Eightfold Path*

In this chapter, let us focus especially on the first two Noble Truths. We'll have opportunities to discuss Nirvana and the elements of the Eightfold Path in more detail in later chapters. Indeed, we have already started discussing the meditation parts of the Path.

The First Noble Truth is that our lives are pervaded by *duhkha*, a term that is often translated as "suffering" but is better rendered as "discontentment" or "unease." Keeping with the image of the Buddha as a spiritual doctor, we could say that *duhkha* is the dis-ease of our lives; it is the existential unease that we feel in the pit of our stomach when we are not being dishonest with or distracting ourselves.

If one is truly happy, perfectly at peace, then there is no need for Buddhism, or, for that matter, for any religious or spiritual teaching and practice. But the first of the Four Noble Truths asks us to face the facts. The first thing one must do at an Alcoholics Anonymous meeting is stand up and confess—most importantly to oneself—that one has a serious problem. You are not going to take the medicine if you are not willing to admit that you are ill. The First Noble Truth is a kind of intervention, a moment of tough love asking us to face up to the problem. Our resistance to admitting that deep down we are discontent is the first barrier on the path to peace.

Remember the first lesson you learned from meditation: how out of control your mind is, and so how much you need to meditate. This is why I like to tell first-time meditators: I hope you had a terrible time! Of course, what I mischievously mean is: I hope that, in sitting still and for once not running away from yourself, you got a glimpse of the unease at the base of your monkey-mind, and that you are now motivated to dig down in search of a more deeply underlying peace and clarity.

Zen meditation is called the "Dharma gate of ease and joy," but to pass through this gate we need to first face up to the fact that we are not at ease and joyful, and we must investigate and discover the reasons for our existential malaise. Why is it that we cannot just sit down and be at peace with ourselves? What is this discontentment that keeps us running around unsettled, fleeing from sitting down and just being and breathing? What is this rumbling dis-ease with our existence, this underlying *duhkha*? Perhaps its antonym will give us a clue. The opposite of *duhkha* is *sukha*, happiness. The job of Buddhas, and of Bodhisattvas who aspire to become Buddhas, is to "take away suffering and provide happiness" (*bakku-yoraku* in Japanese).

But what, after all, is true happiness?[5] All of us can list times in which we feel more or less happy. On closer inspection, we may realize that our moments of happiness are all too momentary. Even the longer periods of happiness we experience are usually at least tinged with the worry that they won't last long enough. Perhaps this is why we seek more intense feelings of pleasure, or semi-conscious states of inebriation, in our attempts to cover over this underlying unease.

I recently heard a man on the radio explain that this is why he and others get hooked on video games. This strikingly self-aware and honest man said that these games are the only way he can find some respite from the dull emotional pain he otherwise feels at all times in the pit of his stomach. He understands this dull pain to be a symptom of an underlying fear of mortality and meaninglessness. And, since he does not think that it is possible for humans to be cured of this anxiety and the dull pain it causes, he thinks that the temporary distraction provided by things like video games is the best medicine available. In other words, he thinks that, since the underlying disease cannot be cured, the best treatment is a diversion that just masks the symptoms for a while. The best we can do is kill time while not paying attention to the ticking of the clock of our senseless mortal lives. In sharp contrast to this pessimistic view, with the Third Noble Truth the Buddha promises a cure, not just a distraction. And, with the Fourth Noble Truth he prescribes moral living and mindful meditation rather than mindless video games, or whatever diversions that were popular in his time for those who wanted to kill precious time.

The Buddha understood the importance of physicians and politically active people who seek to alleviate physical suffering, and he instructed his followers to attend to the physical as well as spiritual welfare of the people. Nevertheless, the Buddha himself was most concerned with addressing our deep feelings of anxiety and unease. Moreover, the Buddha was a spiritual doctor and not just a psychologist. Bouts of depression or panic attacks—what we normally think of as psychological disorders—can be grouped, along with physical pains, as the kind of suffering that can be treated at a hospital or a counseling center by a psychiatrist or a psychologist. We can recover from such psychological disorders without addressing the deeper level of *duhkha* the Buddha was most concerned with, the *duhkha* we all experience, even when we are physically healthy and psychologically in good spirits. Although the content of his teaching differs in important respects from Freud's theories and therapies, the Buddha is more like a psychoanalyst who looks for the deepest underlying causes of our discontent.[6]

Suffering Is Caused by a Mismatch Between Desire and Reality

Before looking at these deeper levels of *duhkha*, let us get clear on the basic reason for every kind of suffering. We suffer because we *don't have* what we *desire to have*, or because we *are not* what we *desire to be*. In other words, suffering is caused by the fact that our desires don't match reality. For example, a little boy craves an ice cream, but he doesn't have an ice cream, and so he cries. Or, a young man wants more than anything to be a millionaire, but he only has two hundred dollars, and so he is miserable. The formula for suffering is always a mismatch between desire and reality: If our desire does not match up with reality, we suffer.

This means that there are two possible strategies for overcoming suffering: we must either change reality or change our desire. Either we need to change reality so that it satisfies our desire or we need to change our desire so that it matches reality.

For example, either the little boy could get his parents to buy him an ice cream or he could learn to stop craving ice cream. In this case, the second option is obviously totally unrealistic, so I would advise the parents to cave in and spoil the kid, at least while I'm trying to enjoy my ice cream at the next table over. In our other example, either the young man could figure out a way to become a millionaire or he could realize that money alone won't make him happy and find an occupation and lifestyle that will. Should this young man give up his dream of becoming rich? He should probably at least think more about why he wants to become rich, and about what else he'll need to do to be happy. A lot also depends on what he would do with the million dollars. Maybe he would use it to make the world a better place, or maybe he would just buy a bunch of freezers and hoard lots of gourmet ice cream.

In any case, the crucial question is which desires we should try to satisfy and which desires we should work on letting go of. How do we decide which strategy to use? In each case of suffering, we have to ask ourselves: Should I try to change reality or should I try to change my desire? Whether or not you are a theist, Reinhold Niebuhr's "Serenity Prayer" is very helpful here. It says: "God, grant me the serenity to accept the things I cannot change, the courage to change the things I can, and the wisdom to know the difference." In the context of Buddhism, we might speak of a "Serenity Practice" rather than a "Serenity Prayer." In fact, the Six Perfections practiced by Mahayana Buddhists included "*patient endurance* of the difficulties in life that cannot be changed" and "*energy* [or *energetic effort*] to change what one can for the better."[7] In any case, the task is the same: to discern which desires should motivate us to change reality and which desires need to be relinquished because satisfying them is unrealistic.[8]

Change Reality or Change Our Minds?

Let me give a few more examples. Let's say you are a teenager and your dream is to become a professional basketball player. You may think that even though your ball-handling skills are not yet good enough, you are willing to work really hard, even twice as hard as your peers, so that in the end you can fulfill your dream. Yet, at some point along the way, you may realize that no matter how hard you train, you won't be able to compete at that level. At that point either you can wallow in self-pity or you can rethink your dream, maybe aiming to become a coach rather than a player. This discernment and flexibility may allow you to modify your desires in a way that leads you to your true calling—and maybe even to a greater happiness than you had imagined.

Let's take an even weightier example. Let's say you are gravely ill. If there is a treatment that can cure your illness, then you would be foolish not to undergo it—even, perhaps, if it involves serious side effects and a prolonged hospital stay. On the other hand, if you are terminally ill and there is simply no way to treat your illness, then accepting this fact, and perhaps moving from a hospital back home or to a hospice where you can better enjoy your last days with your family and friends while you psychologically and spiritually prepare for death, may be the better option.

Here is a different kind of example. Let's say that a group of people go for a picnic in the woods for the first time. Let's say they have decided, for whatever reason, that they are going to do this for lunch every day from now on. They are ready to sit down, but then they notice something they find strange: there are no chairs in nature! Now they have a choice: they can work to change their environment, or they can work to adapt themselves to the already existing environment. In this case, they can cut down some trees and build chairs to sit on, or they can train their bodies to be comfortable sitting on the ground, perhaps in a kneeling or cross-legged position.

Most likely you were raised in a Western or Westernized culture that has, by and large, taken the first route. Everywhere we go there are chairs for us to sit in—offices, schools, airports, and restaurants; even when we go camping we bring folding chairs! As a result, we tend to have rather stiff bodies that cannot comfortably sit on the ground. As children, we all used to have this ability; but after years of sitting in chairs, we have lost our native flexibility. We can call this our "chair karma." Traditional Japanese culture, by contrast, took the other route. People adapted their bodies to the environment, keeping them flexible so that they are comfortable sitting down on a relatively flat surface anywhere. Recently, however, as more Japanese sit in chairs more frequently, they too have started to have stiffer bodies.

Of course, changing the environment rather than adapting to it often seems like the better option. Who would want to give up the conveniences of modern technology? Nevertheless, we should notice that convenience comes at a price. Think of the incredible invention of the automobile. Think of how difficult it must have been in the past to go to school, to work, or to the store. But now think of the costs of this convenience. The most serious cost is obviously the effect our CO_2 emissions are having on climate change. We are starting to talk a lot about that these days—hopefully just in the nick of time.

There are other negative effects of our car culture that we probably don't talk quite enough about. Think about what it has done to our body politic. We commute and career around in private steel boxes on wheels, listening to only the music and news stations we like, rather than take public transportation, mingling with strangers and getting to know them as our fellow citizens. We don't gather in public squares and parks nearly as much as people do in more pedestrian-oriented cultures. Moreover, think about what our car culture has done to our physical bodies and our health. Humans used to be able to walk at a brisk pace for ten miles or more without a second thought. They didn't need to buy gym memberships and make New Year's resolutions to use them. The human body is meant to be in motion for at least a few hours a day, yet many of us spend most of our time sitting in chairs—either at home, at the office, or in the private steel box on wheels that takes us from the one to the other.

Don't get me wrong. I am not recommending that we sell our cars and smash our chairs. And I don't mean to downplay the benefits of changing the world to fit our wants, much less our needs. I just want to point out that there are downsides as well as upsides to this approach, and that sometimes we should think about adapting ourselves to reality rather than trying to change it to fit our desires. This other way of dealing with the mismatch between our desires and reality is especially recommended when some stubborn fact of reality simply cannot be changed no matter how hard we try.

From Suffering to Embracing Change

Okay, now we are at last prepared to start looking more directly at the deeper kinds of psychological and spiritual *duhkha* that the Buddha was most concerned with, and to think about whether this kind of suffering can be addressed by transforming the world or by transforming our minds—that is to say, by altering reality or by altering our attitude toward reality.

The first of these deeper levels of *duhkha* is the fact that we suffer change. We recoil at the thought that everything is impermanent. We don't just want to obtain certain things; we want to hold on to them forever. Yet the harder we grasp them, the tighter our grip, the more we become aware of the sand slipping through our fingers. We cannot ignore that the clock is ticking, and even our times of joy are tinged with an anxious awareness that they, too, will pass.

In fact, even if we could prolong many of the events that make us happy, would we really want to? Sliding full speed down a twisting and turning waterslide is thrilling. But if it went on for more than a minute or two, it would be noxious and even torturous. Spending a night out in New Orleans listening to great music is great fun. But you may also meet some people in their fifties and sixties who have made a lifelong career out of partying like it's still 1999—and, honestly, they don't seem truly happy. Even the joyous embrace of a returning loved one in an airport would get old and awkward if it went on *too* long. We might think and say that we want that hug to last forever. But think about it more carefully: at some point you'd have to get something to eat and go to the bathroom, and it would be pretty weird and uncomfortable to keep hugging while doing those things.

The Buddha realized that we suffer impermanence because we have an inflated desire for permanence. Indeed, when we really think about it, do we really want to be permanent and unchanging? If we really want to last forever just as we are, then we should have ourselves permanently freeze-dried. But that sounds more like eternal death than eternal life.

The wonderfully down-to-earth Vietnamese Zen master Thich Nhat Hanh tells the story of a British man who was getting depressed by all the Buddhist teachings of impermanence, until his fourteen-year-old daughter chided him: "Daddy, please don't complain about impermanence. Without impermanence, how can I grow up?"[9] We resist impermanence and change, but these are what allow us to be the living, breathing, growing, learning, loving beings that we are. To live is to change. To live is to be impermanent. If by eternal we mean unchanging, then "eternal life" is a contradiction in terms.

And so the desire to be permanent, the desire to be rid of impermanence, is a desire that should be let go of, since it is not realistic and since, when we really think about it, permanence is not desirable. We should accept impermanence. Indeed, the more we can embrace it, affirm it, the happier we will be. Experiences are desirable not *despite* but rather *because* they are impermanent.

Think again about the hug in the airport. It brings us joy because we have not seen our loved one in a while and also because we know that it will not last forever. Impermanence brings us back to the present. Our children grow up so fast, and so we need to spend quality time with them now. In truth, each moment is a now-or-never moment. And that is what makes each moment uniquely meaningful and worth fully appreciating.

Japanese culture is especially attuned to the beauty as well as to the sorrows of impermanence.[10] The cherry blossoms burst into bloom, and then just a few days later fall to the ground. Their impermanence intensifies—rather than detracts from—their poignant beauty. The entire nation eagerly waits for them to come into bloom. When they do, hundreds of thousands of people of all ages drop what they are doing to go sit under the cherry trees, sing songs, and soak in their ephemeral charm. Even businesses send young employees out in the morning to stake out prime spots under the trees. The blossoms are thought to be most beautiful as they fall to the ground, fluttering in the wind, singing the swan song of their short lives. Similarly, although we experience all the flickering stars as beautiful, it is even more precious, we feel, to catch a rare glimpse of a shooting star.

Impermanence Is Buddha-nature: Nirvana *in* Rather than *After* Life

It is true that some early Buddhist texts suggest that we need to transcend Samsara, understood as the world of impermanence, in order to attain Nirvana. The Zen tradition, however, teaches that we need to embrace the impermanence of life, learning to let go of the unsettling desire to escape to an imaginary world of permanence, a world that we cannot even really imagine. The thirteenth-century Japanese Zen master Dōgen tells us that Nirvana is to be found in the midst of the birth-and-death world of Samsara. The Buddha-nature is not some timeless realm beyond this one; rather, Dōgen writes, quoting the seventh-century Chinese Zen master Huineng, "impermanence is in itself the Buddha-nature."[11] As long as we crave permanence, it is difficult for us to appreciate this world of impermanence. We cannot change the impermanence of our lives. "To want to live forever," says the fifteenth-century Japanese Zen master Ikkyū, "is to wish for the impossible, the unreal."[12]

We can, of course, wish it were otherwise or hope for an afterlife in which it will be different. I recall watching a very touching scene in a documentary on Mormonism of a family sitting around their dinner table. The father said that he firmly believes that in heaven everything will be just like this, that nothing will be lost. Who cannot sympathize with this ardent wish? I certainly can. My kids were younger then, and part of me wanted them to never grow up. But then I asked myself: What would that really mean? Would one have to sit at the dinner table for all eternity? I'd be miserably stuffed after a few hours, and after a few days my rear end would be unbearably sore, no matter how padded the chairs were. Or would it perhaps mean that in heaven we get to live our lives all over again, innumerable times? Maybe it means we get to relive just all the fun parts over and over. Yet, what about the struggles through which we grow and learn? Do I want to just relive crossing the finish line of that ten-mile race I won when I was fourteen, or do I also want to relive all the pain I went through during the race? The more I think about it, I cannot really imagine what it would mean for my desire for permanence to be satisfied, even if I could convince myself that it were true.

The Buddha did not try to force anyone to believe anything they didn't want to believe. Indeed, he accepted the common belief in life after death, which in his society meant rebirth in an earthly, heavenly, ghostly, or hellish domain.[13] Since it is one's karma—one's volitional thoughts and actions—that determine one's rebirth, the Buddha in effect suggested that we can live as long as we want, since it is the wanting, the craving for continuance, that ensures that we will be reborn in this world or elsewhere. However, he also said that through such continual rebirth we remain in the realm of Samsara, the realm in which our lives are pervaded by *duhkha*, the existential unease we have been discussing. Nirvana entails the extinction of this desire to hold on to the self-perpetuating illusion of the permanence of the ego.

We'll discuss rebirth and Nirvana in some detail in Chapter 23. Let me conclude this chapter by noting that the Buddha characterized the world of Samsara in terms of what he called the Three Marks of Existence: (1) impermanence or incessant change (*anitya*), (2) no-self, egolessness, or insubstantiality (*anatman*), and (3) suffering or existential unease (*duhkha*). The reason for the third characteristic is our refusal to accept the first two. If we were to affirm impermanence and egolessness, Samsara would be converted into Nirvana. We would be able to live joyfully and at peace, and we would be able to bring peace and joy to others.

We have been focusing on the existential unease that is caused by our underlying resistance to change. Yet the deepest level of *duhkha* stems from the fact that we are not the kind of selves we desperately desire to be. We want to be independent and permanent, and yet the fact is that we are interdependent and impermanent. As long as we understand the self as something independent and permanent, then there is no self to be found. Chapter 7 will be devoted to discussing this core teaching of Buddhism, the demanding and debated no-self doctrine.

7

The True Self Is Egoless

In Chapter 6, we discussed the Buddha's diagnosis of *duhkha*, our spiritual disease, the gnawing discontent we feel in the pit of our stomachs whenever there is a gap in our habits of distracting ourselves from ourselves. We talked about how we suffer the impermanence of all the things we care about, especially the impermanence of our own selves.

We Crave to Be What We Are Not

The deepest source of *duhkha* is the fact that we are not at ease with being the kind of beings we in truth are. We suffer from a subtle awareness that we are not the kind of beings we deeply crave to be. In a nutshell, we crave to be *permanent* and *independent*, and yet we constantly bump up against the fact that we are *impermanent* and *interdependent*.[1]

We are changing all the time, and our very existence depends on so much that is beyond our control. Physically, we depend on the air we breathe, the food we eat, even the exact amount of gravity and the temperature range that happen to exist on this planet. Psychologically, we depend on family, friends, neighbors, and compatriots—not to mention our fellow earthlings in other lands who stich our shirts, grow our coffee beans, and buy our products.

In a negative sense, we even depend on our opponents and enemies. U2's Bono can sing about there being "no them, only us." But, sadly, we tend to define our identities by belonging to an Us versus a Them. That's why, soon after the Soviet Union collapsed, Hollywood had to come up with a new villain; in the movie *Independence Day*, the countries of the earth could finally unite only because attacking aliens had become common enemy. Love not only your neighbor but also your enemy, Jesus taught—and, if he had been a snarky rather than a saintly fellow, he might have added: If you can't yet love them, at least thank them for providing the foil needed for your antagonistic identity.

Small children intuitively know how much they depend on their family, although as they grow up they start to yearn for emotional if not always, alas, for financial independence. I was a rebellious teenager at the age of five, the first time I ran away from home. I only got as far as three houses down the block, and, even then, I brought Curious George along to keep me company as I sat pouting

Zen Pathways. Bret W. Davis, Oxford University Press. © Oxford University Press 2022.
DOI: 10.1093/oso/9780197573686.003.0007

under a tree in that neighbor's yard. Fortunately, thanks to impermanence, I was able to grow out of premature assertions of independence. However, I am still struggling to grow out of mature presumptions of being an independent grown-up. I am still working on realizing that I can best be who I am only by nurturing my connections with others.

Perhaps you are further along in the process than I am. But how deeply have any of us truly realized that there can only be an I if there is a We? Have we realized this at the level of received knowledge, at the level of intellectual understanding, or at the truly enlightening level of experiential wisdom? In part, at least, we remain rebellious teenagers with a mistaken idea and ideal of independence. We celebrate our political Declaration of Independence with flags and fireworks, but we fail to fully appreciate the Buddha's spiritual Declaration of Interdependence. We don't want to admit that our existence is dependent on others and on our shared environment. And, let's be honest, we are all resistant to change and almost scared to death of dying.

Recall our formula for suffering: Suffering is caused by the gap between our desires and reality—that is to say, by a mismatch between the way we want things to be and the way things in reality are. Here is a simple three-step logical explanation of how our attachment to the idea of an independent and unchanging ego causes us to suffer:

1. We crave to be permanent and independent beings.
2. The reality is that we are impermanent and interdependent beings.
3. Therefore we suffer from an existential dis-ease (*duhkha*).

Our craving for permanence and independence is based on an ignorance of the way things are. And, insofar as we crave to believe that we are the kind of selves that we are not and cannot be, this ignorance, in turn, is based on craving. Our existential unease is thus caused by a vicious circle, a ferocious feedback loop, between craving and ignorance. Our dis-ease is rooted in a willful ignorance. So says the Buddha's Second Noble Truth.

The gospel, the good news of the Buddha's teaching, is given in the Third Noble Truth: By abandoning craving and eliminating ignorance, we can become enlightened and liberated from the existential unease that plagues us. We can attain the peace of Nirvana.

Knowing Ourselves as the Path to Peace

In Samsara, in living a life based on ignorance and craving, our minds are not at peace. Zen Buddhism teaches that the reason we are not at peace with ourselves is that we have never looked all the way into our own minds. We have never really taken "the step back that turns the light of the mind around on itself." The seventeenth-century Japanese Zen master Suzuki Shōsan says:

> Know yourself by reflecting on yourself. Let your learning be as great as you please, and your erudition as vast, yet you know nothing if you do not know yourself. Until you know yourself, therefore, you cannot know others. Those who know themselves not at all make the foolish self the foundation of their mind. In slandering others, in liking only those who agree with them, in detesting those who do not meekly yield to them, and in raging over every little thing, they torment themselves and torture their minds.[2]

In causing ourselves to suffer, we cause others to suffer, and vice versa in this vicious circle. Because we do not understand ourselves, we do not understand our relations to others. As the Buddha's Second Noble Truth tells us, ignorance and craving combine in this way to keep in motion the wheel of suffering, the Wheel of Life in Samsara. We crave to control others and the world around us because we do not understand who we are and how we are intimately related to them.

Buddhism seeks to cut this Gordian knot of ignorance, craving, and suffering by "shedding light on what lies directly underfoot," dispelling the illusion of a permanent and separate ego and revealing the true nature of the self. Whereas other Buddhist traditions take a more gradual and analytical approach to the question of the self, Zen meditation and kōan practice attempt to cut the knot in one fell swoop with the sword of insight. Zen meditation halls usually feature a statue of Manjusri, the Bodhisattva of Wisdom, who is often depicted wielding the sword of insight—a sword that cuts through the delusion of duality, the illusory sense of being separate from others and from the world. The Zen sword of wisdom thus paradoxically "cuts in one" (rather than "cuts in two") by slicing through our false sense of separateness.

Pacifying the Mind You Cannot Find

One of the most famous kōans tells the story of the enlightenment experience of the Second Chinese Ancestor of the Zen tradition, Huike. It appears as Case 41 in *The Gateless Barrier* collection of kōans. Huike earnestly sought instruction from Bodhidharma, who, after coming from India to China in the late fifth or early sixth century CE, is said to have meditated in a cave for nine years, not having yet found anyone ready to receive transmission of the teaching. Outside the cave in which Bodhidharma sat meditating, Huike stood for days in the cold, snow piling up to his knees. The depth of his existential anguish was such that, legend has it, he finally cut off his own left arm in order to demonstrate to Bodhidharma the sincerity of his search and plea for instruction. Metaphorical or not, this got Bodhidharma's attention.

Huike said, "My mind is not yet at peace. I beg you, my teacher, please give it peace." Bodhidharma replied, "Bring me your mind and I will pacify it for you." Presumably—although the text skips over this important part of the story—Huike then went in search of his mind, spending long days and nights in the meditative quest to know himself. Or perhaps Huike's solitary search had already brought him to the point where he was ready for the next step. In any case, the kōan continues with Huike saying, "I have searched for the mind and yet, in the end, it is ungraspable." To which Bodhidharma responded, "There, now I have thoroughly set it at rest for you."[3]

In searching for the mind, the thing that was supposedly experiencing such existential anguish, Huike could not find it. He could find nothing that he could grasp on to and present to Bodhidharma as the subject who was experiencing, or as the substance that was underlying the suffering.

Yet, how does discovering that the mind is ungraspable bring peace to it? Or, in finding that the mind is ungraspable, did Huike in a sense find the ungraspable mind? Is coming to know that the mind is unknowable after all a kind of knowledge of the mind?

When Bodhidharma arrived in China he was asked, "Who are you?" He responded: "I don't know" or, more literally and simply, "Not-knowing."[4] But if Bodhidharma, the legendary founder of the Zen School, doesn't know who he is, if he doesn't know the true self, then who does? Or is the point that enlightenment, awakening, is not a matter of "knowing"? A poem by the seventeenth-century Japanese Zen master Shidō Bunan reads:

> Originally it cannot be taught or learned;
> When you do not know it
> It is unknown;
> When you know it,
> It is still unknown.[5]

What a strange thing to say: even when one comes to know the true self, it is still unknown! There must be two senses of "knowing" at issue here. The true self cannot be known as an object, since it cannot be objectified. But there must be a second sense of knowing, one that involves knowing that the self cannot be known in the first sense. One knows the subject when one knows that it is not an object.

Yet, how does this knowing or not-knowing bring one peace? How does finding out that the mind is ungraspable, knowing that the mind is unknowable, bring one peace? That is the question of these kōans. The Buddhist philosopher and longtime Rinzai Zen practitioner Takemura Makio writes: "This non-knowing is a matter of illuminating the fact that the self is [to be found] where it is not objectified." Peace is found when we stop looking for the self as if it were an object, and the very place in which it is discovered to be ungraspable as an object is at once the place of awakening to our true subjectivity and agency.[6]

Accepting Pain to Rid Ourselves of Suffering

The ego-self that we are so attached to, the ego-self that suffers and that we desperately want to pacify—when we actually sit down and look for it, it cannot be found. At the base of suffering, there is no sufferer. We might grasp this theoretically, but what is the ungraspable lesson for living?

The seventeenth-century Japanese Zen master Bankei makes a distinction between physical suffering and the kind of existential suffering Buddhism is most concerned with. He says that "if you become confirmed in the unborn Buddha-mind," that is, if you awaken to your true self, "you aren't troubled by the suffering that normally accompanies illness." If "you start to worry about your illness, you create suffering for yourself." Of course, he is not saying that we should pretend that we are not physically suffering. To the contrary, he says that "it's best at such times to give yourself up to the sickness, and to moan when there is pain."[7]

When there is sadness in the wake of a loss, just be sad for the time being. Don't add to the sadness by projecting a "me" that is supposed to be happy right now but is not, a me that is being unfairly assaulted by this sadness. If you find yourself slipping into a downward spiral of becoming depressed about your depression, seek medical attention and give yourself entirely over to the process of recovery. When you are busy, don't resist it, bifurcating yourself into a self that has to work and a self that wants to rest. That only leads to more stress and less productivity. Just immerse yourself in the business to be taken care of. And then, when you rest, just rest; don't split yourself into a trying-to-relax self and a feeling-like-you-should-be-working self. And, of course, when you are happy, just be happy! Don't bifurcate yourself into a self that is enjoying the happiness and a self that doesn't want it to end or a self that is never satisfied—a self that doesn't know what it means to have enough. Just work, just play, just laugh, just cry, just love, just live.

Just dive right into the impermanent flow and interconnectedness of life. That is where the true self is to be found. If by the word "ego" we mean something that remains aloof from life, something unchanging and unaffected, something isolated and unconnected, then in reality there is no such thing as an ego. The true self is egoless. The true self suffers, but it does not suffer its suffering.

The modern philosopher and Zen teacher Hisamatsu Shin'ichi remarked: "Even though I do engage in what people usually refer to as worrying, for me this is not really worrying. . . . This is because it is the worry-free self who is worrying."[8] The true self worries without identifying itself with the worries. The awakened mind is like a mirror that is not tainted by what it experiences. And yet, in the end, the true self is not merely like a mirror that sees the passing of pleasure and pain as what they are without getting involved in them; it is more like a shattered mirror whose bits are inseparable from all that is experienced. The renowned Japanese scholar of Zen Yanagida Seizan explains that the teaching of the "mirror-mind" increasingly gave way to the teaching that the mind—or rather the "no-mind"—is inseparable from the events of the world in which we participate.[9] "The mind and things are one and the same," says the fifteenth-century Japanese Zen master Ikkyū.[10] We'll discuss this further in Chapters 8, 11, and 17. Here we need to back up and discuss the basic Buddhist teaching of *anatman*.

The *Anatman* Doctrine: Selflessness or No-Soul?

According to Zen, the true self is egoless. In order to better understand the crucial distinction between the true self and the delusory ego, we need to delve into one of the most important and challenging teachings of Buddhism: the *anatman* doctrine. The first challenge is the question of how to best translate this term. Should we translate *anatman* as "egolessness," as "selflessness," as "no-self," as "no-ego," or as "no-soul"?

As one can already tell from these very different possible translations, the real challenge is understanding what is meant by this doctrine. Each one of these translations carries different nuances and evokes different reactions in us. For example, to Christians, a teaching of egolessness or selflessness sounds very familiar and commendable. But a doctrine of no-soul sounds like a direct challenge to one of their core beliefs.

The Theravada Buddhist monk and scholar Walpola Rahula, in his landmark and still widely read book *What the Buddha Taught?*, deliberately translates *anatman* as "no-soul" in order to assert that there is a fundamental difference between Buddhism and religions such as Christianity. He says that just as humans have invented the idea of God as a celestial Father out of a desire for self-protection, they have invented the idea of an eternal soul or *atman* out of a desire for self-preservation. Buddhism, according to Rahula, is the only religion, if it is indeed a religion, that faces up to the facts as they are given to us through empirical evidence and rational deliberation rather than blind faith. He writes:

Buddhism stands unique in the history of human thought in denying the existence of such a Soul, Self, or Atman. According to the teaching of the Buddha, the idea of self is an imaginary, false belief which has no corresponding reality, and it produces harmful thoughts of "me" and "mine," selfish desire, craving, attachment, hatred, ill-will, conceit, pride, egoism, and other defilements, impurities and problems. It is the source of all the trouble in the world from personal conflicts to wars between nations. In short, to this false view can be traced all the evil in the world.[11]

That is a powerful challenge to anyone attached to the idea an ego, self, or soul. However, it should be noted that Rahula's views of Buddhism are rooted in the Theravada tradition, a tradition that is criticized, along with other so-called Hinayana or "Lesser Vehicle" schools, by Mahayana or "Greater Vehicle" Buddhist schools such as Zen. The Mahayana schools view the Hinayana teachings as representing a limited understanding of a limited set of the Buddha's teachings.

Also, it should be noted that Rahula has been criticized by recent scholars for downplaying the mythical, ritualistic, and other more recognizably "religious" elements of his own Theravada tradition in order to present it as compatible with modern Western science and psychology.[12] Indeed, his critique of God as an imaginary projection of an all-powerful protector and father figure is surely borrowed from Freud.[13] Nevertheless, Rahula's presentation of a hard-line Theravada interpretation of the *anatman* doctrine should be taken seriously, as should be the challenges to it by scholars of Mahayana Buddhism, for whom the *anatman* doctrine is not only compatible with, but is indeed the other side of the same coin as a Buddhist doctrine of a true self.

In fact, some Christians, such as the Catholic priest and renowned scholar of Zen Buddhism Heinrich Dumoulin, have found there to be significant similarities (as well as differences) between Buddhist and Christian ideas about the self. Responding directly to Rahula's interpretation of the *anatman* doctrine, Dumoulin writes: "This denial of the individual self seems to put Buddhism in clear opposition to Christianity. However, when we look more closely at what is meant by non-self, this opposition is softened."[14] Dumoulin reminds us that "the distinction between empirical ego and true self is also found in Christian religious experience," and that one of Christ's central teachings is that one must "lose one's life in order to win it"—in other words, "the imperative of dying to this phenomenal, provisional ego, in order to attain the true self."[15] In Chapter 12, we will compare this Christian message to what Zen calls the Great Death, through which we must pass if we are to learn to truly live.

The Buddha's Silence and the Ontological Middle Way

Here let us keep our focus on the Buddhist teaching of *anatman*, with the aim of understanding how it is not only compatible with, but actually the other side of the same coin as, the Zen teaching of the true self.

To begin with, insofar as it was the case that "for the Buddha's audience *by definition* the word *ātman/attā* [self] referred to something unchanging," then it can be said that what he meant by the *anatman* doctrine is that "there is nothing in living beings that never changes."[16] However, we should note that even in the Pali Canon, the early collection of sutras and other texts that are the basis of the Theravada tradition, the Buddha did not in fact always unequivocally deny the existence of the self or *atman*. In a famous encounter with a recluse named Vacchagotta, he was asked point-blank: "Is there a self?" The Buddha remained silent. And so the recluse asked, "Then is there no self?" Again, the Buddha remained silent.[17]

What is the point of this famous account of the Buddha's silence? Evidently, the Buddha thought that Vacchagotta would have been misled if he answered either yes or no to the question of whether the self exists. Either way, regardless of whether Vacchagotta was told it exists or does not exist, his mistaken conception of the self would have been confirmed. If the Buddha had answered yes, he would have bolstered Vacchagotta's attachment to a false idea of a substantial and eternal ego. If he had answered no, then he would have plunged him into the mistaken view of nihilism, meaning here the view that there exists nothing at all to which the term "self" could be even provisionally applied. Another mistaken view is annihilationism, the view that while there is an independent ego that persists through this lifetime, it gets annihilated when it dies.

The Buddha's silence in response to Vacchagotta's questions is pregnant with the teaching of what could be called the Ontological Middle Way.[18] Analogous to the Practical Middle Way that steers a course between the extremes of hedonism and asceticism, the Ontological Middle Way steers a course between the extreme views of substantialism or eternalism, on the one hand, and the opposite extreme views of nihilism or annihilationism, on the other. Ontology is an account of what there is in reality. For the Buddha, what exists is neither a world of separate and eternal substances nor a vacuous black hole of nothingness. What exist are interconnected processes.

The Ontological Middle Way

substantialism/ ⟵————interdependent origination ————⟶nihilism/

eternalism   of interconnected processes   annihilationism

The Buddha taught that what exists is not nothing, but neither is it something, if by something we mean independent and enduring entities like the ancient Greek notion of atoms. Although modern physicists still speak of atoms, for etymological reasons they should have renamed the atom after they discovered it could be split, since *a-tom* literally means "what cannot be divided." What physicists now say exists is a dynamic field of interchangeable mass and energy, a field of interconnected processes rather than independent atoms. Not unlike modern physics, the Buddha said that things come about and pass away in processes of "interdependent origination"—a translation of the key Sanskrit phrase *pratitya-samutpada*.

In philosophical terms, both contemporary physicists and ancient Buddhists understand reality in terms of a "process ontology" rather than a "substance ontology." The self, too, is a process—it is a process interlinked with all the other processes in the universe, including, of course, with other "process-selves." In Buddhist lingo, the self is a "life-stream" interconnected with other "life-streams."

Looking for the Self: What Am I?

At this point the Buddha might say, "Don't take my word for it, look and see for yourselves!" So let us take a meditative moment. Pause for a moment and, like Huike, look for the self. Rather than think about what you have been taught to believe, or what you have read or heard somewhere, just introspect: look and see what's there. Who are you? Or, even better, what are you? When you look for your "self," what do you find? Please put down this book and take a few minutes to reflect on this. Look for the self, and see what you find.

* * *

Okay, what did you find? A chain of thoughts—words and concepts—about the self, perhaps? Or memories of something you've heard or read? Maybe you instinctively recited a creed you were raised to believe. In addition to a stream of such thoughts, perhaps what you found when you looked for your "self" included a feeling of uncomfortableness—even a tinge of anxiety—in the face of the question.

There is a great scene in the movie *Anger Management* in which Adam Sandler's character is asked by a therapist played by Jack Nicholson, "Who are you?" The therapist won't accept answers about his occupation or hobbies and presses him to tell the group "who he is," not "what he does." So far, so good. But then the therapist refuses to accept as an answer descriptions of his personality. At this point, our own laughter at Adam Sandler's character starts to change into nervously self-conscious laughter.

Who am I, if not my personality? Yet, come to think of it, my personality can change: I can become more (or less) patient or forgiving, for example. Sometimes we say, "People don't change," but the fact that we occasionally make a point of saying this reveals that we normally think people can and do change. If I mature and become more responsible, or age and become more amiable or irritable, has my "self" then changed? If so, is there some part, some core of me that does not and cannot change? I might believe in the abstract idea of there being an unchanging core of my self. Yet the only self I can find, the only thing I can experience, is a changing set of processes.

Thinking Without a Thinker

The seventeenth-century French philosopher René Descartes famously said, "I think, therefore I am."[19] This is one of the few quotes from a philosopher that actually get parodied and printed on T-shirts and coffee mugs. What does it mean? Descartes tried to doubt everything in order to find something that he absolutely could not doubt, a solid foundation of certainty. With this phrase, he believed he found something indubitable.

But did he? As the American pragmatist philosopher and pioneer psychologist William James later said, when we introspect, we don't in fact find a *thinker*, but rather only a *process of thinking*.[20] Descartes should have said that we can be certain that "thinking is going on" rather than that "I think." The "I" got smuggled into Descartes's thoughts about thinking, and generations of modern philosophers accepted his dubious inference, starting with Hobbes, who agreed that "we cannot conceive of jumping without a jumper, of knowing without a knower, or of thinking without a thinker."[21] Nietzsche is one of the few modern Western philosophers to have directly questioned this claim. He suggests that the reason that we cannot conceive of thinking without a thinker is that the grammar of our Indo-European languages requires a sentence to have a subject.[22] Our language makes us say "I think" just like it makes us say "it rains." The "I" and the "it" are needed because our grammar tells us that sentences need specified subjects and actions need substantial agents. In Japanese, one can just say *atsui*, "hot," rather than "it is hot" or "I am hot," and one can just say *iku*, "going," rather than "I am going." The "I," like the "it," turns out to be a grammatical rather than an ontological necessity, a syntactic filler rather than an empirical fact.[23]

Who is reading the words on this page right now? You might say "I am." If I ask you to point to yourself, you'd probably point to some part of your body—in the United States, people point to their chests; in Japan, people point to their noses. In any case, you are not just your physical appearance. It's what's on the inside that counts, right? Okay, so look and see what is on the inside. Please take another meditative moment and again look for the "I."

* * *

What did you find this time? When you introspectively went fishing for an "I," were you able to catch a substantial self in there anywhere? The eighteenth-century Scottish philosopher David Hume wrote:

> when I enter most intimately into what I call *myself*, I always stumble on some particular perception or other, of heat or cold, light or shade, love or hatred, pain or pleasure. I never can catch *myself* at any time without a perception, and never can observe any thing but the perception.[24]

In other words, when I just look, without any preconceived ideas of what I *should* find or what I *want* to find, when I just look at what I *do* find when I introspect and look for my "self," all that ever shows up is a stream of feelings, perceptions, desires, and thoughts.

The Five Aggregates that Make Up the Life-Stream of the Self

This is what the Buddha calls the Five Aggregates that make up the life-stream of the self: bodily forms, sensations, perceptions, mental formations (including dispositions and volitions), and consciousness of all of the above.[25] These are all interconnected processes, not separate substances. They are always changing. Our trains of thoughts and fleeting feelings are moving much faster even than our bodies are growing, regenerating, and aging. And all these moving parts of the self are interconnected with the Five Aggregates of other life-streams.

The second-century BCE Buddhist philosopher Nagasena explained the *anatman* doctrine to a Greek king using the analogy of a chariot. When we analyze it, we realize that a chariot is nothing but an amalgamation, an aggregate of wheels, axles, floorboard, and other parts. So it is with the self, he said.[26] Biologists tell us that most of our cells live for no more than a few days to about seven years; the building blocks of our bodies are constantly dying off and being more or less replicated. The only cells that live much longer are neurons, but a physicist would tell us that even neurons are made up of constantly changing subatomic particles flashing in and out of existence in a field of interconnected mass and energy. The self is a life-stream, the only constant is the continuity of a pattern, and even the pattern shifts over time.

Is there a self? No, if we mean by "self" an independent and permanent substance. But yes, if we mean by "self" the self-reproducing and shifting pattern of a stream of interconnected processes. The problem is that we misconceive of the *process-self* as a *substance-self*. This is the problem of what the Buddha calls grasping, clinging, or attachment. It is a problem rooted in the feedback loop between ignorance and craving; it is a problem of willful ignorance. We might *say* that we want to know ourselves. But *really* we crave to maintain our ignorance—including an ignorance of this craving that is keeping us in the dark. Our craving to be a substance-self perpetuates the illusion that we are in fact a substance-self.

In his philosophical interpretation of the early Buddhist sutras, Christopher Gowans suggests that the process-self itself depends for its existence on perpetuating this self-misconception of itself as a substance-self. He writes:

> The Buddha taught that substance-selves have no reality in any sense, while process-selves have no independent reality but do have a form of dependent reality. Specifically, the existence of a person's process-self depends on certain beliefs and attitudes the person has, but may and should abandon. In the absence of these, the process-self ceases to exist. This is what happens when *Nibbāna* [Sk. Nirvana] is fully attained.[27]

However, Mahayana Buddhists argue that there is a different kind of motivation that can keep the process-self in a self-perpetuating cycle of rebirth both during this lifetime and between lifetimes; namely, *compassion* instead of *craving* can serve as the motivational glue that maintains the continuity of a life-stream or process-self.[28] We will return to this topic in Chapter 23.

At this point, let us say that the true self is the self that has shed light on itself by cutting the Gordian knot created by the feedback loop between ignorance and craving. The true self wakes up to the fact that it is a process-self and to the fact that there are, in truth, no substance-selves. Can anything more be said of this true self? The eminent Japanese scholars of Indian Buddhism Nakamura Hajime and Saigusa Mitsuyoshi argue that an affirmation of the true self as a *practical agent* accompanies the negation of the ego as a *metaphysical substance* in Buddhism from the beginning.[29] They point to passages where the Buddha says things such as "Only the self shelters the self. . . . By oneself is evil done, by oneself is one made impure. By oneself is evil undone, by oneself is one made pure."[30]

Mahayana Buddhist traditions, and especially Zen, have been less reticent with regard to the true self that is realized by way of negating the illusory ego. They suggest, in particular, that the true self can be characterized as "ungraspable" and as "interconnected." Both of these teachings can be found in the *Diamond Sutra*, which says that "the past mind cannot be grasped, neither can the present mind or the future mind,"[31] and that "bodhisattvas who are wholly devoid of any conception of a separate self are truthfully called bodhisattvas."[32] In Chapter 8 we'll have much more to say about the *interconnected* nature of the true self. Let us conclude this chapter by looking further at what Zen masters have said about the *ungraspable* nature of the true self.

The True Self Is Ungraspable

The ninth-century Chinese Zen master Linji famously speaks of "the true person of no rank who is always going in and out of the face of every one of you."[33] Who you really are is not your status in a company or in society; it cannot be reduced to the ranks you hold or the roles you play. Indeed, it cannot be objectified in any way whatsoever.

We cannot say what the true self is because it is not a "what." The true self is no-thing that can be physically or conceptually grasped. "Neither you nor I can be grasped," says the twelfth-century Chinese Zen master Dahui.[34] The root problem is not just that we are looking for the self in all the wrong places. It is that we are looking for it at all, as if it were some *thing*, some golden golf ball, so to speak, hidden in some crevice of our brain or in some artery of our hearts. The problem is that the subject is objectifying itself. The Third Chinese Ancestor of Zen, Sengcan, says, "Using mind to grasp mind is the original mistake."[35]

Although Zen talks about enlightenment as a matter of *kenshō*, "seeing into one's true nature," many masters have warned that this saying can be misleading if we dualistically separate the act of seeing from the nature seen. The ninth-century Chinese Zen master Huangbo says, "That nature and your perception of it are one."[36] Seeing into one's own nature is *seeing seeing itself*, not seeing an object outside itself.

The twelfth-century Korean Zen master Chinul says: "Self-nature is just your own mind. . . . You are like someone who because he cannot see his own eyes thinks that he doesn't have any eyes. . . . If he realizes that he never lost his eyes, that is the same as seeing his eyes."[37]

Suzuki Shōsan says, "There is a self, but it is not a self. Though distinct from the four elements, it belongs with them. It accompanies the four elements and avails itself of them."[38] Awareness and agency cannot be reduced to the four material elements of the world, or to the Five Aggregates of the ego; and yet neither is some *thing* that can be separated from the processes that make up the ego and its environment.

Linji says that "the mind is without form; it pervades the ten directions and is manifesting its activity right before your very eyes."[39] It is you who are listening to me right now, he repeatedly reminds his audience. Stop seeking for it outside, as if the subject were just another object.

"Haven't you heard that what enters through the gate is not the family treasure?" asked the ninth-century Zen master Yantou. He goes on to say that rather than seeking for the mind outside oneself, "let it flow from your breast, covering heaven and earth!"[40]

"The whole world is you," says the ninth-century Chinese Zen master Xuefeng.[41] Once we realize that we are not an independent substance cut off from the rest of reality, we realize that we are open to everything, that we are indeed defined—or, rather, undefined, unlimited—by this open field of awareness. As the eighth-century Chinese Zen master Shitou tersely puts it: "A sage has no self, yet nothing is not himself."[42]

Although this chapter ends here, we are not done with the question of the true self. In Chapter 8 we'll look further into the interconnected nature of the true self and what it means to say that "the whole world is you." And in Chapter 9 we'll ask: What happens when two persons who have had this realization meet? Do worlds collide? Is the world big enough for more than one true self?

8

We Are One

Loving Others as Yourself

One of the main teachings of the Bible is to "Love your neighbor as yourself." It first appears in Leviticus and is repeated throughout the New Testament.[1] Who is the "neighbor"? Is God just telling his "chosen people" that they should love one another? No, in fact, in Leviticus, God commands his people to love immigrants as well as fellow Jews:

> When an alien resides with you in your land, you shall not oppress the alien. The alien who resides with you shall be to you as the citizen among you. You shall love the alien as yourself, for you were aliens in the land of Egypt.[2]

Jesus goes even further. Not only does he say that we should love foreigners as well as friends, he even tells us to love our enemies:

> You have heard that it was said, "You shall love your neighbor and hate your enemy." But I say to you, Love your enemies and pray for those who persecute you, so that you may be children of your Father in heaven; for he makes his sun rise on the evil and on the good, and sends rain on the righteous and on the unrighteous. For if you love those who love you, what reward do you have? Do not even the tax collectors do the same? And if you greet only your brothers and sisters, what more are you doing than others? Do not even the Gentiles do the same? Be perfect, therefore, as your heavenly Father is perfect.[3]

Some have seen this call to "love your enemies" as Jesus's most innovative as well as most radical teaching. Yet, despite his jab at Gentiles, scholars have pointed out non-biblical as well as biblical precedents. Indeed, five centuries earlier the Buddha taught boundless compassion and lovingkindness. In the *Metta Sutta*, we read:

> As a mother watches over her child, willing to risk her own life to protect her only child, so with a boundless heart should one cherish all living beings, suffusing the whole world with unobstructed loving kindness.[4]

Zen Pathways. Bret W. Davis, Oxford University Press. © Oxford University Press 2022.
DOI: 10.1093/oso/9780197573686.003.0008

Based on such teachings of the Buddha, in the *tonglen* method of Tibetan Buddhist meditation, one cultivates compassion and lovingkindness beginning with one's mother and gradually extending to even those whom one considers to be one's enemies.[5] And the thirteenth-century Japanese Zen master Dōgen says that we should "benefit friend and enemy equally."[6]

What Did Jesus Mean?

It is hard enough to think about loving one's neighbor as oneself, much less one's enemies. You may have heard this teaching a thousand times. But what does it really mean? Did Jesus mean that you should love your neighbor (and even your enemy) in the same manner and to the same degree that you love yourself? Is Jesus recognizing that we are egoistic, that we love ourselves, and telling us that we *also* need to be equally altruistic, that we need to love others just as much as we love ourselves? Is he saying that we should be altruistic to the same degree that we are egoistic?

Or, perhaps, does the "as" in the commandment "Love your neighbor *as* yourself" suggest something even stronger, something even more radically nondualistic? Does it imply that we should empathetically identify with our neighbor, such that the very distinction between loving oneself and loving others dissolves? Is Jesus calling into question the very dichotomy of egoism and altruism? Does his core teaching of love undermine the dualistic opposition of self and other? Is the Divine Love that he embodies—and that he calls on us to commune with—more of a revelation of nonduality than it is a commandment from on high?

If so, Jesus's core teaching strongly resonates with the Zen teaching that when we truly come to know ourselves, we automatically love others, since we no longer see them as "other." The fifteenth-century Japanese Zen master Ikkyū tells us that as his enlightened mind deepened and widened, "that illusive mind that generally separates us from others gradually left me."[7] The seventeenth-century Japanese Zen master Suzuki Shōsan taught:

> Although all things are distinct from one another, the original mind is one. . . .
> For the ignorant person, individual selves are separate from one another. For
> the enlightened person, there is no distinction between "self" and "other." Thus
> the genuine person puts sympathy first, and his compassion is deep.[8]

If something similar to this is also Jesus's teaching, then, like the Buddha, he is saying that wisdom and compassion *naturally* go together. The more we come to know the truth about ourselves, the less we need to be *commanded* to love our neighbors. Not only will the truth set you free, it will also let you love. Opening the mind opens the heart.

Like the ethical teaching of the Golden Rule, this more radical spiritual teaching of overcoming the separation between self and other is not unique to the Buddha and Jesus. Five centuries before Jesus, around the same time as the Buddha lived in India, in China Confucius taught a version of the Golden Rule (see Chapter 16). And a millennium after Buddhism was brought to China, the eleventh-century Neo-Confucian philosopher Cheng Hao wrote: "Benevolent people regard Heaven, Earth, and the myriad things as one body. Nothing is not oneself. If you recognize something as yourself, there are no limits to how far (your compassion) will go."[9]

The Neo-Confucians adopted the notion of being "of one body" with Heaven, earth, and all beings from Zen. And Zen got the idea in part from the foundational Daoist text, the *Zhuangzi*, which contains the following lines: "Heaven and earth are born together with me, and the ten thousand things and I are one."[10] This idea was introduced into Chinese Buddhist thought in the fourth century by Sengzhao, an early Chinese Buddhist philosopher who interpreted Mahayana Buddhist thought in Daoist terms, effectively laying the groundwork for the development of the Zen tradition. He wrote: "Heaven and Earth and I share the same root. The myriad things and I are of the same body."[11]

Sengzhao could weave into Mahayana Buddhism this Daoist idea of being of one body with all beings because Mahayana Buddhism already contained the ideas that all beings interdependently arise, that they are all marked by the same "emptiness," and that sentient beings all share the same capacity for suffering and happiness, deluded dualism and enlightened nondualism. We find such ideas powerfully and poetically expressed by Shantideva, an eighth-century Indian Mahayana Buddhist philosopher. Also using the analogy of different parts of the same body, he writes:

> Just as this body, with its many parts from division into hands and other limbs, should be protected as a single entity, so too should this entire world which is divided, but undivided in its nature to suffer and be happy. . . . [A] pain in the foot is not of the hand, so why is the one protected by the other? . . . In the same way that the hands and limbs are loved because they form part of the body, why are embodied creatures not likewise loved because they form part of the universe?[12]

Tat Tvam Asi: You Are Your Neighbor

In India, a stress on the underlying oneness of all life, and even all reality, is found not only in Mahayana Buddhism but also in many ancient texts of Hinduism.

One of the first Western scholars to learn Sanskrit and study the ancient texts of Hinduism was Paul Deussen. Upon reading the *Upanishads*, the recorded teachings of the ancient Hindu sages, Deussen wrote:

> The Gospels fix quite correctly as the highest law of morality, "love your neighbor as yourselves." But why should I do so, since by the order of nature I feel pain and pleasure in myself, not in my neighbor? The answer is not in the Bible . . . but it is in the [*Upanishads*], in the great formula Tat-tvam-asi which gives in three words metaphysics and morals together.[13]

Tat tvam asi means "that art thou," "you are that." The "that" here indicates *Brahman*, the divine source and unity of all things and all people. And so, Deussen reasoned, *tat tvam asi* gives the answer to the question of why you should love your neighbor: because "you are your neighbor."

Should I love my neighbor only because an all-powerful being commands me to do so, a being who will reward me if I do and punish me if I don't? Should I love my neighbor only so that I can go to Heaven rather than Hell? Should I thus love my neighbor as a means to my own egoistic ends? Or, more profoundly, should I do so because, if I look carefully, I will see God and myself in the face of my neighbor? Some theologians would say that Deussen could have found this answer in the Bible.[14] Indeed, we find the metaphor of different limbs of the same body employed by Paul in thinking of everyone, or at least all Christians, as part of the one body of Christ:

> For just as the body is one and has many members, and all the members of the body, though many, are one body, so it is with Christ. . . . God has so arranged the body . . . that there may be no dissension within the body, but the members may have the same care for one another. If one member suffers, all suffer together with it; if one member is honored, all rejoice together with it.[15]

In any case, let us look further into the answer Deussen found in the *Upanishads*. The famous phrase *tat tvam asi* is a refrain in the lessons Uddalaka gives to his son Shvetaketu in the *Chandogya Upanishad*.[16] Uddalaka uses a number of analogies in order to get his son to awaken to the divine oneness underlying all the differences in the world. For example, he points out the fact that all the different vessels and figures made out of clay differ only in "name and form," but at bottom they consist of the same substance. (He repeats this analogy in terms of different nuggets of the same gold and different tools made out of the same iron.) If Uddalaka were alive today, he'd probably talk to his son about claymation movies. When we watch a claymation movie, we get lost in the details of the story and the relations between the various characters. We forget that they are all made of the same clay. Absorbed in their apparent differences, we forget their essential sameness.

Uddalaka does not deny that people and things really do differ in name and form. His point is that on a deeper level there is an underlying unity of the universe. And then comes the punch line: *tat tvam asi*, that art thou. It is not enough to see, like a scientist, that all objects are made up of the same interchangeable flux of mass and energy. The truly enlightening moment comes when we realize the unity of the seer with all that it sees, the unity of subject and object, the unity of the self and the divine ground of reality—in Hindu terms, the unity of *Atman* and *Brahman*.

Tasting the Oneness of All Life

It may be that "seeing" is not the best of our five senses to use as an analogy for this spiritual realization. It may not be enough to *see* the point. Our word "theory" derives from a Greek word meaning "to look at," that is, to stand back and contemplate something from the outside. Hence, theoretical knowledge may not be able to give us spiritual insight. To really see into something we need to enter into it, to become one with it. That is what *kenshō*, seeing into one's true nature, means in Zen. Zen also speaks of experiencing the "one taste" of reality.[17] Indeed, "*tasting* one's true nature" might be a better metaphorical expression for the enlightening breakthrough experience than "*seeing* into one's true nature."

Sight, in fact, tends to be the most dualistic of our five senses. We can see something from afar without getting involved in it. Hearing is more intimate. After all, we don't have "ear-lids" the way we have eyelids, and so we cannot shut out sounds as easily as we can sights. Believe me, on many an overseas flight I have wished I had ear-lids! I even have a pet evolutionary theory that we used to have them but they atrophied, leaving us with these useless flaps of cartilage that we cannot move, except for a few weird folks who can wiggle their ears. Even the ear-wigglers among us have to buy noise-cancelling headphones if they want to shut out the sounds of the world.

Touch is more intimate still. There is good reason for saying, "You can look, but don't touch!" Smell is, in a way, even more intimate. My students always resent me for reminding them of the fact that when they smell a foul odor, they are actually inhaling little particles being emitted from what they are smelling. Sorry about that!

But surely taste is the most intimate of the five senses. In order to taste something, you have to ingest it, literally "incorporate" it, take it in and allow it to become part of your body. "You are what you eat," we like to say, even though the pun in the original German phrase, "*Man ist was man ißt*," gets lost in translation.

One of Uddalaka's lessons is most instructive in this regard. He tells his son to get a wide pail of water and to put a lump of salt in it. (You can do this experiment at home with one of those backyard plastic kiddie pools.) The next day, after it has dissolved into the water, Uddalaka asks his son if he can *see* the salt. His son says no. Uddalaka then asks him to *taste* the water, and of course he can taste the salt.

Crucially, Uddalaka asks his son to taste it not just in one place, but in several different places in the pail. It is the same taste everywhere. This is why Zen masters also talk about the "one taste" of reality, and of "drinking water and knowing for oneself whether it is hot or cold." We cannot see the salt of life. We cannot tell whether the water of the world is hot or cold by just looking at it. We have to taste it for ourselves.

In English, "I see" can mean "I understand." But if we want to say that we not only understand the *meaning* of what someone is saying but also their *feelings*, we say "I hear you." If his son had told him, "I see what you mean," Uddalaka might have replied: "Yes, son, but have you heard it, touched it, smelled it—and, most importantly, have you tasted it?"

Only when we have managed to *taste* the oneness of all life can we begin to also *see* it in the midst of all of our myriad differences. Only then, says Uddalaka, have we attained that spiritual wisdom in which "we come to know that all of life is one.... One who meditates upon the Self and realizes the Self sees the Self everywhere.... They see the Self in everyone."[18]

The word for "Self" that the Hindu sage Uddalaka uses is *Atman*. Yet, as we discussed in Chapter 7, the Buddha taught the *anatman* doctrine. As in English, in Indian languages such as Sanskrit and Pali, the prefix *a-* or *an-* expresses a privation or negation. And so for centuries monks and scholars have tended to distinguish Buddhism from Hinduism (or, more specifically, Brahmanism) by contrasting the Buddhist *anatman* doctrine with Hindu *atman* metaphysics.

In fact, however, the matter is far from this simple.[19] To begin with, there were and are many different Hindu schools of philosophy and religion, often with very different understandings of what *atman* signifies. What the Buddha was most concerned with refuting, as we have seen, is the notion of *atman* understood as an unchanging and independently existing individual soul-entity.[20] Such a view was widely held at the time by some of the Hindu sages whose teachings appear in the various *Upanishads* as well as by Jainism, a non-Hindu religion established around the same time as Buddhism.[21] Yet what Uddalaka is talking about is the self that unites rather than separates us from others, a self that pervades reality rather than existing in some transcendent realm apart from the world. Even if Uddalaka's stress on oneness does not allow for the complementary stress on difference we find in Zen, we should nevertheless recognize a real kinship between his teaching and at least an important aspect of Zen.

The Three Turnings of the Wheel and Debates
Within Buddhism

There are many sutras and schools of Buddhist philosophy in the background of Zen, some of them more consonant with the various competing Hindu Vedanta philosophies that derive from the *Upanishads* and some of them less so.[22] The development of Buddhism is often described, from a Mahayana perspective, in terms of Three Turnings of the Wheel of the Dharma. The First Turning consists of the early teachings such as those recorded in the Theravada Pali Canon. The Second Turning was initiated by the *Perfection of Wisdom* sutras and was philosophically articulated by Nagarjuna's Madhyamaka School; it develops the teaching of "interdependent origination" and stresses that all things are "empty" (Sk. *shunya*) of essence or independent substantiality. The Third Turning was initiated by sutras such as the *Samdhinirmochana Sutra* and was philosophically articulated by the Yogachara or "Mind-only" (Sk. *citta-matra*) School founded by the half-brothers Vasubandhu and Asanga. This Third Turning occurs in part in response to nihilistic misunderstandings of the philosophy of "emptiness" stressed by the Second Turning, and it provides a more positive phenomenological and soteriological account of an enlightened nondualistic understanding of mind and reality, along with an intricate critique of our unenlightened dualistic conception of an egocentric mind separated from a reified reality.

Another, even more positive set of sutras introduced the idea of the *Tathagatagarbha* (Buddha-embryo or Buddha-womb), an idea that in China was developed into the idea of the Buddha-nature that is often referred to in Zen. These *Tathagatagarbha* and Buddha-nature teachings are often considered to be an extension of the Third Turning of the Wheel of the Dharma.[23] An important source of these ideas is the Mahayana *Mahaparinirvana Sutra*, "which does not consider it impossible for a Buddhist to affirm an *atman* provided it is clear what the correct understanding of this concept is."[24] Such Third Turning ideas of Mind-only and *Tathagatagarbha* also prominently feature in the *Lankavatara Sutra*, which is said to have been favored by Bodhidharma and passed down to the Second Chinese Ancestor of Zen, Huike. However, the Sixth Ancestor, Huineng, promoted the *Diamond Sutra*, and it, together with its Perfection of Wisdom cousin the *Heart Sutra*, have played an even more prominent role in the history of Zen.

There have been centuries of debates within the Mahayana Buddhist tradition between proponents of the Second and Third Turnings. Some scholars and schools have insisted on the preeminence of the Madhyamaka teaching that everything is "empty" of a substantial essence. Other scholars and schools have claimed that the *Tathagatagarbha* and Buddha-nature teachings offer a more positive conception of the pure (i.e., empty of defilements) Buddha-mind that is our true essence.[25] Zen does not so much take a single doctrinal stance in these intra-Buddhist debates as it encourages us to realize through practice the relevant insights of the different teachings.[26]

This is not the place to delve further into the intricate debates among the various schools of Hinduism and Buddhism (for some indications, see the notes to this chapter and Chapter 9). Here, let me just point out some passages from *The Ten Oxherding Pictures* (a Zen classic that will be discussed in Chapter 24), which are clearly reminiscent of Uddalaka's teaching. In the texts appended to the second and third pictures, we read: "It is now clear that the many vessels are composed of a single metal, and that the body of the ten thousand things is your self." And: "Hearing the voice, one gains entry and meets the source wherever one looks. . . . It is like salt in water, or like glue in paint."[27]

Make Me One with Everything

It is popular these days to talk of spiritual oneness—perhaps so popular that it may seem superficial or even saccharine. "We are all one" has almost become a sappy platitude, and so we tend to react to it either by just piously nodding our heads knowingly or by sarcastically smirking dismissively. Perhaps, for some, the power of a song like "One" by U2 or the charity single "We Are the World" breaks through this complacency a bit. Yet, just as often, the idea of oneness gets reduced to the level of jokes we tell at parties. Jokes like the following:

> A Zen master goes to buy a hot dog on the streets of New York, and he says to the vendor, "Make me one with everything."

Try to at least chuckle. The second part of the joke may be a little funnier:

> Having just arrived from Japan and exchanged his yen at the airport, the Zen master only has hundred-dollar bills on him, and so he pays with one of those. The hot dog vendor takes the bill, puts it in his pocket, and goes back to work. The Zen master says, "Hey, what about my change?" The vendor wags his finger and reminds him, "Change comes from within."

Bad jokes aside, what does it really mean, according to Zen Buddhism, to become one with everything, or to realize the oneness of everything? What does Dōgen mean when he tells us to realize that "what Buddhas call the self is the entire earth"?[28] What this does *not* mean is to imagine ourselves being dissolved into a homogeneous blob of smooth (or even crunchy) peanut butter, blinding ourselves to the very real differences between you and me, one snowflake and an-other, a tree and the dog peeing on it.

The ninth-century Chinese Zen master Xuansha taught that "all the universe is one bright pearl." Yet if we misunderstand the one bright pearl as a uniform monism, then Zen masters say that we are "living in the Cave of Demons on Black Mountain." Dōgen tells us that we need to appreciate not just the oneness of the bright pearl of the universe but, at the same time, its "infinite colorations"—for "each of the many facets of its radiant variegations contains the merit of the entire universe."[29]

Indeed, Zen stresses the astonishing uniqueness and irreplaceable singularity of things, persons, and events at least as much and as often as it does the oneness of everything. Zen teachings agree with the U2 lyrics "We're one, but we're not the same." Yet what exactly does this mean?

To begin to answer that crucial question, let us carefully read a statement by the modern Korean Zen master Kusan Sunim, several parts of which could easily be misunderstood. He says that to awaken is to realize that

> this world, mankind, and all the animals are no different from oneself. This is precisely the "Great Self." . . . And as we know that it is not possible to separate any component from the rest of the world, both objects and the relative self cannot really exist. Therefore, the "Great Self" is precisely "no-self."[30]

The paradoxical statement "the 'Great Self' is precisely 'no-self'" is another way of saying that the true self is egoless. In other words, we could even say that *Atman*, correctly understood, is *anatman*, since the self that is being negated in the *anatman* doctrine is the self that sees itself as separate from the rest of the universe. The self that awakens to its unity with the rest of the universe is the true or great self.

When Kusan Sunim says that "both objects and the relative self cannot really exist," by "really exist" he means exist as independent, self-subsisting entities. As long as we think that this is what it means to "really exist," then nothing really exists. But we could turn the matter around and say that since no such independently self-subsisting entities exist, this must *not* be what it means to really exist.

To Exist Is to Coexist

This is the approach taken by the modern Vietnamese Zen master Thich Nhat Hanh, who says that we need to revise the definition of the most basic word in the English dictionary: the verb "to be." I doubt that any of you have ever looked up "is" or "to be" in a dictionary. We may be enthralled by Hamlet's question "To be or not to be," but it never occurred to us that maybe we should question what it means to be in the first place—unless, of course, you are a philosopher interested in questions of ontology, the study of what it means for things to be, and of what kinds of beings there are. Yet what if the apparently transparent meaning of the simple verb "to be" turns out to be not just an abstract matter for professional philosophers but rather a most concrete and pressing existential question for us all?

Nhat Hanh's suggestion is that, based not only on Buddhist philosophy but also on modern physics, we should redefine "being" as "interbeing."[31] "To be is to interbe," he proclaims. In more familiar terms, we could say: To exist is to co-exist. "Interbeing" is Nhat Hanh's reformulation of the key concept of Buddhist philosophy: "interdependent origination" (Sk. *pratitya-samutpada*). Nothing comes about or has its being on its own; everything is empty of "own-being" (Sk. *svabhava*). All things are interconnected; all things inter-are. More precisely, "interbeing" is a translation of a Chinese term that appears frequently in the *Huayan* [Sk. *Avatamsaka*] *Sutra* and in the philosophical writings of the Huayan School of Chinese Buddhism, the school that in many ways laid the philosophical groundwork for Zen. The term is *xiang-ji* (Jp. *sō-soku*), which means "mutually to be."[32] In other words, it means that things that may seem to be separate and even opposed to one another in fact mutually belong to one another.

Take me as an example. Think of all the ways in which I might define myself; all the ways in which I might answer the question: Who are you, what are you? I am a husband, a father, a son, a brother, a friend, a faculty member of a philosophy department, a student and a teacher, a reader and a writer, a listener and a speaker, a resident of Baltimore, a citizen of the United States, an earthling, and so on. Notice that what I have just given you is a list of *relationships* that define me. I am a relational being. If you took away my students, for example, I could no longer be a teacher. (But please don't let them in on this—I don't want them to know that they have that kind of power over my identity!) If you took away the air that I breathe and the food that I eat, I could not exist as the biological entity that I am.

When a loved one dies, we often say that we feel as if part of us is missing; we feel as if their absence has left a hole in our heart. We are not exaggerating, and we are not even just speaking metaphorically, any more than is Emily Dickinson when she writes in a poem: "Each that we lose takes part of us; A crescent still abides."[33] After the loss of a loved one, we feel less complete, less like a full moon and more like a crescent of our former self. We are our relationships. And, the more self-aware we become, the more we realize that the web of relations that defines us extends much further than we thought. "No man is an island," writes John Donne. "Every man is a piece of the continent" of all humankind. Thus, he adds: "Any man's death diminishes me, for I am involved in mankind. And therefore, send not to know for whom the bell tolls. It tolls for thee."[34] A couple of centuries earlier in Japan, the Zen master Ikkyū wrote in a poem: "How long will you see the evening smoke of the [funeral] pyre as another's sorrow?"[35]

In response to being accused of corrupting the youth, Socrates asks in effect: Why the heck would I do that? Why would I want to corrupt the community in which I live, the community that allows me to be who I am?[36] If wealthy people don't take care of the inner-city communities they inhabit, they end up having to flee to the suburbs. But how far and how long can we run away from our communities and our common problems? We could also ask: Why are we polluting the air that we breathe and the water that we drink? If we wish to take care of ourselves, we need to take care of the people with whom, and the environment within which, we exist.

I think education is, or at least should be, largely about breaking down walls and allowing us to understand our interconnectedness. It is much easier to hate people, or to be afraid of them, if you never get to know them. Not being a particularly outgoing person, many times I have been suspicious of someone until I actually talked to them. Seeing into the interconnectedness of all sentient beings activates our innate capacity for empathy and compassion. When my daughter falls down and scrapes her knee, it pains me to witness her pain. When I see, even just on TV, an animal squealing in pain as it is mistreated or slaughtered, I wince and my heart hurts. The more I open my mind to the interconnectedness of all things, the more my heart opens to the sadness and happiness of other sentient beings. When a child laughs, it brightens my world. When a dog circles around me wagging its tail, it infectiously makes me want to dance around and shake my booty too. Keep in mind that the Buddha taught not only compassion for suffering but also "empathetic joy."

The true self is the self that has thoroughly opened itself up to the interconnectedness of everything, the interbeing of all beings, the self who naturally empathizes with all the sorrows and joys of the world. One of the personifications of the true self is Kanzeon, the Bodhisattva of Compassion, who synesthetically as well as empathetically "sees the sounds of the world" (the literal meaning of "Kanzeon").

The Egoless Self Alone Is Venerable

Someone who has experienced this true self has realized that he or she is "of one body with all things." Only those who have experienced their oneness with the universe can say, in the words attributed to the newborn destined to become the Buddha, "I alone am venerable throughout heaven and earth." Why is this not the epitome of narcissism? It is absolutely crucial to distinguish this statement from the self-assertion of a cosmically inflated ego.

In Case 57 of *The Blue Cliff Record*, Zen master Zhaozhou quotes this phrase, "I alone am venerable throughout heaven and earth," in response to a monk's question: "It is said [by the Third Chinese Ancestor of Zen, Sengcan] that 'The real Way is not difficult. It only abhors choosiness and attachment.' Now, what are non-choosiness and non-attachment?"[37] Zhaozhou's response implies that in order to experience oneness with the entire universe, one has to utterly abandon all egoistic desires and fixations. Self-awakening and the arousing of compassion for others are two sides of the same coin, insofar as awakening dissolves the dualistic distinction between self and other.

The contemporary philosopher and Zen teacher David Loy expresses this well when he writes:

> To realize that I am the world—that I am one of the many ways the world manifests—is the cognitive side of the love that an enlightened person feels for the world and its creatures. The realization and the love are two sides of the same coin, which is why Buddhism emphasizes that genuine enlightenment is accompanied by a spontaneous welling-up of compassion for all other sentient beings.[38]

Is There Room for Difference in This Oneness?

Still, you might still be wondering, how could there be room for others in this world of oneness? After all, uniqueness is as important as unity, and if things and events are unique, that means they are different from one another. For us the most significant differences are those between individual people. How does Zen account for that?

This important issue has been touched on and will be addressed more thoroughly in Chapter 9, but let me end this chapter with a few indications of how Zen reconciles the singularity of things and persons with the oneness of the world. Case 40 in *The Blue Cliff Record* is a kōan that deals with this question. It consists of the following encounter dialogue between an enthusiastic disciple and a mature master.

> As the officer Lu Xuan was talking with [the Zen master] Nanquan, he remarked: "The Dharma teacher Sengzhao said, 'Heaven and Earth and I share the same root. The myriad things and I are of the same body.' How marvelous is this saying!" Nanquan pointed to a flower in the garden. He called to the officer and said: "People these days see this flower as though they were in a dream."[39]

Lu Xuan may have personally experienced the oneness of himself and all things. Or he may have just read about it in books. In any case, he was stuck there. He was stuck in what Zen calls a "bad equality" that does not allow for real differences. Nanquan tried to wake him up from his dream of a one-sided oneness in order to get him to realize not only the unique reality and beauty of a flower, but ultimately what Zen calls the "nonduality of equality and differences."

"Equality" originally means "uniformity." It means that things are the same in some important sense. For example, the idea of "equal rights" means that all humans have the same rights. But if we only focus on the equality of people, we ignore their many differences. A Christian would say not only that we are all equally created in the image of God, but also that we are created as unique individuals. Somewhat analogously, a Zen Buddhist would say not only that we are all manifestations of the same Buddha-nature, but also that we are each a uniquely individual manifestation—indeed, that each moment of our lives is a unique event of interconnection with all beings. As the modern Rinzai Zen priest Katayama Suihō puts it, true equality always manifests in and through concrete differences.[40] We may speak of the equality of "humanity" or even of all "life," but these are mere abstract concepts unless manifested in concrete existences. Humanity exists only in individual humans. There is no universal life floating somewhere above singular lives, and, however interconnected these life-streams are, each is, at each moment, an irreplaceably unique confluence of psychophysical formations.

Lu Xuan was fixated on equality and sameness without realizing that true equality and sameness coexist with true individuality and uniqueness. In the language of the ninth-century Chinese Zen master Dongshan's codification of the stages of realization in the Five Ranks, Lu Xuan was stuck at the entry level of dissolving the Skewed within the True—in other words, the Relative within the Absolute, the Apparent within the Real, the Contingent within the Essential, Form within Emptiness, or the Particular within the Universal—and was still far from realizing the ultimate level of integration, the nonduality of these two sides of the same coin of reality.[41] In short, we have to learn to taste the oneness of all life without losing sight of the real differences between individual lives.

The modern Zen philosopher Nishitani Keiji relates a personal experience of watching the sunrise from a hotel balcony and having the "overwhelming experience that the radiance of the sun was focused on me and that the whole world was opening brightly, concentrated on myself alone." And yet, he goes on to say, this experience of "the whole is myself" does not exclude an openness to the fact that a person on the next balcony may be enjoying the same experience.[42]

Indeed, although legend has it that *at the time of his birth* the Buddha-to-be said, "*I alone* am venerable throughout heaven and earth,"[43] legend also has it that *at the time of his enlightenment* he said, "I now see that *all sentient beings* everywhere are endowed with the wisdom and virtues of the Buddha. It is only on account of their deluded thoughts and attachments that they do not realize it."[44] All people are capable of experiencing the oneness of the universe. And all are capable of recognizing that others can experience this too. Moreover, as we will discuss in Chapter 9, we are all capable both of taking center stage and of ceding center stage to others.

9

But We Are Not the Same

Taking Turns as the Center of the Universe

In the last couple of chapters, we have talked about what the self is and is not. We have talked about what it means to think of the self as one with everything. Now we need to talk about how we are unique at the same time as we are united.

We Are United in Our Differences

In Chapter 8, we talked about what it means to love one's neighbor (and even one's enemy) as oneself. We saw how Zen Buddhism stresses the oneness of all life, as do other religious and philosophical traditions such as Daoism, Neo-Confucianism, Hinduism, Stoicism, and Christianity. The more one experiences this oneness, the less one distinguishes between one's own joys and sorrows and those of others. The more I open myself—the more I expand my sense of self—the more the very distinction between egoism and altruism, concern for myself and concern for others, begins to dissolve.

Nevertheless, when Zen master Dōgen quotes the Sixth Chinese Ancestor, Huineng, as saying, "Thus are you, and thus am I," he understands this to mean not only that we all share the same undefiled nature of mind that is "attentively maintained by all Buddhas," but also that we each must manifest this undefiled mind differently through each of our unique acts in concrete circumstances.[1] Realizing the oneness of the Buddha-mind, for Dōgen, has nothing to do with paranormal powers like reading other people's minds.[2]

You and I are, after all, distinct individuals. Our life-streams are interconnected, but they are not identical. Contrary to some popular portrayals and hot dog vendor jokes, Zen does not lose sight of the singularity and uniqueness of persons. Starting from the perspective of my personal life-stream, I am more or less open to others and to the rest of the world, just as you are, starting from your personal life-stream.

Perhaps our streams will one day, as the Hindu sage Uddalaka suggests, flow into the same great ocean.[3] This great communion in the afterlife is a matter of speculation. But here and now, in this life, in the world as we know it, although our life-streams may crisscross, and at certain ecstatic and communal moments even merge, and although in a deep sense we may awaken to the fact that all our

Zen Pathways. Bret W. Davis, Oxford University Press. © Oxford University Press 2022.
DOI: 10.1093/oso/9780197573686.003.0009

life "streams" are forms of the same formless "water," we nevertheless remain different rivers with different names and forms.

And so, as U2's Bono sings, "we're one, but we're not the same." We are interconnected, but we are not identical. We should not deny our differences, but rather be united in our plurality. To borrow the Latin motto of the United States, we should strive to realize that we are *e pluribus unum*, "out of many, one." At the same time, we are *ex uno plures*, "out of one, many." The modern Japanese philosopher Nishida Kitarō, who had practiced Zen and was familiar with Huayan Buddhist philosophy, thought of reality as "one-and-yet-many, many-and-yet-one" (*issokuta, tasokuitsu*). He thought of the ongoing historical development of the world as a ceaseless dialectic in which "the universal determines the individual, and the individual determines the universal."[4] In other words, our natural environment and social world shape us as individuals, and we in turn shape them.

Ramanuja, the eleventh-century Hindu philosopher of "qualified nondualism," points out that unity makes no sense unless it is a unity of different things, just as difference makes no sense unless there is some encompassing unity in which differences can be recognized as differences.[5] For example, we can recognize that blue is different from red because they are both colors. We can say that John and Jill are different persons because they are both persons. The United States is a political union of separate states. The universe is a physical, psychological, and spiritual union of unique things, animals, plants, and persons.

Zen stresses not only the ultimate unity of the universe, but also the irreducible singularity of the different beings—or being-events—that make up the universe. Not only is each person, each life-stream, unique, but each moment of each life-stream, and each being-event of interconnection between life-streams, is unique. Everything, every event of interconnection at every moment, is unique. And every being-event is a unique perspectival expression of the interrelated whole. This lesson of multi-perspectival unity-in-diversity is given most vividly in the simile of the Jeweled Net of Indra, found in the *Avatamsaka Sutra*.[6] The universe is envisioned as a huge net, each knot of which contains a jewel that reflects, and is reflected in, all the others. Dushun, the first patriarch of the Huayan School of Chinese Buddhism, a school that greatly influenced Zen, writes: "This imperial net is made all of jewels: because the jewels are clear, they reflect each other's images, appearing in each other's reflections upon reflections, ad infinitum."[7] Each nondual event of reality holographically mirrors, in its own finite manner and from its own unique perspective, the infinite universe.

For Dōgen, what exists is a flow of singular events of "being-time," and each one is all there ever is:

> As the time right now is all there ever is, each being-time is without exception entire time. A grass and a form-being are both times. Entire being, the entire world, exists in the time of each and every now.[8]

The *Avatamsaka Sutra* makes the same point in terms of space:

> The lands on a point the size of a hairtip
> Are measureless, unspeakable;
> So are the lands on every single point
> Throughout the whole of space.[9]

Dōgen reiterates the point when he says that "there are worlds in all four directions. And you should know that it is not only like this over there, but also right here beneath your feet and even in a single drop [of water]."[10] Each thing, as a singular event of interconnection, is a perspectival opening onto every other such thing in the universe. William Blake unknowingly echoes these East Asian Buddhist holographic thoughts when he beckons us: "To see a World in a Grain of Sand / And a Heaven in a Wild Flower, / Hold Infinity in the palm of your hand / And Eternity in an hour."[11]

It is important to bear in mind that even if each singular event of being-time implies and mirrors the whole universe, it does so in an irreducibly unique and unrepeatable manner. The Zen philosopher Nishitani Keiji writes: "It is not possible for there to be two things that are exactly the same. For there to be two such identical things, there would have to be two worlds that were entirely the same."[12] Everything, every event of interconnection, is preciously unique and unrepeatable and calls for appreciation. A favorite Zen saying among practitioners of the Way of Tea is *ichigo ichie*, which means that each meeting is a once-in-a-lifetime encounter.[13]

And so it turns out that—far from denying differences or proffering a mushy spirituality that would dissolve people together into a homogeneous blob—Zen stresses uniqueness even more, and much more radically than do adolescent Americans obsessing about their individual identities on social media, usually in terms of which groups they identify with. The Zen masters you meet in the literature of the tradition are certainly a motley crew of unusually distinct characters. And the records of their encounters are filled with stories of playful competition and serious trickery, all for the sake of spurring one another along toward deeper insights into their oneness and their differences, into their unity-in-diversity.

A Dharma Battle Between Masters of Absolute Subjectivity

Let us examine an especially revealing—if also rather enigmatic—encounter dialogue, Case 68 in the kōan collection *The Blue Cliff Record*. The kōan consists of a strange exchange between two Chinese Zen masters, Yangshan Huiji and Sansheng Huiran. In order to help us follow the give-and-take of their rather surprising and confusing exchange, let me substitute their names with some more familiar ones: Fred Flintstone and Barney Rubble. Here is the dialogue:

Fred Flintstone asks Barney Rubble, "What is your name?"
Rubble says, "Fred!"
"Fred!" replies Flintstone, "that's my name!"
"Well then," says Rubble, "my name is Barney."
Flintstone roars with laughter.[14]

You are probably thinking: "What the heck kind of dialogue is that? How are we supposed to understand what they are up to, and why does it matter? It sounds more like kids playing around than something that monks in monasteries should spend their time meditating on!" Yet even though the playful exchange ends in roaring laughter, what is at stake in the dialogue is at the same time a deadly serious spiritual matter.

The main points to bear in mind as we think about this dialogue are the following: (1) Fred asks Barney for his name, even though he must have already known it. (2) Barney responds with Fred's name rather than his own. (3) Fred says, "Hey, that's my name!" (4) Barney then declares his own name. (5) The dialogue ends with Fred's roaring laughter.

What is going on here? First of all, why did Fred ask Barney his name if he already knew it? In a remarkable essay on this kōan, Nishitani reminds us that in many traditional societies, knowing someone's personal name was thought to give one a kind of power over them.[15] Indeed, even today, think about how sensitive we are about names. Think about how strange it would feel if a stranger called you by a nickname that only your spouse uses: "How did they know that nickname, and how dare they use it!" Think about how, when we formally introduce people to each other, the traditional custom is to start by giving the name of the person of inferior social status to the person of superior status. Or think about how police officers or border guards demonstrate their authority when they demand that someone show an ID or passport. In fact, with regard to the query "What is your name?" in this kōan, the eighteenth-century Japanese Zen master Hakuin remarks that "it is like a policeman interrogating some suspicious fellow he has found loitering in the dark."[16]

The eleventh-/twelfth-century Chinese Zen master Yuanwu tells us, in his commentary on this kōan, that when Fred asks for Barney's name, he is playfully, but also very seriously, attempting to "rob the name and the being" of his younger colleague.[17] In being made to objectify himself in a name, Barney would in effect be forced to hand over his being to the absolute subjectivity of Fred. In the technical sense in which Zen uses the terms, Fred would assume the position of "master" or "host," and Barney would be relegated to the position of "servant" or "guest."

But Barney knows what Fred is up to, and he tricks him by responding with Fred's name instead of his own. This makes Fred respond: "Hey, that's my name, I'm Fred!" In this way he is made to fall into his own trap. He is led to inadvertently objectify himself, becoming in effect the servant or guest of Barney.

However, the dialogue is not yet over. In response, rather than gloat over his victory, Barney relishes his attainment of the role of master or host by quickly and freely relinquishing it; he voluntarily confesses his own name. "Well then, I'm Barney," he says, offering himself up as a named object in the world of Fred's absolute subjectivity. Fred roars with laughter, but not because he was handed victory in the end. Indeed, one wonders, was he perhaps knowingly playing along the whole time? Like Barney did in the end, did Fred stick his own neck out on purpose, offering Barney the opportunity to take, and then return, the role of host?

What is celebrated with laughter, in the end, is neither victory nor defeat. The real point of the encounter, as the modern Zen master Ōmori Sōgen tells us, is the accomplishment of an exceptionally intense dynamic of "the mutual exchange of host and guest."[18]

The Mutual Exchange of Host and Guest

This Zen phrase, "the mutual exchange of host and guest," was taken up by tea masters who say that the point of the tea ceremony is not just for the tea master to be an excellent host to his or her guests, but rather to make them feel so at home, so much on the same level, that a free exchange of these roles can take place in sharing and conversing over a bowl of tea.

Nishitani's successor in the Kyoto School, Ueda Shizuteru, writes that "the free exchange of the role of host is the very core of dialogue."[19] In a dialogue, sometimes it is proper to speak, while at other times it is proper to listen. When your conversation partner is either too reticent or too talkative, it's hard to engage in the give-and-take rhythm of a good conversation.

Of course, sometimes it is appropriate to talk more than listen, or vice versa. For example, when I give a lecture to a class, I am called on to play the role of host, to command the attention of the students so that I can teach them something. But I also want to hear from them. Not just at the end of lectures but also intermittently during them, I like to toss the ball to the students: How do you think we should understand this idea? How would you respond to this argument? When a student raises her hand, she is signaling that she is ready to play the role of host for a while. At that point I cede the floor and step back into the role of guest and listen. Not only in classes, but in all cooperative activities, sometimes it is proper to take the lead and give instructions, while at other times it is proper to follow the leader and heed her instructions.

"On the ethical plane," writes Ueda, "the emphasis, obviously, falls on the moment of self-negation when the role of host or master is surrendered to the other. But this does not mean a one-sided sacrifice of self. At bottom it is a question of reciprocal exchange in 'giving priority to the other.'"[20] In other words, he is saying, in an ethical relation each person is called on to be other-centered. Only when people are willing to hold the door open for each other is an ethical community possible.

Nishitani writes that a true understanding of the world sees it as a "system of mutual circulation" in which "all things are in a process of becoming master and servant to one another."[21] In the concluding paragraph of his most famous book, *Religion and Nothingness*, Nishitani writes:

> True equality . . . comes about in what we might call the reciprocal interchange of absolute inequality, such that the self and the other stand simultaneously in the position of absolute master and absolute servant with regard to one another. It is an equality in love.[22]

True equality, Nishitani suggests, comes about not when people are shouting at each other, each litigating only for his or her own rights, but rather when we learn to each put the other first, when we allow the other to take center stage. Only through a reciprocal other-centeredness can we learn to play the great game of exchanging roles of host and guest.

Seeing Another as the Center of the Universe

What would it mean to truly experience another person as the center of the universe? The famous Jewish philosopher Martin Buber beautifully illustrates such an experience in his account of what it means to authentically address another as Thou. Buber writes:

> He is no longer He or She, limited by other Hes or Shes, a dot in the world grid of space and time. . . . Neighborless and seamless, he is Thou and fills the firmament. Not as if there were nothing but he; but everything else lives in *his* light.[23]

The great temptation and danger, Buber says, is to treat people like things, establishing what he calls a manipulative "I-it" relation rather than a genuinely interpersonal "I-Thou" relation. For Buber, the ultimate pushback that keeps us from turning everyone into a thing to be used as we please, is God, whom Buber calls "the eternal Thou." The awesome experience of God is an experience of a Thou that absolutely cannot be turned into an It.[24]

The Jewish tradition teaches that the best way to love God is by loving our neighbor. So does Christianity. When Jesus tells us to "love your neighbor as yourself," he says that this is the second of what he calls the two greatest commandments. The first is: "You shall love the Lord your God with all your heart, and with all your soul, and with all your strength, and all your mind."[25]

These are powerful words. But what do they mean? What does it mean to love God? Should we love God like we love our neighbors? In other words, should we love God as ourselves? Or should we love God as wholly other, as a transcendent being up in Heaven far above ourselves? That of course depends on what we mean by all these words, starting with the word "God." A transcendent theism that portrays God as wholly other and above us, as a Father up in Heaven who commands us from on high—rather than, for example, as a Mother Earth who embraces us in Her arms—is a common understanding of God in the Abrahamic traditions of Judaism, Christianity, and Islam. However, there are also other ways in which theologians and mystics in these traditions have understood and experienced God.

Zen and Panentheism

Rather than a dualistic or transcendent theism, the Zen understanding of ultimate reality is closer to a "panentheistic" understanding of God. Not *pantheism*, which equates God with all beings, but *pan-en-theism*. Whereas pantheism means that "all is God," panentheism means that "all is *in* God." Panentheism understands all reality to exist *within* a God who is greater than the sum of His parts. Panentheism (literally "all-in-God-ism") is to be distinguished both from dualistic theism, which maintains the separateness of God and the world, as well as from pantheism ("all-[is]-God-ism"), which tends to completely identify God and the world. Although orthodox Christian theologies have tended to favor a more dualistic theism, there are many Christian theologians, mystics, and philosophers—from Pseudo-Dionysius, Eriugena, Eckhart, and Nicholas of Cusa to Schelling, Emerson, Teilhard de Chardin, Hartshorne, and Moltmann—who have understood God in panentheistic terms (even though the term "panentheism" itself was not formulated until early in the nineteenth century).[26]

The biblical tradition is hardly the only one in which a panentheistic conception of the divine can be found. For example, among the radically divergent Vedanta schools of Hindu philosophy is Ramanuja's panentheistic Vishishtadvaita Vedanta. Better-known in the West is Shankara's Advaita Vedanta School of "nondualism," which is in fact a monism. According to Advaita

Vedanta, the ultimate reality of *Nirguna Brahman* is void of all qualities and distinctions, which are understood as *lila* or *maya*, play or illusion. In sharp contrast, Madhva's Dvaita Vedanta School of "dualism" maintains that *Brahman* is a transcendent personal Lord (*Ishvara*) that is substantially different from the persons and things of this world. Ramanuja's Vishishtadvaita School of "qualified nondualism," in contrast to both of these other schools of Vedanta, posits a panentheistic theology according to which persons and things are finite qualities or modes of the one underlying divine substance, *Brahman*, whom he also speaks of in personal terms as Lord.[27]

One can find a panentheistic conception of God suggested by many passages of the Bible—for example, in the Book of Jeremiah, when God says: "Do I not fill heaven and earth?"[28] Buber professes a panentheistic conception of God when he writes:

> In the relation to God, unconditional exclusiveness and unconditional inclusiveness are one. . . . [F]or entering into the pure relationship [to God] does not involve ignoring everything but seeing everything in the You, not renouncing the world but placing it upon its proper ground. . . . [T]o have nothing besides God but to grasp everything in him, that is the perfect relationship. . . . Whoever goes forth in truth to the world, goes forth to God. . . . God embraces but is not the universe; just so, God embraces but is not my self.[29]

We find a panentheistic conception of God expressed in the New Testament when Paul affirms the idea that "in Him we live and move and have our being,"[30] and in the First Letter of John, which famously says: "God is love, and those who abide in love abide in God, and God abides in them."[31] According to these and many other passages, God is not simply up in the heavens, beyond the world, or outside of us. We are in God and God is in us. God is to be found down on earth as well as up in the heavens—and at the core of our own being.

A Zen Buddhist might even say that God is the kenotic or "self-emptying" core of our being; God is our true self. God is the love that is found within our own hearts, beneath the self-centered passions of the ego. To discover God as Love is, in Buddhist terms, to awaken the Immeasurable Mindsets of lovingkindness, compassion, empathetic joy, and equanimity.

The modern Japanese Zen master Shaku Sōen (English: Soyen Shaku) introduced Zen Buddhism to the United States at the Parliament of Religions in Chicago in 1893. A dozen years later he spent ten months in the United States, giving lectures that were translated into English by his student, D. T. Suzuki. Those lectures were published as a book entitled *Zen for Americans*. The book opens with a chapter titled "The God-Conception of Buddhism." Contrary to popular misconceptions, he says, Buddhism is not atheistic, nor it is pantheistic.

Rather, he suggests, "it may be convenient to borrow the term 'panentheism,' according to which God is *pan kai en* (all and one) and more than the totality of existence."[32]

Buddhism, Shaku Sōen goes on to say, teaches both "the gate of sameness" and "the gate of difference," and it "declares that no philosophy or religion is satisfactory which does not recognize these two gates." The gate of sameness, he suggests, corresponds to "God," while the gate of difference indicates "the world of individual existence." He then makes the crucial point:

> Buddhism recognizes the coexistence and identity of the two principles, sameness and difference. Things are many and yet one; they are one and yet many. I am not thou, and thou art not I; and yet we are of the same essence.[33]

Waves and Water, Mountains and Earth

The classic East Asian Buddhist metaphor for the relation between the universal Buddha-nature that we all share and the mental and physical traits that distinguish us from one another is that of *water* and *waves*. The Vietnamese Zen master Thich Nhat Hanh uses this metaphor to speak of God as well as the Buddha: "When you say that humankind was created by God, you are talking about the relationship between water and wave," not about the relation between a great tsunami and little ripples.[34] The different waves are always moving, intersecting and influencing one another, sometimes clashing, sometimes dancing together. At the same time, they are all waves of the same water; they share the same still depths beneath their sometimes beautiful, sometimes violent splashing about on the surface. The water is in the waves, it is the waves; yet it also transcends their forms in its formless depths. It is not externally transcendent, but rather, as Nishida puts it, "immanently transcendent."

According to Nishida, we should look for God or Buddha not up in the heavens or as an object existing anywhere outside the self, but rather by "illuminating the root origin of the self." The voice of conscience, which shames the small-mindedness of the ego, speaks to us from deeper within.[35] It is this understanding of our relation to God or Buddha in terms of "immanent transcendence," writes Nishida, that Mahayana Buddhism has to offer interreligious dialogue in the modern globalizing world.[36]

The metaphor of water and waves was first developed in the classic Mahayana Buddhist texts the *Lankavatara Sutra* and *The Awakening of Faith in Mahayana*,[37] both of which strongly influenced Zen. One finds this metaphor eloquently employed by the twelfth-century Chinese Zen nun Zhitong. She writes:

Although the entire wave is made of water, the wave is not the water;
Although all of the water may turn into waves, the water is still itself.[38]

Another such metaphor that is used in Zen is that of mountains and the Great Earth. Mountain chains and individual mountains are literally ex-pressions of the same underlying earth. Yuanwu speaks of the "wondrous mountain peaks of solitude" and says that "each one is the whole." Each mountain peak is a singular expression and focal point of the entire earth. What does it mean for one mountain peak to encounter another? Hakuin says that the realization that I am originally of "one body" with others is not a matter of ignoring our differences and individualities; rather, it is like "separate mountain peaks greeting one another."[39]

Each mountain peak can experience itself as a unique focal point that gathers and expresses the entire earth—and also as one relative focal point among other focal points. And so, in Zen, the metaphor of the "mountain peak" can be used to refer not only to the experience of an absolute solitude, but also to the experience of a profound unity with others. With regard to the latter, Nishitani writes: "the marvelous mountain peak is also the place of a Zen *Communio* (that is to say, a religious interrelation)."[40]

Between I and Thou, Bowing Down into the Formless Field

Nishitani and Ueda were both scholars of Christian mysticism as well as cross-cultural philosophers and lay Zen masters, and they both point out the profound parallels between the teachings of Zen and those of Meister Eckhart in particular. One metaphor for God that they are fond of, a metaphor used by Eckhart, Nicholas of Cusa, and many other late medieval and early modern Christian theologians and mystics, says that "God is an infinite sphere, whose center is everywhere and whose circumference is nowhere."[41]

The enlightened person realizes that when I thoroughly let go of my ego—that false sense of self that wishes and foolishly believes itself to be separate from the rest of reality—I can experience myself as the center of the universe, just as I can experience everyone and everything else as the center of the universe. And, crucially, the enlightened person knows when and where and how to take turns being the center of the universe.

To realize oneself as the center of the universe requires, paradoxically, letting go of all self-centeredness. It requires that one recognize that everyone else is also the center of the universe. It requires recognizing that we are each a unique expression of a formless field. As the fifteenth-century Japanese Zen master Ikkyū says, all things and persons come from and return to the formless "original field" of emptiness.[42] All beings are particular manifestations of a universal something that is, quite literally, no-thing. It is not one thing as distinct from another, but rather the formless yet fecund infinite field of interrelations among such finite things. If God or Buddha-nature is an *infinite* sphere, that means that it has no *definite* form. All definite things—whether they be in the shape of people or pineapples—are delimitations of this infinite and dynamically self-forming "no-thing."

You might be thinking, "But isn't a sphere still a definite shape?" You'd be right, and in fact, strictly speaking, an "infinite sphere"—like any shape or form that purports to be infinite—is a contradiction in terms. This is no doubt why some traditions forbid all images of the Infinite as idolatry. Yet, if we want to provisionally use some shape as a symbol for the shapeless Infinite, then a perfectly round circle or sphere—which has no edges or angles, the points along the smooth circumference of which are all equidistant from the center—is probably the best we can do. As will be discussed in Chapters 10 and 24, Zen uses an empty circle as what Nishida calls a "form of the formless."[43]

If all of this seems rather abstract, Ueda helps us bring it back down to earth with a concrete example of what it means for two unique individuals—"two mountain peaks"—to greet one another in such a manner that both their formal differences and their formless commonality are acknowledged. He uses the everyday Japanese greeting of the bow (*ojigi*) to illustrate how mutual self-negation—the emptying of all ego-centered presumptions and agendas—returns us to a communal place wherein we, paradoxically, share no-thing in common. Ueda writes:

> In the encounter with one another, rather than directly becoming "I and Thou" as in the case of a handshake, each person first lowers his or her head and bows. This does not stop at being a mere exchange of formalities. In the depths of "the between," each person reduces himself or herself to nothing. Going from the bottom of "the between" into the bottomless depths that envelop self and other, each returns to a profound nothingness. Both persons, by means of bending their egos and lowering their heads . . . , return for a moment to a place where there is neither self nor other, neither I nor Thou. Then, by raising themselves up, they once again face one another and for the first time become "I and Thou." Having each cut off the roots of unilateral egoism, they become an "I and Thou" in which each is opened to their mutuality.[44]

The Freedom of the True Self in Its Ego-Emptying Openness to Others

Nishitani explains what Ueda calls "unilateral egoism" in terms of the "infinite drive of karma," by which he means the egoistic will to power that propels and perpetuates the stream of unenlightened existence.[45] Insofar as "one ceaselessly strives to expand one's volitional power, one's power of control," one remains self-enclosed. "The manner of being defined by an egoistic will can never go beyond its own self-extension or the expansion of its own power, and thus can never really encounter the other."[46] Only by way of emptying the self, giving the self to others and upholding their being, can we realize a true interconnectedness with them, and only thereby can we attain our own self-standing by being upheld in turn by them.

The true self is not the self-enclosed ego driven by its will to self-expansion and power over others, but rather the self that is open to its interconnection with others. This true self is realized by way of a self-emptying of its egocentric will, and this non-egocentric way of being is implied in the central Buddhist teaching of *anatman* (Jp. *muga*),[47] a term that, as we saw in Chapter 7, is translated in various contexts as "no-self," "no-soul," or "egolessness."

In Zen, it is no contradiction to say that the true self is no-self, insofar as this is understood to mean that the true being of the self is a non-egocentric and dynamic manner of existence, in the literal sense of *ek-sistence*, "standing outside oneself." Insofar as the true self exists—stands outside itself in community with others—it cannot be reified as an independent ego-substance.

Ueda understands the Buddhist teaching of *anatman* as a radical negation of egocentric manners of being a self, as well as of reifying interpretations of the being of the self. Yet, for Ueda, the teaching of *anatman* best serves as an *antidote* to our tendency toward egoistic self-assertion and self-reification, since, *taken on its own*, the doctrine can mislead us into the opposite problem of a mere absence or dissolution of our sense of self.

The experience of *anatman* is best understood, says Ueda, as the second moment in the dialectical movement of the true self, that is, of the self that affirms itself only by way of negating itself. The self-identity of such a self can be expressed as "I, in not being I, am I."[48] In other words, Ueda understands the Buddhist teaching of *anatman* as calling attention to the crucial moment of "in not being I" that breaks open the karmically driven closed circuit of the "I am I" and enables the self to truly be itself by way of not remaining enclosed in itself.

The true self is realized as the dynamic entirety of this circling movement that passes through self-negation to self-reaffirmation: I, in not being I, am I. Problems with the self arise when this process is short-circuited, *either* by leaving out the moment of self-negation and misunderstanding oneself as a self-sufficient *cogito* that can monologically say to itself "I am I," *or* by getting stuck in the moment of self-negation—for example, by misunderstanding the doctrine of *anatman* to be a total denial of the existence of the self. (Bear in mind that, as we saw in Chapter 7, the Buddha clearly rejected nihilistic and annihilationist views of the self as misunderstandings of the *anatman* doctrine.)

These two pitfalls—of either *attachment to* or *loss of* self—are related to two heteronomies, two ways of not being autonomous: we are not free so long as we are ruled by internal karmic impulses, any more than we are free when we are ruled by external forces.

As meditators know all too well, the monkey-mind running around in our heads and the distracting bodily urges to fidget are internal sources of unfreedom, just as are fits of road rage and falling asleep at the wheel. Merely having others leave you alone and let you do what you want is just one facet of freedom; as important as it is politically, such external freedom hardly guarantees psychological or spiritual freedom.

Taking Turns Being the Center of Attention

The true dynamic of the self, teaches Ueda, entails two kinds of freedom: freedom-*from*-the-self and freedom-*for*-the-self. Both of these forms of freedom are realized in and through genuinely dialogical encounters with others. Regarding these two types of freedom as they are manifested in dialogue, Ueda writes:

> Freedom-*for*-the-self entails assuming the role of host and speaking; freedom-*from*-the-self entails deferring the role of host to the other and listening. The true self is a matter of the complementary joining together of freedom-from-the-self and freedom-for-the-self. When that complementary conjunction is undone, freedom-for-the-self mutates into attachment to the self, and freedom-from-the-self mutates into loss of the self. The true self—as the complementary conjunction of freedom-for-the-self and freedom-from-the-self—is found precisely in the dialogue between I and Thou.[49]

As we have seen, Ueda uses the Zen terminology of "host" and "guest" when he says: "The free exchange of the role of host is the very core of dialogue."[50] Sometimes it is appropriate to speak (for example, when one is giving a lecture); sometimes it is appropriate to listen (for example, when one is attending a lecture); and sometimes it is appropriate to alternate between speaking and listening (for example, when one is participating in a discussion after a lecture). The ability to freely and responsively alternate between these roles of host and guest depends on our ability to not get stuck or fixated on either one of these roles. We should fixate neither on the role of speaking nor on the role of listening; neither on the position of leading nor on the position of following; neither on the mode of activity nor on the mode of passivity; neither on moments when we step forward to become the center of attention nor on moments when we step back and allow others to take center stage.

A genuinely dialogical relationship—indeed, any kind of relationship that is genuinely mutual—requires a free exchange of the roles of host and guest. In other words, it is a matter of freely and responsively taking turns as the center of the universe.

10

Who or What Is the Buddha?

Shakyamuni Buddha

Up until this point in this book, when I have spoken of "the Buddha" I have most often specifically meant the historical person whose name is Siddhartha Gautama and who is thought to have lived and taught in northern India between 563 and 483 BCE (or perhaps about eighty years later than this). He is sometimes referred to as the historical Buddha or as Gautama Buddha or, since he was from the Shakya clan, as Shakyamuni, the "sage of the Shakyas."

Shakyamuni was the historical founder of the Buddhist tradition. It might be better to use the plural and speak of the Buddhist traditions, since there are various streams and schools of Buddhism and there are significant differences as well as commonalities among them. Regardless of their differences, all Buddhist traditions share in common a reverence for the historical teacher Siddhartha Gautama, who, upon his enlightenment, became Shakyamuni Buddha. In this book I will often continue to write "the Buddha" as a shorthand for "Shakyamuni Buddha." The context should make it clear when I am doing that. However, in Buddhism, and especially in Mahayana Buddhist traditions such as Zen and Pure Land Buddhism, the meaning of "Buddha" is by no means restricted to this historical teacher. In this chapter, we'll explore the various meanings of "Buddha" in the various traditions of Buddhism.

To begin with, let us recall that "Buddha" is not a proper name but rather an appellation that means "awakened one" or "enlightened one." According to all Buddhist traditions, Shakyamuni was neither the first nor the last Buddha. In a Japanese Zen monastery, such as Shōkokuji, where I practice, the lineage of enlightened teachers is regularly chanted, beginning with six mythical Buddhas who preceded Shakyamuni, then proceeding through the names of the Indian, Chinese, and Japanese Ancestors of that particular lineage, and ending with the previous Zen master of that particular monastery. Although in the Zen tradition one does not typically refer to a living master as a Buddha, technically anyone who is fully enlightened is a Buddha, and, since all humans are originally endowed with the Buddha-nature, we are all capable of becoming Buddhas. Indeed, that is the whole point of Zen practice—to wake up to our true nature and become a Buddha in this very body.

Zen Pathways. Bret W. Davis, Oxford University Press. © Oxford University Press 2022.
DOI: 10.1093/oso/9780197573686.003.0010

However, an individual flesh-and-blood person who is fully awakened to their true nature is not the only understanding of the term "Buddha." In fact, the "true nature" or "Buddha-nature" to which one is awakened is not limited to the borders of one's individual body. To awaken to one's Buddha-nature is to awaken to the fact that one's true self is not confined to this lump of flesh, especially if it is misunderstood to be dualistically cut off from the rest of reality. This should be clear from Chapters 7–9. We can best understand how Zen uses the term "Buddha" by way of comparison with how other Buddhist traditions use this term. Let me start by giving a quick overview of the various Buddhist traditions.[1]

The Various Traditions of Buddhism

After Shakyamuni's death or Parinirvana—his ultimate attainment of Final Nirvana—in the fifth century BCE, his teachings were passed down orally for several centuries. Over time, a schism arose leading to a major split between more conservative groups of Buddhists and more liberal and innovative ones. In some ways, the latter can be compared to early Christians who called on their fellow Jews to follow the spirit rather than the letter of the law.

Eventually, around the first century BCE, a movement emerged that referred to itself as Mahayana, or Great Vehicle. Adherents of Mahayana came to derogatorily refer to the more conservative schools as Hinayana, or Lesser Vehicle. It was thought that, whereas adherents of Hinayana aspire only to become Arhats, accomplished sages or "worthy ones" who have liberated themselves from Samsara, adherents of Mahayana aspire to be Bodhisattvas, "enlightening beings" who vow to liberate all sentient beings, not just themselves. Whereas the limited understanding of the Buddha Dharma practiced by Hinayana Buddhists is said to be like a small raft that can carry only the Arhat himself, the full understanding of the Buddha Dharma practiced by Bodhisattvas is like a giant ship that can ferry all sentient beings across the river to the other shore of Nirvana. Or so the critique goes. Keep in mind that this is the Mahayana version of the difference between itself and the schools it calls Hinayana.

The so-called Hinayana schools mostly died out, except for the Theravada or Doctrine of Elders School, which still thrives today in Sri Lanka, Myanmar, Thailand, and elsewhere in Southeast Asia. The Mahayana traditions spread to, and still thrive today in, Central and East Asia. In Tibet and Bhutan, Tantric or Vajrayana schools took root and flourished. In China, Korea, and Japan, Zen and Pure Land Buddhist schools, among others, developed distinct traditions. Theravada and Mahayana schools coexist in Vietnam.

Along with the Arhat versus Bodhisattva ideals, another major difference between the so-called Hinayana schools and the Mahayana schools concerns their understandings of the term "Buddha." These differences are in fact directly related to each other, insofar as the question is, who should aspire to become a Buddha? A Bodhisattva is someone who aspires to become, and is generally well on the way to becoming, a Buddha. According to the Hinayana understanding, only an especially gifted person, and indeed only one such person in an entire eon, is capable of becoming a Buddha. The rest of us can only, and should only, aspire to become disciples of the Buddha of our time and, by following his teachings, to become Arhats. An Arhat is someone who has personally attained liberation by diligently putting into practice the teachings of a Buddha.

The Mahayana traditions, by contrast, teach that everyone should aspire to eventually become a Buddha, which means that, to begin with, everyone should aspire to become a Bodhisattva. To become a Bodhisattva, one needs to arouse the *bodhicitta*, the "mind of enlightenment," which first of all means the sincere aspiration to become a Buddha so that one can best serve to liberate all sentient beings from suffering. In this spirit, Zen practitioners chant daily the Four Great Vows:

However limitless sentient beings are, I vow to liberate them all.
However inexhaustible deluding afflictions are, I vow to extinguish them all.
However innumerable Buddhist teachings are, I vow to learn them all.
However unsurpassable the Buddha Way is, I vow to complete it.[2]

According to the Mahayana schools, the Hinayana goal of becoming an Arhat ironically betrays a still-egocentric concern with one's own liberation. This lingering spiritual selfishness is ironic because, as all Buddhist traditions recognize, opening the eye of wisdom automatically entails opening the heart of compassion. After all, the wisdom one realizes involves insight into the nonduality of self and other, and so, in effect, it ultimately makes no sense to be concerned only with one's own enlightenment.

The Mahayana image of the Bodhisattva is that of someone who is on the verge of entering Nirvana but who, out of compassion, turns back, forsaking their own complete liberation, in order to work tirelessly on behalf of the liberation of all sentient beings from suffering. For the Pure Land Buddhist schools, Amitabha—pronounced Amida in Japanese—only became a Buddha on the condition that it would enable him to most effectively work to liberate others. Amida Buddha is thought to dwell in a celestial Pure Land, from which he sends his rays of wisdom and compassion down into the world. With the mention of Amida Buddha, we come across a second understanding of the term "Buddha." For Pure Land Buddhists, Shakyamuni was a great historical teacher, but Amida is the ultimate Buddha, the higher power or, as they say, the "other-power" required to save us.

If you are getting a little confused at this point, you are not alone. In the 1970s, the BBC filmed a documentary about Japanese Buddhism as part of its monumental series *The Long Search*. Unable to obtain a single unambiguous answer in Japan to the question "Who or what is the Buddha?," they ended up entitling the episode "The Land of the Disappearing Buddha." Here are some of the answers that the narrator, Ronald Eyre, received from representatives of Zen and Pure Land Buddhism in Japan. He was told that the Buddha is "a dead teacher," "a

Figure 10.1 Amida Buddha statue at Kōtoku-in, a Pure Land Buddhist temple in Kamakura

Figure 10.2 *Ensō*: the "single circle" Zen symbol for the ineffable Truth Body of the Buddha

transcendent being that fills the world with the light of his compassion," "you and me," "this stick," "the thingness of a thing," and "an empty circle."

By this point, you are already in a better position than Mr. Eyre apparently was to understand this seemingly odd array of answers. For example, the answer "a dead teacher" was most likely a provocatively irreverent reference to Shakyamuni Buddha by a Zen Buddhist. The answer "a transcendent being that fills the world with the light of his compassion" surely came from a Pure Land Buddhist referring to Amida Buddha. The other answers—"you and me," "the thingness of a thing," "an empty circle"—must have come from Zen Buddhists referring to the universal Buddha-nature, the formless essence of all forms.

The Three Bodies of the Buddha

To get a better handle on these different ways of understanding the term "Buddha," let me introduce the Mahayana doctrine of the Trikaya or Three

Bodies of the Buddha: the Nirmana Kaya or Manifestation Body, the Sambhoga Kaya or Enjoyment Body, and the Dharma Kaya or Truth Body.[3]

Only the first of these three "bodies" refers to a literal flesh-and-blood body. It might be helpful to keep in mind the different ways we use the term "body" in English. We speak of the "body politic" or of an artist's "body of work," and Christians speak of the Eucharistic bread as the "body of Christ." In fact, the Buddhist Trikaya is in some ways comparable to the Christian Trinity of the Father, Son, and Holy Spirit.

Christ the Son in the Christian Trinity is comparable to the Nirmana Kaya or Manifestation Body. This refers to a flesh-and-blood Buddha, the prime example being Shakyamuni Buddha. Such an enlightened person is seen as a manifestation of the wisdom, compassion, and other virtues of the universal Buddha-nature. It is someone who has awakened to who and what they truly are, and who can teach others the path to such an awakening.

The Manifestation Body of the Buddha plays a major role in the Hinayana schools. When they speak of "the Buddha," they almost always mean Shakyamuni Buddha, the historical teacher who was born, attained enlightenment when he was thirty-five years old, taught for forty-five years, and died—or, rather, attained Parinirvana, Final Nirvana. However, Hinayana Buddhist schools also developed a Two Body doctrine in order to explain the difference between the mortal flesh and blood of Shakyamuni Buddha and the immortal virtues and truth or Dharma to which he awakened. When they depict the Buddha in a statue, the physical form represents his Rupa Kaya or Form Body, while the sometimes enormous size of the statue and the special marks, like long earlobes and the protrusion on the crown of his head, signify the virtues and verities of his Dharma Kaya or Truth Body.

We'll see in a moment how the Mahayana tradition developed this notion of the Dharma Kaya so that it came to indicate the ultimate ubiquitous and transpersonal Body of the Buddha, the most important sense of the term "Buddha" for Zen. But first we need to discuss the penultimate Body of the Buddha that plays a major role in other Mahayana schools: the personal and transcendent Sambhoga Kaya.

The Father in the Christian Trinity is in some respects comparable to the Sambhoga Kaya or Enjoyment Body. Not unlike how some Christians think of "our Father who art in Heaven" as a transcendent being dwelling in an otherworldly paradise, some Buddhists think of a Sambhoga Kaya as a Buddha who dwells in a celestial realm—a Pure Land—that transcends life on earth, beyond the realm of finitude and suffering that Christians describe as a "vale of tears" and that Buddhists think of as Samsara. However, a Sambhoga Kaya is not an eternal and omnipotent Creator God who judges us from on high, but rather the celestial embodiment of a Buddha who over eons has accumulated an enormous surplus of karmic merit and who is able to aid others in overcoming obstacles on their way to enlightenment. He appears to, and his enlightening and liberating virtues are "enjoyed" by, earthly Bodhisattvas through their meditative practices of visualization. Pure Land Buddhists believe that all people of "faithful heart" who fully entrust themselves to his grace or "other-power" will be directly transported to his Pure Land after death.

Amida Buddha and the Pure Land

The most famous Sambhoga Kaya is Amitabha or, in Japanese, Amida Buddha.[4] As the literal version of the story goes, a Bodhisattva named Dharmakara became Amida Buddha through eons of spiritual practice. Epitomizing the Bodhisattva spirit of compassion, from the beginning Dharmakara vowed not to become a Buddha unless and until it meant that he could save anyone who sincerely called on his name. He achieved this, it is said, and he now sends down into the world his rays of light—beams of wisdom and compassion—from his Pure Land in the West. Insofar as we call on his name and utterly rely on his grace or "other-power," we can be reborn in this paradise.

Yet the Pure Land is not simply a paradise to be enjoyed. Rather, it is a land that is free of all the physical and psychological obstacles to attaining enlightenment and becoming a Buddha ourselves. In the Pure Land one can, for example, hear Buddhist teachings whenever one wishes and understand them without difficulty. And, presumably, one's legs don't hurt and one doesn't get sleepy during *zazen* in the Pure Land! In short, Amida Buddha's Pure Land is an optimal training ground for people to quickly and easily become Buddhas. Unable to attain enlightenment in this life on earth, at death they rely on Amida Buddha's other-power to allow them to go forth to be reborn in the Pure Land so that they can, in their turn, return as Buddhas to work on behalf of liberating all sentient beings.

This is a rather simplistic sketch of Pure Land Buddhist mythology. As the tradition developed, especially in the radically reformist teachings of the thirteenth-century Japanese Pure Land Buddhist Shinran, the story got retold in less literalistic ways. For example, according to Shinran, Amida Buddha is not just a celestial Sambhoga Kaya but the Dharma Kaya itself. He divides the Dharma Kaya into the "Dharma-body as suchness" and the "Dharma-body as compassionate means." Amida is ultimately the formless "dharmic naturalness" of the cosmos as such and only secondarily, as a compassionate "expedient means," a celestial Buddha who takes on form to aid us in realizing this liberating and formless naturalness.[5]

We'll return to the rich and profound teachings of Shinran's True Pure Land School of Buddhism (also called Shin Buddhism) in Chapter 12. Here, before we turn our attention to the Dharma Kaya—the Truth Body of the Buddha, which is the most important sense of "Buddha" for Zen Buddhists—let's look at a key idea that is important for understanding the Sambhoga Kaya: the idea of "merit transfer." This idea will help clarify how the ideas of "other-power" and "Pure Land" developed.

Merit Transfer, Other-Power, and Pure Land

The idea of "merit transfer" was very important for the development of Mahayana Buddhism. In the beginning it was thought that by doing good deeds and spiritual practices, one can either enjoy the fruit of this good karma in this life or one can save up this merit and spend it on attaining a better rebirth in one's next life. Early on the idea developed that one could also dedicate one's karmic merit to someone else—for example, to assist a deceased loved one to attain a better rebirth.

As with other teachings, Mahayana Buddhists radicalized and universalized the idea of merit transfer. The scholar Paul Williams writes that

> what distinguishes Mahāyāna from non-Mahāyāna transference of merit is that whereas in the latter case the merit is usually transferred to a particular person . . . in [the case of] Mahāyāna inscriptions merit transference is always for the benefit of all sentient beings, usually in order that they may all attain perfect enlightenment.[6]

So, for example, after sutras and other scriptures are chanted by Zen practitioners, a dedication called an *ekō* is chanted. This dedication is meant to "turn around and send outward" whatever merit—or, we might say, liberating energy—has been generated by the chanting, in order to assist all Buddhas and Bodhisattvas in liberating and enlightening all sentient beings everywhere.

Let's now look at how this radicalized and universalized idea of merit transfer leads to the idea of a Buddha working on behalf of all sentient beings by way of establishing a Buddha Land or Pure Land.

According to the earliest recorded teachings maintained by the Hinayana schools, Shakyamuni Buddha claimed to be nothing more than a human being who had awakened to what it really means to be a human being. He can teach us to do the same; he can save us a lot of time and trouble by giving us instructions—but, in the end, we have to do our own work. We have to study, live an ethical life, and meditate by means of our own effort. No one can do these things for us. More than once, including on his deathbed, Shakyamuni taught: "Monks, be islands unto yourselves, be your own refuge, having no other; let the Dhamma [i.e., the truth of the teachings] be an island and a refuge to you, having no other."[7] As the Sixth Chinese Ancestor of Zen, Huineng, teaches more than a millennium later, you should ultimately "take refuge in the enlightenment . . . truth . . . [and] purity of your own minds."[8]

Shakyamuni said that he can show us the path that he has taken to enlightenment and Nirvana, but he cannot walk the path for us. In the *Dhammapada*, one of the earliest collections of his sayings, we read: "You, yourselves, must walk the path. Buddhas only show the way."[9] In other words, Shakyamuni Buddha presents himself as a *guide*, not a *god*. He can walk side by side with his disciples, and he can leave a detailed road map for the rest of us, but he cannot give anyone a piggyback ride to Nirvana.

By contrast, the Mahayana tradition of Pure Land Buddhism says that you can get to Nirvana by taking a piggyback ride on the broad shoulders, the Great Vehicle, of Amida Buddha. Indeed, according to Shinran, the only way anyone has ever been able to get to Nirvana is by the grace, the other-power, of Amida Buddha. It is spiritual arrogance for anyone to think that they could get there by means of their own "self-power."[10]

This reminds me of a Christian story about a man who, before he found Christ, always felt like he was walking alone, leaving only one set of footprints in the sand. After he found Christ, he always felt like there were two sets of footprints; he felt that Christ was his constant companion on every step of the journey of his life. But then the going got tough. He fell on hard times, losing his job, his health, and his loved ones. Looking down, wondering how he could continue to keep walking, he again saw only one set of footprints. Why, he cried out, had Christ left him alone when he needed Him most? But then he heard an inner voice: "I have not left you alone, I am carrying you." This Christian story about relying on a higher power to carry us through the lows of this life resonates deeply with Pure Land Buddhism. Pure Land Buddhists distinguish themselves from other Buddhists by saying, "Whereas they rely on their own efforts, on their own self-power, we wholly rely solely on the other-power of Amida Buddha." In this way Pure Land Buddhism is more recognizably "religious," at least insofar as we define religion in terms of what Friedrich Schleiermacher called "the feeling of absolute dependence."

But how, one might wonder, does it make sense for a Buddhist claim to rely on a higher power? Let's approach this question in terms of the teaching of karma (which we will discuss in greater detail in Chapter 15). The idea of karma entails that, in biblical terms, "you reap what you sow." If you do the work, you get the results. If you study hard, you get good grades. If you slack off, it shows up on your report card. Yet things are not this simple. Our karmic life-streams are intricately intertwined. It is true that if I give in to hatred and in a rage hit someone, I am allowing myself to become a hateful person who is prone to fits of rage, and I will suffer from these negative emotional states and from the negative relationships they cause me to have with others. But it is also obviously true that the person who gets hit gets hurt. By the same token, if I respond to a hurtful word or act with a forgiving smile, I not only benefit myself but also allow the other person to pivot toward a more positive direction. If I help myself by helping others, they are more likely to do the same. Buddhists speak of this kind of "paying it forward" in terms of "merit transfer." In general, merit transfer means that one directs the benefits of one's good deeds, the fruit of one's good karma, to others.

We can understand this better by rather crudely comparing karmic merit to money. If I work hard, I can accumulate a lot of money. I can use that money for my own benefit, or I can use it to benefit others. In fact, I can give away a lot of money only if I first of all make a lot of money. Bill Gates can afford to be a generous philanthropist because he was a successful capitalist. Analogously, if one diligently engages in spiritual disciplines, one can accumulate a lot of karmic merit to give away. A Bodhisattva engages in mediation and other Buddhist practices so that he or she can be the kind of person who has something to offer others. Put in more mundane terms: if you take the time and make the effort to engage in spiritual practices such as meditation (as well as to sleep, exercise, and eat well), you will at least be a more pleasant person to be around, and you will likely also be kinder and more generous.

Think for a moment about the effect a person's mood can have on others. Sometimes a person is so grumpy that just being around them is a downer. On the other hand, there are people who brighten up a room as soon as they walk into it. Their positive energy is contagious. Think of it this way: Our mood is like a bubble that surrounds us wherever we go and more or less affects—we could even say infects—anyone who comes in contact with it. When we share a mood, we pool our emotional energies and create an atmosphere. When one person is in a good mood and another is in a bad mood, either they cancel each other out or one is stronger and converts the other.

Now, imagine if Mother Theresa, Archbishop Desmond Tutu, Mahatma Gandhi, or whoever you think is a very spiritually inspiring person were to walk into a crowded room. Even before they say or do anything, the atmosphere would be instantly transformed just by their presence, by their aura. That aura—the atmosphere of positive energy emitted by their presence—is how we might begin to understand what is meant by a Buddha Land or a Pure Land. I once saw the Dalai Lama speak in a large auditorium. I can't remember the specifics of what he said, but I'll never forget the way his laughter lit up that very big room. The auditorium felt for a time like a Pure Land.

In the presence of such people, we feel the obstacles to our spiritual progress dissolve. Imagine if that person were not just an earthly human being but rather a celestial Buddha that had accumulated eons of positive energy or karmic merit to transfer to those around him or her. Such a being is Amida Buddha, who is constantly emitting his rays of wise and compassionate light, inconspicuously calling on us to open the eyes of our minds and hearts to see and be uplifted by them.

The Truth Body of the Buddha as Our True Self

Zen Buddhists do not usually speak of "other-power," nor do they think of the Buddha in terms of a celestial Sambhoga Kaya. They might say that they rely on "self-power," but, in contrast to Pure Land Buddhism's critical use of this term, they do not think of this self-power as a form of ego-power. They think of it as the power that naturally emanates from the true self, not as the willful force of the fabricated ego.[11] This true self neither is outside oneself nor is limited to the borders of our physical bodies. The true self is our Buddha-nature. In other words, the Truth Body of the Buddha, the ultimate truth of who and what the Buddha is, is the ultimate truth of who and what we are.

In some Mahayana schools, such as the Japanese esoteric school of Shingon, the Dharma Kaya is personified as Vairochana or, in Japanese, Dainichi Buddha. Dainichi literally means "Great Sun." As in Platonism, the sun is understood as an analogy for the source of all light and life, the source of all mental and physical existence. A Shingon Buddhist engages in various esoteric practices thought to tap into the creative and compassionate energy of Dainichi Buddha.[12] Zen Buddhists, however, understand the Dharma Kaya in transpersonal rather than personal terms. The Dharma Kaya is the formless source or Source-Field of all forms, including but not limited to personal forms. It is the water underneath and within all the waves of existence.

To some extent, the Dharma Kaya could be compared with the Holy Spirit. This is the aspect of the Christian Trinitarian God that is immanent—within the world—rather than wholly transcendent, like the Father; yet neither is it limited to a flesh-and-blood person such as Christ or Shakyamuni. Like the Holy Spirit, the Dharma Kaya permeates the world and its workings can be awakened to in our own hearts. Indeed, the Dharma Kaya is our own Buddha-nature, our own true self. However, whereas the Dharma Kaya is the formless ultimate reality from which the forms of both celestial and earthly Buddhas emanate as compassionate "expedient means," a Christian would not say this of the Holy Spirit in relation to the Father and Son. In the language of Meister Eckhart's Christian mysticism, the Dharma Kaya is more like the transpersonal Godhead (*Gottheit*)—the ground or "silent desert" of "Nothingness"—from which all three Persons of the Trinity emanate.[13]

We will further compare and contrast Zen, Pure Land Buddhism, and Christianity in Chapter 12, and we'll make some additional comparisons between Zen and Meister Eckhart in Chapter 13. Before that, in Chapter 11, we will continue to discuss Zen's understanding of the word "Buddha." We'll talk about what Zen masters mean when they say that "Mind is Buddha," and we'll discuss what is perhaps the most shocking statement made in any religious tradition—namely, Zen master Linji's admonition: "If you encounter the Buddha, kill the Buddha!"

11

Mind Is Buddha

So, If You Encounter the Buddha, Kill Him!

In Chapter 10, we looked at how the word "Buddha" is understood in various Buddhist traditions, including Pure Land Buddhism as well as Zen. In Chapter 12, we'll delve deeper into Pure Land Buddhism in relation to Christianity as well as Zen. In this chapter, we'll look more closely at the ways in which the term "Buddha" is understood in Zen. For our initial guide, we'll examine the eighteenth-century Japanese Zen master Hakuin's *Song in Praise of Zazen*, a text chanted regularly in Rinzai Zen monasteries and meditation meetings.[1]

Ice and Water: Unenlightened Beings Are Originally Buddhas

Hakuin's *Song in Praise of Zazen* begins with a striking yet puzzling claim: "Unenlightened beings are originally Buddhas." This sounds like a contradiction in terms. After all, a Buddha, by definition, is an enlightened being. Moreover, "originally" here means not simply "at a prior point in time" but also "from the beginning," "all along," and so, basically, still now. The term that I am translating as "unenlightened beings" can also be translated as "sentient beings" or "living beings." But it means especially *unenlightened* human beings. I think Hakuin wants the opening line of his *Song* to appear encouraging yet also enigmatic, promising yet also paradoxical. And so it is best translated as "Unenlightened beings are originally Buddhas." Unenlightened beings have never been and could never be anything other than enlightened beings. What a strange, paradoxical, thing to say!

Fortunately, the next lines of Hakuin's *Song* help us resolve the paradox: "Just like water and ice, there is no ice separate from water, and there is no Buddha outside of unenlightened beings." Using the classical Chinese philosophical concepts of *ti*, *xiang*, and *yong*—or substance, form, and function—we could say that Buddha is the formless body or substance that can take on different forms or qualities and thus can function in different manners. In modern scientific terms, for example, the substance H_2O can take on the different qualities and functions

Zen Pathways. Bret W. Davis, Oxford University Press. © Oxford University Press 2022.
DOI: 10.1093/oso/9780197573686.003.0011

of a liquid, a gas, or a solid. Although water, steam, and ice are all H_2O, these different forms of H_2O appear very different and function very differently.

If Hakuin were writing today, he might have said that Buddha-nature is like H_2O and Buddhas are like water. The scientific analogy can only take us so far, however, since a Buddha is someone who is awakened to their Buddha-nature and thus able to manifest the most natural qualities and functions of this nature. A chemist would not say such things of water in relation to H_2O. The qualities and functions of water are not any more or less natural or awakened than are those of ice and steam. In any case, let us learn what we can from Hakuin's illuminating analogy, even if, like all analogies, it should not be taken too literally or pushed too far.

Hakuin is comparing Buddhas to water and unenlightened beings to ice. Unenlightened beings are both the same as and different from Buddhas. They are the same body or substance, but they differ in form and function. Unenlightened beings are H_2O in the hardened and isolated form of ice cubes, whereas Buddhas are H_2O in its most natural formless and fluid state of liquid water. Water is not opposed to taking any form, as the situation requires. And it is also not attached to any form. Water is able to move freely in between any would-be obstructions. As the *Daodejing* tells us, water's flexibility, softness, and willingness to "put itself in the lower position" are actually the sources of water's great strength and efficacy.[2] Flowing water rounds off the edges of even the hardest rocks. And it dissolves even the most frozen formations of ice.

As metaphorical ice cubes, unenlightened beings are attached to their respective forms and falsely see themselves as separate substances. Hence, they constantly bump up against one another, causing one another to suffer in myriad ways. And they constantly suffer from the inevitable erosion and metamorphosis of their own forms. The practice of Buddhism is a matter not of turning one substance into another, but rather of returning the hardened forms of our egos to their native virtue of fluid flexibility. The practice of Zen is a matter of melting the ice cubes of our egos, dissipating hard-and-fast distinctions between self and other, egoism and altruism. It is not a matter of sitting around not doing anything, an ineffective and irresponsible quietism. To the contrary, it is a matter of becoming fluid and flexible and thus responsive and effective.

The core practice of Buddhism, according to the Zen tradition, is *zazen*, seated meditation. In his *Song*, Hakuin claims that *zazen* is the source and perfection of all other Buddhist practices. Yet it is important not to misunderstand *zazen* as an alchemical practice of transforming one substance into another, of transforming an unenlightened being into a substantially different enlightened being. From the beginning we are already Buddhas; *zazen* is a practice of realizing this—of awakening to and actualizing this fact.

In a famous kōan, the eighth-century Chinese Zen master Nanyue comes across his student Mazu sitting in meditation all day in his hermitage. Nanyue asks him why he is meditating. Mazu answers that he is sitting with the intention of becoming a Buddha. Nanyue then picks up a tile and starts rubbing it with a stone. Mazu eventually asks him what he is doing. Nanyue responds that he is polishing the tile to make a mirror. "How can you make a tile into a mirror by polishing it?" Mazu asks. "How can you become a Buddha by sitting in meditation?" Nanyue replies.[3]

Nanyue goes on to say that Mazu should not "cling to the sitting posture," since "Buddha isn't limited to any fixed form." Nevertheless, as Hakuin and other Zen masters have stressed, seated meditation is the best way to realize that which cannot be limited to any fixed form or prescribed posture. Sitting still and sinking deeply into meditation, we let down our guard. We let down the icy walls that separate us from others—and, ultimately, we let dissolve the separation that we maintain between ourselves as unenlightened beings and the Buddha that we want to become. We may need to begin by sitting with the intention of becoming a Buddha, but we ultimately need to let go of even this intention and the separation it, ironically, exacerbates.

Hakuin's *Song in Praise of Zazen* continues: "Not knowing how close it is, unenlightened beings seek it far away from themselves—what a pity! It is as though they were standing in the midst of water crying out in thirst!" The water of the Buddha is all around us. We are in it, we are of it. It is to be found right in the midst of our everyday lives, and yet we look for it as though it were some faraway precious and mysterious thing.

Zen masters sometimes compare their teachings to "selling water by a river." Plenty of pristine water is right there for the taking, but we think we have to purchase it in small amounts from special people. One time I was in Iceland with some colleagues ordering a meal at a restaurant. On the menu was listed "glacial water." Although it was a bit expensive, we were all eager to try the famed Icelandic glacial water. Fortunately, the amused waiter took pity on us and told us that *all* the water in Iceland comes directly from glaciers. We ordered the free tap water, and it was delicious. However, I am sure that, even after being told this, some tourists still order the expensive "glacial water." Sometimes we are not ready for the full truth, so set are we in our preconceptions and expectations. Sometimes we insist on being sold water by a river. In fact, to some extent we all need to do this until we are ready to realize that we already are the Buddhas that we seek to become.

After saying that we are like people crying out in thirst while standing in the midst of fresh water, Hakuin alludes to a famous parable from the *Lotus Sutra* in which the son of a rich man abandons his father and runs away from home.[4] Completely forgetting where he came from, he falls into poverty and misery.

Eventually, he inadvertently approaches his father's house looking for work. He sees his father from a distance and is intimidated by his wealth and prestige. Thinking himself unworthy even to do menial jobs at such a household, he flees. His father, however, immediately recognized him and sends a messenger out to retrieve him. But the son resists, fearing that he is being arrested and forced into service.

Using "skillful means," his father lets him go and later sends another messenger disguised as a menial laborer. The messenger offers the son a job removing excrement from the household. After twenty years of dutifully doing this grueling work, slowly gaining self-esteem along the way, the son is asked by his ailing father to take charge of managing his riches. The son does this honorably, without any thought of wrongdoing, and yet he is still not able to entirely get over thinking of himself as lowly and unworthy. Then one day his father publicly announces that he is his true son and the rightful heir of the household, and the son is finally able to acknowledge who he is—who, indeed, he has all along been. The point of the parable, we are told, is that "this old man with his great riches is none other than the [Buddha], and we are all like the Buddha's sons." When we finally recognize this, we are able to inherit the household of the Buddha, no longer thinking of ourselves as unworthy servants.

The point is that we are all Buddhas, the Buddha is our true self, yet our ignorant egos are standing in the way of realizing this. We thus see the Buddha as something outside ourselves, something that we can believe in (or not), something that we can pray to and serve (or not), maybe even something that we can one day become—but not as something that, deep down, we already are.

Smashing Idols: If You Encounter the Buddha, Kill Him!

As long as we see the Buddha as something outside ourselves, we can never see into the Buddha as our own true nature. This is why the founder of the Rinzai (Ch. Linji) Zen tradition, the ninth-century Chinese Zen master Linji, shockingly teaches: "If you encounter the Buddha, kill the Buddha!"[5]

It is hard to imagine any religious tradition affirming such an apparently blasphemous, sacrilegious, and indeed murderous statement with regard to its most sacred figure! And yet Linji's point is that the so-called Buddha that you would encounter on the road somewhere, the Buddha that you would see as something or someone outside yourself walking down the street, is not the real Buddha. And so, in effect, he is telling us to smash all idols of the Buddha.

The difference between an idol and an icon, the difference between a false substitute and a genuine symbol, is crucial to all religious traditions. Jews and Muslims are stricter than Christians in forbidding all images of God. When

I visited the Taj Mahal, I was struck by the beauty of the geometric designs and by the absence of any representational figure, much less an anthropomorphic one. As sacred as an image may be, it remains a mere symbol for something that cannot be fully expressed or captured by either its material or its form. And it is all too easy to substitute an attachment to the form of a symbol for an appreciation of the formless truth it is imperfectly indicating.

In fact, for centuries after the Buddha died, it was forbidden to make images of him. It was not until the first century BCE that Buddhists began to make sculptures and other images of the Buddha. They were inspired by Greek art and motivated by a compassionate desire to offer people a "skillful means" for approaching formless truths by way of beautiful and didactic forms.

In the BBC documentary mentioned in Chapter 10, "The Land of the Disappearing Buddha," part of the series *The Long Search*, the modern Japanese Zen master Ōmori Sōgen, after practicing the martial art of swordfighting, bows to an image in an alcove. The narrator asks him, "Is that the Buddha you are bowing to?" The Zen master answers that it is a form of Buddha: namely, Kannon, the Bodhisattva of Compassion. He then adds: "When I bow to it, I bow to something in myself. That something I call compassion." The image outside himself is merely a reminder of what, ultimately, he finds working in and through his own heart.

The First Letter of John famously says that "God is love."[6] It does not just say that God loves; it says that God *is* love. If we take this seriously, it implies that to speak of "God's love" is redundant. So is speaking of the "love of God," regardless of whether "God" is understood to be the subject or object of this phrase. A Christian might ask herself, "Is God a divine being who loves, or is God another word for love?" If God *is* love, as John says, then the love I feel in my heart is itself God. John in fact goes on to say that "if we love one another, God lives in us and his love is perfected in us."[7] This love that I feel is thus not merely *for* God or *from* God; it *is* God. And if this love is the truest part of my self, then, it could be said, my true self is none other than God. (We'll return to such theological questions in Chapter 12.)

Recall that the ninth-century Chinese Zen master Yantou says: "Haven't you heard that what enters through the gate is not the family treasure?"[8] In other words, whatever comes from the outside is not your true self. Buddha is nothing outside of one's own heart and mind. One's true heart-mind is the Buddha. Hakuin writes:

> Buddha means, "one who is awakened." Once you have awakened, your own mind itself is Buddha. By seeking outside yourself for a Buddha invested with form, you set yourself forward as a foolish, misguided man. It is like a person who wants to catch a fish. He must start by looking in the water, because fish live

in water and are not found apart from it. If one wants to find Buddha, one must look into one's own mind, because it is there, and nowhere else, that Buddha exists.[9]

The Buddha-Mind Is Unselfconscious

Zen master Shidō Bunan, the teacher of Hakuin's teacher, composed the following poem:

> People are perplexed
> When asked what Buddha is;
> No one knows
> It is his own mind.[10]

Elsewhere he writes: "People themselves are Buddha, yet they do not know it." However, in this case he enigmatically adds: "If they know it, they are far from the Buddha-mind; if they don't know it, they are deluded."[11] It seems that we are damned if we do and damned if we don't know that we are Buddha. In fact, we may be more damned if we do know this. Again Shidō Bunan: "One who knows is an ordinary man, and one who knows not is a Buddha."[12] You may recall from Chapter 7 that, when asked who he is, Bodhidharma answered, "I don't know" or, more literally, "Not-knowing."[13] Not only is a certain kind of reflective and objective "knowing" not enough, it actually gets in the way of enlightenment.

Moreover, this kind of reflective and objective "knowing" can get in the way of compassionate action. The modern Korean Zen master Seung Sahn sums up his entire teaching with these words: "So I hope from moment to moment you only go straight, don't know, which is clear like space, try, try, try for ten thousand years, nonstop, get enlightenment, and save all beings from suffering."[14] Shidō Bunan tells us, "When one is compassionate and unaware of it, one is a Buddha."[15] Likewise, the thirteenth-century Zen master Dōgen tells us, "When Buddhas are truly Buddhas, there is no need for them to be conscious of themselves as Buddhas."[16] Being self-conscious of oneself as a Buddha is sort of like saying to oneself at a party, "I am really dancing so well, so natural and free"— that kind of self-consciousness is a sure way to get out of the groove and trip over one's own feet!

Recall that in Chapter 7 we made a distinction between two senses of "knowing." The true self, we said, cannot be known as an object; it cannot be objectified. But there must be a second kind of non-objectifying, nondualistic knowing in which one becomes aware of one's true nature. This second kind of nondualistic knowing, or wisdom, is what occurs in *kenshō*, that is, in the enlightening experience of "seeing into one's true nature." The fourteenth-century Japanese Zen master Daitō Kokushi teaches: "The heart-mind itself is verily the Buddha. What is called 'seeing one's nature' means to realize the heart-mind Buddha."[17]

Now we can better understand why the Zen School has also been called the Buddha-mind School. Yet what exactly is the Buddha-mind that we can awaken to and realize as our true self? Hakuin refers us to the traditional Mahayana Buddhist doctrine of the "Four Types of Wisdom." The Buddha-mind is said to manifest in these four ways: as "the Great Perfect Mirror Wisdom, the Universal Nature Wisdom, the Marvelous Observing Wisdom, and the Perfecting-of-Action Wisdom."[18]

The first of these is the perfectly still, clear, and pure mind awakened to in deep states of meditation. When all the "clouds" of our swirling thoughts and feelings, desires and regrets, wishes and worries dissipate, the "moon" appears in the open sky and "the universe is filled with its boundless light."[19] The second wisdom of the Buddha-mind is the ability to see all things equally in this impartial light. All things are interconnected, and each one reflects the whole universe from its own vantage point. The third type of wisdom is the ability to discern differences: each thing is an utterly unique focal point of the universe, related to, yet different from, everything else. The fourth type of wisdom is the ability to put the awareness of both equality and difference into action: "Coughing, spitting, moving the arms, activity, stillness, all that," Hakuin says, "is done in harmony with the nature of reality."[20]

The One Mind as the Truth Body of the Buddha

The Buddha-mind that manifests itself most clearly through these Four Types of Wisdom is what the ninth-century Chinese Zen master Huangbo calls the "One Mind." At the base of our small minds is this one, expansive mind. Huangbo writes:

> All the Buddhas and all sentient beings are nothing but the One Mind, besides which nothing exists. . . . The One Mind alone is Buddha, and there is no distinction between Buddha and sentient beings except that sentient beings are attached to forms and so seek externally for Buddhahood.[21]

The twelfth-century Chinese Zen master Dahui tells us that "this Mind can put names on everything, but nothing can put a name on it."[22] Although it has been called many names, he goes on to say, such as "True Suchness, Buddha-nature, Enlightenment and Nirvana," in truth it remains the nameless origin of all names and all that can be named.

This is why the Zen tradition prefers to use metaphorical language, reminding us that we cannot speak of ultimate matters in literal terms. Thus Mazu, for example, writes:

> Though the reflections of the moon are many, the real moon is only one. Though there are many springs of water, water has only one nature. There are myriad phenomena in the universe, but empty space is only one.[23]

Here the moon, water, and empty space are all metaphors for the One Mind. This One Mind is the Dharma Kaya, the Truth Body of the Buddha. Zen master Eisai, who introduced the Rinzai School to Japan in the twelfth century, sings the praises of this One Mind with the following words:

> How great is the Mind! The height of the heavens is such that it is impossible to reach its end; and yet the Mind rises above the heavens. The thickness of the earth is such that it is impossible to measure its extent; yet the Mind rises up from beneath the earth. . . . The many thousands of worlds are innumerable, comparable to the number of grains of sand in the Ganges River; and yet the Mind encompasses these worlds. You might speak of the great void and the primal energy that fills it, and yet the Mind envelops the great void and is pregnant with the primal energy. . . . Great indeed is the Mind.[24]

A modern Japanese Rinzai Zen master, Asahina Sōgen, teaches that "in the Buddha-mind there is neither death nor life, neither sin nor defilement. And so the Buddha-mind is always pure, always at rest, always peaceful." It is unlimited in time and space and "fills the universe." "Human beings are born, dwell, and breathe within this wondrous Buddha-mind." It is there before we are born, while we are alive, and after we die. Sitting in meditation, relentlessly inquiring into who it is that hears, we can awaken to this Buddha-mind as "the great root of our heart-mind."[25]

Nondualism: Neither Idealism Nor Materialism

The Buddha is not a divine being who transcends but rather the One Mind that embraces the world. And yet, even the expressions "Buddha-mind" and "One Mind" say too much and too little. As the true nature of all reality, not just half of reality, the One Mind as the Truth Body of the Buddha is the source and abode—the Source-Field—of body as well as mind, of physical matter as well as psychological mind. Although it has been called the Buddha-mind School, the philosophy of Zen is ultimately neither an idealism nor a realism, neither a mentalism nor a materialism. It is, rather, a nondualism that both undercuts these dichotomies and undergirds these distinctions.

The modern Zen philosopher Nishitani Keiji comments on the story of the tenth-century Zen master Fayan Wenyi who was converted from a "consciousness-only" school of Buddhist philosophy to a Zen experience of nondualism when he was asked whether a big rock lying in the garden in front of him was inside or outside of his mind. Fayan eventually realized that saying either inside or outside would not do justice to a direct and nondual experience of the rock. In such an experience, the rock is neither inside nor outside of the mind; the rock is the mind at that moment. Nishitani concludes that Zen's nondualism can be captured no more by a one-sided subjective idealism than by an equally one-sided naive materialism.[26]

The universe is both mind and matter, and to realize our unity with the universe requires us to see how both our minds and our bodies participate in the One Mind and One Body of reality. Dōgen, that most philosophical of Zen masters, on the one hand says that "the Mind-nature . . . embraces the entire universe. . . . All dharmas . . . are alike in being this One Mind."[27] On the other hand, he affirms that "the entire earth is the True Human Body."[28] The One Mind is the True Body of the Buddha. They are two ways of talking about the same thing.

Dōgen teaches that "there are two approaches to studying the Buddha Way: to study with the mind and to study with the body." Yet, these two paths converge insofar as, on the one hand, one discovers that "mountains and rivers, the great earth, the sun, moon, and stars are the mind . . . walls, tiles, and pebbles are the mind" and, on the other hand, one realizes that "the whole world in all ten directions is this true human body."[29]

The whole truth of this nondual reality cannot be grasped objectively. Indeed, such grasping always constricts its object and divorces it from the subject. It can be endlessly analyzed intellectually, but such analysis only breaks it apart into pieces that can never be entirely stitched back together without remainder, at least as long as the subject who is analyzing and reconstructing remains aloof from the object being analyzed and reconstructed. The One Taste of this nondual reality must be awakened to holistically.

The practice of *zazen* is physical as well as psychological; it is a holistic practice of body-heart-mind-spirit. The breath mediates these dimensions of the self as well as the inner and outer dimensions of self and world. Meditating on the breath holistically reminds us of the whole of reality.

Kōans on the Question "What Is the Buddha?"

In conclusion to this chapter, let me present you with some famous kōans that deal with the question "What is the Buddha?" Keep in mind that kōans, and also commentary on them, are not trying to conceptually clarify an already settled doctrine. Rather, they repeatedly push you to go one step further on a never-ending journey, a journey of deepening and developing experiential wisdom.

After Mazu had become a famous Zen master, a monk once asked him, "What is Buddha?" Mazu answered, "Mind is Buddha." In a comment appended to this kōan, however, the thirteenth-century Chinese Zen master Wumen chides: "Don't you know that one has to rinse out his mouth for three days if he has uttered the word 'Buddha'? If he is a real Zen man, he will stop his ears and rush away when he hears 'Mind is Buddha.'"[30]

In fact, in a later kōan in Wumen's collection, *The Gateless Barrier*, in response to the same question, "What is Buddha?" Mazu this time answers, "No mind, no Buddha." Wumen approves, commenting: "If you can see into it here, your Zen study has been completed."[31] The modern Japanese Zen master Shibayama Zenkei explains: "Earlier, [the monk] had come to Master [Mazu] seeking Buddha outside himself, and in order to break through his illusion [Mazu] told him, 'Mind is Buddha.' Now that [Mazu] sees that many disciples have become attached to 'Mind is Buddha' he says, 'No mind, no Buddha' in order to smash and wipe away their attachment to 'Mind is Buddha.'"[32]

Mazu himself had commented on his apparently contradictory teachings. In response to another monk who asked, "Why do you teach that 'Mind is Buddha'?" Mazu replied, "It is in order to stop a baby crying." "What is it like when the baby stops crying?" asked the monk. "No mind, no Buddha," answered Mazu.[33] One of Mazu's successors remarked: "'Mind is Buddha' is the phrase for one who wants medicine while he has no disease. 'No mind, no Buddha' is the phrase for one who cannot do away with the medicine when his disease has been cured."[34]

From the beginning, we are Buddhas. However, not realizing this, we seek for the Buddha outside ourselves. The dis-ease we experience is of our own making. And even when we find a good teaching, we turn that medicine into a poison by objectifying the Mind and attaching ourselves to the concept of Buddha. No wonder that when another successor of Mazu, Nanquan, was asked if there was any teaching that has not been taught to the people, he said, "Yes, there is." When asked what that teaching is, he replied, "It is neither mind, nor Buddha, nor [sentient] beings."[35]

However, we should take care not to misunderstand this apparent claim of ineffability either. We should not take it to mean that ultimate reality is so transcendent that it cannot be grasped by our mortal minds or expressed by our mundane words. When the ninth-century Chinese Zen master Dongshan was asked by a monk, "What is Buddha?," he immediately replied, "Three pounds of flax!"[36] Presumably, he was at that moment weighing this material. There is no-where that the Buddha can be captured, but that also means that there is no-where it cannot be found; it is always now-here. Three pounds of flax happens to be the amount needed to make a monk's robe, and so Dongshan was perhaps implying that "Buddha" is a dressing that can help a monk become who he truly is. Yet, as a kōan, Dongshan's response has generally been taken to be a direct expression of the manifestation of absolute reality here and now.

The ninth-/tenth-century Chinese Zen master Yunmen gives the most shocking answer to the question "What is Buddha?" He responds, "A shit-stick!"[37] Scholars debate the exact meaning of this vulgar term. But whether it is understood as a dried piece of feces or as a stick that was used like toilet paper, it is surely something that stinks and repulses us. Yunmen is telling us that if the Buddha-nature is everywhere, it must be found even in the vilest thing. He is telling us that in order to awaken to this universal Buddha-nature, we need to let go of our egoistic judgments that dualistically divide reality into what attracts and what repels us.

Yunmen is also telling us that, ultimately, we should be no more attached to the concept of Buddha than we are to a used piece of toilet paper. Once we realize Buddha, we need to "go beyond Buddha," *butsu-kōjō*, as an advanced type of kōan is called. Once we get the point of Zen, we need to get rid of what is called "the stench of Zen." We might say: If you encounter the Buddha in the bathroom, flush him down the toilet.

Keep in mind that the path of Zen proceeds by way of subtraction, not addition. Although shopping malls, online markets, and even some temples are filled with trinkets and trophies of Addition Zen, real Zen is Subtraction Zen. Zen is not about adding new ideas and identities. It is a matter of freeing us from our fixations on the ones we already have. By this point I trust it has started to make sense how the flip side of Subtraction Zen is Vow-Vehicle Zen—in other words, how egoless wisdom and endless compassion are two sides of the same *kokoro* or Buddha-heart-mind.

In Chapter 12, we'll confront once again our most entrenched attachment—namely, our attachment to our egos. We'll see that, in Zen as in Christianity, in order to truly live we must undergo a great spiritual death and rebirth.

12

Dying to Live

Zen, Pure Land Buddhism, and Christianity

Are Zen Buddhism and Christianity Compatible?

I teach in the philosophy department of a Jesuit, Catholic university, which hired me in part to teach courses on Buddhism and other Asian philosophies and religions. Loyola University Maryland has also been very supportive of my leading a Zen meditation group on campus in a chapel that was remodeled so that it doubles as a Japanese-style *zendō* or meditation hall. In fact, before I moved back from Japan to take this job at Loyola, a Jesuit priest, Fr. Greg Hartley, had already been leading a Zen meditation group on campus for years.

Over the past century, there have been many Christians who have taken up the practice of Zen meditation without leaving the Church. In fact, there have been a number of Catholic priests who have become Zen teachers. They have written books with titles such as *Living Zen, Loving God* and *Zen Spirit, Christian Spirit.*[1] Many Protestant clergy and laypeople have also claimed that their Christian faith is not only compatible with, but indeed deepened by, their practice of Zen Buddhism.

The modern Zen master Yamada Kōun used to tell his Christian students that he wanted them to practice Zen not in order to become Buddhists, but in order to become better Christians. Specifically, he reportedly told Fr. Robert Kennedy, who became a Zen teacher without ceasing to be a Catholic priest, that "he did not want to make me a Buddhist but he wanted to empty me in imitation of 'Christ your Lord' who emptied himself, poured himself out, and clung to nothing." "Whenever Yamada Roshi instructed me in this way," recalls Kennedy, "I thought that this Buddhist might make a Christian of me yet!"[2]

To be sure, there are many other Christians and Buddhists who have been less sanguine about the compatibility of these traditions. Walpola Rahula, the hard-line Theravada monk and scholar we met in Chapter 7, claims: "Man's position, according to Buddhism, is supreme. Man is his own master, and there is no higher being or power that sits in judgment over his destiny."[3] Like Feuerbach, Rahula thinks that humans have created the idea of God in their own image, rather than the other way around.[4] Like Freud, Rahula thinks that humans have dreamed up

Zen Pathways. Bret W. Davis, Oxford University Press. © Oxford University Press 2022.
DOI: 10.1093/oso/9780197573686.003.0012

and cling to the illusion of a powerful father figure who commands and judges, protecting his obedient children and punishing his disobedient ones.[5]

Rahula would probably say something similar about the idea of Amida Buddha in Pure Land Buddhism. Amida Buddha's compassion for all living beings is sometimes compared to a mother's love for her children. Unlike the biblical God, Amida is not a punitive Father—after all, the natural workings of karma take care of justice in the world. But, like the biblical God, Amida is popularly thought of as a kind of transcendent being by whose grace or other-power alone we can be saved.

The Mahayana Buddhist traditions in general have been much more willing than so-called Hinayana Buddhist traditions like Theravada to incorporate ideas of transcendent Buddhas and Bodhisattvas who can help us along on our way to Nirvana, in some cases via rebirth in a Pure Land. However, these anthropomorphic images of higher powers do not have the absolute status that the personal, transcendent Creator God does in the biblical traditions. In Chapter 10, we saw how, for Shinran, Amida Buddha is ultimately the formless "dharmic naturalness" of the cosmos and only secondarily, as a compassionate "expedient means," a celestial Buddha who takes on form to aid us in realizing this liberating and formless naturalness.[6]

To give another example, in the Tantric meditation practices of Tibetan Vajrayana Buddhism, a practitioner first visualizes in precise detail the image of a certain Buddha or Bodhisattva as a personification of a certain virtue, such as compassion. After one is able to hold the image of that figure clearly in mind, the next step is to identify oneself with it in order to embody the virtue it represents. Finally, in the last step, one meditates on the emptiness—the lack of independent substantiality—of the figure one has become.[7] In short, images of transcendent beings in Buddhism are generally held to be powerful but still provisional means on the way to the attainment of Buddhahood.

Early Encounters and Misunderstandings Between Christians and Buddhists

In Japan there is a tradition of esoteric Buddhism called Shingon, founded by Kūkai in the ninth century, which stems from some of the same Indian sources as do the Tibetan Vajrayana schools. As we saw in Chapter 10, for Shingon Buddhists the Dharma Kaya is the Cosmic Buddha called Dainichi (Sk. Vairochana), the Great Sun Buddha that is the source of all light and life in the world. Indeed, all reality is thought to be the manifestation of Dainichi.[8]

It is not surprising that when the first Christians arrived in Japan in the mid-sixteenth century, these Jesuit missionaries led by Francis Xavier were told by their Japanese interpreter that "Dainichi" is the best translation for "God" (Ln. *deus*). Accordingly, for two years Xavier roamed the streets of Japan calling out, in Japanese, "Pray to Dainichi [Buddha]!"[9]

These early Christian missionaries thought that the Japanese must have already received a partial or corrupted version of the Gospel of Christianity. The Japanese, for their part, thought that the missionaries had come from the western land of the Buddha, India, and brought with them new doctrines of Buddhism. This honeymoon period of mutual appreciation based on mutual misunderstanding ended after the missionaries were confronted with Buddhist—and in particular Zen—doctrines of "emptiness" and "nothingness." The pivotal Buddhist doctrine of "no-self," moreover, sounded to these Christians like an antithesis to their core belief in an eternal soul. Evidently, there was no place in their intellectual and theological vocabulary for an affirmative understanding of these terms. Perhaps they could have looked deeper into the Christian mystical tradition. In any case, horrified, the missionaries then sought to *convert* rather than *reform* what they perceived as this country of strangely devout nihilists.

For centuries following this fateful first encounter in Japan, Buddhism—and specifically its doctrines of no-self and emptiness—became an object of both fascination and fearful condemnation for Western philosophers and theologians.[10] Only in the twentieth century was the prejudiced misunderstanding of these teachings gradually amended. Still today, no-self and emptiness remain the most intellectually and emotionally challenging doctrines of Buddhism for Westerners to wrap their heads and hearts around. And Buddhism is still often treated as a curiously oxymoronic "atheistic religion."

A few years ago, I was giving a lecture on cosmopolitanism at a Catholic university in Bogotá, Colombia. At one point I mentioned that, five centuries before Jesus, the Buddha founded the first truly cosmopolitan religion, proclaiming the spiritual equality of all people regardless of caste, class, or ethnic or political affiliation. One of my hosts, however, could not contain herself and blurted out in the middle of my lecture, "But Buddhists don't believe in God!" "Well," I responded, "evidently they don't need to in order to believe in universal love and compassion." On second thought, however, if "God is love," as the Bible says, then maybe Buddhists do believe in God after all.

Rediscovering the Question: What Is God?

What does it mean to believe in God? When we ask questions like this, we assume a lot. To begin with, we assume that we understand what we are asking. In this case, we assume that we know what the word "God" means and what it would mean to "believe in" or have "faith in" Him, Her, It, or Them—usually

Him. Is God male rather than female? A Father rather than a Mother? How could we tell? Surely God doesn't have reproductive organs or a sexual orientation. Even if His maleness is just a metaphor, does that nevertheless mean that men are created more in the metaphorical image of God than are women?[11]

In fact, in Genesis we read: "Then God said, 'Let us make humankind in our image, according to our likeness.'"[12] The Hebrew word for "God" here is "Elohim," which is a plural; hence the language of "let *us* make humankind in *our* likeness." Theologians and biblical scholars debate why God speaks in the plural in Genesis and elsewhere throughout the early books of the Bible. One theory—controversial with conservatives yet with solid archeological as well as textual evidence—is that Jews originally thought of God as a married couple, as a Mother and a Father.[13] Apparently, when the Jews exchanged this notion of a Divine Pair for a more strictly monotheistic and manly conception of God, they opted for theological matricide rather than patricide. In the biblical traditions, the Heavenly Father has almost completely overshadowed Mother Earth, and patriarchal priesthoods have condemned—in murderous witch-hunts as well as in more subtly suppressive forms—as pagan heresy all forms of worshiping and rituals of embodying the ancient Great Goddess.[14]

According to the prominent modern Jewish philosopher Emmanuel Levinas, in Judaism "the feminine will never take on the aspect of the Divine."[15] The personal form proper to the biblical God is that of a Father, not a Mother, and thus human society is a paternal rather than a maternal community. Patriarchal prejudice can of course be found in other religious traditions, including those of Asia (for some comments on patriarchy in Zen, see Chapters 14 and 16). Nevertheless, in Asian traditions the female principle was never suppressed to the same degree and magnitude as it was in biblical traditions. In Daoism, the cosmogenic origin is understood to be "the mother of the world." The *Daodejing* claims that the *Dao*, though originally nameless, when named is "the mother of the ten thousand things."[16] In Hinduism, Brahman, the ultimate Godhead, is often thought to transcend all qualities, including male or female. When approached in less absolute terms, Brahman is sometimes personified as male (e.g., Vishnu), sometimes as female (e.g., Kali), and sometimes as androgynous or as a male/female pair (e.g., Shiva or Shiva/Shakti). According to Sikhism, God is neither male nor female, but can manifest as either gender.

The *yab-yum* (literally "father-mother") iconography that depicts the sexual union of a divine couple is one of the primary symbols of enlightenment in Tantric Buddhism. The male figure represents compassion and skillful means, while the female figure represents wisdom. The sexual intercourse between the two represents the primordial union of these two aspects of enlightenment. In Mahayana Buddhism more generally, Buddhas are mostly male, yet Prajnaparamita, the Perfection of Wisdom, is personified as the "Mother of all

Buddhas." In Tibet, the female Bodhisattva or Buddha Tara is a central figure of devotion and Tantric practices of visualization. Known as "the mother of liberation," she is said to have emerged as a tear from the eye of Avalokiteshvara, the Bodhisattva of Compassion. Originally male in India, in East Asia Avalokiteshvara is often portrayed as androgynous or as female and called Kannon in Japanese. It is interesting to note that persecuted Christians in the Tokugawa period (1600–1868) concealed their worship of Mother Mary—who has long served as the primary surrogate for the female aspect of divinity in Catholicism—by disguising Mary as Kannon and fashioning "Maria-Kannon" images.

One of the source terms for Buddha-nature, *Tathagatagarbha*, can be understood both as the "womb of the Buddha" and as the "embryo of the Buddha," a fecund ambiguity based on the fact that the Sanskrit term *garbha* can mean both "womb" and "embryo." These senses are combined in the Womb Mandala employed by Kūkai's Shingon Buddhism, which depicts how, "as a mother enfolds and nurtures a child in her womb, so the energy of compassion nurtures and protects one's innate enlightenment."[17] The Japanese Pure Land reformer "Shinran refers to Amida as the Compassionate Mother, even though Amida originated in India as a male buddha."[18] He sometimes refers to Shakyamuni as Father and Amida as Mother, or to the Light of Amida as Mother and the Name of Amida as Father.[19]

The modern Japanese philosopher Nishida Kitarō, who practiced Zen and had a deep appreciation for Christianity as well as Pure Land Buddhism, writes of the Absolute encountered in the depths of one's self as both "God the Father and Buddha the Mother."[20] In fact, Nishida's philosophy of the "Place of Absolute Nothingness" (see Chapter 21) favors the female image of the divine as an engendering and embracing matrix. In contrast to Western metaphysics and theology, which "pursued the direction of the Father," Nishida says that he intends to "pursue the direction of the Mother" and therewith "the profound and true significance of nothingness [which] was not discovered in Greek philosophy."[21]

Questioning the gender of God is just one of the ways in which studying various religious traditions has provoked and enabled me to keep thinking about how the word "God" has been, and might be, understood. Raimon Panikkar, a Jesuit theologian and pioneer of "intrareligious dialogue" within oneself as a condition for genuine interreligious dialogue with others, has helped me critically think about the metaphor of absolute monarchy used to speak of God in relation to His "kingdom" in the biblical traditions. Biblical monotheism flourished, Panikkar notes, in "places and times in which societies were ruled by emperors and kings." Hence, God was thought of not only as an authoritarian Father, but also as "King of kings, Lord of lords and Emperor of the universe." Humans, for their part, were depicted as either obedient servants or as sinful rebels.

When only a few years had passed after Constantine's edict allowing freedom of worship to christians [sic] and protection to christianity [sic], emperor Theodosius went a step further, substituting the earthly emperor by a heavenly one so that if earlier it was a crime not to worship Caesar, now it was a higher crime not to worship the celestial Emperor whom the christians [sic] adored.[22]

Rereading the story of Exodus and the conquest of the Promised Land in light of the political and military metaphor of a Divine King and Celestial Commander-in-Chief, I could not help but ask: Is it any wonder that a God who commanded the genocide and enslavement of conquered peoples of Canaan would later be understood to command Crusades and other supposedly holy wars against so-called heretics and infidels?[23] Must God be pictured as an at times merciless masculine monarch? Are there no other ways to understand God, in the Bible as well as in other religious traditions?

The burning question for me has become not "Does God exist?" but rather "What does the word 'God' even mean?"[24] I was raised Christian, regularly attending an Episcopalian church; though I confess that the spark of faith never really caught fire in me. Nevertheless, church services did inspire me to become intensely interested in the "big questions" of religion and philosophy. In high school, the first two books I bought were a history of Western philosophy and an introduction to Zen. In hindsight, my encounter with those two books left the first two footprints on the parallel paths down which I have been walking ever since. In college, majoring in philosophy and minoring in religion, I developed the interests that those two books had sparked; I also deepened my knowledge, and my questions, about Christianity. After college, the more I read Christian mystics such as Pseudo-Dionysius and Francis of Assisi, theologians such as Paul Tillich and Raimon Panikkar, and monastics such as Thomas Merton and Bede Griffiths, the less clear and yet the more intriguing the God-question became for me.

After a year of graduate school, I moved to Japan—far away from the clamor of debates in America between theists and atheists, who seem to at least share a certainty about what it is that they are arguing over. It was through reading and listening to Japanese Buddhist philosophers of religion that my eyes were opened to different, and deeper, ways to think about God. Zen Buddhist interpretations of Meister Eckhart were especially mind-blowing—blowing up preconceptions and blowing in fresh and inspiring ideas.

Zen Faith as Trust and as Self-Confidence

Gradually, I also began to question and rethink the meaning of "faith." It is true that Zen does not promote faith in a "higher power," if what we mean by that is a power over oneself that comes from outside oneself. Zen does, however, promote faith in a *deeper power*, in the sense of a power that wells up from the "trans-descendent" depths of oneself. This power is, as it were, beneath rather than above the ego. In Zen, one finds two notions of "faith" (Jp. *shin*): one at the beginning of the path, as "the necessary state of mind for entering the gate of the Buddha Way," and one at the end of the path, as "the ultimate state of mind attesting to the truth."[25] If one understands this as a continuum rather than as two separate senses of faith, it indicates a process through which "faith" (Ln. *fide*) deepens into "confidence."

The ninth-century Chinese Zen master Linji never tires of telling us that what we lack is a particular kind of faith—namely, faith in ourselves. In other words, what we lack is true self-confidence.[26] The thirteenth-century Japanese Sōtō Zen master Dōgen tells us to sit in *zazen* with a firm conviction, with a deep faith, that we are originally Buddhas and all we need to do is to awaken to this fact.[27] And the eighteenth-century Japanese Rinzai Zen master Hakuin—drawing on the terms and teachings of the thirteenth-century Chinese Zen master Gaofeng Yuanmiao—tells us that the first essential requisite for Zen practice is a "great root of faith," followed by a "great ball of doubt" and a "great determination." By "great root of faith," he tells us, is "meant the belief that each and every person has an essential self-nature he can see into."[28] In other words, it is a great trust that practice will lead to *kenshō*. The faith of Zen is the faith that one can awaken to the truth of what one is; and, after this awakening, it is the true self-confidence that naturally accompanies an awakened life.[29]

Zen "trust" or "faith" is thus different from that of other religious traditions; it is not "belief" or "faith" in the sense of a voluntary intellectual assent to a doctrine that one cannot verify with evidence and reason.[30] While this may put Zen at odds with the orthodox understanding and centrality of faith in Christianity, some deep resonances can be found with the apocryphal Gospel of Thomas, which stresses liberating knowledge (Gk. *gnosis*) rather than soteriological faith (Gk. *pistis*).[31] In the Gospel of Thomas, we read:

> They said to him, "Tell us who you are so that we may *believe* in you."
>
> He said to them, "You search the face of heaven and earth, but you have not come to *know* the one who stands before you, and you do not know how to understand the present moment."[32]

In other words, Jesus in the Gospel of Thomas teaches his disciples to *know* rather than to *believe*—and to know "the one who stands before you" as ultimately no different from your own true self. "I am not your master," Jesus says. "Because you have drunk, you have become intoxicated from the bubbling spring that

I have tended." "Whoever drinks from my mouth will become like me; I shall become that person, and the mysteries will be revealed to him."[33]

According to James Heisig, a Catholic priest and comparative philosopher of religion, not only is it possible that the Gospel of Thomas is "a more faithful record" of Jesus's teachings than are found in the canonical gospels, but "everything the Jesus of [the Gospel of Thomas] has to say is congruent with Buddhist teachings on the detached, awakened mind," such that "the text represents the clearest invitation we have among all the early texts of Christianity to a fully Buddhist reading of Jesus and his teachings."[34]

The Kingdom of God and the Pure Land Are Here and Now

In the Gospel of Thomas, Jesus teaches: "I am the one who comes from what is undivided," and "When you make the two into one, and when you make the inner like the outer and the outer like the inner . . . then you will enter [the Kingdom]." The Kingdom of God is not elsewhere in space or later in time; it is right here and now for those who have the eyes to see its nondual reality. "If you bring forth what is within you, what you have will save you," says Jesus in the Gospel of Thomas.[35] The open secret of this ultimate teaching can also be found intimated in the canonical Gospel of John, in which Jesus says, "No one can see the kingdom of God unless they are born again," and in the Gospel of Luke, in which Jesus says, "The Kingdom of God is within you."[36] The modern Japanese Zen master Uchiyama Kōshō quotes the latter passage and comments: "In zazen we can see directly this kingdom within us."[37] The modern Vietnamese Zen master Thich Nhat Hanh concurs: "You don't have to die to enter nirvana or the Kingdom of God. You only have to dwell deeply in the present moment, right now." He goes on to say: "People talk about entering nirvana, but we are already there."[38] We just need to realize it.

The *Vimalakirti Sutra* says something very similar about the Pure Land. It tells us that "an upright mind is the pure land of the bodhisattva"; "it is the failings of living beings that prevent them from seeing the marvelous purity of the land of the Buddha. . . . It is just that your mind has highs and lows and does not rest on Buddha wisdom. Therefore you see this land as impure."[39] The Pure Land is right here and now, if only we have purified eyes to see it.

To be sure, the *Vimalakirti Sutra*, with its metaphorical-psychological interpretation of the Pure Land, is associated more with Zen than with Pure Land Buddhism. In a book called *Finding Our True Home: Living in the Pure Land Here and Now*, Nhat Hanh espouses this Zen interpretation of the Pure Land. He writes:

The notion that the Pure Land is an exterior reality, a place to be found far away in the western direction, is just for beginners. If we deepen our practice, the Buddha and the Buddha's land become a reality in our mind. Our ancestral teachers have always said this. If we practice well, we can experience Amitabha Buddha and the Pure Land wherever we are in the present moment.[40]

While some Pure Land Buddhists may prefer a more literal-cosmological interpretation of the Pure Land, others, such as Taitetsu Unno, maintain that the Pure Land is not a "heavenly home" apart from the here and now, but rather "exists only where and when the *nembutsu* is recited."[41] Reciting the *nembutsu* entails repeatedly chanting "Namu Amida Butsu," meaning "I take refuge in Amida Buddha." When one fully entrusts one's life to the grace or other-power of Amida Buddha, then and there is the Pure Land. Indeed, the identification of the Pure Land with chanting the *nembutsu* with a faithful heart-mind has deep roots in the Pure Land Buddhist tradition, going at least as far back as Shandao, a seminal seventh-century Pure Land Buddhist who had studied the *Vimalakirti Sutra*.

One could compare the Pure Land Buddhist practice—or, as they say, "non-practice," since it is the utter abandonment of practice by means of self-power—of the *nembutsu* to the continual recitation of the Jesus Prayer, "Lord Jesus Christ, have mercy on me," a meditative practice popular in the Eastern Orthodox Church.[42] "Blessed are the poor in spirit, for theirs is the Kingdom of Heaven," says Jesus.[43] To be "poor in spirit" is to be empty of self-will; it is to become an open vessel that can say, "Let Thy Kingdom come, Thy Will be done, on earth as it is in Heaven."[44] Would such utter releasement not lead to an experience of Heaven on earth?

Of course, a Marxist critic might object to the idea (or ideology) that the Kingdom of God or the Pure Land of Amida Buddha can be experienced here and now, since this can become just as much of an "opiate of the people" as saying that you should patiently wait to experience these peaceful abodes up in the sky after you die. Yet, just as the proponents of liberation theology have envisioned the Kingdom of God in this-worldly terms of social justice,[45] some Pure Land Buddhists have sought to wed spiritual and political liberation.[46] And, as we will discuss in Chapter 14, Nhat Hanh—the same Zen master who was just quoted as saying that we can experience the Pure Land in the present moment—is the founder of the modern movement of Engaged Buddhism, and was nominated by Martin Luther King Jr. for the Nobel Peace Prize in light of his non-violent resistance to the war in Vietnam. The message Nhat Hanh has taught for decades—through his deeds as well as his words—is that people can find spiritual peace in the midst of peace activism, and that only if people are at peace with themselves can they truly bring peace to the world.[47]

Zen and Panentheism Redux

It is true that Buddhists, even Pure Land Buddhists, do not believe in a Creator God, a transcendent Being who exists independent of His creation, an almighty Lord who commands, punishes, and rewards us. Among competing biblical theologies, as we saw in Chapter 9, Zen Buddhism is most compatible with panentheism—not pantheism, which means "all is God," but panentheism, which means "all is in God." Whereas pantheism simply equates God with the world, panentheism acknowledges that God is greater and more encompassing than all the beings that exist in Him, Her, or It.

We have seen how many biblical passages lend themselves to a panentheistic interpretation, such as when God says, "Do I not fill heaven and earth?"[48] and when Paul affirms the idea that "in Him we live and move and have our being."[49] In another of Paul's letters we read: "There is one God and father of all, who is above all and through all and in all."[50] In Psalm 139 it is written: "If I go up to the heavens, you are there; if I make my bed in the depths, you are there." God is everywhere: above, below, all around, and within us.

Such a panentheistic conception of the biblical God does not, after all, sound so very different from many Zen pronouncements, even though the latter tend to be expressed in transpersonal rather than personal terms.[51] For example, Zen master Shidō Bunan says: "The True Body fills the universe, / Fills and overflows it; / But rain cannot wet it, / The sun's rays cannot reach it."[52] Whereas Shidō Bunan speaks of the "True Body," Zen master Huangbo speaks of the "One Mind." In any case, what both say of this nondual reality sounds very similar. Huangbo teaches:

> This Mind, which is without beginning, is unborn and indestructible. It is not green nor yellow, and has neither form nor appearance. It does not belong to the categories of things which exist or do not exist, nor can it be thought of in terms of new or old. It is neither long nor short, big nor small, for it transcends all limits, measures, names, traces and comparisons. . . . It is like the boundless void that cannot be fathomed or measured. . . . It is Pure Mind, which is the source of everything and which, whether appearing as sentient beings or as Buddhas, as the rivers and mountains of the world which has form, as that which is formless, or as penetrating the whole universe, is absolutely without distinctions.[53]

Everything that has distinctions, everything that can be defined, is finite. All finite things have as their origin and abode this nameless thing that is not a thing, this no-thing that can only provisionally be called the One Mind, the True Body, or the One True Body-Mind of reality.

Experiencing the Unborn Buddha-Mind in the Midst of Birth-and-Death

Buddhism teaches that everything that is born must die. This is the law of impermanence. Has anyone ever experienced anything that came into being that has not ceased to exist, or will not one day cease to exist? Insofar as we cling to these things, craving for them to last forever, we suffer when they inevitably change and cease to be.

Everything that is conditioned, everything that exists because of the conditions that allow it to exist, will cease to exist when those conditions no longer hold. For example, the human body is able to stay alive because the earth's atmosphere has just the right amount of oxygen and air pressure. If we were suddenly ejected into outer space, our lungs would probably explode, and even if they didn't, our brains would certainly cease to function from a lack of oxygen within a few minutes. Everything that is conditioned exists only so long as those conditions pertain. Everything that is born must die. Everything that grows must grow old and wither. That is the hard pill we have to swallow, the reality check we have to sign.

The good news, the gospel of Buddhism, is that there is something on the other side of the door—a doorway through which we can pass if only we can shed the bulky armor we've vainly attached to the fragile shells of our egos. This something that is not a finite composite and decomposing thing, this something that is no-thing, is what Buddhism calls the Unborn, Unmade, and Unconditioned. In a famous passage from an early sutra, the Buddha teaches:

> There is, monks, an unborn, unbecome, unmade, unconditioned. If, monks, there were no unborn, unbecome, unmade, unconditioned, no escape would be discerned from what is born, become, made, conditioned. But because there is an unborn, unbecome, unmade, unconditioned, therefore an escape is discerned from what is born, become, made, conditioned.[54]

Because there is the Unborn, there is Nirvana. The attainment of Nirvana is the realization of the Unborn. There was a tendency in early Buddhism to understand Nirvana as somewhere beyond Samsara, as a transcendent abode beyond this world of space and time.[55] Even if Nirvana could be provisionally attained in this lifetime, it was thought that Final Nirvana (Parinirvana) could be attained only after leaving the body and everything earthly behind.

The Mahayana tradition, and especially the Zen School, corrected this tendency and brought Nirvana back down to earth. The great second-/third-century Mahayana philosopher Nagarjuna—who is considered to be the Fifteenth Indian Ancestor in the lineage of Zen—taught that Nirvana is not a different place to be, but a different way of being here.[56] Life in this world, for the unenlightened, is Samsara; but for the enlightened, life in this same world is Nirvana.

Zen masters call on us to realize the Unborn here and now. And they tell us that we can fully do this only if we cease perceiving this world of ceaseless change as one of birth and death. As the *Heart Sutra* tells us, in truth there is "not birth or destruction."[57] What is meant by this is that there are no independent and unchanging substances that come into being at a certain time and are destroyed at a later time. There are only transformations, one form morphing into another. The Mind that realizes this is free from the fetters and false ideas of birth and death.

Of course, unless and until we are enlightened, the matter of birth and death is the "one great matter" that needs to be resolved. On a wooden board hung outside Zen meditation halls and struck with urgency several times a day is written: "Great is the matter of birth and death / Life is impermanent and fleeting / Time waits for no one / Take care and don't waste a moment!"

The following story is told of the brief encounter of Yongjia with the Sixth Chinese Ancestor, Huineng, in seventh-century China. Having experienced enlightenment, Yongjia went to Huineng for confirmation. Bursting into Huineng's temple, without paying his respects he walked circles around the master brandishing his staff. "Where do you come from and why do you carry on in this arrogant way," demanded Huineng. "Birth-and-death is a matter of terrible urgency," answered Yongjia, adding, "Death follows birth with great speed." Thereupon Huineng asked him, "Why don't you grasp the Unborn and see that there's no early or late?" To which Yongjia answered, "What grasps the Unborn, and what sees is neither early nor late," a moment later adding, "Even in the midst of motion, our fundamental nature does not move." Huineng approved, and the torch of Zen was passed down to the next generation.[58]

A thousand years later, the seventeenth-century Japanese Zen master Bankei made the Unborn his sole teaching. "What I call the 'Unborn' is the Buddha-mind," says Bankei.[59] In light of the fact that Samsara—the cycle of life, death, rebirth, and re-death in the world of suffering—is translated into Chinese and Japanese simply as "birth-and-death," Bankei teaches:

A man of the Unborn is beyond living and dying [in other words, beyond Samsara]. What I mean by that is: Someone who is unborn is also undying, so he is beyond both birth and death. What I call living and dying at will is when someone dies without being troubled by life and death, the continuous succession of birth-death, birth-death that is samsaric existence. Moreover, living and dying is taking place at every instance throughout the twenty-four hours of the day; dying does not occur only once in your life when you cease breathing. When you're living without being concerned about life or death, you're always living in such a way that whenever death does come, even right now, at this moment, it's no great matter. Now that's what I call "living and dying at will." It means living confirmed in your unborn Buddha-mind.[60]

Rebirth, in Buddhism, is first and foremost "moment-to-moment rebirth" (see Chapter 23). Each moment of change is, in a sense, the death of an old form and the birth of a new one. The boiling water disappears as water in order to become steam. A teenager has to die to his adolescent self in order to be reborn as a young adult, and so on. With our linguistic concepts serving our desiring minds, we latch on to this or that momentary state in a ceaseless process of change as if this momentary state were in itself something permanent—and, as a result, it then frustratingly appears to have been born and to be subject to death. In truth, nothing is born and nothing dies.

Thich Nhat Hanh points out that modern science agrees with Buddhism in this regard. He quotes the French scientist Antoine Lavoisier as saying, "Nothing is created, and nothing is destroyed." And he remarks that this is just what the *Heart Sutra* tells us: "One form of energy can only become another form of energy."[61]

Zen master Dōgen writes that "life itself is as such unborn," and "extinction itself is undying," insofar as there is no independent and substantial thing that comes into and then passes out of existence.[62] There is but a flow of interconnected events, shifting forms conditioning adjacent forms. Our thoughts and feelings come and go as parts of this process. Only the formless Buddha-mind of open awareness is unconditioned, unborn, and so undying.

Commenting on Dōgen's statement "These mountains and waters at this moment are the manifestation of the great way of ancient buddhas," the contemporary Sōtō Zen master Shohaku Okumura (Jp. Okumura Shōhaku) writes: "Timeless reality shows itself within momentary phenomena. . . . This means that moment-by-moment phenomena such as mountains and rivers are the expression of timeless reality, the way of old buddhas." Okumura shows how Dōgen interprets another famous Zen saying—"The blue mountains are constantly walking. The stone woman gives birth to a child in the night"—to "express his understanding of the reality of nikon, this present moment, which is the intersection of impermanence and eternity . . . phenomenal beings and ultimate truth." "In Zen tradition," Okumura Rōshi adds, "it is said that each and every phenomenal being is itself a manifestation of the eternal Dharma body."[63]

We must be careful not to understand the Unborn Buddha-mind and the Eternal Dharma-body as either separate from each other or as separable from the flow of what appears to our intellectual and desiring minds as the samsaric world of life and death. Dōgen warns against the so-called Senika heresy, which holds that there is an individual eternal soul that is dualistically separable from the mortal body.[64] Nirvana is not a heaven separate from this earthly realm of birth-and-death. Rather, Dōgen says,

Just understand that birth-and-death [in other words, samsara] itself is nirvana, and you will neither hate one as birth-and-death, nor cherish the other as being nirvana. Only then will you be free of birth-and-death. . . . It is a mistake to think that you pass from life into death. . . . When there is life, there is nothing at all apart from life. When there is death, there is nothing at all apart from death. Therefore, when life comes, you should just give yourself to life; when death comes, you should give yourself to death.[65]

In a text called "Total Activity," Dōgen quotes the eleventh-/twelfth-century Chinese Zen master Yuanwu Keqin as saying that "birth is the manifestation of total activity, and death is the appearing of total activity." Dōgen comments:

This being so, birth does not hinder birth, and death does not hinder birth. Both the entire earth and the entire sky appear in birth as well as in death. . . . [I]n birth there is the total activity of all living beings, and in death there is the total activity of all living beings.[66]

When we are alive, we enliven and are enlivened by the whole web of the world that conspires to support our existence. When we die, the whole world as perspectivally manifested through our experience expires with us. When we are alive, we are alive. When we die, we die. Nothing is more straightforward. If only we could just affirm these straightforward facts with an equally straightforward heart-mind, living fully while we are alive and dying purely when we die, then we'd realize that Samsara is Nirvana.

Okumura Rōshi relates how his teacher, Uchiyama Kōshō Rōshi, impressed upon him that impermanence is only one side of reality. The other side is eternity. And yet, "the reality of our life is before separation, before any dichotomy, before the distinction between permanence and impermanence." Uchiyama Rōshi expressed this nondual reality of impermanence/eternity, of Samsara/Nirvana, in a poem written during a period of deathly illness:

> Though poor, never poor,
> Though sick, never sick,
> Though aging, never aging,
> Though dying, never dying.
> Reality prior to division—
> Herein lies unlimited depth.

Okumura Rōshi comments that Uchiyama Rōshi was in fact financially poor; "he was often sick, and he was aging, and he was dying. That was the undeniable reality of his life. Yet he also said his life was really rich. Because he lived together with the entire universe, he was never sick, he was never aging, and he was never dying. This is the other half of reality for Uchiyama Rōshi."[67] Here is another poem Uchiyama Rōshi wrote as he prepared himself for death:

> Water isn't formed by being ladled into a bucket
> Simply the water of the whole Universe has been ladled into a bucket
> The water does not disappear because it has been scattered over the ground
> It is only that the water of the whole Universe has been emptied into the
>   whole Universe
> Life is not born because a person is born
> The life of the whole Universe has been ladled into the hardened "idea"
>   called "I"
> Life does not disappear because a person dies
> Simply, the life of the whole Universe has been poured out of this hardened
>   "idea" of "I" back into the Universe[68]

Inspiring and even liberating as these thoughts may be in our rare moments of serenity and clarity, the truth is that most of us constantly—at least unconsciously or semi-consciously—suffer from worrying about death while we are alive. We do not simply live here and now, communing with the universe; rather, haunted by thoughts of our personal mortality, we run ahead in anticipation of the death of our individual egos. The German philosopher Martin Heidegger even claims that this anxious anticipation of death is the defining trait of being human.[69] Heidegger thought that we either authentically face up to our inevitable death and suffer a disorienting anxiety or, most of the time, suppress this rumbling angst by keeping ourselves distracted, inauthentically letting what "they" say on social media and elsewhere determine who we are, what we desire and value, and how we live.

Or we take up a different tactic and soothe ourselves with hopeful ideas of an afterlife. Some even take—or sell—the promise of an afterlife to be the very essence of religion. We want our egos to live forever. But what do religions like Christianity really teach about life and death? Does Christianity simply promise our anxious egos that they can live forever? Or, rather, does not its core teaching say that we must die to our egos in order to be reborn in the eternal life of Christ?

Ego-Death and Spiritual Rebirth

In a speech late in life, Heidegger quotes the seventeenth-century Augustinian friar Abraham a Sancta Clara as saying, "A man who dies before he dies, does not die when he dies."[70] Reading this, the Zen philosopher Nishitani Keiji writes: "This sentence would not sound strange if it had come from the mouth of a man of Zen."[71]

In fact, Nishitani could have quoted the following poem by the eighteenth-century Rinzai Zen master Hakuin, a poem that echoes almost perfectly the saying by Abraham a Sancta Clara:

> O young folk—
> if you fear death,
> die now!
> Having died once,
> You won't have to die again.[72]

Many such sayings from the mouths of Zen masters can be found. For example, as Nishitani does note, Zen master Shidō Bunan famously teaches:

> Become a dead man, remaining alive;
> Become thoroughly dead.
> Then do what you like, according to your own mind;
> All your deeds are then good.[73]

Another common Zen saying is "First, the Great Death; after cutting off completely, then coming back to life."[74] One must undergo the Great Death, the death of the ego, in order to be reborn as the true self. As the eighth-century Layman Pang puts it: "To preserve your life you must destroy it; Having completely destroyed it, you dwell at ease."[75] Real Zen is for Real Life, and yet to attain Real Life we must first undergo the Great Death.

Analogous ideas of ego-death and spiritual rebirth can be found in all the great religions, including of course Christianity. Indeed, it is a core teaching of Jesus. In the Gospel of Matthew, he says: "Whoever does not take up the cross and follow me is not worthy of me. Those who find their life will lose it, and those who lose their life for my sake will find it."[76] This teaching, that each of us must take up the cross and be crucified—that each of us must die to the old Adam in order to be reborn in the true life of Christ—is repeated throughout all four Gospels.[77] The Prayer of St. Francis begins with the words, "Lord, make me an instrument of your peace," and concludes, "And it is in dying that we are born to eternal life."[78] This is not only, and not even primarily, talking about dying and going to Heaven; it is talking about ego-death and a rebirth into a life lived in "imitation of Christ." The prophetic pragmatist philosopher Cornel West says of the inimitable preacher Martin Luther King Jr. that he "understood radical love as a form of death—a relentless self-examination in which a fearful, hateful, egoistic self dies daily to be reborn into a courageous, loving, and sacrificial self."[79]

Baptism, indeed, can be understood as a ritual drowning of the ego and res-urrection as the true self.[80] Perhaps we could even say that in the Christian tra-dition, Christ, as the incarnation of divine love, is the true self. This seems to be implied when St. Paul famously says: "I have been crucified with Christ; and it is no longer I who live, but it is Christ who lives in me."[81]

With this core Christian teaching, we do not seem to be very far at all from Zen master Dōgen's teachings about life and death and about enlightenment as a matter of "dropping off the body-mind." Dōgen writes:

> When you let go of both your body and your mind, forget them both, and throw yourself into the house of Buddha, and when functioning begins from the side of the Buddha drawing you in to accord with it, then, with no need for any expenditure of either physical or mental effort, you are freed from birth-and-death and become Buddha.[82]

It has been said that this particular text, and especially this passage, may have been composed by Dōgen for a Pure Land Buddhist audience rather than a Zen Buddhist audience, since its language of letting actions come "from the side of the Buddha" rather than from one's own efforts resonates with Pure Land Buddhism's teaching of reliance on "other-power" rather than "self-power."

Be that as it may, Zen and Pure Land Buddhism are not as far apart as they are sometimes made out to be. On the one hand, self-power in Zen is decidedly not ego-power; it is ultimately the power of the true self that wells up following the Great Death of the ego.[83] On the other hand, in Pure Land Buddhism, the more one lets go of the ego-power that it calls self-power, the less "other" becomes what it calls "other-power."[84]

In a famous poem, the Pure Land Buddhist devotee Asahara Saichi gives us an indication of what happens when one *completely* entrusts oneself to the natural workings of other-power:

> In other-power, there's no self-power and no other-power.
> All is other-power.
> Namu Amida Butsu.[85]

Since "other" is a relative concept, when "self" drops out of the picture the other is no longer other; it is all that remains. Both before the birth and after the existential death of the fabricated ego, there is no sense in speaking of a Buddha that transcends the ego. In a poem dedicated to Pure Land Buddhist devotees, Zen master Shidō Bunan thus writes: "Unless you recite the name [of the Buddha], there is neither you nor Buddha."[86] Without the one, there is not the other.

Yet why, then, does the second line of Saichi's poem read: "All is other-power"? Does the "other" in this line, in fact, betray a remaining trace of "self," of ego? Is its claim that "All is other-power" then self-contradictory? Should it not say that "almost all" is other-power—except, that is, for the self that is still calling this power *other*? Insofar as one still speaks of an other-power or a higher power, one has not truly undergone the Great Death of ego-power. Insofar as one still has to say, "Let Thy will be done," there is still at least a trace of a "my will" that has not yet died on the cross with Christ.

This is why Meister Eckhart says that "obedience" is still an imperfect releasement (Gm. *Gelassenheit*) unto God's Will, for as long as there is a duality between Lord and servant, there remains a trace of self-will that resists the one Divine Will. "Where there are two," he says, "there is defection." The purely good man is said to be "so much of one will with God that he wills what God wills and in the way that God wills it." Furthermore, in the final "breakthrough," according to Eckhart, "I stand free of my own will and of God's Will and of all his works and of God himself . . . for in this breaking-through I receive that God and I are one."[87] Ultimately, for Eckhart, the complete abandonment of self-will also entails letting go of God's Will. One is then released into what he calls the "pure activity" of living "empty and free" and "without why."[88] In his most radical (and perhaps heretical) teachings, Eckhart may be closer to Zen Buddhism than he is to either the orthodox teachings of Christianity or those of Pure Land Buddhism, both of which preserve a distinction between the self and the higher or other power that it is called on to serve and be saved by. This tends to be the case even in the most self-abnegating and nondualistic teachings of these traditions.

A story told by the modern Rinzai Zen master Yamada Mumon about the thirteenth-century Pure Land Buddhist Ippen Shōnin's visits to Zen master Hattō Kokushi bears retelling here. On their first meeting, Ippen showed the Zen master a verse that he had written about his practice of the *nembutsu*, the practice of entrusting himself to Amida Buddha's other-power by repeatedly chanting "Namu Amida Butsu," "I take refuge in Amida Buddha." Ippen's verse was:

In chanting, there is neither self nor Buddha,
Only the sound Namu Amida Butsu.

Yamada Rōshi recounts the ensuing dialogue as follows:

To this Hattō Kokushi replied, "That shows your practice is still shallow. Try sitting on it some more." At this Ippen Shōnin reflected, "My verse indeed is immature. The sound of Namu Amida Butsu and the me who hears that sound are two. Since there are two things, the sound and that something which is not the sound, it then becomes necessary to say 'Only the sound of Namu Amida

Butsu.' Yes, of course, that is still immature." So saying, he pondered this for another three years and then showed his verse to Hattō Kokushi when they met
again. This time his verse was:

In chanting, there is neither self nor Buddha
Namu Amida Butsu, Namu Amida Butsu.

Hattō Kokushi replied, "Well, I guess that's all we can expect from you." Ippen
Shōnin asked, "Kokushi, what would you have written?" The Kokushi replied,

In chanting, there is neither self nor Buddha
Over the back pond, the wind is sighing.

Yamada Rōshi comments: "Chanting 'Namu Amida Butsu, Namu Amida Butsu' is
certainly a form of *samadhi*," of meditative concentration. "But," he goes on to say:

it is necessary at some point to destroy this consciousness so that you can see
that the actuality of the wind sighing over the pond is itself *nembutsu*. You must
see that the wind in the pines is *nembutsu*, that the murmuring of the valley
stream itself is *nembutsu*.[89]

I'm sure that Yamada Rōshi would agree that we can go yet one step further: at
some point we need to just see that the wind is the wind, the pond the pond, and
the murmuring stream the murmuring stream.

Dōgen writes: "A fish swims like a fish . . . a bird flies like a bird."[90] A poem of his
entitled "Original Face" reads: "In spring, flowers / In summer, cuckoo birds / In autumn, the moon / And in winter, the settled snow is cold and clear."[91] One's Original
Face, one's true self, is illuminated by the myriad phenomena of the world, each in its
"dharma position," each in its proper time and place. The Buddhist philosopher and
Zen practitioner Takemura Makio comments: "The Original Face is said to be none
other than, at this or that time, the snow, moon, and flowers." The flower spoken
of here "is not a flower set over against the ego-self. It is rather the flower, the self,
[which appears] in a horizon that transcends the structural opposition between I-
things or ego–flower. At that time, the self is none other than the world itself."[92]

Takemura points out that Dōgen's poem was likely inspired by Wumen's poem
appended to the kōan, "Everyday Even Mind is the Way." Wumen's poem reads:

Hundreds of flowers in spring, the moon in autumn,
A cool breeze in summer, and snow in winter;
If there is no vain cloud in your mind
For you it is a good season.[93]

"The willows are green, the flowers are red" is an often repeated Zen verse for what in the end, once the vain clouds in our minds dissipate, is all that needs to be said about them. Ultimately, there is no need to see all these things "in the light of God or Amida," "as God's creations," "as the *nembutsu*," "as manifestations of the Cosmic Buddha," or even "as one's Original Face." In their suchness, things simply are such as they are. Thich Nhat Hanh writes:

> When I touch a tree, when I look at a bird, when I contemplate the water in the creek, I admire them not because they have been created by God and not because they have the Buddha nature. I admire them because they are trees, they are rocks, they are water. I bow to a rock because it is a rock.[94]

Who Is It Who Says, "It Is No Longer I Who Live"?

We will return to the proximity of Eckhart and Zen in Chapter 13. In conclusion to this chapter let us note how, in response to Saichi and Paul, a Zen Buddhist might pose the following kōan: When Saichi says, "All is other-power," *who is speaking*? When Paul says, "It is no longer I who live, but Christ who lives in me," *who is speaking*? It cannot be Paul, who purportedly lives no more. But neither can it be Christ, who is named in the third person rather than speaking in the first person. Nishitani once posed this Zen-kōan-like question to a group of German theologians, who were reportedly unable to answer him.[95]

Is it perhaps the true self who is speaking, the true self who is before and beyond the duality of Paul and Christ, the duality of ego-self and Buddha-other, and thus the duality of self-power and other-power? This, indeed, would be the Zen answer. Of course, for it truly to be the Zen answer, one would have to embody and demonstrate the true self, not just name and objectify it. And, if we are being brutally honest with ourselves, this is extremely difficult, almost impossible, to do. Conceptually, it makes sense, but it is all too easy to turn the *concept* of the "true self" into just another projection and possession of the ego. Existentially, to really be able to solve this kōan of "Who is speaking?" one would have to actually undergo the Great Death of the ego.

Until then—that is, until Zen Buddhists are capable of completely dying to their egos and so dying into a life of selfless service—they should, and often do, acknowledge the provisional yet pivotal role that the expedient means of relying on higher powers can play on the spiritual path.

13

Zen as Trans-Mysticism

Everyday Even Mind Is the Way

The fourteenth-century Christian mystic Meister Eckhart once said: "I pray to God that he may make me free of God." He also said: "The highest and final letting go, of which humans are capable, is letting go of God for the sake of God."[1] Much like Zen kōans, these statements boggle the mind—yet also, for many, inspire the spirit.

We have begun to get a sense for the apparently contradictory things Zen masters have said about the Buddha. Here is another famous Zen saying by Daitō Kokushi, a Japanese Zen master who happens to have lived at the same time as Meister Eckhart:

> For countless eons Buddha and I are separated from one another,
> Yet we are not divided for a moment.
> Standing opposite one another all day long,
> We are not opposed for an instant.[2]

In other words, he seems to be saying, I am both infinitely other than, and yet ultimately one with, the Buddha. This statement, it could be said, makes room for both bowing down to and "killing" the Buddha. On the one hand, as a finite ego humbly aware of the karmic constrictions of his cloudy mind, Daitō bows down to the Buddha and to the enlightened Ancestors of the Zen tradition. On the other hand, as one who has experienced the Great Death of the ego, Daitō can say, "I cut aside all Buddhas and Ancestors."[3] And he can write the following enlightenment poem:

> I've broken through Cloud Barrier—
>   the living way is north south east and west.
> Evenings I rest, mornings I play,
>   no other no self.
> With each step a pure breeze rises.[4]

Bowing to the Buddha at the Base of One's Own Mind

Nowhere is the conjunction of these seemingly incompatible attitudes and actions more striking than in the case of the nineteenth-century Chinese Zen

Zen Pathways. Bret W. Davis, Oxford University Press. © Oxford University Press 2022.
DOI: 10.1093/oso/9780197573686.003.0013

master Huangbo. As we saw in Chapter 11, Huangbo taught: "The One Mind alone is Buddha, and there is no distinction between Buddha and sentient beings except that sentient beings are attached to forms and so seek externally for Buddhahood."[5] "If you would only rid yourselves of the concepts of ordinary and enlightened," he says, "you would find that there is no other Buddha than the Buddha in your own Mind."[6] Huangbo is thus a strong advocate of what his successor Linji calls "killing the Buddha" that you would encounter outside yourself[7]—in other words, smashing all idols, casting away all objectifications of the Buddha as someone or something other than one's true self.

And yet this same Huangbo was known for having a lump on his forehead from touching his head to the floor so often in his lifelong practice of making prostrations to the Buddha. There is a story about a novice monk who was puzzled by the apparent contradiction between Huangbo's radically iconoclastic teaching and his custom of what seemed like pious icon worshiping. The story goes like this:

> The novice noticed Huangbo enter the hall of worship and make a triple prostration to the Buddha, whereupon he asked: "If we are to seek nothing from the Buddha, Dharma, or Sangha, what does Your Reverence seek by such prostrations?"

> "Though I seek nothing from the Buddha," replied Huangbo, "or from the Dharma, or from the Sangha, it is my custom to show respect in this way."

> "But what purpose does it serve?" insisted the novice, whereupon he suddenly received a slap.

> "Oh," he exclaimed, "How uncouth you are!"

> "What is this," cried Huangbo. "Imagine making a distinction between refined and uncouth!" So saying, he administered another slap.[8]

This story appears all the more dramatic when we learn that the novice Huangbo slapped was in fact a future emperor. Since slapping someone of that status was certainly against the rules in the strictly hierarchical society of medieval China, this adds yet another twist to the story. In effect, Huangbo was brashly breaking conventions in order to teach the novice monk and future emperor the importance of observing conventions—in the appropriate context and with the appropriate mindset.

Before one is enlightened, one bows down to the Buddha because one has not yet realized that one is the Buddha. After enlightenment, one bows down to the Buddha because that is still the appropriate thing to do. Not only is it an ongoing reminder to oneself of what one truly is—a Buddha who compassionately bows down in service to everything and everyone—it is also a teaching to those around one of how they too can realize and remember this. Recall from Chapter 11 that after the modern Japanese Zen master Ōmori Sōgen bowed to an image of Kannon, the Bodhisattva of Compassion, he said: "When I bow to it I bow to something in myself. That something I call compassion."

The Disappearing and Reappearing Buddha

The episode of the BBC documentary series *The Long Search* in which Ōmori Rōshi said this is titled "The Land of the Disappearing Buddha." When the narrator of the documentary visits a Zen monastery in Kyoto, the first question he asks the abbot, Zen master Kobori Nanrei, is about the fact that in the monastery—or at least in the room of the interview—there hangs a drawing of an empty circle rather than an image of a personal form of the Buddha. "Has the Buddha disappeared in this house?" the narrator asks the Zen master. The Zen master smiles and replies: "Well, there is Buddha for those who do not know what he is really. There is no Buddha for those who know what he is really." Were he there, Meister Eckhart probably would have smiled and nodded in understanding.

The first half of Kobori Rōshi's statement means: For those who have not yet realized that the Buddha is, in truth, their own formless self, the Buddha is depicted in the form of a person before whom one can bow down. The practice of prostrations was explained by the fourteenth-century Japanese Zen master Bassui in this manner: "As for the practice of bowing down before the Buddhas, this is merely a way of horizontalizing the mast of ego in order to realize the Buddha-nature."[9] Bassui implies that once the "mast of ego" has been brought down, that is to say, once we cease sailing the ship of our lives according to the winds of our egoistic whims, the currents of the vast sea of the Buddha-nature, our true self, will naturally take us where we need to go. Once the mast of ego has been leveled, we see the Buddha no longer as outside us, but rather as our true self. Our interconnected individual lives are waves on the great ocean of the Buddha-nature.

And yet, one might still be puzzled about why Huangbo continued to bow to the Buddha his whole life. Huangbo's contemporary, Zen master Zhaozhou, gives us an important clue in his instruction: "Don't dwell where the Buddha is, and run quickly past where the Buddha is not."[10] Zen is not atheistic any more than it is theistic. It rejects religious ideas and images no more than it clings to them. We can, after all, become attached to the idea of having no attachments. A monk once asked Zhaozhou: "How about when one arrives carrying not a single thing?" In other words, what more is there to do once one has let go of all attachments? Zhaozhou responded: "Cast that down!"[11] In other words, let go of your attachment to the idea of having let go of all attachments!

Accordingly, we could supplement Kobori Rōshi's statement so that it says: There is Buddha for those who do not know that their true self is Buddha. There is no Buddha for those who first realize that their true self is Buddha. And there is once again Buddha, when and where appropriate, for those who have gone beyond Buddha.

An advanced type of kōan is called *butsu-kōjō*, "going beyond Buddha." To go beyond Buddha is to go beyond both self-power and other-power. Zen master Bankei says: "My religion has nothing to do with either 'self-power' or 'other-power.' It's beyond them both."[12] What lies beyond both relying on one's own power and relying on a higher power? What Zen calls the "naturalness" of the Everyday Even Mind.

The Mountain Is, Is Not, and After All Is a Mountain

Before elaborating on this core teaching of the Everyday Even Mind, let me note that my supplementation of Kobori Rōshi's statement about the Buddha, so as to make it a three-step rather than a two-step process, corresponds to the *Diamond Sutra*'s many statements to the effect that "A is not A, therefore it is called A."[13] D. T. Suzuki refers to this as "the logic of is/not (*soku-hi*)."[14] It is only by way of negating our linguistic and conceptual reifications of persons and things as static and isolated entities that we can understand them in their dynamic interconnectivity, and only then we can provisionally and perspectively name them in a manner that is appropriate to a particular context.

The most famous example of this three-step logic of is/not is the ninth-century Chinese Zen master Qingyuan Weixin's account of his path to enlightenment. He tells of how, upon seeing a mountain, at first he naively thought, "This is a mountain." Then, after having attained a degree of insight while training under a Zen master, he thought, "This is not a mountain." Finally, though, after reaching what he calls "the ultimate resting abode," he once again thought, "This is a mountain."[15]

At first, we see a mountain through our preconceived ideas of what a mountain is, and we assume that this is the only way to perceive and conceive of a mountain. Then we realize that our human sense organs and cognitive capabilities combined with our particular cultural and linguistic conditioning and our individual egocentric proclivities shape the way in which, at any given time, we perceive and cognize a mountain.[16] We realize that how we experience a mountain at any given time is just one among any number of ways in which it could be experienced. Finally, however, we realize that, here and now, in the present context, it is appropriate to see and say that a mountain is a mountain.

"What's that?" asks a child, pointing out the train window at Mt. Fuji. "That's a mountain," his mother responds. "What should I do when I enter the Buddha Hall?" asks a novice monk. "Bow down to the image of the Buddha," responds a Zen master, who teaches by example as well as with words.

Remember, Zen is about recovering the "beginner's mind." It is not a sacred path that transcends the mundane world and leaves it behind. It is, in the end, about discovering that "Everyday Even Mind is the Way."

Everyday Even Mind Is the Way

When he was a student, Zhaozhou once asked his teacher, Nanquan, "What is the Way, the *Dao*?" Nanquan answered, "Everyday Even Mind is the Way."[17]

The Buddha-mind that is attuned to the Way of the world should not be understood as some special supra-mundane state of consciousness. I was once asked by a newcomer to The Heart of Zen Meditation Group whether through Zen meditation he could experience mystical states of consciousness. I replied, "Yes, unfortunately you can. But don't worry—if you don't pay them any attention, they'll disappear soon enough." From the puzzled and disappointed look on the newcomer's face, I could tell that this was not the answer he expected or desired. But I think it was the answer he needed to hear.

Altered states of consciousness can indeed arise during or after intense periods of Zen meditation. They may be euphoric or alarming, merely odd or completely overwhelming. Even advanced practitioners can mistake them for genuine breakthrough or *kenshō* experiences. They are not. They might be caused simply by not getting enough sleep or by prolonged sensory deprivation. Or they may be caused by the sudden resurfacing of repressed memories or other unresolved mental and emotional issues. One may need to deal with such psychological matters through therapy rather than meditation, and, if so, I would advise one do that, especially before engaging in the spiritual rigors of kōan practice.

Altered states of consciousness and mystical experiences are called *makyō* in Zen, a term that literally translates as "devilish states." They can be an indication that one has attained a certain intensity of concentration, but they should not distract one or fool one into thinking they are the real aim of Zen meditation. In fact, they are neither good nor bad, any more than a burp or a fart is necessarily good or bad. They just happen. While you are meditating, just let them come and let them go, just as you would a burp or a bright idea, a fart or a fantasy.

Mystical Zen is *makyō* Zen. It is another form of artificial Addition Zen. It is just another feather in your cap, another robe wrapped around your ego. Real

Zen is Subtraction Zen. That's why I usually tell newcomers to The Heart of Zen Meditation Group that I hope they get nothing out of the practice, or indeed less than nothing. I hope they leave each meditation session with less than they came with—less baggage cluttering up their minds and hearts. Zen practice is about getting back in touch with the extraordinariness of the ordinary, the miracle of the mundane. It is about fully appreciating and fully engaging in—not striving to transcend or flee from—our everyday lives.

In the *Song of Enlightenment*, an eighth-century text attributed to the Chinese Zen master Yongjia, we read: "Just let everything go . . . then drink and eat as you please, in Nirvana."[18] A century and a half later, Linji, that most radical and uncompromising of Zen masters, says:

> Followers of the Way, as to the Buddha Dharma, no effort is necessary. You only have to be ordinary, with nothing to do—pooping, peeing, getting dressed, eating food, and lying down when you're tired. Fools laugh at me, but the wise understand.[19]

Later he adds:

> Followers of the Way, true Buddha has no figure, true Dharma has no form. All you're doing is devising models and patterns out of phantoms. . . . I say to you there is no Buddha, no Dharma, nothing to practice, nothing to become enlightened to. It's just that you don't believe this and you keep on seeking outside yourselves. . . . Just be ordinary.[20]

Just eat when you're hungry, sleep when you're tired, and go to the bathroom when you need to. "But don't we already do these things?" you might be wondering. Yes, but not really. In one sense we are always here and now, but in another sense, not really. Usually we are lost in mulling over the past or worrying about the future, lost in the web of gossip streaming through our smartphone screens and swirling around in our heads. With all our obsessions and hang-ups, we are far from "just letting everything go" and "just being ordinary."

Of course, we need to recollect and plan and stay informed—these too are ordinary activities for humans. But we should do so while remaining aware of where we are: in the present. Since the present is always moving, this is more like skillfully surfing a fluid wave than it is like standing stiffly in a frozen pond. We are always getting stuck somewhere in our fixations on the past, future, or what we futilely try to hold still as the present. Paradoxically, we are unsettled because of our fixations. We are not, as Linji puts it, "at home on the road."

The difference between the true ordinary mind of an enlightened person and the ordinarily unsettled and anxious mind of an unenlightened person is in fact indicated in the Chinese phrase *ping chang xin* (Jp. *byō jō shin*), which literally means "even and constant mind." Although this phrase is often simply translated as "Ordinary Mind" or as "Everyday Mind," I think it is best to translate it more literally as "Everyday Even Mind."

When one takes a deep breath right before stepping onto a stage to give a speech, or before stepping onto the platform during a diving competition, one is trying to maintain or regain something like the steady and unperturbed Everyday Even Mind that Zen masters are talking about. My teacher Tanaka Hōjū Rōshi once said, in a speech given to high school students, that what is meant by the Zen expression "Everyday Even Mind" is a mind that is placid like a waveless surface of water, a mind that is bright like a spotless mirror.[21] This mind is able to reflect and respond to the vicissitudes of everyday life with spontaneity, sincerity, creativity, and compassion because it is not obsessed with its agendas or anxious about its expectations.

In short, by Everyday Even Mind is meant *both* the equanimity that does not get egoistically attached to or fixated on anything *and* the engaged everyday mind that is thereby able to fully and fluidly attend to the infinitely complex and ceaselessly shifting Way of the world.

How can we attain this Everyday Even Mind? What are the speaker onstage and the diver on the platform doing when they take a deep breath? What are Zen practitioners doing when they meditate on the breath? How are they trying to attain what is not an object that can be physically or mentally grasped?

After being told that "Everyday Even Mind is the Way," Zhaozhou's follow-up questions to Nanquan express his puzzlement about how to proceed. He asks, "Then should we direct ourselves toward it or not?" Nanquan responds: "If you try to inquire after it, you go away from it." Zhaozhou then asks, "If we do not inquire after it, how can we know that it is the Way?" Nanquan replies, "The Way does not belong to knowing or not-knowing. Knowing is illusory awareness; not-knowing is mute blankness."

How, then, are we to proceed? As is so often the case with Zen kōans, it seems that we are damned if we do, damned if we don't. If we try to grasp the Everyday Even Mind, the grasping mind turns it into an object of knowledge. But if we don't somehow come to know it, then we simply remain mired in mindless ignorance. Once again, we see that enlightenment involves a kind of intuitive wisdom rather than an objectifying knowledge.

"If you really attain to the indubitable Way," Nanquan finishes, "it is wide open like the great void. How, then, can there be yes and no, right and wrong?" With these words Zhaozhou is suddenly enlightened. He realizes, we could say, that he had been pursuing the Buddha Way as if it were some object of knowledge, some fixed right way that should be affirmed as opposed to a wrong way that should be avoided. Now he realizes that the Way is the wide-open Everyday Even Mind that allows us to make such distinctions and judgments in the first place—and to do so in the appropriate manner, time, and place.

Everyday Chores Are the Way

Zhaozhou went on to become a famous Zen master, and he sought to return his students again and again to the Everyday Even Mind. In a story that has become a famous kōan, a monk, having just entered Zhaozhou's monastery, requests instruction. In going straight to the master rather than just a senior monk, he is no doubt asking for the highest teaching, and probably also wanting to test the master to see if staying in this monastery would be worth his while. Zhaozhou asks the monk whether he had already eaten breakfast. The monk replies that he has. "Then," says Zhaozhou, "wash your bowls."[22]

On one level, speaking metaphorically as Zen masters often do, Zhaozhou may have been asking whether the monk had already had an initial experience of awakening—he is asking whether he already had his breakthrough breakfast, so to speak. If so, then he needs to "wash his bowls"—in other words, he needs to wipe his mind clean of the pride of having attained something. He needs to practice getting rid of the "stench of Zen." He needs to practice "going beyond Buddha."

At the same time, in a more direct and literal sense, Zhaozhou's instruction to "wash your bowls" indicates that enlightenment is ultimately to be found right in the midst of the chores of everyday life. In a Japanese Zen monastery, rice porridge is served for breakfast, and one washes one's bowl right then and there with a pickled radish and a splash of hot tea. Both metaphorically and literally, removing every last grain and smudge of sticky rice from one's bowl is as much a part of the practice as anything else.

Zen as a Path of Trans-Mysticism

It should be clear by now that Zen is not ultimately a matter of "mysticism," if one means by that term some transcendent or otherworldly experience that transports one beyond the humdrum of the mundane world. The path of Zen leads, rather, to a wholehearted and fully mindful engagement in the extraordinarily ordinary activities of everyday life. If there is anything "supernatural" about Zen, it is not a matter of taking us "above and beyond the natural world" but rather a matter of becoming "supremely natural."

Accordingly, the modern Japanese philosopher and lay Zen master Ueda Shizuteru interprets Zen as a path of what he calls "non-mysticism." Ueda was also a foremost scholar of the fourteenth-century Christian mystic Meister Eckhart. In fact, he first coined his expression "non-mysticism" while writing on Eckhart before he applied it to Zen. Although he was initially struck by the profound parallels between the two, in the end Ueda suggested that Zen goes even further than does Eckhart in shedding the residues of an otherworldly mysticism.

When Ueda began publishing his collected writings in 2001, I had the privilege of joining other scholars who were former students of his in meetings to discuss each volume with him. For one of these meetings I was asked to make a presentation on the volume entitled *Non-Mysticism: Eckhart and Zen*, and I was fortunate enough to be able to visit Professor Ueda at his house and discuss this topic with him further. As a brash young scholar and Zen practitioner, I had the nerve to suggest to him that what he calls "non-mysticism" might be better rendered "de-mysticism" or "trans-mysticism." My reasoning was that he does not think that Eckhart and Zen are simply unrelated or opposed to mysticism, which the term "non-mysticism" might be mistaken to mean. Rather, he thinks that, for Eckhart as well as Zen, mysticism does not go far enough. True and thoroughgoing mysticism, Ueda maintains, leads to its own dissolution—that is to say, it leads back to a direct engagement with the here and now of everyday life. Listening as always with a generous and even mind, Professor Ueda thought about my suggestion for a moment and then magnanimously agreed with it. And so I use the term "trans-mysticism" to explain his illuminating account of the circuitous path of Zen, a path that, in the end, brings us back to the everyday.[23]

The path of Zen's trans-mysticism consists of the following four steps:

1. An ecstatic transcendence of the ego
2. A mystical union with God or Buddha, understood as what both Eastern and Western philosophers have called "the One"
3. A breakthrough beyond the One into an Absolute Nothingness, understood not as an inert void but rather as a dynamic plentitude of potentiality, a formless origin of all forms
4. A return to a wholehearted and unmediated engagement in the here and now of everyday life

Mysticism consists of the first and second steps only. What is distinctive about trans-mysticism is that it goes beyond these to include the third and fourth steps. This path of trans-mysticism entails a "double negation"—that is to say, a twofold process of letting go. To begin with, one must let go of one's habitual identification with the self-encapsulated ego, and in the end, one must let go of even the mystical experience of union with the divine.

The first step, the transcendence of the ego, is common to all forms of religious experience. The second step, the experience of union with the divine, is often considered to be the hallmark of mystical experience. The third step, the break-through beyond mystical union to an Absolute Nothingness, can be understood as a self-overcoming of mysticism. And the fourth step, the return to egoless activity in midst of the everyday world, completes this self-overcoming process of trans-mysticism.

We can understand this entire movement of trans-mysticism in terms of a series of "ecstasies." Although today many tend to think of sex, drugs, and maybe rock-'n'-roll when they hear the word "ecstasy," in fact this is a word that was originally used by mystics to describe their experience of *ek-stasis* or literally "standing outside oneself." The Japanese translation of "ecstasy" is *datsu-ji*, which literally means "shedding the self." By shedding the shell of the ego, by stepping outside the walls of self-centeredness, mystics enter into a communion or even a union with something greater than just themselves. Christian mystics have called this an experience of *unio mystica*, a mystical union with the divine, an experience in which, as Eckhart puts it, "I receive that God and I are one."[24]

This experience of union with the divine is indeed the peak of mysticism, according to Ueda. Yet both Meister Eckhart and Zen take the ecstatic momentum still further, such that Eckhart talks about "breaking through" the persona of God to what he calls the "silent desert of the Godhead," the ineffable origin and ground of reality that lies beyond all distinctions, beyond the Trinity and even beyond the distinction between Creator and created.[25] Since it is utterly beyond or beneath anything that can be defined or described, Eckhart sometimes calls this abyssal ground of the Godhead "nothingness" rather than "being."[26]

Zen also prefers to speak of the ultimate ground or nature of reality in terms of "nothingness" rather than "being." Ueda follows his Kyoto School predecessors in speaking of an "Absolute Nothingness" that underlies or envelops even the distinction between "being" and "relative nothingness."

We meet this Absolute Nothingness in the first kōan of *The Gateless Barrier* collection. In this famous kōan, in response to a monk's question about whether a dog has the Buddha-nature, Zhaozhou says, "No!" In Chinese pronounced *wu* and in Japanese *mu*, this "no" can also mean "nothing" or "nothingness." In his comments on this kōan, Wumen instructs practitioners to "concentrate yourself into this 'nothing' with your 360 bones and 84,000 pores, making your whole body one great inquiry." He also warns us not to "attempt nihilistic or dualistic interpretations."[27] This "nothing" is not opposed to being; rather, we could say, it is the very ground of being—an unfathomable, abyssal ground. It is beyond or beneath all beings, even "God" or the "One."

Just as Eckhart seeks to go beyond a mystical union with God the Father to experience a union with the "nothingness" of the Godhead as the very ground of all beings and the distinctions among them, including even the distinction between oneself and God, the path of Zen leads through a "killing of the Buddha" as an external being to an Absolute Nothingness that undercuts and underlies even the distinction between the One and the Many.

As the great Jesuit historian of Western philosophy Frederick Copleston recognized, Greek philosophy revolves around the question of the One and the Many.[28] How is the oneness of the universe related to the many things that exist in it? The mystical Neoplatonic philosopher Plotinus spoke of the One as the divine ground from which all the many things of the universe emanate. Eckhart echoes Plotinus in thinking of the experience of union with God as an experience of oneness with the One. However, like Zen, his path of trans-mysticism does not stop even there. In letting go of God for nothing—again, not for a nihilistic or relative nothing but rather for the Absolute Nothingness that underlies even the distinctions between Creator and created, Buddha and unenlightened beings, the One and the Many—we have nowhere else to go, and thus are returned to an unmediated engagement in the here and now of the ultimate reality of everyday life. The ultimate answer to the great spiritual question of the meaning of life is in the end found, according to Eckhart, in the "pure activity" of living "empty and free" and "without why" in the midst of the mundane.[29]

Nevertheless, Eckhart persists in preaching that we should learn to see all things "in God" or "in the light of God."[30] Zen goes a step further, pushing us to drop all references to the Buddha as anything outside of the everyday world. Indeed, Zen urges us to return from a mystical or meditative experience of oneness with the One to an undistracted mindfulness of the Many. In Case 45 of *The Blue Cliff Record*, a monk asks Zhaozhou, "All things return to the One; but where does the One return to?" Zhaozhou responds, "When I was in the province of Qingzhou, I made a cloth shirt. It weighed seven pounds."[31]

The monk in this kōan already had a sense that the path of Zen—the path of what we are calling trans-mysticism—does not end with an experience of the oneness of all things, with an experience of a *unio mystica* with the ground of all beings. And yet, he wondered, what could lie beyond or beneath that? This is where the monk had gotten stuck. He had not yet realized that a penetrating experience of the One leads us right back into the midst of the Many.

The One is not opposed to the Many. God or Buddha is not someone or something standing outside of the world. Ultimate reality is right here and right now; the divine is right in the midst of the everyday. The problem is that *we* are not really here and now. The problem is not that we are stuck in the mundane world of the everyday. The problem is that we are always looking elsewhere—outside ourselves and beyond the world—for answers to the question of why. We want to truly live, yet we are distracting ourselves from the truth of our lives. As Hakuin says, we are crying out in thirst while standing in the midst of water. The ultimate "without why" resolution of the great question of the meaning of life is right in front of our noses, right under our feet, all the time—for example, while standing in line at Target waiting to buy a cotton T-shirt that weighs seven ounces.

14

Engaged Zen

From Inner to Outer Peace

In Chapter 13, we discussed the kōan in which Zhaozhou instructs a monk to wash his bowls. The monk was looking for some special teaching, but Zhaozhou pointed out to him that enlightenment is ultimately to be found right in the midst of the chores of everyday life. The eighth-century Layman Pang said: "My daily activities are not unusual, I'm just naturally in harmony with them. . . . [My] supernatural power and marvelous activity—Drawing water and carrying firewood."[1]

Zen is not about acquiring supernatural or supernormal powers. Some people have practiced meditation for years with the aim of becoming able to levitate. But even if you were able to miraculously hover a few inches off the ground, or fly around like Superman, what spiritual good would that physical feat do you? If levitating or flying is what you are interested in, buy a hovercraft or a helicopter.

The Way of Zen does not lead to floating above or flying away from everyday life. It is rather a matter of putting our feet on the ground and awakening, step by step, to the present moment, to the wondrousness of mundane matters and the weightiness of everyday errands.

Dōgen Learns How to Cook

The utmost importance of wholeheartedly engaging in commonplace duties, such as cleaning and cooking, is something the thirteenth-century Japanese Zen master Dōgen first learned in China from his encounters with two monks. Despite their seniority and advanced age, these *tenzo* or monastery cooks were wholly committed to doing their job of procuring and preparing food for their monastic communities.

Why, the young Dōgen wondered, did these senior monks not leave such menial tasks to their juniors? Why did they not dedicate their time to practicing meditation or studying the words of ancient masters? One of the monks laughed at Dōgen's questions, telling him that he apparently understood neither practice nor words. Needing to get back to his monastery to do his duties, the cook left Dōgen to ponder these matters.

Zen Pathways. Bret W. Davis, Oxford University Press. © Oxford University Press 2022.
DOI: 10.1093/oso/9780197573686.003.0014

Months later, Dōgen met up again with this monk, who could tell that he was now ripe and ready for some answers. To Dōgen's question, "What are words?" the cook replied, "One, two, three, four, five." And to the question, "What is practice?" he responded, "In the whole world it is never hidden."[2]

You are likely thinking, "These are the kinds of answers that just leave one with more questions!" But notice the orientation they give us. The monk was telling Dōgen, and now us, to look not in the direction of the increasingly complex and mysterious, but rather back to the apparently simple words we use to carry out seemingly humdrum activities, such as measuring cups of rice. After all, what could be more important than properly preparing the food that keeps us alive? And what could be more precious than showing a toddler how to count her toes?

The modern Japanese Zen master Uchiyama Kōshō paraphrases Dōgen's enigmatic conversation with the monastery cook like this: "Dōgen Zenji asked, 'What is the meaning of our day-to-day activities?' The tenzo replied, 'This and that—everything!' Dōgen Zenji countered, 'Just what is practice?' The tenzo came back, 'Everything you encounter in your life is your practice.'"[3]

When the cook counts "one, two, three, four, five," he is in effect saying that there is no one magical word symbolizing some mysterious truth about the universe. Rather, truth is found in unique things and events, which are as infinite and as interconnected as are numbers.

"There is nothing in the world that is hidden." This is a traditional Zen saying indicating that the truth is right in front of our eyes at all times and in all places. The Way of Zen is to be found not at the end of a long journey but rather right under our feet. The Way of Zen is not hidden; it is just that we have yet to completely open our eyes and fully feel the path on which we are treading.

Vimalakirti and the Mahayana Affirmation of Lay Life

One of the distinguishing characteristics of Mahayana Buddhism is that it breaks down the dichotomy between priesthood and laity, that is, between home-leavers and home-havers. An affirmation of the spiritual depth of everyday lay life is exemplified in the legends and sayings of Layman Pang—in fact, the Pang family, since his wife and daughter sparred with him on equally enlightened terms during their daily activities.[4]

In the early centuries of Buddhism, and in so-called Hinayana schools such as Theravada up until relatively recently, meditation was for the most part practiced exclusively by monks and nuns. Laypeople would practice things like charity, especially in support of monks (and sometimes nuns), as well as morality: right speech, action, and livelihood. By doing these supposedly preparatory practices, laypeople were thought to accumulate karmic merit, such that they would eventually be reborn as someone ready to leave home and devote themselves to the ultimately liberating practice of meditation. Only if one was free from the worldly chores of everyday lay life, it was assumed, could one become a serious spiritual practitioner.

The Mahayana reform movement called this way of thinking about lay life into question. The *Vimalakirti Sutra*—a sutra composed around 100 CE that became one of the most important for the Zen tradition—turns the privileging of priesthood on its head by having a layperson be the teacher of monks. In the story of this sutra, the layperson Vimalakirti has fallen ill, and the Buddha sends his attendant monks to pay their respects and to learn from him.

The figure of the lay teacher Vimalakirti epitomizes the idea of the Bodhisattva as an enlightened and enlightening being who, out of boundless compassion, remains in the world to work toward liberating all sentient beings from suffering. "Because all living beings are sick," Vimalakirti says, "therefore I am sick." "If all living beings are relieved of sickness, then my sickness will be mended."[5] Since a Bodhisattva is someone who has the wisdom to see into the nonduality of self and other, someone who "loves beings as though they were his children," it would simply make no sense to save oneself and leave others behind.

The Buddha sends both his Hinayana disciples and his Mahayana Bodhisattvas to Vimalakirti to inquire about his illness. He symbolically sends them down from his Buddha Land in the sky into the "dusty world" in which this enlightened layperson lives so that, among other things, they can be taught that the Pure Land of the Buddha is in truth a state of mind, not an otherworldly realm.[6] Vimalakirti teaches them to free themselves from otherworldly aspirations and to find true spirituality in bodily existence and in the midst of the mundane activities of everyday life. He tells them that they should not despise the body and bodily desires; rather, he says, without reifying and becoming attached to them, use them to relieve rather than to create suffering.[7]

A goddess appears in Vimalakirti's room and teaches Shariputra, the wisest of the Hinayana disciples, not to denigrate women's bodies in particular.[8] More than a thousand years later, Dōgen tells his Zen community that they should "not discriminate between men and women," that women are just as capable as men of attaining the highest enlightenment and becoming strong guiding teachers.[9] Eight hundred years after Dōgen, female Zen masters are finally being recognized, including Westerners such as Charlotte Joko Beck, author of *Everyday Zen: Love and Work*, and Joan Halifax, a pioneering peace activist and end-of-life counselor.[10] Yet we are still learning this crucial lesson of gender equality in spiritual as well as material matters. Today, Buddhist teachers are working to root out our prejudices based on race, class, and sexual orientation as well as gender, within our meditation centers as well as in our societies at large.[11]

Meditation Retreats Are Not Escapes

Vimalakirti teaches Bodhisattvas that they must not think of remaining in the world in order to liberate others as a sacrifice of their own liberation, since such work in the world is in fact the highest form of liberation. Meditation should not be understood or experienced as an escape from the world. Ironically, as Vimalakirti puts it, "To become infatuated with the taste of meditation is the bondage of the bodhisattva. To be born in this world as a form of expedient means is the liberation of the bodhisattva."[12] We need to be liberated not from the world of everyday life, but rather from the desire to escape it.

The eighteenth-century Japanese Zen master Hakuin stresses the need for "post-satori training," training after an initial breakthrough enlightenment experience, which he says requires "continuous and unremitting devotion to hidden practice [and] scrupulous application." When asked what this means, he replied:

> It certainly doesn't mean sneaking off to some mountain and sitting like a block of wood on a rock or under a tree "silently illuminating" yourself. It means immersing yourself totally in your practice at all times and in all your daily activities—walking, standing, sitting, or lying down. Hence, it is said that practice concentrated in activity is a hundred, a thousand, even a million times superior to practice done in a state of inactivity.[13]

Of course, despite Hakuin's insistence on post-satori practice-in-motion, practice-in-stillness does play an important role in Zen, especially, but not only, in pre-satori training. In fact, at times we all need to recharge our batteries. We need to occasionally retreat from our busy routines and clear our hearts and minds. Meditation retreats are an exceptional—and exceptionally concentrated—way to do this. But we must be careful not to fall into the trap of escapism, especially as one gets past the initial physical and mental difficulties of meditation and begins to experience the deep peace and joy that it brings.

The contemporary Vietnamese Zen master and founder of Engaged Buddhism,[14] Thich Nhat Hanh, tells us that "meditation is not an escape from society. Meditation is to equip oneself with the capacity to reintegrate into society, in order for the leaf to nourish the tree."[15] The American Zen master Robert Aitken concurs when he says that "the true Zen Buddhist center is not a mere sanctuary, but a source from which ethically motivated people move outward to engage in the larger community."[16]

Vimalakirti goes yet a step further in breaking down any supposed dichotomy between meditation and everyday living when he reprimands Shariputra for sitting in quiet meditation under a tree in the forest. "Shariputra," he says, "you should not assume that this sort of sitting is true quiet sitting!" He continues,

"Not rising out of your meditative state of stillness and peace and yet showing yourself in the ceremonies of daily life—that is [true] quiet sitting."[17]

Half a millennium later, the Sixth Chinese Ancestor of Zen, Huineng, echoes this teaching when he says, "The single practice of meditation means at all times, whether walking, standing, sitting, or lying down, always practicing with a straightforward mind."[18] Huineng goes on to quote the *Vimalakirti Sutra*'s statement that "a straightforward mind is the Pure Land." As we saw in Chapter 12, Thich Nhat Hanh is in full agreement with this understanding of the Pure Land, and he has devoted his life to working for outer as well as inner peace in the world.

Being at Peace and Bringing Peace to Others

Vimalakirti's criticism of Shariputra's attachment to practicing quiet and restful meditation in the forest is an important corrective to a tendency to view meditation merely as a means of escaping the noisiness and unrest of city life. Nevertheless, Thich Nhat Hanh wisely recognizes that in order to truly bring peace to the world, we need to be at peace ourselves. In order to *bring peace*, we need to *be peace*. And for this, most of us need, at least occasionally, to retreat from the street to the cushion and cloister. In between such retreats, however, to the street we must return, now with more to offer.

It is interesting to note that Vimalakirti is presented not just as a layperson but as a *rich* layperson. It is said that he uses his immeasurable riches to bring relief to the poor. On a metaphorical level, it is said that the great wealth possessed by Bodhisattvas is the holy Dharma, the teachings that they unstintingly give to others.[19] Bodhisattvas practice the Perfection of Giving (see Chapter 18). There are three main types of giving involved in this practice: the giving of material things, the giving of teachings, and the greatest gift of all, the gift of "fearlessness." A Bodhisattva teaches others how to be free of the distressing anxieties of life, especially the fear of death. The greatest gift, in other words, is to be taught how to attain true peace of mind.

When I was a child, my favorite part of the Sunday church service was when we would stand and say to those around us, "Peace be with you!" In the Gospel of John, Jesus says: "Peace I leave with you; my peace I give you. I do not give to you as the world gives. Do not let your hearts be troubled and do not be afraid."[20] We find here yet another striking parallel between Jesus's teachings and those of Buddhism.

Thich Nhat Hanh is among the Zen masters who view the core teachings of Christianity and Buddhism as complementary, as long as we look deeply into them and, more importantly, sincerely put them into practice. As the subtitle of one of his books suggests, Jesus and Buddha are spiritual siblings, not religious rivals.[21]

Paul Knitter is a leading comparative theologian who has come to affirm this interreligious kinship from the other side. In his provocatively entitled book *Without Buddha I Could Not Be a Christian*, Knitter explains the thought process and practice through which, in the end, he became a Buddhist, not by abandoning Christianity but in order to deepen his understanding of and commitment to it. Knitter's engagement with Buddhist teachings and practices led him to re-read the Christian scriptures and to reinterpret their meaning in light of his own experience. He points out that the only definition of God found in the New Testament is John's pronouncement that "God is love,"[22] and he finally concludes that God is not so much a Transcendent Other as He is an Interconnecting Spirit or "dynamic energy field of InterBeing" in which "we live and move and have our being."[23]

Theologians can debate the orthodoxy of Knitter's biblical interpretations and religious "double belonging." In any case, the final chapter is one of the most engaging parts of his book. Entitled "Making Peace and Being Peace," it draws on Knitter's long experience as a social activist in El Salvador and elsewhere as well as on his study and practice of both Christianity and Buddhism. He writes: "Generalizing grossly, what Buddhists mean by practice is more interior and personal, while what Christians mean is more external and social." Whereas Buddhists stress wisdom, Christians stress charity. "Of course," he immediately adds, "as both Buddhists and Christians acknowledge, each needs the other: wisdom calls for compassion, and compassion requires wisdom."[24]

The difference in emphasis or orientation is said to be that whereas Christians foreground working for justice, Buddhists foreground becoming peaceful oneself so that one can spread that peace to others. For a Buddhist, if one wishes to bring peace to the world, one must first learn how to be peaceful. Hence the title of one of Thich Nhat Hanh's landmark books, *Being Peace*. In that book Nhat Hanh writes:

> If we are not happy, if we are not peaceful, we cannot share peace and happiness with others, even those we love, those who live under the same roof. If we are peaceful, if we are happy, we can smile and blossom like a flower, and everyone in our family, our entire society, will benefit from our peace. . . . [W]ithout being peace, we cannot do anything for peace. . . . I hope we can bring a new dimension to the peace movement. The peace movement is filled with anger and hatred. It cannot fulfill the path we expect from them. A fresh way of being peace, of doing peace is needed. That is why it is so important for us to practice meditation, to acquire the capacity to look, to see, and to understand. . . . Peace work means, first of all, being peace.[25]

Elaborating on this Buddhist perspective, Knitter writes: "Yes, both action and contemplation, both making peace and being peace, are equally important." But while "action and contemplation form a constantly moving circle in which one feeds into the other, the entrance point for the circle is contemplation."[26] In other words, one must, through spiritual practices such as meditation, learn how to *be peace* before one can truly *bring peace* to the world.

A powerful quotation often attributed to Gandhi echoes this idea: "We must be the change we wish to see in the world."[27] This great social justice activist—this advocate of firm yet non-violent resistance who drew his interreligious inspiration from Jesus's Sermon on the Mount as well as from the Hindu *Bhagavad Gita*—taught that we cannot bring peace to others unless we can bring peace to ourselves. If we want to rid the world of imperialism and other causes of injustice, Gandhi says, first "we must acquire greater mastery over ourselves and secure an atmosphere of perfect calm, peace, and good will."[28]

Peace and Justice: Which Is Primary?

The idea that we need to *be peace* in order to *bring peace* may cut against the grain of our inclination to not waste time by sitting around "navel gazing," but rather to get out there and do something to change the world for the better. Activists often chant "No justice, no peace!" Bob Marley and Jimmy Cliff sing, "How is there going to be peace when there is no justice?" That other, more rebellious reggae pioneer Peter Tosh goes so far as to sing: "I don't want no peace, I need equal rights and justice." The great non-violent civil rights activist Martin Luther King Jr., however, cautions that we need both: "I don't think there can be justice without peace, and I don't think there can be peace without justice."[29]

Of course, it is important to fight for equal rights and justice, and this requires upsetting the stability of the status quo when it safeguards peace for some at the expense of oppressing and marginalizing others. The fight for justice, after all, has the aim of eventually establishing a truer and more universal peace.

Yet, sometimes we lose sight of that ultimate purpose of our fight, and we end up wanting retributive justice more than, or even instead of, peaceful coexistence. We want to right the wrongs that have been done to us and to others even more than we want to heal the wounds of the world. We want to punish our evil enemies rather than make amends with them, much less learn to love them. After saying that the "Hindu-Moslem-Christian-Jewish-Buddhist belief about ultimate reality is beautifully summed up in the first epistle of Saint John" in the passage that says "God is love," King warns: "We can no longer afford to worship the God of hate or bow before the altar of retaliation. . . . We still have a choice today: non-violent co-existence or violent co-annihilation."[30]

Bernie Glassman was an American Zen master who for decades pioneered the combination of Zen practice with social activism.[31] On a retreat with Glassman, Paul Knitter confessed to being torn between feeling like he needed to sit in meditation and wanting to get up and go to El Salvador to try to help stop the death squads. Glassman responded, "They are both absolutely necessary." And then he left Knitter with a kōan-like admonishment: "But you won't be able to stop the death squads until you realize your oneness with them."[32] In effect, Glassman was echoing Jesus's core teaching: If we don't learn to love not just our neighbors and our compatriots but also even our enemies as ourselves, we cannot truly bring peace to the world. By fighting for justice with hatred in our hearts, we inevitably sow the seeds of resentment and revenge, in the end creating more enemies and perpetuating the cycle of violence. You cannot, after all, punch your way to peace.

Knitter tells the story of how, at a meeting of the Interreligious Peace Council in Israel and Palestine in 2000, a Tibetan monk and scholar, referring to his own experience with Chinese oppression, attempted to explain that achieving peace in the Middle East requires that we "feel compassion for all who are suffering, on both sides." This does not mean, the Buddhist monk explained, that we don't make judgments of right and wrong, but it does mean that we stop labeling our enemies as evil people and start to have compassion for people who make mistakes based on an egocentric viewpoint that is ultimately rooted in ignorance.[33] Unfortunately, Knitter tells us, such Buddhist contributions to the peace talks in Israel and Palestine were met with little more than "stunned silence."

Jesus shockingly taught that we should love our enemies and "turn the other cheek" rather than demanding "an eye for an eye."[34] Gandhi taught "non-cooperation with evil, with an evil system, and not with the evil doer. My religion teaches me to love even an evildoer."[35] Learning from both of them, King taught that we must "love the person who does an evil deed, although we hate the deed that he does."[36] These are indeed tough-love lessons on true love. While none of us may be fully up to the task, such teachings are especially likely to fall on deaf ears when offered to someone who is directly suffering, and perpetuating, cycles of violence in the name of justice.

The American philosopher and Zen teacher David Loy reminds us that "one of the main causes of evil in this world has been human attempts to eradicate evil," and he brings this teaching closer to home for many of us when he critically analyzes the "war on terror" intended to "eradicate the evil persons," the Islamic militants, who attacked the United States on 9/11. Righteous indignation in what is perceived as a binary struggle of good versus evil easily morphs into self-righteous rage in a battle of Us versus Them; mutual demands of an eye for an eye threaten to end up leaving the whole world blind. Loy writes:

The Buddhist solution to suffering does not involve requiting violence with violence, any more than it involves responding to greed with greed, or to delusion
with delusion. From a Buddhist perspective, the deaths of some three thousand
innocent people in New York and Washington cannot justify a bombing campaign that leads to the deaths of an even larger number of innocent Afghanis.
Rather, the Buddhist solution involves breaking that cycle by transforming
greed into generosity, ill will into loving-kindness, and delusions into wisdom.[37]

Of course, this is all easier said than done. We can learn to recite the best of
Buddhist, Hindu, Jewish, Christian, or Islamic teachings, but learning to live
them is a lifelong task that most of us never come close to fulfilling. And yet,
sometimes people are miraculously capable of turning the other cheek and of
forgiving. In 2006 a shooter killed five young girls outside an Amish school-
house in Pennsylvania before turning his gun on himself. "On the day of the
shooting, a grandfather of one of the murdered Amish girls was heard warning
some young relatives not to hate the killer, saying, 'We must not think evil of this
man.'" An Amish neighbor is said to have comforted and extended forgiveness
to the family of the killer just hours after the shooting.[38] In those most difficult of
circumstances, in those most trying of times, these Amish Christians practiced
what they preach.

Sallie King, author of *Socially Engaged Buddhism*, also attended the
Interreligious Peace Council meetings in Israel and Palestine in 2000. She recalls
that the Buddhist participants "particularly rejected the idea that justice, conceived as the vanquishing of the other side, was a prerequisite for the achievement of peace."[39]

The call for justice is often a cry for "retribution," a word that is sometimes used
as a euphemism for "revenge." Why, Nietzsche asks, does St. Thomas Aquinas say
that "in order that the bliss of the saints may be more delightful for them . . . it
is given to them to see perfectly the punishment of the damned"?[40] Why does
the last book of the Christian Bible, Revelation, insist that sinners will "drink
the wine of God's wrath, poured unmixed into the cup of his anger, and they
will be tormented with fire and sulfur in the presence of the holy angels and in
the presence of the Lamb"?[41] Perhaps God's wrath is an expression of His tough
love. But Nietzsche's question is, why would the saints, angels, and even Christ
himself take pleasure in watching such scenes of torture? Is this, he asks, simply
a revengeful reversal of the Romans taking pleasure in watching Christians be
devoured by lions in the Colosseum? Whereas Nietzsche calls for honesty about
the "will to power" that he believes drives all our actions, from the most inhu-
mane to the most humane, the Buddha, like Jesus, calls for a conversion from
egoistic willfulness to a egolessly non-willful way of being, a conversion to compassion, love, and forgiveness as the path to genuine peace.[42]

We have pondered some deep resonances between the teachings of Christianity and Buddhism, and in Chapter 15 we'll consider even more. But the biblical idea of eternal damnation makes no sense to Buddhists. The Buddhist concept of Hell—whether it is understood metaphorically or literally—is a temporary realm where one is rehabilitated. In general, rather than see evil in the world that needs to be punished, Buddhists see ignorance that needs to be enlightened.

Of course, we must never lose sight of the fact that the pain and suffering of victims of violence are very real. It is vitally important to prevent people from perpetrating such violence, and the need for such deterrence can indeed justify imprisonment and other punishments. But pain and suffering are only multiplied by acts of counterviolence, including any "cruel and unusual" form of punishment that makes no attempt to rehabilitate.

The Buddha famously taught: "Hatreds do not ever cease in this world by hating, but by love."[43] Two and a half millennia later, this timeless teaching reverberates in Gandhi's teaching that humankind "has to get out of violence only through non-violence. Hatred can be overcome only by love."[44] Martin Luther King Jr., that great student and successor of Gandhi's philosophy of non-violent resistance, in a sermon entitled "Loving Your Enemies" explicates this core teaching of Christianity thus:

> Returning hate for hate multiplies hate, adding deeper darkness to a night already devoid of stars. Darkness cannot drive out darkness; only light can do that. Hate cannot drive out hate: only love can do that.[45]

Like Gandhi, King not only talked the talk but also walked the walk, even when that meant non-violently walking into an angry and misguided mob of violent police officers. King was awarded the Nobel Peace Prize in 1964, and in 1967 he nominated Vietnamese Zen master Thich Nhat Hanh for the same, having been inspired by his person and peace activism to speak out against the Vietnam War in that last year of his life.[46]

One could say that the choral message of Buddha, Jesus, Gandhi, King, and Nhat Hanh is that only love conquers hate. Yet—since to speak of "conquering" is still to speak in an antagonistic manner that can inadvertently pull us back onto a slippery slope that leads toward hateful revenge—they might say rather that only love quenches hate. Only love generates love. And, in the end, only peace engenders peace. Of course, struggles for social justice cannot wait for us all to first attain perfect peace in our inner hearts and minds. Yet only if we constantly practice cultivating and sharing inner peace, at the same time as we heed urgent calls for immediate action and activism, can we ever hope to bring true and lasting outer peace to the world.

15

The Dharma of Karma

We Reap What We Sow

In Chapter 14, we talked about the Zen path of bringing peace to the world by way of cultivating peace in ourselves. Insofar as our hearts and minds are filled with anger and hatred, our fight for justice will inevitably end up evoking anger and hatred in the hearts and minds of those whom we think of as our evil enemies. And the self-defeating result of our fight for justice will be a perpetuation of the cycle of violence.

Near the end of Chapter 14 I quoted the Buddha's famous words: "Hatreds do not ever cease in this world by hating, but by love." Elsewhere in the *Dhammapada*, the Buddha says: "Overcome anger by love, overcome evil by good."[1] In his eye-opening collection *Jesus and Buddha: The Parallel Sayings*, Marcus Borg places these passages from the *Dhammapada* next to Jesus's repetition of this revolutionary teaching many centuries later: "Love your enemies, do good to those who hate you, bless those who curse you, pray for those who abuse you."[2]

The many parallels between the teachings and stories of the Buddha and Jesus—which do not always have clear precedents in the Jewish tradition—are indeed astonishing. Some scholars think the resonances are too strong to be coincidental, and so there must have been some kind of influence involved. There has even been speculation that Jesus spent his "lost years" between the ages of twelve and twenty-nine living and learning in India. A few eccentrics have gone so far as to claim that Jesus was resuscitated—rather than resurrected—after the crucifixion and returned to India, and that there is a grave in Kashmir where Jesus is buried. Needless to say, such theories are roundly rejected by mainstream biblical scholars. Yet, less controversially, some reputable scholars have suggested that Jesus could have been exposed to the teachings of Buddhist missionaries either directly or indirectly through the Essenes, the Jewish sect in whose community he probably spent some time.[3]

As skeptical as one might be about these scholarly conjectures, if you think about it, it would be even more astonishing—and revealing—if the parallels between their teachings were in fact merely coincidental. This would mean that Jesus awakened to many of the same truths as did the Buddha, who lived far away and five centuries earlier.

Zen Pathways. Bret W. Davis, Oxford University Press. © Oxford University Press 2022.
DOI: 10.1093/oso/9780197573686.003.0015

Karma as Natural Causality Rather than
Supernatural Intervention

In any case, in our enthusiasm for the similarities between the sayings of the Buddha and those of Jesus we should not lose sight of the significant differences between what became the doctrines of Buddhism and Christianity. We can discern both similarities and differences with Buddhism in the following passage from Paul's epistle to the Romans:

> Do not repay anyone evil for evil, but take thought for what is noble in the sight of all. If it is possible, so far as it depends on you, live peaceably with all. Beloved, never avenge yourselves, but leave room for the wrath of God; for it is written, "Vengeance is mine, I will repay, says the Lord." No, "if your enemies are hungry, feed them; if they are thirsty, give them something to drink; for by doing this you will heap burning coals on their heads." Do not be overcome by evil, but overcome evil with good.[4]

On the one hand, as we have seen, Buddhists would fully agree with the idea that we should not repay evil with evil but rather overcome (or, better, quench) evil by means of good. Yet, on the other hand, the idea of the "vengeance" or "wrath" of God is foreign to the philosophical core of Buddhism.[5] Buddhists do not believe in a God on high who judges and rewards or punishes us for our actions. Buddhists have an easier time understanding God's love than they do God's wrath. Indeed, the idea that "God *is* love" is close to the idea that Buddha is the enlightened mind and compassionate heart, the awakened heart-mind that manifests the Four Immeasurable Mindsets of lovingkindness, compassion, empathetic joy, and equanimity.

A Christian would say that God's wrath is not opposed to His love; rather, it is a kind of tough love that rights wrongs and restores justice. Buddhists also think that there is a force of cosmic justice at work in the world, but for them it is a *natural process* of cause and effect rather than a *supernatural intervention* by a transcendent deity. The Buddhist word for the natural processes of cause and effect that bring about cosmic justice in the world is "karma."

In some respects, the Dharma (teaching) of karma is akin to the biblical idea that you reap what you sow. We find this doctrine, for example, in Paul's letter to the Galatians:

> Do not be deceived: God is not mocked, for you will reap whatever you sow. If you sow to your own flesh, you will reap corruption from the flesh; but if you sow to the Spirit, you will reap eternal life from the Spirit. So let us not

grow weary in doing what is right, for we will reap at harvest time, if we do not give up.[6]

In fact, however, this agricultural metaphor of reaping what we sow works better to explain the natural workings of karma than it does to explain the rewards and punishments meted out by a supernatural deity. For a Buddhist, there is nothing supernatural or miraculous about karma. To ask Buddhists whether they believe in karma would be like asking them if they believe in cause and effect.

Karma as Intentional Mental, Verbal, and Physical Acts

Like "Zen," "karma" is one of those Buddhist words that have been adopted into our everyday English vocabulary. Yet, again like "Zen," our loose use of the word sometimes strays rather far from how it is understood in the Buddha Dharma, the teachings of Buddhism. The Dharma of Karma is a teaching of causality; in other words, it is a teaching that our actions have both causes and effects that we should pay attention to. We need to be mindful of where our actions come from and what they lead to.

Originally, the word "karma" simply meant "action." Yet all actions have consequences; all actions are causes and all causes have effects. According to Newton's third law of motion, all physical actions lead to an equal and oppo-site reaction. The Buddha, however, was more interested in psychology than in physics. When he says that all of our actions have consequences, he is talking about our actions in *thought* and *speech* as well as with the *body*. The Dharma of Karma is concerned with mental and verbal as well as physical actions. In all cases, it is the "intention" or "will" that motivates one's actions that counts. The Buddha said, "It is will, O monks, that I call karma; having willed, one acts through body, speech, or mind."[7]

The Buddha would disagree with the saying "Sticks and stones may break my bones but words can never hurt me." As we all know, words can be very hurtful. Indeed, intentionally hurt feelings can be even harder to heal than an acciden-tally bruised body. The Buddha accordingly paid much attention to the mental karma of intentions and the verbal karma of speech. "Right speech" in the Buddha's Eightfold Path includes refraining not only from lying, but also from using rude and abusive speech, from belittling others, and from gossiping. The Buddha taught that we should speak not only truthfully but also kindly. Zen master Dōgen includes "loving speech," along with generosity, beneficial action, and nondual cooperation, among the Bodhisattva's Four Methods of Guidance. "Loving speech," he says, "means that when you see sentient beings, you arouse the heart of compassion and offer words of loving care. It is contrary to cruel or violent speech."[8]

Despite many popular treatments of karma, both in the ancient East and in the modern West, the basic Buddhist idea of karma is not that of an external supernatural force guaranteeing that "what goes around comes around," like we see in the amusing television show *My Name Is Earl*, in which the main character is trying to make up for all the bad things he has done before he gets run over by a bus or struck by lightning. If what goes around does in fact come around—as my cousin's new boyfriend whispered to me forty years ago when I playfully kicked him under my grandfather's Christmas dinner table—this happens according to the natural physical, psychological, and sociological laws of the universe.

However, the complexity of the universe—including the incalculable web of past actions that collectively influence the present—means that we can never fathom why something particular happens to a particular person at a particular time. The point of the teaching of karma is not to fully explain the present, much less to perfectly predict the future. The point is to understand that our actions have effects—not only on others but also, and even more directly, on ourselves.

We Make Habits and Habits Make Us

You reap what you sow. According to the Buddhist teaching of karma, this means that you become how you act. I find it helpful to think of it this way: *We make our habits, and our habits in turn make us.* Philosopher and Zen teacher David Loy makes the same point when he writes:

> We construct ourselves by what we choose to do. My sense of self is a precipitate of my habitual ways of thinking, feeling, and acting. Just as my body is composed of the food I eat, so my character is built by my conscious decisions. According to this approach, people are "punished" or "rewarded" not for what they have done but for what they have become, and what we intentionally do is what makes us what we are.[9]

Loy reiterates this understanding of karma by saying that "we are punished not *for* our sins but *by* them."[10] Yet, it may be best to avoid using the terms "punishment" and "sin" altogether here, since Buddhists think of bad karma not in terms of disobediently transgressing the commands of a transcendent Judge, but rather in terms of perpetuating and proliferating unwholesome "deluding afflictions" that cause us and those we affect to suffer.

In any case, the idea of karma as actions that shape our habits and thus our character is not unfamiliar to the Western philosophical tradition. Our English word "habit" derives from the Latin *habitus*, which in turn was used to translate the Greek term *hexis*. *Hexis* is the word Aristotle uses for our "moral character," since we learn moral virtues by habitually doing certain actions. For example, he says, "we become just by the practice of just actions, self-controlled by exercising self-control, and courageous by performing acts of courage."[11] It thus makes all the moral difference, he concludes, which habits we are inculcated in from childhood. We are not born virtuous, but rather become virtuous, or unvirtuous, by means of our habitual actions.

Let us look at the case of an unvirtuous moral characteristic. What does it mean, for example, to be a liar? In a recent congressional hearing, the man giving testimony had been convicted of lying the last time he testified before Congress. The question on everyone's mind was, "Can we trust this man to tell the truth this time?" Anticipating this question, the man said, "I have lied, but I am not a liar." One of the legislators responded by saying, in effect, "No, you lied, and by definition that means you are a liar."

Putting aside the facts of this particular case, let us think about the legislator's claim. If one has lied, does this necessarily mean that one is a liar? Or is it possible to lie and not be a liar? On the one hand, it makes sense to say that someone who sings is a singer, and someone who writes is a writer. On the other hand, does that mean that everyone who has ever sung in the shower is a singer and everyone who has ever scribbled on a notepad is a writer?

If the legislator's logic is correct, then *everyone* is a liar, since everyone over the age of three has told a lie at some point in life. If someone states that they have never lied, we can be sure that this statement is a lie. Contrary to the legislator's claim, and again putting aside the facts about the person who was testifying, I think it does make sense to say, "I have lied, but I am not a liar." Indeed, I would say this about myself.

So what *does* it mean, then, for someone to be a liar? I think it means that they lie *habitually*. The more one lies, the more one is inclined to lie. It becomes second nature. That's karma at work. A path through a field is made by walking, and a path made in the past determines where we will likely walk in the present and future. Of course, it only determines where we will *likely* walk. We may, after all, with some effort, clear a new path.

Another example I like to use with my college students is the karmic habit of drinking coffee, since many of them stop by Starbucks on their way to class. When she was twelve years old my daughter started going to Starbucks with friends after school. "How can you afford to buy anything there?" I asked her. She told me that they sell "syrup water" for fifty cents. I'm not sure if the kids had hacked the Starbucks menu system or if this was part of a long-term customer recruitment campaign. If the latter, it is a brilliant marketing ploy to get kids to make a habit of going there while they are young. Sell a kid some cheap syrup water and you make just a few pennies. But teach a kid to hang out in Starbucks and you've created a coffee-craving customer for life. At least my daughter has not fallen into the tobacco company trap of smoking candy-flavored electronic cigarettes. I did not tell my daughter to stop going to Starbucks, but I did tell her about a student of mine who shows up to class every day with not one but *two* large, and expensive, drinks from Starbucks. My frugal daughter's eyes widened. It was a lesson in karma: be aware of the internal and external forces shaping your behavior, so that you can make free and responsible shopping and self-shaping decisions.

Situated Freedom: Steering the Sailboats of Our Lives

Let's say that at some point in your life, you start drinking a cup of coffee in the morning. There are various social, psychological, and biological factors that influenced you in your decision to form this habit. But, a Buddhist would say, nothing entirely forced you to do it. There was at least an element of free choice involved. To some extent you chose not to resist the biological urges, social pressures from peers, and seductive advertisements.

Let's say that at some point you start drinking two, three, or even four cups of coffee a day. Guess what you are going to crave tomorrow when you wake up? That's "coffee karma" at work. Your self-created habit in turn created that craving. Perhaps it even becomes an addiction. Do you want to be addicted to coffee? No. Are you free to instantly stop craving those cups of coffee? No. Who did this to you? You did. Well, not just you—those targeted ads on social media probably had something to do with it.

The good news is that you still do have some freedom to change course. Think of the karmic effects of past actions as being like the momentum a large sailboat has as it moves in a certain direction across the ocean. The wind and the waves correspond to all the conditions of the present situation, including the effects that other people's actions have on you. You may be moving in a wholesome direction, but a strong wind blows you off course. Or you may be moving in an unwholesome direction, but luckily the winds of fortune happen to help bring you back on course. In any case, how you trim the sails and steer the rudder of your life-sailboat is up to you.

Of course, you cannot turn a large sailboat around on a dime, much less suddenly stop it from moving. But you can, working with the winds and waves and momentum, shift its direction and even, with time and effort, turn your life-sailboat around and head to safety. In the case of your coffee addiction, you cannot suddenly stop craving it. If you try to quit cold turkey, you may experience headaches and, even worse, you'll give people around you headaches with your grouchiness. But you can wean yourself down to two cups and then one cup a day. With a bit of professional counseling, you could even learn to switch to herbal tea.

Contrary to some past and present popular misconceptions, karma is not a teaching of determinism. It is rather a teaching of *situated freedom*. The eminent scholar of early Buddhism Richard Gombrich claims that "the key to the Buddha's thought is the doctrine of karma and the idea that we are all responsible for ourselves," and that "the entire Buddhist ideology depends on the proposition that karma is on the one hand conditioned but on the other not strictly determined."[12] Quoting the words of the Buddha, the Theravada Buddhist monk and scholar Nyanaponika Thera emphasizes what he calls "the freedom inherent in the karmic situation." He says that "the lawfulness which governs karma does not operate with mechanical rigidity but allows for a considerably wide range of modifications in the ripening of the fruit."[13] He goes on to write:

> The fact that karmic results are modifiable frees us from the bane of determinism and its ethical corollary, fatalism, and keeps the road to liberation constantly open before us. . . . Any individual's moral choice may be severely limited by the varying load of greed, hatred and delusion and their results which he carries around; yet every time he stops to make a decision or a choice, he is potentially free to throw off that load, at least temporarily.[14]

Of course, often when we think we are making a free choice, really we are just acting on unconscious urges or desires that have probably been shaped by peer pressure or advertising. The doctrine of karma teaches us not only about how situated genuine freedom really is, but also about how difficult it is. Philosopher Christopher Gowans writes, "The heart of the Buddha's position is that causal conditioning in the sense of creating powerful inclinations is consistent with choices and actions contrary to those inclinations." Karma is thus "not a form of determinism," he says, since "the Buddha thinks we are always free to choose the morally better or worse course. . . . To some extent our character may be determined by past actions, but our character never fully determines our actions."[15]

Buddhists speak of karma not only in terms of "causes," but also in terms of "conditions." An apple seed will grow into an apple tree only with the right conditions of soil, sun, and rain. The teaching of karma is meant to alert us to the web of causes and conditions that affect our lives, not so that we become fatalists, but so that we can best exercise our situated freedom.

The modern Vietnamese Zen master Thich Nhat Hanh writes that "our habit energies [Sk. *vasana*] are often stronger than our volition," which is why we "say and do things we don't want to and afterwards we regret it." Western theologians and philosophers have called this the problem of "weakness of will." Theists call on the grace of God to give them the strength to do what they know is the right thing to do. As a Zen Buddhist, Nhat Hanh speaks rather of the power of mindfulness: "Mindfulness is the energy that allows us to recognize our habit energy and prevent it from dominating us."[16]

The seventeenth-century Japanese Zen master Bankei stresses the freedom inherent in the working of karma in order to clearly reject any sort of fatalism or making of excuses when he teaches: "Whether you steal or not is determined by you yourself, not by any karma." With a bit more nuance, he says:

> No mother ever gave birth to a thief. . . . People turn into thieves by watching others exercising their bad habits and imitating them, stealing things of their own accord, because of their own greed. Now how can that be called inborn? . . . A thief may rationalize his problem by laying the blame on his karma, telling you that he cannot help himself. . . . You don't steal because of your karma. Stealing itself is the karma. Suppose theft were caused by karma, suppose stealing were inborn, it's still possible for a thief to realize that what he's been doing is wrong and to stop stealing.[17]

I think the Dharma of Karma can help us think about both sides of the stealing story: about the causes and conditions that created the situation in which, and the personal character with which, people are inclined to steal; and about people's freedom to resist those inclinations, to chart a new course, and to contribute to reshaping the situation for themselves and others.

The Fox Kōan: Freedom Within Karmic Causality

The most famous kōan about karma is the so-called Fox Kōan, which notably is placed second in *The Gateless Barrier* collection of kōans. Although it is sometimes considered to be an advanced and "difficult to pass" kōan, I think Zen master Wumen placed it second in *The Gateless Barrier* for a good reason. The first kōan in the collection is the *Mu* kōan, which is the most famous "initial barrier" kōan (see Chapter 22). If a practitioner really breaks through that barrier, he or she feels totally liberated, utterly free from the bounds and bonds of the ego.

I think the Fox Kōan is meant to bring one back down to earth and, specifically, to keep one from falling into the trap of what has come to be known as "wild fox Zen." In the story of the kōan, an ancient abbot of a monastery condemned himself to be reborn as a wild fox for five hundred lifetimes by saying that an enlightened person "does not fall into karmic causality." He was finally freed from the fox body after being taught that an enlightened person "does not obscure karmic causality."[18]

The central question of the kōan is the relation between "not falling into karmic causality" and "not obscuring karmic causality." To think that one has transcended the world of karmic causality, so that one does not need to pay attention to the causes and effects of one's actions, is in fact to blindly fall into karmic causality in the worst way. Thinking one is simply free from karmic influences, one becomes oblivious to the ways such influences work to shape one's thoughts, words, and deeds. Drunk on one's newfound feeling of freedom, and thinking one has transcended all karmic conditioning once and for all, one plunges headlong into the pitfall of wild fox Zen. Every serious Zen practitioner has to beware of this perilous pitfall, precisely because it lies near the path that must be trodden.

To not obscure karmic causality, to not be oblivious to its workings, is neither to fall into nor to not fall into karmic causality. The point of this especially tricky kōan is that we are free not by transcending karmic causality, but rather by awakening to its ubiquitous workings. Only by maintaining an awareness of the karmic forces at work in the world and—most importantly—in and on oneself can one keep one's hand on the rudder of one's situated freedom. A good sailor, after all, steers her boat not by ignoring but by attentively working with the momentum, wind, and waves.

Self-Determination and Living Without Expectations

Because karma is not a deterministic teaching, because it is a teaching of situated freedom, that also means it is a teaching of personal responsibility and self-determination. We make our habits, and our habits in turn make us. That means that we are responsible for who we become. In a sense, this is a very self-empowering idea. You are what you make of yourself.

Abraham Lincoln reportedly once said that "every man over forty is responsible for his face." I remember looking around in church as a child and marveling at the smiles etched into some older people's faces and the scowls etched into others'. If you laugh a lot, you'll get laugh lines. If you frown a lot, you'll get frown lines. That's facial karma at work. The Buddha himself taught that habitual anger and irritableness "lead to ugliness," both in this life and in the next.[19]

Of course, Lincoln's and the Buddha's statements could easily be misapplied. Surely there are some people with beautiful faces but less than beautiful personalities, and vice versa. Sometimes I feel sorry for children who are being spoiled because of their good looks, since it will be harder for them to keep or acquire that true beauty that is more than skin deep. Lincoln and the Buddha were presumably talking about the manner in which one's personality is expressed in one's habitual facial expressions, not about the shape of one's nose or the structure of one's cheekbones. Still, these statements indicate how the self-empowering teaching of karma can and has been misused, not only on popular TV shows but also by whole Buddhist populations.[20]

It is important to bear in mind that the Buddha taught that the precise working out of the results of karma is one of the "unthinkables." That is to say, exactly what cause, or set of causes, led to this or that effect is one of the facts in the universe that are incomprehensible.[21] He taught that the web of karmic causes and effects is so complex that it is impossible to calculate what caused a specific thing to happen—for example, why a person was born with a special ability or with a disability. Unfortunately, Buddhists have not always heeded the Buddha's warning.

On a popular level, Buddhists have often been preoccupied not only with avoiding the consequences of bad karma, but also with stockpiling karmic merit for benefits in this life and the next. In Zen, such thoughts of earning karmic merit are relegated to a relatively superficial level of teaching and practice. According to a famous and foundational legend, when Bodhidharma arrived in China, he was asked by Emperor Wu how much karmic merit the emperor had accumulated by having many temples built, sutras copied, and monks ordained. Bodhidharma replied, "No merit."[22] True merit, he implied, comes from acting freely and responsibly without any egocentric calculations of merit. This phrase, "no merit," has become a basic teaching in Zen, one that often appears on scrolls of calligraphy.

Yet this was apparently not all that Bodhidharma had to say about the Dharma of Karma. In a canonical though less often read text attributed to him, we are taught to accept bad as well as good fortune as the results of our past karma. Let's look at two passages from this text. The first one reads:

> When experiencing suffering, a practitioner of the Way should reflect: "For innumerable eons, I have preferred the superficial to the fundamental, drifting through various states of existence, creating much animosity and hatred, bringing endless harm and discord. Though I have done nothing wrong in this life, I am reaping the natural consequences of past offenses, my evil karma. It is not meted out by some heavenly agency. I accept it patiently and with contentment, utterly without animosity or complaint."[23]

The second passage reads:

> If you experience such positive rewards as wealth and fame, this results from past causes. . . . Not to be moved by even the winds of good fortune is ineffable accord with the Way. Thus it is called the practice of accepting one's circumstances.[24]

The modern Rinzai Zen master Harada Shōdō quotes the following poem by the eighteenth-century Sōtō Zen master Ryōkan in order to illustrate what this radical acceptance of one's circumstances entails:

> To meet with disaster at the time of disaster is fine just as it is. / To meet with illness at the time of illness is fine just as it is. / To meet with death at the time of death is fine just as it is.[25]

To be clear, this Zen teaching of utterly accepting even disaster, illness, or death does *not* mean that we should not try to do anything and everything we can to prevent and alleviate such calamities. On the contrary, we can change reality, when it can be changed, only by accepting it in the sense of facing up to it. Wishing bad things had not happened is only going to compound one's suffering and distract one from doing something about it. Only by accepting that "this is way things are right now" can we go about realistically working to improve the situation.

Sometimes we can improve the situation, but sometimes we cannot. We all need to be ready to accept death when the time comes. That is no doubt the ultimate task and test. To work up to it, we can start by taking a deep breath and accepting that we are stuck in a traffic jam or have come down with a cold. I think that one of the secrets to happiness—as well as to discerning what we can change and what we cannot—is to accept that what is happening is, in fact, what is happening.

A second secret to happiness is as difficult as it is liberating. It is to have, in one's innermost heart, no expectations. Every expectation sets us up for disappointment. Think about it: even if an expectation is fulfilled, we merely break even. By contrast, if one works hard or gives freely without any expectation of reward, then one can truly appreciate as a gift the good results that may come one's way. This is why Bodhidharma sought to free Emperor Wu from his obsession with earning merit. This is why Dōgen says that the most genuine Zen practitioners "seek the Way without expecting a reward," for the seeking is the Way and it is its own reward.[26]

Why Do Bad Things Happen to Good People?

In the text from which we have been reading, Bodhidharma goes so far as to say that one should take responsibility even for one's misfortunes. This is hard to swallow, metaphysically and ethically as well as existentially. Does it really make sense to accept responsibility for all the bad things that happen to one? To be sure, Bodhidharma does not say that we should tell others to do this. In effect, he teaches us not to say "*you* reap what *you* sow," but rather always only "*I* reap what *I* sow." The focus is always on my own responsibility for my own karma and my own circumstances. Still, it is hard to refrain from generalizing his point, which problematically leads to pointing at others and their circumstances. When bad things happen to good people, as they often do, it does not seem right to think that they deserve it.

The more one thinks about it, the fact that bad things happen to good people is hard to explain in any manner whatsoever. If it is not the ripening of the fruit of their past karma, how else could we explain why bad things happen to people? Is it the Will of God? But why would a good God cause so much undeserved pain and suffering? Because of original sin? Does that mean that there are no good people? Is the child with cancer paying for something Adam and Eve did? Or do bad things happen just because of bad luck? Is our fate then just a matter of chance? Is there no meaning to anything that happens? Is there, after all, no cosmic justice at work in the world?

There may be no really satisfying answer to the question of why bad things happen to good people. The Buddha and the Bible explain why bad things happen to bad people, but they don't really explain why they happen to good people. Why did God create sinners? Or, why did people start acting badly and producing unwholesome karmic effects to begin with?

In fact, the Buddha did not attempt to give an answer to the question of the origin of the universe and the beginning of bad karma. He taught us to attend to the already existing workings of karma the best we can in order to become free and responsible. He also taught us not to try to calculate why specific things happen to specific people, or why the chains of bad karma started churning in the first place. Buddhism does not have the same "problem of evil" that biblical monotheism does, and so Buddhists have not been obsessed with theodicy—that is, with the attempt to explain why there is so much suffering in a world that is created by an all-powerful, all-knowing, and all-loving deity. Christian theologians have suggested such reasons as the need for obstacles on the path toward the perfection of our souls, or the limits of our abilities to fathom the wisdom of the Will of God.[27]

The Buddha just said that, from time immemorial, we have been producing and reproducing bad karma on the basis of ignorance. He also said that while the cycle of ignorance and suffering is beginningless, it is not endless, or at least it need not be. We can put an end to ignorance and thus to needless suffering. This is the promise of Nirvana.

Beyond Blaming the Victim: Karmic Interconnections

In conclusion to this discussion of karma, we need to return to a particular misuse of this teaching that the Buddha warned us about: pointing the finger at others. Moreover, we need to dare to question the text attributed to Bodhidharma and extend this critical consideration to the problem with pointing the finger at oneself. After all, as Nyanaponika Thera puts it, "each individual life-stream is interwoven with many other individual life-streams through the interaction of their respective karmas," and so it does not really make sense to blame an individual, including oneself, for everything that happens to him or her.[28] In many cases, that would be, as we say, to "blame the victim."

Rather than say "*you* reap what *you* sow," and better even than keeping the focus on "*I* reap what *I* sow," it is more helpful and wholesome to think in terms of "*we* reap what *we* sow." And, frankly, the distribution of the effects of our individual and collective actions is clearly not always fair.

Let us take an especially poignant case in point. In a letter to the editor of a Buddhist magazine, Jack Harris, a practicing Buddhist, wrote that he cannot accept the idea that all the negative things that happen to people are the result of their own past karma. Based on his childhood experience of having been sexually assaulted by what he calls "an afflicted individual wearing the garb of a Catholic priest," Harris delivers a powerful critique of this simplistic understanding of karma as, in effect, blaming the victim.

Nevertheless, Harris does not reject the teaching of karma. Rather, he thoughtfully urges us to understand it in the more nuanced manner that the Buddha originally intended. He writes:

> In my own healing process I've come to view the notion of karma as part of an interdependent web of causation. While I'm not responsible for the violence waged on my body . . . I am responsible for how I live out and process those experiences over the course of my life. . . . I often liken karma to ripples in a pond and see my pond as connected to [others'] ponds by creeks and rivers and inlets and bays. The negative actions of one person create ripples in a pond that in some cases become roaring waves that obliterate all in [their] path. The challenge for those of us who become victims . . . of afflicted, greedy, and grasping individuals is to restore our own pond to calmness . . . so that our ripples don't storm out of the creek and overwhelm the next person's pond.[29]

Harris's sage advice reflects a deep understanding of the Dharma of Karma. If followed, it would prevent victims not only from blaming themselves, but also from becoming themselves victimizers—a sadly common spiral of violence.

I wish not only that the "afflicted individual wearing the garb of a Catholic priest" would have better understood the awful effects of his utterly un-Christian actions, but also that certain recent masters of "wild fox Zen" in the United States who have had hurtful sexual relations with students would have more deeply understood the Dharma of Karma.[30] I also wish they would have taken more seriously the ethical teachings of Zen that we will discuss in Chapter 16.

16

Zen and Morality

Following Rules to Where There Are No Rules

The Moral Part of the Path

In Chapter 15, we saw how the Dharma of Karma is a teaching of cause and effect. It teaches us, for example, to attend to how our present state of mind is conditioned in large part by our mental and emotional habits. Karma means action, not just physical action, but also actions of speech and thought. Each thought we have is a karmic act. This is why practicing positive thinking shapes one's mindset and, eventually, one's character. Habitual negative thinking, unfortunately, does this as well.

The Buddha taught "right effort" as one of the limbs of the Eightfold Path.[1] He breaks right effort down into four parts: (1) not giving rise to unwholesome thoughts and emotions; (2) removing those unwholesome thoughts and emotions that we already have; (3) arousing wholesome thoughts and emotions; and (4) cultivating those wholesome thoughts and emotions that we already have. Right effort thus belongs with right mindfulness and concentration in the mental training part of the Eightfold Path.

While we purify our minds with right effort, mindfulness, and concentration, we purify our verbal and physical actions with right speech, action, and livelihood, which together make up the moral training part of the Eightfold Path. Right view and right intention make up the wisdom part of the Path. Summarizing these three parts of the Eightfold Path, Zen joins other schools of Buddhism in speaking of the Three Learnings: morality, meditation, and wisdom.

Early Buddhists compiled the Buddha's moral instructions, largely consisting of monastic regulations, into a group of texts called the Vinaya. Along with the Buddha's sermons (sutras) and later commentaries on the philosophical principles of his teachings, called the Abhidharma, the Vinaya is one part of the Tripitaka or "Three Baskets" of the early Buddhist Canon.

The moral regulations boil down to the "precepts," the basic rules for behavior that monastics and lay Buddhists vow to maintain. In the version of the Vinaya adopted by East Asian Buddhist traditions, monks are expected to abide by 253 such rules, and nuns by 348. Despite the fact that the Buddha taught that women are just as capable as men of attaining enlightenment, this discrepancy between

Zen Pathways. Bret W. Davis, Oxford University Press. © Oxford University Press 2022.
DOI: 10.1093/oso/9780197573686.003.0016

the number of male and female monastic regulations reflects a persistent patriarchal bias of the Buddhist tradition.

As mentioned in Chapter 14, Zen master Dōgen reminded his peers of the spiritual equality of women and men. To his thirteenth-century Japanese audience, he denounced seeing women merely as sexual objects and what he called the ridiculous and crooked custom of not allowing nuns and laywomen into certain secluded areas of Buddhist temples. Dōgen emphatically taught that when looking for a genuine Zen teacher, one should not discriminate between male and female. He writes: "Why are men special? . . . Both men and women attain the Way. You should honor attainment of the Way. Do not discriminate between men and women."[2] Four centuries later the Rinzai Zen master Bankei plainly makes the same point: "Men and women are not the same in appearance. We all know that. But there's not a whisker of difference between them when it comes to their buddha-minds."[3]

Unfortunately, discrimination against women in the Zen tradition, as in other Buddhist traditions, has persisted to this day. One of the refreshingly reformist movements currently under way, especially in the West, is to echo and amplify the teachings of gender equality to be found in the Zen tradition, and to critique the tradition where it has not lived up to its own ideals.[4]

Questioning the Golden Rule: Beyond Egoistic Conceptions of Good and Evil

Dōgen stands out not only for the complexly philosophical nature of many of his writings, but also for his clear emphasis on morality. Especially in his later years, Dōgen stressed the moral causality of karma, the practice of repentance along with meditation, and the importance of taking the precepts.

Dōgen was not the first Zen master in Japan to stress the importance of the moral precepts. The teacher of Dōgen's first Zen teacher, Myōan Eisai, who introduced Rinzai Zen to Japan at the end of the twelfth century, claimed that the precepts are the foundation for Zen practice.[5] Eisai made this claim in light of what he saw as a moral laxity in Japanese Buddhism at the time. In particular, Eisai was critical of a self-styled Zen teacher named Dainichi Nōnin. Nōnin stressed the antinomian and apparently amoral aspects of Zen, such as Linji's teaching that people should just act naturally, eating when hungry and lying down when tired. Dōgen criticized Nōnin's false understanding of what it means to act naturally, citing his Chinese Zen teacher Rujing's denunciation of "the heresy of naturalism."[6]

Another potentially misleading—if misunderstood—teaching of Zen in this regard is the key kōan of the Sixth Chinese Ancestor, Huineng: "Think not of good, think not of evil. At this very moment, what is your Original Face before your father and mother were born?"[7] This kōan pushes practitioners to awaken to their true self, the pure awareness of their open mind and heart, rather than identifying themselves first and foremost with the particulars of their biology and psychology, and especially rather than identifying themselves with their egoistically judgmental minds. The modern Japanese Rinzai Zen master Hirata Seikō says that this is the point of *zazen*; situated in the middle of the Three Learnings of morality, meditation, and wisdom, it is the pivotal role of Zen meditation to purify the mind of all oppositions and relativities, even those of good and evil, in order to enable the non-egoistic discernments of morality and wisdom to function in the concrete and fluid contexts of our lives.[8]

When Huineng says that to awaken to one's Original Face one needs to put aside all thoughts of good and evil, he is saying that we have to relinquish our egoistic judgments of what is good for me and bad for me, judgments that are based on a dualistic separation of oneself from others. Huineng is not saying that one should never again think of good and evil. Rather, he implies that we need to make such judgments from a nondualistic and non-egoistic awareness rather than a dualistic and egoistic distortion of the context in which we are making them. The open heart-mind of our true self, our Buddha-nature, is prior to the constrictions imposed on our unenlightened heart-minds by our egocentric and ethnocentric prejudices. When Huineng traveled north and first encountered the Fifth Chinese Ancestor, Hongren, the master tested him by saying, "You're from [the southern province of] Lingnan and so you're a barbarian. How could you become a Buddha?" Huineng impressed him with his answer: "Although people are southerners and northerners, the Buddha-nature has neither south nor north."[9]

Ethnocentrism is, sadly, as old and as ubiquitous as egocentrism. And all too often, they not only affect our immoral attitudes and actions but also infect our sense of morality itself. How much evil, after all, has been inflicted on others by imposing on them one's own egocentric or ethnocentric conception of the good? This is why I have always been somewhat ambivalent about the Golden Rule, at least in the formulation of it we get in the Bible: "Do unto others as you would have them do unto you."[10] I prefer the formulations of the Golden Rule by Confucius and the Buddha. Confucius says, "Do not impose upon others what you yourself do not desire."[11] And the Buddha says, "Hurt not others with what pains yourself."[12] In fact, this is akin to the version we are given by Hillel, a rabbi who lived a few years before Jesus. He says, "That which is hateful to you do not do to another; that is the entire Torah, and the rest is its interpretation."[13]

The reason why I prefer the more cautious "negative formulations" of the Golden Rule by Confucius, Buddha, and Hillel is that it is easier for us to understand what people *would not want* us to do to them than it is for us to understand what they *would want* us to do. For example, I am quite sure that a new acquaintance does not want me to hit him in the face each time we meet, but I might not know whether he wants a kiss on the cheek, a hug, or a bow from a respectful distance. Many Americans like to give and receive hugs, but most Japanese people definitely don't, and so a gregarious show of affection can easily be taken as an awkward and uncomfortable imposition.

To take a much more egregious example, Western imperialist powers have thought it was the "white man's burden" to bring civilization to other lands, and the results of our cultural assimilationist programs have been mixed at best and extraordinarily cruel at worst. For example, Capt. Richard H. Pratt's slogan "Kill the Indian, and save the man" was used to justify brutally stripping Native American schoolchildren of their native languages and cultures in order to sup- posedly uplift them by forcing them to conform to the ways of the whites.[14]

The lesson to be learned is that only to the extent that we are able to put aside our ethnocentric as well as egocentric standards of judgment are we capable of being open to others, of listening to them and learning about their likes and needs. And only then are we able to appropriately respond to them—a response that will inevitably involve learning as well as teaching. This is why it is ethically necessary to suspend our egocentric and ethnocentric conceptions of good and evil and return to the open heart-mind of our Original Face.

Nevertheless, from Nōnin to contemporary mavericks posing as Zen mas- ters and other stripes of spiritual gurus who claim that their self-serving and harmful acts are "beyond good and evil," the teachings of Huineng and Linji have been subject to misunderstanding and misuse. Fortunately, Zen masters from Eisai and Dōgen in medieval Japan to Robert Aitkin[15] and Reb Anderson[16] in modern America have been there to remind us of the sense and significance of the precepts and other moral teachings of Zen.

The sixteenth-century Korean Zen master So Sahn gives one of the strongest statements of the moral prerequisites for practicing Zen mediation:

> Practicing Zen meditation while remaining immersed in sexual concerns is like cooking sand for a meal. Practicing Zen meditation while yet not avoiding killing any living thing is like a person who plugs his own ears and then shouts something important to himself. Practicing Zen meditation with a mind that would steal is like trying to fill a leaky bowl. And a liar who practices Zen med- itation is a person who would try to use feces for incense. Even for the one who has much wisdom, such failings can only lead you to the way of demons.[17]

The Basic Moral Precepts

Whereas Eisai promoted taking the detailed Hinayana as well as the Mahayana precepts, Dōgen paired the precepts down to the most important, the sixteen

"Bodhisattva Precepts" that he thought lay as well as monastic Buddhists ought to take. (Rinzai Buddhists today take a somewhat similar set of precepts.)

The Bodhisattva Precepts consist of taking refuge in the Buddha, the Dharma (the Buddhist teachings), and the Sangha (the Buddhist community); the Three Pure Precepts of observing prohibitions, doing good deeds, and benefitting all living beings; and the Ten Grave Precepts, namely, not to kill, steal, misuse sex, lie, deal in intoxicants, criticize the faults of lay or monastic Bodhisattvas, praise oneself and disparage others, be stingy with the Dharma or material goods, become angry, or revile the Three Jewels (the Buddha, Dharma, and Sangha).[18]

The first five of the Ten Grave Precepts are the basic moral guidelines that laypeople as well as monastics are expected to abide by in all Buddhist traditions. Sometimes called the Five Lay Precepts, these prohibit killing, stealing, sexual misconduct, false speech, and intoxication. The modern American Zen master John Daido Loori, an heir to both Sōtō and Rinzai Zen traditions, rephrases these prohibitions so as to foreground their positive implications. Showing both sides of each precept coin, he renders them as follows: (1) Affirm life; do not kill. (2) Be giving; do not steal. (3) Honor the body; do not misuse sexuality. (4) Manifest truth; do not lie. (5) Proceed clearly; do not cloud the mind.[19]

These precepts are meant to guide Zen practitioners in skillful thought, speech, and action. They are not commandments dictated by an external judge, but rather tried-and-true lessons for how to act so as to liberate oneself and others from suffering.

Ultimately, There Are No Fixed Rules

As important as the precepts are in Zen, it does not condone a literalistic legalism. The precepts and other prescriptions for behavior in Zen are not meant to be fixed rules that one should unwaveringly follow regardless of time and place. While many of Dōgen's writings are devoted to prescribing detailed monastic guidelines for everything from preparing food to washing one's face and using the toilet, these are not meant to be legalistic rules for a community of anal-retentive fundamentalists. For all Dōgen's increasing stress in his later years on moral precepts and monastic rules, he does not waver from his conviction that, as Hee-Jin Kim puts it, "these norms were not fixed values to which we legalistically conform, but living expressions of the bodhisattva's free and pure activities in accordance with circumstances and occasions."[20]

In the end, Dōgen continues to affirm the ninth-/tenth-century Chinese Zen master Yunmen's statement that "in expressing full function, there are no fixed methods,"[21] which itself echoes the claim by the Third Chinese Ancestor, Sengcan, that "when one attains to the ultimate state, there are no fixed rules."[22]

To be sure, at first, and for a long time—maybe even for multiple lifetimes—we need rules, we need guidelines. Until we are able to discover that the spirit of the law emanates from within, from our own Buddha-nature, we need the letter of the law to provisionally guide us from without. Yet we should not get stuck at the level of doing good and not doing evil simply because that is what someone else is telling us to do and not to do. We should not be content to simply follow the rules of an externally decreed prescriptive and proscriptive morality. Insofar as we open the eye of wisdom, we open the heart of compassion—and, to that extent, our moral actions are increasingly done naturally and even effortlessly, rather than artificially and forcefully.

From Prescription to Description

Dōgen makes this point most strikingly in his interpretation of the "Verse of Common Precepts of the Seven Buddhas." A translation of the ancient Pali version of this famous verse as it appears in the *Dhammapada*, one of the earliest records of the Buddha's teachings, reads: "To shun all evil. To do good. To purify one's heart. This is the teaching of the Buddhas."[23]

Dōgen agrees that, in the beginning, one hears the first line as an imperative: "Do no evil!" However, he then creatively plays on the ambiguities of Chinese and Japanese grammar to claim that, in the end, the proper way to read the phrase is not as a *prescription* but rather as a *description*: the non-doing of evil.

Dōgen similarly reads "do good" as a portrayal of enlightened acts rather than an imperative to improve one's behavior. And finally, given that the initial character in the third line of the Chinese translation of the text can mean "naturally," Dōgen's reading suggests that this line can be understood as "the mind is naturally purified."[24] As the contemporary Japanese philosopher and Sōtō Zen priest Arifuku Kōgaku comments, for Dōgen "the good is not just something that should be done, it is something that is naturally done."[25]

In short, the point of Dōgen's creative hermeneutics here is that while the precepts initially appear as moral *prescriptions* to be voluntarily followed, through practice one realizes that they are *descriptions* of enlightened actions done naturally. Although an unenlightened person experiences the precepts as restrictive, Dōgen says that such teachings and practices "have never hindered the Buddhas and Ancestors."[26]

Thomas Kasulis elaborates on Dōgen's point by imagining how he would treat the biblical phrase "Thou shalt not kill." Dōgen would probably say that in the beginning, one would take this as a divine command. "After some time, however, the efficacy of one's spiritual cultivation is such that one is no longer capable of murder. At that point, one suddenly sees the phrase as a description: '[You are now such a person that] you will not kill.'"[27]

Ultimately, as Bodhidharma's rephrasing of the precepts illustrates, they are not prescriptive but rather descriptive of the functioning of the self-nature of the enlightened mind. For example, instead of the prescription "Do not kill," Bodhidharma says, "Self-nature is subtle and mysterious. In the realm of everlasting Dharma, not giving rise to concepts [or views] of killing is called the Precept of Not Killing."[28] Thoughts or intentions of killing, stealing, lying, and so forth simply do not enter a Buddha's mind. In other words, they do not enter the Buddha-mind that is our true self. It is only because we have not yet awakened to our original Buddha-mind, our true self-nature, that we separate ourselves from others, a separation that gives rise to greed and hatred, which in turn give rise to thoughts and acts of stealing, killing, and so forth, in either a literal or metaphorical sense of these egoistic deeds. The more we awaken to our original self-nature or Buddha-mind, the less need we have for external prescriptions to guide our actions.

Compassionately Breaking the Moral Rules

The ultimate moral and spiritual compass in Mahayana Buddhism is the vow to liberate all sentient beings from suffering. This is the first of the Great Vows recited daily by Zen Buddhists: "However limitless sentient beings are, I vow to liberate them all." Whether a particular act is good or not, and whether a certain precept is a helpful guide to conduct in a particular situation, can be determined in terms of whether it helps or hinders the fulfillment of this Great Vow.

The more one becomes motivated by this Great Vow, the more this moral compass is discovered within, and the less need one has for external prescriptions and proscriptions. This also means that the more one naturally embodies the spirit of the law, the less bound one is to the artificial letter of the law. Along with other Zen masters and the rest of the Mahayana Buddhist tradition, Dōgen affirms that Bodhisattvas may at times need to break the precepts out of compassionate use of "skillful means" in their endeavor to liberate all sentient beings.[29]

The modern Korean Zen master Seung Sahn says that, since in Mahayana Buddhism the precepts are kept not in order to help oneself but to serve all sentient beings, this means that "in some situations, breaking the precepts can help others much better than holding the precepts." What is most important is compassion and clarity of mind. "If your mind is clear, then keeping the precepts is correct practice, and breaking the precepts is also correct practice," he says, giving the example of lying to a hunter in order to save a poor rabbit's life.[30]

The most famous account of skillful or expedient means is found in the *Lotus Sutra*'s parable about a father who saves his children from a burning house by telling them that their favorite toy carts are waiting for them outside.[31] The point of this parable is that a Bodhisattva can, and indeed should, use the expedient means of telling a noble lie for the sake of ultimately conveying a liberating truth.

From a Mahayana point of view, the Hinayana moralist's "attachment to the precepts" turns medicine into poison. How often have rigid rules, set in stone sometime in the distant past, gotten in the way of our ability to respond appropriately to present circumstances? A wonderful story about two Zen monks illustrates the priority of context-sensitive compassion over rule-bound morality. It goes like this:

> Tanzan and Ekido were once traveling together down a muddy road. A heavy rain was still falling. Coming around a bend, they met a lovely girl in a silk kimono and sash, unable to cross the intersection. "Come on, girl," said Tanzan at once. Lifting her in his arms, he carried her over the mud. Ekido did not speak again until that night when they reached a lodging temple. Then he no longer could restrain himself. "We monks don't go near females," he told Tanzan, "especially not young and lovely ones. It is dangerous. Why did you do that?" "I left the girl there," said Tanzan. "Are you still carrying her?"[32]

The moral of the story, so to speak, is to not let moral rules get in the way of doing good. Moral rules are generally helpful as abstract guidelines for good acts, but our acts themselves always take place in concrete contexts.

Moral Dilemmas: When Rules Conflict

In the concrete contexts of our lives, we sometimes find ourselves in what ethicists call "double binds." For example, we don't think that people should lie, but we also don't think that people should allow friends to be harmed. So, what should we do if a murderer arrives at our doorstep and asks whether our friend is hiding inside? Of course, most of us would say that in such a situation it is better to break the rule against lying than to let our friend be killed. To be sure, some of the moral dilemmas that we study in a college ethics class—like how to choose whom to put on the limited space of a lifeboat—are real head-scratchers. But this one seems to be a no-brainer. And yet, believe it or not, one of the most famous ethical philosophers of all times, Immanuel Kant, argued that we should not lie even to the murderer on the doorstep![33]

So much the worse for the persuasiveness of Kant's ethical theory, we might think. But what about those more difficult dilemmas? What about the "runaway trolley" case, in which we are able to save five workers only if we sacrifice another person by pushing him onto the tracks so as to derail the trolley before it runs over them? In fact, military commanders make this kind of "lesser of two evils" judgment all the time.[34]

The *Skill in Means Sutra* tells a rather shocking story of the Buddha as a Bodhisattva in a former life.[35] As a ship captain in the story, the future Buddha learns that a bandit has boarded the ship and plans to kill all five hundred passengers. The only three possible courses of action are (1) to not do anything and let the bandit murder the five hundred passengers; (2) to tell the passengers so that they could preemptively kill the bandit; or (3) to kill the bandit himself.

As with all such pedagogical parables, we are not allowed to ask: "Why can't he just tie the bandit up?" In order to think about rather than evade the dilemma, we have to accept the story's premise that these are the only three possibilities. The future Buddha decides on the third course of action and kills the bandit himself. His reasoning was not just that killing one person is less bad than letting five hundred be killed, but also that it is better to suffer the karmic consequences of killing a person himself rather than to let others commit this act and suffer the karmic consequences.

The Limits of Pacifism

So, despite all that was said in Chapter 14 about its promotion of peace, it turns out that Buddhism does not teach absolute pacifism. Come to think of it, neither did that great teacher of non-violent resistance, Gandhi, who once said: "I do believe where there is a choice only between cowardice and violence, I would advise violence." What prompted this remark was a question from Gandhi's eldest son, who asked what he should have done if had he been present when Gandhi was almost fatally assaulted in 1908. Gandhi told his son that, were he to find himself in such a situation, he should use physical force to stop the assailant rather than run away. Despite his firm belief that "non-violence is infinitely superior to violence" and that "forgiveness is more manly than punishment," if it were not possible to do so non-violently, Gandhi told his son, "it was his duty to defend me even by using violence."[36]

Gandhi's favorite book was the *Bhagavad Gita*, the most widely read and treasured of all Hindu scriptures. This may seem odd, however, insofar as the story of the *Bhagavad Gita* seems to condone war—indeed, a cataclysmic war between cousins. In the beginning of the *Bhagavad Gita*, Arjuna, the main protagonist, falls to his knees and drops his weapons just as he is preparing to signal the start of the conflict. Looking across at the opponents he was preparing to fight, he could not bring himself to kill his own kith and kin. The reader is meant to realize that all wars are wars between relatives. Blinded by racism and nationalism, we forget that there is only one human race. Adam and Eve—as names for our earliest human ancestors—were Africans.

But if the point that all wars are wars among relatives is powerfully and poignantly driven home by the setting of the *Bhagavad Gita*, why then does Krishna, the avatar or incarnation of God on earth, tell Arjuna to get up and fight? All of Krishna's spiritual teachings, on which Gandhi based his life and his teachings of non-violence, culminate in convincing Arjuna to rise up and march forth into this bloodbath.

Gandhi's answer is that the battle scene is not a literal one but rather a metaphor; the real battle is between the forces of good and evil in one's own heart.[37] There is indeed some textual support for this allegorical interpretation. At one point Krishna tells Arjuna to "let the Atman [i.e., the true self] rule the ego. Use your mighty arms to slay the fierce enemy that is selfish desire."[38]

However, the orthodox interpretation in the Hindu tradition is that the war was a literal one and that Arjuna was a warrior; however difficult it was for him, it was his duty to fight in an unavoidable war for a just cause.[39] Thus, in contrast to Gandhi's allegorical interpretation, the *Bhagavad Gita* has traditionally been interpreted as a scriptural basis for what political philosophers call "just war theory."

Yet, I wonder if we have to choose between Gandhi's allegorical interpretation and the orthodox literal one. Perhaps the real point of the text is that we have to engage in an inner struggle between the good and evil in our own hearts in order to know when and where to fight for a just cause, when and where violence is really unavoidable or the lesser of two evils.

Non-violence (Sk. *ahimsa*) is a cardinal virtue in all three of the major religions that originated in ancient India: Hinduism, Buddhism, and Jainism. It is the Jains who have taken this teaching the most seriously—or at least to the most literal extremes. The strictest of Jains wear a veil over their mouths and sweep the ground in front of them in order to avoid accidentally inhaling or stepping on any tiny insects.[40] Many of us can respect the sentiment, but most of us are not going to go that far out of our way to avoid harming any living creature. I confess that I've slapped a fair number of mosquitoes in my backyard, even though—much to the chagrin of my borderline entomophobic daughter—whenever feasible I do practice catch-and-release with insects crawling or flying around our home.

I am not an absolute vegetarian. I was in the past, but stopped after I got really sick from eating vegetables that had been cooked together with meat in, of all places, a Zen temple in Japan. I still eat mostly vegetarian meals, but occasionally I'll have seafood and, less often, poultry. I generally do not eat red meat, and especially try to avoid any meat from animals that were raised and slaughtered on factory farms. What matters to me is not just whether an animal died in order to feed me, but how it was slaughtered or slain, how it was raised in captivity or lived in the wild, and, of course, how sentient a creature it was. We humans like to oversimplify everything with general labels and absolute rules, but eating a squid caught in the ocean is hardly comparable to eating veal from a calf raised in a cage.

I remember witnessing, as a child, a deer take its last breath while staring right at me. I heard a frightened fawn rustling in the bushes, not knowing what to do as its mother lay there dying in front of these savage bipedal beasts, and I realized that my father had accidentally shot a doe out of season. I remember helping to tie that mother's still bleeding carcass on the hood of our car, and I remember later helping to carve up, cook, and eat its flesh. That was the first and last time I went deer hunting. But for several years I did continue to go bird hunting with my father, and to fish. And I increasingly began to wonder about where to draw the line. I am still pondering this question.

Some years ago, while preparing to teach a course in environmental ethics, I recall being deeply touched by an account of a Native American custom in which a father teaches his son to look into the eyes of the deer they have shot as it takes its last breath, and to recite a prayer of gratitude to it for its sacrifice. How different, I thought, this is from modern parents who let their kids grow up eating hamburgers without ever really knowing, much less directly experiencing, where they come from.

Before eating their vegetarian meals, Zen monastics chant a verse of gratitude and a vow to put the nourishment to good use. At the start of a meal most Japanese people put their palms together and say *itadakimasu*, a respectful expression of gratitude that literally means "I humbly receive." As they say this, kids are taught to think of all the things, plants, animals, and people that enabled that food to be there for them.

The Buddha himself was not, in fact, an absolute vegetarian. He did instruct monks not to encourage others to kill animals on their behalf, but he also told them to eat whatever was put in their begging bowls. Indeed, the Buddha is thought by many to have died from eating some rotten pork that was served to him. Given the pragmatic nature of the Buddha's teachings, it is not surprising that in some lands in which people depend on eating animals for survival, such as Tibet, carnivorous Buddhist cultures have developed.

The key question for Buddhists, I think, is how to *minimize* the suffering caused by violence, since the complete abolition of violence is unrealistic, and since to insist on absolute non-violence can actually get in the way of working to minimize suffering.

Minimizing Violence

In order to illustrate this point, let me relate an episode from the Zen monastery of Shōkokuji, where I practice. Many years ago, I stood up from meditation during a retreat one day and felt a large creature crawl across my bare foot. It was a poisonous centipede, called a *mukade*, about seven or eight inches long. The monastery at the time was experiencing an infestation of them, and later that evening a monk mercifully told me that it was all right to move if one crawls on me during meditation—a rare exception to a strict rule! (No such exception, alas, is made for slapping the mosquitoes that feast on our faces—and I'm convinced that those bloodthirsty critters knowingly take advantage of this monastic mandate!)

At the time I was working on the kōan "Nanquan Kills the Cat," a story in which an abbot kills a cat in order to teach a lesson to some monks who were quarreling over which group of them the cat supposedly belonged to.[41] Now, despite endless arguments among scholars, this kōan is not really about whether it is all right to sacrifice an animal in order to enlighten humans. In regard to this kōan the ethically conscious Zen teacher Robert Aitken writes: "The people who object to its violence are those who refuse to read fairy tales to their children."[42] Kōans are like parables that are not meant to be taken too literally. Their purpose is to teach and test, not to report factual events.

In any case, in the context of commenting on this kōan, Tanaka Hōjū Rōshi related to me how some of the monks at Shōkokuji were grumbling and even snickering about his decision to use insecticide to rid the monastery of the poisonous centipede infestation. They were apparently unable to square that decision with the first of the Ten Grave Precepts, the commitment not to kill. Yet, would it have been better to let the monks be bitten? Given the pain and poison that this would involve, I think that Tanaka Rōshi made the right decision.

Much more disturbing are the accounts gathered by Sōtō Zen priest and scholar Brian Victoria in his scathing exposés, *Zen at War* and *Zen War Stories*.[43] During the first half of the twentieth century, many Zen masters and institutions supported the Japanese troops and sent them off to kill and die on the battlefields of unjust wars of imperialistic aggression against their Asian neighbors. We'll return to this deeply troubling issue at the end of Chapter 17. Here, as an American, let me just add that I also think that the American imperialism that originally provoked and inspired the Japanese was morally condemnable. And so was the American decision to drop the atomic bombs that killed more than a hundred thousand civilians—not only in order to quickly end the war, but also in order to demonstrate to the Soviet Union our capacity and willingness to go to such extremes of indiscriminate mass killing.

I think we have to conclude that Zen practice and even enlightenment, on their own, are no more of a guarantee than are democracy and a high level of academic education that human beings will make the right ethical decisions. These lessons from the recent past teach us that we should both meditate and think long and hard before deeming it necessary to use violence in order to minimize violence. They also warn us not to presume that we are further along than we in fact are on the path toward becoming a wise and compassionate Bodhisattva for whom there are no fixed rules.

17

Being in the Zone of Zen

The Natural Freedom of No-Mind

In Chapter 15 we learned that, according to Zen, freedom is not really a matter of being *free from* karmic causality but rather a matter of *freely participating in* karmic causality. In Chapter 18, we'll see how Zen suggests that this is a matter of "natural freedom," a *freedom in nature* rather than *freedom from nature*. In the present chapter, we'll be talking about what it's like to experience the freedom of moving in intuitive attunement with the fluid forces at work in ourselves and the world.

Recovering the Open Mind of a Child

The eighteenth-century French philosopher Jean-Jacques Rousseau begins the first chapter of one of his most famous works with the lines "Man is born free; and everywhere he is in chains. One thinks himself the master of others, and still remains a greater slave than they."[1] Rousseau is talking about the way in which social customs, especially those that foster a constant competition for prestige, inhibit our native freedom and naturally cooperative spirit. Critics accuse him of romantically idealizing the supposedly childlike innocence of human beings in the so-called state of nature. Yet, setting aside the anthropological question of how pure and innocent people in stone age communities were, and for that matter the developmental psychology question of how pure and innocent children are, if we take Rousseau's point less literally, is he not on to something? Is there something about us, something in us, that got lost even before it was ever really found, something that has gotten covered over since time immemorial, something that still waits to be dis-covered?

In a Dharma talk given on Christmas Eve, the beloved modern Vietnamese Zen master Thich Nhat Hanh speaks of "helping the child within us to be reborn again and again, because the spirit of the child is the Holy Spirit, it is the spirit of the Buddha."[2] The open mind of the child, he goes on to say, is free of discrimination and is able to live in the present moment. The famous modern Japanese Rinzai Zen master Yamada Mumon was fond of quoting Jesus's words: "Truly

Zen Pathways. Bret W. Davis, Oxford University Press. © Oxford University Press 2022.
DOI: 10.1093/oso/9780197573686.003.0017

I tell you, unless you change and become like little children, you will never enter the kingdom of heaven."[3] In connection with this teaching from Jesus, Yamada Rōshi quotes a poem by the maverick fifteenth-century Japanese Zen master Ikkyū that reads: "A small child gradually accumulates knowledge / Sadly distancing himself from the Buddha."[4]

As we grow up, we accumulate all kinds of knowledge, or know-how, in our relentless pursuit of what I call the Four P's: pleasure, profit, power, and prestige. We learn to judge things according to whether they help or hinder us in attaining these things. Our minds are filled—clouded and clogged—with plans for procuring the Four P's. Zen masters speak of regaining a natural freedom and compassion that have gotten covered over and clogged up not just by social conventions but also by psychological forces, especially the greed and hatred that are rooted in the primal delusion that our egos and our interests are separate from those of others.

Zen meditation, Yamada Rōshi says, is a matter of returning to the open mind and heart of a small child. It is a practice of emptying the mind, of returning to what Zen calls a state of "no-mind" (Ch. *wuxin*; Jp. *mushin*). What Zen means by the no-mind is an open mind that is able to respond to everything because it is not fixated on anything, a mind that moves freely and fluidly and does not get stuck anywhere. The Sixth Chinese Ancestor of Zen, Huineng, is said to have fully attained enlightenment upon hearing these words from the *Diamond Sutra*: "Arouse the mind that does not linger anywhere."[5] Awaken the open and fluid mind that does not get stuck anywhere, that does not attach itself to, or get fixated on, anything.

The sixteenth-/seventeenth-century Japanese Zen master Takuan says that "a mind full of attachments arises from a mind stopped": "anytime there is a stopping on any object whatsoever, this is 'the mind getting stuck on an object.'" For example, he says: "If there are any thoughts in your mind, even though you're listening to someone else speaking, you don't really hear because your mind has stopped on a thought." On the other hand, if you empty, open, and clear your mind, if you attain what Takuan calls "the mind of no-mind," then "it will act whenever you need it [and] exactly how you need it."[6]

Zen masters are counseling us not to become *childish* in our thinking, but rather to become *childlike* in the sense of recovering the original purity and openness of our hearts and minds. They speak of this open and fluid awareness as a state of "no-mind" and "no-thought" (Ch. *wunian*; Jp. *munen*); it is a nondualistic awareness that precedes and underlies the dualistic mind that separates itself from everything else and then fills itself with thoughts of gain and loss, self and other, and with valuations of what's good and bad for me as a supposedly independent and unchanging ego.

Karma Yoga and the Zone of Zen

The problem is not just that we are egoistic or selfish. The problem is not just that we tend to care too much about ourselves and not enough about others. The problem is also that by losing our no-mind we also, figuratively and literally, trip over our own feet and, in the end, make ourselves ineffective and unproductive as well as lonely and miserable.

The *Bhagavad Gita*, the Hindu classic, also teaches us that our obsessive thoughts about the selfish outcomes of our actions get in the way of actually performing those actions successfully. It is by "renouncing the fruits of our actions," teaches Krishna, that we can fully engage in the activity of the present. This is the teaching of "karma yoga" that Gandhi based his life on. Paradoxically, Krishna promises us that the fruits of our actions will be all the more plentiful if we stop obsessing over them.[7]

This can be illustrated by the phenomenon of "choking" in sports. Why do soccer stars sometimes blow penalty kicks? Why do tennis champions sometimes double-fault on match point? Why is it that a basketball player who can sink nine out of ten free throws in practice, only makes one of two when the game is on the line? It is the same reason people get stage fright or fail to perform well on tests. They become self-conscious and fall out of "the zone."

"Being in the zone" is indeed the closest expression we have for what Zen means by the state of no-mind. When tennis players are able to forget about everything else and just concentrate on the serve, when they can let go of fearing or fantasizing about the outcome and just "be the ball," that's when aces happen and tournaments are won.[8] As soon as the pianist starts thinking about her hands and the keys and the audience and especially about the potential success or failure of her performance, it becomes impossible to immerse herself in the performance of the piece and just—to paraphrase T. S. Eliot—be the music while the music lasts. I tell students that they need to study for a final exam or write a term paper like they dance at a good party. It is precisely worrying about the grade they are going to get that gets in the way of wholly immersing themselves in learning the material or letting the writing flow.

The Point of Life Is to Play: The Journey Is the Autotelic Destination

A philosophy student from Kyoto University once visited Zen master Yamada Mumon. The student asked, "What is the goal of life?" Yamada Rōshi replied straightaway, "To play." Studying, working, driving, cooking, or any other activity, so long as it only aims to get somewhere else, to achieve something else, cannot be the goal of life. When we have achieved a goal, reached a destination, or resolved a problem and have some free time, what do we do? We play. Play is its own end. To be sure, even when we play we all too often remain distracted by unfinished business. But when we're really enjoying ourselves, we just play for the sake of playing. In the best of times with our children, we laugh and play like children ourselves. In Zen, Yamada Rōshi tells us, this complete and joyful absorption in the activity at hand is called the "*samadhi* (or meditative state) of play."[9]

It is important to understand that Yamada Rōshi is not talking about playing as opposed to studying, working, and so on. He is talking about playing right in the midst of carrying out those tasks. He is teaching us that we should make every goal-oriented activity at the same time both a means and an end itself. The journey aims to reach a destination, but also, on a deeper level, the journey itself is the destination.

The psychologist Mihaly Csikszentmihalyi speaks of being in the zone in terms of what he calls "the flow experience," and he argues that this experience is the key to human happiness.[10] We tend to always defer happiness to a later point in time; we are always on the way to where we want to be. Every activity we do is for the sake of something else, rather than for the sake of itself. Rather than seeing the purpose—the end or *telos*—of our current activity as lying in the future, the flow experience of being in the zone happens when our actions are "autotelic"—in other words, when they are experienced as ends in themselves.

None of this means that we should stop thinking about the future or about the results of our actions. Planning and attending to causal connections can themselves be done either in or out of the Zone of Zen. Autotelic actions can, at the same time, be teleologically oriented. The flow experience can still be goal-oriented. In fact, it usually always is, and not just in sports like soccer where one is quite literally goal-oriented. The difference is that one remains fully in the present each step of the way as one charges toward the goal. After all, when you think about it, paradoxical as it may at first sound, nothing has ever happened in the past or in the future. Every action takes place in the present. And so the present is always where the action is, even when those actions aim at the future. That is why the true destination is in each step of the journey and not just at a certain point on a map or in time.

If you were to ask marathon runners whether they would, if they could, push a magic button that would instantly transport them to the finish line, they might be tempted on occasion to say yes. But choosing to push the magic button every time would defeat the whole point of being a runner. They are, after all, runners, not just finishers. If someone asked you whether you would push a magic button that would instantly transport you to the end of a very successful life, would you do it? Probably not. The point is to live here and now, no matter that each here and now is also a step on the way to somewhere else. Even our planning for the future and our reminiscing about the past are, after all, present experiences.

The American pragmatist philosopher John Dewey claims that "art" should not be understood as just one specific type of activity and experience, limited to the "fine arts" that are supposedly ends in themselves without any use-value. Rather, art should be understood as the most fulfilling type of activity and experience. He defines "art" as "any activity that is simultaneously both" "instrumental and consummatory"—in other words, both goal-oriented and autotelic, both the journey and the destination.[11]

Dewey and Csikszentmihalyi are, in effect, both reaffirming and critically revising what Aristotle said long ago. For Aristotle, happiness is found in the degree to which human beings are engaged in activities that are autotelic, activities that are self-sufficient and pleasurable ends in themselves. For Aristotle, however, activities that are purely ends and not also means are higher, and produce greater happiness, than do activities that are at once both means and ends. He claims that the greatest self-sufficient happiness is found in the activity that he deemed to be most proper to human beings: intellectual contemplation.[12] By contrast, for Dewey, Csikszentmihalyi, and Zen, there is a great variety of activities in which human beings can be truly happy, and these activities can be at the same time both autotelic and goal-oriented. Moreover, for Zen, the highest human activity is not intellectual contemplation but rather compassionate deeds dedicated to liberating sentient beings from suffering. In fact, in such activities, rooted in meditation and done in a state of no-mind and no-thought, the rigid distinction between means and ends ultimately breaks down.

Beyond the Dichotomies of Work Versus Play, Autotelism Versus Altruism

The cross-cultural philosopher and lay Zen master Nishitani Keiji writes that, on what he calls the experiential "Field of Emptiness," "all our work takes on the character of play." All our activities are then "without aim or reason outside of themselves and become truly autotelic and without cause or reason, a veritable *Leben ohne Warum* [living without why]." Yet, he goes on to say that "even autotelism is still impure, not quite true."[13] As long as even a trace of egoistic self-consciousness remains, autotelism can relapse into the willful "infinite drive" of karma, the self-perpetuating cycle of solipsistic self-love that drives the never satisfied ego-self forward in its endless (because impossible) quest to be self-sufficient.[14] It is only when autotelic activity is purified of this egoistic self-consciousness that it can pass over into the "sheer, elemental doing" that Zen calls "playful *samadhi*," which transcends the dichotomy between "labor that toils for the sake of something else and play that is divertissement for its own sake."[15]

Kant pointed out that ethical persons recognize not only themselves but also all other people as ends in themselves.[16] According to Nishitani, this means that "the person as autotelic cannot come about without at the same time acknowledging others as autotelic."[17] Yet, for Nishitani, this ethical standpoint of personhood does not go far enough. The ethical standpoint must ultimately give way to a religious conversion. This is "a complete conversion from the standpoint where the self is an autotelic person to the standpoint where the self is a means for all other things."[18]

Nevertheless, this is not simply an abandonment of autotelism or autonomy, but rather a radicalization of these. For here, "the absolute self-negation that sees the telos of the self not in the self but in all things and the absolute self-affirmation that sees the original selfness of the self in all things are one."[19] In other words, when the self no longer misidentifies itself as an independent ego-subject but awakens to its interconnection with all things, the dichotomies between self-negation and self-affirmation, between autotelic play and other-oriented service, and between egoism and altruism drop away. Nishitani envisions a community of such awakened persons living in a relation of "mutually circulating interpenetration" in which "absolute subordination and absolute autonomy come about in unison."[20]

Zazen as a Gateway into the Zone of Zen

With that inspiring—albeit also challenging—vision of a mutually supportive communal life of autotelic service in mind, let us step back to where we are and to the question of how we might begin to move toward concretely comprehending and actualizing it. How can we even begin to personally experience the autotelic Zone of Zen, in which we are immersed in the flow of life, of swimming in concert with its currents and being fully present each stroke of the way? Here again it is *zazen*, Zen meditation, that provides the straightest path and the main gateway into this Zone of Zen.

When we first sit in meditation, our minds are restless, running forward into the future, back into the past, or across the room into someone else's business. Concentrating on the breath, we non-judgmentally become aware of this restlessness. We acknowledge but do not get upset about the fact that we have the urge to fidget or even to get up and go do something else—about the fact that we feel unfree, bound up with the chains of these restless thoughts and emotions.

Here's a tip for a timer: rather than use a clock or a stick of incense, I often tell myself that I am going to sit until I have no urge whatsoever to get up; until I have no desire to be doing anything else; until I feel utterly free and at peace doing just what I am doing—sitting, breathing, being fully at rest in the present. "Easier said than done," you may be thinking. Yes, but commit to it, and over time it will happen. And, I promise, it is a powerful experience, one that you can then start to bring into all the activities of your life.

Zazen, you'll recall from Chapter 3, is not just "seated meditation" in the literal sense but, more deeply and importantly, a matter of letting the heart-mind be seated. It is a matter of finding and centering oneself in an inner stillness that remains undisturbed in the midst of movement. It is a matter of becoming the eye of the storm, the hub of the wheel that stabilizes and steers the most vigorous, effective, and creative of activities. In a poem on *zazen*, the fourteenth-century Japanese Rinzai Zen master Daitō Kokushi wrote: "Look at the horses racing along the Kamo River! That's zazen!"[21] Yamada Mumon says, "No matter what you are doing, if you are putting your whole spirit into it and forgetting yourself in the process, that is *zazen*." He goes on to give as examples the various spiritual disciplines or "Ways" of Japanese culture, such as the "Way of Tea," in which one speaks of "the one taste of tea and Zen."[22]

We have seen that Huineng teaches: "The single practice of meditation is maintaining a straightforward mind at all times, whether walking, standing, sitting, or lying down."[23] What Huineng calls "no-thought," and what later Zen masters refer to as "no-mind," does not exclude thinking; rather, says Huineng, "no-thought is not to think even when involved in thought."[24] The problematic kind of thought involves "the dualism that produces the passions." In other words, we separate ourselves from things and reify them into isolated entities, and then we react to these illusory reconstructions with attachment or revulsion. However, Huineng says, "if you give rise to thoughts from your self-nature, then, although you see, hear, perceive, and know, you are not stained by the manifold environments, and are always free."[25]

In *The Zen Doctrine of No-Mind*, D. T. Suzuki translates *mushin* as "the Unconscious." Yet this translation is likely to be misleading, since, as Suzuki explains, *mushin* is neither a coma-like state of unconsciousness nor what psychoanalysts mean by the subconscious, but rather a nondualistic-consciousness or, in plainer English, an *unselfconsciousness*. In this sense Suzuki speaks of "everyday acts . . . done naturally, instinctively, effortlessly, and unconsciously."[26] Thomas Kasulis points out that no-mind or no-thought is "not an unconscious state at all" but rather a heightened state of nondualistic awareness "in which the dichotomy between subject and object . . . is overcome."[27]

The Hot Cognition of *Wuwei*: Use the Force, Luke!

In his book *Trying Not to Try: The Art and Science of Spontaneity*, Edward Slingerland connects the latest developments in Western cognitive science with the ancient wisdom and practices of East Asia. He suggests that Zen "meditation downregulates the conscious, cold-cognition centers of our brain, thereby creating room for hot cognition to do its thing."[28] He also suggests that kōans are meant to "free the embodied mind from the limitations of cold cognition and shock the student into a state of *wu-wei*."[29]

Wuwei (Jp. *mu-i*) is an important Zen term that derives from Daoism. The Chinese characters literally mean "no-doing" or "non-action," but in Daoism and Zen the word does not mean an absence or negation of any and all activity. Far from it; *wuwei* in fact refers to highly effective activity that is done effortlessly and harmoniously rather than artificially and forcefully. It is, as it were, the ancient Chinese word for activity done "in the zone."

Slingerland reveals how modern cognitive science confirms and helps explain what Daoist and Zen masters have long taught and demonstrated. Although Western philosophers from Plato through Descartes have tended to conceive of the mind in terms of a disembodied rational thinking process, we now know that this "cold cognition" is just the tip of the iceberg of our embodied and emotionally imbued processes of "hot cognition." By identifying and concerning ourselves only with cold cognition, which tends to dualistically separate our conscious minds from our material bodies and the world in which they are enmeshed, we have lost touch with the intuitive wisdom of the "embodied mind," the mind rooted in and in tune with the body, without which we could not walk and talk, much less sing and dance.[30] Most importantly, we have lost touch with what connects us with others and the universe at large.

When Christians take the sacrament of Communion, they ingest the body and not just a disembodied spirit of Christ. Through this ritual of Communion, they holistically remind themselves that their bodies as well as minds are united in the incarnation of God. Although St. Paul is sometimes accused of introducing an Orphic and Platonic soul-body dualism into Christianity, he does emphasize the communion of all in Christ when he teaches: "There is no longer Jew or Greek, there is no longer slave or free, there is no longer male and female; for all of you are one in Christ Jesus."[31]

Analogously, when Zen practitioners sit in *zazen*, they are dropping off their dualistically egoistic body-minds and holistically realizing their oneness with the Body-Mind of the Buddha. As discussed in Chapter 11, Zen master Dōgen teaches that while we can practice either with the mind or with the body, in truth these pathways into the Buddha Way converge as we discover that the One Mind that we awaken to is also the One Body in which we somatically participate.[32]

Slingerland says that "the distinguishing feature of *wu-wei* is the absorption of the self into something greater,"[33] and this "focus on caring—on getting beyond the self" is what he thinks is missing or downplayed in some truncated individualistic understandings of "the flow experience." He says that his own "most common wu-wei experiences . . . have always tended to involve activities that put [him] in contact with the natural world."[34]

Slingerland notes that George Lucas was clearly influenced by East Asian teachings of *wuwei* and no-mind when he came up with the idea of the Force for his *Star Wars* movie series. When Obi-Wan Kenobi tells Luke Skywalker to "let go" and "use the Force," and when Luke turns off his computer and closes his eyes to do so, he is switching, as it were, from the rational "cold cognition" of the self-conscious mind to the intuitive "hot cognition" of the embodied mind.[35]

While the self-conscious mind leads us to think of ourselves as cut off from the rest of reality, the embodied mind—or no-mind—puts us back in touch with the energy or "force" that connects us with everyone and everything. Nishitani speaks of the Field of Emptiness as a "field of force," a magnetic force that binds all things together in a "mutually interpenetrating relation," a "force by virtue of which all things enable one another to exist."[36] To get back in touch with this force field that harmoniously integrates rather than defensively excludes, we have to get back in touch with the open-hearted and open-minded core of ourselves. This clear and sincere heart-mind freely functions as the openly attentive as well as fluidly focusing no-mind, or it gets covered over and clogged up by our distracted and dualistically self-conscious ego-minds.

Just Live, Without Why

One of Zen's most often repeated kōan questions is, "Why did Bodhidharma come from the west?" In other words, what was on his mind, what was his intention, in undergoing the arduous journey by means of which he transmitted Zen from India to China? The answer to this "why" must indeed express the very essence of Zen, since Bodhidharma is the figure of the enlightened heart-mind that strives to liberate by enlightening all sentient beings. And yet, Zen master Linji tells us that if Bodhidharma had had any intent, "if he had had any purpose, he couldn't have saved even himself."[37]

In the most profound sense, Bodhidharma came "without why." His travels and deeds were unselfishly and unselfconsciously autotelic; they were ends in themselves rather than just being steps on the way to somewhere else. He enlightens and liberates the same way that he sleeps when tired and eats when hungry. He brings peace to others because he is at peace with himself. As my Zen and philosophy teacher Ueda Shizuteru demonstrated, there are deep resonances here with the radical Christian teachings of Meister Eckhart, who tells us that, ultimately, to be truly united with God means to be "empty and free" and to live "without why."[38] As long as we say, "Let not my will but thy Will be done," there is still a separation, we are still trying to follow—and, to some extent, still resisting, and thus keeping ourselves separated from—an external command. The true life of "trans-mysticism" (see Chapter 13) is a matter of living spontaneously, naturally, without why.

My first teacher at Shōkokuji monastery, Tanaka Hōjū Rōshi, used to say at the most crucial moments, "*tada, tada*," "just . . . , just . . ." Ultimately, the meaning of life is found only by living fully in the moment, which means living wholly without why. Even when engaged in all our various goal-oriented activities, the real goal is found only by immersing ourselves in each step of the process. This is why, as we saw in Chapter 12, Dōgen says that Nirvana can be—indeed can *only* be—found in the "total activity" (Jp. *zenki*) of each moment of birth-and-death:

> When there is life, there is nothing at all apart from life. When there is death, there is nothing at all apart from death. Therefore, when life comes, you should just give yourself to life; when death comes, you should give yourself to death.[39]

Dealing with the Dark Side of the Force

Of course, while living "without why," wholly immersed in the autotelic activity at hand, may be a deep spiritual teaching, it is also a tall order. Most of us are capable of it only in fleeting moments, and we need to be patient with our hankering after reasons, goals, and hopes.

Moreover, it must be acknowledged that this powerful teaching can and has been co-opted by less enlightened and enlightening persons. I used to think that Nike must have cribbed their advertising slogan, "Just do it," from Zen. In fact, however, they were inspired by the words of a cold-blooded murderer before he was shot by a firing squad.[40] This raises an unnerving question: When this man killed people, did he "just do it" in the manner of an athlete or a musician during their peak performances? What, if anything, would this have to do with the no-mind of Zen?

When Obi-Wan Kenobi tells Luke Skywalker to "use the Force," we should bear in mind that he is also quite literally telling him to use lethal force. Indeed, you may have first become acquainted with the Zen ideas of no-mind and *wuwei* by practicing—or at least watching movies about—a martial art such as karate.[41] Or perhaps you read Eugen Herrigel's longtime bestseller, *Zen in the Art of Archery*. Herrigel seems to have indirectly learned some Zen lessons while practicing this martial art in Japan for a few years in the 1920s. The main lesson he learned was that actions are most effective when done in a nondualistic state of no-mind, in which the self is not separate from the bow, or the arrow from the target. Herrigel claimed that his archery teacher expressed this experience as "It shoots" and "It hits"—although, oddly, the grammar Herrigel attributes to his Japanese teacher is German rather than Japanese.[42] In any case, whatever he learned about Zen through his practice of the martial art of archery did not prevent Herrigel from becoming at least a self-serving—if not ardent—Nazi a decade after his return to Germany.[43]

More disturbing is the fact—documented and denounced by Rinzai Zen priest Ichikawa Hakugen, by Sōtō Zen priest Brian Victoria, and by the scholar and Zen practitioner Christopher Ives—that many Zen masters supported Japanese militarism leading up to and during the Pacific War, and that they applied traditional Zen teachings such as no-mind to the psychological training of soldiers. Many of these soldiers no doubt went on to fight bravely and honorably, but at least some of them went on to commit atrocious war crimes on and off the battlefield.[44] Closer to home, Zen practitioner Ronald Purser relates these past militaristic misapplications of Zen by the Japanese to the present instrumentalization of mindfulness techniques by the United States military.[45]

As the violence perpetrated by cults and crusades has repeatedly revealed, half-baked spirituality can be a doubly dangerous thing. In general, I think that if we look at everything in history that has gone on under the name of its doctrines and that has been supported by its institutions, we must conclude that religions have brought out both the best and the worst of human nature. How much suffering has been *relieved* by religious ceremonies and charities, meditation practices and prayer services? And how much suffering has been *caused* by so-called holy wars, persecutions, inquisitions, and abuses of power? Why is it that religious leaders, and even whole institutions, can tip so easily over into being forces of evil rather than forces of good?

Slingerland suggests that the idea in *Star Wars* that the Force has a "dark side" evinces a Christian influence on George Lucas's imagination. That may be the case, yet this idea can nevertheless help us critically reflect on how the cultivation of no-mind has been used to inflict, rather than alleviate, suffering—not only in the fictional universe of *Star Wars* but also in the historical reality of samurai warlords and kamikaze commanders.

The great second-/third-century Buddhist philosopher Nagarjuna tells us that misunderstanding the teaching of emptiness is like grabbing a snake by the wrong end—if you grab it by the tail rather than the head, it will twist around and bite you![46] Something similar could be said of the practice of no-mind. Robert Aitkin thinks that Zen master Takuan failed to properly grasp the teachings of emptiness and no-mind when he tells a sword master to "forget about what you are doing, and strike the enemy," and that the sword, the one who wields it, and the one who is struck down by it are "all of emptiness."[47] David Loy also incisively criticizes the "militaristic perversion of Buddhism" by medieval and modern Japanese Zen masters and agrees with Brian Victoria that the basic tenets of Buddhism "must be considered to take the position of absolute pacifism." "It is inconceivable," Loy writes, that Shakyamuni Buddha "could have lived as a samurai, or that he would have approved of any such use of his teachings."[48]

These modern Western Zen Buddhists are exemplary in demonstrating how faithfully adopting a tradition should not be understood to preclude critically reforming it. It is hard not to agree with their abhorrence of all forms of violence and their embrace of absolute pacifism. And yet, as they are well aware, the Zen tradition warns us of the dangers of absolutizing any "view," even the most harmless-sounding ones such as pacifism. After all, should we have not gone to war against Nazi Germany? And don't we still want to praise someone who forgets him- or herself and spontaneously fights back against a terrorist or an assailant, saving lives by putting his or her own at risk? As we saw in Chapter 16, in the *Skill in Means Sutra* the Buddha-to-be opted to kill a murderer in order to prevent him from killing five hundred innocent people.

Unless we are absolute pacifists, condemning equally the use of the Force by Luke Skywalker as well as by Darth Vader, unless we think *all* uses of force by the police—not just the illegal and systemically racist ones that rightly provoke righteous protests, but also the brave and by-the-book ones that justly earn honors—are as culpable as the violent acts of some of the criminals they arrest, then we have to admit that there is a place for teaching the Way of Zen to sword masters as well as to tea masters. Indeed, wouldn't it be especially important for those whose profession at times requires them to use physical force to receive spiritual instruction?

In fact, the no-mind of spontaneous freedom that Takuan teaches the sword master does seem to contain significant ethical implications. It is necessary to cast off the dualistic discriminations of the ego, not in order to attain a mere blank state of non-discrimination, but rather in order to discriminate—that is, to make practical distinctions and ethical judgments—*naturally and non-egoistically*. This freedom from unnatural and egoistic discrimination, and freedom for natural and non-egoistic discrimination, is I think what Takuan means when he says: "Without looking at right and wrong, he is able to see right and wrong well; without attempting to discriminate, he is able to discriminate well."[49] Zen master Shidō Bunan says that a person who has undergone the Great Death—that is to say, a person who has died to the petty ego and "attained the great Way"—"naturally sees the right and wrong in others, and is able to lead them to the Way of Buddha."[50]

Zen masters have tended to stress that we find the ultimate source of practical wisdom, the source of making proper ethical judgments, not by intellectually disengaging ourselves from the embodied, everyday world and transcending it to a supernatural realm of reason, but rather by means of a holistic practice of intimately engaging ourselves in the vagaries and vicissitudes of life, by way of nondually attuning ourselves to the fluid principle—the natural Way—that pervades the singular events of the here and now. However, while it is true that cerebral intellection can foster and serve dualistic and egoistic discrimination, so can thoughtless action. Indeed, when karmically habituated to a willful and unwholesome personal and social manner of acting, it starts to seem spontaneous and natural.[51] And so, must not a truly holistic as well as wholesome Zen Way somehow connect and coordinate the complementary pathways of careful critical thinking and spontaneously natural action?

Speaking of the two networks of our nervous system, those of intuitive "hot cognition" and deliberative "cold cognition," Slingerland says:

> The [ultimate] goal of wu-wei is to get these two selves working together smoothly and effectively. For a person in wu-wei, the mind is embodied and the body is mindful; the two systems—hot and cold, fast and slow—are completely integrated. The result is an intelligent spontaneity that is perfectly calibrated to the environment.[52]

I take all this to mean that there is a proper way of being in the Zone of Zen both when one is acting and when one is deliberating—and also, crucially, when one is moving back and forth between these modes of nondualistic and egoless nomind. The most important difference is not between thinking and acting, but rather between thinking and acting in a holistically engaged manner, on the one hand, and thinking and acting in a dualistically egoistic manner, on the other.

As we saw in Chapter 16, moral precepts, while originally taken as *prescriptions* for how a Zen practitioner *should try to act*, ultimately become *descriptions* of how a Zen adept *naturally does act*. Morality, according to Zen, derives neither from a supernatural command, nor merely from rational reflection, but ultimately from getting back in touch with what we might call the *Dao* or Way of Nature. Zen teaches that true freedom is not freedom from nature; it is freedom in nature, a freedom of naturalness or a natural freedom. In Chapter 18, I'll elaborate on this idea before discussing other virtues, in particular generosity, that Zen suggests can be learned by returning to a more intimate connection with the natural world.

Holistic Zen Practice Needs to Incorporate Philosophical Reflection

Let me conclude this chapter by emphasizing and elaborating on the point that if Zen practice is to become truly holistic as well as ethically and politically responsible, it needs to increasingly incorporate intellectual methods of study and thinking alongside its less cerebral and discursive psychosomatic practices such as *zazen*. (In Chapter 21, we'll delve deeper into this crucial contemporary issue in the context of further discussing D. T. Suzuki and especially the pioneer bridge-building contributions of the Zen-practicing philosophers of the Kyoto School.)

Although I have a somewhat more positive view of the intellectual and scholarly resources to be found in the Zen tradition itself, I largely agree with Dale S. Wright that "one of the greatest dangers to the Zen tradition is its ever-present temptation to be disdainful of conceptual thinking."[53] However, Wright interprets what the Zen tradition calls "without thinking" (or, more literally, "non-thinking") and "no-thought" as literally and solely the suspension of thought in "spontaneous, unreflective" action. This conflates what Zen calls "non-thinking" (*hi-shiryō*) with what it calls "not-thinking" (*fu-shiryō*) (on this crucial distinction, see Chapter 22). As we have seen, Huineng says that "no-thought is not to think *even when involved in thought*."[54] What he means by "no-thought" is thus not the cessation of *all* thinking, but rather the cessation of *dualistic and egoistically judgmental* thought, even when engaged in—*and precisely in order to be capable of*—nondualistic and non-egoistic thinking. Nevertheless, I concur with Wright that contemporary Zen practice should be further extended "to include practices that are relevant to the cultivation of moral excellence, as well as to other reflective powers that are essential to admirable forms of human life."[55]

D. T. Suzuki has been accused of inspiring and even proffering an anti-intellectual interpretation of Zen (see Chapter 21), and yet he was in fact among the first to intrepidly and publically recognize the need for Zen monks and priests to study as well as meditate. Although Brian Victoria has been criticized for his excessively polemical treatment of Suzuki's relationship to war,[56] he nevertheless does recognize the boldness of Suzuki's criticism of the Japanese Zen establishment in this regard soon after the war ended. For example, in 1946 Suzuki wrote:

> With *satori* [enlightenment] alone, it is impossible [for Zen priests] to shoulder their responsibilities as leaders of society. Not only is it impossible, but it is conceited for them to imagine they could do so. . . . [B]y itself *satori* is unable to judge the right and wrong of war. With regard to disputes in the ordinary world, it is necessary to employ intellectual discrimination. . . . Furthermore, *satori* by itself cannot determine whether something like communism's economic system is good or bad.[57]

Indeed, in order to critically think about the ideals as well as the realities of political and economic systems such as communism and neoliberal capitalism, democratic socialism and laissez-faire libertarianism, and about all the other ethical and political choices we regularly make (or let be made) and the dilemmas we often face (or fail to face), Zen Buddhists need to more thoroughly include such critical thinking—scholarly investigation and philosophical reflection—among the vital pathways of their practice.

18

Zen Lessons from Nature

Samu and the Giving Leaves

As we saw in Chapters 16 and 17, according to Zen, in order to properly make moral judgments, it is necessary to cast off the dualistic discriminations of the ego so that one can make practical distinctions and ethical judgments *freely and naturally*. Freedom and responsibility, according to Zen, are found not by way of transcending the forces and flows of nature, but rather by way of getting back in touch with them. By contrast, for example, the influential German philosopher Immanuel Kant thought that our physical and emotional nature is responsible for our naturally selfish passions, which must be restrained and ruled over by our supernatural reason. The rational rules of morality, argues Kant, are generally at odds with our physical desires and emotions, and so we must suppress and control our desires with the rational mind. In short, for Kant, to be free is to be liberated from our natural inclinations.[1]

Yet, according to Zen and other schools of traditional Japanese thought, it is immorality that is unnatural. Moreover, freedom is not something gained by separating ourselves from nature; it is rather an expression of a genuine naturalness. It is not a freedom from nature, but rather a freedom in nature, a freedom of naturalness or a natural freedom.[2]

The modern Japanese philosopher Kuki Shūzō sees this Zen ideal of natural freedom as a general characteristic of Japanese culture. He writes:

> In the Japanese ideal of morality, "nature" in the sense of what is "so of itself" has great significance. . . . If one does not reach the point of naturalness, then morality is not seen as completed. This is quite distinct from the West. Indeed, in Western conceptual configurations nature is often thought of as standing in opposition to freedom. By contrast, in Japanese practical experience there is a tendency for nature and freedom to be understood as fused together and identified. Freedom is something that naturally springs forth of itself. Freedom is not born as the result of a strained self-assertiveness. When the heart-mind of heaven and earth naturally comes forth of itself just as it is, that is freedom.[3]

In this chapter, we'll see how Zen suggests that other virtues, in particular generosity, can be learned by returning to a more intimate relation with the natural

Zen Pathways. Bret W. Davis, Oxford University Press. © Oxford University Press 2022.
DOI: 10.1093/oso/9780197573686.003.0018

world. In Chapter 19, we'll see how this natural freedom also involves a naturally artistic creativity. Zen monasteries are not only places for meditating in silence and stillness; they are also places for dynamic artistic activity and wholehearted working in cooperative communion with nature.

Samu: Meditative Work

Zazen and working on kōans are only some of what goes on in a Zen monastery. Much of the time monks, nuns, and lay practitioners dwelling there are engaged in *samu* or meditative work. When Buddhism was adopted by the Chinese, it was also adapted to fit the Confucian work ethic and the Daoist emphasis on living in harmony with nature. Both of these adaptations inform the role that *samu* plays in Zen practice.

The lay Zen master and cross-cultural philosopher Ueda Shizuteru tells us that, in addition to long periods of meditation (*zazen*) and the brief yet highly concentrated interviews with the teacher—called *sanzen* or *dokusan*—in which one's understanding of kōans is tested, the third basis of Rinzai Zen practice is *samu*.[4] Whereas *zazen* is an essentially silent and still as well as solitary practice, even when done with a community, in kōan interviews with the teacher a practitioner engages in an intensely dynamic mode of one-on-one interpersonal encounter. *Samu* is a practice of engaging wholeheartedly with the task at hand—cleaning, cooking, gardening, and so forth—in the concentrated yet fluid state of no-mind that we discussed in Chapter 17. *Samu* also involves cooperating with one's co-workers and communing with the natural world. In this chapter, our discussion of *samu* will include some of the Zen lessons to be learned from a recovery of a cooperative communion with nature.

First, a word or two about how the practice of *samu* developed is in order. When Buddhism was brought from India to China, certain practices changed, just as alterations are now occurring as Buddhism is being adopted and adapted by Westerners. The Chinese people were not used to the Indian custom of supporting mendicants and monastics, who were forbidden to work for a living so that they could concentrate their time and energy on their spiritual practice and teaching. Chinese Zen masters reevaluated what they perceived to be an unnecessary division made between physical work and spiritual practice. They taught that physical work itself could be an important form of spiritual practice. And so, in Zen monasteries *samu* became an integral part of the routine.

A famous saying in Zen is "A day without work is a day without food." This saying, I recall, was always printed on the envelopes of the chopsticks we would distribute to the hundreds of parishioners who would gather at Shōkokuji for a special meal served by the monastery on the summer and winter solstices. A few of us lay practitioners would join the monks on these occasions for a long day of *samu* in service to this community.

The saying "A day without work is a day without food" is attributed to the eighth-century Chinese Zen master Baizhang. As the story goes, the monks were concerned about the health of their aging teacher, who continued to labor in the fields come rain or shine. And so, one day they hid his farming tools from him. Unable to find them, he refused to eat that day. Needless to say, the monks returned his tools to him the following day.[5]

It was Baizhang who first established the rules and regulations of Zen monasteries, in which manual labor is practiced in tandem with sitting meditation, kōan study, and sutra chanting. In Zen monasteries today, except during the intensive meditation retreats calls *sesshin*, monastics generally spend more time in the active practice of *samu* than they do in the stillness of *zazen*. They grow and prepare most of their own food, chop their own firewood, and of course weed and rake their own gardens.

Many years ago, after an intense retreat during which we sat so many hours each day that I thought that my legs were going to drop off—and not in the enlightening sense of "dropping off of the body-mind" that Dōgen speaks of!—I asked a seasoned monk what he found most difficult in his training. I remember being surprised to hear him say that what he found most physically challenging about life in the monastery was not the long hours of *zazen* but rather the long hours of *samu*. Since then, I have come to better appreciate his comment.

A couple of summers ago, I returned to spend several weeks in the monastery of Shōkokuji. During this stay, other than a week of mostly sitting in meditation during a *sesshin*, I spent much of my time sweltering and sweating in the garden. In December of that year, I returned to spend another couple of weeks mostly on the monastery grounds working with fallen leaves in freezing temperatures. Again, in the summer of the following year, after participating in another *sesshin*, I stayed on for a week and mainly worked in the garden, during another record-breaking heat wave. And that December, I returned to rake the leaves once more.

I have practiced *samu* at Shōkokuji and elsewhere many times over the past three decades, but maybe never quite so intensely as during these recent stays. Kobayashi Gentoku Rōshi, the current abbot, evidently felt that I needed to spend more time doing *samu* than *zazen* during these recent stays. In fact, he said as much. There were things I could learn, he said, not only by getting my head out of the books, but also by getting my butt off the meditation cushion. This recent *samu* experience not only reminded me of much that I had forgotten, but also awakened me to much that I had never fully realized.

Figure 18.1 Cleaning the floor at Shōkokuji monastery, Kyoto, December 2019.

Figure 18.2 Harvesting plumbs at Shōkokuji monastery, Kyoto, June 2019.

The Giving Leaves

Returning to my desk after one of these December sojourns at Shōkokuji, I was inspired to write down the following reflections. With an allusion to Shel Silverstein's famous children's book *The Giving Tree*,[6] I entitled these reflections "The Giving Leaves." Here is what I wrote:

> Raking the carpet of fallen maple leaves one December morning at Shōkokuji, a Zen monastery in Japan, it dawned on me. They never stop giving. Nothing ever does.
>
> The maple leaves are famous in the fall for their beautiful hues of yellow, orange and red. The counterpart of the cherry blossoms in the spring, they are celebrated across the country by locals and tourists alike who flock to the temples, shrines, and parks to soak in their autumnal charm.
>
> But then they fall to the ground and, after a few days of providing a still pleasingly rustic and rustling ground-covering, they get rained on—and it begins to sink in that it's going to take many hours of back-straining raking to clean them up.
>
> In a Zen monastery, this becomes the focus of *samu*, meditative work, for a week or so. With my bamboo broom in hand and my antiquated pull-cart in tow, I set out to rake the leaves around 7 AM, having been up since 4 AM doing other forms of Zen practice.
>
> Having spent a lot of time in Zen monasteries washing dishes and cleaning toilets, picking weeds and planting vegetables, I was used to experiencing such so-called menial labor as meaningful exertion, at least when done in a monastic context and with a meditative mindset.
>
> And yet, this time it was more than that. This time it suddenly became clear to me that while we usually only appreciate the maple leaves as gifts of nature at certain times and in certain ways, in fact they never stop giving.
>
> To be sure, I had noticed before how strikingly beautiful the fresh green maple leaves are in the spring, when they embody the vibrant new life of that season. And I had enjoyed swashing through them after they had fallen to the ground in the late autumn—at least before they were rained on and when it was not my job to rake them up.
>
> But now, what I realized was that these fallen leaves were providing me with an opportunity to do meditative work, just as a noisy neighbor offers an opportunity to practice patience and diplomacy, and a screeching toddler with a dirty diaper offers an opportunity to practice replacing annoyance and aversion with compassion and caregiving.

Yet that is not all the fallen and soggy leaves were providing. Far from it. In the monastery, nothing is wasted. The monks grow most of their own food (except for rice, which they would traditionally receive on begging rounds from local farmers). They even grow and make their own tea. They plant, protect, pick, and prepare all their own vegetables, which are mostly what go into their bowls. They don't just go to the supermarket for their groceries, much less do they rely on eating out or ordering take out.

Unlike most of us, the monks are not alienated from all that nature provides and all the labor that goes into growing and preparing the food that keeps us alive. Before they eat, they chant their humble appreciation for the food in their bowls, and they vow to put the nutrients they are receiving to good use. They also symbolically set aside a few grains of rice for the "hungry ghosts" who, with their huge bellies and tiny throats, symbolize all those whose appetites outsize their abilities to satiate themselves.

Over the years, I have worked many hours in the monastery's vegetable garden. But this time, raking the leaves, it dawned on me that the cycle does not begin with planting seeds, or even with weeding and tilling the soil. For one cannot take the soil itself for granted. The soil has to have nutrients to sustain the life of the plants, which in turn provide the nutrients that sustain our lives. Where do those nutrients in the soil come from? In this case, from the maple leaves.

My job that week in December was to rake the hundreds of thousands of fallen leaves, but not just to clear them off the beautiful moss gardens that surround the monastery, allowing those gardens to bestow once again their serene luster. More vitally, the purpose of raking the leaves was to prepare the fertilizing compost for the following year.

The leaves are gathered and stacked. Each layer of leaves is covered with a liberal dusting of *okara*, a byproduct of tofu production. After more leaves are put over the *okara*, and water applied, one stomps around on the layer of leaves to compress them. The bacteria that turn the leaves into nutritious fertilizer feed off this combination of protein, moisture, and limited oxygen. Six months later, the leaves will have metamorphized and they'll be ready to feed the plants that in turn feed us.

Having only ever really appreciated the maple leaves in their springtime vibrancy and autumnal splendor, I now realize that they never stop giving. And I have started to pay more attention to the ways in which other things around me—other things that I had only appreciated in certain ways and at certain times—also never stop giving.

I began to realize that the burden is on me to know how to receive and pass on their gifts. I began to realize that I was being called on—by everything and everyone around me—to participate in this universe of cyclical and ceaseless giving.

Participating in the Big Potlatch of Nature

Reflecting back on writing those words, I recall that the great American Zen poet Gary Snyder spoke of the natural world—or, as he prefers to say, the *wild* world— as "the big potlatch." Incidentally, more than a half century ago Snyder first prac- ticed Zen in Japan at the same monastery in Kyoto, Shōkokuji.[7] After settling back down in his native Pacific Northwest of the United States, he combined his study of the Way of Zen with his study of Native American ways of appreciating and participating in the wider world of wild nature. In one of his most celebrated works, *The Practice of the Wild*, Snyder writes:

> Most of humanity—foragers, peasants, or artisans . . . have understood the play of the real world, with all its suffering, not in simple terms of "nature red in tooth and claw" but through the celebration of the gift-exchange quality of our give-and-take. "What a big potlatch we are all members of!" To acknowledge that each of us at the table will eventually be part of the meal is not just being "realistic." It is allowing the sacred to enter and accepting the sacramental as- pect of our shaky temporal personal being.[8]

We need to learn how to better—more generously and gratefully—participate in this great circulation of giving and taking. This is a lesson we can glean from Silverstein's *The Giving Tree*. Some see the tree in this story as representing a parent and the boy a child. But the tree in the story has also been understood to represent nature, while the boy represents humankind.

As the boy grows up and eventually grows old, the tree gives and gives: apples to eat and later to sell, branches to swing on and later to make a house with, a trunk to cut down and carve out to make a boat with, and finally a stump for the boy-grown-old to sit and rest on. The utterly unselfish tree never asks for any- thing in return. It finds its happiness in providing for the boy's happiness. But the boy does not return the favor. The giving is a one-way street.

One of the striking things about Silverstein's book, in my mind, is the fine line it walks between teaching and preaching. Like all great parables and children's tales, it tells a story and lets us ponder the point. The tree in the story never blames the boy. It just continues to find new ways to grant him happiness. And yet, after playing with the tree as a child, the boy grows into a restless and ego- centric man. Perhaps you could say that the tree spoils the boy, and that it should have taught him with a tougher form of love. In any case, the boy never learns to give back, to participate in the great potlatch of life.

"Potlatch" is a Pacific Northwest Native American word for the lavish gift- giving feasts at which rich people give away much of their wealth, ensuring that goods continue to be circulated among the entire community and neighboring tribes. Considered wasteful and contrary to capitalistic values of accumulation ("greed is good"), it was strictly banned by European conquerors in the nineteenth century. And yet, as the French anthropologist Marcel Mauss points out in his book *The Gift*, practices of potlatch and similar gift-giving customs in tribal societies around the globe serve to build and maintain relationships between human beings. It is, on the contrary, hoarding that weakens the bonds among humans, creating a wealth gap that breeds resentment and false feelings of superiority.[9] If love makes the world go around, love in the form of gift-giving keeps the goods of life circulating.

The Perfection of Giving Without Expectations

We all more or less realize that giving is important. But what does it really mean to give? The tree in *The Giving Tree* teaches by example. It never says to the boy, "You need to give back," even though that is a lesson that readers easily glean from the story. One of the most profound lessons of the book is perhaps that in order to truly give, or give back, we need to give without expecting a return gift, like the tree.

Do we ever really do this? Don't we always expect something in return—at least a thank-you or even just a smile of recognition? Don't we always want to be compensated in some way, if not from the person we gave something to or did something for, then at least a pat on the back from a witness to our generosity?

Yet it is that expectation of getting something in return that spoils our giving; that expectation is the taint of impurity in our generosity. As the French philosopher Jacques Derrida puts it, the return gift annuls the initial gift. As soon as there is a return gift, the event of pure giving is changed into an economy of exchange. Even thinking "I am giving" is a self-congratulation that annuls the gift at the very moment it is being given.[10]

Christmas presents, birthday cards, donations to charity, even just holding the door open for someone—all these usually come with strings attached. We expect something in return: a return gift, a thank-you note, a pat on the back, our name in the credits. We are not unreservedly *giving*, but rather more or less calculatedly *exchanging* one thing for another.

In order to purely participate in the great potlatch of life, we would need to let go of our expectations of a return gift *even when there usually is one*. The point of potlatch is that it aims to be excessive. Of course, this might all be done for show. Perhaps, since one is expected to give, one is just avoiding shame by obeying the custom. And, in any case, one gains prestige and power by being recognized as a great giver. But if this were all there is to it, then potlatch too would be just another form of transactional exchange rather than a genuine event of giving in excess of expectations.

One sees both sides of this in Japanese culture, where gifts of cash and perishable goods are constantly being circulated among family, friends, co-workers, and other acquaintances. For example, at our wedding reception in Japan, my wife and I received lots of envelopes with generous amounts of cash in them from her relatives. Following the custom of *hangaeshi*—literally "returning half"—we took half of the money out of each of the envelopes, set aside a certain amount of that to help cover our reception costs, and made a return gift of the rest to those relatives. Was theirs a true gift? Was ours? Or were we all just following the social rules of transactional exchange?

From the outside, it is impossible to tell if someone is truly giving. Economically evaluated, or cynically seen, every gift can be viewed as a transactional exchange. On the other hand, we could say that from the inside, every occasion of exchange can be experienced as an opportunity for participating in a pure event of giving. Every expenditure of time, money, and energy can be converted into a Bodhisattva practice of the Perfection of Giving. What matters, after all, is not whether or not there *is* a return gift, but whether or not we *expect* one when we give.

If and when we are able to truly give without expectation of a return, then if and when a return does in fact come, we are able to truly appreciate it as a gift. To live and to give without expectations, to give every act one's all without expecting a reward—that might just be the key to true happiness and a truly meaningful life. Of course, we should respect and protect other people's rights and entitlements, and it is often proper to stand up for our own. But, even while fighting for justice and demanding results, to remain—in our innermost hearts—without expectations is a highly demanding but also deeply liberating spiritual practice.

Hindus call this "karma yoga."[11] As we saw in Chapter 17, in the *Bhagavad Gita* Krishna teaches that this practice of immersing oneself totally in activities that benefit the world without obsessing over the "fruits of the act"—in other words, without always thinking, "What's in it for me?"—is the key to spiritual liberation. What's more, he promises, the karma yogi ends up experiencing the greatest fruits of her actions precisely because she is not obsessed with or attached to them.

In Mahayana Buddhism, pure giving without the expectation of return is called the Perfection of Giving. It is the first of the Six Perfections practiced by Bodhisattvas. The other five are the Perfections of Morality, Patience, Vigor, Meditation, and Wisdom. The Six Perfections largely reiterate the teachings of the Eightfold Path, but they place upfront and emphasize the practice of giving.

The Perfection of Giving is different from what we ordinarily think of as giving in that, like the other Perfections, it is based on the Perfection of Wisdom, which means the insight into emptiness or interdependent origination. Specifically, the practitioner of the Perfection of Giving understands that the giver, the gift, and the receiver are all empty of independent substantiality or "own-being"—that is to say, giver, gift, and receiver all depend on each other for their very existence; none of them could exist on their own. The Bodhisattva fully participates in such nondual events of pure giving. And he or she identifies with those events in their entirety.

Scholar of Buddhism Donald Mitchell writes:

> For giving to be a "perfection," it should be practiced with a selfless attitude based on insight into the nonduality of oneself and others. That is, when one has transcended the perceived separation between oneself and another person, then one's giving to that person becomes an action where oneself and the other are united in the pure act of giving and receiving.[12]

Surely, we all have some familiarity with empathetic engagement in acts of more or less pure giving. My wife and I recently gave our daughter a cute new blanket, and there was just a shared moment of joy when she threw it over her smiling face and marched upstairs to put it on her bed. My experience of the giving leaves at the monastery reminded me that these wondrous nondual events of giving are happening around us all the time, inviting us to participate ever more perfectly in them.

Natural Gateways into Zen

The Zen tradition often emphasizes the lessons to be learned from the natural world. In this regard, Zen draws deeply on Daoism and also resonates with the indigenous Japanese tradition of Shintō. There are more than three hundred temples and shrines in Kyoto, each one an oasis of natural beauty and a site of spiritual communion with nature. Shintō shrines are often built around or near a magnificent tree or rock, and a trickling stream sometimes runs through them. In China, Zen monasteries were traditionally built on mountaintops, and head temple complexes in Japan, even those in the middle of metropolises, are still referred to as "main mountains" (*honzan*).

Upon entering a monastery, a monk asked the ninth-century Chinese Zen master Xuansha, "Please show me where to enter the Way." Xuansha responded, "Do you hear the valley stream?" "Yes," replied the monk. "Enter there!" he instructed.[13] The enlightening sounds of nature are often extolled by Zen masters. For example, the thirteenth-century Japanese Zen master Dōgen says, "The sounds of the valley streams are the Buddha's long, broad tongue." He also says,

"When you practice correctly, the sounds and forms of the valley streams and the sounds and forms of the mountains generously deliver eighty-four thousand verses of the Buddha's teaching."[14] And so when Xuansha told the monk to enter the Way of Zen by listening to the sound of the valley stream, we could say that he was teaching him the doctrine of "insentient beings preach the Dharma."

Yet, Xuansha was not just interested in teaching the monk a doctrine about Zen. He was encouraging him to experience Zen directly. And he was trying to awaken him to the fact that Zen can be experienced anywhere and at any time—at that particular moment, he turned the monk's attention to the sound of the valley stream, which the monk was perhaps tuning out in his search for a mystical teaching about some supernatural thing.

Not always, but often, Zen masters direct their students' attention to natural things: the oak tree in the garden, the blue mountains walking, the sound of the valley streams. All beings are the Buddha-nature, teaches Dōgen: "grass and trees" are the Buddha-nature[15] and "the present mountains and waters are actualizations of the Way of the ancient Buddhas," he says.[16]

Human beings are generally deluded about this fact. Other natural beings, by contrast, are not deluded and thus have no need for enlightenment. They simply and freely give themselves over to their interconnected lives among the rest of the worldwide web of reality, taking what they need and giving back what they don't without a first, much less a second thought. The Buddha Way does not lead to a transcendence of nature; it entails rather a return to naturalness, and natural phenomena themselves help teach us this Way.

The thirteenth-/fourteenth-century Japanese Zen master Musō Kokushi teaches:

> Hills and rivers, the earth, plants and trees, tiles and stones, all of these are the self's own original part. . . . Out of the realm of the original part have arisen all things: from the wisdom of Buddhas and saints to the body-and-mind of every sentient being, and all lands and worlds.[17]

When the self awakens to its own "original part," the open core and ubiquitous Source-Field of its being, it realizes its participation in the dynamically interconnected whole of nature.

Of course, the ways in which we humans are called upon to participate in the Way of Nature are not the same as the ways in which other beings participate. We may learn something about stillness and sturdiness from watching a frog sit on a rock, yet we are neither frogs nor rocks: not only do we need softer meditation cushions, but we are capable and called on to do many things that frogs and rocks cannot and need not do.

Dōgen cautions against falling into what his teacher Rujing called the "heresy of naturalism," the ancient version of a licentious Hippie Zen according to which we should just follow our supposedly natural whims without bothering to engage in spiritual and ethical practices.[18] In Chapter 16, we discussed the importance of ethical practice in Zen, and in Chapter 23 we will return to Dōgen's key teaching of "the oneness of practice and enlightenment." In Chapter 19, we'll discuss how the *naturalness* proper to human beings paradoxically needs to be *cultivated*, and how this cultivated naturalness is at the heart of the Zen-inspired Ways of Japanese art.

19

Zen and Art

Cultivating Naturalness

As we saw in Chapter 18, Zen teaches that we have much to learn about being human from getting back in touch with the naturalness of the non-human world. In this chapter, we'll discuss the Zen-inspired artistic "Ways" called *dō*, the Japanese pronunciation of the Chinese character for *dao*, as in Daoism. We'll see how these Ways involve a paradoxically arduous "cultivation of natural-ness." And we'll see how they are understood as vehicles for awakening and cul-tivating such virtues as spontaneity, creativity, and graceful efficacy. We'll then look at Zen gardens as an art form through which humans cultivate their place within the rest of the natural world. After that, the philosophical and spiritual implications of two key concepts of Zen aesthetics will be examined: *kire-tsuzuki* (cut-continuance) and *wabi-sabi* (rustic simplicity). Following some reflections on the nondual relation between time and eternity as displayed by *ikebana*, the Way of Flower Arrangement, the chapter will end with a Zen explanation and appreciation of the intimate relation between form and emptiness, sound and silence, as conveyed in rock gardens, brush paintings, and Japanese flute music.

Cultivating Naturalness

Zen teaches that genuine creativity requires a cultivation of natural spontaneity. "But wait a minute," you might be thinking. "Isn't it paradoxical to speak of a *cultivation* of *naturalness*? Isn't culture opposed to nature? Isn't art by definition artificial? And if something is natural, doesn't that mean that it is born or found that way, such that there is no need for something or someone to *become* natural? Isn't it self-defeating to *practice* being natural?"

These are good questions. Yet, it is perhaps one of the great paradoxes of human nature that we have to practice in order to recover and develop an in-nate naturalness and spontaneous creativity. Think of the graceful naturalness of a professional figure skater, or of a master sushi chef, or of anyone who has perfected their craft. And then peel back the curtain and watch a documentary that shows the years of arduous discipline it took them to achieve that seemingly effortless ease.

Zen Pathways. Bret W. Davis, Oxford University Press. © Oxford University Press 2022.
DOI: 10.1093/oso/9780197573686.003.0019

What does it mean that we have to *strive* to become *effortless*, that we have to *practice* to become *natural*, that we have to *cultivate* a capacity for *spontaneity*? To begin with, it means that we have to rethink our tendency to set up a dichotomy between art and culture, on the one hand, and nature and naturalness, on the other.

In the Japanese tradition, art and culture are not typically seen as essentially opposed to nature and naturalness. The modern Zen philosopher Hisamatsu Shin'ichi lists "naturalness" (Jp. *jinen*)—along with asymmetry, simplicity, austere sublimity, subtle profundity, tranquility, and freedom from attachment—as one of the distinctive characteristics of Zen art. Hisamatsu is careful to distinguish this naturalness from mere unrefined "naïveté or instinct." The artistic naturalness at issue here is "never forced or strained," and yet that does not mean that it simply occurs in nature without human intention or effort. "On the contrary," Hisamatsu says, "it is the result of a full, creative intent that is devoid of anything artificial or strained." It is the outcome of "an intention so pure and so concentrated . . . that nothing is forced." It "results when the artist enters so thoroughly into what he is creating that no conscious effort, no distance between the two, remains." It is a naturalness that lies on the thither, rather than the hither, side of arduous efforts of cultivation and training. Hisamatsu concludes that it "is not found either in natural objects or in children. True naturalness is the 'no mind' or 'no intent' that emerges from the negation both of naïve or accidental naturalness and ordinary intention."[1]

Culture allows us to actualize our humanity, and cultivation requires refraining from acting according to the arbitrary beck and call of every childish impulse and desire. And yet, the process of acculturation and humanization is not simply a departure from nature; it is, rather, the development of a specifically human capacity for participating in nature. This development requires a double negation: first a negation of uncultivated nature, and then a negation of cultivated artificiality.

This may all seem a bit confusing when we think about it abstractly, yet it makes more sense if we consider concrete examples. When I see an expert skier glide gracefully down through the moguls on a steep slope, she resembles a professional dancer smoothly harmonizing her hips and shoulders with the music. The movements of the skier and dancer seem so effortless and natural. But when I try to imitate them, I feel clumsy and my movements appear forced and artificial. Only after much practice would I begin to feel natural and in tune with the moguls or music. The same process happens in learning to play a musical instrument or to paint with watercolors. Only after much painstaking practice does the process begin to feel effortless and natural—and only then can real creativity happen. We cannot force creativity. When it happens, it just happens. In fact, it can feel like we are *in-spired*, almost literally as if a spirit has entered us and taken over the controls. In any case, it feels as though we are participating in a process greater than our controlling egos.

The Japanese philosopher Nishida Kitarō—who practiced Zen for many years—called this "pure experience," by which he meant experience that is especially free of the taint of subject-object duality that our discriminative thinking habitually imposes on experience. Among the examples he gives are those of "a climber's determined ascent of a cliff and a musician's performance of a piece that has been mastered through practice."[2] At such moments, as Nishida later puts it, we discover that we are "creative elements of a creative world."[3]

In Japan, the cultural art forms known as Ways provide patterns and practices for cultivating natural spontaneity, harmony, beauty, efficiency, effectiveness, and creativity. These include, among others, the Ways of Tea, Flower Arrangement, Calligraphy, Incense, Karate-dō, Kendō, Jūdō, and Aikidō.[4] The masters and practitioners of these Ways often understand them to be rooted in Zen. The Ways are seen as various concrete manifestations or offshoots of the state of mind or "no-mind" awakened and cultivated most directly and purely in the practice of *zazen*. The Way of Zen is, as it were, the religious root from which all these artistic branches stem, the spiritual source from which these cultural streams flow.

When I first lived in Japan in my early to mid twenties, alongside Zen I practiced the Way of Karate rather intensively for several years. I would often go to a karate dōjō in the morning and to a Zen temple in the evening. Gradually I learned to see that the connections between the two went beyond the fact that my karate practices began and ended with bows and a brief meditation. I learned to experience karate as a Way of cultivating the ability to move freely in the Zone of Zen without self-consciously tripping over my own feet or fearfully freezing up and failing to evade the high-flying feet of my sparring partner.

Stages on the Ways: Conforming, Rebelling, Creating

I also learned about the stages involved in cultivating natural spontaneity and creativity by practicing the Way of Karate. Before one is ready to spar freely, one has to learn the set "forms," the *kata*, of the karate school in which one is training. The first thing that I learned was that the Way of Karate demanded that I let go of my all too American insistence on doing things "my way." At first, and for a long time, one has to conform to the forms by modeling oneself on the movements of the teacher and senior students.

There was one senior student in particular whom I would try to imitate as best I could, since her performance of the forms seemed so flawless. However, once I started to participate in tournaments, I was surprised to discover that she did not receive very high scores in the black belt division of the *kata* competition.

One day I asked my teacher why this senior student did not score highly in tournaments. Surprisingly, he told me that it was because she had not yet made the forms truly her own and thus did not demonstrate enough uniqueness or originality. "Uniqueness, originality?" I thought. "But I have been trying hard to let go of my American obsession with uniqueness and originality so that I can conform to the traditional forms, so that I can model myself on the molds that were set in stone by past masters." I wasn't exactly wrong, but I had only grasped the first step of the process.

I learned that conforming or imitating is only the first of three stages in the process of karate and indeed all the Japanese Ways. In Japanese, these three stages are called *shu*, *ha*, and *ri*.[5] These terms literally mean "preserving," "breaking with," and "departing from." We can rephrase them in terms of "conforming," "rebelling," and "creating."

To begin with, one has to put one's egoistically assertive artificiality aside and conform to the set patterns of the tradition. This stage generally takes many years, and, frankly, most practitioners never really go beyond it. But eventually, if one sticks with the practice long enough, and when the time is ripe, one breaks the rules—in the sense that one violates the letter of the law in order to better express its spirit. In fact, one *must* do this in order to truly *appropriate* the tradition, which literally means to make it one's own. I recently saw a bilingual advertisement in a Tokyo airport that says, "To break the rules, you must first master them." A more literal translation of the Japanese version would be: "Master the forms. In order to break them." In any case, this saying implies that after one has mastered the rules, one has to rebel against them in order to become creative.

However, rebellion is still a subtle form of bondage. Rebels are still defined by—and thus bound to—that against which they rebel. The final stage of "departing from" is where true originality can be found. Here one is bound neither to one's egoistic whims, nor to forms or rules set in stone, nor even to rebelling against anything. In the Way of Karate as in other Ways, when a master truly reaches this level, a new form is created and perhaps even a new school is born.

These stages are strikingly similar to what Nietzsche calls the "three metamorphoses of the spirit," for which he used the three figures of the camel, the lion, and the child.[6] The camel is the "weight-bearing spirit" who takes on the heavy load of tradition. The camel is obedient and takes on all the discipline and teachings it can bear. Only then is it ready to head out alone into the desert, where it becomes a lion who shakes off the heavy load of tradition and struggles against the "great dragon" of "thou shalt" with the self-confidence of "I will!" This, we could say, is the stage of spiritual adolescence, a rebellious stage in which one should not remain stuck—but through which one must pass.

I was once a rather rebellious teenager myself, and my kids are now rather rebellious teenagers, so I know firsthand the difficulties, but also the importance, of this transitional stage. A longtime participant in The Heart of Zen Meditation Group, Janet Preis, insightfully expressed an understanding of this stage in a conversation about going through it with her own teenage lioness. She said that in order for her daughter to learn to go her own way, it was necessary for her to turn her back on her mother and walk out the door. We should not—and cannot—stop our teenagers from rebelliously turning their backs on us, or from walking out the door in order to learn to walk on their own two feet. Having done our best to give them guidance so long as they let us, and ground rules so long as they are needed, in the end we need to give them the go-ahead to find their own way. (My cubs would tell you that I'm still working on this!)

It is important to pass through a period of rebellion; but it is even more important not to get stuck there. In Nietzsche's terms, the lion is capable of saying no to the old but not yet yes to the new. For this third metamorphosis of the spirit, a kind of spiritual rebirth is necessary. "The child," Nietzsche says, "is innocence and forgetting, a new beginning, a game, a self-propelled wheel, a sacred 'Yes.' For the game of creation . . . a sacred 'Yes' is needed."[7]

With his allegory of the three metamorphoses of the spirit, Nietzsche is clearly reflecting on his own struggles with Christianity, the religion in which he was raised as the pious son of a Lutheran pastor. Nietzsche's figure Zarathustra heralds the "overman" who would completely overcome Christianity and rethink religion. But did Nietzsche himself get stuck in the rebellious lion stage? He worried intensely about whether he was able to rid himself of "the spirit of revenge" against the faith of his upbringing.[8] In Chapter 12, I talked about how I developed a deeper appreciation for Christianity only after I drifted away from it as a teenager and then later learned to see some of its core teachings from the outside and with Zen Buddhist eyes.

In any case, and to return to the topic of this chapter, I suspect that the three stages I have described can be appreciated by anyone who has struggled with learning a craft and who knows what it is like to discover a genuine originality and creativity only after passing through a period of arduous training. To attain a naturally creative spontaneity, one has to work through the paradox of "trying not to try." It takes strict discipline to become genuinely free. Just acting according to whatever superficially feels natural won't do if one wants to become internally as well as externally free. If we just act on our arbitrary whims, we are merely repeating the karmic impulses we have become habituated to.

The three stages can be seen in the discipline of monastic training as well as in the Japanese Ways that are inspired by Zen. The modern Japanese Rinzai Zen master Hirata Seikō, after stressing the role of regulations and forms in Zen monastic training and more generally in East Asian education, notes that it is important not to get stuck in the forms and fall into a rigid formalism. It is for that reason that Zen speaks of the process of "entering and then exiting formalities," of immersing oneself in and then breaking out of regulatory frameworks.[9] In working on a kōan, for example, one has to learn to see with the eyes and hear with the ears of the Zen Ancestors in the stories before one is able to make the kōan one's own and present one's response to it in full confidence. And only after passing many kōans could one eventually become capable of creating one's own.

Also, consider the practice of *zazen*, which at first feels rather artificial. One has to sit and breathe in a certain manner, and one is not allowed to move, despite urges to fidget, adjust one's posture, or scratch an itch. Yet, once one gets used to it, *zazen* feels like the most natural thing one does—it truly feels like "the Dharma Gate of ease and joy." Sitting down, one feels at peace; standing up, one feels refreshed, reenergized, and ready to creatively reengage.

Zen Gardens: Art as Part of Nature

Let's turn now to the relation between art and nature. One of the salient characteristics of Zen is the degree to which, and the way in which, not only nature and naturalness but also art and beauty are deeply connected with spirituality. In Zen, art, nature, and spirituality are intimately interwoven. This is why Zen temples and monasteries always include gardens.

In a sense, Zen gardens can be understood as an art of literally re-presenting nature: not representing in the sense of reproducing it in an essentially different medium, but rather re-presenting the macrocosm of the natural world in a carefully curated microcosmic space. Many famous Zen rock gardens—more officially called "dry mountains-and-waters gardens"—are designed as microcosmic re-presentations of the macrocosmic natural world: raked sand evokes oceans and rivers, rocks replicate islands and mountains, and so forth.[10]

These gardens do not replicate nature in an artificial medium. They are themselves part of nature. Moreover, the human artists who cultivate these gardens, and also the spectators who view and commune with them, are not supernatural aliens but rather natural beings recovering a sense of their place in the natural world. Zen gardens are, as it were, nature re-presenting itself to itself through the natural artistry and appreciation of its human manifestations.

Just as a dualistic understanding of the relation between nature and humanity is foreign to Zen, a strict dichotomy between nature and culture is alien to Zen art.[11] This struck me clearly once when a Zen master invited my family to tour the insides of Kinkakuji and Ginkakuji, the famous Temples of the Golden Pavilion and Silver Pavilion in Kyoto. The sliding doors of the rooms open wide onto the meticulously cultivated gardens, which in turn open onto the uncultivated mountain forests beyond the temple grounds.

Figure 19.1 Author with Kobayashi Gentoku Rōshi at Shōkokuji, Kyoto, June 2018.

Japanese gardens often use a technique called *shakkei*, meaning "borrowed scenery" or "borrowed landscape." The natural environment is allowed to appear as the background and even as an extension of the garden; conversely, the garden appears as a part of the whole of the natural world. When one sits in the temple of Entsūji in northern Kyoto, its sliding doors open onto the cultivated garden in the foreground, with the backdrop of Mt. Hiei looming beyond its hedges. This ancient Zen garden thus opens onto the mountain atop which lies Enryaku-ji, the temple complex and headquarters of Tendai Buddhism. Incidentally, I used to live at the foot of Mt. Hiei and would often hike the trails, wondering if they were the ones down which Eisai and Dōgen descended, turning their backs on their Tendai parentage and destined to creatively transplant the Rinzai and Sōtō schools onto Japanese soil. On my hikes I would also marvel at the manner in which temples and shrines are nestled among the trees and small streams, human habitats harmoniously integrated into and immersed within the *rest* of nature.

Borderlines that Connect as Well as Separate

As we learned in Chapters 8 and 9, nondualism for Zen should not be misunderstood as disallowing or even downplaying differences. Rather, it means that the borders that separate things are at the same time the membranes that connect them. On the one hand, the border between the inside of a Japanese temple or traditional house and the garden outside is clearly marked, usually with an *engawa* or narrow wooden veranda on which one can sit to view the garden. On the other hand, this is a porous border; sliding doors open so as to allow the circulation of air between the inside and outside regions of the world. Something similar can be said for the fences, walls, or hedges that demarcate where the cultivated garden ends and the uncultivated environment begins.

This aesthetic of neatly demarcated borders that connect as well as separate is called *kire-tsuzuki*, or "cut-continuance." As the contemporary Kyoto School philosopher Ōhashi Ryōsuke has shown, this aesthetic pervades Japanese art and culture.[12] It can be seen, for example, in the borderlines between tatami mats, lines that both connect one mat to another and separate them. The aesthetic of cut-continuance can also be seen in the sharp and distinct, yet also clearly connected, movements made by a Noh theater actor or by a karate practitioner performing the forms.

The world is made up of singular and distinct things, persons, and events that are, at the same time, intimately interconnected. The tea room and the garden are separate and yet connected. Each one is not the other, and yet each one cannot fully be what it is without the other. The Kyoto School philosopher and lay Zen master Nishitani Keiji uses the metaphor of adjacent rooms in a house to explain how walls connect as well as separate spaces. A room is shaped by its four walls, but each of these walls also belongs to an adjacent room.[13] He uses this metaphor of adjacent rooms both separated and connected by walls to talk specifically about the relation between Zen and art. Yet I am sure that he would agree with me that the point can be generalized, such that we can use it to talk about all relations, including relations between individual human beings and relations between human society and the rest of the natural world. For example, the hedges between my backyard and my neighbor's backyard belong to both of us, and we both need to water their roots and trim their branches. As humanly cultivated parts of nature, hedges also serve as a hinge between the human and the non-human worlds, enabling us to stay in touch with the cosmos that encompasses us.

Humans are distinct parts of the interconnected natural world. We are not the trees, and yet we cannot breathe—and so cannot be—without the trees. Our homes protect us from the elements, but they are also made of the elements. Windows and doors are made to open onto, as well as shut out, the outside world. Taking care of our garden requires appreciating that it is part of the surrounding natural environment; it is a way of thinking globally and acting locally. The natural art of Zen gardens teaches us these lessons.

Wabi Sabi: The Rustic Simplicity of the Imperfect and Impermanent

The Zen arts also remind us of the impermanence of all things and of the interconnectedness of life and death. They remind us that we cannot truly live unless we acknowledge our own fragility and mortality along with the ephemeral uniqueness of all that we hold dear.

As mentioned in Chapter 6, since ancient times the Japanese have celebrated the poignant beauty of the cherry blossoms not despite their ephemerality, but rather because of it. Bursting into bloom for just a few short days, the cherry blossoms are most beautiful as they flutter to the ground. Nearly everyone takes time out of their busy lives to sit and sing under the trees, bathing in their transient beauty and being touched by their annual display of *mono-no-aware* or "the pathos of things."

A more specifically Zen aesthetic is that of *wabi-sabi*, a phrase infamously difficult to translate. *Wabi-sabi* can be sensed in the rustic simplicity and solitude of a weathered mountain hut as well as in the handmade and well-worn implements of the tea ceremony, such as a chipped ceramic tea bowl that is cherished for its unique imperfections and aged earthiness. *Wabi-sabi* has become famous around the world despite the fact—or probably rather because of the fact—that it goes against the grain of the modern materialistic infatuation with the mass production and consumption of shiny new technological devises. Steve Jobs was fascinated by Zen and Japanese aesthetics, but the iPhone, despite its beautiful simplicity and planned obsolescence, hardly reflects the rustic nature and natural imperfections of an artifact with *wabi-sabi*. Andrew Juniper writes that the

> term *wabi sabi* suggests such qualities as impermanence, humility, asymmetry, and imperfection. These underlying principles are diametrically opposed to those of their Western counterparts, whose values are rooted in a Hellenic worldview that values permanence, grandeur, symmetry, and perfection.[14]

Indeed, the aesthetic sensibility of *wabi-sabi* affirms what Buddhism calls the Three Marks of Existence: the *insubstantiality* and *impermanence* of all things, and the *sorrow* that accompanies a yearning to transcend this ephemeral and imperfect world. Yet, as the Japanese philosopher Tanaka Kyūbun points out, *wabi-sabi* also expresses a radical reaffirmation of our mortal lives once we let go of any world-negating aesthetic or spiritual aspirations toward otherworldly transcendence.[15]

The aesthetic of *wabi-sabi* reminds us to appreciate the lives of things and our own lives because of—rather than despite—the fact that they are fragile and ephemeral. It manifests a mature spirituality that does not flee from the impermanence and imperfection of our lives and all that we care about. Nor does it sink into melancholy and world-negation; rather, it cultivates a keen appreciation of the interconnectedness of the mundane and the marvelous, of solitude and solidarity, of beauty and impermanence, and, ultimately, of life and death.

When the eighteenth-/nineteenth-century wandering Zen monk Ryōkan was asked by a family to write in calligraphy a saying that would bring them good fortune, he wrote the single character for "death." Exasperated, the family asked him why he would write something apparently so inauspicious. He explained: "When people are mindful of death, they don't waste time or squander their wealth."[16] Like Ryōkan's calligraphy of the character for "death," when we drive by a cemetery sign that says *memento mori*, "remember death," we should understand this as a reminder to live our lives to the fullest, to appreciate each moment as a precious and irreplaceable opportunity to attend to what matters most.

Ikebana: A Living-Dying Flower as a Moment of Eternity

The Japanese art of flower arrangement, called the Way of Flowers (*kadō*) or, more often, *ikebana*, also provides us with a beautiful lesson in impermanence. *Ikebana* literally means "enlivening flowers," and yet, paradoxically, it does this by first of all cutting them off from their roots and, in effect, killing them. Nishitani claims that this paradox goes to the heart of *ikebana* as an art form whose "essential beauty lies precisely in its being transitory and timely," as opposed to "buildings, sculptures, paintings, and so forth" that "are all made to withstand this thing we call time."[17] The latter kind of art form is an artificial extension of the natural will of all things to endure, to live forever and not die. And yet, to present life without the shadow of death is to misrepresent the whole truth of life.

> Although the life of nature contains temporality as part of its essence, it resists and conceals that essence. Nature exists as if it were trying to slip away from time. In contrast, the flower with its roots cut has, in one stroke, returned to its

original, essential fate in time. . . . The flower thus poised in death is cut off from its time in life to exist as if in a timeless present. . . . Breaking through the surface of time, it becomes a moment in eternity.[18]

Thus, as opposed to "the kind of art that seeks eternity by denying temporality," *ikebana* "tries to unveil eternity by becoming radically temporal." "This momentariness of a higher order expresses eternity. Finitude, though thoroughly finite, becomes a symbol of eternity. Time, though thoroughly temporal, becomes an eternal moment."[19]

The "eternity" Nishitani speaks of here is not a personal immortality or the immutability of any form whatsoever. All persons are born and die; all forms arise and fall. And yet, in the background of these living and dying persons, rising and falling forms, is a formless fecundity, an impersonal wellspring of personality. Nishitani's teacher, Nishida Kitarō, calls this the "Eternal Now" that envelops and manifests itself in the ceaseless flow of time. East Asian art, Nishida says, "is generally considered impersonal because this background is an essential part of the art. It reverberates in a formless, infinite echo, in faint traces of a voiceless infinity." In contrast, he adds, Western art tends to be "completely shaped," filling up the apparently inert "void" of the canvas or space. There are, of course, exceptions. Nishida points out that this "backdrop of eternity" can be sensed in Michelangelo's "unfinished sculptures," which show smooth personal forms emerging from unhewn impersonal stone; and also in Goethe's poetry, which allows the finite human individual to disappear into and appear out of an infinite background.[20]

Forms of Emptiness, Sounds of Silence

The Zen arts are often tangible, visible, and audible reminders of the interconnectedness of form and emptiness. The most famous Buddhist sutra chanted throughout East Asia is the *Heart Sutra*, and its most famous line is "Form is emptiness, emptiness is form."[21] There are several ways to understand what this means, starting with the basic understanding that all things are empty of "own-being," meaning that nothing has its being on its own; in other words, all things are interconnected.

The Vietnamese Zen master Thich Nhat Hanh reminds us that to be empty of one thing means to be full of another: a cup that is empty of water is full of air. All things are empty of own-being; but that also means that they are full of inter-being.[22] Emptiness is thus not opposed to the distinct forms of things; it is, rather, the way in which those forms are—or, as it were, inter-are. As every artist concerned with the composition of a painting knows, one form can be what it is only in relation to the empty space and/or other forms around it.

Nhat Hanh also employs a common Mahayana metaphor to explain another way of understanding the relation between form and emptiness. He says: "Form is the wave and emptiness is the water."[23] In one sense, wave and water are distinct; and yet, in another sense, they are the same. The wave is a form of the water, which in itself is formless. Because the water is formless, it can take on any form. As we saw in Chapter 9, this metaphor of water and waves is a key to Zen's understanding of the nondual relation between individuality and universality. As I put it in Chapter 13, our interconnected individual lives are understood to be like different waves interacting on the same great ocean of the Buddha-nature.

The fifteenth-century Japanese Zen master and poet Ikkyū speaks of emptiness as a formless "original field" from which everything arises and to which everything returns. He says: "All forms—of plants, trees, and land—come from emptiness, and so as a provisional metaphor it is called the original field."[24] As we will discuss in Chapter 21, the modern Zen philosophers of the Kyoto School speak of the "Place of Absolute Nothingness" and the "Field of Emptiness."

In the Western tradition, "emptiness" and "nothingness" have usually been understood only negatively, as a mere privation or lack of being, or as an inert vacuity. It is for this reason that nineteenth-century Europeans misunderstood Buddhism as a nihilistic pessimism and condemned it as a "cult of emptiness" or "cult of nothingness."[25] They did not understand that in Zen the Field of Emptiness is a fecund matrix that engenders and encompasses all forms. In fact, this is not entirely unlike the way some mystics in the biblical traditions have spoken of God or the Godhead "in whom we live and move and have our being" as a sublime "Nothingness" whose plentitude cannot be reduced to the finite form of any being (see Chapters 9, 12, 13).

Zen understands nothingness or emptiness as a creative source of beings, as a formless yet fecund origin of forms, and as a place, field, or matrix that allows things and persons to be and to inter-be, rather than as a mere absence of being or as an inert void.[26] The philosophical background of this Zen understanding of nothingness and emptiness can be found in Daoism as well as in Mahayana Buddhism. The *Daodejing* tells us that "the myriad beings are born from being, and being is born from nothingness."[27]

The best way to gain an initial—and perhaps, in the end, also deeper—appreciation of this understanding of emptiness or nothingness as a creative Source-Field may be through art rather than philosophy.[28] Often we can sense and feel what we cannot yet—or cannot ultimately—understand with our intellects. And so, let me conclude this chapter with an image of the famous rock garden at Ryōanji in Kyoto, and with the suggestion that, along with it, you also look at some "mountains and waters" landscape paintings by Guoxi, Mayuan, Sesshū, Sōami, and other classical East Asian artists. If possible, while viewing these images listen to some traditional Japanese flute (*shakuhachi*) music. I think you will be able to appreciate how such art forms demonstrate how silence and emptiness can be experienced not as mere absences of sound and form, but rather as both the creative wellspring from out of which they arise and the peaceful abode back into which they return.

Figure 19.2 Viewing rock garden at Ryōanji, Kyoto, December 2018.

20

Zen and Language

The Middle Way Between Silence and Speech

Chapter 19 ended with some references to images and music that demonstrate how visual forms and audible sounds can be experienced as expressive determinations of a silent yet fecund origin, of an amorphous matrix that both pulsates with creative potentiality and pacifies with restful tranquility. In this chapter, we'll take up the closely related issue of how Zen both indicates the limits of language and celebrates its creative delimitations.

Let's begin by reading the most famous haiku by the seventeenth-century Zen poet Matsuo Bashō, a poem thought by many to have been written in commemoration of his experience of enlightenment:

> The old pond
> A frog leaps in
> The sound of water![1]

The old pond may have been just that: an old pond by which Bashō was sitting, perhaps in meditation. At the same time, the old pond can be understood as an image for the primordially silent and formless field, aboriginally empty yet filled with the potential to manifest in this or that singular interconnected event of reality—such as the sudden splash of a leaping frog.

Another haiku by Bashō relates the silence of a cliff to the piercing sound of a cicada:

> Oh quietude—
> Seeping into the cliff
> The call of a cicada[2]

Note how the sounds of the frog's splash and the cicada's call allow us to become aware—at least retroactively, and perhaps even simultaneously—of the stillness of the old pond and the quietude of the cliff. Another Zen poem makes this point with the clear cry of a bird within the reticent vastness of the surrounding mountain.

Zen Pathways. Bret W. Davis, Oxford University Press. © Oxford University Press 2022.
DOI: 10.1093/oso/9780197573686.003.0020

> A solitary bird calls out
> The mountain grows all the more
> Darkly mysterious[3]

Poetry has always been highly valued as a linguistic vehicle for spiritual insight and expression in Zen. Not only haiku, but also longer forms of poetry have been written by Zen monastics and lay practitioners down through the ages.[4] In addition to poetry, the recorded teachings, dialogues, and commentaries of Zen masters fill many volumes.

And yet, at the same time, Zen masters claim to "not rely on words and letters" and often warn against getting entangled in textual exegeses and doctrinal disputes. They promote instead the direct path of silent meditation, and often prefer to teach in person with a few pithy "living words" or even with non-verbal actions, rather than with verbose written discourses (such as this book!).

Zen's Ambivalent Stance(s) Toward Language

Zen's stance or stances toward language can thus appear to be highly ambivalent, paradoxical, and even at times contradictory. On the one hand, Zen masters repeatedly instruct their students to go beyond words—sometimes "using words to get rid of words" and sometimes resorting to shouts and even blows. One must, they stress, holistically experience enlightenment oneself, not just read about someone else's experience of it. Reading about someone else's lunch won't fill your stomach. On the other hand, Zen has produced more texts than perhaps any other Buddhist tradition. How can we understand this paradox?

To begin with, we should note that Buddhism has no bible. It has a canon, or several canons, defined and interpreted differently by the different traditions and schools. But it has no single infallible book of revelation. It has hundreds of sutras, each proclaiming to be, in some sense, the words of the Buddha. And it has thousands of commentaries, philosophical treatises, and other types of writings. The Japanese edition of the East Asian Buddhist Canon contains more than five thousand individual texts. The Zen tradition alone has produced hundreds of volumes—and counting.

Zen does not proclaim that in the beginning was the Word. Rather, in the beginning was Reality, and Reality can never be fully captured in words. Thich Nhat Hanh is surely one of the most eloquent of modern Zen masters; and yet he too stresses: "The world of concepts is not the world of reality. . . . Words are inadequate to express the truth of ultimate reality." He does go on to acknowledge the importance of employing language as a "finger pointing to the moon," as a skillful means for "liberating us from the prejudices and attachments to knowledge."[5] Other Zen masters have not always been so patient with the limits of language; Huineng is depicted as tearing up sutras, and Dahui reportedly burned the printing blocks of his teacher's celebrated kōan collection, *The Blue Cliff Record*, since this intricate text was inadvertently causing students to lose the Way as they became sidetracked by and caught up in the "entangling vines" of words and letters.

With intentional irony, the main Rinzai kōan collection compiled in Japan is entitled *The Collection of Entangling Vines*.[6] In his preface to *The Gateless Barrier*, which along with *The Blue Cliff Record* is the most famous collection of kōans, the thirteenth-century Chinese Zen master Wumen paradoxically writes:

> These talks would serve to stir up waves where there is no wind, or to gash a wound in a healthy skin. Even more foolish is one who clings to words and phrases and thus tries to achieve understanding. It is like trying to strike the moon with a stick, or scratching a shoe because there is an itchy spot on the foot. It has nothing to do with the Truth.[7]

Even if it is hyperbole for Wumen to say that clinging to the written words of Zen masters, including his own, has "nothing to do with the Truth," he is stressing a point that Zen masters never tire of making: One cannot intellectually read or write one's way to enlightenment. It demands a more wholehearted and holistically embodied-spiritual practice.

At the same time, Wumen and other Zen masters also tell us not to get attached to silence either. Some, like the prolific thirteenth-century Japanese Zen master Dōgen, even stress that we should affirm the entangling vines of languages as a vital part of the web in which our lives are interwoven with all things.[8] After all, one might wonder, if it were only concerned with direct non-verbal experience and silent transmission, then why has the Zen tradition produced so many texts?

Wumen tells us, in his commentary on one of the kōans in *The Gateless Barrier*: "If you understand the first word of Zen / You will know the last word. / The last word or the first word— / 'It' is not a word."[9] We can understand this to mean that because there is no first word, there is no last word; because there is no foundational text, there is no final text. Since "it" can never be finally and fully captured in any text, it must always be expressed afresh in every new context. And so, every new Zen master must leave behind a new record of teachings, sayings, stories, poetry, or encounter dialogues, since every new enlightening experience gives rise to a new expression—or at least a creative reiteration of old one—in a new situation.

One of the most patiently pedagogical of Zen texts is *Dialogues in a Dream*, a record of the fourteenth-century Japanese Zen master Musō Soseki's teachings given to Ashikaga Tadayoshi, the brother and governing partner of the first

Muromachi *shōgun*. At the end, Tadayoshi asks whether he can distribute a copy of his record of the dialogues to other people with an interest in the Way. Musō Soseki responds in a nuanced manner as follows:

> The guidance of a Zen monk is not like that of scholastics, who teach doctrines they have memorized or written down on paper. The Zen monk simply expresses in a direct and immediate way whatever the situation calls for. This is called "face-to-face guidance." . . . [T]he ancient masters all forbade the recording of their statements. However, if nothing was ever to be written down, then the paths of guidance would be severed. Thus the Zen school has resigned itself to publishing records of the ancients, though this is not its true intention.[10]

Musō Soseki may have had in mind the ninth-century Chinese Zen master Huangbo, who hesitated to allow his lay disciple to record and distribute his teachings. In response to being handed a poem, Huangbo responded: "If things could be expressed like this with ink and paper, what would be the purpose of a sect like ours?"[11] Huangbo and Musō stress that linguistic teachings cannot convey the whole truth, since they are always situational, spatially and temporally delimited, and because they are always tailored to the person to whom they are imparted in light of their current place on the path.

And yet, such demarcations and disclaimers are only part of the story of Zen's stance or stances toward language. Indeed, striking affirmations of the expressive power of written as well as spoken words abound in the Zen tradition. They include the following saying: "Zen is like spring and words are like the flowers. Spring abides in the flowers and all the flowers are spring. Flowers abide in spring and all of spring is the flowers."[12] The fifteenth-century Japanese Zen poet Ten'in Ryūtaku simply and bluntly states: "Outside poetry there is no Zen, outside of Zen there is no poetry."[13]

Can we reconcile these apparently contradictory claims about the limits and ubiquity of language, about its impotence and power? Can nothing be expressed, or can everything be expressed? Are we to remain silent, or are we to speak? The ninth-century Chinese Zen master Deshan thrust this dilemma upon us and presses us for an answer: "Thirty blows if you can speak; thirty blows if you can't!"[14]

Using Words to Point Beyond Words

We would probably not be able to evade Deshan's blows. Nevertheless, it should be clear by now that in order to understand Zen, we must be able to understand both the limits of language and its expressive power.

The Zen tradition often foregrounds the former—namely, the teaching that we need to first free ourselves from our linguistic strictures. It is said in this regard that words are at best like fingers pointing at the moon, not the enlightening moon itself. We tend to get fixated on the finger, like a dog who just sniffs and licks your hand, not understanding that you are trying to point to something. Another analogy used to make this point is "a painting of a rice cake." Just as it is only a real rice cake that can satisfy your physical hunger, only the experience of enlightenment will satisfy your spiritual hunger. An explanation can at best whet your appetite for the actual experience.

Hence, it is said in the Zen tradition that from the time of his enlightenment to the end of his life, as he traveled about for forty-five (or forty-nine) years giving all the talks that became the sutras, "the Buddha taught not a single word." The chapter on Nirvana in Nagarjuna's seminal text, *Mulamadhymakakarika*, ends with the lines:

> This halting of cognizing everything, the halting of hypostatizing, is blissful.
> No Dharma whatsoever was ever taught by the Buddha to anyone.[15]

In the *Lankavatara Sutra*, which Bodhidharma is said to have brought with him to China, the Buddha says:

> The Dharma transcends language. Therefore, Mahamati, neither I nor any other buddha or bodhisattva speaks a single word. . . . Still, if we did not say anything, our teaching would come to an end. . . . Therefore, Mahamati, bodhisattvas are not attached to words but expound the teaching of the sutras according to what is appropriate. Because the longings and afflictions of beings are not the same, I and other buddhas teach different teachings to beings with different levels of understanding.[16]

In other words, all words are matters of "expedient means," provisional fingers pointing at ineffable reality, which ultimately cannot be said to arise or cease, "because even the categories of existence and nonexistence do not apply."[17]

Zen masters frequently use contentless indicators, such as the word "suchness," to gesture toward the experience of reality "such as it is," without the distorting filters of linguistic concepts. This technique of using words to point beyond words can be traced back to the seminal sixth-century text *The Awakening of Faith in Mahayana*, in which we read:

> All explanations by words are provisional and without [absolute] validity, for they are merely used in accordance with illusions and are incapable [of denoting Suchness]. . . . The term Suchness is, so to speak, the limit of verbalization

wherein a word is used to put an end to words. . . . It should be understood that all things are incapable of being verbally explained or thought of; hence the name Suchness.[18]

Ultimately, the text claims, we can only say that reality is such as it is. Yet, this is not to say that we should remain silent and refuse to think; rather, in our use of linguistic and conceptual distinctions, we should maintain a recognition of them as provisional. Words perspectivally reveal—and tend to isolate, dichotomize, and de-temporalize—certain momentary aspects of reality only by way of simultaneously concealing others.[19]

A Special Transmission Beyond Texts and Teachings

A stress on the non-linguistically-delimited direct experience of enlightenment is expressed in the definition of Zen attributed to Bodhidharma:

> Not relying on words and letters,
> A special transmission outside all doctrines;
> Pointing directly to the human heart-mind,
> Seeing into one's true nature and becoming a Buddha.[20]

Of course, Zen teachers do not say that you should not read or listen to their teachings. The modern Japanese Zen master Yamada Mumon says that "it is only because there is a teaching that there is something transmitted separate from it." He suggests that the teachings are necessary but not sufficient for enlightenment. Disabusing his listeners and readers of an anti-intellectual misunderstanding of Zen, he says: "First, we must study the sutras and ponder the records left by the teachers of the past in order to determine where our own nature is." "Sometimes," he continues, "you hear it said that Zen monks do not have to read books or study. When did this misleading idea get started? . . . The ancient teachers engaged in all branches of scholarship and studied all there was to study."[21]

On the other hand, Yamada Rōshi goes on to say, "Just through scholarship alone, they were not able to settle what was bothering them. It was then that they turned to Zen." The study of teachings and texts is important, but, in the end, one has to go through and beyond the words of others to a firsthand and holistic experience of awakening. Words are important, even necessary—but they are not sufficient. In effect he is saying that Zen is not anti-intellectual, but it is trans-intellectual.

The special transmission that cannot be reduced to a doctrine and that does not rely on language is said to have been passed down from one Zen Ancestor to the next, from Shakyamuni Buddha to present-day Zen masters. Case 6 in

The Gateless Barrier tells the story of the transmission from Shakyamuni Buddha to the First Indian Ancestor of Zen, Mahakashyapa, in the Flower Sermon. As the story goes, one day the Buddha sat down to give a sermon in his usual manner. This time, however, he simply held up a flower without saying a word. The audience was mystified, except for Mahakashyapa, who smiled. The Buddha then said:

> I have the all-pervading True Dharma, incomparable Nirvana, exquisite teaching of formless form. It does not rely on words and letters and is transmitted outside all doctrines. I now hand it to Mahakashyapa.[22]

This special transmission is said to have been subsequently passed down from one Ancestor to the next, such as when Bodhidharma, who is said to have brought Zen from India to China a thousand years later, acknowledged his successor Huike after he demonstrated his understanding by means of bowing and standing in silence.[23]

The seventeenth-century Japanese Zen master Shidō Bunan, in the following words, tells us that the ultimate truth cannot be taught in words:

> When you penetrate the fundamental origin
> You go beyond all phenomena.
> Who knows the realm beyond all words
> Which the Buddhas and Ancestors could not transmit?[24]

Indeed, he tells us, the ultimate truth cannot be "transmitted" at all. There is no sacred object or mystical formula to be handed down. Teachers can only verify whether their students have themselves experienced enlightenment. So-called Dharma transmission is really a matter of *recognition*, not a bestowal or transference of something.

The Sixth Chinese Ancestor of Zen, Huineng, told the monk who pursued him that, if he wished, he could take the robe and bowl, since they are mere symbols of recognition. When the monk said that he was after the Dharma, not just these symbols, Huineng instructed him to not think of good or evil and to directly realize, at this very moment, his "Original Face," his true self. With this, the monk is said to have had a great awakening. However, his awakening was evidently still incomplete, insofar as he went on to ask: "Besides these secret words and meanings, is there a still deeper meaning or not?" Huineng told him: "What I have just told you is no secret. If you will reflectively illuminate your Original Face, the secret is in you yourself."[25]

The twelfth-century Chinese Zen master Dahui, who advocated the kōan practice of "looking at phrases" rather than the practice of "silent illumination," nevertheless stressed that *the point of words is to point beyond words*. This meant, for Dahui, to point back behind the differentiations of words to the Mind that is the undifferentiated source of differentiations. "This Mind," he says, "can put names on everything, but nothing can put a name on it." Even such lofty Buddhist names as "Suchness," "Buddha-nature," "Enlightenment," and "Nirvana" are at best provisional names for this ultimately unnamable Mind.[26]

No amount of intellectualizing about reality can help you solve the great problem of life and death, the problem of Samsara. Dahui admonishes armchair intellectuals, saying:

> Your whole life you've made up so many little word games, when the last day of your life arrives, which phrases are you going to use to oppose birth and death? To succeed you must know clearly where we come from at birth and where we go at death.[27]

A typical Zen answer to the question of where we come from at birth and go at death might be the Great Ocean of the One Mind or the Truth Body of the Buddha. Yet these too are just words, just fingers pointing at the moon, just verbal indications of enlightenment or Nirvana, not the liberating experience of awakening itself. Even words such as "ineffable" and "silence" are just that, words.

Traveling the Middle Way Between Silence and Speech

We have seen how Zen demands that we go beyond language. And yet, it also insists that we must speak. Even a silent experience of ineffability is, at best, just one side of the whole truth. Dahui pushes us to go beyond a one-sided negation of words, saying: "This Matter can neither be sought by the mind nor obtained by no-mind. It can neither be reached through words nor penetrated through silence."[28]

The Third Chinese Ancestor of Zen, Sengcan, ends his famous poem, *Inscription on Trust in Mind*, by reminding us that "the Way is beyond all words."[29] One can detect the influence of Daoism here on the early development of Zen in China. The paradoxical opening lines of the *Daodejing* tell us, "The Way that can be told is not the abiding Way."[30] And yet, we might well wonder, if you can't tell us about the real Way, then why write the rest of the book? Indicating the limits of language obviously cannot be the whole story of the teachings of Daoism or Zen.

The ninth-century Chinese Zen poet Bai Juyi criticized some Zen teachers of his day for a one-sided rejection of language, pointing out that "abandoning the written word completely is not the Middle Way." Bai Juyi also criticized some

Daoists for erring in this direction, playfully yet pointedly writing the following verse about the words of Laozi, the legendary author of the *Daodejing*:

> "Those who speak don't know;
> those who know don't speak"—
> I'm told those are Laozi's words,
> but if we believe that Laozi knew,
> how is it he wrote five thousand words?[31]

The sixteenth-century Korean Zen master So Sahn tells us:

> If you become attached to words and speech, then even the Buddha's silently raising a flower or Mahakashyapa's wordless smile will be only another trace of the sutras. However, when you attain the truth within your own mind, even all the base chatter or elegant speech of the mundane world become[s] nothing less than this same "special transmission outside the sutras."[32]

A canonical reference to the transcendence of language is found in the *Vimalakirti Sutra*, a highly revered text in the Zen tradition. The climax of this sutra is generally held to be the layperson Vimalakirti's "thunderous silence," with which he demonstrates what it means to "truly enter the gate of nonduality" without using a word or even a syllable.[33]

And yet, the modern Rinzai Zen master Shibayama Zenkei warns us that Vimalakirti's silence must not be misunderstood as silence in opposition to speech.[34] Indeed, earlier in the *Vimalakirti Sutra* itself a wise goddess reprimands the Hinayana representative Shariputra for remaining silent and for claiming that "emancipation cannot be spoken of in words." The goddess teaches him: "Words, writing, all are marks of emancipation. . . . Therefore, Shariputra, you can speak of emancipation without putting words aside."[35]

Dōgen questions the Zen tradition's apparent predilection to privilege silence over speech, suggesting that other responses to Bodhidharma besides Huike's silent stance were also appropriate, including that of Daofu, who said: "I neither cling to nor abandon words and letters; I use them as a means of the Way."[36] In Dōgen's own prolific and profound writings we find both instructions to step back from language into meditative silence as well as pronouncements and demonstrations of the expressive power of language.

In *Universally Recommended Instructions for Zazen*, the first text he composed, Dōgen points us toward the meditation cushion and away from texts and talks when he instructs us to "put aside the intellectual practice of investigating words and chasing phrases, and learn to take the backward step that turns the light [of the mind around] and shines it inward."[37] In his second text, *Negotiating the Way*, Dōgen warns against being led astray by "skillfully turned words and phrases" and becoming "enmeshed in the traps and snares of words and letters," and he again encourages us to "cast everything aside and single-mindedly engage in *zazen*."[38]

And yet, Dōgen later writes that "making utterances and posing questions about the Buddha-nature were ordinary, rice-eating, tea-drinking activities in the lives of Buddhas and Ancestors."[39] He chastises monks who claim that the stories of the masters that have become kōans are "beyond logic and unconcerned with thought," telling us that "the illogical stories mentioned by those bald-headed fellows are only illogical for them, not for Buddha Ancestors."[40] Dōgen goes on to say that those people who claim that these stories are illogical "are more stupid than animals who learn the Buddha Way." "Such people are true beasts," Dōgen says elsewhere, who claim that monks should devote themselves solely to meditation, avoiding both listening to the teaching of the Buddha Dharma and speaking of the Buddha-nature.[41] Far from steering us away from language, Dōgen often stresses our capacity for what he called *dōtoku* or "expressive attainments of the Way." Indeed, his text with that title begins by saying: "All Buddhas and Ancestors are Expressions of the Way."[42] We should note, however, that Dōgen is not just talking about verbal expressions; he goes on to say that even sitting in silence is an expressive attainment of the Way.[43]

While Dōgen affirms the potential of speech as well as silence to express an understanding of the matter of Zen, Wumen warns against the pitfalls of both: "If you open your mouth, you will lose it. If you shut your mouth, you will also miss it. Even if you neither open nor shut your mouth, you are a hundred and eight thousand miles away."[44]

In the end—or, in truth, all along the Way—the point is not whether you speak or remain silent; the point is whether you have awakened to what cannot be permanently captured either in speech or in silence, and yet which can be provisionally expressed by either speech or silence in the proper time and place, as the situation and audience demands. In short, for Zen, silence can be just as problematic as speech, and speech just as effective as silence. Just as there are many kinds of speech, there are many kinds of silence. The question in each case is, what kind of silence and what kind of speech are expressing, developing, and conveying what kind of experience?

Whether Zen experience is expressed through speech or silence, the *sense* of what is said or not said may be only partially or not at all intelligible to those who are not acquainted with the *reference*, that is to say, with the experience expressed. To make a crude—if also creamy—analogy, one may read enough books about the differences between flavors of ice cream to be able to make a lot of intelligible claims about them, but if one has not actually tasted those different flavors of ice cream, one does not really know what one is talking about. They may not have had scoops of ice cream a thousand years ago in China, but they probably did have more than thirty-one flavors of dumplings. And they certainly did have hot and cold water. Cups of hot and cold water may look the same from the outside, but the experience of drinking them is very different. Hence the Zen saying: "To drink water and know for oneself whether it is hot or cold."

We can understand why Zen masters would stress, in different contexts, both the limits of language and its expressive power. *Taken on its own*, a linguistic indication of an enlightening experience is like a "finger pointing at the moon," or a sign saying that the water is hot. Yet *taken in conjunction with (the rest of) the experience itself*, linguistic expressions have the potential not only to convey but also to embody, evolve, and enrich the experience of enlightenment.

Poetizing Both the Limits and the Expressive Delimitations of Language

Zen masters, of course, do not have a monopoly on reflecting on such linguistic and "sigetic" (from the Greek *sigan*, to keep silent) matters. Great poets the world over are often attentive to the limits of language as well as to its expressive power, to the depth and fecundity of silence as well as to the beauty and vitality of words. The German poet Rainer Maria Rilke is certainly among them.

Rilke longed to become capable of what he calls "the kind of speech that may be possible there, where silence reigns."[45] In one of his poems, Rilke writes: "Full round apple, pear and banana, / gooseberry . . . All this speaks / death and life into the mouth." Edging toward the limits of language's power of expression, he goes on to say: "Do not things slowly become nameless in your mouth?"

But then, without abandoning us to the mute experience of swallowing our words along with an ineffable apple, Rilke urges us back toward speech: "Dare to say what you call apple . . . ambiguous, sunny, earthy, of the here and now—: / O experience, sensing, joy—, immense!"[46] Words not only "gently fade before the unsayable,"[47] as Rilke puts it, they also spring forth into ever new vibrant possibilities of expression.

Rilke's self-composed epitaph, etched on his tombstone in Raron, Switzerland, reads:

> Rose, oh pure contradiction, desire and delight
> to be no one's sleep under so many
> eyelids.[48]

Rilke compares the beautiful petals of a rose to eyelids (*Lider*)—under which, however, no one sleeps. *Lider* is used here not only as a metaphor for petals; it is surely also intended to evoke the homonym *Lieder*, songs. Peeling back the petals of Rilke's life and poetry reveals nothing but an empty center. Do we experience this empty center as a resting place, as a source of awakening, as an underlying open-mindedness and open-heartedness, as an ungraspable source of freedom and creativity? Or do we experience it as a horrifying vacuum, as a hollow void encountered where we had expected—where we had desperately desired—to find a substantial core of the self? Did we hope to find someone, rather than no one? The last word of the first line of Rilke's epitaph, *Lust*, can mean both desire and delight. Does Rilke desire not to sleep? Or does he take delight in being the no-one, the no-self, who is both utterly at rest and wide awake? Does the image of the rose, as a symbol of resurrection, express a wish to escape the great sleep of death, or at least to not have one's poetry be forgotten? The poem, like the rose, and like a kōan, leaves us with layers of questions and contradictions. As with all great poems, how we read Rilke's epitaph tells us as much about ourselves as about him. It is as much a mirror that reflects back to us our own insights and attachments as it is a window into the poet's heart and mind.

Rilke apparently attempted to whittle his life and work down to this laconic epitaph, just as Zen masters have traditionally left behind a parting poem on their deathbeds. For example, the fourteenth-century Japanese Zen master Kōhō Ken'nichi left the following death poem:

> To depart while seated or standing is all one.
> All I shall leave behind me
> Is a heap of bones.
> In empty space I twist and soar
> And come down with the roar of thunder
> To the sea.[49]

The exemplary modern Zen philosopher and lay Rinzai master Ueda Shizuteru suggests that not only Zen's so-called death poems or parting verses (*jisei*) but many great poems can, in turn, be whittled down to a single word in them—and often even to an apparently meaningless one. In the case of Rilke's final poem, Ueda focuses our attention on its most inconspicuous word, the "oh" in the first phrase: "Rose, oh pure contradiction."[50] Ueda reads this little word—if it is even a word—as the primal emotive gasp that gives birth to Rilke's death poem. Such primal utterances, often found in haiku and in other forms of Zen poetry, are, as it were, pivotal points between silence and speech.

Zen as a Ceaseless Practice of Exiting and Reentering Language

Ueda's illuminating interpretations of Japanese and Western poetry reveal both the limits and the expressive power of language. Rooted in Zen practice and thought, he shows how we can understand Zen's apparent wavering between stressing either the limits or the expressive power of language not as a problem that plagues Zen, but rather as a dynamic interplay essential to it. He refers to the seventeenth-century Japanese Zen master Bankei as saying, in effect, that one must first "exit language" in order to attain the Dharma Eye with which to "exit into language" in order to understand and express the Dharma in words.[51]

Ueda finds this bidirectional movement away from and back into language epitomized in the twin practices that lie at the core of the Rinzai Zen tradition—namely, *zazen* and *sanzen*, silent meditation and verbal interviews with a teacher. He writes: "*Zazen* is a bottomless stillness and silence, whereas *sanzen* is a cutting edge of movement and speech."[52] The bidirectional movement between these two practices entails a twofold negation: "*Zazen* is a negation of language, and *sanzen* is a negation of silence."[53]

$$\text{Zazen} \longleftarrow \text{negation of speech} \longleftrightarrow \text{negation of silence} \longrightarrow \text{Sanzen}$$

(silent meditation)   (verbal interviews)

Thus, the apparent contradictions in Zen between negating and affirming language, between prohibiting and demanding words, can be understood as exhortations to participate in the interplay of this bidirectional movement. One must go beyond language to experience things afresh, and one must bring this fresh experience of things back into language. Ueda sees this bidirectional movement not only as essential to Zen practice, but also more generally as the dynamic relation between experience and language as such. He speaks of this double movement as a matter of "exiting language and exiting into language."[54]

We saw this double movement out of and back into language exemplified in Rilke's poem about the experience of eating an apple. Usually when we eat an apple, we experience it as just another "apple" that we are eating on just another busy day, perhaps on the way from work to the gym or to pick up the kids. But sometimes, perhaps on a special or unusual occasion, such as while taking a break on a long hike in the woods, we are suddenly struck by its extraordinary flavor and texture, almost as if it were the first time we had ever really tasted such a thing. Suddenly, the all too general word "apple" no longer seems to do justice to the wondrousness of its unique feel and flavor. Words slip away as we enthusiastically offer our hiking companion a bite. "What does it taste like?" our friend asks, demanding a description. Reaching deep, the extraordinary experience inspires us to come up with fresh words, words that not only fit but even enhance our appreciation of the taste and texture and scent of this strange and wonderful thing. The friend shares the experience, and the next thing you know we're trading metaphors like wine connoisseurs communing over a priceless bottle of old fermented grapes.

Philosophers since Aristotle have pointed out that human beings are animals who are distinguished by their capacity for language. As Helen Keller's remarkable story reveals, we cannot truly live as human beings without words. However, it is also true that we cannot live entirely enclosed inside them. "Language is the house of being," Heidegger famously remarks; language domesticates the world for us, makes it intelligible and thus livable.[55] And yet, Ueda in effect replies, a house is a home only in the process of leaving and returning to it; otherwise it is a bird cage or a prison house.[56] While it is true that our experience becomes meaningful only by means of language, it is also true that experience exceeds and thus enables us to revise and revitalize language. We thus live, as Ueda says, in the ceaselessly circulating movement of "exiting language and exiting into language."[57]

Zen practice, especially the Rinzai Zen practice of going back and forth between long periods of silent meditation and intense one-on-one interviews, slows down and intensifies this movement between exiting and reentering language. It is thus no surprise that this Zen tradition has spawned such an amazingly fresh and vibrant body of kōan commentary and poetry.

In Chapter 21, we'll discuss how some members of the Kyoto School, the group of modern Japanese philosophers to which Ueda belongs, were Rinzai practitioners who attempted to extend the linguistic expression of Zen to include philosophy.

21

Between Zen and Philosophy

Commuting with the Kyoto School

Zen's Emphasis on Holistic Practice Rather than Either Faith or Reason

Is Zen a religion, a philosophy, both, or neither? This is a loaded question, because "religion" and "philosophy" are loaded terms—loaded, that is, with Western preconceptions and presuppositions.[1] For example, we tend to assume that religion is based on *faith*, whereas philosophy relies on *reason*. And we discuss and debate the relation between faith and reason, often in terms of religion and science. All these are Western terms, and the apparent disjunction between them reflects the hybrid nature of the Western tradition.

If we want to understand other traditions, we must also reflect on our own, so that we have a sense of the lenses through which we are looking. The Western tradition developed on the bicultural basis of an ancient and medieval marriage between Greco-Roman philosophy and Judeo-Christian religion. In modern times, this couple has gone through a great deal of marital tension and, for some, even a divorce. More than two thousand years after they first met, we are still trying to figure out how "Athens" can get along with "Jerusalem."

By contrast, Asian traditions—including Hinduism, Buddhism, Confucianism, and Daoism—never separated and so never needed to wed (much less divorce) philosophy and religion. While it may seem strange to Westerners that these traditions do not make a clear distinction between these two ways of pursuing wisdom and goodness, it seems just as odd to them that we do. Why not use all the resources at our disposal to fathom the depths of reality and to figure out our place in it?[2]

Zen, of course, has its own hybrid history. We have frequently discussed how Chinese and later Japanese ideas, values, and practices were grafted onto the Zen branch of the tree of Buddhism, a tree originally rooted in Indian soil. But this synthesis has not spawned a faith-versus-reason cleavage. Zen stresses embodied-spiritual *practice* and the *experience* that is enabled through that psychosomatic practice more than either faith or reason. Nevertheless, insofar as Zen practice has been and/or is to become truly holistic, it needs to make

Zen Pathways. Bret W. Davis, Oxford University Press. © Oxford University Press 2022.
DOI: 10.1093/oso/9780197573686.003.0021

room for both faith and reason along with embodied-spiritual practices such as meditation.

Previously (in Chapters 3, 6, and 12) we discussed the meaning and roles played by "faith" (Ch. *xin*; Jp. *shin*) in Zen. In short: To begin with, there is a preliminary role for faith as a matter of *trusting* that the teachings and practices will lead one to open the eye of wisdom and heart of compassion. Ultimately, through study and practice, this preliminary faith blossoms into true *confidence*.[3] In this chapter, our focus will be on the relation between Zen and philosophy.

The tradition of Buddhism certainly contains many recognizably philosophical texts.[4] These include the Abhidharma discourses of early Buddhist scholars, who sought to analyze in great detail the basic patterns and elements of experiential reality; the Yogachara discourses of Mahayana Buddhist phenomenologists, who sought to describe the nature and levels of consciousness as well as to discern the relation of consciousness to what we think of as external reality; and the disputations of the Madhyamaka school of Mahayana Buddhist philosophers, who sought to demonstrate that all conceptualized objects are essentially empty, meaning that they are temporary products of "interdependent origination" and lack independent substantiality or "own-being." Madhyamaka philosophers such as Nagarjuna deftly employ rigorous argumentation to point out the logical inconsistencies of our linguistic reconstructions of reality. While Yogachara discourses have been compared to Western versions of idealism and phenomenology,[5] Madhyamaka discourses have reminded some Western philosophers of the ancient skeptics, others of mysticism and/or idealism, others of Wittgenstein's comment—at the end of the tersely argued text that spawned the school of logical positivism—that "What we cannot speak about must be passed over in silence,"[6] and still others of Derrida's postmodern deconstruction of logocentrism.[7]

As we saw in Chapter 20, Zen masters often use language to point beyond language. And yet, we also saw how, just as often, they celebrate the expressive power of language, especially in poetry and in the encounter dialogues that became kōans. Yet what about philosophy? By the time Zen started developing in China in the sixth century, Chinese Buddhists had already fairly well mastered the complex philosophies of the Buddhist schools that had been imported from India starting some five hundred years earlier. Chinese Buddhists had even started developing some of their own philosophical schools, such as the Huayan school, whose view of the thoroughly interrelational web of reality was especially influential on Zen.[8] It is sometimes said that Huayan provides the philosophical theory for Zen practice.

And yet, Zen does not understand itself to be simply the practical application of a theory. For Zen, this would be to put the cognitive cart before the holistic horse. Abstract theory is seen as derivative of concrete practice, not the other way around. Accordingly, for centuries Zen has emphasized embodied-spiritual practice over merely cerebral intellection. At times, however, this emphasis has unfortunately derailed the holistic path of Zen into the muddy waters of anti-intellectualism. Although the recorded sayings and dialogues of the classical Zen masters reveal that most of them were well versed in the theoretical literature of the Buddhist tradition, as time went by, some less studious and intellectually insightful monks apparently began to think that Zen practice need not involve reading and thinking at all.

In Chapter 20, we saw how the thirteenth-century Sōtō Zen master Dōgen, while affirming the importance of regularly putting down the books and silently sitting, also bemoaned the fact Zen monks were not sufficiently versed in the literature of Buddhism and mistook kōans to be "illogical stories." In the fourteenth century, the Rinzai Zen master Musō Soseki taught:

> The ancients generally began their practice only after a broad education in the Buddhist and non-Buddhist classics. Hence, they were not biased in their understanding. Nowadays . . . one sees people neglectful of their meditation and unlearned in the sutras, treatises, and sacred teachings; people who, having meditated a bit, and attained a level of understanding no greater than that of non-Buddhist or Hinayana practicers, imagine that, since their understanding results from zazen, they are now fully enlightened. . . . It is in an attempt to correct such errors that I regularly lecture on the sutras and treatises.[9]

Six hundred years later, the twentieth-century Rinzai master Yamada Mumon quipped: "Sometimes you hear it said that Zen monks do not have to read books or study. When did this misleading idea get started?"[10] It seems that this "misleading idea" of Zen as entailing an anti-intellectualism goes way back and is still with us today.

D. T. Suzuki on Both the Limits of and Need for Philosophy

More than anyone else, D. T. Suzuki is responsible for having introduced Zen to America and the rest of the world over the course of his long and productive life. His writings on Zen span more than a half century, from the early 1900s to the 1960s.[11] Especially in his earlier works, he often stresses the need to go beyond, or dig down beneath, cerebral intellection.[12] Indeed, throughout his career Suzuki viewed the intellect as subordinate to, or rather as lying on the surface of, something deeper. He sometimes called that which underlies the intellect "the unconscious," adopting this term more from Jung than from Freud, and significantly redefining it to translate Zen's "no-mind" (*mushin*). Suzuki also referred to that which wells up from beneath the surface of the intellect as "the will," in this case drawing on his lifelong friend Nishida Kitarō's early voluntarism, which in turn drew on Fichte and Schopenhauer.

In a text based on a lecture given in 1957, Suzuki writes:

> Whatever we may say about the intellect, it is after all superficial, it is something floating on the surface of consciousness. The surface must be broken through in order to reach the unconscious. . . . But I must remind my readers not to take me for an anti-intellectualist through and through. What I object to is regarding the intellect as the ultimate reality. The intellect is needed to determine, however vaguely, where reality is. And the reality is grasped only when the intellect quits its claim on it. Zen knows this and proposes as a koan a statement having some savor of intellection, something which in disguise looks as if it demanded a logical treatment.[13]

The kōan, he goes on to say, "is not to be solved with the head; that is to say, intellectually or philosophically." It can be solved only when the intellect is exhausted and the "Cosmic (or ontological) Unconscious," the primal energy of the cosmic will, breaks through and manifests as "prajna plus karuna, wisdom plus love."[14]

However, at the same time as Suzuki consistently maintained that the nondual source of wisdom and compassion lies beyond the reach of the analytical intellect, he increasingly stressed the need to develop what he calls "Zen thought" that would philosophically express "Zen experience." As Richard Jaffe points out, "Suzuki was very deliberate in his project to create a modern Zen, or as he put it, 'to elucidate its ideas using modern intellectual methods.'"[15] Suzuki was sharply critical of Yasutani Hakuun Rōshi's overly harsh training methods that focus too much on forcing an initial breakthrough experience. In a letter written in 1964, Suzuki remarks: "I met Yasutani, but he has no philosophy. The initial experience, i.e., satori, is most important [for him], therefore. And [yet] philosophical reflections are not to be neglected or set aside in the understanding of Zen, for they are to be included in Zen proper."[16]

Suzuki even stressed the need to develop a "logic" of Zen, and he praised Nishida's great achievements in this regard. In a letter to Akizuki Ryōmin in which he reflects on his experiences in the United States in the early 1950s, Suzuki writes:

> In Zen today, the compassionate aspect is insufficient. Therefore it lacks opportunities for social engagement. In addition, it has no "logic" (ronri). That's something that Nishida always said. If we are going to get Westerners to accept it, somehow, logic is necessary.[17]

Suzuki would no doubt have applauded the Engaged Zen that has been developing in the United States and elsewhere since the 1960s, which we discussed in Chapter 14. The rest of this chapter is devoted to introducing the attempts to bridge Zen and philosophy by Nishida and some of the other members of the Kyoto School he spawned.

The Kyoto School on the Relation Between Zen and Philosophy

The Kyoto School is a group of twentieth- (and now twenty-first-) century Japanese philosophers who have sought to bring Zen and Pure Land Buddhism into dialogue with Western philosophy and religion.[18] Nishida Kitarō's most prominent successor was Nishitani Keiji, and Nishitani's most prominent successor was Ueda Shizuteru. All three of them were committed Zen practitioners as well as academic philosophers. Both Nishitani and Ueda were recognized as lay Rinzai Zen masters. Other philosophers associated with the Kyoto School who were also accomplished Rinzai Zen practitioners and teachers include Hisamatsu Shin'ichi and Abe Masao (known in the West as Masao Abe).

Allow me to acknowledge my personal connections with the Kyoto School. While living in Kyoto for about a decade, I was able to study with the leading heirs and scholars of the Kyoto School. In particular, I had the great privilege of learning directly from Professor Ueda, who passed away in June 2019 while I was working on this book. As I mentioned in the dedication, it was Professor Ueda who formulated my Zen name, Kanpū, using one of the characters from his own name. The second-greatest gift I received from him was one of his two scrolls of Nishida's calligraphy. The scroll was given to Ueda by Nishida's daughter when Nishitani introduced them. Unfortunately, Nishitani passed away in 1990, the same year that I first moved to Japan, and so I did not get to meet him. However, eleven years after that I published my very first article, which was written in Japanese and on Nishitani's philosophy of Zen.[19]

While living in Kyoto, I tried my best to follow in the giant footsteps of Nishitani and Ueda, which often meant literally commuting a couple of kilometers on foot or by bicycle between Kyoto University and Shōkokuji monastery. This was a pedagogical as well as a physical commute; it was a matter of going back and forth between studying philosophy and practicing Zen at these institutions of higher and deeper learning. Once a month, after a meditation session at Shōkokuji, Professor Ueda would give a talk to a small group of us on a classic text from the Zen tradition. Once every three months, the inner circle of Kyoto School philosophers would gather to sit in a circle on the tatami mat floor of the living room of Nishitani's old home and discuss, page by page, the nineteen volumes of Nishida's *Complete Works*. Needless to say, these were special and formative years for me.

Six months before Professor Ueda passed away, I had the opportunity to thank him at an intimate gathering of family and former students. I told him that, more than anyone, he exemplified and modeled a way of bringing Zen and philosophy together, letting them enrich each other without ever reducing one to the other.[20]

It is important to point out that, for Ueda and these other Zen-practicing Kyoto School philosophers, Zen and philosophy should be *related* but not *conflated*. Ueda once wrote:

> It must be said that there is a fundamental gap between Eastern practice, especially the Zen of non-thinking, and philosophy as an academic discipline of reflection that arose and developed in the West. Nishida Kitarō cast himself into that gap. . . . If the meeting of Christianity and Greek philosophy, as the collision between the principle of faith and that of reason, was an event that pervaded and drove (and still pervades and drives) the spirit of the European world for centuries, the encounter and mutual friction between Buddhism—especially in the honed and concretized form of Zen—and the Western world will undoubtedly continue as a great drama played out in the depths of history for many generations to come.[21]

Ueda inherited this task from Nishitani, who himself once wrote: "[The] problem of Zen and philosophy . . . remains even now to be settled. It is, after all, the task remaining at the core of the spiritual and cultural encounter between East and West."[22]

In the preface to his book *The Standpoint of Zen*, Nishitani explains that, for him, philosophy plays the role of a mediator between post-philosophical Zen and the pre-philosophical life-world. He writes of

> proceeding on a path from the pre-philosophical to philosophy, and then further from philosophy to the post-philosophical. Yet, at the same time, this implies the reverse direction, in other words, a return path from the standpoint of the *practice* of Zen, through the standpoint of philosophy, and back to the place of the pre-philosophical.[23]

Nishitani thought that we can "step back" from unenlightened everyday experience by means of philosophical reflection on the basic principles and structures of that experience. Furthermore, through Zen practice we can step back in a more holistic manner to an experience of what Nishida calls, adapting a Zen phrase, "radical everydayness."[24] We can thus go from unenlightened everyday experience through philosophical reflection to Zen practice and the experience of an enlightened everydayness. Then, moving in the opposite direction, philosophy can discursively reflect on the enlightened experience attained through Zen practice, allowing it to contribute to a critical and meliorative engagement with the unenlightened everyday life-world.

These Zen-practicing Kyoto School philosophers understand their endeavor to be unprecedented. Although it had long engaged with the philosophical strands of the Buddhist tradition, Zen had yet to engage with Western philosophy, which was first introduced to Japan in the late nineteenth century. According to Ueda, whereas the Zen tradition has long excelled at expressing Zen experience in the form of poetry, it was Nishida who first succeeded in developing a philosophy from out of Zen experience.[25] And it is this project that those such as Nishitani and Ueda himself inherited.

When the distinguished German philosopher Otto Pöggeler read Nishida's and Nishitani's works, he had the strange impression that their philosophies were deeply religious, and yet the Western terms "religion" and "philosophy" did not seem to capture exactly what they were engaged in. In particular, what they mean by "religion" struck him as not so much a doctrine of faith as "a holistic return to the source of life."[26] It could be said that, by drawing on their East Asian Buddhist background, these Kyoto School philosophers of religion have been rethinking the very meaning of the terms "philosophy" and "religion."[27]

In a set of lecture notes, Nishida explains how he understands the relation between philosophy and religious experience:

> Philosophy is intellectual knowledge; it is academic learning. But in contrast to the regular sciences, which are based on certain hypotheses or presuppositions, philosophy seeks to dig down further beneath these presuppositions and return to their origin, so as to bring them under the sway of what is immediately given. However, that which is immediate, truly concrete, and originary, is in fact the content of religion. At this point, philosophy and religion converge. But philosophy seeks to illuminate this conceptually, while religion experiences it, and seeks to live it directly. It is therefore the case that great philosophy contains religious content, and great religion contains philosophical reflection.[28]

Nishida Kitarō's Early Philosophy of Pure Experience

In the preface to his first book, *An Inquiry into the Good*, Nishida writes that, for him, "religion . . . constitutes the consummation of philosophy."[29] The book culminates with a section on religion in which he develops a dialectical and panentheistic conception of God. Yet throughout Nishida understands his method to be thoroughly philosophical. He sometimes even calls his method thoroughly scientific, not only because it is rational but also because he attempts to base his reflections purely on unadulterated empirical evidence—indeed, on what he calls "pure experience."

Nishida borrows this expression, "pure experience," from the American pragmatist philosopher and pioneer psychologist William James. James is well known in part for his book *The Varieties of Religious Experience*, in which he recorded and sympathetically interpreted firsthand accounts of religious and mystical experiences. Yet James claims that he himself is constitutionally incapable of mystical experiences and can only speak of them secondhand.[30] He attempted to base his own philosophy strictly on empirical evidence, developing what he calls a philosophy of "radical empiricism."[31]

Nishida agrees with James that not only our everyday preconceptions but also our scientific conceptions about the nature of experience contain unwarranted presuppositions. In particular, we assume that experience is a matter of an internal self becoming conscious of an external world. In other words, we presuppose a subject-object dualism when we reflect back on experience. This unquestioned presupposition then causes us to get caught up in intractable philosophical problems, such as the skeptical doubt about whether an internal self could ever really come to know an external world. Both Nishida and James attempt to look directly at experience without projecting on it this subject-object split. What they find is what they call pure experience, by which they mean experience that is not yet adulterated by retroactively imposed ideas of how experience is supposed to be constituted and conceptualized.

Nishida opens the first chapter of *An Inquiry into the Good* with the following lines:

> To experience means to know facts just as they are, to know in accordance with facts by completely relinquishing one's fabrications. What we usually refer to as experience is adulterated with some sort of thought, so by pure I am referring to the state of experience just as it is without the least addition of deliberative discrimination. The moment of seeing a color or hearing a sound, for example, is prior not only to the thought that the color or sound is the activity of an external object or that one is sensing it, but also to the judgment of what the color or sound might be.[32]

Before he published this work in 1911, Nishida had intensely practiced Zen for a number of years alongside his ongoing study of philosophy.[33] A year or two after the book was published, a student asked him a pointed question after class one day. That student was Morimoto Seinen, who later become a famous Zen master in his own right. He asked Nishida: "Did *An Inquiry into the Good* originate only on the basis of studying the texts of Western philosophy, or was Zen practice or the experience of *kenshō* (a breakthrough enlightenment experience) involved in its origination?" Nishida is said to have clearly answered that his book originated "*from both*."[34]

Be that as it may, in a prefatory note added to a later edition of the book, Nishida tells us that he had already conceived of the kernel idea of the book while he was in high school, before he had begun either practicing Zen or reading James. The basic intuition that he already had then was that "true reality must be actuality just as it is and that the so-called material world is something conceptualized and abstracted out of it."[35] Nishida explains what he means by referring to the German philosopher Gustav Fechner, who

> said that one morning . . . he gazed in the bright sunlight at a spring meadow with fragrant flowers, singing birds, and flitting butterflies and became engrossed in what he called the daytime perspective, in which truth is things just as they are, as opposed to the colorless and soundless nighttime perspective found in the natural sciences.[36]

Both perspectives give us reality, but the "nighttime perspective" gives us only a partial view of reality abstracted or filtered out from the whole, whereas the "daytime perspective" gives us the concrete and undiluted whole of reality.

For Nishida, scientific accounts of reality are true, but they are not the whole truth. Science does not even give us the whole truth of our experience of nature. It is not that science tells us all that can be known about nature as the material world, while we need religion to give us additional supernatural truths about the spiritual world. Nishida was skeptical of this kind of supernatural understanding of spiritual truths, since he regarded both spirit/nature and mind/matter dualisms as illegitimate abstractions from the sole reality of pure experience. He thought that spirit and nature—or mind and matter—are two halves of a whole, and that we only grasp half of reality if we separate one from the other. The truth of religion, and the true meaning of Spirit and God, must be found in the midst of the reality we experience, not up in the heavens or in another, supernatural world.

James would have probably agreed with much of Nishida's early philosophy of pure experience. However, there are significant differences between his radical empiricism and that of Nishida. The most salient difference is that whereas James referred to pure experience as a "blooming, buzzing confusion" that we must organize according to our pragmatic interests,[37] Nishida thought that there is an organizing principle at work within pure experience itself. It is this immanently unifying force at work in the self and throughout the world that Nishida calls God.

Nishida's View of God

In *An Inquiry into the Good*, Nishida says that God is "the unifier of pure experience that envelops the universe."[38] The more we get back in touch with our own pure experience at each moment of our lives, the more we get back in touch with God as "an infinite unifying power that functions directly and spontaneously from within each individual." "In other words," he goes on to say, "our personalities are the particular forms in which the sole reality—which transcends the distinction between mind and matter—manifests itself according to circumstances."[39]

"The universe" in which all our personalities participate is said to be "an expression of God's personality."[40] For Nishida, "the universe is not a creation of God but rather a manifestation of God."[41] Moreover, "the idea of a transcendent God who controls the world from without," he says, "not only conflicts with our reason but also falls short of the most profound religiosity."[42] Nishida does not look for the most profound religiosity in supernatural miracles. Like Einstein, he thinks that the laws of nature are themselves God's revelation, so there is no need for them to be broken for God to be revealed. Rather, Nishida finds the most profound religiosity in what I called in Chapter 13 a trans-mystical experience of the here and now, the experience of what Nishida later calls "radical everydayness."

Although Nishida's view of God or Buddha—and he often uses these terms interchangeably—might seem closer to a monistic pantheism than to a dualistic theism, Nishida rejects both of these labels.[43] In his last essay, written just prior to his death in 1945, he says that his understanding of the relation between God, the world, and the self could perhaps be understood in terms of "panentheism"—meaning, as we saw in Chapters 9 and 12, not simply that "all is God" but rather that "all is *in* God." God is, as it were, greater than the sum of His (or Her or Its) manifestations.[44]

However, Nishida goes on to say that even the idea of panentheism falls short of expressing the dynamically dialectical relation between God and the self. That relation ultimately occurs through what he calls "inverse correspondence." What he means by this expression is that God and the self are both self-negating—in Christian language, kenotic or self-emptying. God and the self enter into each other by way of negating or emptying themselves. God exists by emptying Himself out into the world as an expression of love for all beings. In response, we are called on to empty ourselves, abandoning our egocentricity, to be filled with the communal love and creative power of God. In this way, our individual selves can become unique expressions of God's compassion and creativity.[45]

Nishida's Place of Absolute Nothingness

Nishida's final essay is entitled "The Logic of Place and the Religious Worldview." Although a religious sensibility pervades all of Nishida's works, most of them are focused on other matters of philosophical inquiry—such as epistemology and metaphysics, or philosophy of art, culture, history, politics, mathematics, and science. His abiding concern throughout was to understand all aspects of the world and our lives in relation to the most direct experience of the nondual nature of reality as a unity-in-diversity.[46]

In Nishida's first book, as we have seen, he called this nondual basis of reality the world of "pure experience." Yet he soon dropped this term, saying that, despite his intentions, it lent itself to being misunderstood in terms of a "psychologism."[47] In other words, his early philosophy unwittingly privileged subjective consciousness over material reality and tended to reduce the objective world to "phenomena of consciousness."

Subsequently, Nishida developed a philosophy based instead on what he calls "the Place of Absolute Nothingness."[48] It is not hard to hear echoes of the kōan Nishida passed after many years of meditation: the famous *Mu* kōan that appears as the first case in *The Gateless Barrier*.[49] *Mu* means "no" or "nothing" but, in this kōan and elsewhere in Zen and Daoist texts, it does not mean "no" as opposed to "yes," or "nothing" as opposed to "something." It transcends and envelops all such dualities and distinctions. We will talk more about this and other kōans in Chapter 22. Here let us keep our focus on Nishida's philosophy.

In his relentless philosophical endeavor to dig down beneath the divide between subject and object, without reducing one to the other as do both subjective idealism and material realism, Nishida realized that *all oppositions must take place in some place*. Opposition is still a relation, and to be in any kind of relation two things have to share some place or field in which they can be related. This insight was the kernel of Nishida's "logic of place."[50]

Nishida gives the example of colors. Red is opposed to blue. And yet, both are colors; both exist within the *field* of color. To give another example: up and down, right and left, are opposites; and yet, they are united in that they exist as directions within the same dimension of *space*. The question for Nishida then became, what is the one Place that unites all oppositions, including that of subjective consciousness and objective reality? What is the one Place that unites all the different things and dimensions of the universe? Since this universal Place cannot be one of the particular things it unites or envelops, it is literally no-thing. Accordingly, drawing on his Zen Buddhist background, Nishida calls it the Place of Absolute Nothingness.

By calling it *Absolute* Nothingness, Nishida means to indicate that it is not what he calls "relative nothingness." In other words, Absolute Nothingness is not simply the negation or privation of being. The Place of Absolute Nothingness envelops even the opposition between determinate being and relative nothingness. Why not call it Absolute Being? The main reason is that both Eastern and Western traditions of philosophy have long associated *being* with *form* and *nothingness* with *formlessness*. Definite forms are always, by definition, limited and finite. The ultimate matrix of reality cannot be a finite form; it must be a formless infinite. Moreover, it must be a formless infinite that, by way of self-negation, dynamically manifests itself in finite forms.

In the preface to the book in which he first develops this idea of a self-determining Place of Absolute Nothingness, Nishida writes:

> It goes without saying that there is much to admire in, and much to learn from, the impressive achievements of Western culture, which thought of form as being and of the giving of form as good. However, does there not lie hidden at the base of our Eastern culture, preserved and passed down by our ancestors for several thousand years, something which sees the form of the formless and hears the voice of the voiceless? Our hearts and minds endlessly seek this something; and it is my wish to provide this quest with a philosophical foundation.[51]

Whereas Western philosophical and religious traditions have generally followed the ancient Greeks in "thinking of form as being and of the giving of form as good,"[52] Nishida attempts to develop a philosophy from the East Asian perspective of thinking of the Source-Field of reality and morality as a self-forming formlessness. Nishida thus understands Absolute Nothingness not as an inert void, but rather as a dynamically self-determining Place that gives rise—and gives place—to all things, a self-forming formlessness that creatively manifests itself in finite forms.

One of the closest parallels in the Western tradition may be Plotinus's Neo-Platonism, which thinks of the Many definite forms of reality as emanations of a formless One.[53] In fact, Nishida's junior colleague and fellow Kyoto School philosopher Tanabe Hajime criticized Nishida's middle-period philosophy for what he considered to be a lapse into a Neo-Platonist-like "mystical emanationism" that does not do justice to the concrete and dialectical interactions among things in the world, especially in the sociohistorical world. Subsequently, Nishida expressly distanced himself from Plotinus's Neo-Platonism[54] and increasingly thought of the Place of Absolute Nothingness as a dynamic medium of dialectical interaction between subject and object, self and other, self and society, one society and another, and human beings and the natural environment.[55]

Tanabe was the first of many philosophers influenced by Nishida who developed their own ways of thinking of reality in terms of a dynamically and dialectically self-negating and self-determining Absolute Nothingness. These philosophers came to be known collectively as the Kyoto School. Starting with Tanabe, some of them drew on Pure Land Buddhism more than Zen. Nishida was rooted in Zen but also, especially in his last essay on religion, drew freely on the insights of Pure Land Buddhism as well as Christianity. As mentioned previously, the most prominent of the Kyoto School philosophers who were primarily committed to Zen practice and thought include Hisamatsu Shin'ichi, Nishitani Keiji, Abe Masao, and Ueda Shizuteru.

Abe Masao's Kenotic God and Dynamic Emptiness

In this book I have frequently discussed Nishitani and Ueda, and on occasion have also referred to Hisamatsu. Abe is better known in the West than in Japan, since he spent much of his career in the United States and wrote many of his works in English. He is especially known for his contributions to interreligious dialogue.

Drawing on insights and suggestions from Nishida and Nishitani,[56] Abe explored in particular some intriguing parallels between the Buddhist notion of Emptiness and the Christian conception of God. On the one hand, Abe stresses the self-emptying nature of Buddhist Emptiness—in Nishida's language, the self-negation of Absolute Nothingness. On the other hand, he stresses the Christian idea that, as selfless love, God "empties" Himself of his transcendent divinity, taking finite human form and dying on the cross. Using the Greek word that appears in the Bible for this self-emptying, *kenosis*, and the Sanskrit Buddhist word for emptiness, *sunyata*, Abe entitled one of his most provocative and influential essays "Kenotic God and Dynamic Sunyata."[57]

Near the beginning of that essay, Abe quotes the following passage from Paul's epistle to the Philippians: "Christ Jesus . . . emptied himself, taking the form of a servant, . . . he humbled himself, becoming obedient even unto death, yea, the death on the cross."[58] We, in turn, says Paul, are called upon to take up the cross and be reborn by way of undergoing our own existential ego-death (see Chapter 12).

Abe ignited a debate among theologians over the question of whether God the Father, and not just the Son, empties Himself. Whereas Hans Küng denied that God the Father empties himself, Karl Rahner spoke of "the self-emptying of God, his becoming, the kenosis and genesis of God himself." Rahner says that God "creates by emptying himself, and therefore, of course, he himself is in the emptying."[59]

According to Abe, however, even Rahner does not go far enough in overcoming the dualism between Creator and creature that pervades the Christian theological tradition. Buddhism, especially Zen, and the Kyoto School philosophies inspired by Zen, are said to be more thoroughgoing in their nondualistic understanding of the self-emptying nature of both Buddha and the self. For Abe, this Zen Buddhist understanding of religion is most needed in an age of nihilism.

Nishitani Keiji on Stepping Back Through Nihilism

Abe's teacher Nishitani was the first Kyoto School philosopher to take seriously the problem of nihilism. Like other thinkers, Nishitani associates the rise of modern nihilism with the ramifications of Nietzsche's horrifying—yet also, Nietzsche thought, potentially liberating—proclamation that "God is dead."[60]

Today, we can no longer simply inquire into the nature of God's existence, but must confront the swelling sense that He does not exist at all. Atheists may celebrate the demise of belief in God, while theists may bemoan it, but everyone must come to grips with the fact that modern science and the materialism of our secular society have at least decentered—if not dispensed with—the foundational role of religion for many in the modern world.

To be sure, there has been a rise in religious fundamentalism around the world today—in the extreme right wing of Evangelical America and Hindu India as well as in the radical hijackers of Islam in the Middle East. Such conservative dogmatism or fanatical fideism can be seen as a regressive backlash against the modern onset of nihilism. By contrast, Nishitani views the crisis of nihilism as an opportunity to rediscover a more profound and more genuine religiosity—or what today many would call spirituality.

Nishitani claims that we must not flee from nihilism, closing our eyes and ears and just shouting our dogmatic beliefs to ourselves and at others. Rather, *we must go all the way through the bottom of nihilism.* Only if we "overcome nihilism by way of passing through nihilism," he suggests, can we awaken to the true nature and home-ground of our existence.[61] Nishitani speaks of this home ground in Zen Buddhist terms as the Field of Emptiness. Insofar as we cling to a false sense of being, insofar as we think of the self and other beings as independent and unchanging substances, we are bound to experience the relative nothingness of nihilism as a threat to everything we believe we are and everything we believe we possess.

Yet, if we "trans-descend" from what Nishitani calls the Field of Being through the Field of Nihility all the way to the Field of Emptiness, we can discover that creative and encompassing Place of Absolute Nothingness of which Nishida spoke. In other words, we can discover that the death of a false understanding of God as an otherworldly being allows us to experience the sacred right in the midst of the secular world; we can experience the Godhead as a Field of Emptiness that encompasses and enlivens the interrelated persons, things, and events of the here and now.[62]

How exactly do we go about doing this? That question brings us back from the abstractions of philosophy to concreteness of practice. The problem of nihilism initially became the focus of Nishitani's attention as a problem that he felt painfully as a personal existential crisis. He later became convinced that the problem of nihilism lies "at the root of the mutual aversion of religion and science" and that it "contains something difficult to solve solely from the standpoint of religion, or solely from the standpoint of philosophy," at least insofar as these remain disconnected from each other.[63] Having chosen a career as a professional philosopher, Nishitani recalls that, no matter how much philosophy he studied, he could not rid himself of a certain anxious feeling of disconnectedness from reality; it was as if his feet were not touching the ground, or as if he were a fly bumping up against the glass of a windowpane, unable to actually go outside and directly encounter the world. It was the impotence of theoretical philosophy alone to solve this crisis of disconnectedness that led him to take up the practice of Zen. And, sure enough, after some time of practicing meditation and kōan training, the feeling went away.[64] In this manner, Nishitani relates, "in my case Western philosophy became connected with the 'practice' of Zen."[65] However, Nishitani does not present this journey through Western philosophy to Zen practice merely as an autobiographical account of his personal path, since he took his own existential plight to be a sign of the nihilistic times.

In an essay entitled "The Issue of Practice," Nishitani writes that the modern world has lost an understanding of the importance of holistic ways of practice in which the whole person—body, heart, mind, and spirit—are engaged and educated.[66] We cannot, as it were, simply think our way through nihilism. The step back through nihilism needs to be done with the entirety of the self. Nishitani suggests that while the Japanese and other Easterners have much to learn from the Western intellectual way of philosophical thinking, Westerners have much to learn from Eastern ways of holistic practice.[67] These ways include, of course, Zen meditation—a topic to which we return in Chapter 22.

22

Sōtō and Rinzai Zen Practice

Just Sitting and Working with Kōans

In the last couple of chapters, it seems that we have focused on the philosophy more than the practice of Zen. Yet, we need not draw too sharp a line between these two. Not only can philosophy serve as a cerebral gateway into the more embodied-spiritual practices of Zen, it can also become an intellectual pathway that participates in the Great Way of Zen itself. Indeed, if the practice of Zen is to be truly holistic, it needs to incorporate the mind as well as the body, heart, and spirit. For its part, if philosophical reflection is to be counted among the pathways of Zen, it needs to remain in touch especially with the core practices of *zazen*, seated meditation, and, in Rinzai Zen, *sanzen*, working with a teacher on kōans, the often enigmatic and paradoxical stories, dialogues, sayings, or questions assigned as topics of meditation and used to trigger and test a student's awakening.

Chapters 3 and 4 introduced the basics and discussed a number of important aspects of the practice of *zazen*. This chapter will delve more deeply into the nature and methods of meditation as practiced in the two main Japanese schools of Zen: Sōtō and Rinzai. The Sōtō School stems from the Chinese Caodong School and was brought to Japan by Dōgen in the thirteenth century. The Rinzai School stems from the Chinese Linji School; it was introduced to Japan by Eisai and other Zen masters in the twelfth and thirteenth centuries, and revitalized by Hakuin in the eighteenth century. The first half of this chapter will discuss Dōgen's teachings regarding the strikingly and stringently simple method of *shikantaza* or "just sitting." The second half will then discuss Hakuin's and other Rinzai Zen masters' teachings regarding the method of kōan practice.

Methodological disputes between these two schools date back to the twelfth century, when the Linji (Jp. Rinzai) master Dahui, who advocated the "looking at phrases" method of intensely concentrating on the key word or phrase of a kōan in order to trigger an enlightening breakthrough, criticized the "silent illumination" method of meditation taught by Caodong (Jp. Sōtō) masters such as Hongzhi. According to Dahui, silent illumination is an inert and quietistic practice of silence and stillness that disregards the need for a transformative moment of enlightenment.[1] Although Dahui's critique was very influential, apparently causing even subsequent Caodong masters to refrain from using the expression

Zen Pathways. Bret W. Davis, Oxford University Press. © Oxford University Press 2022.
DOI: 10.1093/oso/9780197573686.003.0022

"silent illumination," in fact it did not do justice to Hongzhi's and other Caodong masters' more subtle and less dramatic understanding of the interplay between "original enlightenment" and "initiated enlightenment," and of the interplay between a meditative merging with the oneness of the "empty field" of the luminous Buddha-mind and interacting with the diversity of phenomenal forms in daily life.[2] Tellingly, Dahui and Hongzhi themselves not only remained on good personal terms but also, despite Dahui's digs, apparently maintained great respect for each other as Zen masters. Hongzhi certainly demonstrated his magnanimous mind when he petitioned for Dahui to be appointed to a prestigious nearby monastery, and when he requested that Dahui take care of his affairs after his death.[3]

The Caodong School continued to thrive alongside the Linji School, and within a century they were both successfully transplanted to Japan. Rinzai Zen was transmitted to Japan from China in the twelfth and thirteenth centuries, and it has thrived in monasteries in Kyoto ever since. The Rinzai School was patronized by the shogunate government, and so it also flourished in Kamakura, near today's Tokyo, and in other major city centers. In these urban settings, Rinzai Zen has exerted a tremendous influence on the development of the artistic Ways such as the tea ceremony, calligraphy, and poetry, as well as the martial arts.

In the early thirteenth century, Dōgen returned from China to establish the Japanese Sōtō School. He eventually moved the center of his school away from Kyoto to a relatively unpopulated region of Japan, and the Sōtō School to this day is popular across the countryside of Japan. Sōtō is sometimes referred to in Japan as "Farmer Zen," while Rinzai is called "Samurai Zen." These monikers reflect not only their different patrons and practitioners, but also Sōtō's more careful and plodding nature and Rinzai's sharper and more dynamic character.[4]

All contemporary Rinzai Zen masters trace their lineage back to Hakuin, who in the eighteenth century revitalized the Rinzai tradition and formalized the kōan curriculum. Most of the kōans themselves derive from "encounter dialogues" and other episodes in the lives of the Chinese masters of the sixth through tenth centuries. These were gathered in the twelfth and thirteenth centuries, the most famous collections being *The Blue Cliff Record* and *The Gateless Barrier*.

Although my own practice and teaching are rooted in Rinzai, I have a deep respect for Sōtō and I often practice *shikantaza*, especially during periods when I am not engaged in kōan practice. I have also studied and written on Dōgen, who is widely, and rightly, considered to be not only one of the most spiritually inspiring but also the most philosophically profound of Zen masters. Throughout this book I have frequently cited Sōtō as well as Rinzai masters, and in this chapter I will present their methods of meditation as distinct yet compatible.

Different methods are appropriate for different people. In general, I would suggest that serious practitioners begin by counting and then following the breaths for a year or two. After that they can discern whether they want—or, rather, feel a deep spiritual need—to engage in the demanding practice of working with kōans, for which they would need to find a qualified teacher. After many years of going as far as they can in a kōan curriculum, they can then settle into the simple yet profound practice of "just sitting." For those not inclined or not able to engage in kōan practice, the long and intense "marathon of sprints" middle step in this process can be skipped.

Dōgen's Just Sitting and Non-thinking

Although training in Sōtō Zen does not involve a kōan curriculum as it does in Rinzai Zen, Dōgen himself highly valued kōans. Legend has it that the night before returning to Japan from China, he copied by hand the entire text of *The Blue Cliff Record*. He also assembled his own collection of three hundred kōans.[5] Many of Dōgen's own writings consist of insightful and creative commentaries on kōan literature.

However, when it came to the practice of *zazen*, Dōgen instructed his students to

> put aside the intellectual practice of investigating words and chasing phrases, and learn to take the backward step that turns the light [of the mind around] and shines it inward.... Give up the operations of the mind, intellect, and consciousness; stop measuring with thoughts, ideas, and views.[6]

Despite his prolific and profound writings on kōans, Dōgen expressly discourages "looking at phrases" *while* sitting in *zazen*. As one settles into "steady, immovable sitting," rather than focus on the central term or phrase of a kōan, Dōgen instructs us to "think of not-thinking. How do you think of not-thinking? Non-thinking."

These pithy and perplexing words are taken from a dialogue between the eighth-century Chinese Zen master Yaoshan and a monk. The dialogue reads:

> Yaoshan, Great Master Hongdao, was sitting. A monk asked him, "In steadfast sitting, what do you think?" Yaoshan said, "Think not-thinking." The monk asked, "How do you think not-thinking?" Yaoshan replied, "Non-thinking."[7]

The word translated as "thinking" here is a compound of two characters pronounced *si-liang* in Chinese and *shi-ryō* in Japanese (思量). The first character, 思, is a very general term that covers a wide range of operations of the mind.

Depending on the context, it can mean "think," "expect," "judge," "consider," "believe," "feel," "regard," "expect," "imagine," "intend," "desire," "care for," and so on. The second character, 量, is more specific. It means "weigh," "measure," "calculate," or "estimate." The compound term thus connotes a kind of discriminative thinking that calculates and evaluates. And so, the kind of thinking we are specifically being instructed not to engage in during *zazen* is the accustomed habit of the mind to look away from itself and toward things, things that it represents as objects standing over against itself as an independent subject. Our habitually egocentric mind then weighs, measures, calculates, and evaluates these objects according to our interests, preferences, and plans.

Yet, how do we let go of this constant stream of egocentric, calculative thinking? Dōgen tells us to "just sit," *shikantaza.* Just sitting entails neither chasing after thoughts nor chasing them off, neither clinging to them nor trying to get rid of them. Rather, one should just let passing sensations, perceptions, thoughts, and feelings come and go as they will. Over time, they will naturally cease to command one's attention, cease to entice one to chase after them, cease to irritate one so that one wants to chase them off. Their force and frequency will dissipate and they may disappear altogether for short or even for extended periods of time.

Shunryu Suzuki (Jp. Suzuki Shunryū)—the revered master who established Sōtō Zen in America—teaches: "Do not try to stop your mind, but leave everything as it is. Then things will not stay in your mind for so long. Things will come as they come and go as they go." He adds that "eventually your clear, empty mind will last fairly long."[8] In any case, just as the open and peaceful blue sky remains there, regardless of whether or not there are passing clouds, non-thinking awareness remains there, regardless of whether we are thinking or trying not to think.

John Daido Loori Rōshi says that non-thinking is "the boundless mind of samadhi that neither holds on to, nor lets go of, thoughts."[9] Becoming directly aware of—which means simply becoming—this clear, empty, open, untainted mind is the core of just sitting. This mind is, at bottom, neither an activity of thinking nor an object of thought; it is an open field of nondual awareness that embraces and enables both thinking and not-thinking.

The question is, how do we awaken to the Big Mind of this underlying and encompassing nondual awareness? How do we cease to identify ourselves with the monkey-mind of our obsessive habits of thought and realize that, at bottom, we are the clear, peaceful, empty mind of non-thinking? Dōgen, following Yaoshan, tells us to "think not-thinking."

If one is told "not to think," the first thing one does, the only thing one knows how to do, is to *think* about not thinking. Yet, when Dōgen tells us to "turn the light of the mind around," he is not telling us to make the mind into a mental object; he is not telling us to turn the seer into something seen, or to make awareness into an object of awareness. Nevertheless, we may indeed have to go through this detour, the "wall gazing" impasse of "thinking not-thinking," in order to occasion the "backward step" with our whole being into a direct experience of what, in the language of thinking, we can only call "non-thinking."

It is important not to confuse *non*-thinking with *not*-thinking. Not-thinking here means either the suppression of thought or a contentless object of thought. Non-thinking is not this kind of blankly staring out into space or zoning out in between daydreams. It is important to bear in mind that non-thinking does not exclude thinking. Non-thinking is not opposed to thinking or, for that matter, to daydreaming or mind-wandering. It is the ultimate "where-from" and "where-in" of these; it is the open field of awareness that encompasses and engenders thinking. It is there when we are lost in thought, and it is there when we are too tired to think. Non-thinking awareness is always there, even though we rarely ever notice it.

It needs to be emphasized that non-thinking is not opposed to thinking, since Zen is sometimes mistaken—by misguided proponents as well as mistaken opponents—as entailing and even promoting an anti-intellectualism. Dōgen himself, remember, was a remarkably creative and critical thinker as well as an avid reader and prolific writer of texts, even while he advocated regularly stepping back from these activities to just sit at rest in the open awareness of non-thinking. Such just sitting does not replace, but rather enables, just reading, just thinking, and just doing all the other important duties and activities of life.

Finally, it is important not to misunderstand and mistakenly practice "just sitting" as a matter of "just sitting around," lackadaisical in one's self-assurance that one is already enlightened. Although Dōgen says we should sit in full faith—full confidence—that, in truth, we are Buddhas, he also repeatedly urges us to "arouse the aspiration for enlightenment" and meditate with wholehearted intensity, "as if putting out a fire on your head."[10]

Just Sitting and Kōan Practice: The Slow Simmer and Pressure Cooker Approaches

Some Rinzai Zen masters have expressed appreciation for *shikantaza* as the highest and hardest kōan, since it gives you nothing in particular to focus on. It demands awakening to what Dōgen calls the *genjōkōan*, the always new presencing of truth here and now. As is often the case with Zen—with life—what seems to be the easiest turns out to be the hardest.

The point of *shikantaza* is not to become enlightened, but rather to realize that you already are enlightened. You do not need to *become* a Buddha, since you already *are* one. And yet, you do need to *realize* this fact; you do need to *awaken* to your original Buddha-nature. And that awakening, that realization, makes all the difference.

Although Dōgen did not like to speak of *kenshō*, of the enlightening experience of suddenly "seeing into one's true nature," he did reportedly have a dramatic awakening experience upon hearing his teacher exclaim that *zazen* is a matter of "dropping off the body-mind."[11] Moreover, in his instructions on *zazen*, Dōgen affirms cases of "sudden enlightenment" when he speaks of "using the opportunity provided by a finger, a banner, a needle, or a mallet, and meeting realization with a whisk, a fist, a staff, or a shout."[12]

Dōgen instructs his students to sit in meditation with the conviction that "they are in essence within the Buddha Way, where there is no delusion, no false thinking, no confusion, no increase or decrease, and no mistake." To arouse this trust, and ultimately to awaken a true self-confidence, he says:

> You do this by sitting, which severs the root of thinking and blocks access to the road of intellectual understanding. . . . If once, in sitting, you sever the root of thinking, in eight or nine cases out of ten you will immediately attain understanding of the Way.[13]

Although in this passage Dōgen speaks of "immediately attaining" enlightenment, the Sōtō practice of *shikantaza* has been traditionally understood as a patient practice of *mokushō* or "silent illumination" of one's Buddha-nature. Slowly but surely, *shikantaza* leads to the realization of the Buddha that one already is.

If *shikantaza* is the slow simmer approach to this realization, kōan practice is the pressure cooker approach. In both approaches, faith or trust in the reality of one's Buddha-nature leads to the confidence that arises from actually awakening to it. In the pressure cooker kōan approach, the "great root of faith" is coupled with the "great feeling of doubt" or "great ball of doubt." Together with "great determination," these make up the three required mindsets for kōan training.[14]

Initial Barrier Kōans: Entering the World of Rinzai Zen

Let us now look at what Rinzai Zen masters Hakuin and Wumen have had to say about working on a kōan such as the *Mu* kōan, the first case in *The Gateless Barrier* and the most famous "initial barrier" kōan used in Rinzai training.[15] In the story of this kōan, a monk asks Zhaozhou whether or not a dog has Buddha-nature. Zhaozhou answers "No!" His one-word response is pronounced *wu* in Chinese and *mu* in Japanese. While *wu* or *mu* normally means "no" or "does not have," here it points beyond all oppositions, including *yes* versus *no* and *has* versus *has not*. In part it is meant to frustrate the intellect, which can operate only by drawing distinctions and weighing opposites. Yet Zhaozhou's utterance is not only meant to short-circuit dualistic discrimination; it is also, and most importantly, a direct demonstration of the nondualistic Buddha-nature itself. It is not enough to understand this non-intellectual answer intellectually, for example as an irrational utterance. *Mu* is not irrational any more than it is rational. It is beyond or beneath even that dualistic distinction.

If you are getting confused, that's good! Once confusion sets in, once the discriminating intellect is frustrated to the point of exhaustion, then the real work can begin. That real work involves generating the "great feeling of doubt." The Great Doubt is not a skeptical stance taken toward an object or doctrine; it is rather a matter of being wholeheartedly plunged into the issue we are trying to resolve at the very heart of our practice. As the modern Japanese Zen master Yamada Kōun puts it, we must concentrate on our practice "to the point that our entire body and mind are like a single mass of inquiry." If we are practicing with the *Mu* kōan, then "we must become a ball of Mu, our spiritual energy solidified into an immovable mass of questioning."[16]

Based on his own experience with the *Mu* kōan, Hakuin teaches:

> When a person faces the great doubt, before him there is in all directions only a vast and empty land without birth and without death, like a huge plain of ice extending ten thousand miles. As though seated within a vase of lapis lazuli surrounded by absolute purity, without his senses he sits and forgets to stand, stands and forgets to sit. Within his heart there is not the slightest thought or emotion, only the single word *Mu*. It is just as though he were standing in complete emptiness. At this time no fears arise, no thoughts creep in, and when he advances single-mindedly without retrogression, suddenly it will be as though a sheet of ice were broken or a jade tower had fallen. He will experience a great joy.[17]

Only by delving all the way into and then suddenly breaking through the frozen purity of a state of complete emptiness, Hakuin says, can one attain "the great penetration of wondrous awakening."

In addition to assigning the *Mu* kōan, Hakuin formulated his own initial barrier kōan: "What is the sound of one hand?"[18] We know the clapping sound that two hands can make, but what sound does one hand make? The answer is not to slap one's hand on the table or to snap one's fingers. After all, if some clever response like this were the answer, how enlightening would that really be? Kōans are not game-like riddles, and kōan practice is no joke. It is, physically and psychologically, an extremely demanding endeavor. Indeed, spiritually speaking, it must become a matter of life and death.

If, when you come up with what you think might be an answer to a kōan, ask yourself whether coming up with that answer changed your life. If it did not, then you can be sure that it is not the answer. Maybe if someone else were to say or do the same thing, it would manifest an enlightening breakthrough for them, but if it is not life-changing for you, then at best you are solving an intellectual puzzle or perhaps just mimicking someone else's answer.

When you are working on a kōan, especially an initial barrier kōan, you need to exhaust the intellect. That is why many kōans are intentionally paradoxical. They often invite you—even trick you—into trying to figure them out *as if* they were intellectual puzzles. And yet, they can never truly be solved that way. They frustrate the analytical, discursive, dualistic intellect. Once the intellect is exhausted and the Great Doubt begins to beset you, this means that you are really getting to work on the kōan—or, rather, that the kōan is really getting to work on you.

Here's how I instruct kōan practitioners. Each time you sit down to meditate, run the kōan through your head a few times, especially the key word or phrase, called a *watō*, which is the pivotal sticking point of the kōan. Breathe this word or phrase in and out like a mantra for a few minutes. Then, don't think about it anymore; rather, put it in the pit of your stomach and sit with it, meditate on it with your whole being and not just with your head. Wake up with it, brush your teeth with it, eat with it, walk with it, work with it—the whole time *letting it work on you*.

You will come to realize that what initial barrier kōans like the "sound of one hand" are prodding you to do is to dig down beneath all dualities. The "one hand" is the absolute oneness that embraces and pervades all dualities and differences. It is the absolute nonduality that does not even stand over against dualities, which would, after all, just create one more meta-duality. It is the one dimension, as it were, in which all differences exist. In order to awaken to it, you need to put all dualistic intellection aside. And yet, when you awaken to it, you realize that it does not annihilate differences, or compete with them in any way. It is, rather, what lets them be in the first place; it is the "first place" in which all oppositions and all the myriad things have always taken place.

An entrance into the world of Rinzai Zen requires one to first break through all dualistic oppositions: oppositions of subject/object, inner/outer, pure/defiled, being/nothingness, speech/silence, and so on. The entire world of relativities in which we live must be transcended—or rather trans-descended, dug down beneath—before it can be reaffirmed.

Another entry kōan used in Rinzai training is "What is your Original Face before your father and mother were born?"[19] Most often, however, the initial barrier through which practitioners are traditionally required to pass is the *Mu* kōan, which appears for good reason as the first kōan in *The Gateless Barrier*.

The title of this kōan collection could also be translated as *Wumen's Barrier* or as *The Barrier (or Checkpoint) with the Gate of Mu*. Wumen, the thirteenth-century Chinese Zen master who compiled and commented on the kōans in *The Gateless Barrier*, instructs us not to "attempt nihilistic or dualistic interpretations" of *Mu* (Ch. *Wu*). In other words, *Mu* is neither a sheer vacuity nor is it the mere opposite of being; it is neither a "no" as opposed to a "yes" nor a "has" as opposed to a "has not." Rather than attempt to understand *Mu* intellectually and dualistically from a distance, you must wholeheartedly "rouse the word *Mu*" by "concentrating yourself into this *Mu* with your 360 bones and 84,000 pores, making your whole body one great ball of doubt."

Yet, Wumen does not tell us to simply become *mu* on the meditation cushion and stay there. This would, after all, be a form of what Zen calls "emptiness sickness" in which one gets stuck hiding out in a "demonic cave of darkness." Rather, like Hakuin, he says that after "inside and outside have naturally become welded into a single block . . . all of a sudden it will break open, and you will astonish heaven and shake the earth."[20]

The Rinzai Zen Kōan Curriculum

It is important to point out that while the initial barrier kōans we have been discussing are crucial, insofar as it is by breaking through them that one first attains *kenshō*, a taste of enlightenment, they are but a first step on the very long road of an extensive kōan curriculum in Rinzai Zen. Initial barrier kōans are also called *hosshin* or Truth Body of the Buddha kōans, since they enable one to experience the ultimate truth of nonduality in which the self and the rest of the universe are rooted.

After one has passed an initial barrier kōan, one is assigned many *sassho*. This term is often loosely translated as "checking questions," but really these are more like follow-up kōans in their own right. Some of these are *kikan* kōans, which require one to demonstrate the "dynamic functioning" of the nondual reality one has awakened to. A more advanced genre of kōans is called *gonsen* or "investigation of words." No longer ensnared by words, one learns to understand and employ them as what Dōgen calls "expressive attainments of the Way."

Early kōans push one to go beyond and beneath words and doctrines, in order to experience more directly the nondual reality they are meant to express—like being asked to *actually taste a food* rather than just *read about how it tastes*. Later kōans are often more concerned with cultivating an experiential understanding of what we might call the "intuitive logic" of Zen teachings. Here, one could say, the intellect is reengaged, yet in a manner that allows it to remain rooted in, and inseparable from, the whole of one's awakened self.

Victor Sōgen Hori, a philosopher and scholar of religion who spent thirteen years as a Rinzai Zen monk in Japan, points out that the "first half of kōan training puts major emphasis on *kyōgai*," the existential state of being and behaving that one must demonstrate as an answer to a kōan, and a lesser emphasis on the *hōri* or "Dharma rationale" articulated in kōans, whereas "the second half [of kōan training] reverses these emphases."[21]

In other words, while all kōans require one to *experience* and *express* the ultimate nondual truth of both the oneness and differences of reality, at first the emphasis is put on attaining the nondual experience, whereas later the emphasis shifts to being able to properly express an appropriate understanding and articulation of it in various contexts. Moreover, as the longtime Rinzai Zen practitioner and scholar Takemura Makio writes, "The kōan system is not just meant to enable one to attain awakening. Rather, it is meant to guide one along the path of realizing the way of life of a Bodhisattva."[22]

The Necessary Role of the Teacher in Kōan Practice

If and when you ever become interested in engaging in kōan practice, you will need to find a teacher to work with. The right teacher or "true teacher" (*shōshi*) must be both a truly qualified teacher and also the right teacher for you. He or she must be an authorized teacher whose personality and style are a good fit for you. Zen monks in training are called *unsui*, which literally means "clouds and water." Like rain clouds, these monks traditionally wandered from monastery to monastery in search of the right teacher. When the right teacher is found, and the conditions of the Zen center are right, lightning strikes and the rain waters flow.

Throughout this book, I have discussed various kōans in order to explain the philosophy and practice of Zen. Kōans can be appreciated on various levels, philosophical as well as spiritual. They can be taken as material for intellectual inquiry, or as matters of existential exigency. They can be fruitfully pondered in solitude, or discussed in a college classroom. However, if one wishes to wholeheartedly work on kōans as a spiritual "life or death" pathway of practice, it is essential to do so under the guidance of a qualified Zen teacher.

The relationship between a Zen teacher and student is said to be like that of a mother hen and a baby chick that is trying to hatch out of an egg.[23] The practice of *zazen* is then like a baby chick sitting under the watchful eye of its mother hen in the nest of a monastery or Zen center. When the time is ripe, the chick will peck from the inside at the same time as the mother hen pecks from the outside. Only by working together in this manner can the chick break out of its shell of dark delusion and into the light of day.

When I was in college, I had a very knowledgeable professor who taught Asian religions. I took all of his classes, and even learned yoga and meditation from his wife. However, neither he nor she was a Zen teacher. Looking back, I do not think it was appropriate for him to have given his students an assignment that involved meditating on a Zen kōan. Without proper guidance, I threw myself into working on the famous *Mu* kōan. I not only sat for hours in meditation, but also, as instructed, tried to keep this kōan in mind from morning to night. One morning, I suddenly woke up psychologically paralyzed for a few minutes on my dorm room bed, with a vivid hallucination of a huge dog sitting on top of me and panting right in my face! It was a very intense experience—but of course it had absolutely nothing to do with Zen awakening. At that moment I needed an actual Zen teacher.

I later learned that such experiences are called *makyō* or "devilish states." They are a kind of byproduct of intensive meditative concentration. They can be pleasurable or uncomfortable, even euphoric or terrifying, but in any case, one should fixate on them no more than one should on an itchy nose or rumbling stomach. Such *makyō* experiences can be caused by the resurfacing of painful memories or repressed emotions. My experience of the dog was no doubt related to the fact that, as child, I was once pinned down and bitten in the face by a neighbor's German shepherd. Other *makyō* experiences may be caused by sensory deprivation or a heightened awareness of light or sound due to intense concentration. In any case, while they may present issues one should deal with on a physical or psychological level, they are certainly not the aim of Zen meditation. Nevertheless, meditators often mistake *makyō* for *kenshō*, byproducts of meditative concentration for enlightening breakthroughs. Part of the role of the teacher is to disabuse one from making this mistake.

To work on a kōan requires working with a teacher. The teacher will never give you the answer, which would defeat the purpose. But he or she can give you gentle or stern course corrections, encouragement, and support—albeit often in the form of tough love!

The Experience of Being Tested on Kōans

Good Zen teachers will never spoon-feed you. They will teach you in the style that Confucius suggested when he said:

> I will not open the door for a mind that is not already struggling to understand, nor will I provide words to a tongue that is not already struggling to speak. If I hold up one corner of a problem, and the student cannot come back to me with the other three, I will not attempt to instruct him again.[24]

This is like a math teacher who gives students just one variable of an equation and tells them that, for homework, they need to figure out the other three on their own—and if they can't, or if they are not at least willing to stay up all night struggling to do so, they needn't bother coming back to school. This insistence on student initiative and ingenuity may be very different from the rote memorization that came to be associated with Confucian scholastic education, but it is very much the approach used in Rinzai Zen kōan practice to this day.

When a kōan practitioner goes to the teacher for a one-on-one interview, called *sanzen* or *dokusan*, he or she goes to be *tested* rather than *taught*. The teacher assigns you the kōan, and you have to come up with the answer on your own. Moreover, you cannot *explain* the answer; you have to *embody* it, *perform* it. This embodied performance may be verbal or not, but it must always be presented with your whole being.

Often the teacher will quickly just ring the bell, signaling that, at that instant, the interview is over and immediately you should stop whatever you are saying or doing, bow, and leave the interview room. The same ring of the bell, in fact, signals to the next student that it is time for his or her interview.

This is what the experience of going for an interview is like: At a designated time, a signal is given and practitioners leap up from their meditation cushions and race to line up to be interviewed by the teacher. Sometimes there are too many people for the teacher to be able to interview everyone, in which case if you lose the race you lose the opportunity to be interviewed that time around. Practitioners kneel in line waiting for their turn, at a considerable distance from the interview room in order to maintain privacy.

When it is your turn and when you hear the bell rung by the teacher, signaling that the previous interview is over, you ring a bell announcing that you are on your way. After winding through the hallways from the waiting room to the interview room, you make bows and enter. Once you are seated in front of the teacher, you state the kōan you have been assigned and then present your answer. Sometimes the teacher will offer you some feedback. Often, however, the teacher will just ring the bell and perhaps, in order to urge you onward, give you a few encouraging slaps on the back. Then it's back to the meditation hall.[25]

23

Death and Rebirth—Or, Nirvana
Here and Now

As we approach the end of this book, it's time to talk once more, in depth, about the end of life. We first broached the tremendous topic of death in Chapters 5 and 6. Midway through this book, in Chapter 12, we discussed the Great Death that Zen tells us that we need to undergo in order to truly live. In this chapter, we'll revisit this pivotal topic of spiritual death and rebirth by way of addressing Buddhist teachings about literal death and rebirth.

Death as the Business of Japanese Buddhism

For various social and historical as well as religious reasons, death has become the business of Buddhist temples in Japan. Most Japanese go to Shintō shrines on other occasions, such as to celebrate the birth of a child or to pray before taking a college entrance exam. And it has become fashionable to have a Christian wedding ceremony, even though only around 1 percent of Japanese people are actually Christians. Yet, when it comes to death—to funeral and memorial services—almost all Japanese go to Buddhist temples and call on Buddhist priests.

From a Western perspective, the Japanese may appear to be rather religiously promiscuous. In the same calendar year, a typical Japanese family might attend a Shintō festival, a Christian wedding, and a Buddhist funeral. From their point of view, Westerners can seem dogmatic and exclusionary in their religious commitments. If all religions deal with the big questions and great mysteries of life and death, why would any one religion presume to have a monopoly on clear and certain answers?[1]

Of course, death is hardly the only thing Japanese people associate with Buddhism. If a Japanese person is inclined to take up a spiritual practice such as meditation, he or she most likely goes to a Buddhist temple. Buddhist temples and their gardens are also very popular destinations among Japanese people of all ages for more or less reverential "spiritual tourism." Nevertheless, many Japanese people associate Buddhist temples and priests predominantly with funerals and with the memorial services that are conducted periodically for months and years after a death in the family. When it comes time to seek solace in the face of

Zen Pathways. Bret W. Davis, Oxford University Press. © Oxford University Press 2022.
DOI: 10.1093/oso/9780197573686.003.0023

mortality and after the loss of a loved one, most Japanese feel most comfortable with Buddhist rituals and teachings.

It is also true that, quite literally, death is the *business* of Buddhist temples in Japan, including Zen temples.[2] Most of their income comes from conducting funerals and memorial services. Yet, while the term "funerary Buddhism" (*sōshiki bukkyō*) is usually used in a pejorative sense, by sincere Buddhists as well as by secular critics, these services undoubtedly do provide real comfort and community to grieving families. Doctrinally speaking, they are thought to transfer karmic merit to the departed person so that he or she goes to a better place.

The Six Realms of Rebirth in Samsara

Traditionally in Buddhism, this "better place" has been thought of as one of the higher of the Six Realms of Rebirth in Samsara. The higher three realms are those of human beings, heavenly beings, and, more ambivalently, fighting spirits.[3] The lower three realms are those of animals, hungry ghosts, and hell beings. It is thought that one must transmigrate through these Six Realms of Rebirth for many lifetimes before one has accumulated enough karmic merit to be reborn as a human being in a social situation and psychological state conducive to finally attaining the liberation of Nirvana. Nirvana is thought to be, in some sense, beyond the Six Realms of Rebirth in Samsara altogether.

Wheel of Life paintings depict the Six Realms of Rebirth in Samsara held in the clutches of Yama, the personification of death and karmic retribution. Going around clockwise from the top left, the Wheel depicts the realms of human beings, heavenly beings, fighting spirits, hungry ghosts, hell beings, and animals. The Wheel of Life in Samsara is driven by the Three Poisons—greed, hatred, and delusion—which are depicted in the hub of the Wheel as a pig, a snake, and a rooster chasing each other around and around.

The effects of karma are depicted in a band around the hub of the Wheel that shows people falling down and rising up between the realms. The accumulation of a lot of good karmic merit can lead to being reborn as a heavenly being. However, heavenly beings tend to become so egocentrically wrapped up in their own pleasurable state that they eventually fall down into lower realms. One may fall into the realm of fighting spirits: jealous demigods who are obsessed with competition and gaining power over others. Or one may fall into the realm of hungry ghosts: pitiful creatures whose appetites far surpass their meager abilities to satisfy those excessive desires. They are usually depicted with huge bellies but only tiny mouths and throats.

Aggressively angry and callously cold beings are reborn in the flaming and frozen areas of the hell realm. Yet hell beings suffer so intensely that eventually they not only burn off their own bad karma, but also generate good karma by becoming empathetically aware of the sufferings of others. Heaven and hell are thus not permanent afterlife destinations in Buddhism. They are places where one reaps the benefits and suffers the consequences of one's karma. In heaven, one reaps long-lasting but not everlasting rewards. Hell is filled with intense suffering, but this suffering is not just retribution; it is also for the sake of rehabilitation. It is thus not eternal damnation.

Only as a human is there the right balance of suffering and freedom-from-suffering to enable one to be both motivated and capable of engaging in the spiritual practice that leads to liberation from Samsara. Outside of the Wheel of Life in Samsara altogether are pictured the Buddha and Nirvana. They are depicted in the upper right and left corners of the painting.

The Wheel of Life is painted on the outside walls of many Tibetan and Bhutanese monasteries in order to educate people in the basics of Buddhism. Yet it is not often found in Japan. In fact, Japanese Buddhists don't think or talk much at all about rebirth in the Six Realms. When they do talk about the afterlife, they tend to speak of becoming a Buddha, attaining Nirvana, or going to the Pure Land—expressions that they often use rather vaguely to mean roughly the same thing.

Perhaps such vagueness is appropriate when talking about the great mysteries of death and the afterlife. Etched into my memory is a conversation about death I had with my mother just a few months before she suddenly passed away. A devout Christian who was deeply interested in meditation and mysticism, she told me—with emotionally watery eyes yet also with a strangely peaceful smile and calm voice—that she was okay with the mystery of death. A decade later, the lay Zen master Ueda Shizuteru said something similar to me and a couple of senior colleagues when we visited him in his retirement home about nine months before he passed away. He spoke of letting go and letting be, of what the German mystic Meister Eckhart called *Gelassenheit*. He calmly spoke of releasing himself unto the dark and amorphous unknown of death.

Rebirth Without an Eternal Soul

"Wait a minute," you might be thinking, "it might make sense for mystically inclined Christians to say they are okay with the mystery of what happens after death, but how can Buddhists believe in an afterlife at all if they don't believe in an eternal soul?" In fact, Japanese Buddhists do use a term, *reikon*, that can be translated as the "soul" of the deceased person—and yet, if pressed, a Japanese Buddhist priest would tell you that this does not refer to an independent and unchanging entity.[4] If this is particularly difficult for us to understand, that is because we are so used to thinking of selves or souls as independent and unchanging entities. And so, it is difficult for us to imagine what it would mean for there to be an afterlife without an eternal soul that remains unchanged as it gets transported from one place to another.

Buddhist philosophers ask us to look at this matter the other way around. If a soul were to be truly independent and unchanging, then it could not be saved, because it would be stuck in whatever state it happens to be in. The seminal second-/third-century Mahayana Buddhist philosopher Nagarjuna logically demonstrates that it is precisely the emptiness of the self—its lack of an unchanging essence—that makes the transformative path to Nirvana possible.[5] The contemporary Tibetan Buddhist teacher Traleg Kyabgon points out that, according to Buddhism,

> what is transferred from one life to the next is not an unchanging psychic principle, but different psychic elements all hanging together, *samskaras*—memories, various impressions, and so on, none of which is unchanging in itself. . . . If, on the contrary, [the mind] were a fixed thing, it would be unable to change, and whatever nature it had would necessarily remain, making a transformation of consciousness impossible.[6]

Indeed, it is because the mind is mutable that it can mature. If the mind could not change, we could not change our mind; we could never transform an ignorant bundle of mental processes into an enlightened one.

Come to think of it, St. Augustine acknowledged not only that the soul is *dependent* on God for its existence, but also that, unlike God, the soul must be *modifiable* over time; otherwise conversion—which for him meant turning away from earthly desires toward love of God—would not be possible.[7] Christians sometimes speak of this conversion as a matter of dying to the old Adam in order to be reborn in the true life of Christ. And so, it turns out that souls are neither independent nor unchanging entities in Christianity either.

For Buddhists, the rebirth that is thought to happen after death is not entirely unlike the constant rebirth we undergo during this life.[8] This "moment-to-moment rebirth" is going on all the time. My personality is constantly developing along with my thoughts and emotions, just as the cells of my body are constantly dying off and being replaced—not to mention the smaller molecules that make up cells, and the even smaller processes of particle physics that make up molecules. On a larger scale, my childhood self had to disappear in order for my adult self to come into existence.

Keeping up with this incessant change can be difficult. A few years ago I came to the realization that part of my irritation with the new rebellious attitude of my teenage son was based on the fact that I was grieving the loss of the more docile and dutiful child he had once been. Yet that sweet little boy had to mutate into a "terrible teen" if he was ever going to grow up—which, of course, the more mature part of me wants him to do. And so, I realized, practicing a bit of mindfulness, that I need to let go of my attachment to the adorable little boy who is no more in order to appreciate the fine young man he is in the process of becoming. Admittedly, I am still having trouble keeping up with the pace of his growing up!

Changes can be looked at from the perspective of discontinuity or from the perspective of continuity. If we focus on the greatest ruptures of discontinuity, we can speak of physical, psychological, or spiritual "death." If we turn our attention to their aspects of complementary continuity, we can also speak of "rebirth."

In Chapter 12, we discussed the teachings of spiritual death and rebirth in Christianity and Pure Land Buddhism as well as in Zen. In addition to noting Jesus's core teaching that we need to lose our life in order to gain true life,[9] we quoted the seventeenth-century Augustinian friar Abraham a Sancta Clara as saying, "A man who dies before he dies, does not die when he dies."[10] And we compared this with the eighteenth-century Japanese Zen master Hakuin's poem written on a scroll under the single character for death:

> O young folk—
> if you fear death,
> die now!
> Having died once,
> You won't have to die again.[11]

Undergoing a spiritual death and rebirth is at the heart of all the great religious traditions. It is the only way to enter the Kingdom of Heaven in Christianity, and it is the only way to resolve the one great matter of life and death here on earth for Zen Buddhists.

We may understand, at least intellectually, that this spiritual death and rebirth is the most important matter, and yet we cannot keep ourselves from wondering: "Okay, but what does happen when our physical bodies die?" Christian preachers such as Abraham a Santa Clara and Zen masters such as Hakuin have different responses to that question. Christians can debate whether the eternal soul leaves the lifeless corpse behind or whether this dualistic idea is an early Orphic-Platonic corruption of the original Christian teaching of "the resurrection of the body."[12] Our concern here is with the Zen response.

As we saw in Chapter 12, the thirteenth-century Sōtō Zen master Dōgen warns against the so-called Senika heresy, which holds that there is an individual eternal soul that is separable from the mortal body.[13] The fifteenth-century Rinzai Zen master Ikkyū also warns against this dualistic view:

To the eye of illusion it appears that though the body dies, the soul does not. This is a terrible mistake. The enlightened man declares that both perish together. Buddha is also an emptiness. Sky and earth all return to the original field.[14]

What does this mean? Let's approach such provocative and peculiarly Zen responses to the question of death and the afterlife by way of first looking further into more traditional Buddhist responses.

Transmigration Through the Six Realms in This Life as Well as Between Lives

In a *sutta* from the Pali Canon called *The Greater Discourse on the Destruction of Craving*, Shakyamuni Buddha clearly rejects the "pernicious view" that "it is this same consciousness that runs and wanders through the round of rebirths," a view held by a monk who was the "son of a fisherman" and who the Buddha says is "caught up in a vast net of craving."[15] Buddhists have traditionally thought that after the demise of the physical form of the body, and, according to some schools, after passing through what Tibetan Buddhists call the intermediate stage of *bardo* with a more subtle bodily form, the bundle of the other four of the Five Aggregates that we discussed in Chapter 7—the interdependent and ever-changing collection of psychological processes that makes up the mental and emotional aspects of our life-stream—eventually finds an appropriate new physical body in which to be reincarnated.[16]

Usually, this rebirth as reincarnation in this sense is determined by karma. Karma can be good or bad, but, insofar as karma is at bottom based on ignorance and egoistic craving, it propels one to be reborn in one of the Six Realms of Rebirth in Samsara. Even a great philanthropist, insofar as he or she gives out of a desire to be recognized as a giver, will at best be reborn as a heavenly being, which is merely the happiest form of life in Samsara.

However, according to Mahayana Buddhist traditions there is a different reason, a different *motivation* for some beings to be reborn in Samsara. Enlightened beings, Buddhas and Bodhisattvas, are no longer driven by karma, but they can—and, indeed, naturally would—voluntarily choose to be reborn in Samsara out of the compassionate desire to endlessly work toward liberating all sentient beings from suffering.[17] This is why Wheel of Life paintings often include a Buddha or Bodhisattva in each one of the Six Realms of Rebirth in Samsara.

Tibetan Buddhists talk a lot about rebirth, both the rebirth of normal unenlightened people and that of enlightened beings such as the Dalai Lama, who is thought to be a reincarnation of the Bodhisattva of Compassion. By contrast, Zen Buddhists rarely talk in detail or in literal terms about rebirth or reincarnation. Indeed, on a couple of occasions when I mentioned Tibetan Buddhism to one Japanese Rinzai Zen master, he tilted his head and wondered out loud about what he sees as Tibetan Buddhists' excessive concerns with, and literalistic beliefs about, rebirth.

Shohaku Okumura (Jp. Okumura Shōhaku), a leading contemporary Japanese Sōtō Zen master, comes straight out and says: "Many people believe in transmigration from one lifetime to another. I don't believe in this." And yet, he goes on to say, "I know we transmigrate within this life." As have many Zen masters past and present, Okumura Rōshi explains transmigration through the Six Realms in terms of moment-to-moment rebirth in this life. He explains:

> Sometimes we feel like heavenly beings, sometimes like hell dwellers. Often, we are like hungry ghosts, craving satisfaction, constantly searching for more. When our stomachs are full and we have nothing to do, we become sleepy and lazy like animals. Sometimes we are like asuras or fighting spirits. As human beings we work to acquire fame and profit. Even when our stomachs are full, we are not satisfied. We need something more, such as fame or wealth. Heavenly beings are like millionaires whose desires are completely fulfilled. They look happy but I think such people are rather bored. . . . Within this constant transmigration there is no peaceful basis for our lives. This way of life is a vain attempt to satisfy our egos.[18]

Okumura Rōshi is giving here a *metaphorical-psychological* interpretation of the Six Realms of Rebirth rather than a *literal-cosmological* one. As we saw in Chapter 12 with regard to the concept of the Pure Land, this metaphorical-psychological interpretation is nothing new. It is not a modern reinterpretation of a traditional doctrine, but has long been a part of the Buddhist tradition.

Such metaphorical-psychological interpretations have frequently been favored by past and present Zen masters in particular. For them, explanations and descriptions of life in the Six Realms of Rebirth in Samsara, as well as other-worldly accounts of the Pure Land, Buddhahood, and Nirvana, are best understood metaphorically in terms of possible ways of experiencing life here and now.

A Zen Master's Confession of Ignorance

Although all Buddhist sects in Japan are in the funeral business, it is fair to say that this is easier for Pure Land priests than it is for Zen priests to reconcile with their teachings and practices, since Pure Land Buddhism speaks of "going forth to be reborn in Amida Buddha's Pure Land," whereas Zen speaks of "becoming a Buddha in this very body."

Shakyamuni Buddha himself famously refused to answer questions about whether a Buddha exists after death or not. He told his disciples that he had left that issue unaddressed "because it is unbeneficial, it does not belong to the fundamentals of the spiritual life, it does not lead . . . to enlightenment, to Nibbāna [Sk. Nirvana]."[19] We need to be reminded of our impermanence and we need to face up to our mortality, not primarily so that we can prepare for the afterlife, but so that we can undergo the great spiritual death that allows us to live fully here and now. When Confucius was asked about death, he replied: "We do not yet understand life—how could we possibly understand death?"[20] Analogously, when asked questions about death, Zen masters are likely to turn the questioner's attention back to life.

Once, a philosophy student from Kyoto University visited the famous modern Rinzai Zen master Yamada Mumon. At first, they just sat silently looking at each other for about twenty minutes. Then Yamada Rōshi suddenly shouted, "Aren't you going to say something?" To which the student blurted out, "What happens when someone dies?" Yamada Rōshi replied, "His body gets cold." Student: "What happens after that?" Yamada: "It probably gets cremated." Student: "What then?" To this last question Yamada Rōshi simply said: "I don't know what happens after that."[21]

It was only then that the student turned his attention from death back to life and asked, "What is the goal of life?" In Chapter 16 we discussed Yamada Rōshi's provocative and profound answer: "To play." Not only does this famous Zen master tell us that the point of life is to play, he admits that he doesn't know what happens after one dies. "What a refreshingly honest answer!" one might think. Or, one might wonder: "What good is Zen then, at least as a religion, if it cannot provide us with knowledge about what happens after we die?"

But does anyone really know what happens after we die? Of course, one may *believe* in a Heaven and a Hell, or in rebirth as a human or other kind of being; or one may not believe in such things. But does anyone really *know*? One may desperately desire there to be an afterlife, and one may give this desperate desire a nice name like "hope" or "faith" rather than a naughty one like "craving" or "attachment." In any case, we have to admit that we don't really know what happens to us after death—or even if anything at all does happen to us.

I think the harder and deeper question about death is this: Once we admit that no one really knows what happens, what comportment should we take toward death? Is there a *wisdom* in the face of death that is not a matter of *knowledge* about the afterlife?

Personal Experiences with the Great Kōan of Death

When my Zen teacher Tanaka Hōjū Rōshi died, Ueda Shizuteru Sensei asked us, "Where did he go?" After pausing for a moment, he told us that this was the kōan that Tanaka Rōshi had left us with. A decade later, just two weeks before Ueda Sensei himself died, he in effect gave me his answer to this kōan—but not in words, not as a doctrine of knowledge. He held his palms together, bowed deeply over the edge of his hospital bed, and then silently yet very intently and intensely gazed into my eyes. There was a wisdom conveyed in his gaze that surpasses all understanding. However, as with all kōans, it does little good to have been given the answer. One has to realize it for oneself.[22]

In Zen, resolving the great matter of life and death requires facing up to mortality. In order to truly live, we have to come to terms with the termination of life as we know it. The kōan that Hakuin struggled hardest with was: "When Nanquan died, where did he go?" He finally attained a major breakthrough after he was standing in the middle of the road totally absorbed in this kōan and an impatient "madwoman" suddenly knocked him over with a broom.[23]

The most dramatic breakthrough I've personally experienced in my Zen practice was with the kōan "If I were sliced right in two, how would I be saved?" It was one of dozens of follow-up kōans I was given after the *Mu* kōan. It took me a long time to pass the *Mu* kōan—indeed, even after a circuitous struggle to find the answer, I was made to repeat it for many months until I truly became it, until it became me, until there was no more me but just it, until it too was no more. I then passed rather easily several follow-up kōans. But then I got stuck, really stuck, on the "sliced right in two" kōan. I grappled desperately with it for many months and through many intensive retreats.

Then, one day I proceeded to the interview room in a state of complete absorption, not knowing which way was up, down, left, or right, unaware of any temporal distinction between before and after or any spatial difference between here and there. Faith, doubt, and determination were all rolled up into a Great Ball of Unknowing. And then it happened. There, in front of Tanaka Rōshi, but really neither in front of or behind anyone or anything, I suddenly broke through the kōan—or, rather, it broke through me. I felt as though a huge weight was suddenly lifted off my entire being. I was infused with a buoyant lightness, and everything shone in a vibrant new light. For once, at last, everything was no longer about me, and I was free.

A couple of hours later I walked out of the monastery into the spring breeze, floating in lightness, basking in the light—for the first time in my life fully appreciating the preciousness of everyone and everything, the absolute value of each as a unique event in the wonderful web of reality. Everything was bathed in the warm embrace of a limitless light, including this particular sentient being that provides the vast openness of the universe one of its myriad places of perception and interconnection.

Then a strange coincidence occurred. I usually rode my bicycle home from the monastery, but that day I had an errand to run in downtown in Kyoto, and so I took the subway. A few moments after getting in the subway car, Tanaka Rōshi suddenly appeared beside me. In the ten years I practiced under his direction, this was the only time I ever ran into him in the subway or, indeed, anywhere outside the monastery. With a gleam in his eye and grinning from ear to ear, he asked, "How do you feel?" With a huge smile of my own, I replied, "Wonderful!" Nothing more needed to be said. We shared a laugh. It was the purest, most deeply felt laugh of my life.

The intensity of the experience gradually faded over the next few days. Yet my life has never really been the same since. Even though my heart and mind still often get quite clouded, an awareness of the clear sky I suddenly woke up to on that day more or less remains. Since then I have understood what the fourteenth-century Japanese Rinzai Zen master Daitō Kokushi meant by his poem "Penetrating the clouds to the sky beyond, even on a rainy night I see the moon."[24]

Many years later I read that the modern Sōtō Zen master Sawaki Kōdō Rōshi used to say, "In our zazen we see things from our coffin." Okumura Shōhaku Rōshi tells us that what he meant by this was that "we are as if already dead. We have no opinions, no desires" and like a "dead person cannot disagree, argue, or complain to the people around the casket."[25] With the ego and its agendas out of the way, such "just sitting" (*shikantaza*), as Okumura Rōshi elaborates elsewhere, is "a practice in which we let go of the individual karmic self that is constantly seeking to satisfy its own desires. In zazen the true self, the self that is one with the entire universe, is manifest."[26] This, I think, is what the founder of Japanese Sōtō Zen, Dōgen, meant when he spoke of *zazen*, and of his enlightening experience during *zazen*, both as "dropping off the body-mind" (*shinjin datsuraku*) and as "the *samadhi* of self-receiving-and-employing" (*jijuyū zanmai*). This occurs when one no longer experiences oneself as physically and mentally separate from the rest of the world, but rather awakens to one's place, receives and performs one's role within the whole matrix of reality.[27] Although the Sōtō School does not use kōans to trigger breakthrough experiences of *kenshō*, the practice and experience of "just sitting," and of acting from that bottomless basis, were unmistakably and qualitatively deepened and clarified for me that spring day at Shōkokuji.

Although the kōan practice of Rinzai Zen is designed to optimize their enabling conditions, it is impossible to predict if and when enlightening breakthroughs will happen, or how profound and life-changing they will be. Perhaps a subtle breakthrough may occur spontaneously on a stroll in the woods or on a sidewalk, or a more dramatic one may be triggered by a terrific or tragic experience or by the ingestion of a mind-altering chemical substance. As Michael Pollan suggests in *How to Change Your Mind*,[28] the use of psychedelic substances may induce states of consciousness that perhaps resemble at least some aspects of experiences of *kenshō*—though usually mixed with a heavy dose of the distracting "devilish states" or *makyō* that we discussed in Chapter 22. Pollan reports that his psychedelic "journeys have shown me what the Buddhists try to tell us but I have never really understood: that there is much more to consciousness than the ego, as we would see if it would just shut up."[29] What Pollan is referring to as the "ego" is what some neuroscientists call "the default mode network," the part of the brain that filters and narrates experience so that it is egocentrically interpreted to be all about "me" as separate from, and as the center of, the rest of the world. Reportedly, brain imagery of experienced meditators and of persons tripping on psychedelic substances look in some ways alike. Specifically, both exhibit "a quieting of the default mode network." And "when activity in the default mode network falls off precipitously, the ego temporarily vanishes, and the usual boundaries we experience between self and world, subject and object, all melt away."[30] Pollan also reports on recent studies that suggest that the use of psychedelics, in combination with psychotherapy, may be surprisingly effective in treating addiction, depression, and the fear of death in terminal cancer patients.

I must say, however, that the breakthrough Zen experiences I have had were qualitatively different from any of the drug-induced experiences that I have either had myself or read reports about. Based on my own youthful experiments as well as on the reportage of writers like Aldous Huxley and Pollan, I agree that the use of psychedelic substances can jar one into seeing that "the mountain is not a mountain"—in other words, they can catapult the mind out of its habitual "box," its egocentric, ethnocentric, linguistically and culturally overdetermined way of conceptualizing and categorizing experience.[31] Nevertheless, the sense of being swept away on an out-of-control hallucinatory "trip" to outer space—or, as it were, into "inner space"—is decidedly foreign to the bare-feet-on-the-ground sense of utter clarity, freedom, and responseability that characterizes a genuine *kenshō* experience.[32] I do not doubt that the resurfacing of memories and lucid dream-like experiences that occur on a psychedelic trip may have great therapeutic value for psychoanalysis, and arguably they would be too hastily dismissed or at least sidelined with the perhaps overgeneralizing term *makyō* in the context of Zen training. Yet chemically induced mystical states of consciousness should not distract Zen practitioners from the trans-mystical path that leads to an awakening of the Everyday Even Mind. Whether chemically or otherwise induced, such out-of-the-blue mystical experiences can easily leave one disoriented, without clear connection to the here and now of everyday life, and without the clear sense of freedom and response-ability to say—when and where appropriate—that "the mountain is after all a mountain" (see Chapter 13).

In any case, without the discipline of a practice, the effect of such experiences would be difficult to integrate into the rest of one's life—not to mention, in the case of using drugs, the serious side effects that cloud rather than clear the mind. The kōan curriculum practiced in Rinzai Zen is a method not only of priming one for the occurrence of breakthrough experiences, but also of allowing one to stay in touch with them, to deepen one's appreciation and understanding of them, and to integrate them into one's daily life.

Especially in the case of initial barrier kōans, the priming of the pump is a matter of generating and cultivating the Great Doubt (see Chapter 22). And so, it is important to get stuck—to get really stuck—on at least some of them, like I was for many months on the "sliced right in two" kōan.

In retrospect, I realize that I was stuck on my own fear of death—a deep-seated fear that I did not even really know I had. To be sure, once in graduate school I literally woke up in a cold sweat when I viscerally realized what the German philosopher Martin Heidegger is talking about when he says that human existence is, at its usually unconscious existential core, being-toward-death.[33] Or there was that time when I was walking right by a burning corpse on the bank of the Ganges River and a stream of urine suddenly shot out of it—another shocking experience of mortality seared into my memory. In retrospect, at those times I needed a Zen teacher like Hakuin to assign me a "death kōan" to work on.[34]

When one is stuck on a kōan, it seems utterly impossible to pass. In hindsight, however, kōans always seem so simple and straightforward. It is we who make them difficult. We project our ideas on them or we flee from really confronting them because we sense that they are asking us to confront our own deepest anxieties.

Zen does not pander to our fears, to our cravings, or even to our hopes and dreams. And so, the kōans on which practitioners get stuck the longest are usually the ones that are the most important for them to deal with. Only by getting really stuck on a kōan is one plunged into the Great Doubt—and, as Hakuin says, "At the bottom of great doubt lies great awakening. If you doubt fully you will awaken fully."[35]

Yet, rarely if ever does someone fully awaken in just one breakthrough experience. Hakuin himself spoke of having numerous kenshō experiences, some more penetrating and life-changing than others. Hence, in the Rinzai kōan curriculum designed by Hakuin, one circles back again and again to the same core issues. Among them, of course, is the great matter of mortality.

Many years after experiencing a breakthrough with the "sliced right in two" kōan, I was directly confronted yet again with a death kōan. This time it was Case 29 in the Blue Cliff Record, which reads:

A monk asked Dasui, "When the flames of the great fire at the end of the cosmic eon destroy all things, will 'it' [that is, the Buddha-nature, my true self] also be destroyed or not?" Dasui replied, "It will be destroyed." The monk asked, "If so, does that mean that 'it' will perish along with everything else?" Dasui replied, "Yes, it will perish with everything else."[36]

Like me, the monk was stuck on his fear of death. He was apparently wishing that the teachings of the Buddha-nature and the true self were promises of personal immortality. Perhaps he was slipping into the Senika heresy, hoping that the ineffable "it" that Zen masters apophatically indicate refers to an eternal psychic substance that survives the destruction of everything physical. His hope betrayed a stubborn remainder of ego-attachment, and so Dasui gave him a lesson in tough love.

Zen Masters Tell Us to Go to Hell

"Abandon all hope, ye who enter here." According to Dante, these lines are written over the gates of Hell.[37] Zen masters, by contrast, have high hopes for going to Hell. For them, out of bottomless compassion, we should want to go to Hell. When asked by a college student in America if he thought people go to Heaven after they die, the modern Rinzai Zen master Fukushima Keidō replied: "Only the ego wants to go to Heaven!"[38]

When Zen masters do talk about life after death, they generally talk in parables about being reborn wherever they can be of the most service. The ninth-century Chinese Zen master Zhaozhou said that when he dies, he "will go straight down to Hell." An astonished monk asked, "How can it be that such a holy man of great merit will go to Hell?" Zhaozhou responded, "If I don't go to Hell, how could I save someone like you?"[39]

In some cases, Zen masters speak instead of being reborn as a beast of burden. When Zhaozhou's teacher, Nanquan, was asked by a disciple where he would go after he died, he responded: "I am going to the foot of the hill to be reborn as an ox," apparently so that he could work in the fields in service of the poor farmers.[40] A similar story is told of Zhaozhou's contemporary Guishan Lingyou, who told his disciples that he would be reborn as an ox, and that if they wanted to meet him they should look for an ox who is toiling and sweating under a heavy load.[41]

As a young child Hakuin heard a Buddhist priest read letters in which Nichiren Shōnin describes "in graphic detail the torments of the Eight Scorching Hells." Mortally terrified, he eventually decided to leave home and become a monk in order to escape falling into such hellfires.[42] Later, when his teacher Shōju Rōjin asked Hakuin why he had become a monk, Hakuin replied it was because he was afraid of falling into Hell. Shōju scornfully retorted, "You're a self-centered rascal, aren't you!" Many years later, when Hakuin asked his student Tōrei the same question, Tōrei answered, "To work for the salvation of my fellow beings." Hakuin laughed and said that Tōrei's reason was much better than his own.[43]

Hakuin's autobiography, *Wild Ivy*, begins with the lines:

> Anyone who wants to achieve the Way of enlightenment must drive forward the wheel of the Four Great Vows. But even when you gain entry through the Gate of Nonduality, if you lack the Mind of Enlightenment, you will still sink back into the paths of evil.[44]

The Four Great Vows, as we saw in Chapter 10, begin with the great compassionate vow to liberate all sentient beings from suffering. As discussed in Chapters 2, 8, 9, and 11, the more enlightened one becomes to the delusory nature of the dichotomous border walls we build between self and other, the more this compassionate vow is understood to be nondualistic rather than altruistic. Nevertheless, a mature understanding of nonduality sees the relation between self and other as a matter of "neither one nor two," rather than as a monistic oneness without distinctions.

When he first came to Shōju Rōjin in order to have confirmed what he mistakenly thought was his ultimate attainment of enlightenment, Hakuin was actually stuck in the inert homogeneity of a half-baked understanding of the Gate of Nonduality. "You're doing Zen down in a hole!" Shōju barked at him.[45] Stuck in a "demonic cave of darkness," Hakuin did not yet have the Mind of Enlightenment that he speaks of in the opening lines to his autobiography. This is the *bodhicitta*, the wholehearted aspiration to attain enlightenment not just for oneself but for the sake of liberating all sentient beings.

The foregoing stories stress this central message of Mahayana Buddhism: the great compassionate vow to dedicate one's life to liberating all sentient beings from suffering. Mahayana Buddhism is not simply about overcoming craving and ignorance; it is, ultimately, about awakening the compassionate heart that, necessarily, accompanies the wise mind that sees into the interconnectedness of all beings.

A monk once remarked to Zhaozhou that Shakyamuni Buddha must have been entirely free from all passionate desires. Zhaozhou responded, "No, he had the greatest passionate desire in this whole world." "Why do you say that?" asked the astonished monk. Zhaozhou replied, "Shakyamuni had the great passionate desire to save all sentient beings, didn't he?"[46]

Being at Home on the Way: Practice is Enlightenment

Many religions tend to have an otherworldly orientation; they tend to value the afterlife in heaven even more than this life on earth. Not so with Zen Buddhism. In fact, all schools of Mahayana Buddhism call for a return to this world. Even those Pure Land Buddhists who focus their attention on "going forth" (Jp. ōsō) to be reborn after death in the Pure Land understand the Pure Land to be a place where one can quickly and easily become a Buddha. And one becomes a Buddha not merely for one's own sake, but so that one can "return" (gensō) to work on behalf of liberating all sentient beings from suffering.

The Pali Canon of the Buddha's teachings, which is the textual basis for the so-called Hinayana school of Theravada Buddhism, makes a distinction between two kinds of Nirvana: "Nirvana with remainder"—namely, with a remainder of karmic conditioning and so a body-mind made up of the Five Aggregates (bodily forms, sensations, perceptions, dispositions/volitions, and consciousness); and "Nirvana without remainder" of this karmically conditioned life-stream or process-self living in this world. "Nirvana without remainder" is also called Final Nirvana (Parinirvana) and occurs at the time of what appears to be death.[47] The Theravada monk and scholar Walpola Rahula is speaking of "Nirvana with remainder" when he says, "Nirvana can be realized in this very life; it is not necessary to wait till you die to 'attain' it."[48] However, "Nirvana without remainder," Final Nirvana, is described in the Pali Canon mostly via negativa, that is to say, by way of saying what it is not like (namely, not like any of our experiences with the bodily senses or the mind in this world of space and time). It is said that Final Nirvana is ultimately attained with the "dissolution of the body"—indeed, the dissolution of all the Five Aggregates along with the four elements and all sense-objects. This does seem to suggest that an otherworldly transcendence is the ultimate goal.[49]

The Mahayana tradition is especially critical of the Hinayana idea that, as Rahula puts it, "the Buddha or an Arahant [Sk. Arhat] has no re-existence after his death."[50] This view is criticized as entailing a kind of escapism and even, ironically, a kind of spiritual selfishness. Eschewing escapist desires for and visions of Nirvana, Mahayana Buddhism explicitly breaks down the very duality between Samsara and Nirvana.[51] It does this first of all with the idea and ideal of "non-abiding Nirvana," which means that enlightened beings abide in Nirvana no more than they do in Samsara. To borrow a Christian phrase, they remain "in the world but not of the world," working tirelessly on behalf of enlightening all sentient beings.

In fact, Mahayana sutras and philosophical treatises go even further in deconstructing any binary distinction between Nirvana and Samsara. The Lankavatara Sutra states that "the difference between Samsara and

Nirvana . . . does not exist," and that Nirvana is a transformation of the most fundamental level of consciousness rather than a transcendence of the world.[52] In a different Buddhist context, Nagarjuna famously proclaims: "There is no distinction whatsoever between Nirvana and Samsara. . . . What is the limit of Nirvana, that is the limit of Samsara."[53] Philosopher Jay Garfield explains Nagarjuna's point as follows:

> Nirvana is not someplace else. It is a way of being here. . . . Nirvana is only Samsara experienced as a buddha experiences it. It is the person who enters Nirvana, but as a state of being, not as a place to be.[54]

Okumura Rōshi agrees with such a this-worldly understanding of Nirvana when he writes:

> The Buddha taught that there are two different ways of living. If we are blind to the reality of egolessness and impermanence, our life becomes suffering. If we waken to this reality and live accordingly, our life becomes nirvana.[55]

This is not giving a novel or unorthodox teaching. The scholar Rupert Gethin finds what he calls "the principle of *the equivalence of cosmology and psychology*" in the earliest strata of the history of Buddhist thought.[56] And Okumura Rōshi is in effect reiterating the teaching of the founder of the Japanese Sōtō School, Dōgen, who wrote:

> Just understand that birth-and-death in Samsara itself is Nirvana, and you will neither hate the one as being birth-and-death in Samsara, nor cherish the other as being Nirvana. Only then can you be free of birth-and-death in Samsara.[57]

The founder of the Linji (Jp. Rinzai) School, the ninth-century Chinese Zen master Linji admonishes his monks for their otherworldly orientation: they "all have a mind to seek buddha, to seek dharma, to seek emancipation, to seek escape from [Samsara]. Foolish fellows! When you've left [Samsara] where would you go?"[58] If Nirvana is to be found anywhere, it must be found in the here and now.

Yamada Mumon Rōshi teaches that Nirvana is a wide-open mind that is able to accept all that is natural and smile at all times, even when the going gets tough and when one realizes that the tough work to be done in this world never ceases.[59] He says, "To be right in the very middle of ceaselessly churning daily life, just this is the pure land of serenity and nirvana."[60] True Nirvana is found where one is wholeheartedly engaged in everyday life, where one no longer has the need to draw any rigid dichotomies, even between Nirvana and Samsara. As the *Heart Sutra* tells us, it is precisely because Bodhisattvas are no longer bound to the distinction between attaining Nirvana and remaining stuck in Samsara that they attain true Nirvana—or, according to a slightly different interpretation, they see through the very idea of Nirvana as the final delusion, insofar as we inevitably imagine Nirvana to be an escape from Samsara.[61]

According to Zen, the Buddha Way does not take us away from life in this world. Our true home is not to be found at the end of the journey. Linji teaches that we need to learn how to be "a person who is endlessly on the road, yet has never left home."[62] This, we could say, is the original ninth-century Chinese version of today's bumper-sticker slogan, "The journey itself is the destination."

In his voluminous lectures on Dōgen late in life, the modern Japanese philosopher and lay Rinzai Zen master Nishitani Keiji remarks that "there is not the slightest difference between the fundamental spirit of Linji's saying [about being at home on the road] and that of Dōgen's teaching of 'the oneness of practice and enlightenment.'"[63] This, indeed, was Dōgen's central teaching.[64] The point of practice is not to reach the destination of enlightenment later in life, much less in the afterlife. Practice is not a step on the way to enlightenment; practice itself is enlightenment. Even a moment of truly just sitting in meditation, Dōgen says, is a moment of enlightening self and others.[65] Every moment of letting the heart-mind be seated, of finding the peaceful still point in the midst of the most efficacious, creative, and compassionate action, is a moment of Nirvana.

"Early Buddhist translators used the Chinese term [*dao*, meaning 'way'] to denote both the path of Buddhist practice (Sk. *mārga*) and the enlightened wisdom that results from it (Sk. *bodhi*)."[66] This translation not only evinces the Daoist influence on Chinese Buddhism; it also, more specifically, sets the course for the specifically Zen understanding of "sudden enlightenment" as a matter of waking up to the Way on which we are walking.

The Chinese character for Zen "practice" (Ch. *xing*; Jp. *gyō* 行) literally means "to go." While this word is used in other contexts in the sense of walking on a path that leads to a goal, at which point one would cease walking, this is not how practice is understood in Zen. Zen practice is a matter of living each moment to the fullest, to realize the goal of life in each moment of life—and the goal of life, after all, is not to cease living. The goal of life is rather to realize that being alive entails being on the go, ceaselessly walking the Way. The English word "practice" is fittingly ambiguous. For example, in one sense one practices medical procedures in order to become a doctor. Yet, once one has become a doctor, one does not cease to "practice medicine," since that activity is precisely what it means to be a doctor. Analogously, a scholar does not stop studying, an athlete does not stop training, and a Zen Buddhist does not stop practicing Zen Buddhism.

Dōgen taught:

> Students, even if you gain enlightenment, do not stop practicing, thinking that you have attained the ultimate. The Buddha Way is endless. Once enlightened you must practice all the more.[67]

Even Shakyamuni and Amida Buddha, it is said, are still engaged in this practice of enlightenment, this practice of enlightening self and others. They are at Home on the Way, at peace in the hustle and bustle of the marketplace or wherever they are needed to work on behalf of liberating and bringing peace to all sentient beings. Paradoxically, the end of practice is to realize that there is no end of practice. Real Zen is this endless realization.

24
Reviewing the Path of Zen
The Ten Oxherding Pictures

Figure 24.1 The Ten Oxherding Pictures of Zen

Zen Pathways. Bret W. Davis, Oxford University Press. © Oxford University Press 2022.
DOI: 10.1093/oso/9780197573686.003.0024

In order to reflect on the path of Zen as a whole, in this concluding chapter I will comment on a classic and beloved text of the tradition: *The Ten Oxherding Pictures*.[1] The text consists of a set of ten pictures together with a title, a preface, and a poem appended to each one. The pictures are shown here in the order of left to right, with rows proceeding from top to bottom. Here are the titles and a brief description of each picture:

1. *Searching for the Ox*: A young man is walking in search of the ox, unsure of where to look.
2. *Seeing Its Traces*: The man has now found and is following the footprints of the ox.
3. *Seeing the Ox*: The man sees the ox, or at least part of it.
4. *Catching the Ox*: The man has tethered the ox and is struggling to control it.
5. *Taming the Ox*: The ox has become docile and is being gently led by the man.
6. *Returning Home Riding the Ox*: The man is riding atop the ox, leisurely playing a flute.
7. *Ox Forgotten, Person Abides*: The ox has disappeared and the man sits outside a mountain hut.
8. *Person and Ox Both Forgotten*: An empty circle.
9. *Returning to the Root, Back to the Source*: A tree in bloom by a stream.
10. *Entering the Town with Outstretched Hands*: A joyful old sage, with a large belly and a large sack slung over his shoulder, reaches out offering something in a gourd to a younger man. (In some renditions, only the older sage appears.)

The original pictures and poems were composed by the twelfth-century Chinese Zen master Kuoan Shiyuan. The general introduction and the prefaces to each picture were written by Kuoan's successor, Ziyuan. Kuoan and Ziyuan belonged to the Linji School, which became the Rinzai School in Japan.

Kuoan's original pictures no longer exist, but over the centuries many artists have recreated them. The most famous rendition is that of the fifteenth-century Japanese artist Tenshō Shūbun, who established the Japanese tradition of ink wash painting. Shūbun was a monk at Shōkokuji, the monastery where I practice in Kyoto. His rendition was the favorite of my teacher, Ueda Shizuteru, who is renowned for his philosophical interpretations of *The Ten Oxherding Pictures*.[2]

Curiously, Kuoan's *Ten Oxherding Pictures* did not become popular in China. Instead, another, slightly earlier version of oxherding pictures by Puming, who was probably a Caodong (Jp. Sōtō) Zen master, became the most popular version in China and also in Korea.[3] Later I'll discuss some of the major differences between these two versions. In fact, a number of different versions of oxherding pictures were created by Chinese Zen masters starting in the eleventh century.[4]

It seems that at this point in the development of the Zen tradition, there was felt a need to reflect on the entire path of Zen practice. Of course, discussions and depictions of stages of the path (Sk. *marga*) had already long been a part of the Buddhist tradition in India and elsewhere in Asia. In Tibet, there is a series of pictures that uses an elephant rather than an ox.[5] It starts with a monk chasing after an elephant that is being led by a monkey, and later a rabbit appears on its back. The elephant represents the mind, the monkey represents restlessness, and the rabbit represents lethargy. Eventually, the elephant is tamed and the monkey and rabbit disappear. As happens with the ox in Puming's version of the oxherding pictures, the color of the elephant gradually changes from black to white, representing a progressive purification of the mind. This is also the case in the version of oxherding pictures by Qingjiu, a version that Ziyuan ambivalently critiques in his introduction to Kuoan's version.[6]

In Zen, the mind is thought to be *originally* pure, and the point of practice is to *suddenly awaken* to this original purity underneath the coverings of deluding afflictions, rather than to *gradually purify* the mind of them. Doctrinally speaking, Zen has distinguished itself from other Buddhist schools that teach a path of gradual enlightenment by insisting on this sudden nature of enlightenment. Actually, in the eighth and ninth centuries there was heated debate within Zen between the Northern School's doctrine of gradual enlightenment and the Southern School's doctrine of sudden enlightenment.[7] In the end, the Southern School won out and the Northern School died out. Some eminent Zen masters—most notably the ninth-century Chinese Huayan and Zen master Zongmi and the twelfth-century founder of Korean Zen, Chinul—developed a synthetic doctrine of "sudden enlightenment followed by gradual cultivation."[8] Yet, ever since sudden enlightenment became the orthodox teaching of Zen, many Zen masters have been somewhat hesitant to speak of stages on the path of Zen.

However, the best Zen masters past and present—including those who composed the various versions of the oxherding pictures—have realized that it is important not to fall into the trap of positing an overly simplistic dichotomy between a gradual path and sudden enlightening experiences. On the one hand, a momentary flash of insight can become nothing more than a fading memory if it is not deepened and developed through post-enlightenment practice. And, on the other hand, a gradual path can, after all, lead to sudden—often unexpected and unforeseeable—breakthroughs.

In the case of Kuoan's pictures, the biggest breakthrough comes in picture 8, when everything suddenly disappears, leaving only an empty circle. Before that, in picture 7, the ox suddenly disappears. Since the ox did not come on the scene until picture 3, which depicts the first breakthrough moment, this means that the ox is actually pictured in only four of Kuoan's *Ten Oxherding Pictures*. This contrasts with Puming's ten pictures, in which the ox appears in all but the last, the empty circle. Also, whereas in Puming's version the color of the ox gradually changes from black to white, and whereas in yet another version by a master named Fuyin the ox turns—or, as he says, "returns"—from white to black,[9] the ox is always black in Kuoan's version.

What Does the Ox Represent?

"Hold on," you might be thinking. "Why are we talking about an ox and oxherding in the first place? I thought this book was about Zen, not tending livestock!" Actually, you are more likely thinking: "I know that the ox must be a metaphor for something, but for what?"

The standard answer is that the ox represents our true self, our Buddha-nature. We'll have to complicate this answer later on, but we can begin with the understanding that the quest the oxherder embarks on in picture 1 is a search for the true self; it is a journey of self-realization. The oxherder is *the seeking self*, while the ox is *the self that is sought*. In other words, the *deluded self* wants to awaken to its *true self*, and so sets out in search of it.

The oxherder finds footprints of the ox in picture 2, and then first catches a glimpse of it in picture 3. In the next three pictures, he catches the ox, tames it, and rides it home. We'll discuss the really strange stuff that happens after that later. To begin with, let's think about why the true self is pictured as an ox. Perhaps, as some commentators have suggested, the fact that cows are sacred animals in Hindu India is relevant. Yet, more directly relevant is surely the fact that taming an unruly ox is used as a simile for the practice of meditation in a number of early Buddhist sutras as well as in earlier Zen texts.[10]

Ueda points out that the calmness and confidently plodding nature of the ox makes it a good metaphor for the meditative mind. Moreover, an ox's great strength can become dangerous if one upsets and loses control of it, just as the untamed mind is unwieldy and destructive.[11] We should also bear in mind the vital role that oxen played in the agricultural life of China at the time. A farmer's ox was his prized possession. To lose one's ox, after all, would be tantamount to losing one's livelihood. And so, *The Ten Oxherding Pictures* begins with the oxherder realizing that he has lost his most important belonging; he has lost sight of the very source that sustains his life.

Pictures 1 and 2: Starting to Search, Finding Traces

As we discussed in Chapter 2, the spiritual path in general, and the path of Zen in particular, begins with waking up to the problem of self-alienation, to the fact that we do not truly know ourselves. In his preface to the first picture, Ziyuan tells us that we have turned our backs on our own true self; we have covered over our own originally enlightened mind. Awakening to the fact of our delusion is the crucial first step, and it is with that step that *The Ten Oxherding Pictures* begins. In the first picture, the oxherder realizes that he has lost the ox; the deluded self realizes that he is deluded, realizes that he has alienated himself from his own true self. He is still lost, but since now he knows that he is lost, he has become a seeker.

In a later Japanese version of oxherding pictures, the seventeenth-century Sōtō monk Geppa added two more pictures at the beginning, entitling them "Arousing Aspiration" and "Leaving Home."[12] These preliminary pictures dramatize and stress the importance of first waking up to the problem of self-alienation and setting out in search of the true self.

Although in the first of Kuoan's pictures the oxherder has already set out in search of the ox, he does not yet know where to search. He does not know which path to take, or even in which direction to proceed. This is why, in picture 1, the oxherder's body is facing one direction, yet he is looking over his shoulder in the other direction. When we set out on the spiritual journey, we might be highly motivated to find our true self, but we are probably not sure how to go about searching for it, or even exactly what it is that we are searching for.

And so, we read a lot of books and listen to a lot of teachers. Finally, we come across some texts and teachings that ring true. Reading these texts and listening to these teachings, we sense that they are speaking to something inside us; they begin to stir awake a slumbering self-awareness deep within. We are, in fact, always able to *appreciate* more than we are yet able to really *understand*. Just as we can appreciate good food, art, and music without being much of a chef, artist, or musician ourselves, we can appreciate good spiritual teachings without being a spiritual teacher ourselves. When reading or listening to authentic spiritual teachings, we may have the distinct feeling that they are illuminating a path that we should follow in order to better understand ourselves. Such texts and teachings are represented by the *footprints* of the ox, which in picture 2 the oxherder has now found and is eagerly following. These texts and teachings are not the ox itself, but they are evidence that the ox exists, they tell us something about its nature, and they lead us in the right direction to find it ourselves.

In Ziyuan's preface to picture 2, we read: "Relying on the sutras, you understand the principles; by studying the teachings, you come to know the traces left behind." Traces of what? Traces left behind by those who have awakened to the true self. These traces are tracks that you can follow, tracks that tell you which way to go on the path toward self-awakening. Ziyuan tells us quite specifically what these traces, the texts, teach: "It is now clear that the many vessels are composed of a single metal, and that the body of the ten thousand things is your self." In other words, through reading texts and listening to teachings, you come to understand that, despite all the differences among the myriad things we experience, there is a pervading oneness to reality, and that pervading oneness is your true self.

In Chapter 8, we saw how the ancient Hindu sage Uddalaka made a similar point using the simile of many pots made of the same clay, or different nuggets made of the same gold, or different tools made out of the same iron.[13] Later, in China, the Huayan Buddhist philosopher Fazang uses the analogy of a statue of a golden lion. The shapes that make up the figure of the lion are like the myriad forms of reality, whereas the pervasive gold is like the formless emptiness they all share in common.[14] A modern physicist might say that the pervasive "clay" or "gold" of reality is the quantum field of fluctuations of interchangeable mass and energy. In any case, as Ziyuan makes clear, it is crucial that one realizes that we are not just talking about a unifying field of *external* or *objective* reality. In other words, it is crucial to realize that "the body of the ten thousand things is your self." Here Ziyuan is paraphrasing a famous saying of the seminal Chinese Buddhist philosopher Sengzhao: "Heaven and Earth and I share the same root. The myriad things and I are of the same body."[15]

This is what the oxherder has come to understand at the stage of picture 2. And yet, this remains for him an abstract intellectual understanding. Recall the three levels of wisdom we discussed in Chapter 3: received wisdom, intellectual wisdom, and experiential wisdom. Although it may make sense to you that all things are made up of the same one reality—that there is a unity to the universe and that you too are part and parcel of this unity—this may still be an intellectual idea in your head, not a holistic and thus transformational awakening experience.

In his preface to picture 2, Ziyuan says that at this stage the oxherder is still not able to "distinguish right from wrong" or to "differentiate true and false." This suggests that an intellectual understanding of the unity of the universe all too easily falls into a one-sided grasp of oneness, an abstract conception of a One reality that is opposed to the Many things of the world, a uniform sameness that obliterates rather than makes room for differences—including differences that call on us, in various concrete contexts, to distinguish right from wrong and true from false. In Chapter 8, we saw Nanquan point to a flower in order to wake a scholar up from his dream-like infatuation with an abstract idea of oneness. That scholar was perhaps like the young man in picture 2.

The ultimate experiential awakening to a true understanding of oneness is depicted in picture 8, the empty circle, together with pictures 9 and 10. The oneness of the circle is an openness that makes way for, makes room for, the myriad things and people of the world, which indeed reappear within the open circle in the last two pictures.

Picture 3: Glimpsing the True Self

We have gotten way ahead of ourselves. As we will see, ultimate awakening is depicted in the trilogy of the last three pictures. Yet initial awakening—one's first experience of *kenshō* or seeing into the true nature of the self—takes place in picture 3, which shows the young man catching a glimpse of the ox. When the oxherder first lays eyes on his lost ox, he is overjoyed. This experience can be quite dramatic. As the text suggests, it often occurs in an extraordinary experience of the most ordinary of things, like hearing a pebble strike a stalk of bamboo, or seeing a peach blossom, to mention two famous examples. In any case, such experiences are not a matter of seeing something outside the self; they are a matter of seeing the self in everything and everything in the self. The most famous example is Shakyamuni's breakthrough upon seeing the morning star. At that enlightening moment, according to Yamada Mumon Rōshi, Shakyamuni must have thought, "I am shining!"[16]

In his preface to picture 3, Ziyuan uses the metaphor we discussed in Chapter 8: it is like tasting salt dissolved in water. The salt cannot be seen from the outside, but if we dive in and open our mouths, we taste it clearly and we taste it everywhere. If we open our hearts and minds to everything around us, we cease to experience ourselves as separate from the rest of reality and empathetically identify with everything.

Yet, at this stage we have merely glimpsed the true self. We have not yet erased the dualistically deluded ego and overcome self-alienation, which means that, despite the dramatic nature of this unusual experience—indeed, because it remains an unusual experience—we easily slip back into viewing ourselves as separate from everything else. The journey home has just begun. Having found the ox, the oxherder must now catch and tame it.

Pictures 4–6: Catching and Taming the Ox-Mind

The oxherder catches the ox in picture 4, but now there is a struggle taking place. In Kuoan's appended verse we read: "With your last bit of spiritual strength you take hold of the ox; yet its mind is headstrong, its body powerful, and it won't quickly or easily be broken." Ziyuan's preface to this picture states: "More stubborn than ever and still wild, if you wish to tame it you must use your whip."

At this point we have to repeat the question: what does the ox represent? We started by saying that it represents our true self, our Buddha-nature. Indeed, this is what almost all traditional and modern commentaries say. And yet, we have just seen the text of picture 4 refer to the ox as "more stubborn than ever and still wild," such that it needs to be "broken" and "tamed." Does it make sense to say such things about the true self or Buddha-nature?

Ueda says no. He says that, although the text attributes stubbornness and wildness to the ox, really these are characteristics of the oxherder at this stage. In fact, Ueda says, if you look closely at Shūbun's rendition of picture 4, it is unclear who is trying to flee from whom, and who is pulling whom. Is it perhaps the ox that is pulling the still resistant oxherder onto the homeward-bound path of awakening?[17]

If we stick with the standard interpretation of the ox as representing the true self, this does seem to be the best way to view what is going on here. However, there is another compelling interpretation given by the modern Chinese Zen master Sheng-yen. He suggests that "the ox represents the mind and its activities." As a matter of fact, the ox is referred to in many commentaries as the "ox-mind," and it is not a stretch to understand this to mean the mind in all its *unenlightened* as well as *enlightened* activities.

If we understand the ox to represent the mind in *all* its activities, writes Sheng-yen, "on the one hand, the ox may be seen as the great white ox of enlightened Buddha-nature. Seeking, discovering, taming, and riding the ox home would then signify the process of awakening to and actualizing one's true nature to the point where it is fully integrated with all aspects of life." "On the other hand," he goes on to say, "the ox is characterized as wild and unruly, and must be forcibly restrained from wandering off into the weeds of desire and deluded thinking. This image seems more suggestive of the mind of vexation than the mind of enlightenment."[18] We need not choose between these views of the ox, says Sheng-yen, since it is the same mind that can be either deluded about or enlightened to its own true nature.

This interpretation has the merit of retrieving an instructive aspect of Puming's and other versions of oxherding pictures that show the color of the ox changing from black to white over the course of the training. It is the same ox, the same mind, but its underlying purity is uncovered as the deluding afflictions are removed. A later version of the oxherding pictures portrays the ox as white from start to finish.[19] This was evidently a critique of the apparent *gradualness* of versions such as Puming's and a reminder that the Buddha-nature is pure from the beginning; one just needs to *suddenly* wake up to its purity. Fair enough, but a merit of the oxherding pictures, in all their versions, is arguably that they reconcile the sudden and gradual approaches to enlightenment. As Ōtsu Rekidō Rōshi, a modern Rinzai Zen master and former abbot of Shōkokuji monastery, puts it: "The breakthrough must indeed be abrupt and sudden. But the practice after this breakthrough, in order to preserve that which has been gained, must be gradual."[20]

To be sure, there are dramatic breakthroughs, experiences of *kenshō*, which fundamentally change one's life and one's understanding of one's self. In Kuoan's version, as we have noted, such *kenshō* experiences occur first in picture 3, next in picture 7, and ultimately in picture 8, which opens the door to and includes, as we will see, pictures 9 and 10. And yet, it is also undeniable that there is a *path* to be practiced and stages to be gone through. After all, one should not just wait, but should do all that one can to prepare for enlightening breakthroughs to happen. When they do happen, they will certainly surprise you. They may appear like bolts of lightning that suddenly come out of nowhere, rather than like raindrops patiently collected in a pail. Some paintings of picture 3 portray this well when they have the ox suddenly appear to one side of or even behind the oxherder on his path of practice. Shakyamuni Buddha was always clear that Nirvana is "unproduced," and so it is not the product or result of the path. The path leads one to discover Nirvana—and to realize that it was always already there.[21]

I like to compare the relation between methodical practice and sudden breakthroughs to walking out onto the thin ice of a frozen lake and then suddenly falling through the ice. Aiming for the center of the frozen lake, we methodically take one step after another. Aiming for enlightenment, we regularly engage in meditation and other forms of practice. Yet, when the moment comes and the ice breaks, we suddenly realize that the water of the Buddha-nature was always right underfoot. Although the ice may be the thinnest at the center of the lake, the real goal is not to reach the center, but rather to break through the ice and plunge into the water. This can potentially happen anywhere at any time. However, a methodical practice of walking toward the center of the lake is the best way to cultivate the conditions for a sudden breakthrough to occur.

And so, we need to diligently practice; we need to patiently train the mind, tend the ox. Four centuries before the various versions of oxherding pictures were composed, the eighth-century Chinese Zen master Mazu is said to have asked a monk tending the fires in the kitchen what he was doing. The monk replied, "Tending the ox." "How does one do that?" asked Mazu. "When he strays into the grass, I pull his nose back onto the path," the monk answered. "You really do know how to tend the ox!" Mazu replied.[22] This precursor dialogue would seem to support versions of the oxherding pictures that portray a gradual whitening of the ox. However, as we saw in Chapter 11, Mazu is also known for being instructed by his teacher, Nanyue, that one can no more become a Buddha by methodically sitting in meditation than one can make a mirror by polishing a tile.

Kuoan's version of the oxherding pictures has the great merit of clearly depicting both the gradual and sudden aspects of training and awakening. Accordingly, the ambiguity of the symbolism of the ox in Kuoan's pictures may well have been intentional. This ambiguity is especially at play in the middle stages of the path—the stages depicted in pictures 4, 5, and 6—where it appears that the practitioner is both taming and being tamed by the ox. In picture 4, we witness an intensely ambivalent struggle. In picture 5, the oxherder is leading the now docile ox. Yet, in picture 6, he is leisurely riding on the back of the ox, playing a tune and letting the ox take him wherever he wishes, for wherever that is will be home. Effort is giving way to effortlessness as practice becomes a way of life.

In the many years it generally takes a Zen practitioner to go from stage 4 to stage 6, the great effort of practicing-to-become-enlightened transforms into the effortlessly efficacious practice-of-enlightenment. This enlightened effortlessness is wonderfully depicted in the popularly painted picture 6. Needless to say, this is not a matter of lazily zoning out, but rather a matter of living fully engaged in the Zone of Zen.

Picture 7: Forget About the Ox, Remember Your Self

A major—though still not complete—breakthrough happens in picture 7, which is entitled "Ox Forgotten, Person Abides." In this picture, the ox has disappeared, and the oxherder sits alone outside a mountain hut, at peace with himself and the world. Ziyuan's preface to this picture begins with these words: "The Truth is not two; the ox was just posited as a provisional topic." The Truth, the Dharma, is the ultimate truth about reality that Buddhist teachings are meant to express. For Zen, this is the true self, the self that understands itself to exist as a part of—rather than to subsist apart from—the worldwide web of reality.

The root delusion—the cause of our cravings and attachments and the suffering they perpetuate—is our karmic habit of experiencing ourselves as separate from others and the rest of the world. To awaken to the true self is thus to "return to the root and source" of reality, as the title of picture 9 announces. At that stage, we have really gotten over ourselves; we have gotten our egos totally out of the way so that the myriad things of the world can shine forth in all their splendor.

But at the stage of picture 7, we have not yet gotten that far. At this stage, we have forgotten the ox, but not yet the self. Nevertheless, this picture represents an important breakthrough: the realization that the ox was, after all, just a finger pointing at the moon. Once we know what it was pointing at, we can put the finger down, and indeed we should put the finger down so that it does not block our view of the moon. In Shūbun's depiction of picture 7, a man on a mountaintop is directly beholding the moon, a traditional symbol of enlightenment.

Ziyuan uses another traditional metaphor to make the point: it is like the fisherman realizing that what he is really after is the fish, not the fancy new fishing net he recently acquired. We often get so wrapped up in our collection of spiritual paraphernalia that we forget the spiritual practice it is meant to facilitate. Like a camper more interested in browsing the latest camping gear inside a store than in actually going out into the great outdoors, we spend a lot of time and money shopping online for imported incense and exquisite images. Such paraphernalia can, of course, inspire and facilitate a lot of real practice—but only if we do not mistake the net for the fish.

In picture 7, the oxherder has a crucial realization—namely, the insight that in order to find oneself, one has to stop looking outside the self, as if the self were one object alongside others. One must, as the thirteenth-century Japanese Zen master Dōgen says, "learn to take the backward step that turns the light [of the mind around] and shines it inward," illuminating, as it were, the illuminating mind itself.[23]

The ninth-century Chinese Zen master Linji admonishes his students for objectifying the mind and looking for it outside themselves: "Turn your own light inward upon yourselves! A man of old said: 'Yajñadatta [thought he had] lost his head, but when his seeking mind came to rest, he was at ease.'"[24] Linji is referring here to a story that appears in the *Shurangama Sutra*, which tells of a man who fell in love with the image of his face in a mirror, but then became distraught when he found that, without the mirror, he could see the rest of his body but not his head; and so he went madly about seeking his "lost head."[25]

The lesson is that we paradoxically find ourselves only when we realize that the mind that seeks is not some*thing* that can be found. That is like using a torch to look for fire, or like using a flashlight to look for a flashlight. I've never done those silly things, but I have looked all over for my glasses before realizing that I was wearing them. The eighth-century Chinese Zen master Baizhang "compared the search for enlightenment to searching for an ox while riding on its back."[26] And the thirteenth-century Chinese Zen master Wuxue Zuyuan exclaims: "It's you who are the Buddha, but you just won't see— / Why go riding on an ox to search for an ox?!"[27]

Ueda points out that although in the first six pictures the ox represents the true self, it nevertheless represents the true self *from the standpoint of the deluded, self-alienated self*.[28] The struggle between the oxherder and the ox is a struggle with and within ourselves.[29] As we progress from picture 4 to picture 6, the dualism between the oxherder and the ox is gradually overcome. But it is only in picture 7 that the oxherder is able to dispense with the image of the ox altogether and just be himself. No longer needing to be an oxherder—a seeker or a tamer—he sits alone at peace with himself and the world.

Pictures 8–10: The Tricycle Trilogy of the True Self

One can imagine the story ending with picture 7. Indeed, some spiritual paths do end with a sage at peace with himself on a mountaintop. Such solitary sages leave the world behind or, at least, leave it as it is. For Zen, this is to have climbed to the top of a hundred-foot pole and yet to be unable or unwilling to leap off—to leap, that is, back into the world filled with dust as well as flowers.[30]

It is worth noting here that the ultimate temptation Siddhartha experienced came *after* his enlightenment, after, that is, he sat at the base of the Bodhi Tree for seven days "experiencing the happiness of liberation." Mara—the personification of temptation—said to him, "If you have discovered the path, / The secure way leading to the Deathless, / Be off and walk that path alone; / What's the point of instructing others?"[31] Compounding this temptation to travel a solo path and stay on the mountaintop of Nirvana alone, the newly awakened Buddha thought: "If I were to teach the Dhamma [Sk. Dharma], others would not understand me, and that would be troublesome for me. . . . Those dyed in lust, wrapped in darkness will never discern this abstruse Dhamma which goes against the worldly stream, subtle, deep, and difficult to see." Yet at that point the god Brahma—here symbolizing the compassion that accompanies wisdom—pleaded with the Buddha, saying: "There are beings with little dust in their eyes who are wasting through not hearing the Dhamma. There will be those who will understand the Dhamma." Listening to this plea and "out of compassion for beings," the Buddha rose and began his forty-five-year teaching career.[32] These texts from the Pali Canon foreshadow the development of the Mahayana Bodhisattva ideal and its critique of the so-called Hinayana ideal of the Arhat who seeks his own salvation and leaves the world behind. As Karen Armstrong puts it, "The Dhamma demanded that [the Buddha] return to the marketplace and involve himself in the affairs of a sorrowing world."[33]

There is yet another danger lurking at the stage depicted by picture 7 of *The Ten Oxherding Pictures*—namely, the danger of mistaking an ironically inflated and spiritually self-satisfied ego for the true self.[34] We have all heard of, and some of us have met, holier-than-thou sages who have succumbed to the temptation to get stuck at this lofty stage, losing the luster of their limited enlightenment by metaphorically tying themselves up with—if not literally wearing around their necks—golden chains. Yet Zen spirituality truly begins with the overcoming of this state of being stuck in the clouds of spiritual transcendence. Real Zen is found only where the path up the mountain doubles as a path down the mountain. The path of Zen is, in truth, the ceaseless circulation of the upward and downward journey, the never-ending to and fro of ascending and descending. The enlightened and enlightening figure in picture 10 models this as he commutes between his rustic hut and the bustling city.

This path of the most profound spiritual circulation is portrayed in the last three pictures taken together. As Ueda explains, whereas pictures 1–7 tell the story of a linear progression to higher and higher levels of self-realization, the last three pictures are all on the same level. The true self is not simply portrayed in any single one of these last three pictures; the true self is the endless movement, the ceaseless circulation among them.[35]

It is possible to relate the last three pictures to a Zen interpretation of the doctrine of the Three Bodies of the Buddha discussed in Chapter 10.[36] The empty circle of picture 8 would indicate the formless Truth Body, understood as the originally pure mirror-mind that is capable of nondually embracing and illuminating all the forms of the world. The peaceful freedom and naturalness of the stream flowing and tree blooming "of their own accord" in picture 9 would present an utterly open-minded experience of these illuminated phenomena as a thoroughly this-worldly conception of the Enjoyment Body. And the compassionate activity depicted in picture 10 would present the Manifestation Body tirelessly and joyously working on behalf of liberating all sentient beings.

It is also possible to understand the last three pictures as each foregrounding one or two of the Four Immeasurable Mindsets of lovingkindness, compassion, empathetic joy, and equanimity (introduced in Chapter 5). The empty circle of picture 8 presents the absolute evenness of the mind of equanimity, the mirror-mind that sees the equality of everything and everyone such as they are without attachment or aversion, without bias or prejudice. A circle is indeed defined by the fact that every point on the circumference is equidistant from the center. Yet in this case the center is everywhere and the non-egocentric heart-mind is the open circle's equanimous awareness. Such non-egocentric awareness enables an empathetically joyful experience of all the natural beauty and wondrous interconnections of the world, as depicted in picture 9. It also opens the no longer egocentric heart-mind to all the psychological and spiritual as well as physical sufferings of sentient beings, and thus the doorway to an engagement in the world motivated by lovingkindness and compassion, as illustrated in picture 10. It could also be said that all four of these Immeasurable Mindsets are gathered in picture 10, where the enlightened and enlightening figure, without attachment or aversion, compassionately liberates others from suffering and joyously celebrates with them the wonders of living a life of naturalness within human society, which is in turn situated within the wider community of the natural world and, ultimately, within the empty circle of the Buddha-nature, the formless source and abode—the Source-Field—of all forms.

Having indicated their interconnectedness, let us now focus on each of these last three pictures, highlighting in turn one wheel of the tricycle trilogy of the true self.

Picture 8: The Empty Circle: Infinite Possibility, Freedom, and Openness

"First, the Great Death; after cutting off completely, then coming back to life."[37] This classic Zen saying is portrayed in the last three pictures. Picture 8 is entitled "Person and Ox Both Forgotten." It is just an empty circle, not a picture of anything at all. It is a great negation, an absolute emptying, of all forms. Ōtsu Rōshi relates picture 8 to what the ninth-century Chinese Zen master Linji calls "taking away both person and surroundings," dropping off both subject and object—in this case, forgetting both the searching self and the searched-for Buddha-nature.[38]

It is said that there are at least a hundred ways to draw this circle, and countless ways to understand it.[39] While the ways to understand the circle may be infinite, one of those ways is to understand it as a symbol of infinity. Infinity here means infinite possibility, a formlessness pregnant with all possible forms. When I see the empty circle, I see freedom and creative potentiality, the absence of any boundaries and the open source of all innovation. I also see a formless symbol of the open mind of wisdom and the open heart of compassion.

As we discussed in Chapter 21, the Western tradition has tended to associate being with form and form with the good, and so has conditioned us to be horrified by what we see in picture 8 as a vacuum of nothingness, a white hole, as it were, of inert and vacant emptiness. In East Asia, by contrast, the empty circle—or, as it is usually called, "the single circle"—is seen as a sign of perfection, a well-rounded completeness without any jagged edges remaining.[40] In fact, one of the first Western philosophers, Parmenides, spoke of the one true reality as a homogeneous "well-rounded sphere."[41] Yet, in stark contrast to his conception of an unchanging and undifferentiated One, the empty circle of Zen dynamically makes room for the teeming multiplicity of forms.

The empty circle is often drawn so as to leave it open, reminding us that it symbolizes a dynamic Way that never reaches a static completion (see image in Chapter 10). The empty circle can thus be understood and experienced as the creative source as well as the peacefully encompassing abode—the Source-Field—of all the multifarious things we experience. As Ōtsu Rōshi puts it, the "complete nothingness is the originary place from which all thoughts and every kind of knowledge originates," and "the unhindered life of Zen flows in the circulation between" the indivisible nondual essence indicated by picture 8 and the manifestation of the manifold diversity of phenomena portrayed in picture 9.[42]

As we saw in Chapter 8, Zen teaches that "all the universe is one bright pearl." Yet, if we misunderstand the one bright pearl as synonymous with the homogeneous monism of Parmenides's well-rounded sphere, then we are stuck "in the cave of demons on black mountain." Dōgen thus urges us to appreciate not just the oneness of the one bright pearl of the universe but, at the same time, its "infinite colorations," for "each of the many facets of its radiant variegations contains the merit of the entire universe."[43]

Picture 9: Forms of Nature Within the Formless Circle

Puming's and Qingjiu's versions of the oxherding pictures understandably end with the empty circle. However, according to Kuoan and the Japanese Zen tradition that has cherished his version, those versions stop short of expressing the affirmation of a dynamic and pluralistic world of forms, not to mention the compassionate engagement to which the Zen path ultimately leads. Puming's version goes beyond the stage of forgetting the ox yet keeping the self, but it does not explicitly go beyond depicting the peak experience of letting go of all attachments to forms and enjoying the peace of Nirvana. Kuoan and the Japanese Zen tradition have thus insisted on adding two more pictures—two more steps, as it were, in the round dance of the true self that takes place in a ceaseless movement among pictures 8, 9, and 10.

In terms of the famous couplet of the *Heart Sutra*, picture 8 shows us that "form is emptiness," whereas picture 9 shows us the other side of the same coin, the converse and complementary truth that "emptiness is form." In Zen parlance, whereas picture 8 displays "true emptiness" (Jp. *shinkū*), picture 9 displays "wondrous being" (*myōu*). These two go together since it is precisely because things are empty of independent substantiality that they can be as they truly are in their dynamic interconnectedness. As for picture 10, the modern Rinzai Zen master Akizuki Ryōmin follows D. T. Suzuki in saying that it expresses the "wondrous activity" (*myōyū*) that issues from a realization of the nonduality of true emptiness and wondrous being.[44]

Ueda understands picture 8 in terms of what his predecessors in the Kyoto School, Nishida Kitarō and Nishitani Keiji, call the Place of Absolute Nothingness and the Field of Emptiness. We discussed these ideas in Chapter 21. Ueda himself uses a traditional Mahayana Buddhist expression to say that the circle represents the "Empty Space" (Jp. *kokū*) that allows all form-things to exist in their interrelations and that encompasses all our finitely meaningful worlds.[45] In his German writings Ueda translates this term as *die unendliche Offenheit* (the Infinite Openness) and as *die unendliche Weite* (the Infinite Expanse).[46]

The empty circle makes room for everything. It is always there as the formless background, even though we hardly ever notice it, since our intentional consciousness functions by foregrounding this or that set of forms. Ueda points out that in Kuoan's version of the oxherding pictures, the empty circle was in fact there from the beginning and remains there till the end. All the events before and after picture 8 take place within it, even though, before the inherently indescribable experience indicated by picture 8, we did not realize this. "In fact," writes Ueda, "from the beginning the true self was portrayed not as the ox but rather, insofar as it was portrayed at all, as the circle." And every determinate thing that appears within this all-embracing empty expanse is, as it were, a "self-determination of the true world of this single circle."[47]

Enlightenment is a matter of waking up to what has always been there. In the first lines of his preface to picture 1, Ziyuan writes: "It has never been lost, why the need to search for it? It is because you have turned your back on your own awakening that you have become alienated from it." We have turned our back on ourselves. We have mistaken ourselves for isolated egos, and as a result have distorted our view of other persons and objects in the world. And so, we needed to turn away from our distorted view of the world and to search for our true self. It was helpful to have an image of the true self—in this case an ox—for a while, but then came the time when it was necessary to let go of this heuristic device.

In picture 7, the seeker found his higher, truer self. But, in picture 8, even that needed to be let go of. No more inner, no more outer, now he can finally just let things be as they are. Picture 9, which simply depicts a mountain stream flowing under a tree in bloom—without an objectified self in sight—shows how it is easiest to do this in nature. It is relatively easy to let beautiful flowers and meandering brooks show themselves in all their natural splendor without getting in their way. As the open heart-mind of the empty circle, the true self formally withdraws from the scene, getting completely out of the way so as to make room for the forms of nature to present themselves. Not only can meditation, the practice of clearing the heart-mind, enable us to appreciate the wonders of nature, but, conversely, as we saw in Chapter 18, appreciating the wonders of nature can enable us to clear the heart-mind and to awaken and cultivate such virtues as freedom and generosity.

Alas, it is much harder to be enlightened, and to enlighten others, amid the hustle and bustle of the human world. It is much easier to forget about one's troubles and to commune with nature on the spacious balcony of a beach house or mountain retreat center than it is to be at peace in—and to bring peace to—a subway car crammed full of stressed-out commuters. Nevertheless, a line from *The Blue Cliff Record* may inspire us to flow with the cool waters of the mountain stream down into the heat of the city: "Peaceful meditation does not require mountains and rivers: when you have extinguished the mind, fire itself is cool."[48]

Picture 10: The Bodhisattva Returns from the Mountaintop to the City Center

Picture 10 shows an old sage coming down from the mountain, returning to the marketplace and (in Shūbun's rendition) greeting a young man. It is a Zen depiction of the Bodhisattva return to the world to work on behalf of liberating and enlightening others. The figure with outstretched hands who appears in this last picture is a traditional forerunner not only of the modern proponents of Engaged Buddhism, but indeed of all those persons, past and present, who bring the peace they have found to others; of all those who share the wisdom they have attained; of all those who have become vehicles of the great vow to enlighten and liberate all sentient beings. The long journey of the oxherder had reached a premature peak when he, no longer needing the provisional symbol of the ox, became a solitary sage on a mountaintop. In the end, however, his journey leads to a sacrifice of that solitude in order to bring solace to others.

"Going to bars and fish markets, he turns all into Buddhas," Ziyuan tells us. "He does not use any secret sagely powers to do this," Kuoan says, but merely by entering the marketplace bare-chested and barefooted, covered in dirt and ash—and smiling from ear to ear. His contagious laughter creates an atmosphere of infectious peace and joy that surrounds him wherever he goes.

The enlightened and enlightening figure in picture 10 is traditionally associated with Budai, a tenth-century Chinese Zen monk who was nicknamed the "Laughing Buddha." Known in the West also as the "Happy Buddha," in the East he came to be thought of as a prefiguration of Maitreya, the Buddha of the future. As legend has it, Budai was a wandering monk who would give away anything that was given to him. Budai's name literally means "cloth sack," and the sack he carries on a staff slung over his shoulder serves as a kind of clearinghouse for donations. Like us, he owns nothing. Unlike us, he realizes this. He understands that things are given to us so that we may, in turn, give them onward to others.

The Budai-like figure in picture 10 does not make a show of his Bodhisattva blessings. We are told that he "hides his light," concealing his sageness under the dirt and ashes of his service. He has passed through the furnace of the empty circle of picture 8. In his preface to that imageless picture Ziyuan strikingly writes: "Letting go of worldly feelings and emptying out thoughts of holiness, he does not linger where the Buddha is, and he runs quickly past where the Buddha is not."[49] This means that he is neither a fundamentalistic Buddhist nor an iconoclastic nihilist. He has shed all attachment to—and all the trappings of—holiness, and yet he does not make a show of this shedding either. In other words, he has washed off "the stench of Zen" that at some point in our practice we all get and have to get rid of. Like a bird flying across a clear blue sky, he embodies pure Subtraction Zen with no lingering residues of the paraphernalia of parasitic Addition Zen. Yet, neither does he throw away whatever might be useful to others; he makes a show of iconoclasm no more than he clings to iconography.

It should be evident by now that the other side of the coin of Subtraction Zen is Vow-Vehicle Zen. By way of clearing our minds and emptying our hearts of all our attachments and acquisitiveness, we free ourselves up for becoming pure vehicles of the great Bodhisattva vow to enlighten and liberate all sentient beings. Insight into emptiness is awakening to interconnectedness, and thus the loving heart is opened along with the awakened mind. Such is the nonduality of wisdom and compassion that is the core teaching of Zen Buddhism.

With the ego out of the way, the wise and compassionate Peaceful Wind of the Buddha Way can blow right through us to all those who are affected by our lives. While picture 8—the empty circle of egoless wisdom—presents the pure formless form of Subtraction Zen, picture 10—the circle full of interactivity—depicts the concomitant compassion of Vow-Vehicle Zen. The enlightened and enlightening true self continually commutes between these two sides of the same coin of wisdom/compassion. Absolute detachment opens the door to whole-hearted engagement. Freedom from egocentric attachment to any form enables nondualistic interaction with all forms.

In Shūbun's famous rendition, the Budai-like figure in picture 10 is shown with outstretched hands, offering gifts to the young boy in the scene—including, of course, the greatest gift of pointing the boy down the pathway toward his own enlightening journey. He is, as it were, passing the enlightening torch to the next generation of oxherders. The Budai-like figure in picture 10 is a portrayal of the true self. At the same time, the true self is this entire scene. And he knows it. In a clearly self-aware yet utterly unselfconscious manner, he identifies himself not only with his finite form but also, indeed first and foremost, with the open field in which we are all interconnected.

Finding, Forgetting, and Opening the Self

Let us conclude our review of the path of Zen by relating *The Ten Oxherding Pictures* to the key passage from Dōgen's *Genjōkōan* that we discussed at the end of our preview of the path of Zen in Chapter 2:

> To study the Buddha Way is to study the self.
> To study the self is to forget the self.
> To forget the self is to be enlightened by the myriad things of the world.
> To be enlightened by the myriad things of the world is to let drop off the
>   body-mind of the self and the body-mind of others.[50]

The first line can be paired with pictures 1–7: "To study the Buddha Way is to study the self." Buddhism is not really about learning doctrines and rituals; it is about coming to "know thyself."

The second line can be paired with picture 8: "To study the self is to forget the self." This is the experience of utterly "dropping off the body-mind," letting go of all our attachments to the physical things and psychological thoughts we have possessively and egoistically identified ourselves with.

The third line can be paired with picture 9: "To forget the self is to be enlightened by the myriad things of the world." With the false fabrications of our isolated egos out of the way, the interconnected events of the world can naturally shine forth without egoistic distortion.

Finally, the fourth line can be paired with picture 10: "To be enlightened by the myriad things of the world is to let drop off the body-mind of the self and the body-mind of others." No longer thinking of oneself as selfishly separated from others, one inspires others to set out on the path to the same realization. Like the humble sage in picture 10, one not only endlessly continues one's enlightening practice, one also, as Dōgen goes on to say, continually "lays to rest the traces of enlightenment," hiding one's sageness with the dirt and ashes of one's service.

The path of Zen, as depicted in *The Ten Oxherding Pictures*, is, to be sure, an extremely demanding one. It often seems almost as intimidating as it is inspiring. At every stage appears a still higher stage. Beyond every mountain range appears yet another mountain range. And, in the end, if we manage to get that far, the path leads down from the mountains right back to the valley where we started. Passing the torch of the beginner's mind to others, our journey does not end. Only now we realize that the journey itself is the true destination. Now, at last, we are at Home on the Way.

Discussion Questions

Chapter 1: What Really Is Zen? Recovering the Beginner's Open Mind

- What really is Zen, in contrast to how it has been repackaged or watered down in the pop culture of the West?
- What is meant by "emptying one's cup" and recovering "the beginner's mind"?
- What issues should modern Westerners who are interested in Zen bear in mind as they adopt and adapt its teachings and practices?
- What does it mean to understand Zen's stories as "liberating legends" rather than as factual historical records?
- How should Zen Buddhism be understood in the context of interreligious dialogue?

Chapter 2: Previewing the Path of Zen: Know Thyself, Forget Thyself, Open Thyself

- How have philosophical and religious teachings from around the world stressed both the difficulty and the importance of coming to truly know oneself?
- How does Zen's method of "investigating the self" compare with Socrates's quest to "know thyself"?
- What is meant by "karmic editing," and how does Zen meditation alleviate its distorting effects?
- What does Zen master Dōgen mean when he says that "to study the self is to forget the self"?

Chapter 3: Zen Meditation as a Practice of Clearing the Heart-Mind

- Why is meditation so important in Zen Buddhism?

- What is the difference between received, intellectual, and experiential wisdom?
- In what sense is the method of Zen meditation one of "subtraction"?
- How have Zen teachers warned of possible misuses of secularized "mindfulness" techniques?
- What is the ultimate aim, and what are the proximate benefits of practicing Zen meditation?

Chapter 4: How to Practice Zen Meditation: Attending to Place, Body, Breath, and Mind

- Where, when, and for how long should one meditate?
- How should the body be positioned when meditating?
- How does one meditate on the breath?
- What should one do with the mind when meditating?
- Why is it important to maintain physical stillness when practicing *zazen*?
- How should one deal with mental distractions when meditating?
- How does one engage in walking meditation?

Chapter 5: The Buddha's First and Last Lesson: The Middle Way of Knowing What Suffices

- What motivated Siddhartha to set out on the spiritual quest that led him to become the Buddha?
- How did the Buddha distinguish between different types of desires?
- Why did the Buddha reject extreme asceticism as well as extreme hedonism?
- How does the Buddha's Middle Way teach us to be satisfied with what suffices?

Chapter 6: The Buddha's Strong Medicine: Embracing Impermanence

- How did the Buddha summarize his basic teachings in what he called the Four Noble Truths?

- What did the Buddha mean when he said that our lives are pervaded by suffering or "existential unease"?
- What are the root causes of this spiritual suffering, and how did the Buddha present himself as a "spiritual doctor" who could diagnose and offer a prescription for it?
- What does it mean to say that suffering is caused by a mismatch between desire and reality, and what are the two approaches to resolving this problem?
- Why does the Buddha say that we need to embrace change rather than pine for permanence?

Chapter 7: The True Self Is Egoless

- How does the Zen quest to know oneself paradoxically lead to an enlightening "not-knowing" and to an understanding of the "ungraspable" nature of the self?
- What is the *anatman* doctrine of Buddhism, and should *anatman* be translated as "egolessness," as "no-self," or as "no-soul"?
- What debates exist among Buddhist traditions and scholars about how to understand the *anatman* doctrine?
- What is the "Ontological Middle Way" of "interdependent origination," and what is the philosophical difference between a "substance-self" and a "process-self"?
- How does Zen understand the teaching of "no-self" to be compatible with the teaching of "the true self"?

Chapter 8: We Are One: Loving Your Neighbor as Yourself

- What did Jesus mean when he said you should love your neighbor (and even your enemy) as yourself, and how might this be related to Zen teachings of the nonduality of self and other?
- Why might the metaphor of "tasting" be more appropriate than "seeing" to describe the experience of oneness?
- What similarities can be found with teachings of oneness in the Hindu *Upanishads*, and how have such similarities been debated over the course of the historical development of Buddhism?
- Why does Zen think that "to exist is to coexist"?

- How does Zen's teaching of nonduality imply both unity and uniqueness, oneness and difference—and how are these understood to be compatible?

Chapter 9: But We Are Not the Same: Taking Turns as the Center of the Universe

- How does Zen stress our individuality and uniqueness at the same time as it stresses our unity or oneness?

- What is the point of the strange dialogue between Yangshan Huiji and Sansheng Huiran (aka Fred Flintstone and Barney Rubble)?

- Among theological conceptions of God, how does the Zen metaphysics expressed in the metaphor of "water and waves" best accord with "panentheism," that is to say, with the idea that "all is *in* God"?

- What does the modern Zen philosopher Ueda Shizuteru mean when he says that "the free exchange of the role of host is the very core of dialogue"?

- What does it mean to say that we can take turns being the center of the universe?

Chapter 10: Who or What Is the Buddha?

- Other than the historical person Siddhartha Gautama, what else does the word "Buddha" refer to?

- What is the Trikaya or "Three Bodies of the Buddha," and how does it compare to the Christian Trinity?

- Who is Amida (Sk. Amitabha) Buddha?

- How does the doctrine of "merit transfer" help explain the development of ideas such as the "other-power" and "Pure Land" of a celestial Buddha?

- How does Zen understand the Buddha as both ultimate reality and the true self, rather than as either a historical person or a transcendent savior?

Chapter 11: Mind Is Buddha: So, If You Encounter the Buddha, Kill Him!

- What does Hakuin mean when he says that "unenlightened beings are originally Buddhas," and how does he explain this with the analogy of water and ice?

- What does Linji mean when he says that "if you encounter the Buddha, kill him"?
- What does it mean to say that "Mind is Buddha"?
- What does it mean to say that the philosophy of Zen is a nondualism rather than either an idealism or a materialism?
- What sense do you make of the various kōans dealing with the question of what the Buddha is?

Chapter 12: Dying to Live: Zen, Pure Land Buddhism, and Christianity

- How have Zen and Christianity been seen as either compatible or incompatible?
- How might Zen and other religious traditions enable us to rethink the meaning of "God"?
- Where are the Kingdom of God and the Pure Land?
- What does Zen mean by the "Great Death," and why is it necessary to pass through this experience in order to awaken to "the Unborn" and thus to truly live?
- How is the idea of a spiritual death and rebirth in Zen comparable to similar ideas in Pure Land Buddhism and Christianity?

Chapter 13: Zen as Trans-Mysticism: Everyday Even Mind Is the Way

- Why do Zen Buddhists bow to the Buddha if they think that the Buddha is their own mind?
- What is meant by the Zen teaching that "Everyday Even Mind is the Way"?
- When a monk asked a Zen master for the ultimate teaching, why did the master tell him to go wash his breakfast bowls?
- What does it mean to say that Zen is a path of "trans-mysticism"?

Chapter 14: Engaged Zen: From Inner to Outer Peace

- How does Mahayana Buddhism, as exemplified in the *Vimalakirti Sutra*, break down the barrier between monastic and lay life, and how does it stress the spiritual significance of everyday life in the midst of society?

- What is "Engaged Buddhism"?
- Why should a meditation retreat not be thought of as an escape from the troubles of society?
- What does it mean to say that we need to *be peace* in order to *bring peace*?
- How should we understand the relation between peace and justice?

Chapter 15: The Dharma of Karma: We Reap What We Sow

- How does the Dharma (i.e., teaching) of Karma provide a non-theistic way of thinking about cosmic justice?
- What does it mean to say, "We make our habits, and our habits in turn make us"?
- Why is the teaching of karma not a determinism or fatalism, but rather a teaching of "situated freedom"?
- How can the teaching of karma be misused so as to "blame the victim," and how should karma be understood so that it does not lead to this problem?

Chapter 16: Zen and Morality: Following Rules to Where There Are No Rules

- Why does Huineng say that we should "not think of good and evil" in order to realize our "Original Face"?
- What are the Precepts in Buddhism, and what role do they play in Zen?
- How does Dōgen suggest that, in the course of practice, "do good" becomes a *description* rather than a *prescription*?
- Why are Bodhisattvas allowed to break moral rules in their use of "skillful means"?
- Why does Zen teach "minimizing violence" rather than an absolute pacifism?

Chapter 17: Being in the Zone of Zen: The Natural Freedom of No-Mind

- How does what Zen calls "no-mind" and "non-doing" relate to what we call "being in the zone" or "the flow experience"—or, for that matter, to Luke Skywalker's use of the Force?

- How can meditation enable us to get into the Zone of Zen in all the activities of our lives?
- How does the Zone of Zen relate to what Hindus call *karma yoga*, to what Daoists call *wuwei*, and to what cognitive scientists call "hot cognition"?
- What are the possible dangers of a half-baked "just do it" state of mind, and how has Zen been misused for military purposes?
- Why does critical thinking need to be more thoroughly incorporated into a truly holistic practice of Zen?

Chapter 18: Zen Lessons from Nature: *Samu* and the Giving Leaves

- How does Zen think of freedom as "freedom *in* nature" rather than as "freedom *from* nature"?
- How did the practice of *samu* or "meditative work" get incorporated into Zen, and how does it bring practitioners into a more intimate relation with nature?
- What does Zen, and Mahayana Buddhism in general, call the "Perfection of Giving," and how might we learn this virtue from a more attentive interaction with the natural world?
- How have Zen masters indicated that we can learn about Zen from the natural world around us?

Chapter 19: Zen and Art: Cultivating Naturalness

- Why does Zen think that, paradoxically, we need to *cultivate naturalness*, and how do the Japanese "Ways" of art and the martial arts allow us to do this?
- How do Zen gardens enable us to experience the relationship between human art and the natural world in a nondualistic manner?
- How does the Japanese aesthetic of "cut-continuance" demonstrate that the borderlines between things both connect as well as separate them?
- How does the aesthetic of *wabi-sabi* enable us to discover spiritual lessons as well as a poignant beauty in the rustic simplicity of imperfect and impermanent things?
- What can the Japanese art of flower arrangement, *ikebana*, reveal to us about the relations between life and death and between time and eternity?

- How do Zen-inspired art and music allow us to experience formlessness and silence as the creative Source-Field of form and sound?

Chapter 20: Zen and Language: The Middle Way Between Speech and Silence

- How is the relation between sound and silence presented in haiku and other forms of poetry?
- How can we reconcile the fact that Zen speaks of going beyond language with the fact that it has produced such a vast body of literature?
- Why does Zen think it is important to indicate the limits of language?
- How does Zen celebrate the expressive power of language?
- What does Ueda Shizuteru mean by the ceaseless dynamic of "exiting language and exiting into language"?

Chapter 21: Between Zen and Philosophy: Commuting with the Kyoto School

- How should we understand the relation between Zen experience and philosophical thinking?
- What is the Kyoto School, and how have some of its members connected the practice of Zen to the study of philosophy and religion?
- What does Nishida Kitarō mean by "pure experience" and the "Place of Absolute Nothingness"?
- How has Abe Masao ignited a theological and interreligious debate about the "self-negating" or "self-emptying" nature of God?
- How does Nishitani Keiji suggest that Zen can help us discover a deeper spirituality in an age of nihilism?

Chapter 22: Sōtō and Rinzai Zen Practice: Just Sitting and Working with Kōans

- What are the differences between the methods of meditation in the Japanese Sōtō and Rinzai schools?
- How can the differences between Rinzai and Sōtō methods be traced back to debates in twelfth century China between advocates of "looking at phrases" and "silent illumination" approaches to Zen meditation?

- What does "just sitting" mean, and how does the "non-thinking" it involves relate to "thinking," "not-thinking," and "thinking not-thinking"?
- What is a kōan—what does one do with it, and what does it do to one?
- What is a "first barrier" kōan, and what other types of kōans are there?

Chapter 23: Death and Rebirth—Or, Nirvana Here and Now

- How is death the business of Zen temples in Japan, and what does Zen really teach about death and the afterlife?
- What are the traditional Buddhist teachings about "moment-to-moment" rebirth in this life and rebirth between lives?
- What are the Six Realms of Rebirth in Samsara, and how can they be understood in a metaphorical as well as a literal sense?
- How might working on a "death kōan" bring about a life-changing experience?
- Why do Zen masters tell us to go to Hell?
- How does Zen teach that Nirvana is to be found in the here and now?

Chapter 24: Reviewing the Path of Zen: *The Ten Oxherding Pictures*

- What does it mean to speak of stages in the practice of Zen, given its doctrine of sudden rather than gradual enlightenment?
- What does the ox represent, and what does it mean to search for it, see its traces, catch it, tame it, and ride it home?
- Why does the ox disappear in the seventh picture?
- What does the empty circle of the eighth picture represent, and why does the path of Zen not simply end there?
- What does it mean to speak of the last three pictures together as a "tricycle trilogy of the true self"?
- Who is the older man in the last picture, and why does the story end with him coming down from the mountain and entering the city?

Notes

Preface

1. Let me clarify that, while I am authorized to teach Zen and direct a Zen center, I am not a "Zen master." This English expression roughly translates *rōshi*, a term that literally means "elder teacher" but in the Rinzai School is strictly used as a title only for the very few monks and extremely few laypersons who have completed the entire kōan curriculum and received *inka shōmei*, the ultimate "seal of certification" of enlightenment. To my knowledge only one Westerner, Jeff Shore, has completed this training and received *inka shōmei* in a Japanese Rinzai Zen monastery, though many have received this and other titles in the various traditional and modern Zen schools transplanted to Western countries and more or less adapted to fit the needs of their new environments.
2. *Nishida Kitarō zenshū* [Complete works of Nishida Kitarō] (Tokyo: Iwanami, 1987–89), vol. 15, p. 47. See the passage quoted in Chapter 21.
3. *Hisamatsu Shinichi chosakushū* [The collected works of Hisamatsu Shin'ichi] (Tokyo: Risōsha, 1970), vol. 1, p. 435. Unless otherwise noted, all translations in this book are my own.
4. A Zen approach to questions of epistemology (the study of knowledge) is indicated in parts of Chapters 2, 3, 9, 11, 15, 20, and 21. For more explicit and in-depth treatments of this topic, see the following articles of mine: "The Philosophy of Zen Master Dōgen: Egoless Perspectivism," in *The Oxford Handbook of Japanese Philosophy*, edited by Bret W. Davis (New York: Oxford University Press, 2020), pp. 201–12; "Zen's Nonegocentric Perspectivism," in *Buddhist Philosophy: A Comparative Approach*, edited by Steven M. Emmanuel (West Sussex: Wiley-Blackwell, 2018), pp. 123–43; and "Knowing Limits: Toward a Versatile Perspectivism with Nietzsche, Heidegger, Zhuangzi and Zen," *Research in Phenomenology* 49 (2019): 301–34.

Acknowledgments

5. For the transcript of a talk on incorporating these experiential and holistic forms of pedagogy into classes, see Bret W. Davis, "The Life of the Body-Heart-Mind-Spirit: Cross-Cultural Reflections on Cura Personalis," Nachbahr Award Talk, Loyola University Maryland, October 2, 2015, https://www.loyola.edu/-/media/department/center-humanities/documents/nachbahr-lectures/bret%20davis%20nachbahr%20talk%2010%202%202015.ashx?la=en For articles on how such holistic practices in

non-Western traditions provoke us to rethink the methods and aims of "philosophy," see Bret W. Davis, "Beyond Philosophical Euromonopolism: Other Ways of—Not Otherwise than—Philosophy," *Philosophy East and West* 69, no. 2 (April 2019): 1–28; and Bret W. Davis, "Buddhist Philosophy as a Holistic Way of Life: Studying the Way with Body and Mind (*Shinjin Gakudō*)," in *Key Concepts in World Philosophies*, edited by Sarah Flavel and Chiara Robianno (New York: Bloomsbury Academic, 2022).

Chapter 1

1. Edward Said's landmark *Orientalism* (New York: Vintage, 1978) focuses on how Western scholars, authors, and artists have portrayed Middle Eastern cultures as exotic and erotic, yet intellectually and culturally inferior to the West. J. J. Clarke points out how the Orientalism directed at South and East Asia has had similar problems, yet also some more ambivalently positive aspects. Many Enlightenment thinkers looked to China, and Romantic thinkers to India, for philosophies that could serve as what he calls a "corrective mirror" for self-critique. Of course, as Clarke duly recognizes, even though much of the Orientalism directed at South and East Asia has praised rather than denigrated its object, it has by no means been free of distortions and questionable motivations. J. J. Clarke, *Oriental Enlightenment: The Encounter Between Asian and Western Thought* (New York: Routledge, 1997), pp. 37–70; see also Bret W. Davis, "Step Back and Encounter: From Continental to Comparative Philosophy," *Comparative and Continental Philosophy* 1, no. 1 (2009): 9–22.
2. Nyogen Senzaki, *101 Zen Stories* (1919), as reprinted in Paul Reps and Nyogen Senzaki, *Zen Flesh, Zen Bones* (New York: Anchor Books, 1957), p. 5.
3. *The Discourse on the Inexhaustible Lamp of the Zen School*, by Zen Master Torei Enji with commentary by Master Daibi of Unkan, translated by Yoko Okuda (Boston: Charles E. Tuttle, 1996), p. 196, translation modified.
4. Shunryu Suzuki, *Zen Mind, Beginners Mind* (New York: Weatherhill, 1970), p. 21.
5. Hans-Georg Gadamer, *Truth and Method*, 2nd ed., translated by Joel Weinsheimer and Donald Marshall (New York: Crossroad, 1989), p. 270.
6. See Plato's *Meno* 80–81.
7. Bernard Faure, *Chan Insights and Oversights: An Epistemological Critique of the Chan Tradition* (Princeton: Princeton University Press, 1993). See also by the same author *The Rhetoric of Immediacy: A Cultural Critique of Chan/Zen Buddhism* (Princeton, NJ: Princeton University Press, 1991). Despite their often polemical tenor and intent, Faure's works are among the more philosophically sophisticated and provocative critiques of Zen.
8. John R. McRae, *Seeing Through Zen: Encounter, Transformation, and Genealogy in Chinese Chan Buddhism* (Berkeley: University of California Press, 2003).
9. A classic account of this "traditional narrative" is Heinrich Dumoulin, *Zen Buddhism: A History*, 2 vols., translated by James W. Heisig and Paul Knitter (New York: Macmillan, 1990, 1994). A new edition of this work was published in

2005 by World Wisdom. In his introduction to the new edition of the first volume, which treats the prehistory of Zen in India and the early history of Zen in China, John R. McRae criticizes Dumoulin for uncritically repeating the historical inaccuracies of the traditional narrative of the early history of Zen. He concludes that Dumoulin's book "is *not* a reliable source for understanding Zen Buddhism in India and China," and that "the legendary accounts Dumoulin so painstakingly compiled need to be understood in terms of mytho-poetic creation rather than historical narration" (xxxix–xl). In his introduction to the new edition of the second volume, which treats the medieval and early modern history of Zen in Japan, Victor Sōgen Hori, an academic scholar who also trained as a Zen monk in Japan for many years, questions the overly polemical motives as well as the epistemological biases of academic scholars such as McRae and Faure who seek to debunk Zen's historical narratives as "ideology-posing-as-history." Hori reminds us that all religions tend to "present their myth as if it were history," since "the point of religious writing is not to write secular history but to express that religion's version of spiritual truth" (xvii). Based on his experience with both the practice and scholarship on Zen, Hori insightfully comments on the ideological and epistemological commitments involved in *both* the practitioner's "insider's view" *and* the scholar's "outsider's view," and on the unremarked parallels between the two. He concludes that Dumoulin's *History* was "the last substantial work to attempt the Middle Way, embodying a scholar's respect for historical research and a monks respect for Zen as a religion" (xx). Peter D. Hershock's works are among the all too rare attempts to interweave philosophical, practical, and historical approaches to Chan/Zen, as well as the critical "outsider's perspective" of a scholar with the sympathetic "insider's perspective" of a practitioner. See his engaging books on the history of Chinese Chan and Japanese Zen: *Chan Spirituality* (Honolulu: University of Hawai'i Press, 2004); and *Public Zen, Personal Zen: A Buddhist Introduction* (Lanham, MD: Rowman & Littlefield, 2014). Starting with his *Liberating Intimacy: Enlightenment and Social Virtuosity in Ch'an Buddhism* (Albany: State University of New York Press, 1996), Hershock stresses the irreducibly social nature of Zen enlightenment, a topic that will be addressed in Chapters 8, 9, and 14–16 in the present book. John C. Maraldo, an important scholar who is trained in philosophical hermeneutics and is familiar with both the practice of and critical-historical scholarship on Zen, has penned a painstaking critical response and alternative to recent polemical trends in scholarship on the history of Zen: *The Saga of Zen History and the Power of Legend* (Nagoya: Chisokudō Publications, 2021). In chapter 8 of his book, as a possible model for studying Zen, Maraldo references recent anthropological methods of "engaged ethnography," which, overcoming the colonialistic fear of "going native," "prescind from assuming the epistemic superiority of the scholar's stance over traditional understanding" and thereby open up a genuinely reciprocal exchange between anthropologists and the traditions they study while participating in. As an example of this reciprocal approach, Maraldo refers to Paula Arai's *Bringing Zen Home: The Healing Heart of Japanese Women's Rituals* (Honolulu: University of Hawai'i Press, 2011). Hori's works are also exemplary in this regard; see Victor Sōgen Hori, "Rinzai Kōan Training: Philosophical Intersections," in *The Oxford Handbook of Japanese Philosophy*, edited by Bret W. Davis (New York: Oxford University Press, 2020), pp. 231–46. The pioneers of this twofold approach are those Zen-practicing philosophers of the Kyoto School, in whose lineage I studied and practiced and who are frequently referenced in this book (see especially Chapter 21). I should note that while Maraldo's book and mine were written simultaneously and independently, we shared penultimate drafts. I was encouraged to read that Maraldo considers the present book to be a "careful and considerate introduction to Zen that surmounts the division between insider and outsider" (*The Saga of Zen History*, p. 280n17).

10. Bernard Faure, "Bodhidharma as Textual and Religious Paradigm," *History of Religions* 25, no. 3 (1986): 187–98.

11. See Andy Ferguson, *Zen's Chinese Heritage: The Masters and Their Teachings* (Somerville, MA: Wisdom Publications, 2000).

12. McRae, *Seeing Through Zen*, p. 60. See also *Readings of the Platform Sutra*, edited by Morten Schütter and Stephen F. Teiser (New York: Columbia University Press, 2012), chapters 1, 2, and 3.

13. McRae, *Seeing Through Zen*, p. 60. Excellent treatments of the teachings of the *Platform Sutra* are provided by Peter N. Gregory and Brook Ziporyn in *Readings of the Platform Sutra*, chapters 4 and 7.

14. Steven Heine, *Zen Skin, Zen Marrow: Will the Real Zen Buddhism Please Stand Up?* (New York: Oxford University Press, 2008). Hershock also insightfully discusses the "deepening rift between what might be called objective/external and subjective/internal approaches to most effectively and accurately presenting Zen," attempting to "move in the direction of closing the gap" by "offering what aims to be a more 'nondualist' approach to Zen" (*Public Zen, Personal Zen*, xv–xvi). Like Maraldo, Hershock suggests that traditional Zen "histories" should not be seen merely as retrospective factual documents or reduced to politically motivated machinations, since their pedagogical and liberating intent is primarily prospective and co-creative; in other words, Zen (hi)stories can be understood not so much "as records of things past but rather as rehearsals of meanings still in the process of being composed" (ibid., 247). In any case, Hershock argues that "the tension between *documenting* and *demonstrating* Zen" is in fact nothing new; it "can be seen as having been a perennial factor in Zen's vitality and sustained relevance. . . . Seen in this way, the presence in the contemporary West of tensions in how Zen is understood can be seen as a sign of maturation—a sign that Zen is being aptly localized" (ibid., 235). See also in this regard Dale S. Wright's books: *Philosophical Meditations on Zen Buddhism* (New York: Cambridge University Press, 1998); and *What Is Buddhist Enlightenment?* (New York: Oxford University Press, 2016). Unlike more cynical and polemical scholars, Wright is interested in critically developing rather than debunking Zen. Nevertheless, Wright's constructive criticism involves not only refuting previous Western "romantic" interpretations of Zen Buddhism but also rejecting or substantially revising any traditional teachings and practices that he judges to be incompatible with certain contemporary Western cultural, scientific, and philosophical views and values that he treats as axiomatic. Heine and Wright have edited together a number of volumes, all published by Oxford University Press, which gather work from many of the most prominent

scholars of the Zen tradition: *The Kōan* (2000), *The Zen Canon* (2004), *Zen Ritual* (2008), *Zen Classics* (2006), and *Zen Masters* (2010).

15. Gadamer, *Truth and Method*, pp. 303–4, 361.

16. McRae, *Seeing Through Zen*, p. 10.

17. See Paul Ricoeur, *Freud and Philosophy: An Essay on Interpretation*, translated by Denis Savage (New Haven: Yale University Press, 1970), pp. 20–36; and Paul Ricoeur, *Hermeneutics*, translated by David Pellauer (Malden, MA: Polity Press, 2013), pp. 6–8.

18. See Ricoeur, *Freud and Philosophy*, pp. 524–51; and Paul Ricoeur, "Religion, Atheism, and Faith," in *The Conflict of Interpretations*, edited by Don Ihde (Evanston, IL: Northwestern University Press, 1974), pp. 440–67.

19. Ricoeur is hardly the only philosopher to use atheist critiques to purify rather than dismiss Christianity. See Merold Westphal, *Suspicion and Faith: The Religious Uses of Modern Atheism* (New York: Fordham University Press, 1998). Other noteworthy scholars in this regard include Derridian decontructionists such as John Caputo, and Thomas Altizer, the provocative proponent of "death of God theology." For an insightful critique of Altizer's interpretation and use of Buddhism, see the chapter by Janet Gyatso in *Thinking Through the Death of God: A Critical Companion to Thomas J. J. Altizer*, edited by Lisa McCullough and Brian Schroeder (Albany: State University of New York Press, 2004). Richard Kearney, a student of Ricoeur's, is another important contemporary philosopher who has pursued "the religious meaning of atheism"—the project, that is, of returning to "a postreligious theism in the wake of Freud and Nietzsche." See his *Anatheism: Returning to God After God* (New York: Columbia University Press, 2010). What Kearney calls "anatheism" (literally "after-God-ism") is a "wager" on faith in a God of hospitality and love after the death of the egocentric/ethnocentric god of power, protection, and punishment who is denounced by critics from Nietzsche to Dawkins and Dennett.

20. The now canonical *Heart Sutra*, for example, must be understood *both* as a radical critique of a formulaic and reifying understanding of basic Buddhist doctrines *and* as a more radical expression of the core intent of those same doctrines. See *The Heart Sutra*, translation and commentary by Red Pine (Emeryville, CA: Shoemaker & Hoard, 2004); and Donald S. Lopez Jr., *The Heart Sūtra Explained: Indian and Tibetan Commentaries* (Albany: State University of New York Press, 1988).

21. *Zen Sourcebook: Traditional Documents from China, Korea, and Japan*, edited by Stephen Addiss with Stanley Lombardo and Judith Roitman (Indianapolis, IN: Hackett Publishing, 2008), p. 9.

22. See the famous painting by the twelfth-century artist Liang Kai.

23. *Zen Sourcebook*, p. 49.

24. See *Having Once Paused: Poems of Zen Master Ikkyū (1394–1481)*, translated by Sarah Messer and Kidder Smith (Ann Arbor: University of Michigan Press, 2015), pp. 91–119.

25. *The Roaring Stream: A New Zen Reader*, edited by Nelson Foster and Jack Shoemaker (Hopewell, NJ: Ecco Press, 1996), p. 332.

26. Robert Sharf is a sharp and erudite critic, yet unfortunately one whose extensive research and analytical knife are often wielded in a rather polemically one-sided

manner. He professes that a "hermeneutic suspicion" is "the mark of critical scholarship," and that, just as in the case of investigating claims of alien abduction, scholars of religion should "look for other explanations"—especially ideological ones—rather than relying on first-person phenomenological accounts of experience. "In the end," Sharf concludes, "the Buddhist rhetoric of experience is both informed by, and wielded in, the interest of personal and institutional authority." Robert Sharf, "Experience," in *Critical Terms for Religious Studies*, edited by Mark C. Taylor (Chicago: University of Chicago Press, 1998), pp. 107, 111–12; see also Robert Sharf, "Buddhist Modernism and the Rhetoric of Meditative Experience," *Numen* 42, no. 3 (1995): 228–83. Zen practitioners should take such skeptical and reductive critiques seriously—more seriously, at least, than those critiques take their motives, practices, and experiences. There are certainly forces of individual and institutional self-preservation and self-promotion at work in our places of liberatory practice. But surely Zen practice and experience cannot be wholly reduced to the play of such egoistic and ideological forces. For a critical response to Sharf by a scholar who is also a longtime Zen practitioner and priest, see Hori, "Rinzai Kōan Training: Philosophical Intersections," pp. 241–43.

27. Maraldo, *The Saga of Zen History*, pp. 85–87.

28. Yanagida Seizan, *Shoki Zenshū shisho no kenkyū* [Studies in the historical writings of the early Chan school] (Kyoto: Hōzōkan. 1967), pp. 17–18; as quoted in in Maraldo, *The Saga of Zen History*, p. 123. Incidentally, I once attended a talk in Kyoto by Yanagida on D. T. Suzuki, and his combination of warm admiration and careful critique was entirely different in nuance and tone from the harshly dismissive rhetoric of many of Suzuki's Western critics, most of whom nevertheless claim Yanagida as the main inspiration for their scholarship.

29. John R. McRae, "Translator's Introduction," *The Platform Sutra of the Sixth Patriarch* (Berkeley: Numata Center for Buddhist Translation and Research, 2000), pp. xiii–xiv; as quoted in Maraldo, *The Saga of Zen History*, pp. 157–58. In contrast to more singlemindedly dedicated debunkers such as Alan Cole, the approaches of scholars such as McRae and Faure to (hi)stories of the Zen tradition is more nuanced and multifaceted. Nevertheless, writes Maraldo, in general "scholars of Chan have not considered legend a methodological category distinct from myth.... It may be the task of critical historians to discern when legends belie history and when they underlie it. But the audience of legends rarely concerns itself with such judgement.... Legends resist reduction to fiction and devious falsification on the one hand, and strict adherence to factual truth on the other. The legendary quality of premodern Chan writing invites us to read the texts within an epoché, a suspension of judgment about their historical truth or falsity according to our criteria" (*The Saga of Zen History*, pp. 207, 219, 221).

30. Maraldo, *The Saga of Zen History*, p. 293.

31. The Jesuit priest and Zen master Robert Kennedy writes: "For Zen Buddhists, the historical life of the man Gotama [i.e., Siddhartha Gautama] is not of primary importance. If he never lived at all, the self-confidence of accomplished Zen practitioners would not be shaken." He goes on to say that "the Christian experience of the historical Jesus differs," and quotes a theologian who writes: "God has so taken possession

of this one concrete human life that in it and through it (God) acts effectively and definitively for the eternal welfare of the whole human race." Nevertheless, "in spite of this dogmatic difference," Kennedy maintains, "Christians can learn from the Buddhist experience." Robert E. Kennedy, *Zen Spirit, Christian Spirit: The Place of Zen in Christian Life* (New York: Continuum, 1995), pp. 123–24. The modern Japanese Rinzai Zen master Hirata Seikō confirms this difference with Christianity, writing that "for we Zen Buddhists, whether Bodhidharma or Shakyamuni existed or not is irrelevant, since if the experience Bodhidharma spoke of can be truly experienced right now with this five-foot body of mine, that means that Bodhidharma actually exists." Hirata Seikō, *Zen kara no hassō* [Thoughts from Zen] (Kyoto: Zenbunka Kenkyūsho, 1983), pp. 12–13. John Daido Loori Rōshi reportedly said something similar: "If research proves that the Buddha never existed as a historical person, it wouldn't matter. The teachings, tested and practiced for twenty-five centuries, speak for themselves" (quoted in Barbara O'Brian, *The Circle of the Way: A Concise History of Zen from the Buddha to the Modern World* [Boulder, CO: Shambhala, 2019], p. 4).

32. See David L. McMahan, "Repackaging Zen for the West," in *Westward Dharma: Buddhism Beyond Asia*, edited by Charles S. Prebish and Martin Baumann (Berkeley: University of California Press, 2002), pp. 218–29; and McMahan's landmark book on this topic, *The Making of Buddhist Modernism* (New York: Oxford University Press, 2008). McMahan defines "Buddhist modernism" as "forms of Buddhism that have emerged out of an engagement with the dominant cultural and intellectual forces of modernity," and in particular with a Protestant Christian understanding of religion, scientific rationalism, and Romanticism. In its "cross-pollination" with Western modernity, a "new form of Buddhism" has originated as "a cocreation of Asian, Europeans, and Americans" who have carried out a "detraditionalization, demythologization, and psychologization" of the various traditions of Buddhism (*The Making of Buddhist Modernism*, pp. 5–6, 241).

33. The parallels between the interconnected event or field ontology of physics on the one hand and Asian philosophies such as Buddhism and Daoism on the other have often been noted. The pioneer—although problematically syncretistic—treatment is Fritjof Capra, *The Tao of Physics: An Exploration of the Parallels between Modern Physics and Eastern Mysticism*, 4th ed. (Boston: Shambhala, 2000). For a collection of essays on mysticism by the founders of quantum physics themselves, see *Quantum Questions: Mystical Writings of the World's Greatest Physicists*, edited by Ken Wilber (Boston: Shambhala, 2001). While noting intriguing connections, Wilber and the physicists stress, however, that the "objective" approach of science should never be conflated with, or thought of as a substitute for, the "subjective" approach of mystics and phenomenologists of religious experience, even if these may turn out to be in some respects complementary approaches to the same nondual reality. On the relation between neuroscience and Zen, see the many books by James H. Austin, starting with his *Zen and the Brain* (Cambridge, MA: MIT Press, 1998). On various connections made between Buddhism and the cognitive and physical sciences, see *Buddhism and Science: Breaking New Ground*, edited by B. Alan Wallace (New York: Columbia University Press, 2003). For a critical history of the connections drawn between

Buddhism and science, see Donald S. Lopez Jr., *Buddhism and Science: A Guide for the Perplexed* (Chicago: University of Chicago Press, 2008). For a philosophical critique of Buddhist modernism, especially with regard to claims of verification by cognitive science, see Evan Thompson, *Why I Am Not a Buddhist* (New Haven: Yale University Press, 2020).

34. McMahan, *The Making of Buddhist Modernism*, p. 254. See also Jeff Wilson, *Mindful America: The Mutual Transformation of Buddhist Meditation and American Culture* (New York: Oxford University Press, 2014), p. 4.

35. McMahan, *The Making of Buddhist Modernism*, p. 260.

36. Thich Nhat Hanh, *Being Peace* (Berkeley: Parallax Press, 1987), p. 84.

37. Thich Nhat Hanh, *Zen Keys: A Guide to Zen Practice* (New York: Doubleday, 1995), p. 102.

38. See Nishitani Keiji, *Religion and Nothingness*, translated by Jan Van Bragt (Los Angeles: University of California Press, 1982), pp. 139–40, 154–55, 251.

39. Stephen Batchelor, *Buddhism Without Beliefs* (New York: Riverhead Books, 1997); and *Secular Buddhism* (New Haven: Yale University Press, 2017). For an insightful critique of Bachelor's "secular Buddhism," see Wright, *What is Buddhist Enlightenment?*, chapter 3.

40. Robert E. Kennedy, *Zen Spirit, Christian Spirit: The Place of Zen in Christian Life* (New York: Continuum, 1995), p. 14. See the beginning of Chapter 12. For a severe critique of Yamada Kōun's synthetic and streamlined modern Sanbō Kyōdan (now called Sanbō Zen) school, which has been hugely influential in the West yet remains marginal in Japan, see Robert Sharf, "Sanbōkyōdan: Zen and the Way of the New Religions," *Japanese Journal of Religious Studies* 22, nos. 3–4 (1995): 417–58. Although Sharf accuses this school of uprooting Zen from its Buddhist scholastic and monastic moorings, it has spawned not only important figures of interfaith dialogue and "diapraxis" such as Robert Kennedy and Rubin Habito but also seminal American Zen masters such as Robert Aitken and insightful Zen teachers, Buddhist philosophers, and social critics such as David Loy.

41. See Daisetz Teitaro Suzuki, *Mysticism Christian and Buddhist* (New York: Dover, 2002). For Ueda Shizuteru's understanding of the proximity between Eckhart and Zen, see Chapter 13.

42. D. T. Suzuki, *Essays in Zen Buddhism, First Series* (New York: Grove, 1961), p. 268.

43. In *Nostra Aetate*, the Second Vatican Council's "Declaration on the Relation of the Church with Non-Christian Religions," passed in 1965, we read: "The Catholic Church rejects nothing that is true and holy in these [other] religions. She regards with sincere reverence those ways of conduct and of life, those precepts and teachings which, though differing in many aspects from the ones she holds and sets forth, nonetheless often reflect a ray of that Truth which enlightens all men. Indeed, she proclaims, and ever must proclaim Christ 'the way, the truth, and the life' (John 14:6), in whom men may find the fullness of religious life, in whom God has reconciled all things to Himself." See also *Dominus Iesus*, signed in 2000 by Cardinal Joseph Ratzinger (who later became Pope Benedict XVI) when he was the Prefect of the Congregation for the Doctrine of the Faith (the institution in charge of defending

the faith, formerly known as the Inquisition), in which is written: "If it is true that the followers of other religions can receive divine grace, it is also certain that *objectively speaking* they are in a gravely deficient situation in comparison with those who, in the Church, have the fullness of the means of salvation."

44. See Catherine Cornille, *The Im-Possibility of Interreligious Dialogue* (New York: Crossroad, 2008), pp. 191–93. Working self-consciously and self-critically from a Christian standpoint, Cornille provides a thoughtful reflection on the difficult, yet not impossible, requirements for opening up religions to a genuine and mutually enriching interreligious dialogue.

45. Suzuki, *Essays in Zen Buddhism, First Series*, p. 268. For trenchant critiques of Suzuki as ostensibly peddling a nationalistic "reverse Orientalism," see Faure, *Chan Insights and Oversights*, chapter 2; and Robert H. Sharf, "Whose Zen? Zen Nationalism Revisited," in *Rude Awakenings: Zen, The Kyoto School, and the Question of Nationalism*, edited by James W. Heisig and John C. Maraldo (Honolulu: University of Hawai'i Press, 1994), pp. 40–51. For a more measured critique of Suzuki's modernist interpretation of Zen, see McMahan, *Buddhist Modernism*, pp. 122–34. For an excellent, sympathetic, yet balanced presentation of Suzuki's long and prolific career of introducing Zen to the West and the wider world, see Richard M. Jaffe's introduction to D. T. Suzuki, *Selected Works of D. T. Suzuki, Volume I: Zen* (Oakland: University of California Press, 2015), pp. xi–lvi. For a summary account of the seminal debate between Suzuki and the Chinese scholar Hu Shi, in which Hu insisted "on the study of Chan's history for understanding the seemingly irrational teachings of Chan, in contrast to Suzuki's insistence on their transhistorical meaning and truth," see Maraldo, *The Saga of Zen History and the Power of Legend*, pp. 103–13.

46. John B. Cobb Jr., *Beyond Dialogue: Toward a Mutual Transformation of Christianity and Buddhism* (Eugene, OR: Wipf and Stock, 1982). Other noteworthy Christian approaches to mutually transformative interreligious dialogue with Buddhism include the following: William Johnston, *The Still Point: Reflections on Zen and Christian Mysticism* (New York: Fordham University Press, 1982); Raimundo Panikkar, *The Silence of God: The Answer of the Buddha* (Maryknoll, NY: Orbis Books, 1989); Joseph S. O'Leary, *Religious Pluralism and Christian Truth* (Eugene, OR: Wipf and Stock, 1996); James W. Heisig, *Dialogues at One Inch Above the Ground: Reclamations of Belief in an Interreligious Age* (New York: Crossroad, 2003); and Paul F. Knitter, *Without Buddha I Could Not Be a Christian* (London: Oneworld Publications, 2009). From the Buddhist side, see Masao Abe, *Buddhism and Interfaith Dialogue*, edited by Steven Heine (Honolulu: University of Hawai'i Press); Eiko Hanaoka, *Zen and Christianity: From the Standpoint of Absolute Nothingness* (Kyoto: Maruzen, 2009); and Thich Nhat Hanh, *Going Home: Jesus and Buddha as Brothers* (New York: Riverhead Books, 1999). See also Chapters 7–15, 21, and 23 in the present book. A very informative account of the history of Buddhist-Christian relations is available in German: Michael Von Brück and Whalen Lai, *Buddhismus und Christentum: Geschichte, Konfrontation, Dialog*, 2nd ed. (Munich: Beck, 2000).

47. I would go so far as to say that a dialogical encounter with another religious tradition is not wholly sincere and fully engaged unless one is open to at least the

possibility of being converted to it. Defensive apologetics and eristic debate are insufficiently self-critical and truth-oriented to allow for a truly open-minded interreligious dialogue. I agree with Raimon Panikkar that "if *interreligious* dialogue is to be real dialogue, an *intrareligious* dialogue [i.e., an inner dialogue within myself] must accompany it; that is, it must begin with my questioning myself and the *relativity* of my beliefs (which does not mean their *relativism*), accepting the challenge of a change, a conversion, and at the risk of upsetting my traditional patterns" (Raimon Panikkar, *The Intrareligious Dialogue* [New York: Paulist Press, 1999], p. 74). However, as Catherine Cornille points out, to set as a condition an openness to the possibility of conversion would be overly demanding for most would-be participants in interreligious dialogue (*The Im-Possibility of Interreligious Dialogue*, pp. 89–90). Furthermore, Cornille stresses the need for commitment to one's own religious tradition as well as "doctrinal humility" and empathetic openness to learning new truths from other religious traditions that can enrich the ongoing development of one's own. She compellingly argues that it is necessary to find and maintain a "proper balance between openness and commitment" in order to participate in interreligious dialogue. Yet, there is disagreement over where this proper balance lies. Panikkar and Paul Knitter, for example, lean further in the direction of openness and even "multiple religious belonging" than Cornille's relatively more conservative approach allows for (see Cornille's excellent anthology on this topic, *Many Mansions: Multiple Religious Belonging and Christian Identity*, edited by Catherine Cornille [Eugene, OR: Wipf and Stock, 2002]). Moreover, there are various degrees and kinds of engagement in, and commitment to, various aspects of a religious tradition (its doctrines, rituals, community, etc.), not to mention a wide range of hermeneutical stances that can be taken toward its teachings. There is an entire spectrum of stances between exclusive identification with a single tradition on the one hand and eclectic New Age syncretism on the other. Some of these in-between stances can be called "multiple religious belonging," but others may be more synthetic and even end up producing new religious traditions such as Bahá'í. A genuinely pluralistic interreligious dialogue needs to take into account not just the plurality of religions and religious identities, but also the plurality of ways of being involved in one or more religious tradition.

Chapter 2

1. Ueda Shizuteru, *Watashi to wa nanika* (Tokyo: Iwanami, 2000); Shizuteru Ueda, *Wer und was bin ich: Zur Phänomenologie des Selbst im Zen-Buddhismus* (Freiburg: Verlag Karl Alber, 2011).
2. *Zenshū nikka seiten* [Daily scriptures of the Zen School] (Kyoto: Baiyō Shoin, 1998), p. 78.
3. *Daodejing*, chapter 33, in *Readings in Classical Chinese Philosophy*, 2nd ed., edited by Philip J. Ivanhoe and Bryan W. Van Norden (Indianapolis, IN: Hackett, 2005), p. 179.

For a pithy deep dive into the Daoist background of Zen, see David Hinton, *China Root: Taoism, Ch'an, and Original Zen* (Boston: Shambhala, 2020). Although Hinton unfortunately goes overboard in his contentious claims that Chan is "anti-Buddhist" and that Japanese (and by extension American) Zen completely lost touch with the decisively Daoist foundations of Chan, his linguistic and conceptual interpretations of the significant Daoist portion of the roots of this fruitfully hybrid tradition are nevertheless engaging and often illuminating.

4. *The Essential Vedanta*, edited by Eliot Deutsch and Rohit Dalvi (Bloomington, IN: World Wisdom, 2004), p. 166.

5. Martin Luther King Jr., *The Radical King*, edited and introduced by Cornel West (Boston: Beacon Press, 2015), p. 26.

6. Mahatma Gandhi, *The Essential Gandhi: An Anthology of His Writings on His Life, Work, and Ideas*, edited by Louis Fischer (New York: Vintage, 2002), p. 275.

7. Benjamin Franklin, *Autobiography: Poor Richard Letters* (New York: D. Appleton, 1904), p. 195.

8. Ralf Waldo Emerson, "Gnothi Seauton," https://archive.vcu.edu/english/engweb/ transcendentalism/authors/emerson/poems/gnothi.html.

9. 1 Corinthians 3:16. Throughout this book translations of passages from the Bible are mostly taken from the New Revised Standard Version, sometimes amended in light of other translations, such as the International Standard Version.

10. Saint Augustine, *The Confessions*, translated by Maria Boulding, edited by John Rotelle (Hyde Park, NY: New City Press, 1997), book VI, 1, p. 134. Granted, theological versions of the quest to "know thyself" may stress the ability of God to know us better than we can know ourselves. One finds this expressed in Psalm 139: "You have searched me, Lord, and you know me. . . . Such knowledge is too wonderful for me, too lofty for me to attain."

11. William C. Chittick, *The Sufi Path of Knowledge: Ibn al-Arabi's Metaphysics of Imagination* (Albany: State University of New York Press, 2010), p. 345. The great twelfth-/thirteenth-century Sufi philosopher Ibn al-Arabi elaborates: "When you enter into His Paradise you enter into yourself. Then you will know yourself with a gnosis other than that by which you knew your Lord by knowing yourself. Thus, you will be possessed of two kinds of gnosis, first knowing Him as knowing yourself, second, knowing Him through you as Him, not as you." Ibn Arabi, *The Bezels of Wisdom*, translated by R. W. J. Austin (New York: Paulist Press, 1980), p. 108.

12. Plato, *Phaedrus*, 229e–230a, in *Euthyphro, Apology, Crito, Phaedo, Phaedrus*, translated by Harold North Fowler (Cambridge, MA: Harvard University Press, 1914), pp. 421–23.

13. See Plato's *Apology*, 20–21.

14. *Daodejing*, chapter 71, in *Readings in Classical Chinese Philosophy*, p. 198.

15. *Daodejing*, chapter 48, my translation.

16. In fact, Kasulis has recently retold the story in print in the first person. He also specified that the Zen master was Kobori Nanrei Rōshi of Ryōkōin, a subtemple of Daitokuji in Kyoto. See Thomas P. Kasulis, *Engaging Japanese Philosophy* (Honolulu: University of Hawaiʻi Press, 2018), p. 574.

17. Thomas Kasulis, *Zen Action/Zen Person* (Honolulu: University of Hawai'i Press, 1981), p. ix.

18. In case you are curious, although I don't know what became of the motorcycle, my hair was spotted by my aunt Susan being woven into a woman's locks a couple of weeks later on a local Houston television show. "Can you believe this hair came from a guy in Galveston!" the hairdresser reportedly said.

19. Faith does play an important role in Buddhism, including in Zen: faith as preliminary trust and ultimately faith as true self-confidence. See Chapters 3, 6, 12, 21.

20. See Plato's *Symposium*, 174d–175b.

21. See Plato's *Phaedo*, 63e–668c. See Plato's *Symposium* for Socrates's account of how the philosopher should ascend a path from a physical love of beautiful bodies to a metaphysical love of the disembodied Form of Beauty.

22. See Nishitani Keiji, "The Standpoint of Zen," translated by John C. Maraldo, *The Eastern Buddhist* 17, no. 1 (1984): 1–26. The first half of this remarkable essay explains Zen's "investigation into the self" by way of comparing and contrasting it with Socrates's quest to "know thyself," and compares and contrasts Zen's "great doubt" with Descartes's method of doubt. The second half examines the "direct pointing at the mind" to which Zen's self-investigation leads.

23. For more on this issue, see the Preface, the end of Chapter 17, and Chapter 21.

24. Cage wrote: "What I do, I do not wish blamed on Zen, though without my engagement with Zen . . . I doubt whether I would have done what I have done." John Cage: *Silence* (Middletown, CT: Wesleyan University Press, 1961), p. xi.

25. <IBT>Shohaku Okumura, *Realizing Genjokoan: The Key to Dogen's Shobogenzo* (Somerville, MA: Wisdom Publications, 2010)</IBT>, p. 49.

26. Ibid., p. 65.

27. On Zen's perspectivism, see the articles cited in note 4 of the Preface.

28. *Zhuangzi: The Essential Writings*, translated by Brook Ziporyn (Indianapolis, IN: Hackett, 2009), pp. 26–27, 49. On the formative role of meditative practices in the Daoist tradition, see Harold D. Roth, *Contemplative Foundations of Classical Daoism* (Albany: State University of New York Press, 2021).

29. Kosho Uchiyama, *Opening the Hand of Thought: Foundations of Zen Buddhist Practice*, translated and edited by Tom Wright, Jisho Warner, and Shohaku Okumura (Somerville, MA: Wisdom Publications, 2004), p. 50.

30. "The Presencing of Truth: Dōgen's *Genjōkōan*," translated by Bret W. Davis, in *Buddhist Philosophy: Essential Readings*, edited by Jay Garfield and William Edelglass (Oxford: Oxford University Press, 2009), pp. 256–57, translation slightly modified.

31. Dōgen is said to have attained enlightenment upon hearing his teacher, Rujing, admonish a sleeping monk with this phrase: "To practice Zen is to drop off the body-mind!" Rujing reportedly meant by this that "when practicing singleminded intense sitting, the five desires will depart and the five defilements will be removed." The five desires are for "wealth, sex, food and drink, fame, and sleep." The five defilements are "craving, anger, sleep, regret, and doubt." Rujing is apparently drawing on a text by the great second-/third-century Buddhist philosopher Nagarjuna in this understanding of meditation. See Takashi James Kodera, *Dogen's Formative Years in China: An*

Historical and Annotated Translation of the Hōkyō-ki (Boulder, CO: Prajna Press, 1980), pp. 124, 180n43. Dōgen's own understanding of and use of the phrase "dropping off the body-mind" goes beyond this sense of shedding defilements to indicate a liberating letting go of all attachments to a reified misconception of our physical and psychological selves as dualistically cut off from the other people and things that we, in truth, intimately coexist with.

32. Dōgen, *Treasury of the True Dharma Eye: Zen Master Dogen's Shobo Genzo*, edited by Kazuaki Tanahashi (Boston: Shambhala, 2012), p. 475. Compare this with the quote from Martin Luther King Jr. in the final note of Chapter 14.

33. Ibid., p. 881.

34. Ibid., p. 476.

Chapter 3

1. Dōgen, *The Heart of Dōgen's Shōbōgenzō*, translated by Norman Waddell and Masao Abe (Albany: SUNY Press, 2002), p. 11, translation modified.

2. *Hōkyōki*, in Takashi James Kodera, *Dogen's Formative Years in China: An Historical and Annotated Translation of the Hōkyō-ki* (Boulder, CO: Prajna Press, 1980), p. 124.

3. See T. Griffith Foulk, "'Just Sitting'? Dōgen's Take on Zazen, Sutra Reading, and Other Conventional Buddhist Practices," in *Dōgen: Textual and Historical Studies*, edited by Steven Heine (New York: Oxford University Press, 2012), pp. 75–106.

4. My translation. Compare *Zen Sourcebook: Traditional Documents from China, Korea, and Japan*, edited by Stephen Addiss with Stanley Lombardo and Judith Roitman (Indianapolis IN: Hackett, 2008), p. 10. Scholars have pointed out that this saying, as with much of the lore of early Zen, was retroactively formulated in the Song dynasty, first appearing in print in the eleventh-century transmission of the lamp texts. See Steven Heine, *Zen Skin, Zen Marrow: Will the Real Zen Buddhism Please Stand Up?* (New York: Oxford University Press, 2008), pp. 39–40.

5. See Rupert Gethin, *The Foundations of Buddhism* (New York: Oxford University Press, 1998), p. 36; and David V. Fiordalis, "Learning, Reasoning, Cultivating: The Practice of Wisdom and the *Treasury of Abhidharma*," in *Buddhist Spiritual Practices: Thinking with Pierre Hadot on Buddhism, Philosophy, and the Path*, edited by David V. Fiordalis (Berkeley, CA: Mangalam Press, 2018), pp. 245–89. Pierre Hadot has shown how "spiritual exercises" were central to the holistic "philosophy as a way of life" practiced by ancient Greek and Roman philosophers, in contrast to the more limited textual and intellectual practices of modern academic philosophers. See Pierre Hadot, *Philosophy as a Way of Life: Spiritual Exercises from Socrates to Foucault*, edited by Arnold I. Davidson, translated by Michael Chase (Oxford: Blackwell, 1995). For comparisons with Buddhism and with the Zen-practicing philosophers of the Kyoto School, see Bret W. Davis, "Buddhist Philosophy as a Holistic Way of Life: Studying the Way with Body and Mind (*Shinjin Gakudō*)," in *Key Concepts in World Philosophies*, edited by Sarah Flavel and Chiara Robianno (New York: Bloomsbury Academic, 2022); and Bret

W. Davis, "Commuting Between Zen and Philosophy: In the Footsteps of Kyoto School Philosophers and Psychosomatic Practitioners," in *Transitions: Crossing Boundaries in Japanese Philosophy*, edited by Francesca Greco, Leon Krings, and Yukiko Kuwayama (Nagoya: Chisokudō Publications, 2021), pp. 71–111.

6. Sarah Shaw points out that, even though they are sometimes downplayed in the Theravada tradition and especially in modernized forms of Vipassana and mindfulness methods of meditation, practices aimed at calming the mind (P. *samatha*), practices which lead to rarified states of meditative absorption (P. *jhana*; Sk. *dhyana*—the word from which Ch. *chan* and Jp. *zen* derived), play a central role in the Buddha's instructions for meditation in the Pali Canon. We should bear in mind, after all, that what she calls the "ancient pairing" of mindfulness (P. *sati*) and concentration (P. *samadhi*) appears as the seventh and eighth limbs of the Eightfold Path. See Sarah Shaw, *Mindfulness: Where It Comes from and What It Means* (Boulder, CO: Shambhala, 2020), esp. chapters 6 and 15. Be that as it may, the Theravada Buddhist tradition maintains that concentration is a step on the way to the ultimately liberating practices of insight. The classical text in this regard is the fifth-century Buddhaghosa's *The Path of Purification (Visuddhimagga)*, translated by Bhikkhu Ñāṇamoli (Onalaska, WA: BPS Pariyatti Editions, 1991). This text explains the path of Buddhism as beginning with "purification of virtue," then proceeding to "purification of consciousness" by means of practices of "concentration" (P. *samadhi*), and culminating in a "purification by knowledge." This final purification issues in "understanding" (P. *panna*) or "insight" (P. *vipassana*), which, according to Buddhaghosa and the Theravada tradition, alone opens the door to Nirvana. While the Pali Canon provides the source materials for this conception of the path as reportedly taught by the Buddha, scholar of early Buddhism Richard Gombrich has compellingly argued that this doctrine, which subordinats meditative concentration to intellectural insight, is a product of editing and commentary on the part of early Theravada scholastics rather than a view that can be unequivocally attributed to the Buddha himself. In fact, a number of early sutras suggest either that concentration and insight must be practiced in tandem or that enlightenment and Nirvana may be attained by either path. "Retracing an Ancient Debate: How Insight Worsted Concentration in the Pali Canon," in Richard F. Gombrich, *How Buddhism Began: The Conditioned Genesis of the Early Teachings*, 2nd ed. (New York: Routledge, 2006), chapter 4.

7. *The Platform Sutra: The Zen Teachings of Hui-neng*, translated by Red Pine (Emeryville, CA: Shoemaker & Hoard, 2006), p. 10.

8. *Samyutta Nikāya* 45:8, in *In the Buddha's Words: An Anthology of Discourses from the Pāli Canon*, edited by Bhikkhu Bodhi (Somerville, MA: Wisdom Publications, 2005), p. 239.

9. Kosho Uchiyama, *Opening the Hand of Thought: Foundations of Zen Buddhist Practice*, translated and edited by Tom Wright, Jisho Warner, and Shohaku Okumura (Somerville, MA: Wisdom Publications, 2004), p. 50.

10. Ibid., pp. 59–60.

11. Dōgen, *Fukanzazengi* (Universally Recommended Instructions for Zazen), translated by Carl Bielefeldt and T. Griffin Foulk, with the Rev. Taigen Leighton and the

Rev. Shohaku Okumura, reprinted in *Engaging Dōgen's Zen: The Philosophy of Practice as Awakening*, edited by Tetsuzen Jason M. Wirth, Shūdō Brian Schroeder, and Kanpū Bret W. Davis (Somerville, MA: Wisdom Publications), pp. 195–96.

12. In case these newcomers wish to practice Zen meditation as Christians, I tell them that the great fourteenth-century Christian mystic Meister Eckhart taught that "God is not found in the soul by adding anything but by a process of subtraction," and that "if God is to make anything in you or with you, you must beforehand have become nothing" (Meister Eckhart, *Selected Treatises and Sermons*, edited and translated by James M. Clark and John V. Skinner [New York: Harper & Brothers, 1958], pp. 54, 194). On Eckhart and Zen, see Chapter 13.

13. *Zhuangzi: The Essential Writings*, translated by Brook Ziporyn (Indianapolis, IN: Hackett, 2009), pp. 8, 30–32, 112. See also Bret W. Davis, "Heidegger and Daoism: A Dialogue on the Useless Way of Unnecessary Being," in *Daoist Encounters with Phenomenology*, edited by David Chai (New York: Bloomsbury Academic, 2019), pp. 161–96.

14. See Nishitani Keiji, *Nishitani Keiji chosakushū* [Collected works of Nishitani Keiji] (Tokyo: Sōbunsha, 1986–95), vol. 18, p. 19.

15. *Zen no goroku* [The Written Records of Zen], vol. 16, edited by Kajitani Sōnin, Yanagida Seizan, and Tsujimura Kōichi (Tokyo: Chikuma Shobō, 1974), p. 147. The author of this text is unknown, but Yanagida surmises that it was written by Yuantong Faxiu, an eleventh-century Chinese Zen master in the lineage of Yunmen (ibid., p. 232).

16. See the webpage of the Umass Memorial Health Center for Mindfulness, https://www.umassmemorialhealthcare.org/umass-memorial-center-mindfulness; and Jon Kabat-Zinn, *Full Catastrophe Living: Using the Wisdom of Your Body and Mind to Face Stress, Pain, and Illness*, rev. ed. (New York: Bantam, 2013).

17. Evan Thompson, *Why I Am Not a Buddhist* (New Haven, CT: Yale University Press, 2020), pp. 118–39. Thompson criticizes especially the scientific claims of proponents of modern mindfulness.

18. See Ronald Purser and David Loy, "Beyond McMindfulness," *Huffington Post*, last updated August 31, 2013, https://www.huffpost.com/entry/beyond-mcmindfulnes s_b_3519289; Ronald E. Purser, *McMindfulness: How Mindfulness Became the New Capitalist Spirituality* (London: Repeater, 2019); and Robert Meikyo Rosenbaum and Barry Magid, eds., *What's Wrong with Mindfulness (and What Isn't): Zen Perspectives* (Somerville, MA: Wisdom Publications, 2016). For an excellent historical account of the mindfulness movement in America since the 1970s, see Jeff Wilson, *Mindful America: The Mutual Transformation of Buddhist Meditation and American Culture* (New York: Oxford University Press, 2014). In her book *Mind Cure: How Meditation Became Medicine* (New York: Oxford University Press, 2019), Sōtō Zen Buddhist priest and scholar Wakoh Shannon Hickey reveals how this recent mindfulness movement can in fact be traced back to the use of meditation in the "individualistic strand" of the Mind Cure or New Thought movement in the United States at the end of the nineteenth century and the beginning of the twentieth. Hickey points out that the earlier "community-oriented strand" of this movement—which consisted of groups

often led by either white women or African American men—had incorporated elements of Buddhist and Hindu practices of meditation into their overall projects of social-political as well as personal liberation. However, "as meditation became increasingly medicalized, individualized, and commodified, the social concerns of the early New Thought and Emmanuel Movement churches fell by the wayside" (p. 102). "In the journey from Mind Cure to Mindfulness, as meditation became medicalized, individualized, and commodified, at least three important things got lost along the way: the ethical frameworks in which the disciplines of meditation and yoga historically have been embedded, the benefits and challenges of long-term spiritual community, and systemic analysis of suffering" (p. 187).

19. Wilson points out that what Japanese Buddhists call "*genze riyaku*, meaning this-worldly or practical benefits," have always been a part of the Buddhist tradition. In particular, this form of "expedient means" has allowed Buddhism to be adopted into new cultures. What is novel about the modern Western adoption of Buddhism is not that it promises practical benefits but that it promotes the practical benefits of meditation (mindfulness) rather than of receiving blessings, purchasing amulets, and so on (*Mindful America*, pp. 4–6, 105–9). Teachings of how to attain "the welfare and happiness visible in this present life" (P. *dittha-dhamma-hitasukha*) are as old as Buddhism itself (see *In the Buddha's Words: An Anthology of Discourses from the Pāli Canon*, edited by Bhikkhu Bodhi [Somerville, MA: Wisdom Publications, 2005], chapter IV), yet these typically invoked virtuous speech, action, and livelihood rather than the more advanced mental disciplines of mindfulness and concentration. As the spiritual practice of meditation is brought out of the monastery and into the marketplace, the question is whether it will be reduced to its practical benefits or whether those practical benefits will serve as a step on the path toward a more serious ethical and spiritual practice.

20. On adapting mindfulness practices so that they are suitable to people dealing with trauma, see David A. Treleaven, *Trauma-Sensitive Mindfulness* (New York: W. W. Norton & Company, 2018). Intensive practices of meditative concentration would seem to be especially dangerous for persons prone to psychosis. The Japanese psychiatrist Kimura Bin suggests that mental health requires maintaining a dynamic balance between individuated existence and staying in touch with the pre-individuated field of the interconnected natural processes from out of which our sense of individual identity arises. While the schizophrenic is unable to first achieve a stable sense of individuated existence, the Zen practitioner, on the other side of this achievement, seeks to shed an overly reified and dualistic sense of independence and fixed identity in order to get back in touch with an aboriginal field of naturalness, freedom, creativity, and compassionate interconnectivity (see Kimura Bin, "Self and Nature – An Interpretation of Schizophrenia." *Zen Buddhism Today* 6 [1988]: 1–10). While the Buddhist teachings of no-self and impermanence, together with meditative practices of dissolving a fixation on a fictitiously independent and permanent ego, can be experienced as spiritually liberating by persons who have already achieved a stable self-identity and sense of self-worth and agency, they would likely exacerbate the suffering of a schizophrenic. While psychotherapists have indeed successfully applied

meditation techniques in treating patients dealing with a wide range of mental health issues, including addiction, anxiety, and depression (see *Mindfulness and Psychotherapy*, 2nd ed., edited by Christopher K. Germer, Ronald D. Siegel, and Paul R. Fulton [New York: The Guilford Press, 2013]), mental health care professionals still disagree on whether most cases of negative psychological experiences triggered by practices of meditation—often, but not only, by insufficiently prepared newcomers who plunge into an intense period of practice—can be accounted for as manifestations of underlying mental health issues. See David Kortava, "Lost in Thought: The Psychological Risks of Meditation," *Harpers Magazine* (April 2021). In any case, meditation teachers and centers should be aware of potential adverse side-effects and prepared to respond to them appropriately, which often entails encouraging participants to seek medical attention and/or psychological counseling rather than to "just keep sitting through it." Willoughby Britton, assistant professor of psychiatry and human behavior at Brown University, has created Cheetah House, a non-profit organization for addressing adverse psychological experiences with meditation (https://www.cheetahhouse.org/about). Brown University's Contemplative Studies Initiative (https://www.brown.edu/academics/contemplative-studies/), founded by scholar of Daoism and Rinzai Zen priest Harold Roth, has pioneered the pedagogical incorporation of meditative practices into higher education. And since the Mindfulness Center at Brown (https://www.brown.edu/public-health/mindfulness/) is now a leading institution for research on and training in mindfulness programs such as MBSR (Mindfulness Based Stress Reduction), we can expect Brown University to serve as a hub for researchers and practitioners to carry out a much needed interdisciplinary dialogue on the provenances, purposes, methods, and effects of various meditative disciplines. Another key organization for this exciting and exigent dialogue is the recently founded International Society for Contemplative Research (ISCR).

21. Sarah Shaw writes that in traditional Buddhist practices mindfulness "may not be judgmental, but it does exercise discrimination"—or we might say discernment or what Aristotle called practical wisdom (Gk. *phronesis*)—insofar as it "brings an intuitive ethical sense of the rightness of a particular action in a particular moment and in a particular situation" (*Mindfulness: Where It Comes from and What It Means*, pp. 181, 89). John D. Dunne provides a non-partisan comparison of "classical, nondual, and contemporary" practices of mindfulness in "Buddhist Styles of Mindfulness: A Heuristic Approach," in *Handbook of Mindfulness and Self-Regulation*, edited by Brian D. Ostafin (New York: Springer, 2015), pp. 251–70. For a more in-depth treatment of nondual practices of meditation, such as Tibetan Mahamudra, see also John D. Dunne, "Toward an Understanding of Non-Dual Mindfulness," *Contemporary Buddhism* 12 (2011): 77–88. Kagyu Mahamudra and its Nyingma cousin Dzogchen are the Tibetan Buddhist practices of meditation that most closely resemble Zen meditation. For a remarkably clear explication of Mahamudra, see Traleg Kyabgon, *Mind at Ease: Self-Liberation Through Mahamudra Meditation* (Boulder, CO: Shambhala, 2004). For an excellent collection of traditional and modern writings on Dzogchen, see *The Dzogchen Primer: Embracing the Spiritual Path According to the Great Perfection,*

edited by Marcia Binder Schmidt (Boston: Shambhala, 2002). For a contemporary philosophical analysis of a seminal eighth-century debate in Tibet between a Chinese Zen monk, Heshang Moheyan, and an Indian Buddhist scholar, Kamalaśīla, in which the latter severely censures the former's teaching of a non-discursive and nondualistic practice of meditation and promotes instead discursive forms of meditation understood as extensions of doctrinal study and rational intellection, see Tom J. E. Tillemans, "Yogic Perception, Meditation, and Enlightenment: The Epistemological Issues in a Key Debate," in *A Companion to Buddhist Philosophy*, edited by Steven M. Emmanuel (West Sussex: Wiley-Blackwell, 2013), pp. 290–306. Tillemans mainly follows the partisan mainstream Tibetan account of the debate, told from the reportedly victorious side of Kamalaśīla, but he ends by discussing a fourteenth-century Tibetan Dzogchen teacher's critique of the limits of the "dualistic mind" and its "dichotomizing thought," and his advocacy instead of a nondualistic "primordial gnosis," which strikingly resemble the teachings of the Chinese Zen monk that have been deemed heretical in Tibetan Buddhism since the notorious debate in the eighth century.

22. Purser, *McMindfulness*. Despite the fact that he has not undertaken a serious study (much less practice!) of Buddhism, Slavoj Žižek's psychoanalytic and Neo-Marxist critique of "Western Buddhism" as serving as a contemporary "opium of the people" that enables people to cope with, and thus in effect remain complicit in, exploitative capitalist systems should be taken seriously. See Slavoj Žižek, *On Belief* (New York: Routledge, 2001), pp. 12–13. For an explication of and response to Žižek's critique and misunderstandings of Buddhism more generally, see Eske Møllgaard, "Slavoj Žižek's Critique of Western Buddhism," *Contemporary Buddhism* 9, no. 2 (2008): 167–80.

23. The classical text of Vipassana meditation is *Satipatthana Sutta* 1:55–63, in *In the Buddha's Words: An Anthology of Discourses from the Pāli Canon*, edited and introduced by Bhikkhu Bodhi (Somerville, MA: Wisdom Publications, 2005), pp. 281–90. For a modern commentary, see Joseph Goldstein, *Mindfulness: A Practical Guide to Awakening* (Boulder, CO: Sounds True, 2013).

24. See Robert Sharf, "Mindfulness and Mindlessness in Early Chan," *Philosophy East and West* 64 (2014): 933–64, at 941–45. An early and very influential book in this vein is Nyanaponika Thera, *The Heart of Buddhist Meditation: A Handbook of Mental Training Based on the Buddha's Way of Mindfulness* (New York: Samuel Weiser, 1973), first published in 1953. A more recent and widely read introduction is Bhante Henepola Gunaratana, *Mindfulness in Plain English* (Somerville, MA: Wisdom Publications, 2015). Lucid and informative accounts of the history of mindfulness in the context of various meditative practices in the Buddhist traditions can be found in Sarah Shaw's *Introduction to Buddhist Meditation* (New York: Routledge, 2009) and *Mindfulness: Where It Comes from and What It Means*. Chapter 15 of the latter provides a very concise account and judicious evaluation of modern Theravada and secular methods of mindfulness.

25. See Dunne, "Buddhist Styles of Mindfulness."

26. Sharf, "Mindfulness and Mindlessness in Early Chan," pp. 945–50.

27. *Zhuangzi: The Essential Writings*, p. 12. See Bret W. Davis, "Knowing Limits: Toward a Versatile Perspectivism with Nietzsche, Heidegger, Zhuangzi and Zen," *Research in Phenomenology* 49 (2019): 301–34.

28. *The Record of Linji*, translated by Ruth Fuller Sasaki, edited by Thomas Yūhō Kirchner (Honolulu: University of Hawai'i Press, 2009), p. 155, translation modified.

29. Ibid., p. 186.

30. See Bret W. Davis, "Zen's Nonegocentric Perspectivism," in *Buddhist Philosophy: A Comparative Approach*, edited by Steven M. Emmanuel (West Sussex: Wiley-Blackwell, 2018), pp. 130–31.

Chapter 4

1. For an excellent collection of cross-cultural investigations into the conceptual and practical importance of the breath, see *Atmospheres of Breathing*, edited by Leon Škof and Petri Berndston (Albany: State University of New York Press, 2018).

2. *The Roaring Stream: A New Zen Reader*, edited by Nelson Foster and Jack Shoemaker (Hopewell, NJ: Ecco Press, 1996), p. 301.

3. Shunryu Suzuki, *Zen Mind, Beginners Mind* (New York: Weatherhill, 1970), p. 36.

4. Ibid., p. 32.

5. Ibid., p. 35.

6. Ibid., pp. 34, 128.

7. *The Roaring Stream*, p. 302.

8. My translation. See *The Platform Sutra: The Zen Teachings of Hui-neng*, translated by Red Pine (Emeryville, CA: Shoemaker & Hoard, 2006), p. 6; *The Platform Sūtra of the Sixth Patriarch*, translated by Philip B. Yampolsky (New York: Columbia University Press, 1967), p. 130. It should be kept in mind that the *Platform Sutra* was composed from the perspective of the Southern School successors of Huineng, and in critique of Shenxiu and his rival Northern School. For an excellent collection of essays on the complicated composition and seminal content of this text, see *Readings of the Platform Sutra*, edited by Morten Schütter and Stephen F. Teiser (New York: Columbia University Press, 2012).

9. *The Platform Sutra*, Pine's translation, p. 7.

10. My translation. Compare Pine's translation, p. 8, and Yampolsky's translation, p. 132.

11. In a later version of the text that became the standard in the tradition, the third line of Huineng's verse is changed to the famous phrase "Originally there is not a single thing." This teaching of emptiness implies that even the remnant of a duality between a pure and unchanging mirror and impure and changing images needs to be let go of. Even the empty mirror needs to be emptied out into the world. As the eminent Zen scholar Yanagida Seizan explains, after Huineng the teaching of the mirror-mind increasingly gave way to the teaching that the mind—or rather the "no-mind," as will be discussed in Chapter 17—is inseparable from the things and events of the world (*Zen shisō* [Zen thought] [Tokyo: Chūkō Shinshō, 1975], pp. 81–106). In the

comments appended to Case 40 of *The Blue Cliff Record*, Xuedou is quoted as saying, "Mountains and rivers do not exist within the vision of a mirror." Yuanwu adds the comment: "Don't view mountains and rivers . . . with a mirror. To do so produces a dualism. It's just that mountains are mountains, waters are waters, each dharma abides in its dharma position, and the features of the mundane world constantly abide as they are." My translation. Compare *The Blue Cliff Record*, translated by Thomas Cleary and J. C. Cleary (Boston: Shambhala, 1992), p. 248.

12. *The Diamond Sutra*, chapter 14, my translation from the Chinese. See Yampolsky's translation of the *Platform Sutra*, p. 133n41; and Pine's translation of the *Platform Sutra*, p. 111.

13. *The Platform Sutra*, translated by Pine, p. 11, translation modified. Compare Yampolsky's translation, p. 136.

14. Here are some suggestions for further reading on the theory and practice of Zen meditation: Two very accessible step-by-step instructions are John Daishin Buksbazen, *Zen Meditation in Plain English* (Somerville, MA: Wisdom Publications, 2002); and John Daido Loori, *Finding the Still Point: A Beginner's Guide to Zen Meditation* (Boston: Shambhala, 2007). Also recommended is Robert Aitken, *Taking the Path of Zen* (San Francisco: North Point Press, 1982). For a lucid translation of eight classical texts on meditation from the Zen tradition, see Thomas Cleary, *Minding Mind: A Course in Basic Meditation* (Boston: Shambhala, 2009). For a landmark collection of essays on the basics of Zen practice by leading teachers in the transmission of Sōtō and Rinzai Zen to America, see *On Zen Practice: Body, Breath, Mind*, edited by Taizan Maezumi and Bernie Glassman (Somerville, MA: Wisdom Publications, 2002). On Rinzai Zen meditation, see Omori Sogen, *An Introduction to Zen Training*, translated by Dogen Hosokawa and Roy Yoshimoto (Boston: Tuttle, 2001), and Meido Moore, *The Rinzai Zen Way: A Guide to Practice* (Boulder, CO: Shambhala, 2018). On Sōtō Zen meditation, see Kosho Uchiyama, *Opening the Hand of Thought: Foundations of Zen Buddhist Practice*, translated and edited by Tom Wright, Jisho Warner, and Shohaku Okumura (Somerville, MA: Wisdom Publications, 2004).

Chapter 5

1. See the Buddha's first sermon, "Setting the Wheel in Motion," *Samyutta Nikāya* 56:11, in *In the Buddha's Words: An Anthology of Discourses from the Pāli Canon*, edited by Bhikkhu Bodhi (Somerville, MA: Wisdom Publications, 2005), p. 75.

2. If the average American were to jump right into week-long retreat in a Zen monastery, it would certainly feel like an excruciatingly painful practice of extreme asceticism—but so would trying to run a full marathon at on the first day one decides to take up jogging. It may be the case that many Zen monasteries tilt too far in the direction of asceticism, even more than is necessary as a corrective to our more hedonistic lifestyle. But it is no doubt true that many of our lifestyles tilt too far in the direction

of indulging various desires, an indulgence that multiplies and distorts our natural desires into unnatural cravings.

3. On the life of the Buddha, see Sherab Chödzin Kohn, "The Life of the Buddha," in *The Buddha and His Teachings*, edited by Samuel Bercholz and Sherab Chödzin Kohn (Boston: Shambhala, 2003), pp. 3–44; and Karen Armstrong, *Buddha* (New York: Penguin, 2001).

4. T. S. Eliot, *The Waste Land and Other Writings*, with an introduction by Mary Karr (New York: Random House, 2001), p. 54n308.

5. *Saṃyutta Nikāya* 35:28, in *In the Buddha's Words*, p. 346.

6. Kohn, "The Life of the Buddha," p. 9.

7. Benjamin Franklin reportedly remarked: "The constitution only gives you the right to pursue happiness. You have to catch it yourself." Although the quote is most likely apocryphal, it is said to be "in keeping with Franklin's general convictions." Darrin M. McMahon, *Happiness: A History* (New York: Grove Press, 2006), pp. 331–32.

8. See Daniel Kahneman and Angus Deaton, "High Income Improves Evaluation of Life but Not Emotional Well-Being," Center for Health and Well-being, Princeton University, 2010, https://www.princeton.edu/~deaton/downloads/deaton_kahneman_high_income_improves_evaluation_August2010.pdf.

9. *Subha Sutta* 24–27, in *The Middle Length Discourses of the Buddha: A Translation of the Majjhima Nikāya*, 2nd ed., translated by Bhikkhu Ñāṇamoli and Bhikkhu Bodhi (Somerville, MA: Wisdom Publications, 1995), pp. 816–17; see also p. 375. For a practice-oriented treatment by a teacher of Tibetan Buddhism, see B. Alan Wallace, *The Four Immeasurables: Practice to Open the Heart* (Boulder, CO: Snow Lion, 2010). For a modern Vietnamese Zen master's commentary, see Thich Nhat Hanh, *The Heart of the Buddha's Teaching* (Berkeley, CA: Parallax Press, 1998), chapter 22.

10. *Zengaku daijiten* [Large dictionary of Zen studies] (Tokyo: Daishūkan, 1985), p. 464.

11. See David R. Loy, *The Great Awakening: A Buddhist Social Theory* (Somerville, MA: Wisdom Publications, 2003), p. 28. Loy insightfully develops this Buddhist path of personal transformation into a social critique of consumerism and corporate greed and an alternative vision of a society based on the wisdom of the Middle Way; see especially chapters 2–4 in that book. See also David R. Loy, *Money, Sex, War, Karma: Notes for a Buddhist Revolution* (Somerville, MA: Wisdom Publications, 2008).

12. The relation between moderation, modesty, and self-knowledge is thematized in Plato's *Charmides*. For Aristotle, *sophrosyne* is "a mean in regard to pleasures," specifically the mean between the excess of self-indulgence and that of deprivation. Unlike the case with finding and practicing the golden mean of a virtue such as courage (which he defines as the mean between cowardice and recklessness), with regard to sense desires Aristotle says humans tend to err only in one direction—namely, that of excessive indulgence of them. Aristotle, *Nicomachean Ethics*, translated by Martin Ostwald (New York: Macmillan, 1962), pp. 77–82. The extreme Indian ascetics of the Buddha's time are an exception to Aristotle's rule, as are people suffering from afflictions such as anorexia. Workaholics who don't relax and sleep enough also err in this direction.

13. *Daodejing*, chapter 33, my translation.

14. *The Dhammapada*, translated by Ananda Maitreya (Berkeley, CA: Parallax Press, 1995), p. 56 (chapter 15, verse 6). I don't know whether either of these famous novelists were familiar with any of these traditional Asian teachings, but when Kurt Vonnegut said to Joseph Heller that the billionaire whose party they were at probably made more money in one day than Heller had made over the years from his best-selling novel *Catch 22*, Heller responded: "I've got something he can never have . . . The knowledge that I've got enough." *The New Yorker*, May 16th, 2005.

15. Translated by James W. Heisig in his article "Sufficiency and Satisfaction in Zen Buddhism: Recovering an Ancient Symbolon," *Studies in Formative Spirituality* 14, no. 1 (1993): 55–74. Quoted passages are from pp. 62, 67–68.

16. Ibid., p. 68.

17. "Sona Sutta: About Sona" (AN 6.55), translated from the Pali by Thanissaro Bhikkhu, Access to Insight, November 30, 2013, https:// accesstoinsight.org/tipitaka/an/an06/ an06.0055.than.html.

Chapter 6

1. "Setting the Wheel in Motion," *Saṃyutta Nikāya* 56:11, in *In the Buddha's Words: An Anthology of Discourses from the Pāli Canon*, edited by Bhikkhu Bodhi (Somerville, MA: Wisdom Publications, 2005), pp. 75–78. For a good explication, see Rupert Gethin, *The Foundations of Buddhism* (New York: Oxford University Press, 1998), chapter 3.

2. See *Alagaddūpama Sutta* 13 and *Mahātanhāsankhaya Sutta* 14, in *The Middle Length Discourses of the Buddha*, translated by Bikkhu Ñānamoli and Bhikku Bodhi (Somerville, MA: Wisdom Publications, 1995), pp. 228–29, 352–53.

3. In a famous and often-cited text, the *Kālāma Sutta*, the Buddha instructs a group of people who are confused by all the different teachers promoting their own doctrines and disparaging those of other teachers. The Buddha says to them: "It is fitting for you to be in doubt. . . . Do not go by oral tradition, by lineage of teaching, by hearsay, by a collection of texts, by logic, by inferential reasoning, by reasoned cogitation, by the acceptance of a view after pondering it, by the seeming competence of a speaker, or because you think, 'The ascetic is our teacher.' But when you know for yourselves, 'These things are unwholesome; these things are blamable; these things are censured by the wise; these things, if undertaken and practices, lead to harm and suffering,' then you should abandon them" (*In the Buddha's Words: An Anthology of Discourses from the Pāli Canon*, edited by Bhikkhu Bodhi [Somerville, MA: Wisdom Publications, 2005], p. 89). In effect, the Buddha is telling them to rely not on received wisdom, nor even on intellectual wisdom, but rather on the experiential wisdom that is rooted in holistic and direct personal experience. However, note that he includes their experience of the fact that "these things are censured by the wise." Part of our personal experience, after all, is our interpersonal contact with teachers who impress us with their demeanor and actions as well as with their compelling reasoning and wise words, and not merely with their rhetorical skills or institutional authority. Such teachers and

their teachings inspire us to trust them, and it is not surprising that the Buddha lists "faith" as one of the required virtues for making progress on the path, and "doubt" as one of the great hindrances (see, for example, ibid., pp. 96, 100, 125, 271–72). On the important roles that several senses of "faith" play in the different schools of Buddhism, see William Edelglass, "Aspiration, Conviction, and Serene Joy: Faith and Reason in Indian Buddhist Literature on the Path," and Bret W. Davis, "Faith and/or/ as Enlightenment: Rethinking Religion from the Perspective of Japanese Buddhism," both in *Asian Philosophies and the Idea of Religion: Paths Beyond Faith and Reason*, edited by Sonia Sikka and Ashwani Peetush (New York: Routledge, 2020), pp. 13–35, 36–64. See also Chapters 3, 12, 21, and 22 in the present volume.

4. *Majjhima Nikāya* 63, *Cūlamālunkya Sutta* 5; in *The Middle Length Discourses of the Buddha*, translated by Bikkhu Ñānamoli and Bhikku Bodhi (Somerville, MA: Wisdom Publications, 1995), pp. 534–35; also in *In the Buddha's Words*, pp. 231–32.

5. The Dalai Lama co-authored a book with Howard C. Cutler called *The Art of Happiness: A Handbook for Living* (New York: Riverhead Books, 1998), which inspired not only some serious reflections on the Buddhist view of happiness but also attempts by some less scrupulous popular writers and positive psychologists to loosely link Buddhism with their understanding of the pursuit of individual happiness. For a good example of the former, see Matthieu Ricard, "A Buddhist View of Happiness," in *The Oxford Handbook of Happiness*, edited by Susan A. David, Ilona Boniwell, and Amanda Conley Ayers (New York: Oxford University Press, 2013), pp. 344–56. For an incisive examination of the divergences between the modern Western pursuit of individual happiness and the key role altruism plays in the Buddhist path toward liberating all sentient beings from suffering, see William Edelglass, "Buddhism, Happiness, and the Science of Meditation," in *Meditation, Buddhism, and Science*, edited by David L. McMahan and Erik Braun (New York: Oxford University Press, 2017), pp. 62–83. Also see Dzongsar Jamyang Khyentse, *Not for Happiness: A Guide to the So-Called Preliminary Practices* (Boston: Shambhala, 2012). Like the Dalai Lama, yet from Bhutan rather than Tibet, Dzongsar Jamyang Khyentse is a Vajrayana Buddhist lama. His critique is implicitly aimed not just at the popular effects of the Dalai Lama's book on happiness, but also at potential compromises made in the Bhutanese government's celebrated project of promoting "Gross National Happiness" rather than just gross national product. See Bret W. Davis, "Cultural Identity and the End of Happiness: Two Dilemmas and Other Lessons from Bhutan," for an edited volume in preparation.

6. Some Zen teachers have brought the insights of psychotherapy and Zen Buddhism to bear on each other. See David Loy, *Lack and Transcendence: The Problem of Death and Life in Psychotherapy, Existentialism, and Buddhism* (New York: Humanities Books, 1996); Barry Magid, *Ordinary Mind: Exploring the Common Ground of Zen and Psychotherapy* (Somerville, MA: Wisdom Publications, 2002); and Barry Magid, *Ending the Pursuit of Happiness: A Zen Guide* (Somerville, MA: Wisdom Publications, 2008). See also *Psychoanalysis and Buddhism*, edited by Jeremy D. Safran (Somerville, MA: Wisdom Publications, 2003); and *Buddhism and Psychotherapy Across Cultures*, edited by Mark Unno (Somerville, MA: Wisdom Publications, 2006).

7. Donald W. Mitchell, *Buddhism: Introducing the Buddhist Experience* (New York: Oxford University Press, 2002), p. 61. The other four of the Six Perfections are generosity, morality, meditation, and wisdom.

8. Stoic philosophers also thought this kind of discernment is the key to human happiness. Epictetus opens his *Handbook* with the statement: "Some things are up to us and some are not up to us. Our opinions are up to us, and our impulses, desires, aversions—in short, whatever is our own doing. Our bodies are not up to us, nor are our possessions, our reputations, or our public offices, or, that is, whatever is not our own doing." Claiming that "what upsets people is not things themselves but their judgments about the things," Epictetus stresses our need to practice accepting the things that cannot be changed, concluding: "Do not seek to have events happen as you want them to, but instead want them to happen as they do happen, and your life will go well." Epictetus, *The Handbook (The Encheiridion)*, translated by Nicholas P. White (Indianapolis, IN: Hackett, 1983), pp. 11, 13 (sections 1, 5, and 8). Although in the Western tradition this Stoic ethic greatly influenced the development of the Christian spirituality of "Let not my will but Thy Will be done" (see Luke 22:42), in modern times Western culture has, it is fair to say, by and large taken the more active road of trying to change reality to satisfy our consumerist and technological desires.

9. Thich Nhat Hanh, *The Heart of Understanding: Commentaries on the Prajnaparamita Heart Sutra* (Berkeley, CA: Parallax Press, 2009), p. 15.

10. See Charles Shirō Inouye, *Evanescence and Form: An Introduction to Japanese Culture* (New York: Palgrave Macmillan, 2008).

11. Dōgen, *The Heart of Dōgen's Shōbōgenzō*, translated by Norman Waddell and Masao Abe (Albany: State University of New York Press, 2002), pp. 75–76.

12. *Japanese Philosophy: A Sourcebook*, edited by James W. Heisig, Thomas P. Kasulis, and John C. Maraldo (Honolulu: University of Hawai'i Press, 2011), p. 174.

13. For a clear introduction to the topic of rebirth from a Tibetan Buddhist perspective, see Reginald A. Ray, "Rebirth in the Buddhist Tradition," in *The Buddha and His Teachings*, edited by Samuel Bercholz and Sherab Chödzin (Boston: Shambhala, 2003), pp. 301–11. For both traditional Buddhist views and specifically Zen teachings regarding death, rebirth, and Nirvana, see Chapter 23.

Chapter 7

1. The philosopher and Zen teacher David Loy compellingly argues that underlying even our fear of death is the anxiety caused by our repressed awareness of the fact that at the core of our being there is a "lack" of any substantial essence. In vain we struggle to make up for this lack by trying to possess and identify with objects, ideas, or experiences such as money, fame, or sex. However, "nothing in our notoriously impermanent world can fill up the bottomless pit at the core of my being—bottomless, because there is really no-thing there that can be filled up. . . . According to Buddhism, such personal 'reality projects'—these ways we try to make ourselves

feel more real—cannot be successful, for a very different approach is needed to overcome our sense of lack. Instead of trying to ground ourselves somewhere on the 'outside,' we need to look 'inside.' Instead of running away from this sense of emptiness at our core, we need to become more comfortable with it and more aware, in which case it can transform from a sense of lack into the source of our creativity and spontaneity." David R. Loy, *The Great Awakening: A Buddhist Social Theory* (Somerville, MA: Wisdom Publications, 2003), p. 164, and see also 22, 27, 30, 35; David Loy, *Lack and Transcendence: The Problem of Death and Life in Psychotherapy, Existentialism, and Buddhism* (Amherst, NY: Humanity Books, 1996); and David R. Loy, *Money, Sex, War, Karma: Notes for a Buddhist Revolution* (Somerville, MA: Wisdom Publications, 2008), pp. 15–23.

2. *Japanese Philosophy: A Sourcebook*, edited by James W. Heisig, Thomas P. Kasulis, and John C. Maraldo (Honolulu: University of Hawai'i Press, 2011), p. 184.

3. Zenkei Shibayama, *The Gateless Barrier: Zen Comments on the Mumonkan*, translated by Sumiko Kudo (Boston: Shambhala, 2000), p. 285, translation modified.

4. *The Blue Cliff Record*, translated by Thomas Cleary and J. C. Cleary (Boston: Shambhala, 1992), p. 1.

5. *The Roaring Stream: A New Zen Reader*, edited by Nelson Foster and Jack Shoemaker (Hopewell, NJ: Ecco Press, 1996), p. 295.

6. Takemura Makio, *Zen no shisō wo shiru jiten* [Encyclopedia for understanding Zen thought] (Tokyo: Tōkyōdō Shuppan, 2014), p. 86.

7. *Zen Sourcebook: Traditional Documents from China, Korea, and Japan*, edited by Stephen Addiss with Stanley Lombardo and Judith Roitman (Indianapolis, IN: Hackett, 2008), pp. 234–35.

8. Quoted in Minobe Hitoshi, "Hisamatsu Shin'ichi's Awakening to the True Self," translated by Bret W. Davis, in *The Oxford Handbook of Japanese Philosophy*, edited by Bret W. Davis (New York: Oxford University Press, 2020), p. 260.

9. Yanagida Seizan, *Zen shisō* [Zen thought] (Tokyo: Chūkō Shinshō, 1975), pp. 81–106.

10. *Japanese Philosophy: A Sourcebook*, p. 176.

11. Walpola Rahula, *What the Buddha Taught*, 2nd ed. (New York: Grove Press, 1974), p. 51.

12. See William Edelglass, "Aspiration, Conviction, and Serene Joy: Faith and Reason in Indian Buddhist Literature on the Path," in *Asian Philosophies and the Idea of Religion: Paths Beyond Faith and Reason*, edited by Sonia Sikka and Ashwani Peetush (New York: Routledge, 2020), pp. 13–35.

13. See Sigmund Freud, *Totem and Taboo* and *The Future of an Illusion*, in *The Freud Reader*, edited by Peter Gay (New York: W. W. Norton, 1989), pp. 504–6, 695–99, 703–4, 712. On Freud's critique of biblical religion and what Christians (and by implication adherents to other religions) can learn from it, see Paul Ricoeur, *Freud and Philosophy: An Essay on Interpretation*, translated by Denis Savage (New Haven, CT: Yale University Press, 1970), pp. 20–36, 524–51; and Merold Westphal, *Suspicion and Faith: The Religious Uses of Modern Atheism* (New York: Fordham University Press, 1998), part 2.

14. Heinrich Dumoulin, *Understanding Buddhism* (New York: Weatherhill, 1994), p. 30.

15. Dumoulin, *Understanding Buddhism*, p. 42.

16. Richard Gombrich, *What the Buddha Thought* (London: Equinox, 2009), p. 9.

17. *Saṃyutta Nikāya* 44:10, in *The Connected Discourses of the Buddha*, translated by Bhikkhu Bodhi (Somerville, MA: Wisdom Publications, 2000), pp. 1393–94. Commented on in Walpola, *What the Buddha Taught*, p. 62–64; and in Dumoulin, *Understanding Buddhism*, pp. 34–36.

18. See *Saṃyutta Nikāya* 12:17, in *The Connected Discourses of the Buddha*, p. 547.

19. René Descartes, *Discourse on Method* and *Meditations on First Philosophy*, 3rd ed., translated by Donald A. Cress (Indianapolis, IN: Hackett, 1993), p. 19.

20. William James, *The Principles of Psychology*, chapter 9, reprinted in William James, *The Essential Writings*, edited by Bruce Wilshire (Albany: State University of New York Press, 1984), p. 44.

21. *The Philosophical Writings of Descartes*, trans. John Cottingham, Robert Stoothoff, and Dugald Murdoch (Cambridge: Cambridge University Press, 1985), vol. 2, p. 122.

22. Friedrich Nietzsche, *Beyond Good and Evil*, translated by Walter Kaufmann (New York: Vintage, 1966), pp. 23–24.

23. See Fujita Masakatsu, "The Significance of Japanese Philosophy," translated by Bret W. Davis, *Journal of Japanese Philosophy* 1 (2013): 5–20.

24. David Hume, *A Treatise of Human Nature*, 2nd ed., edited by L. A. Selby-Bigge (New York: Oxford University Press, 1978), p. 252.

25. On the Five Aggregates and the no-self doctrine, see Rahula, *What the Buddha Taught?*, pp. 20–26; Rupert Gethin, *The Foundations of Buddhism* (New York: Oxford University Press, 1998), pp. 133–62; Peter Harvey, *An Introduction to Buddhism: Teachings, History, and Practices* (Cambridge: Cambridge University Press, 1990), pp. 49–53; and Paul Williams with Anthony Tribe, *Buddhist Thought: A Complete Introduction to the Indian Tradition* (New York: Routledge, 2000), pp. 56–62. For some noteworthy philosophical treatments of this topic, see Christopher W. Govans, *Philosophy of the Buddha* (New York: Routledge, 2003), 63–116; Mark Siderits, *Buddhism as Philosophy* (Indianapolis, IN: Hackett, 2007), chapter 3; and Jay L Garfield, *Engaging Buddhism: Why It Matters to Philosophy* (New York: Oxford University Press, 2015), chapter 4.

26. Nāgasena, *Milindapañha*, 27; *The Questions of King Milinda*, translated by T. W. Rhys Davids (Oxford: Oxford University Press, 1890), pp. 44–45.

27. Govans, *Philosophy of the Buddha*, p. 63.

28. See Reginald A. Ray, "Rebirth in the Buddhist Tradition," in *The Buddha and His Teachings*, edited by Samuel Bercholz and Sherab Chödzin (Boston: Shambhala, 2003), pp. 307–8; and Shohaku Okumura, *Realizing Genjokoan: The Key to Dogen's Shobogenzo* (Somerville, MA: Wisdom Publications, 2010), pp. 110–11.

29. Nakamura Hajime and Saigusa Mitsuyoshi, *Baudda: Bukkyō* [Bauddha: Buddhism] (Tokyo: Shōgakkan, 1996), pp. 186–89.

30. *The Dhammapada*, translated by Ananda Maitreya (Berkeley, CA: Parallax Press, 1995), pp. 45–46 (chapter 12, verses 4 and 9).

31. Thich Nhat Hanh, *The Diamond That Cuts Through Illusion: Commentaries on the Prajñaparamit Diamond Sutra* (Berkeley, CA: Parallax Press, 1992), p. 19 (chapter 18).

32. *The Diamond Sutra and The Sutra of Hui-neng*, translated by A. F. Price and Wong Mou-lam (Boston: Shambhala, 1990), p. 38 (chapter 17).

33. *The Record of Linji*, translation and commentary by Ruth Fuller Sasaki, edited by Thomas Yūhō Kirchner (Honolulu: University of Hawai'i Press, 2009), p. 4.

34. *Zen Sourcebook*, p. 119.

35. *Zen Sourcebook*, p. 16.

36. *Zen Sourcebook*, p. 36.

37. *Zen Sourcebook*, p. 138.

38. *Japanese Philosophy: A Sourcebook*, p. 184.

39. *The Record of Linji*, p. 11.

40. *The Roaring Stream*, p. 125.

41. *The Roaring Stream*, p. 141.

42. *The Roaring Stream*, p. 150.

Chapter 8

1. Leviticus 19:18; Matthew 19:19, 22:39; Mark 12:31, 12:33; Luke 10:27; Romans 13:9; Galatians 5:14; James 2:8.

2. Leviticus 19:33–34.

3. Matthew 5:43–48.

4. The Buddha, "Unlimited Friendliness: The Metta Sutta," in *The Buddha and His Teachings*, edited by Samuel Bercholz and Sherab Chödzin (Boston: Shambhala, 2003), p. 142.

5. Gyalwa Gendun Gyatso, the Second Dalai Lama, "Exchanging Oneself for Others," in *The Buddha and His Teachings*, edited by Samuel Bercholz and Sherab Chödzin (Boston: Shambhala, 2003), pp. 157–64.

6. Dōgen, *Treasury of the True Dharma Eye: Zen Master Dogen's Shobo Genzo*, edited by Kazuaki Tanahashi (Boston: Shambhala, 2012), p. 475.

7. *The Roaring Stream: A New Zen Reader*, edited by Nelson Foster and Jack Shoemaker (Hopewell, NJ: Ecco Press, 1996), p. 273.

8. *Japanese Philosophy: A Sourcebook*, edited by James W. Heisig, Thomas P. Kasulis, and John C. Maraldo (Honolulu: University of Hawai'i Press, 2011), p. 185.

9. *Readings in Later Chinese Philosophy: Han Dynasty to the 20th Century*, edited by Justin Tiwald and Bryan W. Van Norden (Indianapolis, IN: Hackett, 2014), p. 201.

10. *Zhuangzi: The Essential Writings with Selections from Traditional Commentaries*, translated by Brook Ziporyn (Indianapolis, IN: Hackett, 2009), p. 15 [2:31–32].

11. *Taishō Shinshū Daizōkyō*, edited by Takakusu Junjirō and Watanabe Kaigyoku (Tokyo: Taishō Issaikyō Kankōkai, 1924–32), 45:159b28–29.

12. Śāntideva, *The Bodhicaryāvatāra*, translated by Kate Crosby and Andrew Skilton (New York: Oxford University Press, 1995), pp. 96, 98 [8:91, 99, 114].

13. Quoted in *The Upanishads*, translated by Eknath Easwaran (Tomales, CA: Nilgiri Press, 1987), pp. 277–78.

14. The Jewish philosopher Emmanuel Levinas stresses that in Judaism the relation to God is to be found in the relation to the neighbor, and that the face of the other person expresses God's command not to kill. See his *Totality and Infinity: An Essay on Exteriority*, translated by Alphonso Lingis (Pittsburgh: Duquesne University Press, 1979), pp. 78–79; and his *Difficult Freedom: Essays on Judaism*, translated by Seán Hand (Baltimore: Johns Hopkins University Press, 1990), pp. 16, 19, 26. However, he insists on the alterity of other persons and on the transcendence of God rather than on their nonduality with the self. For a critical comparison with the Mahayana Buddhist philosophy of Nishida Kitarō, see Bret W. Davis, "Ethical and Religious Alterity: Nishida After Levinas," in *Kitarō Nishida in der Philosophie des 20. Jahrhunderts*, edited by Rolf Elberfeld and Yōko Arisaka (Freiburg: Alber Verlag, 2014), pp. 313–41.

15. 1 Corinthians 12:12, 24–25. Paul was likely influenced by Stoicism's use of this metaphor. The Roman emperor and Stoic philosopher Marcus Aurelius counsels us to think of ourselves as a "limb [Ln. *melos*] of a larger body," rather than just as a "part" (*meros*) of a larger whole, so that helping others becomes "its own reward" since you "realize who you're really helping" (*Meditations*, VII.13, trans. Gregory Hays).

16. *The Upanishads*, pp. 182–88.

17. *Zengaku daijiten* [Large dictionary of Zen studies] (Tokyo: Daishūkan, 1985), p. 35.

18. *The Upanishads*, pp. 183, 190.

19. Eminent Japanese scholars of Indian Buddhism Nakamura Hajime and Saigusa Mitsuyoshi write: "It must be said that to consider the negation of the *atman* (i.e., *anatman*) that is taught by Buddhism to be a straightforward antithesis to [the doctrine of the *Atman* in] the *Upanishads* is a gross oversimplification, or indeed a clear mistake." Nakamura Hajime and Saigusa Mitsuyoshi, *Baudda: Bukkyō* [Bauddha: Buddhism] (Tokyo: Shōgakkan, 1996), p. 182. For studies that focus on how the Buddha critically distances his teaching from those of the Brahminism of the Upanishads (in particular the *Brihadaranyaka Upanishad*, with which the Buddha seems to have been very familiar), as well as Jainism, see Richard F. Gombrich, *How Buddhism Began: The Conditioned Genesis of the Early Teachings*, 2nd ed. (New York: Routledge, 2006), especially chapter 2; and Richard Gombrich, *What the Buddha Thought* (London: Equinox, 2009), especially chapters 3–5. Gombrich argues that the Buddha was primarily concerned with providing soteriological teachings about action (especially intentional mental action) and that he distinguished his teachings from those of the Upanishads that taught liberation by means of a mystical knowledge (gnosis) of the identity of an unchanging essential Self (*Atman*) with an unchanging Absolute (*Brahman*).

20. A specific concept of *atman* that can be found in many of the *Upanishads* (which were written over many centuries and contain a wide variety of teachings) and which is indeed consistently rejected by Buddhism is defined in Japanese as *jō-itsu-shu-sai*, meaning a "permanent-individual-owner-controller." The Buddha clearly taught that attachment to the false idea of an independent and permanent substance-ego was a root cause of suffering. And yet the Buddha also repeatedly stressed the moral and spiritual freedom and responsibility of the agent-self (called by some schools *pudgala*

in order to distinguish it from *atman*, though other schools equated the two terms and rejected both). In some Mahayana sutras and discourses, a positive notion of the "Great *Atman*" (Jp. *daiga*) or the "True *Atman*" (Jp. *shinga*) of the Buddha is explicitly affirmed in order to counteract nihilistic misinterpretations of the teachings of *anatman* (Jp. *muga*), emptiness, and Nirvana. See Nakamura Hajime, *Bukkyō-go daijiten* [Large dictionary of Buddhist terms] (Tokyo: Tōkyō Shoseki, 1975), vol. 1, pp. 157–58; *Bukkyō jiten* [Dictionary of Buddhism], edited by Nakamura Hajime et al. (Tokyo: Iwanami, 1989), pp. 100, 530; and Taya Raishun, Ōchō Enichi, and Funahashi Issai, *Bukkyō-gaku jiten* [Dictionary of Buddhist studies] (Kyoto: Hōzōkan, 1955), pp. 49–50.

21. On the soul-body dualisms of the so-called Senika heresy and Jainism, see note 64 of Chapter 12. On rebirth, see Chapter 23.

22. See Chapter 9 for a sketch of the three main Vedanta philosophies. The *Lotus Sutra* speaks of a Buddha whose life span is incalculably long; as the compassionate "father of the world," he constantly teaches by "expedient means" according to the aptitude of persons. See *The Lotus Sutra*, translated by Burton Watson (New York: Columbia University Press, 1993), esp. chapter 16. In East Asia, the Buddha of the *Lotus Sutra* came to be understood not just as immeasurably long-lived but indeed eternal; and, moreover, this "eternal Buddha" is linked with the Buddha-nature doctrines found in the *Awakening of Faith in the Mahayana* and in such sutras as the *Lankavatara Sutra* and the Mahayana *Mahaparinirvana Sutra*. See Paul Williams, *Mahāyāna Buddhism: The Doctrinal Foundations* (New York: Routledge, 1989), p. 151. While some Buddhists and Buddhologists in the distant and well as recent past have criticized the ideas of the *Tathagatagarbha* (Buddha-embryo or Buddha-womb) and Buddha-nature as evincing a belated Hindu influence and the infiltration into Buddhism of an un-Buddhist *Atman/Brahman* doctrine, the matter is far from this simple. In the *Mahaparinirvana Sutra*, for example, we find an attempt to articulate the "positive side" of the Buddha's teaching without, however, simply reasserting the existence of a substantial ego. In one place we read: "I [the Buddha] have never said that all beings do not have self; I said always that beings all have the Buddha-nature. Is not the Buddha-nature self? . . . This Buddha-nature is, truth to say, no self. For the sake of beings, I say self." And in another place it is said that: "There can be [non-Buddhists] who talk about the eternal self or the 'not-is' of the self. This is not the case with the Tathagata. He says that there is the self; or, at times, there is not. This is the middle path." *The Mahayana Mahaparinirvana-Sutra*, translated by Kosho Yamamoto (Tokyo: Karinbunko, 1974), vol. 2, p. 660, and vol. 1, p. 168.

23. Williams provides a good introduction to these developments, in East Asia as well as India and Tibet, in his *Mahāyāna Buddhism: The Doctrinal Foundations*; see also Paul Williams with Anthony Tribe, *Buddhist Thought: A Complete Introduction to the Indian Tradition* (New York: Routledge, 2000).

24. Williams and Tribe, *Buddhist Thought*, p. 163.

25. Williams points out a crucial passage in the *Shrimala Sutra* in which the Buddha-nature or *Tathagatagarbha* "is empty, void, but not empty in the Madhyamaka sense of lacking inherent existence," but rather void of all defilements. He later writes

that "the tension between the two approaches to [emptiness] can be traced to an opposition between the Madhyamaka view of emptiness as an absence of inherent existence in the object under investigation, and the *tathāgatagarbha* perspective on emptiness, so influential in Chinese Buddhism including Chan, which sees emptiness as radiant pure mind empty of its conceptual accretions." Williams, *Mahāyāna Buddhism*, pp. 101, 195. The proponents of so-called Critical Buddhism, Matsumoto Shirō and Hakamaya Noriaki, offer the latest concerted effort to criticize the doctrine of *Tathagatagarbha* or Buddha-nature, which they interpret—or misinterpret—as a metaphysical substance. This allows them to argue that it is un-Buddhist insofar as it does not accord with the essential Buddhist doctrine of interdependent origination. For an excellent collection of essays by Matsumoto, Hakamaya, and other noteworthy scholars involved in the controversy they provoked, see *Pruning the Bodhi Tree: The Storm over Critical Buddhism*, edited by Jamie Hubbard and Paul L. Swanson (Honolulu: University of Hawai'i Press, 1997). Although he does not refer to the Japanese Critical Buddhists, Jungnok Park, a disaffected former Korean Zen (Jogye) monk who studied Buddhology at the University of Oxford, also criticizes, from what he takes to be an authoritative empiricism and rationalism of early Buddhism, the doctrines of *Tathagatagarbha*, Buddha-nature, and other notions of a true self as they developed in India and especially in China. See Jungnok Park, *How Buddhism Acquired a Soul on the Way to China* (Bristol, CT: Equinox Publishing, 2012). While the philology of these critics is usually very impressive and often illuminating, the hermeneutical and philosophical fruits of their labors are sometimes spoiled by the critical—or polemical—agenda that steers their research. In her chapter in *Pruning the Bodhi Tree* and in chapter 5 of her *Buddha Nature* (Albany: State University of New York Press, 1991), Sallie B. King demonstrates that the concept of Buddha-nature implies a soteriological strategy and a dynamic nondualism (rather than a substantialistic and homogeneous monism) that is fully in accord with other basic Buddhist teachings such as emptiness and interdependent origination. The foremost expert on the notions of *Tathagatagarbha* and Buddha-nature in Japan, Takasaki Jikidō, explains how the *Ratnagotravibhāga* responds to the question of why, when the *Heart Sutra* and other texts preach the non-existence or emptiness of all beings, the Buddha later preached the doctrine of the universal existence of the Buddha-nature. Takasaki summarizes the five reasons this text gives in response as follows: (1) to encourage practice, for everyone has the potential to gain enlightenment; (2) to stress equality, for *all* sentient beings have the Buddha-nature; (3) to eliminate the false view of the ultimate reality of the personal ego; (4) to counteract the nihilistic interpretation of emptiness; and (5) to encourage respect for everyone as an embodiment of the Buddha-nature. Elaborating on the first and third of these reasons, Takasaki stresses that the Buddha-nature refers to the "originally pure nature of the mind" (Sk. *prakrtivyavadana*; Jp. *jishōshōjōshin*) and the wisdom of the Buddha (awakened mind), and not to a substantial entity. He also argues that the relevant texts, including those by Zen masters such as Dōgen, are well aware of the dangers of reifying this concept and the need to stress its compatibility with the doctrines of *anatman*, interdependent origination, and emptiness. Takasaki Jikidō, *Busshō to wa nanika* [What is Buddha-nature?] (Kyoto: Hōzōkan, 1997), esp. pp. 41, 78–82.

26. On the various interrelated teachings of "emptiness" found in Zen, see Bret W. Davis, "Forms of Emptiness in Zen," in *A Companion to Buddhist Philosophy*, edited by Steven Emmanuel (West Sussex: Wiley-Blackwell, 2013), pp. 190–213. I have discussed the doctrine of Buddha-nature, and the debates surrounding it, in Bret W. Davis, "Does a Dog See into Its Buddha-nature? Re-posing the Question of Animality/Humanity in Zen Buddhism," in *Buddha Nature and Animality*, edited by David Jones (Fremont, CA: Jain, 2007), pp. 83–126.

27. My translation. Compare Yamada Mumon, *Lectures on The Ten Oxherding Pictures*, translated by Victor Sōgen Hori (Honolulu: University of Hawai'i Press, 2004), pp. 29, 37.

28. Dōgen, *Treasury of the True Dharma Eye: Zen Master Dogen's Shobo Genzo*, edited by Kazuaki Tanahashi (Boston: Shambhala, 2012), p. 879.

29. Dōgen, *The Heart of Dōgen's Shōbōgenzō*, translated by Norman Waddell and Masao Abe (Albany: State University of New York Press, 2002), pp. 33, 36.

30. Quoted in Robert E. Buswell, *The Zen Monastic Experience* (Princeton, NJ: Princeton University Press, 1992), p. 154.

31. See Thich Nhat Hanh, *Zen Keys: A Guide to Zen Practice* (New York: Doubleday, 1995), pp. 41, 105–7; and Thich Nhat Hanh, *The Heart of Understanding: Commentaries on the Prajñaparamita Heart Sutra*, rev. ed. (Berkeley, CA: Parallax Press, 2009), pp. 3–8.

32. Thich Nhat Hanh, *Being Peace* (Berkeley, CA: Parallax Press, 1987), p. 87. Indirectly, Nhat Hanh uses "interbeing" as a translation of two Vietnamese words of Chinese origin, *tiep hien*, which he tells us mean "to be in touch" or "to continue" and "the present time" or "to make real, to manifest, realization" (ibid., pp. 85–86).

33. *The Complete Poems of Emily Dickinson*, edited by Thomas H. Johnson (New York: Bay Back Books), p. 663. For an illuminating commentary, see Thomas P. Kasulis, *Engaging Japanese Philosophy* (Honolulu: University of Hawai'i Press, 2018), p. 26.

34. John Donne, *Devotions upon Emergent Occasions*, Meditation 17.

35. Ikkyū, *Skeletons*, in *An Anthology of Rinzai Zen*, translated by Thomas Cleary (New York: Grove Press, 1978), p. 85.

36. See Plato's *Apology* 25–26.

37. *Two Zen Classics: Mumonkan and Hekiganroku*, translated with commentary by Katsuki Sekida (New York: Weatherhill, 1977), p. 306, translation modified.

38. David R. Loy, *The Great Awakening: A Buddhist Social Theory* (Somerville, MA: Wisdom Publications, 2003), p. 99.

39. My translation. Compare *Two Zen Classics*, p. 255.

40. See Katayama Suihō, *Zen to tetsugaku no aida* [Between Zen and philosophy] (Tokyo: Kōsei Shuppan, 2018), pp. 17–21.

41. See Isshū Miura and Ruth Fuller Sasaki, *The Zen Koan: Its History and Use in Rinzai Zen* (New York: Harcourt Brace, 1965), pp. 62–72; and Ross Bolleter, *Dongshan's Five Ranks: Keys to Enlightenment* (Somerville, MA: Wisdom Publications, 2014).

42. Nishitani Keiji, "Encounter with Emptiness," in *The Religious Philosophy of Nishitani Keiji*, edited by Taitetsu Unno (Berkeley, CA: Asian Humanities Press, 1989), pp. 2–3.

43. See case 57 of *The Blue Cliff Record; Two Zen Classics*, p. 306, emphasis added.

44. See case 67 of *Record of Serenity*; Gerry Shishin Wick, *The Book of Equanimity: Illuminating Classic Zen Koans* (Somerville, MA: Wisdom Publications, 2005), p. 210, translation modified and emphasis added. The statement is originally from the *Avatamsaka Sutra* (*Taishō Shinshū Daizōkyō*, 10.272c4–7).

Chapter 9

1. See Dōgen, *Treasury of the True Dharma Eye: Zen Master Dogen's Shobo Genzo*, edited by Kazuaki Tanahashi (Boston: Shambhala, 2012), pp. 260–64.

2. See ibid., pp. 748–50.

3. "As the rivers flowing east and west merge into the sea and become one with it, forgetting they were ever separate rivers, so do all creatures lose their separateness when they merge at last into pure Being." *The Upanishads*, translated by Eknath Easwaran (Tomales, CA: Nilgiri Press, 1987), pp. 184–85.

4. *Nishida Kitarō zenshū* [The complete works of Nishida Kitarō] (Tokyo: Iwanami, 1987–89), vol. 7, p. 264.

5. John Koller, *Asian Philosophies*, 7th ed. (New York: Pearson, 2018), p. 158–59.

6. See *The Flower Ornament Scripture: A Translation of the Avatamsaka Sutra*, translated by Thomas Cleary (Boston: Shambhala, 1993), pp. 215, 226, 232. See also Francis H. Cook, *Hua-yen Buddhism: The Jewel Net of Indra* (University Park: Pennsylvania State University Press, 1977).

7. Tu Shun, "Cessation and Contemplation in the Five Teachings of the Hua-yen," in Thomas Cleary, *Entry into the Inconceivable: An Introduction to Hua-Yen Buddhism* (Honolulu: University of Hawai'i Press, 1983), p. 66. In his *Engaging Japanese Philosophy* (Honolulu: University of Hawai'i Press, 2018), Thomas Kasulis reveals how a "holographical" mereology—i.e., an account of the relation between the whole of the universe and its parts according to which each of the parts is a perspectival microcosm of the macrocosm—is reiterated throughout the history of Japanese philosophy, including of course in the writings of Zen masters such as Dōgen.

8. Dōgen, *The Heart of Dōgen's Shōbōgenzō*, translated by Norman Waddell and Masao Abe (Albany: State University of New York Press, 2002), p. 50.

9. *The Flower Ornament Sutra*, p. 892.

10. Dōgen, "The Presencing of Truth: Dōgen's *Genjōkōan*," translated by Bret W. Davis, in *Buddhist Philosophy: Essential Readings*, edited by Jay Garfield and William Edelglass (Oxford: Oxford University Press, 2009), p. 257. On Zen's perspectivism, see the articles cited in note 4 of the Preface.

11. William Blake, *The Poetry and Prose of William Blake*, edited by D. E. Erdman (New York: Doubleday, 1970), p. 118.

12. *Nishitani Keiji chosakushū* [Collected works of Nishitani Keiji] (Tokyo: Sōbunsha, 1986–95), vol. 14, p. 126.

13. Kusumoto Bunyū, *Zengo nyūmon* [Introduction to Zen terms] (Tokyo: Daihōrinkaku, 1982), p. 128.

14. My translation (using substitute names). Compare *The Blue Cliff Record*, translated by Thomas Cleary and J. C. Cleary (Boston: Shambhala, 1992), p. 381.

15. Nishitani Keiji, "The I-Thou Relation in Zen Buddhism," translated by Norman Waddell, in *The Buddha Eye: An Anthology of the Kyoto School and its Contemporaries*, edited by Frederick Frank, rev. ed. (Bloomington, IN: World Wisdom, 2004), pp. 39–53, at 46. In this remarkable essay Nishitani discusses the kōan we are examining. For a treatment of this topic in Nishitani's thought, see Bret W. Davis, "Encounter in Emptiness: The I-Thou Relation in Nishitani Keiji's Philosophy of Zen," in *The Bloomsbury Companion to Japanese Philosophy*, edited by Michiko Yusa (New York: Bloomsbury Academic, 2017), pp. 231–54.

16. As quoted in Nishitani, "The I-Thou Relation in Zen Buddhism," p. 46.

17. Ibid.

18. Ōmori Sōgen, *Hekiganroku* [The blue cliff record] (Tokyo: Tachibana Shuppan, 1995), vol. 2, pp. 133–34. On Zen master Linji's development of the notions of "host" and "guest" from the Huayan Buddhist notions of "principle" and "satellite," see Bret W. Davis, "Zen's Nonegocentric Perspectivism," in *Buddhist Philosophy: A Comparative Approach*, edited by Steven M. Emmanuel (West Sussex: Wiley-Blackwell, 2018), pp. 123–43. For an interpretation of Linji's "Four Classifications" (see note 38 of Chapter 24) in the context of interpersonal dialogue, and for a more extensive treatment of Case 68 of *The Blue Cliff Record*, see Davis, "Encounter in Emptiness."

19. Ueda Shizuteru, "'Tomo-ni' to 'hitori'" ["Together" and "alone"], in *Ueda Shizuteru shū* [Ueda Shizuteru collection] (Tokyo: Iwanami, 2002), vol. 10, p. 281.

20. Shizuteru Ueda, *Wer und was bin ich? Zur Phänomenologie des Selbst im Zen Buddhismus* (Freiburg: Verlag Karl Alber, 2011), p. 36; Ueda Shizuteru, "Emptiness and Fullness: Śūnyatā in Mahāyāna Buddhism," translated by James W. Heisig and Frederick Greiner, *The Eastern Buddhist* 15, no. 1 (1982): 37.

21. Nishitani Keiji, *Religion and Nothingness*, translated by Jan Van Bragt (Los Angeles: University of California Press, 1982), p. 149.

22. Ibid., p. 285.

23. Martin Buber, *I and Thou*, translated by Walter Kaufmann (New York: Charles Scribner's Sons, 1970), p. 59; see also ibid., p. 126.

24. Ibid., pp. 57, 123.

25. Luke 10:27; Matthew 22:37; Mark 12:30–31.

26. The term "panentheism" was coined as an English translation of Karl Krause's (1781–1832) German term *Allingottlehre*, but it was not commonly used before Charles Hartshorne propagated it in the mid-twentieth century. See John W. Cooper, *Panentheism: The Other God of the Philosophers* (Grand Rapids, MI: Baker Academic, 2006), p. 26. Cooper's illuminating survey of the history of panentheism concludes with a dogmatic refutation of panentheism from an orthodox Calvinist perspective. Recently a number of scholars have seen panentheism as a way of reconciling theology and science. See *In Whom We Live and Move and Have Our Being: Panentheistic*

Reflections on God's Presence in a Scientific World, edited by Philip Clayton and Arthur Peacocke (Grand Rapids, MI: William B. Eerdmans, 2004).

27. See Koller, *Asian Philosophies*, 150–61; and Christopher Bartley, *An Introduction to Indian Philosophy* (New York: Bloomsbury Academic, 2015), chapters 11–13.

28. Jeremiah 23.24

29. Buber, *I and Thou*, pp. 127, 143. Buber's panentheism was presumably inspired by Hasidic sources like the "Song of Unity," which says: "Everything is in Thee and Thou art everything; Thou fillest everything and dost encompass it" (as quoted in Karen Armstrong, *A History of God: The 4,000 Year Quest of Judaism, Christianity and Islam* [New York: Ballantine Books, 1993], p. 243). Incidentally, Buber shows more appreciation for Mahayana Buddhism than for the historical Buddha's teachings. See *I and Thou*, pp. 140–41.

30. Acts 17:28.

31. 1 John 4:16

32. Soyen Shaku, *Zen for Americans*, translated by D. T. Suzuki (La Salle, IL: Open Court, 1906), p. 26, "*pan kai en*" written in Greek letters in the original.

33. Soyen Shaku, *Zen for Americans*, p. 27.

34. Thich Nhat Hanh, *Going Home: Jesus and Buddha as Brothers* (New York: Riverhead Books, 1999), p. 7.

35. Nishida Kitarō, "The Logic of Place and the Religious Worldview," *Last Writings: Nothingness and the Religious Worldview*, translated by David A. Dilworth (Honolulu: University of Hawai'i Press, 1987), p. 77, translation modified.

36. Ibid., pp. 99, 120–21. According to Nishida, while the relation between God or Buddha and the self may be approached in terms of "panentheism," it must ultimately be understood in terms of a spiritual dialectic of mutual self-negation or self-emptying, a relation Nishida calls "inverse correspondence." See ibid., pp. 67–70, 85–87, 108, 118. Nishida's conception of God/Buddha will be discussed in Chapter 21.

37. *The Lankavatara Sutra*, translated by Daisetz Teitaro Suzuki (London: Routledge & Kegan Paul, 1932), p. 42. *The Awakening of Faith*, translated by Yoshito S. Hakeda (New York: Columbia University Press, 1967), pp. 41, 55.

38. *Zen Sourcebook: Traditional Documents from China, Korea, and Japan*, edited by Stephen Addiss with Stanley Lombardo and Judith Roitman (Indianapolis, IN: Hackett, 2008), p. 64.

39. *Nishitani Keiji chosakushū*, vol. 12, pp. 261–62.

40. Ibid., pp. 262–63.

41. See Nishitani, *Religion and Nothingness*, pp. 146, 158, 263. Nishitani inherits a fondness for this definition of God from his teacher and the founder of the Kyoto School, Nishida Kitarō. See *Nishida Kitarō zenshū*, vol. 7, p. 208, and vol. 11, pp. 130, 423. The expression seems to have first appeared in "the rather obscure and extremely brief *pseudo-Hermetic Liber XXIV philosophorum* (*Book of the XXIV Philosophers*), dating from the twelfth century." Karsten Harries, *Infinity and Perspective* (Cambridge, MA: MIT Press, 2001), p. 59.

42. Ikkyū, *Skeletons*, in *An Anthology of Rinzai Zen*, translated by Thomas Cleary (New York: Grove Press, 1978), pp. 81–89.

43. *Nishida Kitarō zenshū*, vol. 4, p. 6.

44. *Ueda Shizuteru shū*, vol. 10, pp. 107–108.

45. Nishitani, *Religion and Nothingness*, p. 236.

46. *Nishitani Keiji chosakushū*, vol. 17, pp. 9–10. I have explained this egocentric "will" that ex-ists, goes outside itself, only in order to appropriate others into its own expanded domain in terms of "ecstatic incorporation." See Bret W. Davis, *Heidegger and the Will: On the Way to Gelassenheit* (Evanston, IL: Northwestern University Press, 2007), esp. pp. 9–12. On Nishitani's thought in this regard, see Bret W. Davis, "Nishitani After Nietzsche: From the Death of God to the Great Death of the Will," in *Japanese and Continental Philosophy: Conversations with the Kyoto School*, edited by Bret W. Davis, Brian Schroeder, and Jason M. Wirth (Bloomington: Indiana University Press, 2011), pp. 82–101.

47. *Nishitani Keiji chosakushū*, vol. 17, pp. 14–15.

48. *Ueda Shizuteru shū*, vol. 10, pp. 23–24. This can be related to "the logic of is/not" that D. T. Suzuki gleans from the *Diamond Sutra*; commented on in Chapter 13.

49. *Ueda Shizuteru shū*, vol. 10, pp. 281–282.

50. Ibid., p. 281.

Chapter 10

1. Some of the best introductions to the various traditions of Buddhism include Peter Harvey, *An Introduction to Buddhism: Teachings, History, and Practices* (Cambridge: Cambridge University Press, 1990); and Donald W. Mitchell, *Buddhism: Introducing the Buddhist Experience* (New York: Oxford University Press, 2002). On the Mahayana traditions, see Paul Williams, *Mahāyāna Buddhism: The Doctrinal Foundations* (New York: Routledge, 1989). Also recommended is the pair of anthologies edited by Takeuchi Yoshinori et al.: *Buddhist Spirituality: Indian, Southeast Asian, Tibetan, Early Chinese* (New York: Crossroad, 1994); and *Buddhist Spirituality: Later China, Korea, Japan, and the Modern World* (New York: Crossroad, 1999).

2. My translation. For some alternative translations, see Kazuaki Tanahashi, *Zen Chants: Thirty-Five Essential Texts with Commentary* (Boston: Shambhala, 2015), pp. 30, 122. On the practice of chanting in Zen, see the Meditation Checkup at the end of Lesson 20 in Bret W. Davis, *Real Zen for Real Life* (Chantilly, VA: The Teaching Company, 2020).

3. For more information on the Trikaya doctrine, see Harvey, *An Introduction to Buddhism*, pp. 125–30; Mitchell, *Buddhism*, pp. 123–25; and Williams, *Mahāyāna Buddhism*, pp. 167–84. For a detailed study of the historical and textual development of the doctrine, see Guang Xing, *The Concept of the Buddha: Its Evolution from Early Buddhism to the Trikāya Theory* (New York: RoutledgeCurzon, 2005).

4. For more details on Amitabha/Amida Buddha and Pure Land Buddhism, see Harvey, *An Introduction to Buddhism*, pp. 125–30; Mitchell, *Buddhism*,

pp. 108–12, 206–11, 254–62; and Williams, *Mahāyāna Buddhism*, pp. 251–76. One of the best scholarly introductions to Shinran's Pure Land Buddhist thought is Yoshifumi Ueda and Dennis Hirota, *Shinran: An Introduction to His Thought* (Kyoto: Hongwanji International Center, 1989). One of the most accessible and engaging introductions to the spirituality of Shinran's school of True Pure Land (or Shin) Buddhism is Taitetsu Unno, *River of Fire, River of Water: An Introduction to the Pure Land Tradition of Shin Buddhism* (New York: Doubleday, 1998).

5. *The Collected Works of Shinran*, translated by Dennis Hirota et al. (Kyoto: Jōdo Shinshū Hongwanji-ha, 1997), vol. 1, pp. 461, 530. See Bret W. Davis, "Naturalness in Zen and Shin Buddhism: Before and Beyond Self- and Other-Power," *Contemporary Buddhism* 15, no. 2 (July 2014): 433–47.

6. Williams, *Mahāyāna Buddhism*, p. 208.

7. "Attadiipaa Sutta: An Island to Oneself" (SN 22.43), translated from the Pali by Maurice O'Connell Walshe, Access to Insight (BCBS Edition), November 30, 2013, http://www.accesstoinsight.org/tipitaka/sn/sn22/sn22.043.wlsh.html. See also "Maha-parinibbana Sutta: Last Days of the Buddha" (DN 16), translated from the Pali by Sister Vajira and Francis Story. Access to Insight (BCBS Edition), November 30, 2013, http://www.accesstoinsight.org/tipitaka/dn/dn.16.1-6.vaji.html, at 2:33; and *The Dhammapada*, translated by Ananda Maitreya (Berkeley, CA: Parallax Press, 1995), pp. 45–46 (chapter 12, verses 4 and 9).

8. *The Platform Sutra: The Zen Teachings of Hui-neng*, translated by Red Pine (Emeryville, CA: Shoemaker & Hoard, 2006), p. 19.

9. *The Dhammapada*, translated by Ananda Maitreya (Berkeley, CA: Parallax Press, 1995), p. 76 (chapter 20, verse 4).

10. See *The Collected Works of Shinran*, vol. 1, p. 550; and Thomas Kasulis, *Engaging Japanese Philosophy* (Honolulu: University of Hawai'i Press, 2018), pp. 192–93.

11. See Davis, "Naturalness in Zen and Shin Buddhism."

12. See Kūkai, *Major Works*, translated, with an account of his life and a study of his thought, by Yoshito S. Hakeda (New York: Columbia University Press, 1972); Taikō Yamasaki, *Shingon: Japanese Esoteric Buddhism*, translated by Richard and Cynthia Peterson, edited by Yasuyoshi Morimoto and David Kidd (Boston: Shambhala, 1988); and John W. M. Krummel, "Kūkai's Shingon: Embodiment of Emptiness," in *The Oxford Handbook of Japanese Philosophy*, edited by Bret W. Davis (New York: Oxford University Press, 2020), pp. 145–57.

13. See Bernard McGinn, *The Mystical Thought of Meister Eckhart* (New York: Crossroad, 2001), chapter 5.

Chapter 11

1. In what follows, translations of passages from Hakuin's *Song in Praise of Zazen* are my own. For full translations of the text, see *Zen Sourcebook: Traditional Documents*

from China, Korea, and Japan, edited by Stephen Addiss with Stanley Lombardo and Judith Roitman (Indianapolis, IN: Hackett, 2008), pp. 250–51; and Shodo Harada, *The Path of Bodhidharma*, translated by Priscilla Daichi Storandt (Boston: Tuttle, 2000), pp. 69–70.

2. See *Daodejing*, chapters 8, 43, and 66.

3. *Entangling Vines: A Classic Collection of Zen Koans*, translated by Thomas Yūhō Kirchner (Somerville, MA: Wisdom Publications, 2013), p. 122.

4. *The Lotus Sutra*, translated by Burton Watson (New York: Columbia University Press, 1993), pp. 81–86.

5. My translation. Compare *The Record of Linji*, translation with commentary by Ruth Fuller Sasaki, edited by Thomas Yūhō Kirchner (Honolulu: University of Hawai'i Press, 2009), p. 22.

6. 1 John 4:8.

7. 1 John 4:12.

8. *The Roaring Stream: A New Zen Reader*, edited by Nelson Foster and Jack Shoemaker (Hopewell, NJ: Ecco Press, 1996), p. 125.

9. *The Essential Teachings of Zen Master Hakuin*, translated by Norman Waddell (Boston: Shambhala, 2010), p. 61.

10. *The Roaring Stream*, p. 295, translation modified.

11. *Japanese Philosophy: A Sourcebook*, edited by James W. Heisig, Thomas P. Kasulis, and John C. Maraldo (Honolulu: University of Hawai'i Press, 2011), p. 190.

12. *Japanese Philosophy: A Sourcebook*, p. 193.

13. *The Blue Cliff Record*, translated by Thomas Cleary and J. C. Cleary (Boston: Shambhala, 1992), p. 1.

14. Zen Master Seung Sahn, *The Compass of Zen* (Boston: Shambhala, 1997), p. 353.

15. *Japanese Philosophy: A Sourcebook*, p. 193.

16. Dōgen, "The Presencing of Truth: Dōgen's *Genjōkōan*," translated by Bret W. Davis, in *Buddhist Philosophy: Essential Readings*, edited by Jay Garfield and William Edelglass (Oxford: Oxford University Press, 2009), p. 256.

17. *The Roaring Stream*, p. 251.

18. *Hakuin on Kenshō: The Four Ways of Knowing*, edited with commentary by Albert Low (Boston: Shambhala, 2006), p. 17.

19. *Hakuin on Kenshō*, p. 30.

20. Ibid.

21. *Zen Sourcebook*, pp. 37–38, translation slightly modified.

22. Ibid., p. 120.

23. *The Roaring Stream*, p. 45.

24. Myōan Eisai, *A Treatise on Letting Zen Flourish to Protect the State*, translated by Gishin Tokiwa, in *Zen Texts* (Berkeley, CA: Numata Center for Buddhist Translation and Research, 2005), p. 71, translation modified.

25. Asahina Sōgen, *Hekiganroku teishō* [Lectures on The Blue Cliff Record], rev. ed. (Kyoto: Sankibō Busshorin, 1997), pp. 592, 594. Asahina Rōshi shares with Eisai not only an emphasis on the spiritual teaching of the Buddha-mind but also a willingness to put Zen at the service of protecting the state. For a critique of Asahina Rōshi's

politics, see Brian Victoria, *Zen at War* (New York: Weatherhill, 1997), pp. 162–66. On this troubling issue, see the final sections of Chapters 16 and 17.

26. "Nishitani Keiji's 'The Standpoint of Zen: Directly Pointing to the Mind,'" translated by John C. Maraldo, edited with an introduction by Bret W. Davis, in *Buddhist Philosophy: Essential Readings*, edited by Jay Garfield and William Edelglass (Oxford: Oxford University Press, 2009), pp. 99–101.

27. Dōgen, *The Heart of Dōgen's Shōbōgenzō*, translated by Norman Waddell and Masao Abe (Albany: State University of New York Press, 2002), pp. 22–23.

28. Dōgen, *Treasury of the True Dharma Eye: Zen Master Dogen's Shobo Genzo*, edited by Kazuaki Tanahashi (Boston: Shambhala, 2012), p. 878.

29. Dōgen, *The Treasury of the True Dharma Eye*, pp. 423–26, translation modified.

30. Zenkei Shibayama, *The Gateless Barrier: Zen Comments on the Mumonkan*, translated by Sumiko Kudo (Boston: Shambhala, 2000), p. 214.

31. Ibid., p. 235.

32. Ibid., p. 236.

33. Ibid.

34. Ibid.

35. Ibid., p. 196.

36. Ibid., p. 134.

37. Ibid., p. 154.

Chapter 12

1. Ruben L. F. Habito, *Living Zen, Loving God* (Somerville, MA: Wisdom Publications, 2004); Robert E. Kennedy, *Zen Spirit, Christian Spirit: The Place of Zen in Christian Life* (New York: Continuum, 1995).

2. Kennedy, *Zen Spirit, Christian Spirit*, p. 14.

3. Walpola Rahula, *What the Buddha Taught*, 2nd ed. (New York: Grove Press, 1974), p. 1.

4. Ludwig Feuerbach, *The Essence of Christianity*, translated by George Eliot (Amherst, NY: Prometheus Books, 1989).

5. Rahula, *What the Buddha Taught*, p. 51. For references to texts by and on Freud in this regard, see note 13 of Chapter 7.

6. *The Collected Works of Shinran*, trans. Dennis Hirota et al. (Kyoto: Jōdo Shinshū Hongwanji-ha, 1997), vol. 1, pp. 461, 530.

7. See Peter Harvey, *An Introduction to Buddhism: Teachings, History, and Practices* (Cambridge: Cambridge University Press, 1990), p. 267; and John Powers, *A Concise Introduction to Tibetan Buddhism* (Ithaca, NY: Snow Lion Publications, 2008), pp. 76–79.

8. See the sources cited in note 12 of Chapter 10.

9. Urs App, *The Cult of Emptiness: The Western Discovery of Buddhist Thought and the Invention of Oriental Philosophy* (Rorschach: UniversityMedia, 2012), p. 14.

10. See App, *The Cult of Emptiness*; and Roger-Pol Droit, *The Cult of Nothingness: Philosophers and the Buddha*, trans. David Streit and Pamela Vohnson (Chapel Hill: University of North Carolina Press, 2003). On the no-self doctrine, see Chapters 7 and 8 of the present volume. The doctrine (or doctrines) of emptiness is discussed in various places (see index); for an in-depth study, see Bret W. Davis, "Forms of Emptiness in Zen," in *A Companion to Buddhist Philosophy*, edited by Steven Emmanuel (West Sussex: Wiley-Blackwell, 2013), pp. 190–213.

11. For a trenchant critique by a radical feminist theologian, see Mary Daly, *Beyond God the Father: Toward a Philosophy of Women's Liberation*, rev. ed. (Boston: Beacon Press, 1993).

12. Genesis 1:26.

13. Michael Coogan, *God and Sex: What the Bible Really Says* (New York: Twelve, 2010), p. 163–88. See also Karen Armstrong, *A History of God: The 4,000 Year Quest of Judaism, Christianity and Islam* (New York: Ballantine Books, 1993), pp. 50–54. Elaine Pagels writes that "the absence of feminine symbolism for God" sets Judaism, Christianity, and Islam "in striking contrast to the word's other religious traditions," including the teachings of Gnostic Christianity, many of whose "texts speak of God as a dyad who embraces both masculine and feminine elements." Elaine Pagels, *The Gnostic Gospels* (New York: Vintage Books, 1979), pp. 48–49.

14. See Merlin Stone, *When God Was a Woman* (New York: Harcourt, 1978); and *Womanspirit Rising: A Feminist Reader in Religion*, 2nd edition, edited by Carol P. Christ and Judith Plaskow (New York: HarperOne, 1992).

15. Emmanuel Levinas, *Difficult Freedom: Essays on Judaism*, translated by Seán Hand (Baltimore: Johns Hopkins University Press, 1990), p. 37.

16. *The Daodejing of Laozi*, translated by Philip J. Ivanhoe (Indianapolis, IN: Hackett, 2003), chapters 1, 40, 52. See Ellen M. Chen, "Dao as the Great Mother and the Influence of Motherly Love in the Shaping of Chinese Philosophy," *History of Religions* 14, no. 1 (August 1974): 51–64.

17. Taikō Yamasaki, *Shingon: Japanese Esoteric Buddhism*, translated by Richard and Cynthia Peterson, edited by Yasuyoshi Morimoto and David Kidd (Boston: Shambhala, 1988), p. 128.

18. Mark Unno, quoted in Jeff Wilson, "The Buddha of Infinite Light and Life," *Tricycle: The Buddhist Review*, Spring 2009.

19. *The Essential Shinran: A Buddhist Path of True Entrusting*, edited by Alfred Bloom (Bloomington, IN: World Wisdom, 2007), p. 83.

20. Nishida Kitarō, "The Logic of Place and the Religious Worldview," *Last Writings: Nothingness and the Religious Worldview*, translated by David A. Dilworth (Honolulu: University of Hawai'i Press, 1987), p. 77, translation modified.

21. *Nishida Kitarō zenshū* [The complete works of Nishida Kitarō] (Tokyo: Iwanami, 1987–89), vol. 12, pp. 7, 16–17. See Bret W. Davis, "Ethical and Religious Alterity: Nishida After Levinas," in *Kitarō Nishida in der Philosophie des 20. Jahrhunderts*, edited by Rolf Elberfeld and Yōko Arisaka (Freiburg: Alber Verlag, 2014), pp. 313–41.

22. Raimon Panikkar, *The Rhythm of Being: The Gifford Lectures* (Maryknoll, NY: Orbis Books, 2010), pp. 127–28. On Panikkar's rethinking of theology in terms of the

"rhythm of Being" as a nondualistic, perichoretic dance among the three dimensions of reality, the "cosmotheandric" trinity of World, Man, and God, see ibid., pp. 37–54, 105–106, and chapters 5 and 6. On Panikkar's conception of intrareligious and interreligious dialogue, see Raimon Panikkar, *The Intrareligious Dialogue* (New York: Paulist Press, 1999); and Bret W. Davis, "Sharing Words of Silence: Panikkar After Gadamer," *Comparative and Continental Philosophy* 7, no. 1 (2015): 52–68.

23. See Deuteronomy 2:34, 3:6, 7:1–2, 13:15, 20:13–17; Joshua 6:17–24; and 1 Samuel 15:3.

24. After writing this I came across the following passage by a Christian theologian who has endeavored to rethink God in the language of Buddhist rather than Greek philosophy: "We [Christians] have been more anxious for proof that there is a God than for an understanding of what is meant by the word *God*." Joseph S. O'Leary, "Toward a Buddhist Interpretation of Christian Truth," in *Many Mansions: Multiple Religious Belonging and Christian Identity*, edited by Catherine Cornille (Eugene, OR: Wipf and Stock, 2002). pp. 40–41. See also the discussion of interreligious dialogue in Chapter 1 of the present volume.

25. *Zengaku daijiten* [Large dictionary of Zen Studies] (Tokyo: Daishūkan, 1985), p. 603.

26. *The Record of Linji*, translated by Ruth Fuller Sasaki, edited by Thomas Yūhō Kirchner (Honolulu: University of Hawai'i Press, 2009), p. 155.

27. Dōgen, "Guidlines for Studying the Way," in *Moon in a Dewdrop: Writings of Zen Master Dōgen*, edited by Kazuaki Tanahashi (San Francisco: North Point Press, 1985), p. 42.

28. *The Essential Teachings of Zen Master Hakuin*, translated by Norman Waddell (Boston: Shambhala, 2010), p. 62.

29. Some further comments on "faith" in Zen are provided in Chapters 3, 6, 21, and 22. For an in-depth study of this topic, see Bret W. Davis, "Faith and/or/as Enlightenment: Rethinking Religion from the Perspective of Japanese Buddhism," in *Asian Philosophies and the Idea of Religion: Paths Beyond Faith and Reason*, edited by Sonia Sikka and Ashwani Peetush (New York: Routledge, 2020), pp. 36–64.

30. See *The Essential Augustine*, edited by Vernon J. Bourke (New York: Hackett, 1974), p. 19.

31. See Elaine Pagels, *Beyond Belief: The Secret Gospel of Thomas* (New York: Vintage Books, 2003); and Davis, "Faith and/or/as Enlightenment."

32. The Gospel of Thomas, in Pagels, *Beyond Belief*, p. 239, emphasis added.

33. Ibid., pp. 229, 241.

34. James W. Heisig, *Jesus' Twin: A Dialogue with the Gospel of Thomas* (New York: Crossroads, 2015), pp. 15, 159.

35. The Gospel of Thomas, in Pagels, *Beyond Belief*, pp. 235, 241, 231, 237.

36. John 3:3; Luke 17:20–21.

37. Kosho Uchiyama, *Opening the Hand of Thought: Foundations of Zen Buddhist Practice*, translated and edited by Tom Wright, Jisho Warner, and Shohaku Okumura (Somerville, MA: Wisdom Publications, 2004), p. 111.

38. Thich Nhat Hanh, *The Heart of the Buddha's Teaching* (Berkeley, CA: Parallax Press, 1998), pp. 120, 142.

39. *The Vimalakirti Sutra*, trans. Burton Watson (New York: Columbia University Press, 1997), pp. 26, 29–30.

40. Thich Nhat Hanh, *Finding Our True Home: Living in the Pure Land Here and Now* (Berkeley, CA: Parallax Press, 2001), p. 23.

41. Quoted in Jan van Bragt, "Salvation and Enlightenment: Pure Land Buddhism and Christianity," *Nanzan Bulletin* 14 (1990): 30.

42. The most famous account of the Jesus Prayer is the anonymous book by a nineteenth-century Russian author: *The Way of a Pilgrim*, translated by R. M. French, foreword by Huston Smith (New York: HarperOne, 1965).

43. Matthew 5:4.

44. Matthew 6:10.

45. See Gustavo Gutierrez, *A Theology of Liberation: History, Politics, and Salvation*, rev. ed., translated by Caridad Inda and John Eagleson (Maryknoll, NY: Orbis Books, 1988), pp. 10–12.

46. On some modern Pure Land Buddhists who were inspired by Marxism, see Melissa Ann-Marie Curley, *Pure Land, Real World: Modern Buddhism, Japanese Leftists, and the Utopian Imagination* (Honolulu: University of Hawai'i Press, 2017). On premodern peasant uprisings led by Pure Land Buddhists, see Thomas Kasulis, *Engaging Japanese Philosophy* (Honolulu: University of Hawai'i Press, 2018), pp. 269, 410. On Marx's critique of religion and what Christians (and by implication adherents of other religions) can learn from it, see Merold Westphal, *Suspicion and Faith: The Religious Uses of Modern Atheism* (New York: Fordham University Press, 1998), part 3.

47. To be sure, there are cases where the abstract idea of spiritual equality has served to excuse and even promote acquiescence to status quo social inequality. The modern proponents of so-called Critical Buddhism have effectively brought attention to such problems. See Hakamaya Noriaki, "Thoughts on the Ideological Background of Social Discrimination," translated by Jamie Hubbard, in *Pruning the Bodhi Tree: The Storm over Critical Buddhism*, edited by Jamie Hubbard and Paul L. Swanson (Honolulu: University of Hawai'i Press, 1997), pp. 339–55. See also James Mark Shields, *Critical Buddhism: Engaging with Modern Japanese Buddhist Thought* (Burlington, VT: Ashgate, 2011).

48. Jeramiah 23:24.

49. Acts 17:28.

50. Ephesians 4:6.

51. John W. Cooper distinguishes between "personal and nonpersonal or Ground-of-being panentheism." John W. Cooper, *Panentheism: The Other God of the Philosophers* (Grand Rapids, MI: Baker Academic, 2006), p. 28. The Zen understanding of reality is more akin to the "nonpersonal" species, according to which "the Divine is the Ground—the ultimate cause, source, and power—of personhood and interpersonal communion but is not itself personal" (ibid.). However, Zen resonates more with panentheists like Eckhart and Schelling who speak of a Nothingness, an *Ungrund* (unground), or an abyss that underlies and undercuts even such distinctions as Divine Ground vs. Mundane Manifestations, and it speaks of this in terms of an

Interrelational Field rather than as a Substantial Ground. (Cooper briefly addresses the Zen or Zen-inspired thought of Masao Abe and Alan Watts in ibid., 232–33.)

52. *The Roaring Stream: A New Zen Reader*, edited by Nelson Foster and Jack Shoemaker (Hopewell, NJ: Ecco Press, 1996), p. 294.

53. *The Roaring Stream*, pp. 91–93.

54. *Udāna* 8:3; 80–81; in *In the Buddha's Words: An Anthology of Discourses from the Pāli Canon*, edited and introduced by Bhikkhu Bodhi (Somerville, MA: Wisdom Publications, 2005), p. 366.

55. See note 49 of Chapter 23.

56. See Nāgārjuna, *The Fundamental Wisdom of the Middle Way: Nāgārjuna's Mūlamadhyamakakārikā*, translated with commentary by Jay L. Garfield (New York: Oxford University Press, 1995), pp. 332–33.

57. *The Heart Sutra*, translation and commentary by Red Pine (Emeryville, CA: Shoemaker & Hoard, 2004), pp. 90–96.

58. *The Roaring Stream*, p. 22.

59. *Zen Sourcebook: Traditional Documents from China, Korea, and Japan*, edited by Stephen Addiss with Stanley Lombardo and Judith Roitman (Indianapolis, IN: Hackett, 2008), p. 231.

60. *Zen Sourcebook*, p. 233.

61. Thich Nhat Hanh, *The Heart of Understanding: Commentaries on the Prajñaparamita Heart Sutra*, rev. ed. (Berkeley, CA: Parallax Press, 2009), p. 20.

62. Dōgen, *The Heart of Dōgen's Shōbōgenzō*, translated by Norman Waddell and Masao Abe (Albany: State University of New York Press, 2002), p. 106.

63. Shohaku Okumura, with contributions by Carl Bielefeldt, Gary Snyder, and Issho Fujita, *The Mountains and Waters Sūtra: A Practitioner's Guide to Dōgen's "Sansuikyo"* (Somerville, MA: Wisdom Publications, 2018), pp. 61–63, 77, 82.

64. Dōgen, *The Heart of Dōgen's Shōbōgenzō*, pp. 21, 63. Okumura informs us that "Senika, who appears in the Mahayana Mahaparinirvana Sutra [chapter 39], is a non-Buddhist who converses with Shakyamuni about the nature of the mind/body relationship. In the discussion Senika propounds the theory of an eternal self that exists beyond the body, but later accepts the teaching of anatman as it is presented by the Buddha and becomes a Buddhist monk." Shohaku Okumura, *Realizing Genjokoan: The Key to Dogen's Shobogenzo* (Somerville, MA: Wisdom Publications, 2010), p. 284n22. Senika's soul-body dualism resembles the metaphysics of Jainism, which maintains that an individual soul (Sk. *jiva*) is trapped inside a karmically produced body, and that the point of spiritual practice is to liberate the soul from the body (for a clear synopsis, see John Koller, *Asian Philosophies*, 7th ed. [New York: Pearson, 2018], pp. 31–38). This also resembles the Orphic idea that the soul (Gk. *psyche*) must be liberated from the "tomb of the body" (Gk. *sema-soma*), a view apparently endorsed by Plato (see Plato's *Gorgias* 493a, *Cratylus* 400c, *Phaedo* 62b, and *Phaedrus* 250c). On Shakyamuni Buddha's clear rejection of such a view, see *Mahātanhāsankhaya Sutta*, in *The Middle Length Discourses of the Buddha: A Translation of the Majjhima Nikāya*, 2nd ed., translated by Bhikkhu Nānamoli and Bhikkhu Bodhi (Somerville, MA: Wisdom Publications, 2001), pp. 349–61.

65. Dōgen, *The Heart of Dōgen's Shōbōgenzō*, p. 106.

66. Dōgen, *Treasury of the True Dharma Eye: Zen Master Dogen's Shobo Genzo*, edited by Kazuaki Tanahashi (Boston: Shambhala, 2012), p. 451, translation modified.

67. Okumura, *The Mountains and Waters Sūtra*, pp. 79–81.

68. Okumura, *Realizing Genjokoan*, p. 125.

69. See Martin Heidegger, *Being and Time*, translated by Joan Stambaugh, revised by Dennis J. Schmidt (Albany: State University of New York Press, 2010), pp. 227–55. See also the section entitled "From Being-Towards-Death to the Great Death: An Exhortation from Zen," in Bret W. Davis, *Heidegger and the Will: On the Way to Gelassenheit* (Evanston, IL: Northwestern University Press, 2007), pp. 56–59.

70. Martin Heidegger, *Gesamtausgabe* (Frankfurt: Vittorio Klostermann, 2000), vol. 16, p. 605.

71. Keiji Nishitani, "Reflections on Two Addresses by Martin Heidegger," in *Heidegger and Asian Thought*, edited by Graham Parkes (Honolulu: University of Hawai'i Press, 1987), p. 152. This is not to say it would mean exactly the same thing if it came from the mouth of a man of Zen. In Chapter 23, we'll return to Zen's eschewal of other-worldly orientations of religions such as the Christianity espoused by Abraham a Sancta Clara.

72. *Japanese Death Poems: Written by Zen Monks and Haiku Poets on the Verge of Death*, compiled with an introduction and commentary by Yoel Hoffmann (Tokyo: Charles E. Tuttle, 1986), p. 6.

73. For an alternative translation, see *The Roaring Stream*, p. 290.

74. Kusumoto Bunyū, *Zengo nyūmon* [Introduction to Zen terms] (Tokyo: Daihōrinkaku, 1982), p. 104.

75. *The Roaring Stream*, p. 68.

76. Matthew 10:38–39.

77. See Matthew 16:25, Mark 8:35, Luke 17:33, and John 3:1–8 and 12:25.

78. Harvey D. Egan, *An Anthology of Christian Mysticism*, 2nd ed. (Collegeville, MN: Liturgical Press, 1996), p. 220.

79. Cornel West, "Introduction: The Radical King We Don't Know," in Martin Luther King Jr., *The Radical King*, edited and introduced by Cornel West (Boston: Beacon Press, 2015), p. xvi.

80. This is why Anabaptist Christians, such as the Amish, believe that baptism should be undertaken by fully consenting adults rather than involuntarily by babies.

81. Galatians 2:19–20.

82. Dōgen, *The Heart of Dōgen's Shōbōgenzō*, pp. 106–7.

83. The Buddhist philosopher and Rinzai Zen practitioner Takemura Makio writes in this regard that "*zazen* is in fact a matter of letting go of self-power and giving oneself over to the working of a life that transcends the self. Hence, as ways of thoroughly casting off self-power, Zen and Pure Land Buddhism join hands." Takemura Makio, *Zen no shisō wo shiru jiten* [Encyclopedia for understanding Zen thought] (Tokyo: Tōkyōdō Shuppan, 2014), p. 33.

84. See Bret W. Davis, "Naturalness in Zen and Shin Buddhism: Before and Beyond Self- and Other-Power," *Contemporary Buddhism* 15, no. 2 (July 2014): 433–47.

85. Quoted in Yoshifumi Ueda and Dennis Hirota, *Shinran: An Introduction to His Thought* (Kyoto: Hongwanji International Center, 1989), p. 226, translation modified.

86. *Japanese Philosophy: A Sourcebook*, edited by James W. Heisig, Thomas P. Kasulis, and John C. Maraldo (Honolulu: University of Hawai'i Press, 2011), p. 193.

87. Meister Eckhart, *Deutsche Predigten und Traktate*, edited with modern German translations by Josef Quint (Munich: Carl Hanser, 1963), pp. 110, 308–9, 389.

88. See Bret W. Davis, *Heidegger and the Will*, chapter 6, "Releasement to and from God's Will: Excursus on Meister Eckhart After Heidegger," especially pp. 127–36.

89. Yamada Mumon, *Lectures on* The Ten Oxherding Pictures, translated by Victor Sōgen Hori (Honolulu: University of Hawai'i Press, 2004), pp. 41–42.

90. Dōgen, *Moon in a Dewdrop: Writings of Zen Master Dôgen*, edited by Kazuaki Tanahashi (New York: North Point Press, 1985), p. 219.

91. My translation from the original Japanese as quoted in Takemura Makio, *Zen no tetsugaku* [Philosophy of Zen] (Tokyo: Chūsekisha, 2004), p. 29. Dōgen's poem plays a central role in Takemura's illuminating philosophical interpretation of Zen (see also ibid., pp. 113, 135, 151).

92. Ibid., p. 31; see also ibid., p. 52.

93. Zenkei Shibayama, *The Gateless Barrier: Zen Comments on the Mumonkan*, translated by Sumiko Kudo (Boston: Shambhala, 2000), p. 140.

94. Thich Nhat Hanh, *Going Home: Jesus and Buddha as Brothers* (New York: Riverhead Books, 1999), p. 30

95. See Hans A. Fischer-Barnicol's account in *The Letters of Martin Buber: A Life of Dialogue*, edited by Nahum N. Glatzer and Paul Mendes-Flohr, translated by Richard and Clara Winston and Harry Zohn (New York: Schocken Books, 1991), p. 663. Nishitani's question has deep roots in the Zen tradition. When the Chinese Zen master Yinyuan came to Japan and established the Ōbaku School there in the 17th century, he introduced the Ming dynasty (1368–1644) Chinese Zen practice of what was called the *nembutsu kōan*, which entails meditating on the question, "Who, right now, is chanting Amida's name?" See Peter D. Hershock, *Public Zen, Personal Zen: A Buddhist Introduction* (Lanham: Roman & Littlefield, 2014), pp. 136–137. The 16th century Chinese Zen master Yunqi Zhuhong's taught the use of this *nembutsu kōan*, saying that "Reflecting back on '*Who is the person reciting the buddha-name?*' has the same intent as studying Zen. With this "fundamental kōan" in mind, he instructed, "Turn the light around and observe for yourself, until you know the ultimate locus of this mindfulness of buddha." *Pure Land, Pure Mind: The Buddhism of Masters Chu-hung and Tsung-pen*, translated by J. C. Cleary (New York: Sutra Translation Committee of the United States and Canada, 1994), pp. 84, 67.

Chapter 13

1. Meister Eckhart, *Deutsche Predigten und Traktate*, edited with modern German translations by Josef Quint (Munich: Carl Hanser, 1963), pp. 214, 202.

2. Nishida Kitarō, the founder of the Kyoto School, was fond of this saying. See Nishida Kitarō, "The Logic of Place and the Religious Worldview," *Last Writings: Nothingness and the Religious Worldview*, translated by David A. Dilworth (Honolulu: University of Hawai'i Press, 1987), p. 70. And so was his most famous student, the lay Zen master and philosopher Nishitani Keiji. See Nishitani Keiji, *Religion and Nothingness*, translated by Jan Van Bragt (Berkeley: University of California Press, 1982), p. 102; see also *Nishitani Keiji chosakushū* [Collected works of Nishitani Keiji] (Tokyo: Sōbunsha, 1990), vol. 11, pp. 59–60.

3. Kenneth Kraft, *Eloquent Zen: Daitō and Early Japanese Zen* (Honolulu: University of Hawai'i Press, 1992), p. 192, translation modified.

4. Ibid., 187.

5. *Zen Sourcebook: Traditional Documents from China, Korea, and Japan*, edited by Stephen Addiss with Stanley Lombardo and Judith Roitman (Indianapolis, IN: Hackett, 2008), pp. 37–38, translation slightly modified.

6. *The Roaring Stream: A New Zen Reader*, edited by Nelson Foster and Jack Shoemaker (Hopewell, NJ: Ecco Press, 1996), p. 93.

7. *The Record of Linji*, translation with commentary by Ruth Fuller Sasaki, edited by Thomas Yūhō Kirchner (Honolulu: University of Hawai'i Press, 2009), p. 22.

8. *The Roaring Stream*, pp. 90–91, translation modified.

9. As quoted in Phillip Kapleau, *The Three Pillars of Zen: Teaching, Practice and Enlightenment* (New York: Anchor Books, 1989), pp. 182–83.

10. Quoted in *Jūgyūzu—Zazengi* [The Ten Oxherding Pictures—the principles of Zen meditation], edited with commentary by Akizuki Ryōmin (Tokyo: Shunjūsha, 1989), p. 101. See also Yuanwu's opening remarks on Case 95 in *The Blue Cliff Record*, and a similar saying by Ziyuan in his preface to the tenth of *The Ten Oxherding Pictures* (see the penultimate section of Chapter 24 in the present volume).

11. *Shōyōroku* [Ch. Congronglu], edited by Yasutani Hakuun (Tokyo: Shunjūsha, 1973), p. 321.

12. *Zen Sourcebook*, p. 234.

13. See especially chapters 13 and 17 of the *Diamond Sutra*; also see Thich Nhat Hanh's commentary in *The Diamond That Cuts Through Illusion: Commentaries on the Prajñaparamit Diamond Sutra* (Berkeley, CA: Parallax Press, 1992), chapter 6.

14. See Michiko Yusa, "D. T. Suzuki and the 'Logic of Sokuhi,' or the 'Logic of Prajñāpāramitā," in *The Dao Companion to Japanese Buddhist Philosophy*, edited by Gereon Kopf (Dordrecht: Springer, 2019), pp. 589–616; and Mori Tetsurō, "D. T. Suzuki's Logic of Is/Not as Zen Praxis," translated by Bret W. Davis, in *The Oxford Handbook of Japanese Philosophy*, edited by Bret W. Davis (New York: Oxford University Press, 2020), pp. 249–56.

15. *Taishō Shinshū Daizōkyō*, edited by Takakusu Junjirō and Watanabe Kaigyoku (Tokyo: Taishō Issaikyō Kankōkai, 1924–32), 51:614b–c. See Masao Abe, *Zen and Western Thought*, edited by William R. LaFleur (Honolulu: University of Hawai'i Press, 1985), p. 4.

16. On Zen's perspectivism, see the articles cited in note 4 of the Preface.

17. Here and below I am using my own translation of this kōan, Case 19 in *The Gateless Barrier*. Compare Zenkei Shibayama, *The Gateless Barrier: Zen Comments on the Mumonkan*, translated by Sumiko Kudo (Boston: Shambhala, 2000), p. 140.

18. *The Roaring Stream*, p. 24, capitalization added.

19. *The Record of Linji*, translation with commentary by Ruth Fuller Sasaki, edited by Thomas Yūhō Kirchner (Honolulu: University of Hawai'i Press, 2009), pp. 11–12, translation modified.

20. Ibid., p. 20, translation modified.

21. *Nenge Roku* [The record of Zen master Tanaka Hōjū Rōshi], edited by Tanaka Kanjū (Kyoto: Daitsūin, 2014), p. 31.

22. *The Gateless Barrier*, p. 67.

23. The following summary account is based on Bret W. Davis, "Letting Go of God for Nothing: Ueda Shizuteru's Non-Mysticism and the Question of Ethics in Zen Buddhism," in *Frontiers of Japanese Philosophy 2*, edited by Victor Sōgen Hori and Melissa Anne-Marie Curley (Nagoya: Nanzan Institute for Religion and Culture, 2008), pp. 226–255, which is, in turn, based mainly on Ueda Shizuteru, *Hishinpishugi—Ekkuharuto to Zen* [Non-mysticism: Eckhart and Zen], volume 8 of *Ueda Shizuteru shū* [Ueda Shizuteru collection] (Tokyo: Iwanami, 2002). See also the updated edition of Ueda's first book, written in German and published in 1965 on the basis of his doctoral dissertation at the University of Marburg: *Die Gottesgeburt in der Seele und der Durchbruch zur Gottheit: Die mystische Anthropologie Meister Eckharts und ihre Konfrontation mit der Mystik des Zen-Buddhismus* (Freiburg: Verlag Karl Alber, 2018). For some of his writings available in English translation on this topic, see Ueda Shizuteru, "'Nothingness' in Meister Eckhart and Zen Buddhism: With Particular Reference to the Borderlands of Philosophy and Theology," translated by James W. Heisig, in *The Buddha Eye: An Anthology of the Kyoto School and Its Contemporaries*, edited by Frederick Frank (Bloomington, IN: World Wisdom, 2004), pp. 157–69; and Ueda Shizuteru, "Ascent and Descent: Zen in Comparison with Meister Eckhart," translated by James W. Heisig, Part I in *The Eastern Buddhist* 16, no. 1 (1983): 52–73; Part II in *The Eastern Buddhist* 16, no. 2 (1983): 72–91.

24. *Meister Eckhart: The Essential Sermons, Commentaries, Treatises, and Defense*, translated by Edmund Colledge and Bernard McGinn (Mahwah, NJ: Paulist Press, 1981), pp. 202–3.

25. Eckhart, *Deutsche Predigten und Traktate*, p. 316.

26. See Meister Eckhart, "Saul Rose from the Ground," in Reiner Schürmann, *Meister Eckhart: Mystic and Philosopher* (Bloomington: Indiana University Press, 1978), pp. 122–28; and Ueda, "'Nothingness' in Meister Eckhart and Zen Buddhism." Jewish Kabbalists have also referred to the essential nature of God as "Nothing (*ayin*)." "The highest form of divinity that the human mind can conceive is equated with nothingness because it bears no comparison with any of the other things in existence." Karen Armstrong, *A History of God: The 4,000 Year Quest of Judaism, Christianity and Islam* (New York: Ballantine Books, 1993), p. 248. However, Ueda distinguishes the Zen understanding of nothingness from a negative theological one, insofar as the latter

serves as a cloak for an ineffably transcendent being. See Davis, "Letting Go of God for Nothing," p. 236.

27. *The Gateless Barrier*, p. 19.

28. Frederick Copleston, S.J., *A History of Philosophy* (New York: Image Books, 1993), vol. 1, p. 76.

29. See Bret W. Davis, *Heidegger and the Will* (Evanston, IL: Northwestern University Press, 2007), chapter 6, "Releasement to and from God's Will: Excursus on Meister Eckhart after Heidegger," especially pp. 127–36.

30. See Eckhart, *Deutsche Predigten und Traktate*, 89–90; and Ueda, "'Nothingness' in Meister Eckhart and Zen Buddhism," p. 160.

31. *The Blue Cliff Record*, translated by Thomas Cleary and J. C. Cleary (Boston: Shambhala, 1992), p. 270, translation modified.

Chapter 14

1. *The Roaring Stream: A New Zen Reader*, edited by Nelson Foster and Jack Shoemaker (Hopewell, NJ: Ecco Press, 1996), p. 65.

2. See "Instructions for the Tenzo (Tenzokyōkun)," in *Dōgen's Pure Standards for the Zen Community: A Translation of Eihei Shingi*, translated by Taigen Daniel Leighton and Shohaku Okumura (Albany: State University of New York Press, 1996), pp. 40–42.

3. Zen Master Dōgen and Kōshō Uchiyama Rōshi, *How to Cook Your Life: From the Zen Kitchen to Enlightenment*, translated by Thomas Wright (Boston: Shambhala, 2005), p. 83. See also the illuminating philosophical interpretation given in Thomas Kasulis, *Engaging Japanese Philosophy* (Honolulu: University of Hawai'i Press, 2018), pp. 214–37.

4. See *The Roaring Stream*, pp. 64–69.

5. *The Vimalakirti Sūtra*, translated by Burton Watson (New York: Columbia University Press, 1997), p. 65.

6. Ibid., pp. 26–31.

7. Ibid., pp. 37, 67–72.

8. Ibid., pp. 90–91.

9. Dōgen, *Treasury of the True Dharma Eye: Zen Master Dogen's Shobo Genzo*, edited by Kazuaki Tanahashi (Boston: Shambhala, 2012), pp. 72–77.

10. Charlotte Joko Beck, *Everyday Zen: Love and Work* (San Francisco: HarperOne, 2007). Joan Halifax, *Being with Dying: Cultivating Compassion and Fearlessness in the Presence of Death* (Boston: Shambhala, 2009).

11. See Zenju Earthlyn Manuel, *The Way of Tenderness: Awakening Through Race, Sexuality, and Gender* (Somerville, MA: Wisdom, 2015); Angel Kyodo Williams and Rod Owens, with Jasmine Syedullah, *Radical Dharma: Talking Race, Love, and Liberation* (Berkeley, CA: North Atlantic Press, 2016); and *Buddhism and Whiteness: Critical Reflections*, edited by George Yancy and Emily McRae (Lanham, MD: Lexington Books, 2019).

12. *The Vimalakirti Sūtra*, p. 70.

13. *Wild Ivy: The Spiritual Biography of Zen Master Hakuin*, translated by Norman Waddell (Boston: Shambhala, 1999), pp. 34–35.

14. See Thich Nhat Hanh, *Interbeing: Fourteen Guidelines for Engaged Buddhism*, 3rd ed. (Berkeley, CA: Parallax Press, 1987). For an inspiring collection of brief essays by leading figures of this movement, see *True Peace Work: Essential Writings on Engaged Buddhism*, 2nd ed. (Berkeley, CA: Parallax Press, 2019). For an excellent scholarly treatment of the main ideas and arguments, see Sallie B. King, *Being Benevolence: The Social Ethics of Engaged Buddhism* (Honolulu: University of Hawai'i Press, 2005).

15. Thich Nhat Hanh, *Being Peace* (Berkeley, CA: Parallax Press, 1987), p. 48.

16. Robert Aitken, *The Mind of Clover: Essays in Zen Buddhist Ethics* (San Francisco: North Point Press, 1984), p. 3.

17. *The Vimalakirti Sūtra*, p. 37, translation modified.

18. *The Platform Sutra: The Zen Teachings of Hui-neng*, translated by Red Pine (Emeryville, CA: Shoemaker & Hoard, 2006), p. 11, translation modified.

19. *The Vimalakirti Sūtra*, pp. 34 and 98.

20. John 14:27.

21. Thich Nhat Hanh, *Going Home: Jesus and Buddha as Brothers* (New York: Riverhead Books, 1999).

22. 1 John 4:8.

23. Paul F. Knitter, *Without Buddha I Could Not Be a Christian* (London: Oneworld Publications, 2009), pp. 18–20.

24. Ibid., p. 167.

25. Nhat Hanh, *Being Peace*, pp. 3, 80.

26. Knitter, *Without Buddha I Could Not Be a Christian*, p. 184.

27. Gandhi's family reportedly affirmed that Gandhi often said this, although these exact words do not appear in any of his writings. The earliest in-print use of the phrase "Be the change you want to see happen" has been traced back to a 1974 book chapter entitled "The Love Project" by a Brooklyn high school teacher named Arleen Lorrance. See https://quoteinvestigator.com/2017/10/23/be-change/.

28. Mahatma Gandhi, *The Essential Gandhi: An Anthology of His Writings on His Life, Work, and Ideas*, edited by Louis Fischer (New York: Vintage, 2002), p. 146. On Gandhi's insistence on "self-purification," "reform from within," and attaining peace by peaceful means, see also ibid., pp. 164–66, 174, 215, 267, 293–94.

29. Martin Luther King Jr., *The Radical King*, edited and introduced by Cornel West (Boston: Beacon Press, 2015), p. 98.

30. King, *The Radical King*, pp. 216–17.

31. See Bernie Glassman, *Bearing Witness: A Zen Master's Lessons in Making Peace* (New York: Bell Tower, 1998); and the website for the Zen Peacemakers international organization he founded: https://zenpeacemakers.org. See also The Buddhist Peace Fellowship (http://www.buddhistpeacefellowship.org), as well as its journal, *Turning the Wheel: The Journal of Socially Engaged Buddhism*.

32. Knitter, *Without Buddha I Could Not Be a Christian*, p. 173.

33. Ibid., p. 183.

34. Matthew 5:38–40.

35. Gandhi, *The Essential Gandhi*, p. 177; see also ibid., pp. 83, 167–68.

36. King, *The Radical King*, p. 58. King explains that his method of non-violent resistance "does not seek to defeat or humiliate the opponent, but to win his friendship and understanding. . . . [T]he attack is directed against forces of evil rather than against persons who happen to be doing the evil" (pp. 49–50).

37. David R. Loy, *The Great Awakening: A Buddhist Social Theory* (Somerville, MA: Wisdom Publications, 2003), pp. 105–7.

38. "West Nickel Mines School Shooting," Wikipedia, accessed June 30, 2021, https://en.wikipedia.org/wiki/West_Nickel_Mines_School_shooting#Incident.

39. Sallie B. King, *Socially Engaged Buddhism* (Honolulu: University of Hawai'i Press, 2009), p. 37.

40. *Summa Theologiae*, III, Supplementum, Q. 94, Art. 1, as translated by Walter Kaufmann in *Basic Writings of Nietzsche* (New York: Random House, 1968), p. 485. On Nietzsche's critique of Christianity and what Christians (and by implication adherents of other religions) can learn from taking it seriously, see Merold Westphal, *Suspicion and Faith: The Religious Uses of Modern Atheism* (New York: Fordham University Press, 1998), part 4. Quoting John Howard Yoder's warning against the "egocentric altruism" that makes of oneself "the incarnation of a good and righteous cause for which others may rightly be made to suffer," Westphal writes: "Is there a better explanation of the mutual terrorism that has defined the Arab-Israeli conflict, or, to bring the matter closer to home, of Hiroshima and Nagasaki?" (Westphal, *Suspicion and Faith*, p. 255). In Chapter 16 we'll discuss the Zen teaching that we need to drop all our egocentric and ethnocentric conceptions of good and evil in order to recover a non-judgmental awareness that is open to all the myriad perspectives on the concrete and fluid contexts in which non-egocentric judgements need to be made.

41. Revelation 14:9–11.

42. To be sure, in his own manner Nietzsche also affirmed such virtues and sought to chart an alternative course to their realization. On the complexity, depth, and deep ambivalences in Nietzsche's thought, especially in relation to Buddhism, see Bret W. Davis, "Zen After Zarathustra: The Problem of the Will in the Confrontation Between Nietzsche and Buddhism," *Journal of Nietzsche Studies* 28 (2004): 89–138; and Bret W. Davis, "Nietzsche as Zebra: With Both Egoistic Antibuddha and Nonegoistic Bodhisattva Stripes," *Journal of Nietzsche Studies* 46, no. 1 (2015): 62–81.

43. Alternative translation: "Animosity does not eradicate animosity. Only by loving kindness is animosity dissolved." *The Dhammapada*, translated by Ananda Maitreya (Berkeley, CA: Parallax Press, 1995), p. 2.

44. Gandhi, *The Essential Gandhi*, pp. 293–94.

45. King, *The Radical King*, p. 59.

46. See "Beyond Vietnam: A Time to Break Silence," in King, *The Radical King*, pp. 201–17. In the following passage from the concluding chapter of King's last book, *Where Do We Go from Here: Chaos or Community?*, written in 1967, the clear resonances with, and perhaps even influences from, Thich Nhat Hanh's Zen Buddhist teaching of engendering peace among all people and nations by waking up to the ontological and ethical reality of our "interbeing" are plainly apparent: "From time immemorial

men have lived by the principle that 'self-preservation is the first law of life.' But this is a false assumption. I would say that other-preservation is the first law of life. It is the first law of life precisely because we cannot preserve self without being concerned about preserving other selves. The universe is so constructed that things go awry if men are not diligent in their cultivation of the other-regarding dimension. 'I' cannot reach fulfillment without 'thou.' The self cannot be self without other selves. . . . All men are interdependent. . . . In a real sense, all life is interrelated. The agony of the poor impoverishes the rich; the betterment of the poor enriches the rich. We are inevitably our brother's keeper because we are our brother's brother. Whatever affects one directly affects all indirectly" ("The World House," reprinted in *The Radical King*, pp. 86–87).

Chapter 15

1. Alternative translation: "Where there is anger, apply loving kindness. Where there is evil, offer good." *The Dhammapada*, translated by Ananda Maitreya (Berkeley: Parallax Press, 1995), p. 63 (chapter 17, verse 3).

2. Luke 6:27; Marcus Borg, ed., *Jesus and Buddha: The Parallel Sayings* (Berkeley, CA: Ulysses Press, 1997), pp. 18–19.

3. Much of what has been written on this controversial topic is overly laden with either a defensive eclesiastical agenda or an aggressive anti-eclesiastical agenda, and some of it is of notoriously questionable scholarship. For a clear and fairly cautious assessment of the claims, see James M. Hansen, "Was Jesus a Buddhist?," *Buddhist-Christian Studies* 25 (2005): 75–89.

4. Romans 12:17–21.

5. In Tibet and elsewhere, Vajrayana Buddhists do employ Tantric practices that entail visualizing deities, some of whom are wrathful in nature. Yet, the visualizion is a skillful means of transmuting the energy of a practitioner's deluded afflictions into the positive energy of their enlightened nature. For example, Yamantaka, Conqueror of Death, is the wrathful form of the Bodhisattva of Wisdom, Manjusri. "The anger which the *yi-dam* [tutelary deity] shows is not that of a vengeful god, but, hate-free, it aims to open up the practitioner's heart by devastating his hesitations, doubts, confusions and ignorance. . . . By visualizing such a fearful form, . . . the practitioner can clearly see the danger in his own tendency to anger, and can transmute it into a wisdom." Peter Harvey, *An Introduction to Buddhism: Teachings, History, and Practices* (Cambridge: Cambridge University Press, 1990), pp. 261–62.

6. Galatians 6:7–9.

7. *Anguttara Nikāya* III.415, as quoted in Harvey, *An Introduction to Buddhism*, p. 40.

8. Dōgen, *Treasury of the True Dharma Eye: Zen Master Dogen's Shobo Genzo*, edited by Kazuaki Tanahashi (Boston: Shambhala, 2012), p. 475, translation modified.

9. David R. Loy, *The Great Awakening: A Buddhist Social Theory* (Somerville, MA: Wisdom Publications, 2003), p. 7.

10. Ibid., p. 133.

11. Aristotle, *Nicomachean Ethics*, translated by Martin Ostwald (New York: Macmillan, 1962), p. 34.

12. Richard Gombrich, *What the Buddha Thought* (London: Equinox, 2009), pp. 13, 60. See also Traleg Kyabgon, *Karma: What It Is, What It Isn't, Why It Matters* (Boulder, CO: Shambhala, 2015), pp. 34, 47–48.

13. Nyanaponika Thera, "Karma and Its Fruit," in *The Buddha and His Teachings*, edited by Samuel Bercholz and Sherab Chödzin Kohn (Boston: Shambhala, 2003), p. 123.

14. Ibid., p. 126. David Loy makes the case for an empowering rather than fatalistic understanding of karma in "How to Drive Your Karma," in David R. Loy, *Money, Sex, War, Karma: Notes for a Buddhist Revolution* (Somerville, MA: Wisdom Publications, 2008), pp. 53–63.

15. Christopher W. Gowans, *Philosophy of the Buddha* (New York: Routledge, 2003), pp. 87, 105.

16. Thich Nhat Hanh, *The Heart of the Buddha's Teaching* (Berkeley, CA: Parallax Press, 1998), p. 24.

17. *Japanese Philosophy: A Sourcebook*, edited by James W. Heisig, Thomas P. Kasulis, and John C. Maraldo (Honolulu: University of Hawai'i Press, 2011), pp. 197–98.

18. Zenkei Shibayama, *The Gateless Barrier: Zen Comments on the Mumonkan*, translated by Sumiko Kudo (Boston: Shambhala, 2000), pp. 32–33. In the background of this kōan is the traditional Buddhist doctrine that one is liberated from the bonds of karma when one attains enlightenment or Nirvana (see Kyabgon, *Karma*, pp. 73, 82–83). The question is what such liberation means. As with the relations between Samsara and Nirvana, and between the Two Truths (i.e., the Ultimate Truth of Emptiness and the Conventional Truth of Provisional Forms), Zen understands freedom from karma and working with karma to be nondually interrelated.

19. *Majjima Nikāya* III.204–5; *The Middle Length Discourses of the Buddha*, 2nd ed., translated by Bhikkhu Nānamoli and Bhikkhu Bodhi (Somerville, MA: Wisdom Publications, 2001), pp. 1054–55.

20. Dale S. Wright provides a thoughtful and constructive critique of the Buddhist teaching of karma from a contemporary philosophical perspective in chapter 4 of his *What Is Buddhist Enlightenment?* (New York: Oxford University Press, 2016).

21. *Anguttara Nikāya* IV.77. See Nyanaponika, "Karma and Its Fruits," p. 126; and Harvey, *An Introduction to Buddhism*, p. 41.

22. See *Zen Sourcebook: Traditional Documents from China, Korea, and Japan*, edited by Stephen Addiss with Stanley Lombardo and Judith Roitman (Indianapolis, IN: Hackett, 2008), p. 9.

23. Bodhidharma, "Outline of Practice," in Shodo Harada, *The Path of Bodhidharma*, translated by Priscilla Daichi Storandt (Boston: Tuttle, 2000), p. 1. See *Zen Sourcebook*, p. 11; and *The Roaring Stream: A New Zen Reader*, edited by Nelson Foster and Jack Shoemaker (Hopewell, NJ: Ecco Press, 1996), p. 4.

24. Bodhidharma, "Outline of Practice," p. 2.

25. Shodo Harada, *The Path of Bodhidharma*, p. 20.

26. Dōgen, *Treasury of the True Dharma Eye: Zen Master Dogen's Shobo Genzo*, edited by Kazuaki Tanahashi (Boston: Shambhala, 2012), p. 476.

27. See *The Problem of Evil: A Reader*, edited by Mark Larrimore (New York: Blackwell, 2001).

28. Nyanaponika Thera, "Karma and Its Fruit," p. 126. Dale Wright claims: "Although there are a few interesting places in Buddhist philosophy where a collective dimension to karma is broached, in Asanga and Vasubandhu for example, I think that it is true to say that this concept has been overwhelmingly understood in individual terms, that is, that the karma produced by my acts is mine primarily, rather than ours collectively." Wright, *What Is Buddhist Enlightenment?*, p. 84. Although Wright does not provide evidence for this historical claim, Richard Gombrich's account of the earliest Buddhist teachings of karma in *What the Buddha Thought* does stress the idea of invidual responsibility and the intent behind one's ethical actions rather than clan affilition and the proper performance of funerals and other rituals. Traleg Kyagbon also notes that "the Buddha put more emphasis on individual actions than did the more traditional versions of karma, with their emphasis on clan and the interpenetration of karmic consequences between family members" (*Karma*, pp. 32–33). However, in a more nuanced manner he goes on to write: "Individuals are responsible for their actions and create their own karma, and so have to bear the responsibility for those actions, and yet . . . It may arise in a communal setting of some sort, so, in effect, it can practically take the form of shared karmic experience. . . . It can be conceived of as a karmic network, or a web of karma, where each individual experiences suffering or good fortune through mutual karmic history" (ibid., p. 46). He later claims that "blaming the victim" is "completely contrary to the Buddhist view" of karma (ibid., pp. 108–9). In any case, Wright is right to point out that such an individualistic conception of karma ironically "reinforces a picture of the world as composed of a large number of discreet and isolated souls, a view that a great deal of Buddhist thought has sought to undermine." Mahayana Buddhist thought in particular has "recognized that effects radiate out from causes in an ultimately uncontainable fashion, rendering lines of partition between selves and between all entities in the world significantly more porous and malleable than we tend to assume" (*What Is Buddhist Enlightenment?*, p. 85).

29. Jack Harris, "Questioning Karma," *Tricycle: The Buddhist Review*, Spring 2006, p. 12.

30. See Sandra Bell, "Scandals in Emerging Western Buddhism," in *Westward Dharma: Buddhism Beyond Asia*, edited by Charles S. Prebish and Martin Baumann (Berkeley: University of California Press, 2002), pp. 230–42; Mark Oppenheimer, "The Zen Predator of the Upper East Side," *The Atlantic*, December 2014; Mark Oppenheimer, "Joshu Sasaki Roshi, Rinzai Zen Master, Dies at 107: The Influential Teacher Leaves a Mixed Legacy," *Tricycle: The Buddhist Review*, July 30, 2014; and Michael Downing, *Shoes Outside the Door: Desire, Devotion, Excess at San Francisco Zen Center* (Berkeley, CA: Counterpoint, 2002). While these sources are good places to get a sense of the severity of the scandals, it is of course important to read and listen to various perspectives on these lamentable episodes in the still young history of Zen in the West. It is also crucial to note how these and other Zen centers in the West have,

in response, reevaluated the role of ethical precepts, rethought the authority of the teacher, and reconfigured institutions for coed monastic and lay practice. See Zen Studies Society, "Ethical Guidelines," https://zenstudies.org/about/ethical-guideli nes/; Rinzai-ji Zen Center and Mt. Baldy Zen Center, "Statements of Right Conduct," http://www.rinzaiji.org/rinzai-ji/right-conduct/; San Francisco Zen Center, "Ethical Principles," http://sfzc.org/about-zen-center/principles-governance/ethics/ethical-principles; and American Zen Teachers Association, "AZTA Ethics Policy,"https://zenteachers.org/assets/zenteach/sites/default/files/AZTA%20Ethics%20Policy%20Requirement.pdf. The difficult and unresolved task—a communal kōan of sorts—that the contradictory legacies (which differ not only in detail but also in degree of redeemability) of these controversial teachers have left us with entails, on the one hand, the need to separate the baby of their liberating teaching and guidance from the bathwater of their harmful abuses of their authority and, on the other hand, the need to resist temptations to completely reduce their identities and legacies to either one or the other of these aspects. Ken Wilber has endeavored to explain how someone may be very advanced on the spiritual path of Waking Up while remaining stuck at a relatively immature stage on the moral path of Growing Up. For introductions to his Integral Theory in this regard, see his *Integral Meditation: Mindfulness as a Path to Grow Up, Wake Up, and Show Up in Your Life* (Boulder: Shambhala, 2016) and *Integral Buddhism and the Future of Spirituality* (Boulder: Shambhala, 2018). I appreciate Wilber's attempt to parse these two vectors of development, yet tend to think that they are inherently more interrelated than his two-track system suggests. Zen Buddhism did not need to wait for modern Western morality and psychology to have resources for criticizing rogue rōshis! While I also have other reservations about Wilber's triumphalist account of the history of the universe as a uni-directional evolutionary progress of Spirit to ever higher and more inclusive stages, his Integral Theory is nevertheless a noteworthy attempt to combine modern Western accounts of moral and psychological development with Zen Buddhism and other traditional paths of spiritual awakening.

Chapter 16

1. See *Saṃyutta Nikāya* 45:8, in *In the Buddha's Words: An Anthology of Discourses from the Pāli Canon*, edited by Bhikkhu Bodhi (Somerville, MA: Wisdom Publications, 2005), p. 239.
2. Dōgen, *Treasury of the True Dharma Eye: Master Dogen's Shobo Genzo*, edited by Kazuaki Tanahashi (Boston: Shambhala, 2012), p. 77.
3. *Japanese Philosophy: A Sourcebook*, edited by James W. Heisig, Thomas P. Kasulis, and John C. Maraldo (Honolulu: University of Hawai'i Press, 2011), pp. 199–200.
4. For an eye-opening collection of recorded yet long marginalized stories of enlightened women in the history of Zen, with essays by contemporary female Zen teachers, see *The Hidden Lamp: Stories from Twenty-five Centuries of Awakened Women*, edited

by Zenshin Florence Caplow and Reigetsu Susan Moon (Somerville, MA: Wisdom Publications, 2013). See also Jin Y. Park's remarkable study of a twentieth-century Korean feminist who became a famous Zen nun and teacher, *Women and Buddhist Philosophy: Engaging Zen Master Kim Iryŏp* (Honolulu: University of Hawaii Press, 2017; and Michiko Yusa and Leah Kalmanson's illuminating study of a famous Zen practitioner and pioneer Japanese feminist, "Raichō: Zen and the Female Body in the Development of Japanese Feminist Philosophy," in *The Oxford Handbook of Japanese Philosophy*, edited by Bret W. Davis (New York: Oxford University Press, 2020), pp. 613–29.

5. Myōan Eisai, *A Treatise on Letting Zen Flourish to Protect the State*, translated by Gishin Tokiwa, in *Zen Texts* (Berkeley, CA: Numata Center for Buddhist Translation and Research, 2005), pp. 75–77.

6. Dōgen, *Hōkyōki*, in Takashi James Kodera, *Dogen's Formative Years in China: An Historical and Annotated Translation of the Hōkyō-ki* (Boulder, CO: Prajna Press, 1980), p. 119, translation modified.

7. *Entangling Vines: A Classic Collection of Zen Koans*, translated and annotated by Thomas Yūhō Kirchner (Somerville, MA: Wisdom Publications, 2013), p. 34 (Case 2), capitalization added. See also Zenkei Shibayama, *The Gateless Barrier: Zen Comments on the Mumonkan*, translated by Sumiko Kudo (Boston: Shambhala, 2000), p. 166 (Case 23).

8. See Hirata Seikō, *Zen kara no hassō* [Thoughts from Zen] (Kyoto: Zenbunka Kenkyūsho, 1983), pp. 120–21. See also Takemura Makio, *Zen no tetsugaku* [Philosophy of Zen] (Tokyo: Chūsekisha, 2004), pp. 26–27, 112–13.

9. My translation. Compare *The Platform Sūtra of the Sixth Patriarch*, translated by Philip B. Yampolsky (New York: Columbia University Press, 1967), p. 127.

10. Leviticus 19:18; Matthew 7:12; see also Luke 6:31.

11. *Analects* 15:24, in *Readings in Classical Chinese Philosophy*, 2nd ed., edited by Philip J. Ivanhoe and Bryan W. Van Norden (Indianapolis, IN: Hackett, 2005), p. 46.

12. *Udanavarga* 5:18, in W. Woodville Rockhill, *Udanavarga: A Collection of Verses from the Buddhist Canon* (London: Trübner, 1883), p. 27. The Buddha also said: "Feeling for others as for yourself, do not kill others or cause others to kill." *The Dhammapada*, translated by Ananda Maitreya (Berkeley, CA: Parallax Press, 1995), p. 37 (X.2).

13. *Shabbat 31a*, https://www.sefaria.org/Shabbat.33a?lang=bi.

14. Carlisle Indian School Digital Resource Center, "'Kill the Indian, and Save the Man': Capt. Richard H. Pratt on the Education of Native Americans," 1892, http://carlisleindian.dickinson.edu/teach/kill-indian-and-save-man-capt-richard-h-pratt-education-native-americans.

15. Robert Aitken, *The Mind of Clover: Essays in Zen Buddhist Ethics* (San Francisco: North Point Press, 1984).

16. Reb Anderson, *Being Upright: Zen Meditation and the Bodhisattva Precepts* (Berkeley, CA: Rodmell Press, 2001).

17. *Zen Sourcebook: Traditional Documents from China, Korea, and Japan*, edited by Stephen Addiss with Stanley Lombardo and Judith Roitman (Indianapolis, IN: Hackett, 2008), p. 216.

18. See Dōgen, *Treasury of the True Dharma Eye*, pp. 891–894.

19. John Daido Loori, *The Eight Gates of Zen* (Boston: Shambhala, 2002), pp. 133–145.

20. Kim, Hee-Jin, *Eihei Dōgen: Mystical Realist* (Somerville, MA: Wisdom Publications, 2004), p. 223.

21. Dōgen, *A Primer of Sōtō Zen: A Translation of Dōgen's Shōbōgenzō Zuimonki*, translated by Reihō Masunaga (Honolulu: University of Hawai'i Press, 1971), p. 9.

22. Alternative translation: "In the very end, at the ultimate, there's no room for rules and measures." *The Roaring Stream: A New Zen Reader*, edited by Nelson Foster and Jack Shoemaker (Hopewell, NJ: Ecco Press, 1996), p. 14.

23. *The Dhammapada*, p. 52.

24. Dōgen, *Shōbōgenzō: The True-Dharma Eye Treasury*, translated by Gudo Wafu Nishijima and Chodo Cross (Berkeley, CA: Numata Center for Buddhist Translation and Research, 2007–8), vol. 1, p. 137.

25. Arifuku Kōgaku, *Dōgen no sekai* [The world of Dōgen] (Osaka: Ōsaka Shoseki, 1985), p. 271.

26. Dōgen, *Shōbōgenzō: The True-Dharma Eye Treasury*, vol. 1, p. 129, translation modified.

27. Thomas Kasulis, *Zen Action/Zen Person* (Honolulu: University of Hawai'i Press, 1981), p. 96. See also Thomas Kasulis, *Engaging Japanese Philosophy* (Honolulu: University of Hawai'i Press, 2018), pp. 240–42.

28. Robert Aitken, *The Mind of Clover*, p. 22.

29. See Dōgen, *A Primer of Sōtō Zen*, pp. 9, 11; and Dōgen, *Shōbōgenzō: The True-Dharma Eye Treasury*, vol. 1, p. 132.

30. Seung Sahn, *The Compass of Zen* (Boston: Shambhala, 1997), pp. 199–201.

31. *The Lotus Sutra*, translated by Burton Watson (New York: Columbia University Press, 1993), pp. 56–62.

32. Paul Reps and Nyogen Senzaki, *Zen Flesh, Zen Bones* (New York: Anchor Books, 1957), p. 18. The Jewish philosopher Martin Buber would no doubt appreciate this story. Buber writes: "If there is nothing that can so hide the face of our fellowman as morality can, religion can hide from us as nothing else can the face of God." The "once-and-for-all" principles of morality and the dogmas of religion, he says, close us off from "the unforeseeable moment" of "the situation's power of dialogue." Martin Buber, *Between Man and Man*, translated by Ronald Gregor Smith (New York: Macmillan, 1965), p. 18.

33. Immanuel Kant, "On a Supposed Right to Lie from Philanthropy," in *Immanuel Kant: Practical Philosophy*, edited by Mary J. Gregor (New York: Cambridge University Press, 1996), pp. 605–16.

34. Indeed, at this moment while I am revising this manuscript, government officials are having to weigh how to protect people from a dreadful disease on the one hand and from economic ruin on the other.

35. *Skill in Means (Upāyakauśalya) Sutra*, 2nd ed., translated by Mark Tatz (Delhi: Motilal Banarsidass, 2016).

36. Mahatma Gandhi, *The Essential Gandhi: An Anthology of His Writings on His Life, Work, and Ideas*, edited by Louis Fischer (New York: Vintage, 2002), p. 137.

37. See Eknath Easwaran's introduction to *The Bhagavad Gita*, 2nd ed., translated by Eknath Easwaran (Tomales, CA: Nilgiri Press, 2007), pp. 20–21.

38. *The Bhagavad Gita*, p. 109 (chapter 3, verse 43).

39. See Diana Morrison's introduction to chapter 1 of *The Bhagavad Gita*, p. 75.

40. In fact, Jains believe that the entire universe is filled with life, such that even things like rocks have souls (*jiva*) and are subtly sentient. Although it is most important to not harm fully sentient beings such as humans, the principle of non-violence should be applied to how we treat everything. See *Sources of Indian Tradition*, 2nd ed., edited by Ainslie T. Embree (New York: Columbia University Press, 1988), vol. 1, pp. 53–55.

41. Zenkei Shibayama, *The Gateless Barrier*, p. 107 (Case 14).

42. Aitken, *The Mind of Clover*, p. 6. Actually, I did refrain from reading those gruesome Brothers Grimm stories to my kids!

43. Brian Victoria, *Zen at War*, 2nd ed. (Lanham, MD: Rowman & Littlefield, 2006); Brian Daizen Victoria, *Zen War Stories* (New York: RoutledgeCurzon, 2003). See also Christopher Ives, *Imperial-Way Zen: Ichikawa Hakugen's Critique and Lingering Questions for Buddhist Ethics* (Honolulu: University of Hawai'i Press, 2009). For a landmark, and still one of the most well rounded and insightful, scholarly treatments of the ethical and social dimensions of Zen, see Christopher Ives, *Zen Awakening and Society* (Honolulu: University of Hawai'i Press, 1992). For another thoughtful treatment of ethics in Zen, see John C. Maraldo, "The Alternative Normativity of Zen," in *Frontiers of Japanese Philosophy 6: Confluences and Cross-Currents*, edited by Raquel Bouso and James W. Heisig (Nagoya: Nanzan Institute for Religion and Culture, 2009), pp. 190–214.

Chapter 17

1. Jean-Jacques Rousseau, *The Social Contract and Other Writings* (New York: Barnes & Noble Books, 1995), p. 1.

2. Thich Nhat Hanh, *Going Home: Jesus and Buddha as Brothers* (New York: Riverhead Books, 1999), p. 67.

3. Matthew 18:3.

4. Yamada Mumon, *Hannya Shingyō* [The Heart Sutra] (Kyoto: Zen Bunka Kenyūsho, 1986), p. 182.

5. The *Diamond Sutra*, chapter 14, my translation from the Chinese. Alternative translation: "Give rise to that mind that is not caught up in anything." Thich Nhat Hanh, *The Diamond That Cuts Through Illusion: Commentaries on the Prajñaparamit Diamond Sutra* (Berkeley, CA: Parallax Press, 1992), p. 13. On this part of the story of Huineng, see *The Platform Sutra of the Sixth Patriarch*, translated by Philip B. Yampolsky (New York: Columbia University Press, 1967), p. 133n41; and *The Platform Sutra: The Zen Teachings of Hui-neng*, translated by Red Pine (Emeryville, CA: Shoemaker & Hoard, 2006), p. 111.

6. *Japanese Philosophy: A Sourcebook*, edited by James W. Heisig, Thomas P. Kasulis, and John C. Maraldo (Honolulu: University of Hawaiʻi Press, 2011), pp. 178–81.

7. *The Bhagavad Gita*, translated by Eknath Easwaran, 2nd ed. (Tomales, CA: Nilgiri Press, 2007), p. 105.

8. See the many personal accounts documented in Michael Murphy and Rhei A. White, *In the Zone: Transcendent Experience in Sports* (New York: Penguin Books, 1995).

9. Yamada Mumon, *Hekigan monogatari* [Blue cliff stories] (Tokyo: Daihōrinkaku, 1965), pp. 127–28, 370.

10. Mihaly Csikszentmihalyi, *Flow: The Psychology of Optimal Experience* (New York: Harper Perennial Modern Classics, 2008).

11. John Dewey, *Experience and Nature*, edited by Jo Ann Boydston (Carbondale: Southern Illinois University Press, 1988), p. 271.

12. See Aristotle, *Nicomachean Ethics*, translated by Martin Ostwald (New York: Macmillan, 1962), pp. 14–17, 288–91.

13. Nishitani Keiji, *Religion and Nothingness*, translated by Jan Van Bragt (Berkeley: University of California Press, 1982), p. 252–53.

14. See ibid., pp. 234–35.

15. Ibid., p. 253.

16. Immanuel Kant, *Foundations of the Metaphysics of Morals*, 2nd ed., translated by Lewis White Beck (New York: Macmillan, 1990), p. 46.

17. Nishitani, *Religion and Nothingness*, p. 274.

18. Ibid., p. 275.

19. Ibid., p. 277.

20. Ibid., p. 275, translation modified.

21. Kenneth Kraft, *Eloquent Zen: Daitō and Early Japanese Zen* (Honolulu: University of Hawaiʻi Press, 1992), p. 187.

22. Yamada Mumon, *Jiko wo mitsumeru* [Looking into the self] (Kyoto: Zen Bunka Kenkyūsho, 1983), pp. 293–294. These artistic Ways will be discussed in Chapter 19.

23. *The Platform Sutra of the Sixth Patriarch*, translated by Philip B. Yampolsky (New York: Columbia University Press, 1967), p. 136, translation modified.

24. Ibid., p. 138.

25. Ibid., p. 139.

26. Daisetz Teitaro Suzuki, *The Zen Doctrine of No-Mind* (London: Rider, 1958), pp. 106–7.

27. Thomas Kasulis, *Zen Action/Zen Person* (Honolulu: University of Hawaiʻi Press, 1981), pp. 47–48.

28. Edward Slingerland, *Trying Not to Try: The Art and Science of Spontaneity* (New York: Crown, 2014), p. 211. For Slingerland's more scholarly work on this topic in classical Chinese philosophy, see his *Effortless Action: Wu-wei as Conceptual Metaphor and Spiritual Ideal in Early China* (New York: Oxford University Press, 2003).

29. Slingerland, *Trying Not to Try*, p. 153.

30. A classic study of how Buddhism and cognitive science can shed light on each other is Francisco J. Varela, Evan Thompson, and Eleanor Rosch, *The Embodied Mind: Cognitive Science and Human Experience* (Cambridge, MA: MIT Press, 1991).

31. Galatians 3:28.

32. Dōgen, *Treasury of the True Dharma Eye: Zen Master Dogen's Shobo Genzo*, edited by Kazuaki Tanahashi (Boston: Shambhala, 2012), pp. 423–26.

33. Slingerland, *Trying not to Try*, p. 47.

34. Ibid., p. 45.

35. Ibid., p. 31.

36. Nishitani, *Religion and Nothingness*, p. 159, translation modified.

37. *The Record of Linji*, translation with commentary by Ruth Fuller Sasaki, edited by Thomas Yūhō Kirchner (Honolulu: University of Hawai'i Press, 2009), p. 28.

38. See Bret W. Davis, *Heidegger and the Will: On the Way to Gelassenheit* (Evanston: Northwestern University Press, 2007), chapter 6, "Releasement to and from God's Will: Excursus on Meister Eckhart After Heidegger," esp. pp. 135–36.

39. Dōgen, *The Heart of Dōgen's Shōbōgenzō*, translated by Norman Waddell and Masao Abe (Albany: State University of New York Press, 2002), p. 106.

40. Jeremy W. Peters, "The Birth of 'Just Do It' and Other Magic Words," *New York Times*, August 20, 2009; Martin Kessler, "The Story Behind Nike's 'Just Do It' Slogan," *Only a Game*, WBUR, November 23, 2018. In fact, the murderer's words were "Let's do it." Nike's advertising executive Dan Wieden combined this phrase with Nancy Reagan's anti-drug slogan, "Just say no," and the Nike slogan was born. Wieden did not mention any inspiration from Zen, and Nancy Reagan likely associated Zen with the drugs she was waging her war against.

41. For an engaging and fair treatment of the fascinating—and at times troubling—relationship between Zen and the martial arts, written by a Christian theologian and karate instructor, see Jeffrey K. Mann, *When Buddhists Attack: The Curious Relationship Between Zen and the Martial Arts* (Rutland, VT: Tuttle, 2012).

42. Eugen Herrigel, *Zen in the Art of Archery*, translated by R. F. C. Hull (New York: Vintage Books, 1971), p. 88.

43. See Shoji Yamada, *Shots in the Dark: Japan, Zen, and the West*, translated by Earl Hartman (Chicago: University of Chicago Press, 2009), chapters 2–4.

44. See Brian Victoria, *Zen at War*, 2nd ed. (Lanham, MD: Rowman & Littlefield, 2006); Brian Daizen Victoria, *Zen War Stories* (New York: RoutledgeCurzon, 2003); Christopher Ives, *Imperial-Way Zen: Ichikawa Hakugen's Critique and Lingering Questions for Buddhist Ethics* (Honolulu: University of Hawai'i Press, 2009).

45. Ronald E. Purser, *McMindfulness: How Mindfulness Became the New Capitalist Spirituality* (London: Repeater, 2019), pp. 203–17.

46. Nāgārjuna, *The Fundamental Wisdom of the Middle Way: Nāgārjuna's Mūlamadhyamakakārikā*, trans. with commentary by Jay L. Garfield (New York: Oxford University Press, 1995), p. 68.

47. Robert Aitken, *The Mind of Clover: Essays in Zen Buddhist Ethics* (San Francisco: North Point Press, 1984), pp. 5–6.

48. David R. Loy, *The Great Awakening: A Buddhist Social Theory* (Somerville, MA: Wisdom Publications, 2003), p. 146.

49. Takuan Sōhō, *The Unfettered Mind*, translated by William Scott Wilson (Tokyo: Kodansha, 1986), p. 81, translation modified.

50. *Japanese Philosophy: A Sourcebook*, p. 193.

51. Contemporary work by social psychologists on how our "implicit bias" or "implicit social cognition" functions is very relevant here. We need "cold cognition" in order to call into question the biases implicit in the spontaneous operation of our "hot cognition." For an excellent account of how Buddhist practice can contribute to alleviating racial discrimination, see Jessica Locke, "Living Our Histories, Shaping Our Futures: Buddhist Practice and Anti-Racist Education for White People," *Insight Journal* 46 (2020): 37–54.

52. Slingerland, *Trying Not to Try*, p. 29.

53. Dale S. Wright, "Enlightenment and the Moral Dimension of Zen Training," in Dale S. Wright, *What Is Buddhist Enlightenment?* (New York: Oxford University Press, 2016), p. 100.

54. *The Platform Sūtra of the Sixth Patriarch*, p. 138, emphasis added.

55. Wright, "Enlightenment and the Moral Dimension of Zen Training," p. 105.

56. See Brian Daizen Victoria, "The 'Negative Side' of D. T. Suzuki's Relationship to War," *The Eastern Buddhist* 41, no. 2 (2010): 97–138; and Kemmyō Taira Satō and Thomas Kirchner, "Brian Victoria and the Question of Scholarship," *The Eastern Buddhist* 41, no. 2 (2010): 139–66. On the controversial political writings of the Kyoto School, see *Rude Awakenings: Zen, The Kyoto School, and the Question of Nationalism*, edited by James W. Heisig and John C. Maraldo (Honolulu: University of Hawai'i Press, 1994); and *Re-politicising the Kyoto School as Philosophy*, edited by Chris Goto-Jones (London: Routledge, 2008); the latter volume includes my article "Turns to and from Political Philosophy: The Case of Nishitani Keiji."

57. Quoted in Victoria, *Zen at War*, pp. 148–49. See also in this regard the reference to Ken Wilber's work in note 30 of Chapter 15.

Chapter 18

1. See Immanuel Kant, *Foundations of the Metaphysics of Morals*, 2nd ed., translated by Lewis White Beck (New York: Macmillan, 1990), p. 70.

2. For an in-depth study of this topic, see Bret W. Davis, "Natural Freedom: Human/Nature Nondualism in Zen and Japanese Thought," in *The Oxford Handbook of Japanese Philosophy*, edited by Bret W. Davis (New York: Oxford University Press, 2020), pp. 685–715.

3. Kuki Shūzō, *Kuki Shūzō zenshū* [Complete works of Kuki Shūzō] (Tokyo: Iwanami, 1980), vol. 3, p. 276.

4. Shizuteru Ueda, *Wer und was bin ich? Zur Phänomenologie des Selbst im Zen Buddhismus* (Freiburg: Verlag Karl Alber, 2011), p. 99. See also Ueda Shizuteru, "The

Practice of Zen," translated by Ron Hadley and Thomas L. Kirchner, *The Eastern Buddhist* 27, no. 1 (1994): 10–29.

5. Andy Ferguson, *Zen's Chinese Heritage: The Masters and Their Teachings* (Somerville, MA: Wisdom Publications, 2000), p. 81.

6. Shel Silverstein, *The Giving Tree* (New York: Harper & Row, 1964).

7. See Gary Snyder, "Spring Sesshin at Shokoku-ji," in *The Gary Snyder Reader: Prose, Poetry, and Translations 1952–1998* (Berkeley, CA: Counterpoint, 1999), pp. 34–40.

8. Gary Snyder, *The Practice of the Wild* (Berkeley, CA: Counterpoint, 1990), p. 20. For a philosophically rich and powerful wake-up call to rediscover our intimate relation with nature before it is too late, by a contemporary cross-cultural philosopher and Sōtō Zen priest, see Jason M. Wirth, *Mountains, Rivers, and the Great Earth: Reading Gary Snyder and Dōgen in an Age of Ecological Crisis* (Albany: State University of New York Press, 2017). David R. Loy's *EcoDharma: Buddhist Teaching for the Ecological Crisis* (Somerville, MA: Wisdom Publications, 2019) is another timely and compelling treatment of this topic by an exemplary philosopher and Zen teacher. Simon James's *Zen Buddhism and Environmental Ethics* (Hampshire, England: Ashgate, 2004) is a clear and informative treatment of this topic.

9. Marcel Mauss, *The Gift: The Form and Reason for Exchange in Archaic Societies*, translated by W. D. Halls, foreword by Mary Douglas (New York: W. W. Norton & Company, 2000). Mauss in fact writes of "the gift-exchange" and "exchange-through-gift," since he holds that all giving is in truth exchanging (see ibid., pp. xvii–vii, 3, 41–42, 46–48, 65, 72–74). The idea of a "pure gift" that does not expect reciprocation is for him an illusion, and a harmful one at that, since he stresses that it is the reciprocity demonstrated in the exchange of gifts that establishes and maintains the bonds of human society. And yet, if we grant that, generally speaking, most gifts must eventually be reciprocated in order to establish and maintain human society, does not the relative purity or impurity of acts of giving *in the moment they are enacted* determine whether such bonds take either the form of a community of sharing and solidarity or the form of a transactional society of self-serving individuals?

10. Jacques Derrida, *Given Time: I. Counterfeit Money*, translated by Peggy Kamuf (Chicago: University of Chicago Press, 1992), pp. 7, 12–14, 23–24. Derrida writes that "a work as monumental as Marcel Mauss's *The Gift* speaks of everything but the gift: it deals with economy, exchange, contract . . . Mauss does not worry enough about this incompatibility between gift and exchange or about the fact that an exchanged gift is only a tit for tat, that is, an annulment of the gift" (24, 37).

11. *The Bhagavad Gita*, 2nd ed., translated by Eknath Easwaran (Tomales, CA: Nilgiri Press, 2007), esp. chapters 3–5.

12. Donald W. Mitchell, *Buddhism: Introducing the Buddhist Experience* (New York: Oxford University Press, 2002), p. 113.

13. This story is used as the epigraph to *The Roaring Stream*. For a more literal translation, see Andy Ferguson, *Zen's Chinese Heritage: The Masters and Their Teachings* (Somerville, MA: Wisdom Publications, 2000), p. 275.

14. Francis Dojun Cook, *How to Raise an Ox: Zen Practice as Taught in Master Dōgen's Shobogenzo* (Somerville, MA: Wisdom Publications, 2002), pp. 69, 80, translation

modified. Shohaku Okumura, with contributions by Carl Bielefeldt, Gary Snyder, and Issho Fujita, *The Mountains and Waters Sūtra: A Practitioner's Guide to Dōgen's "Sansuikyo"* (Somerville, MA: Wisdom Publications, 2018) contains an excellent translation of, and set of commentaries on, Dōgen's classic text on natural phenomena as manifestations of the Buddha.

15. Dōgen, *The Heart of Dōgen's Shōbōgenzō*, translated by Norman Waddell and Masao Abe (Albany: State University of New York Press, 2002), p. 85.

16. Ibid., p. 217, translation modified.

17. As quoted in Nishitani Keiji, *Religion and Nothingness*, translated by Jan Van Bragt (Berkeley: University of California Press, 1982), p. 108.

18. Dōgen, *Hōkyōki*, in Takashi James Kodera, *Dogen's Formative Years in China: An Historical and Annotated Translation of the Hōkyō-ki* (Boulder, CO: Prajna Press, 1980), p. 119, translation modified. See also Dōgen, *Treasury of the True Dharma Eye: Zen Master Dogen's Shobo Genzo*, edited by Kazuaki Tanahashi (Boston: Shambhala, 2012), p. 427.

Chapter 19

1. Shin'ichi Hisamatsu, *Zen and the Fine Arts*, translated by Gishin Tokiwa (Tokyo: Kodansha, 1971), pp. 32–33.

2. Kitarō Nishida, *An Inquiry into the Good*, translated by Masao Abe and Christopher Ives (New Haven, CT: Yale University Press, 1990), p. 6. For more on Nishida's conception of "pure experience," see Chapter 21.

3. *Nishida Kitarō zenshū* [The complete works of Nishida Kitarō] (Tokyo: Iwanami, 1987–89), vol. 8, pp. 314, 339; vol. 10, p. 307.

4. Robert Carter, *The Japanese Arts and Self-Cultivation* (Albany: State University of New York Press, 2008) is an engaging introduction to Japanese artistic and spiritual practice.

5. See Fujiwara Ryōzō, *Shu ha ri no shisō* [The thought of preserving, breaking, and departing] (Tokyo: Bēsubōru-magajinsha, 1993).

6. Friedrich Nietzsche, *Thus Spoke Zarathustra*, translated by Walter Kaufmann (New York: Penguin Books, 1966), pp. 25–27.

7. Ibid., p. 27.

8. See, for example, Nietzsche's *Ecce Homo* (sections 1:6–7), where he compares the Buddha's teaching "Not by enmity [or hatred] is enmity ended; by friendliness [or love] enmity is ended" with his own struggle to free himself from "vengefulness and rancor," and where he nevertheless claims that his "war against Christianity" is not rooted in the kind of *ressentiment* and lust for revenge that he accuses Christianity itself of. For critical assessments, see Ryôgi Ôkôchi, "Nietzsches amor fati im Lichte von Karma des Buddhismus," *Nietzsche-Studien* 1 (1972): 91; Paul Ricoeur, "Religion, Atheism, and Faith," in *The Conflict of Interpretations*, edited by Don Ihde (Evanston, IL: Northwestern University Press, 1974), pp. 447, 457, 466; Bret W. Davis, "Zen After

Zarathustra: The Problem of the Will in the Confrontation Between Nietzsche and Buddhism," *Journal of Nietzsche Studies* 28 (2004): 89–138; and Bruce Ellis Benson, *Pious Nietzsche: Decadence and Dionysian Faith* (Bloomington: Indiana University Press, 2008).

9. Hirata Seikō, *Zen kara no hassō* [Thoughts from Zen] (Kyoto: Zenbunka Kenkyūsho, 1983), pp. 39–40.

10. See François Berthier, *Reading Zen in the Rocks: The Japanese Dry Landscape Garden*, translated with a philosophical essay by Graham Parkes (Chicago: University of Chicago Press, 2000); and Stephen Mansfield, *Japanese Stone Gardens: Origins, Meaning & Form* (Tokyo: Tuttle, 2009).

11. See Bret W. Davis, "Natural Freedom: Human/Nature Nondualism in Zen and Japanese Thought," in *The Oxford Handbook of Japanese Philosophy*, edited by Bret W. Davis (New York: Oxford University Press, 2020), pp. 685–715.

12. Ōhashi Ryōsuke, *Kire no kōzō: Nihon-bi to gendai sekai* [The Structure of the cut: Japanese beauty and the modern world] (Tokyo: Chūōkōron-sha, 1986); Ryōsuke Ōhashi, *Kire: das Schöne in Japan*, 2nd edition, translated by Rolf Elberfeld (Paderborn: Wilhelm Fink, 2014). For an excerpt translated into English, see *Japanese Philosophy: A Sourcebook*, edited by James W. Heisig, Thomas P. Kasulis, and John C. Maraldo (Honolulu: University of Hawai'i Press, 2011), pp. 1192–97.

13. Nishitani Keiji, "Emptiness and Sameness," in *Modern Japanese Aesthetics: A Reader*, edited by Michele Marra (Honolulu: University of Hawai'i Press, 1999), pp. 196–97.

14. Andrew Juniper, *Wabi Sabi: The Japanese Art of Impermanence* (Tokyo: Tuttle, 2003), p. 2.

15. Tanaka Kyūbun, *Nihon-bi wo tetsugaku suru* [Philosophical reflections on Japanese beauty] (Tokyo: Seishi-sha, 2013), p. 110.

16. Quoted in Juniper, *Wabi Sabi*, p. 159.

17. Nishitani Keiji, "Ikebana," translated by Jeff M. Shore, in *Japanese Philosophy: A Sourcebook*, p. 1198.

18. Ibid., p. 1199.

19. Ibid., p. 1200.

20. Nishida Kitarō, "The Eternal in Art and Poetry," translated by James W. Heisig, in *Japanese Philosophy: A Sourcebook*, pp. 659–62.

21. See *The Heart Sutra*, translation and commentary by Red Pine (Emeryville, CA: Shoemaker & Hoard, 2004), pp. 75–85.

22. Thich Nhat Hanh, *Zen Keys: A Guide to Zen Practice* (New York: Doubleday, 1995), pp. 105–7; and Thich Nhat Hanh, *The Heart of Understanding: Commentaries on the Prajnaparamita Heart Sutra* (Berkeley, CA: Parallax Press, 2009), pp. 3–8.

23. Nhat Hanh, *The Heart of Understanding*, p. 13.

24. Ikkyū, *Skeletons*, in *An Anthology of Rinzai Zen*, translated by Thomas Cleary (New York: Grove Press, 1978), p. 87, translation modified.

25. Urs App, *The Cult of Emptiness: The Western Discovery of Buddhist Thought and the Invention of Oriental Philosophy* (Rorschach: UniversityMedia, 2012); Roger-Pol Droit, *The Cult of Nothingness: Philosophers and the Buddha*, translated by David Streit and Pamela Vohnson (Chapel Hill: University of North Carolina Press, 2003).

26. See Bret W. Davis, "Forms of Emptiness in Zen," in *A Companion to Buddhist Philosophy*, edited by Steven Emmanuel (West Sussex: Wiley-Blackwell, 2013), esp. pp. 194–98.

27. *Daodejing*, chapter 40.

28. Good collections and commentaries include Stephen Addiss, *The Art of Zen: Paintings and Calligraphy by Japanese Monks, 1600–1925* (New York: Harry N. Abrams, 1989); and Helmut Brinker, *Zen: Masters of Meditation in Images and Writings*, translated by Andreas Leisinger (Zurich: Artibus Asiae, 1997). François Jullien, *The Great Image Has No Form, or on the Nonobject Through Painting*, translated by Jane Marie Todd (Chicago: University of Chicago Press, 2009) is a fascinating philosophical study of the Daoist landscape painting that greatly influenced Zen art. See also in this regard Bret W. Davis, "Seeing into the Self in Nature: Awakening Through Cao Jun's Paintings," in *Cao Jun: Hymns to Nature*, edited by John Sallis (Boston: McMullen Museum of Art, Boston College, 2018), pp. 25–34. Also of value are the images and the essays collected in the section "Zen and the Arts" in *The World of Zen*, edited by Nancy Wilson Ross (New York: Vintage, 1960).

Chapter 20

1. My translation. Compare *Bashō's Haiku: Selected Poems of Matsuo Bashō*, translated and with an introduction by David Landis Barnhill (Albany: State University of New York Press, 2004), p. 54.

2. My translation. Compare *Bashō's Haiku*, p. 94.

3. Quoted in Ueda Shizuteru, *Zen—kongen-teki ningen* [Zen: originary human being], vol. 4 of *Ueda Shizuteru shū* [Ueda Shizuteru collection] (Tokyo: Iwanami, 2001), p. 230.

4. See, for example, *Cold Mountain: 100 Poems by the T'ang Poet Han-shan*, translated by Burton Watson (New York: Columbia University Press, 1970); David Pollock, *Zen Poems of the Five Mountains* (New York: Crossroad, 1985); and Victor Sōgen Hori, *Zen Sand: The Book of Capping Phrases for Kōan Practice* (Honolulu: University of Hawai'i Press, 2003).

5. Thich Nhat Hanh, *Zen Keys: A Guide to Zen Practice* (New York: Doubleday, 1995), pp. 41, 51.

6. *Entangling Vines: A Classic Collection of Zen Koans*, translated and annotated by Thomas Yūhō Kirchner (Somerville, MA: Wisdom Publications, 2013).

7. Zenkei Shibayama, *The Gateless Barrier: Zen Comments on the Mumonkan* (Boston: Shambhala, 2000), p. 9.

8. Dōgen is undoubtedly the most prolific, profound, and playful philosopher of language in the Zen tradition. See Steven Heine, "Dōgen on the Language of Creative Textual Hermeneutics," in *The Oxford Handbook of Japanese Philosophy*, edited by Bret W. Davis (New York: Oxford University Press, 2020), pp. 215–29. See also, in the

same volume, Rolf Elberfeld, "Philosophical Implications of the Japanese Language," translated by Bret W. Davis, esp. pp. 679–82.

9. *The Gateless Barrier*, pp. 99–100.

10. Musō Soseki, *Dialogues in a Dream*, translated and annotated by Thomas Yūhō Kirchner with Fukuzawa Yukio (Kyoto: Tenryu-ji Institute for Philosophy and Religion, 2010), p. 186.

11. *The Roaring Stream: A New Zen Reader*, edited by Nelson Foster and Jack Shoemaker (Hopewell, NJ: Ecco Press, 1996), p. 90.

12. Quoted in Ueda Shizuteru, *Zen—kongen-teki ningen*, p. 240.

13. *The Roaring Stream*, p. 304.

14. *The Record of Linji*, translation with commentary by Ruth Fuller Sasaki, edited by Thomas Yūhō Kirchner (Honolulu: University of Hawai'i Press, 2009), p. 300.

15. Mark Siderits and Shōryū Katsura, *Nāgārjuna's Middle Way: Mūlamadhyamakakārikā* (Somerville, MA: Wisdom Publications, 2013), p. 304 (25:24).

16. *The Lankavatara Sutra*, translation and commentary by Red Pine (Berkeley: Counterpoint, 2012), p. 219.

17. Ibid., p. 217.

18. *The Awakening of Faith*, attributed to Aśvaghosha, translated by Yoshito S. Hakeda (New York: Columbia University Press, 2006), pp. 39–40; words in brackets included in Hakeda's translation, except for "[absolute]."

19. In this regard Zen is also strongly influenced by Daoism, especially Zhuangzi. See Bret W. Davis, "Knowing Limits: Toward a Versatile Perspectivism with Nietzsche, Heidegger, Zhuangzi and Zen," *Research in Phenomenology* 49 (2019): 301–334.

20. My translation. Compare *Zen Sourcebook: Traditional Documents from China, Korea, and Japan*, edited by Stephen Addiss with Stanley Lombardo and Judith Roitman (Indianapolis, IN: Hackett, 2008), p. 10.

21. Yamada Mumon, *Lectures on* The Ten Oxherding Pictures, translated by Victor Sōgen Hori (Honolulu: University of Hawai'i Press, 2004), p. 30.

22. *The Gateless Barrier*, p. 58, translation modified.

23. *Zen Sourcebook*, p. 10.

24. *Japanese Philosophy: A Sourcebook*, edited by James W. Heisig, Thomas P. Kasulis, and John C. Maraldo (Honolulu: University of Hawai'i Press, 2011), p. 190, translation modified.

25. *The Gateless Barrier*, p. 166 (Case 23), translation modified.

26. *Zen Sourcebook*, p. 120.

27. Ibid., p. 123.

28. *The Roaring Stream*, p. 191.

29. *Zen Sourcebook*, p. 18.

30. See Bret W. Davis, "Heidegger and Daoism: A Dialogue on the Useless Way of Unnecessary Being," in *Daoist Encounters with Phenomenology*, edited by David Chai (New York: Bloomsbury Academic, 2019), pp. 172–75.

31. *The Roaring Stream*, p. 84. See *Daodejing*, chapter 56.

32. *Zen Sourcebook*, p. 212.

33. *The Vimalakirti Sutra*, translated by Burton Watson (New York: Columbia University Press, 1997), pp. 110–11.

34. *The Gateless Barrier*, pp. 230–231, 255–256.

35. *The Vimalakirti Sutra*, p. 88.

36. Dōgen, *Treasury of the True Dharma Eye: Zen Master Dogen's Shobo Genzo*, edited by Kazuaki Tanahashi (Boston: Shambhala, 2012). p. 479, translation modified.

37. Dōgen, *Fukanzazengi* (Universally recommended instructions for zazen), translated by Carl Bielefeldt and T. Griffin Foulk, with Taigen Leighton and Shohaku Okumura, reprinted in *Engaging Dōgen's Zen: The Philosophy of Practice as Awakening*, edited by Tetsuzen Jason M. Wirth, Shūdō Brian Schroeder, and Kanpū Bret W. Davis (Somerville, MA: Wisdom Publications), pp. 195–96.

38. Dōgen, *The Heart of Dōgen's Shōbōgenzō*, translated by Norman Waddell and Masao Abe (Albany: State University of New York Press, 2002), pp. 17–18.

39. Dōgen, *The Heart of Dōgen's Shōbōgenzō*, p. 92, translation modified.

40. Dōgen, *Treasury of the True Dharma Eye*, p. 157, translation modified.

41. Dōgen, *The Heart of Dōgen's Shōbōgenzō*, p. 84.

42. See Dōgen, *Treasury of the True Dharma Eye*, p. 439, translation modified.

43. Ibid., p. 441.

44. *The Gateless Barrier*, p. 182, translation modified.

45. Rainer Maria Rilke, *Duino Elegies*, translated by J. B. Leishman and Stephen Spender (New York: W. W. Norton, 1967), p. 18.

46. Rainer Maria Rilke, *Sonnets to Orpheus*, translated by M. D. Herter (New York: W. W. Norton, 1970), pp. 40–41, translation modified.

47. Ibid., pp. 88–89.

48. My translation.

49. *Japanese Death Poems: Written by Zen Monks and Haiku Poets on the Verge of Death*, compiled with an introduction and commentary by Yoel Hoffmann (Tokyo: Tuttle, 1986), p. 107.

50. See Ueda, *Zen—kongen-teki ningen*, pp. 186ff.; and also Ueda Shizuteru, "Emptiness and Fullness: Śūnyatā in Mahāyāna Buddhism," translated by James W. Heisig and Frederick Greiner, *The Eastern Buddhist* 15, no. 1 (1982): 30ff.

51. Ueda, *Zen—kongen-teki ningen*, p. 240.

52. Ibid., p. 210.

53. Ibid. See also Ueda Shizuteru, "The Practice of Zen," translated by Ron Hadley and Thomas L. Kirchner, *The Eastern Buddhist* 27, no. 1 (1994): 10–29.

54. Ueda Shizuteru, "Language in a Twofold World," translated by Bret W. Davis, in *Japanese Philosophy: A Sourcebook*, edited by James W. Heisig, Thomas P. Kasulis, and John C. Maraldo (Honolulu: University of Hawai'i Press), pp. 768–69.

55. Martin Heidegger, *Pathmarks*, edited by William McNeill (Cambridge: Cambridge University Press, 1998), p. 239.

56. Ueda, *Zen—kongen-teki ningen*, p. 387.

57. I agree with much of Dale Wright's criticism of the mistaken idea that a Zen master or anyone else could live or act in any meaningful way while dwelling in a "pure experience" that would be totally free of all linguistic and cultural conditioning. Yet

I cannot endorse the hermetically enclosed linguistic transcendentalism implied in Wright's claims that "experience always comes fully clothed" in language; that "the words adequate to the experience are already there in association with the experience itself"; and that "by means of language, the world (the given) is focused and organized in advance of every encounter with entities, persons, or situations. Thus when we see something, we have already interpreted it—immediately—as whatever it is." Dale S. Wright, *Philosophical Meditations on Zen Buddhism* (Cambridge: Cambridge University Press, 1998), p. 69; Dale S. Wright, *What Is Buddhist Enlightenment?* (New York: Oxford University Press, 2016), p. 155. If we were to be a priori wholly enclosed in language in this manner, no experience we have could ever break through and alter the linguistic and conceptual framework preprogrammed into us by our culture, language, and tradition. If that were the case, no one could be any more or any less culturally biased or open-minded than anyone else. Wright is skeptical of the Zen tradition's references to meditative silence or other experiences that transcend language, arguing that "every effort to relegate language to a subordinate position is itself linguistically produced, thereby continually placing language in a more fundamental position than its particular message" (*What Is Buddhist Enlightenment?*, p. 164). More plainly put, Wright is claiming that talk of "transcending language" is just that: talk. But that's like arguing that it is self-refuting to say, in English, that there exist languages other than English; or that it's impossible to point to anything other than a finger. Why would it not be possible to indicate something beyond the medium or means used to make that indication? For a similarly one-sided postmodern critique of Zen's indications of the limits of language, see Bernard Faure, *Chan Insights and Oversights: An Epistemological Critique of the Chan Tradition* (Princeton, NJ: Princeton University Press, 1993), chapters 7 and 8. To repeat, I do agree with these critics that Zen enlightenment cannot entail that one would dwell meaningfully in some pure experience untainted by linguistic and cultural conditioning. But I also agree with Ueda that the fabric of such conditioning can be torn through and resewn, ruptured and renewed, through experiences that "exit language and exit into language." I also agree with what Ueda and other commentators have said about the positive roles that language plays in the Zen tradition. Steven Heine has insightfully commented on the at times playful and often provocative, poetic, and creative ways in which language is used in Zen. In seeking a middle way beyond the extremes of what he calls the "Traditional Zen Narrative" view that language is merely a heuristic instrument (a disposable finger pointing at the moon) and the "Historical and Cultural Criticism" accusation that Zen's use of language dissolves into sheer nonsense, Heine argues that "Zen writings are fully expressive of spiritual attainment, rather than merely a prelude to the abandonment of language" (Steven Heine, *Zen Skin, Zen Marrow: Will the Real Zen Buddhism Please Stand Up?* [New York: Oxford University Press, 2008], pp. 29, 40). Elsewhere Heine writes: "Zen is perhaps best known not so much for the negation of speech, which would represent an extreme view, but for inventing a creative new style of expression that uses language in unusual and ingenious fashion to surpass a reliance on everyday words and letters" (Steven Heine, "On the Value of Speaking and Not Speaking: Philosophy of Language in Zen

Buddhism," in *A Companion to Buddhist Philosophy*, edited by Steven Emmanuel [West Sussex: Wiley-Blackwell, 2013], p. 350). I largely agree with this view, but do not think it fully accounts for the ways in which silent meditation and nonverbal actions and experiences (or aspects of experiences) also play important roles in Zen. Heine himself acknowledges both sides in the concluding sentence of the article just quoted from: "Zen's language of non-language, or vice versa, leaves open the possibility for inventive expression and productive silence to intermingle and to be alternatively used or discarded, as appropriate for particular discursive contexts and pedagogical situations" (ibid., 362). Ueda's bidirectional and ceaseless movement of "exiting language and exiting into language" problematizes any static dichotomy between an inside and an outside of language, and in so doing offers a fresh and dynamic alternative that is able to account for both positive and negative attitudes toward language found in the Zen tradition. For a more extensive treatment, see Bret W. Davis, "Expressing Experience: Language in Ueda Shizuteru's Philosophy of Zen," in *Dao Companion to Japanese Buddhist Philosophy*, edited by Gereon Kopf (New York: Springer, 2019), pp. 713–38.

Chapter 21

1. On applying the terms "philosophy" and "religion" to non-Western traditions such as Japanese Buddhism, see Bret W. Davis, "What Is Japanese Philosophy?," in *The Oxford Handbook of Japanese Philosophy*, edited by Bret W. Davis (New York: Oxford University Press, 2020), pp. 1–79; and Bret W. Davis, "Faith and/or/as Enlightenment: Rethinking Religion from the Perspective of Japanese Buddhism," in *Asian Philosophies and the Idea of Religion: Paths Beyond Faith and Reason*, edited by Sonia Sikka and Ashwani Peetush (New York: Routledge, 2020), pp. 36–64.

2. See Bret W. Davis, "Beyond Philosophical Euromonopolism: Other Ways of—Not Otherwise than—Philosophy," *Philosophy East and West* 69, no. 2 (April 2019): 1–28; and Bret W. Davis, "Buddhist Philosophy as a Holistic Way of Life: Studying the Way with Body and Mind (*Shinjin Gakudō*)," in *Key Concepts in World Philosophies*, edited by Sarah Flavel and Chiara Robianno (New York: Bloomsbury Academic, 2022).

3. For an in-depth treatment of this issue, see Davis, "Faith and/or/as Enlightenment."

4. See *Buddhist Philosophy: Essential Readings*, edited by Jay Garfield and William Edelglass (New York: Oxford University Press, 2009); Mark Siderits, *Buddhism as Philosophy* (Indianapolis, IN: Hackett, 2007); Jay L Garfield, *Engaging Buddhism: Why It Matters to Philosophy* (New York: Oxford University Press, 2015); and *A Companion to Buddhist Philosophy*, edited by Steven Emmanuel (West Sussex: Wiley-Blackwell, 2013).

5. See Dan Lusthaus, *Buddhist Phenomenology* (New York: RoutledgeCurzon, 2002); and *Madhyamaka and Yogācāra: Allies or Rivals?*, edited by Jay L. Garfield and Jan Westerhoff (New York: Oxford University Press, 2015).

6. Ludwig Wittgenstein, *Tractatus Logico-Philosophicus*, translated by D. F. Pears and B. F. McGinness (London: Routledge & Kegan Paul, 1961), p. 74. See Andrew P. Tuck, *Comparative Philosophy and the Philosophy of Scholarship: On the Western Interpretation of Nāgārjuna* (New York: Oxford University Press, 1990).

7. See *Buddhisms and Deconstructions*, edited by Jin Y. Park, afterword by Robert Magliola (Lanham, MD: Rowman & Littlefield, 2006).

8. See Garma C. C. Chang, *The Buddhist Teaching of Totality: The Philosophy of Hwa Yen Buddhism* (State College: Pennsylvania State University Press, 2001); Thomas Cleary, *Entry Into the Inconceivable: An Introduction to Hua-yen Buddhism* (Honolulu: University of Hawai'i Press, 1983); Francis H. Cook, *Hua-yen Buddhism: The Jewel Net of Indra* (University Park: Pennsylvania State University Press, 1977); and Bret W. Davis, "Zen's Nonegocentric Perspectivism," in *Buddhist Philosophy: A Comparative Approach*, edited by Steven M. Emmanuel (West Sussex: Wiley-Blackwell, 2018), pp. 123–43.

9. Musō Soseki, *Dialogues in a Dream*, translated and annotated by Thomas Yūhō Kirchner with Fukuzawa Yukio (Kyoto: Tenryu-ji Institute for Philosophy and Religion, 2010), pp. 186–87.

10. Yamada Mumon, *Lectures on* The Ten Oxherding Pictures, translated by Victor Sōgen Hori (Honolulu: University of Hawai'i Press, 2004), p. 30.

11. For some critical assessments of Suzuki's interpretations of Zen, see the sources listed in note 45 of Chapter 1.

12. Exemplary in this regard is "Illogical Zen," in D. T. Suzuki, *An Introduction to Zen Buddhism*, foreword by Carl Jung (New York: Grove Press, 1964), pp. 58–65, originally written in 1914.

13. D. T. Suzuki, "The Koan and the Five Steps," in *Selected Works of D. T. Suzuki*, Volume I, *Zen* (Oakland: University of California Press, 2015), p. 169.

14. Ibid., pp. 171, 173, 175.

15. Richard M. Jaffe, editor's introduction to D. T. Suzuki, *Selected Works of D. T. Suzuki*, Volume I, *Zen*, p. xiv.

16. Ibid., p. liii.

17. Ibid., p. xv. For Suzuki's own efforts to develope a logic of Zen, see Michiko Yusa, "D. T. Suzuki and the 'Logic of Sokuhi,' or the 'Logic of Prajñāpāramitā,'" in *The Dao Companion to Japanese Buddhist Philosophy*, edited by Gereon Kopf (Dordrecht: Springer, 2019), pp. 589–616; and Mori Tetsurō, "D. T. Suzuki's Logic of Is/Not as Zen Praxis," translated by Bret W. Davis, in *The Oxford Handbook of Japanese Philosophy*, edited by Bret W. Davis (New York: Oxford University Press, 2020), pp. 249–56.

18. See Bret W. Davis, "The Kyoto School," *The Stanford Encyclopedia of Philosophy*, Summer 2019 ed., edited by Edward N. Zalta, http://plato.stanford.edu/archives/sum2019/entries/kyoto-school/>. For a more concise introduction, see my entry on "The Kyoto School" in *The Routledge Encyclopedia of Philosophy*.

19. Bret Davis, "Nishitani Keiji ni okeru 'taiho': Nihirizumu o tōshite zettai-teki shigan e" [The "step back" in Nishitani Keiji: through nihilism to the absolute near-side], in *"Kongen" e no tankyū: Kindai Nihon no shūkyō shisō no yamanami* [The search

for "grounds": the range of religious thought in modern Japan], edited by Shōji Hosoya (Kyoto: Kōyō Shobō, 2000), pp. 71–91; a revised version was later published as "Nishitani Keiji no Zen-tetsugaku" [Nishitani Keiji's philosophy of Zen], in *Zen to Kyoto-tetsugaku* [Zen and Kyoto philosophy], edited by Ueda Shizuteru (Kyoto: Tōeisha, 2006), pp. 228–49. Meanwhile, an English version was published as "The Step Back Through Nihilism: The Radical Orientation of Nishitani Keiji's Philosophy of Zen," *Synthesis Philosophica* 37 (2004): 139–59.

20. For some personal reflections on my final few meetings with Professor Ueda, see Bret W. Davis, "Where Did He Go? Ueda Shizuteru Sensei's Last Lesson," *The Eastern Buddhist* 48, no. 2 (2020): 163–68. For an overview of Ueda's thought, see Bret W. Davis, "The Contours of Ueda Shizuteru's Philosophy of Zen," in *Companion to the Philosophy of Ueda Shizuteru*, edited by Ralf Müller, Raquel Bouso, and Adam Loughnane (New York: Springer, 2022).

21. Ueda Shizuteru, *Nishida-tetsugaku e no michibiki* [A guide to Nishida's philosophy] (Tokyo: Iwanami, 1998), pp. 167, 226–27.

22. Keiji Nishitani, "Remembering Daisetz Suzuki," in *A Zen Life: D. T. Suzuki Remembered*, edited by Masao Abe (New York: Weatherhill, 1986), p. 153.

23. *Nishitani Keiji chosakushū* [Collected works of Nishitani Keiji] (Tokyo: Sōbunsha, 1990), vol. 11, p. 8.

24. See Nishida Kitarō, "The Logic of Place and the Religious Worldview," in *Last Writings: Nothingness and the Religious Worldview*, translated by David A. Dilworth (Honolulu: University of Hawai'i Press, 1987), pp. 108–9, where the phrase (*byōjōtei*) I am translating more literally as "radical everydayness" is translated as "a religious celebration of the ordinary and everyday." Nishida coined this expression, in the context of quoting Zen texts, by modifying the expression "Everyday Even Mind" (*byōjōshin*), which was discussed in Chapter 13.

25. Ueda Shizuteru, *Zen no fūkei* [The landscape of Zen], in *Ueda shizuteru shū* [Ueda Shizuteru collection] (Tokyo: Iwanami, 2002), vol. 5, pp. 14–15. See also Ueda Shizuteru, "Zen and Philosophy in the Thought of Nishida Kitarō," translated by Mark Unno, in *Japanese Religions* 18, no. 2 (1993), pp. 162–193.

26. Otto Pöggeler, "Westliche Wege zu Nishida und Nishitani," in *Philosophie der Struktur: 'Fahrzeug' der Zukunft?*, edited by Georg Stenger and Margarete Röhrig (Freiburg: Verlag Karl Alber, 1995), pp. 95–108.

27. See Bret W. Davis, "Provocative Ambivalences in Japanese Philosophy of Religion: With a Focus on Nishida and Zen," in *Japanese Philosophy Abroad*, edited by James W. Heisig (Nagoya: Nanzan Institute for Religion and Culture, 2004), pp. 246–74; and Davis, "Faith and/or/as Enlightenment."

28. *Nishida Kitarō zenshū* [The complete works of Nishida Kitarō] (Tokyo: Iwanami, 1987–89), vol. 15, p. 47.

29. Kitarō Nishida, *An Inquiry into the Good*, translated by Masao Abe and Christopher Ives (New Haven, CT: Yale University Press, 1990), p. xxx.

30. William James, *The Varieties of Religious Experience* (Mineola, NY: Dover, 2002 [1902]), p. 379.

31. William James, *Essays in Radical Empiricism* (New York: Longmans, Green, 1912).

32. Nishida, *An Inquiry into the Good*, p. 3.

33. See Shibata Masumi, "The Diary of a Zen Layman: The Philosopher Nishida Kitarō," translated by Frederick Frank, *The Eastern Buddhist* 14, no. 2 (1981): 121–31; and Michiko Yusa, *Zen and Philosophy: An Intellectual Biography of Nishida Kitarō* (Honolulu: University of Hawai'i Press, 2002), chapters 4 and 5. After years of struggling with it, Nishida finally passed the *Mu* kōan (on this kōan, see Chapter 22). Yet he apparently did not have a major breakthrough experience, writing in his diary that he "did not feel overjoyed." A short time later he stopped formally practicing Zen and dedicated himself entirely to his philosophical endeavors. Nevertheless, his early Zen practice clearly impacted his thinking for the rest of his life. By contrast, Nishitani and Ueda were both lifelong Zen practitioners—and eventually lay Zen masters—as well as prolific scholars and philosophers.

34. *Zen: Morimoto Seinen no sekai* [Zen: the world of Morimoto Seinen], edited by Hantō Taiga (Tokyo: Shunjūsha, 1984), p. 65.

35. Nishida, *An Inquiry into the Good*, p. xxxiii.

36. Nishida, *An Inquiry into the Good*, p. xxxiii, translation modified.

37. William James, *Principles of Psychology* (New York: Henry Holt, 1890), vol. 1, p. 488.

38. Nishida, *An Inquiry into the Good*, p. 164.

39. Ibid., p. 131.

40. Ibid., p. 161.

41. Ibid., p. 158, translation slightly modified.

42. Ibid., p. 155.

43. Nishida, *An Inquiry into the Good*, p. 155.

44. Nishida, "The Logic of Place and the Religious Worldview," p. 70.

45. Ibid., pp. 67–69, 85–87, 108, 118.

46. Although he worked largely outside the orbit of the Kyoto School, Izutsu Toshihiko, one of modern Japan's premier comparative philosophers, interprets the philosophy of Zen in terms of a "field structure of ultimate reality." According to Izutsu, "the philosophical thinking of Zen—and Buddhism in general—is based on, and centers around, the category of relation instead of substantia. Everything, the whole world of Being, is looked at from a relational point of view." The "originally non-articulated Field" articulates itself freely into either "subject" or "object." "It is important to note," he writes, "that in this self-articulation of the Field, the whole Field is involved, not this or that particular sphere of it. Instead of being an abstraction, the 'subject' or 'object' in such a case is a total concretization or actualization of the entire Field." Thus, whether Zen masters stress the "subject" or the "object," this is a matter of stressing a perspectival focal point that always implies the interrelational whole. Toshihiko Izutsu, *Toward a Philosophy of Zen Buddhism* (Boulder: Prajna Press, 1982), pp. 45–46.

47. Nishida, *An Inquiry into the Good*, pp. xxxi–xxxii.

48. For an astute philosophical introduction to this idea, see John C. Maraldo, "Nishida Kitarō's Philosophy: Self, World, and the Nothingness Underlying Distinctions," in *The Oxford Handbook of Japanese Philosophy*, edited by Bret W. Davis (New York: Oxford University Press, 2020), pp. 417–30.

49. Zenkei Shibayama, *The Gateless Barrier: Zen Comments on the Mumonkan*, translated by Sumiko Kudo (Boston: Shambhala, 2000), p. 19.

50. Nishida first worked out his "logic of place" and his basic idea of the Place of Absolute Nothingness in a dense and difficult essay entitled "Place." An annotated translation by John W. M. Krummel and Shigenori Nagatomo can be found in Nishida Kitarō, *Place and Dialectic: Two Essays by Nishida Kitarō* (New York: Oxford University Press, 2012), pp. 49–102.

51. *Nishida Kitarō zenshū*, vol. 4, p. 6.

52. According to the Greeks, for something to be unlimited meant that it was indefinite, formless, chaotic. Anything unlimited or indefinite is also unintelligible, since knowledge requires definition of order and form. In their chart of opposites, the Pythagorians thus aligned "limit" with "good" and "unlimited" with "bad." An intriguing anomaly among the Presocratics is Anaximander, who thought of the *arche*, the originating principle of all things, as the *apeiron*, the "unlimited" or "indefinite." Melissus is another interesting exception to the rule. Unlike Parmenides, he thought that the One must be infinite; however, like Parmenides and unlike Anaximander, he thought that the undifferentiated One alone is real and that the differentiated Many is unreal. *A Presocratics Reader*, 2nd ed., edited by Patricia Curd, translations by Richard D. McKirahan and Patricia Curd (Indianapolis, IN: Hackett, 2011), pp. 16–17, 29, 60, 127–28. Plato thought of true being as the perfect metaphysical Forms of things (see, for example, *Republic* 475–79, 506–9, 522–25, 596–98; *Phaedo* 74–75; and *Symposium* 210–12). According to Aristotle, "Nothing is complete which has no end and the end is a limit" (*Physics* 207a14–15, trans. Hippocrates G. Apostle). Things that are still becoming are thus unlimited in the sense of incomplete; the more complete something is, the more delimited it is. In this sense, prime matter is the most infinite (indefinite) being, while the Unmoved Mover is the most finite (definite). It is for this reason that medieval theologians as late as the thirteenth-century Albert the Great could refer to God as "the most finite being of all" (Ln. *finitissimum omnium*). However, Albert the Great later joined other medieval theologians in the increasingly prevalent tendency to break with the ancient Greeks in thinking of God as infinite rather than as maximally finite. While medieval theologians struggled to reconcile the Greek emphasis on intelligibility and definiteness with divine transcendence and infinity, in Eastern traditions "emptiness" and "nothingness" have often been privileged over being and definiteness. See *Nothingness in Asian Philosophy*, edited by JeeLoo Liu and Douglas L. Berger (New York: Routledge, 2014); and David Chai, *Zhuangzi and the Becoming of Nothingness* (Albany: State University of New York Press, 2019).

In a schematic essay on this topic, Nishida writes that in Greek philosophy "that which has form and determination was regarded as the real" (e.g., Plato's Forms). Judeo-Christian culture, however radically different in various ways it was from Greek culture, and despite negative theology's indications of an unknowable "hidden God" (*Deus absconditus*) as a kind of divine "nothingness," nevertheless primarily considered the *person* of God, as "the most perfect being," to be the basis of reality. In radical contrast to both the Greek and Judeo-Christian origins of Western culture, Nishida says, Indian, Chinese, and Japanese cultures took "the profoundest idea of nothingness as its basis." Finite beings are understood as self-determinations or self-delimitations of this Absolute Nothingness. Nishida Kitarō, "The Forms of Culture of the Classical Periods of East and West Seen from a Metaphysical Perspective," translated by D. Dilworth with Masao Abe, in *Sourcebook for Modern Japanese Philosophy*, edited by David A. Dilworth and Valdo H. Viglielmo with Agustin Jacinto Zavala (Westport, CT: Greenwood Press, 1998), pp. 21–36.

53. Plato's highest Form, that of the Good, is said to be "beyond being" (*The Republic* 509b). Plotinus interprets Plato's Good as "the One" and "the First," yet for him this is not only beyond being but also beyond form: "The First must be without form, and, if without form, then it is no Being; Being must have some definition and therefore be limited; but the First cannot be thought of as having definition and limit, for thus it would be not the Source but the particular item indicated by the definition assigned to it.... [I]t therefore transcends Being." Plotinus, *The Enneads*, translated by Stephen MacKenna, abridged with an introduction and notes by John Dillon (New York: Penguin Books, 1991), p. 397 (V.5.6). In this respect, as well as in the idea that the soul too must become formless in order to return to this formless One beyond being, Plotinus's One is closer than Plato's Good to some of the Kyoto School's ideas of Absolute Nothingness. The following comment by renowned Plato scholar Paul Friedländer on the difference between Plotinus and Plato is revealing in this context: "That the Highest must be without form or shape, that the soul must become formless in order to comprehend it—there is nothing like this in Plato.... It never did or could enter the mind of Plato, a citizen of so form-conscious a world, to let the soul be dissolved in formlessness." Paul Friedländer, *Plato: An Introduction*, 2nd ed., translated by Hans Meyerhoff (Princeton, NJ: Princeton University Press, 1969), p. 83.

54. Nishida writes that "the One of Plotinus stands at an opposite pole to the Eastern sense of nothingness. This is why it did not attain to the standpoint of radical every-dayness" that we find expressed by Zen masters such as Linji (Nishida, "The Logic of Place and the Religious Worldview," p. 109, translation modified).

55. See Sugimoto Kōichi, "Tanabe Hajime's Logic of Species and the Philosophy of Nishida Kitarō: A Critical Dialogue Within the Kyoto School," in *Japanese and Continental Philosophy: Conversations with the Kyoto School*, edited by Bret W. Davis, Brian Schroeder, and Jason M. Wirth (Bloomington: Indiana University Press, 2011), pp. 52–67. On the development of Nishida's thought, see Fujita Masakatsu, "The Development of Nishida's Philosophy: Pure Experience, Place, Action-Intuition," translated by Bret W. Davis, in *The Oxford Handbook of Japanese Philosophy*, pp. 389–415; and John Krummel, *Nishida Kitarō's Chiasmatic Chorology: Place of Dialectic, Dialectic of Place* (Bloomington: Indiana University Press, 2015). On the problems and possibilities of Nishida's philosophy of culture, see Bret W. Davis, "Nishida's Multicultural Worldview: Contemporary Significance and Immanent Critique," *Nishida Tetsugakkai Nenpō* [The journal of the Nishida Philosophy Association] 10 (2013): 183–203.

56. For Nishida's and Nishitani's references to the self-emptying (*kenosis*) of God, see Nishida, "The Logic of Place and the Religious Worldview," p. 70; and Nishitani

Keiji, *Religion and Nothingness*, translated by Jan Van Bragt (Berkeley: University of California Press, 1982), p. 59.

57. Masao Abe, "Kenotic God and Dynamic Sunyata," in *The Emptying God: A Buddhist-Jewish-Christian Conversation with Masao Abe on God, Kenosis, and Sunyata*, edited by John B. Cobb Jr. and Christopher Ives (Maryknoll, NY: Orbis Books, 1990), pp. 3–65. For the dialogue and debate surrounding Abe's thesis of "the self-emptying of God," in addition to *The Emptying God*, see *Buddhist Emptiness and Christian Trinity: Essays and Explorations*, edited by Roger Coreless and Paul F. Knitter (New York: Paulist Press, 1990); and *Divine Emptiness and Historical Fullness: A Buddhist-Jewish-Christian Conversation with Masao Abe*, edited by Christopher Ives (Valley Forge, PA: Trinity Press International, 1995); see also *Masao Abe: A Zen Life of Dialogue*, edited by Donald W. Mitchell (Boston: Tuttle, 1998). I attempted to convey the key points and positions in the debate, which has taken place in English, to a Japanese audience in Bret Davis, "Kami wa doko made jiko wo kūzuru ka—Abe Masao no kenōshisu-ron wo meguru giron" [How far does God empty himself? On the debate surrounding Masao Abe's theory of kenosis], in *Sekai no naka no Nihon no tetsugaku* [Japanese philosophy in the world], edited by Fujita Masakatsu and Bret Davis (Kyoto: Shōwadō, 2005), pp. 245–59.

58. Philippians 2:5–8, as quoted in Masao Abe, "Kenotic God and Dynamic Sunyata," p. 9.

59. As quoted in Masao Abe, "Kenotic God and Dynamic Sunyata," p. 14.

60. Friedrich Nietzsche, *The Gay Science*, translated by Walter Kaufmann (New York: Vintage Books, 1974), pp. 181 (§125) and 279 (§343). On Nishitani's profoundly sympathetic, if also in the end critical, interpretation of Nietzsche, see Nishitani Keiji, *The Self-Overcoming of Nihilism*, translated by Graham Parkes with Setsuko Aihara (Albany: State University of New York Press, 1990), chapters 3–5; Nishitani, *Religion and Nothingness*, pp. 65–66, 211–17, 232–35; and Bret W. Davis, "Nishitani After Nietzsche: From the Death of God to the Great Death of the Will," in *Japanese and Continental Philosophy: Conversations with the Kyoto School*, edited by Bret W. Davis, Brian Schroeder, and Jason M. Wirth (Bloomington: Indiana University Press, 2011), pp. 82–101.

61. *Nishitani Keiji chosakushū*, vol. 20, p. 192.

62. See Nishitani, *Religion and Nothingness*, pp. 95–100, 108–12, 135–40; Davis, "The Step Back Through Nihilism"; and Graham Parkes, "Nishitani Keiji: Practicing Philosophy as a Matter of Life and Death," in *The Oxford Handbook of Japanese Philosophy*, pp. 465–83.

63. *Nishitani Keiji chosakushū*, vol. 20, pp. 193–94.

64. Nishitani Keiji and Yagi Seiichi, *Chokusetsu keiken* [Direct experience] (Tokyo: Shunjūsha, 1989), pp. 57–60.

65. Nishitani Keiji, "Zen to gendai sekai" [Zen and the modern world], in *Zen to tetsugaku* [Zen and philosophy], edited by Nishitani Keiji and Ueda Shizuteru (Kyoto: Zenbunka Kenkyūsho, 1988), p. 29.

66. *Nishitani Keiji chosakushū*, vol. 20, pp. 54–67.

67. See Bret W. Davis, "Commuting Between Zen and Philosophy: In the Footsteps of Kyoto School Philosophers and Psychosomatic Practitioners," in *Transitions: Crossing*

Boundaries in Japanese Philosophy, edited by Francesca Greco, Leon Krings, and Yukiko Kuwayama (Nagoya: Chisokudō Publications, 2021), pp. 71–111; and Davis, "Buddhist Philosophy as a Holistic Way of Life."

Chapter 22

1. See Morten Schlütter, *How Zen Became Zen: The Dispute over Enlightenment and the Formation of Chan Buddhism in Song-Dynasty China* (Honolulu: University of Hawai'i Press, 2008), chapters 5 and 6; and *Swampland Flowers: The Letters and Lectures of Zen Master Ta Hui*, translated by J. C. Cleary (Boston: Shambhala, 2006), pp. 106–8. In his investigation of the sociological context of their soteriological teachings, Schlütter points out that Dahui's more prominent Linji School was in competition with Hongzhi's newly flourishing Caodong School for support from the literati, and that Dahui's method of using the key word or phrase (Ch. *huatou*; Jp. *watō*) of a kōan and Hongzhi's method of silent illumination were probably both geared to these lay practitioners as much as to the monks in their monasteries. One could compare this not only to the spread of both schools of Zen (along with other "single practice" schools such as Pure Land and Nichiren Buddhism) in Japan starting in the twelfth century, but also to the current context in which both Sōtō's practice of "just sitting" and Sanbō Kyōdan's (Sanbō Zen's) stress on the initial breakthrough enlightenment experience (*kenshō*) brought about by intensely meditating on a *watō* such as Zhaozhou's "No!" (Ch. *wu*; Jp. *mu*) have thrived in the United States and elsewhere on account of their simplicity and practicality for the laypersons and lay priests who make up the vast majority of Western Zen practitioners. Comparatively, the Rinzai School, with its extensive and demanding kōan curriculum, has, unsurprisingly, not been as successful in promulgating itself in this new sociological context.

2. See Schlütter, *How Zen Became Zen*, chapter 7; and Taigen Dan Leighten, *Cultivating the Empty Field: The Silent Illumination of Zen Master Hongzhi* (Rutland, VT: Tuttle, 2000), esp. pp. 13–16.

3. Schlütter, *How Zen Became Zen*, p. 135.

4. A third Zen school, Ōbaku, was established in Japan in the seventeenth century by immigrant masters from China and still exists today. Like the Rinzai School, it stems from the Linji School in China. Today, its practice is very similar to that of the Rinzai School, though historically it combined Zen meditation with the Pure Land Buddhist practice of reciting the *nembutsu*. For a good summary historical account of the Ōbaku school in relation to the Sōtō and Rinzai schools, see Part II of Peter D. Hershock's *Public Zen, Personal Zen: A Buddhist Introduction* (Lanham: Roman & Littlefield, 2014).

5. Dōgen, *The True Dharma Eye: Zen Master Dōgen's Three Hundred Kōans*, translated by Kazuaki Tanahashi and John Daido Loori, with commentary and verse by John Daido Loori (Boston: Shambhala, 2005).

6. Dōgen, "*Fukanzazengi* (Universally Recommended Instructions for Zazen)," translated by Carl Bielefeldt and T. Griffin Foulk, with Taigen Leighton and Shohaku Okumura, reprinted in *Engaging Dōgen's Zen: The Philosophy of Practice as Awakening*, edited by Tetsuzen Jason M. Wirth, Shūdō Brian Schroeder, and Kanpū Bret W. Davis (Somerville, MA: Wisdom Publications), p. 196. Some of the material in this section of this chapter has been adapted and condensed from Bret W. Davis, "The Enlightening Practice of Nonthinking: Unfolding Dōgen's *Fukanzazengi*," *Engaging Dōgen's Zen: The Philosophy of Practice as Awakening*, edited by Tetsuzen Jason M. Wirth, Shūdō Brian Schroeder, and Kanpū Bret W. Davis (Somerville, MA: Wisdom Publications), pp. 215–21.

7. Dōgen, *Treasury of the True Dharma Eye: Zen Master Dogen's Shobo Genzo*, edited by Kazuaki Tanahashi (Boston: Shambhala, 2012), p. 303, translation modified.

8. Shunryu Suzuki, *Zen Mind, Beginners Mind* (New York: Weatherhill, 1970), p. 128.

9. John Daido Loori, "Yaoshan's Non-Thinking," in *The Art of Just Sitting: Essential Writings on the Zen Practice of Shikantaza*, edited by John Daido Loori (Somerville, MA: Wisdom Publications, 2002), p. 141.

10. Dōgen, "Guidelines for Studying the Way: *Gakudō Yōjin-shū*," in *Moon in a Dewdrop: Writings of Zen Master Dōgen*, edited by Kazuaki Tanahashi (New York: North Point Press, 1985), pp. 31, 42, translation modified. See also *Hōkyōki*, in Takashi James Kodera, *Dogen's Formative Years in China: An Historical and Annotated Translation of the Hōkyō-ki* (Boulder, CO: Prajna Press, 1980), p. 137. For an excellent collection of traditional and contemporary writings on *zazen* as practiced especially in the Sōtō School of Zen, see Loori, *The Art of Just Sitting*.

11. *The Record of Transmitting the Light: Zen Master Keizan's Denkoroku*, translated by Francis Dojun Cook (Somerville, MA: Wisdom, 2003), p. 254. Traditionally, Dōgen is said to have attained enlightenment when he heard his teacher, Rujing, admonish a monk who was dozing off during meditaiton by shouting at him: "When you practice Zen, you must drop off the body-mind; what is the use of just sleeping?" However, some recent Sōtō Zen teachers and scholars have denied that Dōgen experienced such a decisive enlightenment experience, since that would not accord with his teaching that *zazen* does not aim at anything, including the kind of breakthrough enlightenment experiences that the Rinzai Zen School calls *kenshō* (seeing into one's true nature). See Shohaku Okumura, *Realizing Genjokoan: The Key to Dogen's Shobogenzo* (Somerville, MA: Wisdom Publications, 2010), pp. 86–87. For the evidence that Dōgen did in fact not only experience but also encourage enlightening breakthroughs, see Kodera, *Dogen's Formative Years in China*, pp. 60–62; and Davis, "The Enlightening Practice of Nonthinking," p. 245n67.

12. Dōgen, "*Fukanzazengi* (Universally Recommended Instructions for Zazen)," p. 197.

13. Dōgen, "Guidelines for Studying the Way," p. 42, translation slightly modified.

14. See *The Essential Teachings of Zen Master Hakuin*, translated by Norman Waddell (Boston: Shambhala, 2010), p. 61; and *The Discourse on The Inexhaustible Lamp of the Zen School*, by Zen Master Torei Enji with commentary by Master Daibi of Unkan, translated by Yoko Okuda (Boston: Tuttle, 1996), pp. 15–16, 151–55, 189–90, 516–18.

15. Zenkei Shibayama, *The Gateless Barrier: Zen Comments on the Mumonkan*, translated by Sumiko Kudo (Boston: Shambhala, 2000), p. 19.

16. Kōun Yamada, *Zen: The Authentic Gate* (Somerville, MA: Wisdom Publications, 2015), p. 170.

17. *The Zen Master Hakuin: Selected Writings*, translated by Philip B. Yampolsky (New York: Columbia University Press, 1971), pp. 144–45.

18. See ibid., pp. 163–66.

19. *Entangling Vines: A Classic Collection of Zen Koans*, translated and annotated by Thomas Yūhō Kirchner (Somerville, MA: Wisdom Publications, 2013), p. 34 (Case 2), capitalization added.

20. *The Gateless Barrier*, pp. 19–20, translation modified

21. G. Victor Sōgen Hori, "Kōan and *Kenshō* in the Rinzai Zen Curriculum," in *The Kōan: Texts and Contexts in Zen Buddhism*, edited by Steven Heine and Dale S. Wright (New York: Oxford University Press, 2000), p. 286. See also Victor Sōgen Hori, "The Steps of Kōan Practice," in *Zen Sand* (Honolulu: University of Hawai'i Press, 2003), pp. 16–29; and Victor Sōgen Hori, "Rinzai Kōan Training: Philosophical Intersections," in *The Oxford Handbook of Japanese Philosophy*, edited by Bret W. Davis (New York: Oxford University Press, 2020), pp. 231–45.

22. Takemura Makio, *Zen no shisō wo shiru jiten* [Encyclopedia for understanding Zen thought] (Tokyo: Tōkyōdō Shuppan, 2014), p. 110.

23. See Case 16 of *The Blue Cliff Record*.

24. *Analects* 7:8, in *Readings in Classical Chinese Philosophy*, 2nd ed., edited by Philip J. Ivanhoe and Bryan W. Van Norden (Indianapolis, IN: Hackett, 2005), p. 21.

25. Here are some suggestions for further reading on kōan practice: Isshū Miura and Ruth Fuller Sasaki, *The Zen Koan: Its History and Use in Rinzai Zen* (New York: Harcourt Brace, 1965) is a classic introduction to kōans as used in the Rinzai School of Zen. The original, much longer version of this book, which contains extensive notes and background information, has been republished as *Zen Dust: The History of Koan and Koan Study in Rinzai (Linji) Zen*, rev. ed. (Melbourne: Quirin Press, 2015). *Sitting with Koans: Essential Writings on the Practice of Zen Koan Introspection*, edited by John Daido Loori (Somerville, MA: Wisdom Publications, 2006) is a good collection of modern (and a few traditional) writings.

Chapter 23

1. See Jan Van Bragt, "Multiple Religious Belonging of the Japanese People," in *Many Mansions: Multiple Religious Belonging and Christian Identity*, edited by Catherine Cornille (Eugene, OR: Wipf and Stock, 2002), pp. 7–19. Van Bragt quotes the modern Japanese philosopher Watsuji Tetsurō as writing: "We cannot but recognize a number of religions are true. . . . But precisely because we recognize all these faiths equally, we cannot belong to any one of them. We are on a new quest for God" (16–17). And he

ends with a quote from Yamaori Tetsuo: "Ours has been a worldview that considers exclusive affiliation to a particular sect an essentially irreligious posture" (18).

2. See Jørn Borup, *Japanese Rinzai Zen: Myōshinji, a Living Religion* (Boston: Brill, 2008), pp. 254–73.

3. While the status and power of "fighting spirits" (Sk. *asura*) may in some sense be the result of positive karma, their jealous motivations and aggressive actions are clearly generating negative karma. They do not appear in the early versions of Buddhist cosmology. For guides to the relevant early texts on the realms of rebirth, see *In the Buddha's Words: An Anthology of Discourses from the Pāli Canon*, edited by Bhikkhu Bodhi (Somerville, MA: Wisdom Publications, 2005), pp. 148–51; and Eric Cheetham, *Fundamentals of Mainstream Buddhism* (Boston: Tuttle, 1994), pp. 19–23. For a clear interpretation of the Wheel of Life (or Wheel of Becoming), including the twelve-link chain of the interdependent origination of craving, ignorance, and *duhkha* depicted on the outer rim of the Wheel, see John Koller, *Asian Philosophies*, 7th ed. (New York: Pearson, 2018), pp. 65–74.

4. For a detailed and very critical examination of how such terms crept into Chinese Buddhist discourse, see Jungnok Park, *How Buddhism Acquired a Soul on the Way to China* (Bristol, CT: Equinox, 2012). Park's thesis is that, in contrast to the Indian context, in which people generally already believed in rebirth but needed to be convinced of the compatibility of this doctrine with the Buddha's novel doctrine of no-self, the pre-Buddhist Chinese did not believe in a permanent self and so did not need to be disabused of this notion. What they did need to be convinced of, however, was the doctrine of the cycle of rebirth in Samsara. In order to do this, early Chinese Buddhists used Daoist terms to invent the idea of a soul that survives death. Since the fifth century, Park acknowledges, more astute translators and Chinese Buddhist teachers have attempted to correct this erroneous introduction of a soul into discussions of rebirth and other doctrines, but in his view unsuccessfully. I am not convinced that many past and present East Asian Buddhists, and in particular Zen Buddhists, think of such terms as referring to an independent and unchanging soul-substance, even if on occasion the "expedient means" of certain discourses and rituals may indeed give this impression.

5. See Nāgārjuna, *The Fundamental Wisdom of the Middle Way: Nāgārjuna's Mūlamadhyamakakārikā*, translated with commentary by Jay L. Garfield (New York: Oxford University Press, 1995), pp. 245–50, 309–11.

6. Traleg Kyabgon, *Karma: What It Is, What It Isn't, Why It Matters* (Boulder, CO: Shambhala, 2015), pp. 98, 104.

7. For Augustine, there is a hierarchy of reality (a version of "the great chain of being"), structured according to how susceptible an entity is to change: "Unchangeable spirit is God, changeable spirit [i.e., the soul], having been made, is nature, but is better than body." *The Essential Augustine*, edited by Vernon J. Bourke (New York: Hackett, 1974), p. 49. See also ibid., pp. 43–46, 63–64. Scholar of early Buddhism Richard Gombrich points out that, although in the West the Buddha's *anatman* doctrine is often presented as if it were the antithesis of the Christian doctrine (or doctrines) of the soul, "once we see what the Buddha was arguing against, we realize that it was

something very few westerners have ever believed in and most have never heard of. He was refusing to accept that a person has an unchanging essence," an essence that could be identified with metal functions no more than with bodily functions. Richard F. Gombrich, *How Buddhism Began: The Conditioned Genesis of the Early Teachings*, 2nd ed. (New York: Routledge, 2006), pp. 15–16.

8. See Walpola Rahula, *What the Buddha Taught*, 2nd. ed. (New York: Grove Press, 1974), pp. 33–34; and Reginald A. Ray, "Rebirth in the Buddhist Tradition," in *The Buddha and His Teachings*, edited by Samuel Bercholz and Sherab Chödzin (Boston: Shambhala, 2003), pp. 305–7.

9. Matthew 10:39, 16:25; Mark 8:35; Luke 17:33; and John 12:25.

10. Martin Heidegger, *Gesamtausgabe* (Frankfurt: Vittorio Klostermann, 2000), vol. 16, p. 605.

11. *Japanese Death Poems: Written by Zen Monks and Haiku Poets on the Verge of Death*, compiled with an introduction and commentary by Yoel Hoffmann (Tokyo: Tuttle, 1986), p. 6.

12. See Alan F. Segal, *Life After Death: A History of the Afterlife in Western Religion* (New York: Doubleday, 2004).

13. On the Senika heresy, see note 64 of Chapter 12.

14. *Japanese Philosophy: A Sourcebook*, edited by James W. Heisig, Thomas P. Kasulis, and John C. Maraldo (Honolulu: University of Hawai'i Press, 2011), p. 177.

15. *Mahātanhāsankhaya Sutta*, in *The Middle Length Discourses of the Buddha: A Translation of the Majjhima Nikāya*, 2nd ed., translated by Bhikkhu Nānamoli and Bhikkhu Bodhi (Somerville, MA: Wisdom Publications, 2001), pp. 349–61.

16. The most famous and fascinating account of this process is *The Tibetan Book of the Dead: Liberation Through Understanding in the Between*, translated by Robert A. F. Thurman (New York: Bantam Books, 1994). For some of the Buddha's sutras on karma and rebirth in the Pali Canon, see *In the Buddha's Words*, pp. 155–76; see also Cheetham, *Fundamentals of Mainstream Buddhism*, chapter 12.

17. See Ray, "Rebirth in the Buddhist Tradition," pp. 307–8; and Shohaku Okumura, *Realizing Genjokoan: The Key to Dogen's Shobogenzo* (Somerville, MA: Wisdom Publications, 2010), pp. 110–11.

18. Shohaku Okumura, *Living by Vow: A Practical Introduction to Eight Essential Zen Chants and Texts* (Somerville, MA: Wisdom Publications, 2012), pp. 135–36. Elsewhere Okumura Rōshi writes: "I don't believe in literal rebirth, yet I don't deny its existence either. . . . [T]he only thing I can say about it with surety is 'I don't know.'" He goes on to say, however, that after he turned fifty he began to think about rebirth differently: "As I enter the latter period of my life, I now find that I do hope I will live another life after this one, since this life has been too short to do all I need to in practicing the Buddha Way." Okumura, *Realizing Genjokoan*, p. 117.

19. *Majjhima Nikāya* 63, *Cūlamālunkya Sutta* 8; in *In the Buddha's Words*, p. 233.

20. *Analects* 11:12, in *Readings in Classical Chinese Philosophy*, 2nd ed., edited by Philip J. Ivanhoe and Bryan W. Van Norden (Indianapolis, IN: Hackett, 2005), p. 31, translation modified.

21. Yamada Mumon, *Hekigan monogatari* [Blue cliff stories] (Tokyo: Daihōrinkaku, 2004), pp. 127, 369–70.

22. See Bret W. Davis, "Where Did He Go? Ueda Shizuteru Sensei's Last Lesson," *The Eastern Buddhist* 48, no. 2 (2020): 63–68.

23. *Wild Ivy: The Spiritual Biography of Zen Master Hakuin*, translated by Norman Waddell (Boston: Shambhala, 1999), p. 33; see also *The Zen Master Hakuin: Selected Writings*, translated by Philip B. Yampolsky (New York: Columbia University Press, 1971), pp. 119–120.

24. Kenneth Kraft, *Eloquent Zen: Daitō and Early Japanese Zen* (Honolulu: University of Hawai'i Press, 1992), p. 187.

25. Shohaku Okumura, *The Mountains and Waters Sūtra: A Practitioner's Guide to Dōgen's "Sansuikyo"* (Somerville, MA: Wisdom Publications, 2018), pp. 43–44.

26. Okumura, *Realizing Genjokoan*, p. 81.

27. See Dōgen, *The Heart of Dōgen's Shōbōgenzō*, translated by Norman Waddell and Masao Abe (Albany: State University of New York Press, 2002), pp. 8–30. On the question of whether Dōgen experienced a dramatic awakening experience in China upon hearing his teacher Rujing exclaim that *zazen* is a matter of "dropping off the body-mind," see note 11 of Chapter 22.

28. Michael Pollen, *How to Change Your Mind: What the New Science of Psychedelics Teaches Us About Consciousness, Dying, Addiction, Depression, and Transcendence* (New York: Penguin Books, 2018). On the science of psychedelics, in addition to chapters 5 and 6 of Pollan's book, see also James H. Austin, *Zen and the Brain* (Cambridge, MA: MIT Press, 1998), pp. 418–43.

29. Pollen, *How to Change Your Mind*, p. 288.

30. Ibid., p. 305; see also ibid., pp. 390–91. Pollan suggests that a regular practice of meditation can be used to maintain and cultivate the spiritual insights a psychedelic trip may have triggered (pp. 408–9). That may be the case, but this combination may also distort one's expectations and experiences of meditation.

31. See Pollan, *How to Change Your Mind*, pp. 251–52, 263–65, 271, 288–90, 305, 336–17, 352–53, 379, 389–95. For Aldous Huxley's pioneer work in this regard, see *The Doors of Perception* (New York: HarperCollins, 1956).

32. See "Satori Is Not Like LSD," in Keido Fukushima, *Zen Bridge* (Sommerville, MA: Wisdom Publications, 2017), pp. 91–94. For a trenchant critique of comparisons of drug-induced states with Zen enlightenment, see Brad Warner, *Hardcore Zen: Punk Rock, Monster Movies and the Truth About Reality* (Somerville, MA: Wisdom Publications, 2003), pp. 163–73.

33. See Martin Heidegger, *Being and Time*, translated by Joan Stambaugh, revised by Dennis J. Schmidt (Albany: State University of New York Press, 2010), pp. 227–55. See also "From Being-Towards-Death to the Great Death: An Exhortation from Zen," in Bret W. Davis, *Heidegger and the Will: On the Way to Gelassenheit* (Evanston, IL: Northwestern University Press, 2007), pp. 56–59.

34. See *The Zen Master Hakuin: Selected Writings*, pp. 219–20.

35. Ibid., p. 144.

36. My translation. Compare *The Blue Cliff Record*, translated by Thomas Cleary and J. C. Cleary (Boston: Shambhala, 1992), p. 187.

37. Dante Alighieri, *The Divine Comedy*, translated by John Ciardi (New York: Penguin, 2003), p. 31.

38. Reported to me by Tetsuzen Jason Wirth, a Sōtō Zen priest and cross-cultural philosopher who hosted Fukushima Rōshi on some of his visits to the United States.

39. As quoted in Takemura Makio, *Zen no tetsugaku* [Philosophy of Zen] (Tokyo: Chūsekisha, 2004), p. 191; see also Omori Sogen, *An Introduction to Zen Training*, translated by Dogen Hosokawa and Roy Yoshimoto (Boston: Tuttle, 2001), p. 161.

40. Quoted in Master Sheng-yen, *Hoofprint of the Ox: Principles of the Chan Buddhist Path as Taught by a Modern Chinese Master* (New York: Oxford University Press, 2001), p. 222.

41. Hirata Seikō, *Zen kara no hassō* [Thoughts from Zen] (Kyoto: Zenbunka Kenkyūsho, 1983), pp. 21–22.

42. *Wild Ivy*, pp. 9–17.

43. Recounted by Norman Waddell in his introduction to *Wild Ivy*, p. xxii.

44. *Wild Ivy*, p. 1.

45. Ibid., p. 32.

46. Omori, *An Introduction to Zen Training*, pp. 161–62, translation modified.

47. See Peter Harvey, *An Introduction to Buddhism: Teachings, History, and Practices* (Cambridge: Cambridge University Press, 1990), pp. 61–68; Donald W. Mitchell, *Buddhism: Introducing the Buddhist Experience* (New York: Oxford University Press, 2002), p. 62; Rupert Gethin, *The Foundations of Buddhism* (New York: Oxford University Press, 1998), pp. 75–76.

48. Rahula, *What the Buddha Taught*, p. 43.

49. Ibid., pp. 38–39. In passing Rahula affirms "the Mahāyāna view of Nirvāna as not being different from *Samsāra*. The same thing is Samsāra or Nirvāna according to the way you look at it" (p. 40). But it is unclear how he reconciles this with the idea that the ultimate attainment of Nirvana entails "the dissolution of the body" and indeed the "complete destruction" of the Five Aggregates and the absence of the four elements and all sense-objects (37, 39, 41). In one of the "inspired utterances" (*Udāna* 8.1) recorded in the Pali Canon, the Buddha spoke of Nirvana as "a domain where there is not earth, no water, no fire, no wind, no sphere of infinite space, no sphere of infinite consciousness, no sphere of neither awareness nor non-awareness; there is not this world, there is not another world, there is no sun or moon. I do not call this coming or going, nor standing, nor dying, nor being reborn; it is without support, without occurence, without object. Just this is the end of suffering" (as quoted in Gethin, *The Foundations of Buddhism*, pp. 76–77; for an alternative translation, see *In the Buddha's Words*, pp. 365–66).

50. Rahula, *What the Buddha Taught*, p. 41.

51. For more on the Mahayana ideas of "non-abiding Nirvana" and the nonduality between Samsara and Nirvana, see Mitchell, *Buddhism: Introducing the Buddhist Experience*, pp. 99–101, 118, 135–36, 187–89, 199; and Paul Williams, *Mahāyāna*

Buddhism: The Doctrinal Foundations (New York: Routledge, 1989), pp. 67–68, 181–84.

52. *The Lankavatara Sutra*, translation and commentary by Red Pine (Berkeley, CA: Counterpoint, 2012), p. 91.

53. Mark Siderits and Shōryū Katsura, *Nāgārjuna's Middle Way: Mūlamadhyamakakārikā* (Somerville, MA: Wisdom, 2013), p. 302 (25.19–20), transliteration of "Nirvana" and "Samsara" altered.

54. Nāgārjuna, *The Fundamental Wisdom of the Middle Way*, pp. 332–33, transliteration of "Nirvana" and "Samsara" altered.

55. Okumura, *Living by Vow*, pp. 136–37.

56. Rupert Gethin, *The Foundations of Buddhism* (New York: Oxford University Press, 1998), p. 119.

57. Dōgen, *The Heart of Dōgen's Shōbōgenzō*, p. 106, translation modified. See Chapter 12 for more on this point.

58. *The Record of Linji*, translation with commentary by Ruth Fuller Sasaki, edited by Thomas Yūhō Kirchner (Honolulu: University of Hawai'i Press, 2009), pp. 22–23.

59. Yamada Mumon, *Hannya Shingyō* [The Heart Sutra] (Kyoto: Zen Bunka Kenkyūsho, 1986), pp. 167–70.

60. Yamada Mumon, *Lectures on* The Ten Oxherding Pictures, translated by Victor Sōgen Hori (Honolulu: University of Hawai'i Press, 2004), p. 63.

61. See *The Heart Sutra*, translation and commentary by Red Pine (Emeryville, CA: Shoemaker & Hoard, 2004), pp. 136–40.

62. *The Record of Linji*, p. 143, translation modified. In fact, Linji's kōan-question that is the context of this saying is even more involved and challenging: "One person is endlessly on the road, yet has never left home. Another has left home, yet is not on the road. Which deserves the offerings of humans and gods?" Although generations of teachers and scholars have given various interpretations—including interpretations that favor one over the other or that deride both of the persons described—I follow Nishitani (see the reference in the following note) as well as Yamada Mumon Rōshi and Ōmori Sōgen Rōshi in understanding Linji to be prodding us to become capable of effectively employing both expressions in complementary (as well as contrasting) manners. See Yamada Mumon, *Rinzai-roku* [The Record of Linji], 2nd ed. (Kyoto: Zen-bunka Kenkyūsho, 2012), pp. 43–44; and Ōmori Sōgen, *Rinzai-roku kōwa* [Lectures on the Record of Linji] (Tokyo: Shunjūsha, 2005), pp. 44–46.

63. Nishitani Keiji, *Shōbōgenzō kōwa* [Lectures on the Shōbōgenzō] (Tokyo: Chikuma Shobō, 1987), vol. 1, pp. 69–70.

64. Dōgen, *The Heart of Dōgen's Shōbōgenzō*, pp. 19–20. For an explication, see Bret W. Davis, "The Enlightening Practice of Nonthinking: Unfolding Dōgen's *Fukanzazengi*," in *Engaging Dōgen's Zen: The Philosophy of Practice as Awakening*, edited by Tetsuzen Jason M. Wirth, Shūdō Brian Schroeder, and Kanpū Bret W. Davis (Somerville, MA: Wisdom Publications, 2017), pp. 207–15.

65. Dōgen, *The Heart of Dōgen's Shōbōgenzō*, pp. 11–13.

66. Brook Ziporyn, "The Platform Sūtra and Chinese Philosophy," in *Readings of the Platform Sutra*, edited by Morten Schütter and Stephen F. Teiser (New York: Columbia University Press, 2012), p. 173.

67. *Zen Sourcebook: Traditional Documents from China, Korea, and Japan*, edited by Stephen Addiss with Stanley Lombardo and Judith Roitman (Indianapolis, IN: Hackett, 2008), p. 150.

Chapter 24

1. Throughout this chapter I use my own translations of passages from this text. The best available complete translation can be found in Yamada Mumon, *Lectures on* The Ten Oxherding Pictures, translated by Victor Sōgen Hori (Honolulu: University of Hawai'i Press, 2004). Other translations and commentaries include Daisetz Teitaro Suzuki, *Manual of Zen Buddhism* (New York: Grove Press, 1960), pp. 127–34; Omori Sogen, *An Introduction to Zen Training*, translated by Dogen Hosokawa and Roy Yoshimoto (Boston: Tuttle, 2001), pp. 182–213; Stephanie Wada, with translations by Gen P. Sakamoto, *The Oxherder: A Zen Parable Illustrated* (New York: George Braziller, 2002); John Daido Loori, *Riding the Ox Home: Stages on the Path of Enlightenment* (Boston: Shambhala, 2002); and Jeff Shore, *Zen Classics for the Modern World* (Darby, PA: Diane, 2011), pp. 4–43.

2. Unfortunately, neither Ueda's monograph nor his book co-authored with Yanagida Seizan on *The Ten Oxherding Pictures*, both of which I frequently refer to in this chapter, have yet been translated from Japanese. The best article by Ueda available in English translation in this regard is "Emptiness and Fullness: Śūnyatā in Mahāyāna Buddhism," translated by James W. Heisig and Frederick Greiner, *The Eastern Buddhist* 15, no. 1 (1982): 9–37. The original German version of this article can be found in Shizuteru Ueda, *Wer und was bin ich: Zur Phänomenologie des Selbst im Zen-Buddhismus* (Freiburg: Verlag Karl Alber, 2011), chapter 1. Also in German, a good elucidation of Ueda's interpretation of the *Oxherding Pictures* can be found in Steffen Döll, *Wozu also suchen? Zur Einführung in das Denken von Ueda Shizuteru* (Munich: Iudicium, 2005), chapters 3 and 7.

3. Yanagida Seizan, "Kaidai" [Commentary], in Ueda Shizuteru and Yanagida Seizan, *Jūgyūzu: Jiko no genshōgaku* [The ten oxherding pictures: phenomenology of the self] (Tokyo: Chikuma Shobō, 1992), pp. 273–77. Red Pine suggests that Puming's version was created after Kuoan's, but this seems unlikely. See the preface to *P'u Ming's Oxherding Pictures and Verses*, translated by Red Pine (Anacortes, WA: Empty Bowl Press, 2015).

4. The different versions of oxherding pictures that I refer to in this chapter are collected in Zenkei Shibayama and Gyokusei Jikihara, *Zen Oxherding Pictures* (Osaka: Sōgensha, 1975). D. T. Suzuki's *Manual of Zen Buddhism* contains Puming's version as well as Kuoan's (pp. 135–44). For a beautiful bilingual edition of Puming's version, see Red Pine's *P'u Ming's Oxherding Pictures and Verses*. For a commentary on Zide's (Jp. Jitoku) version of *Six Oxherding Pictures*, which attempts to synthesize and distill Qingjiu and Puming's versions with Kuoan's version, see Zenkei Shibayama, *A*

Flower Does Not Talk: Zen Essays, translated by Sumiko Kudo (Rutland, VT: Tuttle, 1970), pp. 152–203.

5. See Piya Tan, "The Taming of the Bull: Mind-Training and the Formation of Buddhist traditions," https://web.archive.org/web/20130718003156/http://dharmafarer.org/wordpress/wp-content/uploads/2009/12/8.2-Taming-of-the-Bull-piya.pdf.

6. See Yamada, *Lectures on The Ten Oxherding Pictures*, pp. 1–2.

7. See *Sudden and Gradual: Approaches to Enlightenment in Chinese Thought*, edited by Peter N. Gregory (Honolulu: University of Hawai'i Press, 1988).

8. See Peter N. Gregory, *Tsung-mi and the Sinification of Buddhism* (Honolulu: University of Hawai'i Press, 2002), pp. 192–96; and Robert E. Buswell Jr., *Tracing Back the Radiance: Chinul's Korean Way of Zen* (Honolulu: University of Hawai'i Press, 1991), pp. 57–62. Bodhidharma, the semi-legendary figure who is said to have brought Zen from India to China around the end of the fifth or the beginning of the sixth century, taught that while "many paths enter the Way," they can be boiled down to two types: "entering through principle" and "entering through practice." Although most of the text that is attributed to Bodhidharma called "The Two Paths" is devoted to spelling out the details of entering the Way through gradual practice, he is understood to have favored entering the Way directly through principle, and the Zen tradition has followed his lead. "To enter through principle," Bodhidharma writes, "means using techniques to awaken the essence and understanding that all beings have the same true nature, which does not shine clearly because it is covered with the dust of delusion." *Zen Sourcebook: Traditional Documents from China, Korea, and Japan*, edited by Stephen Addiss with Stanley Lombardo and Judith Roitman (Indianapolis, IN: Hackett, 2008), p. 11. It should be noted, however, that even if Bodhidharma did in fact favor the sudden enlightenment approach, in "The Two Paths" he also affirms and teaches a path of gradual enlightenment.

9. Yanagida, "Kaidai," in Ueda and Yanagida, *Jūgyūzu: Jiko no genshōgaku*, p. 273. It is interesting to speculate why Fuyin would have the ox "return" from white to black. In the famous eighth-century text *Santongqie* (Jp. *Sandōkai*) by the Chinese Zen master Shitou, a text chanted regularly in the Japanese Sōtō School, "darkness" refers to the wisdom of non-discrimination and the universal Buddha-nature, whereas "lightness" refers to phenomenal differences. The point of Shitou's text is that dark and light, unity and differences, emptiness and form, or principle and facts must be understood as nondual. See "All Is One, One Is All: Merging of Difference and Unity," in Shohaku Okumura, *Living by Vow: A Practical Introduction to Eight Essential Zen Chants and Texts* (Somerville, MA: Wisdom Publications, 2012), pp. 207–48.

10. See the *Mahagopalaka Sutta* (The Greater Discourse on the Cowherd), in *The Middle Length Discourses of the Buddha: A Translation of the Majjhima Nikāya*, 2nd ed., translated by Bhikkhu Ñāṇamoli and Bhikkhu Bodhi (Somerville, MA: Wisdom Publications, 1995), pp. 313–18. Also see the texts referred to in Red Pine's preface to *P'u Ming's Oxherding Pictures and Verses*, and in Piya Tan, "The Taming of the Bull."

11. Ueda Shizuteru, *Jūgyūzu wo ayumu* [Walking the path of *The Ten Oxherding Pictures*] (Tokyo: Daihōrinkaku, 2003), p. 12.

12. Shibayama and Jikihara, *Zen Oxherding Pictures*, pp. 87–88.

13. *The Upanishads*, translated by Eknath Easwaran (Tomales, CA: Nilgiri Press, 1987), pp. 182–83.

14. Garma C. C. Chang, *The Buddhist Teaching of Totality: The Philosophy of Hwa Yen Buddhism* (State College: Pennsylvania State University Press, 2001), pp. 224–30.

15. *Taishō Shinshū Daizōkyō*, edited by Takakusu Junjirō and Watanabe Kaigyoku (Tokyo: Taishō Issaikyō Kankōkai, 1924–32), 45:159b28–29. The modern Zen master and scholar Akizuki Ryōmin notes similar ideas in the third chapter of the *Lankavatara Sutra* and elsewhere, but says that the sense of Ziyuan's phrase matches in particular that of Sengzhao's statement. Akizuki Ryōmin, *Jūgyūzu, Zazengi* [*The Ten Oxherding Pictures*, the principles of zazen] (Tokyo: Shunjūsha, 1989), p. 43. See the quotation of Sengzhao's phrase in Case 40 of *The Blue Cliff Record*, and my comments on this kōan in Chapter 8. Earlier in Chapter 8, I note a similar passage in the *Zhuangzi* that prefigures the phrase of Sengzhao, whose weaving of Daoist ideas into Buddhism laid the groundwork for the genesis of Zen.

16. Yamada Mumon, *Jiko wo mitsumeru* [Looking into the self] (Kyoto: Zen Bunka Kenkyūsho, 1983), p. 50.

17. Ueda, *Jūgyūzu wo ayumu*, pp. 96–97, 115–16.

18. Master Sheng-yen, *Hoofprint of the Ox: Principles of the Chan Buddhist Path as Taught by a Modern Chinese Master* (New York: Oxford University Press, 2001), p. 203.

19. Shibayama and Jikihara, *Zen Oxherding Pictures*, pp. 60–70.

20. *Der Ochs und sein Hirte: Eine altchinesische Zen-Geschichte erläutert von Meister Daizohkutsu R. Ohtsu mit japanischen Bilder aus dem 15. Jahrhundert*, translated by Kōichi Tsujimura and Harmut Buchner (Pfullingen: Neske, 1958), p. 88.

21. See Donald W. Mitchell, *Buddhism: Introducing the Buddhist Experience* (New York: Oxford University Press, 2002), p. 62; and Walpola Rahula, *What the Buddha Taught*, 2nd ed. (New York: Grove Press, 1974), p. 40.

22. Sheng-yen, *Hoofprint of the Ox*, p. 201.

23. Dōgen, "*Fukanzazengi* (Universally Recommended Instructions for Zazen)," translated by Carl Bielefeldt and T. Griffin Foulk, with Taigen Leighton and Shohaku Okumura, in *Engaging Dōgen's Zen: The Philosophy of Practice as Awakening*, edited by Tetsuzen Jason M. Wirth, Shūdō Brian Schroeder, and Kanpū Bret W. Davis (Somerville, MA: Wisdom Publications, 2017), p. 196.

24. *The Record of Linji*, edited by Thomas Yūhō Kirchner, translated by Ruth Fuller Sasaki (Honolulu: University of Hawai'i Press, 2009), p. 10.

25. See *The Śūrangama Sūtra*, translated by Bhiksu Heng Sure et al. (Ukiah, CA: Buddhist Text Translation Society, 2009), pp. 159–166.

26. Audrey Yoshiko Seo, *Ensō: Zen Circles of Enlightenment* (Boston: Weatherhill, 2007), p. 14.

27. David Pollock, *Zen Poems of the Five Mountains* (New York: Crossroad, 1985), p. 25. See also the story recounted by Ōtsu Rekidō Rōshi in *Der Ochs und sein Hirte*, pp. 94–95.

28. Ueda, *Jūgyūzu wo ayumu*, pp. 11–13, 154.

29. Ibid., pp. 89–90, 133.

30. See Zenkei Shibayama, *The Gateless Barrier: Zen Comments on the Mumonkan*, translated by Sumiko Kudo (Boston: Shambhala, 2000), p. 311 (Case 46).

31. *Saṃyutta Nikāya* 4:24, in *The Connected Discourses of the Buddha*, translated by Bhikkhu Bodhi (Somerville, MA: Wisdom Publications, 2000), p. 216.

32. *Ariyapariyesanā Sutta* 19–21, in *The Middle Length Discourses of the Buddha: A Translation of the Majjhima Nikāya*, 2nd ed., translated by Bhikkhu Ñāṇamoli and Bhikkhu Bodhi (Somerville, MA: Wisdom Publications, 1995), pp. 260–61. See also *Saṃyutta Nikāya* 6:1; and *Mahāvagga* 1:5.

33. Karen Armstrong, *Buddha* (New York: Penguin, 2001), p. 96.

34. See Ueda Shizuteru, "Jiko no genshōgaku: Zen no Jūgyūzu no tebiki toshite" [Phenomenology of the self: with Zen's ten oxherding pictures as a guide], in Ueda and Yanagida, *Jūgyūzu: Jiko no genshōgaku*, pp. 48–55.

35. See Ueda, "Jiko no genshōgaku," pp. 32, 55–70, 89–93.

36. This is also suggested by John Daido Loori in *Riding the Ox Home*, p. 57.

37. Kusumoto Bunyū, *Zengo nyūmon* [Introduction to Zen terms] (Tokyo: Daihōrinkaku, 1982), p. 104. On the Great Death, see Chapter 12.

38. *Der Ochs und sein Hirte*, pp. 109–10. Linji speaks of "Four Classifications" of teaching methods that he employs in order to awaken students to the dynamically perspectival nondual relation between humans and the surrounding world. He states these as follows: "[1] Sometimes I take away the person but do not take away the surroundings; [2] sometimes I take away the surroundings but do not take away the person; [3] sometimes I take away both person and surroundings; [4] sometimes I take away neither person nor surroundings." *The Record of Linji*, p. 7. Ōtsu Rōshi links the third of Linji's classifications to picture 8 of *The Ten Oxherding Pictures*. It would also be possible to link the first classification to picture 9, the second classification to picture 7, and the fourth classification to picture 10.

39. For some excellent examples and an informative introduction to the history of the use of this emblematic and enigmatic Zen symbol, see Seo, *Ensō: Zen Circles of Enlightenment*.

40. I am following Ueda in referring to what is traditionally called "the single circle" (Jp. *ichi-ensō*) as "the empty circle" (*kū-ensō*). The traditional expression stresses oneness, yet it is important not to mistake that oneness for a homogeneous substance that does not allow for differences. Ueda's expression stresses that the dynamically self-emptying quality of this oneness encompasses, rather than erases, the plurality of interconnected and changing events. With reference to a poem from Zen master Bankei, Ueda writes that "the empty circle" is discovered when not only "the bottom of the bucket drops out" but also even "the single circle of the ring is no more." Ueda, *Jūgyūzu wo ayumu*, pp. 166–67; see also Ueda, "Jiko no genshōgaku," pp. 154–59. Even the empty circle is still a finger pointing at the moon, a circumscribed symbol for an undelimited openness—a paradoxically "infinite sphere, whose center is everywhere and whose circumference is nowhere" (see Chapter 9).

41. See G. S. Kirk, J. E. Raven, and M. Schofield, *The Presocratic Philosophers* (Cambridge: Cambridge University Press, 1983), p. 252, where the phrase in question is translated as "the bulk of a ball well-rounded on every side."

42. *Der Ochs und sein Hirte*, pp. 110, 117.

43. Dōgen, *The Heart of Dōgen's Shōbōgenzō*, translated by Norman Waddell and Masao Abe (Albany: State University of New York Press, 2002), pp. 33, 36.

44. Akizuki, *Jūgyūzu, Zazengi*, p. 122. See also the comments by Akizuki Rōshi's student Takemura Makio in his *Zen no shisō wo shiru jiten* [Encyclopedia for understanding Zen thought] (Tokyo: Tōkyōdō Shuppan, 2014), pp. 105–6, 213–14.

45. See *Ueda Shizuteru shū* [Ueda Shizuteru collection] (Tokyo: Iwanami, 2002), vol. 2, pp. 329–345; and Ueda Shizuteru, "Language in a Twofold World," translated by Bret W. Davis, in *Japanese Philosophy: A Sourcebook*, edited by James W. Heisig, Thomas P. Kasulis, and John C. Maraldo (Honolulu: University of Hawai'i Press), p. 769.

46. Ueda, *Wer und was bin ich*, pp. 72–79, 165–170, 190–91, 194–96, 201.

47. Ueda, "Jiko no genshōgaku," pp. 155–56.

48. *The Blue Cliff Record*, translated by Thomas Cleary and J. C. Cleary (Boston: Shambhala, 1992), p. 259.

49. This phrase echoes earlier ones by Zhaozhou and then Yuanwu in his opening comments to Case 95 of *The Blue Cliff Record* (see Chapter 13).

50. "The Presencing of Truth: Dōgen's *Genjōkōan*," translated by Bret W. Davis, in *Buddhist Philosophy: Essential Readings*, edited by Jay Garfield and William Edelglass (Oxford: Oxford University Press, 2009), pp. 256–57, translation slightly modified.

Index

For the benefit of digital users, indexed terms that span two pages (e.g., 52–53) may, on occasion, appear on only one of those pages.

In addition to listing key terms and names as they appear in the pages of this book, this index includes full names and dates for referenced figures in the history of Zen Buddhism, and Japanese pronunciations of the names of Chinese Zen masters. Dates are also provided for some other figures on the periphery of the history of Zen Buddhism. On a selective basis, source language terms in Pali (P.), Sanskrit (Sk.), Chinese (Ch.), Japanese (Jp.), German (Gm.), and Greek (Gk.) are provided, and translations or simple explanations of some terms are provided. In cases where terms include sinographs (Chinese characters) that were simplified in modern Japanese in the mid-twentieth century, the modern Japanese versions used today appear in brackets following the traditional versions. Chinese names and terms are written in the now standard Pinyin rather than in the older Wade-Giles transliteration system. East Asian names are written without a comma in the order of family name first, except in a few cases where an author has used the Western order.

Figures are indicated by *f* following the page number

See also afflictions; *duhkha*; Nirvana; rebirth; suffering

samu (Jp. 作務, meditative work), 237–38, 239*f*, 240

Sanbō Kyōdan (Jp. 三宝教団, Sanbō Zen 三宝禅), 356n.40, 422n.1

Sansheng Huiran (Jp. Sanshō E'nen, c. 830–c. 900), 119

sanzen (Jp. 参禪 [参禅], private interview with a Zen teacher, also called *dokusan* 獨參 [独参]), 237, 273, 290, 300–1

Sawaki Kōdō (1880–1965), 311

SBNR (spiritual but not religious). *See* spirituality

Schelling, Friedrich Wilhelm Joseph, 123, 389–90n.51

Schlütter, Morten, 422n.1

science, 14, 95, 107, 143–44, 281–82, 283, 285, 355n.32, 363n.17

cognitive science, 12, 27, 228–29

neuroscience, 311–12, 355–56n.33

nighttime perspective of, 283

physics, 12, 166, 355–56n.33

psychology, 95

religion and, 275, 288, 289, 355–56n.33

self (Jp. *jiko* 自己), 15, 21, 34–35, 55, 108, 127–29, 151, 272, 377n.22

agent-self (Sk. *pudgala*), 100

attachment to and loss of, 128–29

autotelism, 227

Buddha/God and, 125, 146, 147, 149, 160–61, 170, 171, 173, 174–75, 176, 177, 283, 284, 288, 376n.14, 382n.36

Buddha's silence regarding existence or non-existence of, 96

ego (Sk. *ātman*; Ch. *wǒ*; Jp. *ga* 我; in modern Japanese also *jiga* 自我), 69, 88, 91, 93, 94, 95, 124, 127–28, 171, 183, 226–27, 288

emptiness of, 30, 305

emptying/forgetting/shedding, 21, 29–31, 47, 128, 170, 183, 228, 233–329, 333, 334, 337–38, 391n.83 (*see also* dropping off the body-mind; emptying one's cup/mind)

freedom from/for, 129

Hindu *Atman* vs. Buddhist *anatman*, 108, 376n.19

"I, in not being I, am I," 128

independent and permanent, 91, 97–98

investigation into the self, investigation and clarification of the matter of the self (Jp. *kojikyūmei* 己事究明), xvii, 20–22, 24, 29–30, 37, 48, 91, 97–98, 360n.22

know thyself (Gk. *gnōthi seauton*), 21–23, 24, 73, 91, 337, 360n.22

knowing vs. not- or non-knowing, 92–93, 148

oneness/nonduality with everything, 110–11, 117, 172, 298, 311, 326, 329

original part (Jp. *honbun-nin* 本分人), 246

permanent-individual-owner-controller (Jp. *jō-itsu-shu-sai* 常一主宰), 376–77n.20

process-self, life-stream, 97, 99–101, 115, 117–18, 139–40, 207–8, 307, 316

seeking/sought self, 323, 330

self and others, 30, 104, 122–23, 133, 188, 198–99, 215, 245, 315, 397–98n.46

self-contradictory nature of, 34

true person of no rank (Ch. *wúwèi zhēnrén* 無位真人; Jp. *mu-i no shinnin* 無位の眞人 [無位の真人]), 101

true self (Ch. *zhēnwǒ*; Jp. *shinga* 眞我 [真我] or *shin no jiko* 眞の自己 [真の自己]), 21–22, 31, 69, 92, 93–94, 95–96, 100–2, 113–14, 124, 128–29, 132, 141, 146, 147, 149, 170, 172, 173, 174–75, 176, 177, 210–11, 215, 267, 311, 314, 323–25, 326, 327, 329, 330, 331–32, 334–35, 337, 376–77n.20, 425n.4

true self or Great Self (Ch. *dàwǒ*; Jp. *daiga* 大我) is no-self, 95, 96, 111, 376–77n.20

turning the self inside out, 29–31

ungraspable, unobjectifiable, 101–2, 330

unity of *Atman* and *Brahman*, 107

See also body-heart-mind-spirit; Five Aggregates; *kenshō*; no-self; other-power vs. self-power

selling water by a river, 145

Sengcan (aka Jianzhi Sengcan; Jp. Kanchi Sōsan, d. 606), 100–1, 114, 213, 268

Sengzhao (384–414, seminal Chinese Buddhist philosopher), 105, 114, 325

Senika heresy, 166, 306, 314, 390n.64

Serenity Prayer/Serenity Practice, 83

sesshin (Jp. 接心 or 攝心 [摂心], intensive Zen retreat), 50, 238

Seung Sahn (1927–2004), 148, 215

sex scandals in Zen centers, 400–1n.30

shakkei. See garden

Shaku Sōen (English: Soyen Shaku, 1860–1919), 124–25

shakuhachi (Japanese flute), 259–60

Shandao (613–681, Chinese Pure Land Buddhist), 162

Shankara (8th cent. Hindu philosopher), 21–22, 123–24